Contents

KU-269-628

8 Information and consultation

9 Transnational issues

Abbreviations

Courts

ECJ	European Court of Justice
ECHR	European Court of Human Rights
PC	Privy Council
SC	Supreme Court
HL	House of Lords
CA	Court of Appeal
Ct Sess	Court of Session
NICA	Northern Ireland Court of Appeal
QBD	Queen's Bench Division
Div Ct	(Queen's Bench) Divisional Court
KBD	King's Bench Division
ChD	Chancery Division
NIRC	National Industrial Relations Court
EAT	Employment Appeal Tribunal
ET	Employment Tribunal

Case references

AC	Law Reports, Appeal Cases
All ER	All England Law Reports
Ch	Law Reports, Chancery Division
CMLR	Common Market Law Reports
COET	Employment Tribunal folio number
EAT	Employment Appeal Tribunal unreported case number
ECR	European Case Reports
ET	Employment Tribunal unreported case number
EWCA	Court of Appeal unreported case number
ICR	Industrial Cases Reports
IRLR	Industrial Relations Law Reports
ITR	Industrial Tribunal Reports
KB	Law Reports, King's Bench Division
QB	Law Reports, Queen's Bench Division
SCOET	Scottish Employment Tribunal folio number
SLT	Scots Law Times
TLR	Times Law Reports
UKSC	Supreme Court unreported case number
WLR	Weekly Law Reports

Legislation

EA	Employment Act 2002
EqA	Equality Act 2010
ERA	Employment Rights Act 1996
ERelA 1999	Employment Relations Act 1999
ERelA 2004	Employment Relations Act 2004
ETA	Employment Tribunals Act 1996
TULR(C)A	Trade Union and Labour Relations (Consolidation) Act 1992

Statutory references, unless otherwise stated, are to the Transfer of Undertakings (Protection of Employment) Regulations 2006 SI 2006/246.

Many cases in this Handbook were decided under the Transfer of Undertakings (Protection of Employment) Regulations 1981 SI 1981/1794, which preceded the 2006 Regulations. However, wherever possible, reference is made to the corresponding provision in the later Regulations and not to their antecedents in repealed legislation.

Introduction

When a business is sold by one employer to another, or the responsibility for providing a service transfers from one employer to another, the question arises as to what happens to the dedicated workforce. Do the employees concerned have the right to work for the new employer? And, if so, do they retain the contractual and other employment rights that they enjoyed prior to the transfer or is the new employer entitled to vary their contracts in order to harmonise their terms and conditions with those of any existing employees? These are the main issues with which the Transfer of Undertakings (Protection of Employment) Regulations 2006 SI 2006/246 (TUPE) – the subject of this Handbook – are concerned.

Below, we explain the legislative history and background to the TUPE Regulations, consider the complex matter of their territorial extent, and outline the scheme of this Handbook.

Background

In 1977 rules appeared at European level requiring the UK to legislate to protect employees affected by a business transfer. These were set out in EU Council Directive No.77/187 'on the approximation of the laws of the Member States relating to the safeguarding of employees' rights in the event of transfers of undertakings, businesses or parts of businesses', which, following amendments, was reissued in its entirety as EU Council Directive No.2001/23. In essence, the two main objectives of the Acquired Rights Directive (as it is commonly known) are to ensure that when a relevant transfer of a business takes place:

- the contracts of employment of the employees assigned to the business transfer automatically from the 'transferor' (the old employer) to the 'transferee' (the new employer), with their terms and conditions intact, and

- both the transferor and the transferee inform and consult with representatives of those of their respective employees who might be affected by the transfer.

In order to implement the Directive, the UK Government introduced the Transfer of Undertakings (Protection of Employment) Regulations 1981 SI 1981/1794. These Regulations, which became widely known by the acronym TUPE, were in place for some 25 years, during which time they gave rise to much head-scratching among employment lawyers. Some of the problems in this regard flowed from the need for the Regulations to be interpreted in the light of the Acquired Rights Directive, the scope of which has been obscured somewhat by the European Court of Justice in a series of confusing (and in some instances confused) judgments.

The requirement to update TUPE to implement the 2001 version of the Directive, together with a power contained in S.38 of the Employment Relations Act 1999 to provide increased TUPE protection, presented the Labour Government with an opportunity to bring some clarity to this complex area of law. After an extremely drawn-out process, the Transfer of Undertakings (Protection of Employment) Regulations 2006 SI 2006/246 finally came into force on 6 April 2006. These Regulations introduced a number of important changes to the law, the most important being to bring the vast majority of service provision changes within TUPE's scope and to promote a 'rescue culture' by making it easier for insolvent business to be transferred to new employers.

Changes made in January 2014

The Coalition Government which came to power in 2010 considered that some aspects of the 2006 Regulations went further than the minimum requirements of the Acquired Rights Directive and therefore constituted unnecessary 'gold-plating'. It issued a 'call for evidence' on the effectiveness of TUPE, which was followed in 2013 by a consultation on reforming the 2006 Regulations. Among the more notable changes initially proposed was a repeal of the service provision changes rules, but this proposal was eventually dropped. Nevertheless, the Collective Redundancies and Transfer of Undertakings (Protection of Employment) (Amendment) Regulations 2014 SI 2014/16 ('the Amendment Regulations') introduced a number of important changes to the 2006 Regulations:

- in respect of service provision changes, new Reg 3(2A) was inserted to clarify what had previously been made clear in case law – that, for a transfer by way of a service provision change to take place, the activities carried out under the contract must remain fundamentally the same in the hands of the new contractor

- changes to contractual terms and conditions are prohibited by new Reg 4(4) if the 'sole or principal reason' for the variation is 'the transfer'. Previously, changes were prohibited if the sole or principal reason for the variation was 'the transfer itself' or 'a reason connected with the transfer that is not an economic, organisational or technical reason entailing changes in the workforce' ('an ETO reason'). This second formula has not been dropped entirely, however, as new Reg 4(5)(a) now provides that a change will not be prohibited if it is agreed between the parties and is made for an ETO reason. Unilateral changes which are authorised by a term in the contract are now also expressly permitted, as a result of new Reg 4(5)(b)

- a further exception to the prohibition on changes to terms and conditions is found in new Reg 4(5B). This applies in respect of terms incorporated from a collective agreement, provided that at least one year has passed since the transfer and the employee is left in a no less favourable position overall. In addition, new Reg 4A states that where a transferred contract incorporates such provisions of collective agreements 'as may be agreed from time to time', Reg 4(2) does not transfer any rights, powers, duties and liabilities in relation to any provision of a collective agreement agreed after the date of the transfer if the transferee is not a participant in the collective bargaining for that provision. This enshrines the 'static' approach to terms derived from collective agreements as developed in domestic and EU case law

- a dismissal will now only be deemed automatically unfair by Reg 7(1) if the sole or principal reason for it is 'the transfer'. As with Reg 4, all mention of reasons 'connected to' the transfer has been dropped

- the expression 'entailing changes in the workforce', which appears in both Regs 4 and 7, is now specifically stated to include a change of workplace. This reverses the effect of previous case law and widens the scope to make changes to terms and conditions, or to make employees redundant, on a TUPE transfer

- as a result of new Reg 13A, micro-businesses – i.e. those with fewer than ten employees – are now entitled to consult directly with employees rather than elected employee representatives; and

- employee liability information under Reg 11 must now be provided 28 days before the transfer (previously, the time limit was 14 days).

These changes only apply in respect of transfers occurring on or after 31 January 2014. As a result, there will continue to be cases applying the old provisions for some time – it is not uncommon, particularly in the case of changes to terms and conditions, for a claim to arise years after the transfer. In addition, the changes do not have the same territorial extent as the 2006 Regulations, as we explain under 'Territorial scope' below.

Overview of the TUPE Regulations
The provisions of TUPE are discussed in detail in the following chapters of this Handbook. Briefly, the Regulations provide for two forms of 'relevant transfer': a 'business transfer' and a 'service provision change' (see Chapter 1, 'Identifying a "relevant transfer"'). If either applies, then the following provisions come into play:

- under Reg 4(1) and (2), the contracts of employees who are assigned to the part of a business, or group of employees, that is subject to a relevant transfer will not terminate upon the transfer, but will instead carry on as if they had been agreed between the employees and the new employer (the transferee). All rights, powers, duties and liabilities under or in connection with the employees' contracts of employment made with the old employer (the transferor) pass to the transferee (see Chapter 2, 'Who transfers?', and Chapter 3, 'What transfers?')

- changes to the terms and conditions of transferring employees are restricted by Reg 4(4). The basic position is that changes are void where the sole or principal reason for them is the transfer. But there are exceptions: changes can be agreed where there is an 'economic, technical or organisational reason entailing changes in the workforce'; unilateral changes can be made if authorised by an existing term of the contract; and collectively agreed terms can be altered by agreement once a year has passed since the transfer (see Chapter 5, 'Changing terms and conditions')

- although an employee's contract will automatically transfer under Reg 4, this can be prevented if the employee informs the transferee or transferor that he or she objects to being employed by the transferee – Reg 4(7). The effect of such an objection is the automatic termination of the employee's contract, although this will not amount to a dismissal (see Chapter 2, 'Who transfers?')

- however, an employee's objection to the transfer will not prevent a claim of constructive dismissal in response to a repudiatory breach of contract by the transferor – Reg 4(11). Furthermore, Reg 4(9) establishes that where a transfer involves or would involve a substantial change in working conditions to an employee's material detriment, that employee can resign and regard him or herself as having been dismissed. There is no requirement, for the purposes of Reg 4(9), that the employer's actions even amount to a breach of contract, let alone a repudiatory breach (see Chapter 4, 'Unfair dismissal')

- where the sole or principal reason for an employee's dismissal is the transfer, Reg 7(1) deems it to be automatically unfair for the purposes of the Employment Rights Act 1996 (ERA). If, however, the sole or principal reason for dismissal is 'an economic, technical or organisational reason entailing changes in the workforce', then the dismissal is not deemed to be automatically unfair. Instead, such a dismissal is deemed, for the purposes of the ERA, to be either by reason of redundancy or for 'some other substantial reason', and the fairness of such a dismissal is determined in the ordinary way (see Chapter 4, 'Unfair dismissal')

- Regulations 8 and 9 attempt to promote a 'rescue culture' by making it easier for insolvent businesses to be transferred to new employers. The former prevents the insolvent transferor's pre-existing debts towards the affected employees from passing to the transferee. The latter enables employers and employee representatives to agree changes to terms and conditions of employment if this is done with a view to ensuring the survival of the business and the preservation of jobs (see Chapter 6, 'Transfer of insolvent companies')

- although most of TUPE is concerned with the rights of employees, Reg 11 compels the transferor to supply information about transferring employees to the transferee no later than 28 days before the transfer (see Chapter 8, 'Information and consultation'); and

- Regulation 13 sets out a duty to inform appropriate employee representatives of the transfer and the measures that may be taken in connection with it. If the employer has fewer than ten employees, Reg 13A permits the information to be supplied directly to the employees (see Chapter 8, 'Information and consultation').

Territorial extent

The TUPE Regulations implement the UK's obligations under the Acquired Rights Directive. These require appropriate protections to be put in place for all employees in the UK. As such, it is unsurprising that Reg 1(3) stipulates that the Regulations 'shall extend to Northern Ireland, except where otherwise provided'. Schedule 1 to the Regulations facilitates this by modifying certain provisions in their application to Northern Ireland.

But although the Regulations apply to England, Wales, Scotland and Northern Ireland, they do not have uniform application across the UK. Instead, the unsatisfactory situation that currently prevails is that there are different provisions that need to be taken into account on either side of the Irish Sea. This divergence in TUPE coverage has its roots in the devolution arrangements that apply to Northern Ireland: responsibility for employment law there falls to the Department for Employment and Learning (DfEL), rather than to the Department for Business, Innovation and Skills (BIS), which assumes such responsibility in England, Wales and Scotland. The devolution arrangements mean that S.38 of the Employment Relations Act 1999, the enabling power used to introduce Reg 3(1)(b) and therefore extend TUPE coverage to the vast majority of service provision changes, does not apply to Northern Ireland. As a result, equivalent protection for employees involved in service provision changes had to be set down separately in the Service Provision Change (Protection of Employment) Regulations (Northern Ireland) 2006 SI 2006/177.

More significantly, the devolution arrangements also meant that it was not within BIS's power to extend the 2014 Amendment Regulations to Northern Ireland. Only the DfEL can legislate to implement these changes and, thus far, it has declined to do so. Consequently, the version of the 2006 Regulations that currently applies in Northern Ireland is that which applied to England, Wales and Scotland prior to January 2014. For those involved in business transfers or service provision changes that span Northern Ireland and any other part of the UK, this has added further complication to an already complex process.

Scheme of the Handbook

The scheme of this Handbook is as follows:

- Chapter 1 addresses that most complicated of employment law questions: what is a 'relevant transfer'? It explores the two types of transfer – standard business transfers and service provision changes – to which TUPE applies

- Chapter 2 considers the matter of who will transfer from the transferor to the transferee. In doing so, it sets out the definition of 'employee' for the purposes of the TUPE Regulations, looks at when such an employee will be 'assigned' to the transferring undertaking and discusses the assigned employees' ability to object to the transfer of their employment

- Chapter 3 details the rights, powers, duties, liabilities, acts and omissions that transfer from the transferor to the transferee under TUPE

- Chapter 4 looks at when a dismissal will be rendered automatically unfair owing to its connection with a relevant transfer, and when an employer might be able to avoid an automatically unfair dismissal finding by pointing to an 'economic, technical or organisational reason' for dismissal. It also considers the circumstances in which a constructive dismissal may arise in a TUPE context

- Chapter 5 highlights the types of change to terms and conditions that are expressly permitted and expressly prohibited under the Regulations

- Chapter 6 examines the rules with regard to the transfer of insolvent businesses. In particular, it looks at the specific limitations regarding the transfer of employee debts and liabilities to the transferee and at the special provision permitting employees' terms and conditions of employment to be varied where the transferor is subject to certain insolvency proceedings

- Chapter 7 discusses the impact of a TUPE transfer on an employee's continuity of employment

- Chapter 8 covers the rules governing information and consultation in a TUPE context. It looks at both the duty on the transferor to provide information to the transferee about the employees who are to transfer, and the duty on both transferor and transferee to inform and consult appropriate representatives of employees who may be affected by a relevant transfer

- Chapter 9 considers whether the Regulations apply to a transfer from or to the UK and, if they do, what this might mean in practice. It also broaches the subject of what protection the Regulations bestow on overseas employees

- Chapter 10 discusses the general prohibition on contracting out of employment protection provisions contained in TUPE and considers the limited exceptions that apply

- Chapter 11 explores some of the practical matters – such as due diligence, warranties and indemnities – that should be considered by those involved in a relevant transfer.

The law is stated as at 1 November 2015.

> **This publication aims to provide accurate, authoritative information and comment on the subjects it covers. It is offered to readers on the understanding that the publisher is not in business as a lawyer or consultant.**

1 Identifying a 'relevant transfer'

Business transfers

Service provision changes

Insolvency

The public sector

When does transfer occur?

The Transfer of Undertakings (Protection of Employment) Regulations 2006 **1.1** SI 2006/246 (TUPE) lay down complex rules dealing with enhanced unfair dismissal rights, the preservation of transferring employees' terms and conditions, and the provision of information and consultation. However, none of these rules will take effect without the occurrence of a 'relevant transfer' under Reg 3.

For many years, the identification of a 'relevant transfer' for TUPE purposes was one of the most perplexing matters in the employment law arena. With regard to service provision changes (SPCs) following outsourcing, insourcing or retendering exercises, the shifting sands of European case law concerning the application of the EU Acquired Rights Directive (No.77/187) and its successor (No.2001/23) ('the Acquired Rights Directive'), which TUPE implements in the UK, muddied the waters still further. This confusion led the Labour Government which introduced the 2006 Regulations to make special provision for SPCs by including two definitions of a 'relevant transfer' in Reg 3. The first, Reg 3(1)(a), simply reflects the definition of a 'transfer of an undertaking' contained in the Directive – and hence applies only where the Directive applies. Reg 3(1)(b), however, goes beyond the Directive's requirements to bring many more SPCs within TUPE's scope. The rationale behind this move, as set out in the 2005 Consultation document that preceded the Regulations, was that everyone involved in an outsourcing, retendering, or insourcing exercise 'should know where they stand... so that employers can plan effectively in a climate of fair competition and affected employees are protected as a matter of course'. Although the introduction of Reg 3(1)(b) was intended to simplify matters, it has in fact resulted in a substantial body of case law, much of which has illuminated the numerous circumstances in which an SPC will not amount to a TUPE transfer.

In 2011 the Coalition Government identified Reg 3(1)(b) as a possible example **1.2** of 'gold plating' – i.e. where the transposition of an EU Directive goes considerably further than the minimum requirements. Subsequently, in 2013, the Department for Business, Innovation and Skills (BIS) issued a consultation

1

on amending TUPE, included in which was the proposal to repeal Reg 3(1)(b) and return to a single Directive-led definition of 'relevant transfer'. However, a substantial majority of respondents to the consultation expressed their opposition to this move, and the Government later announced that it had been persuaded to retain Reg 3(1)(b). The upshot of that decision is that there remain two different (although not mutually exclusive) routes by which a 'relevant transfer' covered by TUPE can occur: first, where the Directive-driven definition, contained in Reg 3(1)(a), is satisfied (we refer to this below as a 'business transfer'); and secondly, where a 'service provision change' as defined by Reg 3(1)(b) takes place.

In this chapter we examine both these definitions in detail. We then go on to consider, more specifically, when TUPE might apply in insolvency situations and to transfers within the public sector. Finally, we touch on the matter of when exactly a relevant transfer can be said to take place – an issue of particular concern where a transfer comprises a series of transactions.

Throughout this chapter we refer when relevant to the BIS Guide, 'Employment rights on the transfer of an undertaking' ('the BIS Guide'), which was last updated in January 2014.

1.3 Business transfers

Regulation 3(1)(a) provides that TUPE will apply where there is a 'transfer of an undertaking, business or part of an undertaking or business situated immediately before the transfer in the United Kingdom to another person where there is a transfer of an economic entity which retains its identity'. This cumbersome wording will be familiar to TUPE aficionados. It reflects the definition of a transfer of an undertaking contained in the Acquired Rights Directive, which in turn is based on the extensive case law from the European Court of Justice (ECJ) as to when the transfer rules should take effect.

A preliminary point concerns what to call a transfer under Reg 3(1)(a). One option would be 'transfer of an undertaking', but given that this features prominently in the title of the Regulations, which provide for two distinct types of transfer, it may serve to confuse. In this chapter we shall instead refer to a transfer under Reg 3(1)(a) as a 'business transfer' – the term now adopted in the BIS Guide.

1.4 Breaking Reg 3(1)(a) down, four questions must be answered in the affirmative in order to identify a 'business transfer' under that provision:

- was there a transfer 'to another person'?
- did an 'economic entity' transfer?
- did the economic entity 'retain its identity' after the transfer? and

- was that entity 'situated immediately before the transfer in the United Kingdom'?

We examine these questions in turn below.

Note that, as stated in the introduction to this chapter, outsourcing, insourcing and retendering exercises falling outside the traditional Reg 3(1)(a) definition of a relevant transfer will nevertheless be covered by the TUPE Regulations provided they satisfy the 'service provision change' test set out in Reg 3(1)(b) – see 'Service provision changes' below.

Transfer 'to another person'   1.5
With regard to the method of transfer, Article 1(1)(a) of the Acquired Rights Directive states: 'This Directive shall apply to any transfer of an undertaking... *to another employer as a result of a legal transfer or merger*' (our stress). Transposing this requirement, Reg 3(1)(a) states that TUPE will apply to a 'transfer of an undertaking, business or part of an undertaking or business... *to another person*' (our stress). It has always been accepted that the transfer rules apply to the ordinary sale of a business, conducted between a vendor and a purchaser. However, as we shall see, this is not the only method by which a business transfer can occur. In fact, keen to promote the purpose of the Directive – which is to safeguard employees' rights upon a change of employer – the ECJ has held that the transfer rules can cover an extremely wide range of events, including the termination of a lease and a change of service provider.

Below, we consider the principles to be applied to determine whether a method of transfer is capable of attracting the application of the Directive, and hence Reg 3(1)(a).

Share sales generally not covered. We noted above that Article 1(1)(a) of the   1.6
Acquired Rights Directive expressly applies 'to any transfer of an undertaking... to *another employer*' (our stress). Although the wording of Reg 3(1)(a) differs from that of Article 1(1)(a), stating as it does that a transfer must be 'to another person' rather than 'to another employer', the BIS Guide states: 'To qualify as a business transfer, the identity of the employer must change. The Regulations do not therefore apply to transfers by share take-over because, when a company's shares are sold to new shareholders, there is no transfer of a business or undertaking: the same company continues to be the employer.'

The change in the ownership of the employer brought about by a share sale has no impact in itself on the contractual relations between an employer and its employees. Thus, in Brookes and ors v Borough Care Services Ltd and anor 1998 ICR 1198, EAT, the Appeal Tribunal confirmed that share sales ordinarily fall outside the scope of TUPE, and went so far as to say that TUPE will not apply to a share sale even where the transaction is designed primarily as a means of avoiding liability under the Regulations.

1.7 However, while a share sale itself is not capable of amounting to a transfer, what of the situation where, following a share sale, the purchasing company assumes day-to-day control of its new asset? Two cases have considered this issue. The first was Print Factory (London) 1991 Ltd v Millam 2007 ICR 1331, CA. The claimant, M, had worked for FP Ltd from 1994. In 1999 FP Ltd was sold under a share sale agreement to MC Ltd, which thus became its holding company. In 2005 both companies went into separate administrations, and M was dismissed. On the following day, TPF Ltd purchased MC Ltd from the administrators. M brought a number of claims relating to his dismissal to an employment tribunal, and sought to establish as a preliminary issue that there had been a transfer of his employment in 1999 from FP Ltd to MC Ltd. In the tribunal's view, there had been more than a simple share sale in this case. MC Ltd had taken over the day-to-day running of FP Ltd's business, taking the key management decisions and doing 'far more than a simple shareholder would have done following a simple sale, or... a parent company of a subsidiary would have done in similar circumstances'. Thus, the tribunal stated, although in theory M had still been employed by FP Ltd following that company's sale, he had effectively been employed by MC Ltd. These findings led the tribunal to conclude that this share transfer was covered by TUPE.

On appeal, the EAT overturned the tribunal's decision. In its view, the transaction in question could not be covered by TUPE since, as a matter of law, the subsidiary company, FP Ltd, remained the employer of the employees in question following the share sale. The tribunal had erred in 'piercing the corporate veil' – that is, in looking behind the legal form and concluding that the undertaking in question 'was not in the hands of the legal entity in whose name it was ostensibly run'. The EAT held that 'as a matter of law, it is the corporate entity that runs the business and absent any sham, the courts are entitled to look no further'. Mr Justice Elias, then President of the EAT, commented that 'it may be difficult to justify the different treatment of a transfer of a business and sales of shares regimes, but that distinction is firmly rooted in the law and recent amendments to TUPE have not taken the opportunity to bring the two regimes together'. M appealed to the Court of Appeal.

1.8 The Court of Appeal rejected the EAT's reasoning and reinstated the tribunal's decision that TUPE had applied. Lord Justice Buxton found that, contrary to the findings of the EAT, the tribunal had not 'pierced the corporate veil' in this case. In his view, a piercing of the corporate veil only arises 'when it is established that activity x is carried on by company A, but for policy reasons it is sought to show that in reality the activity is the responsibility of the owner of company A, company B'. That scenario did not pertain here. Rather, the tribunal found that the running of FP Ltd's business (activity x) had actually been carried out by MC Ltd (company B) rather than FP Ltd (company A). The EAT had given insufficient weight to this finding, and had instead concentrated on the legal structure of the two companies concerned. Buxton LJ concluded: 'The legal

4

structure is of course important, but it cannot be conclusive in deciding the issue of whether, within that legal structure, control of the business has been transferred as a matter of fact. That was the conclusion of the employment tribunal, and the EAT demonstrated no proper basis for displacing that conclusion.' Lord Justice Moses agreed, adding that where, following a transfer of shares, a subsidiary is 100 per cent owned by a parent, the question of whether the business has been transferred for the purposes of TUPE is one of fact which must be resolved deploying the experience and expertise of the employment tribunal. He acknowledged that 'the mere fact of control, which will follow from the relationship between parent and subsidiary, will not be sufficient to establish the transfer of the business from subsidiary to parent'. However, in this case the tribunal had 'identified a number of evidential indications, which, in combination, established that control of the business, in the sense of how its day-to-day activities were run, had passed from [FP Ltd] to [MC Ltd]'. It had been entitled to rely on these in concluding that there had been a TUPE transfer in this case.

The second case was Jackson Lloyd Ltd and anor v Smith and ors EAT 0127/13, where JL Ltd carried out the repair and maintenance of properties for providers of social housing. The business was in severe financial difficulties and M Ltd, a subsidiary of MG plc, bought 100 per cent of its shares. In order to preserve JL Ltd's contracts and avoid the risk of triggering a retendering process, the outward appearance was given that JL Ltd remained autonomous, separate and in competition with MG plc. In reality, however, MG plc took over JL Ltd's management, facilities, amenities and functions. An employment tribunal found that, while the share sale to M Ltd did not constitute a relevant transfer, there was a TUPE transfer under Reg 3(1)(a) to MG plc, which took over the day-to-day control of JL Ltd's business. Upholding the tribunal's decision, the EAT commented that Millam (above) is not authority for the proposition that a share sale itself is a transfer, which would be inconsistent with Brookes and ors v Borough Care Services Ltd (above). Rather, in accordance with the approach established in Millam, the tribunal had found that a TUPE transfer took place when day-to-day control of J Ltd's business passed to MG plc.

It therefore seems to remain the case that TUPE will not apply to a share sale **1.9** itself. Accordingly, it will usually be easier from an employer's perspective if a share transfer rather than a business transfer takes place. This is because the special obligations under the TUPE Regulations with regard to unfair dismissal (see Chapter 4, 'Unfair dismissal'), varying terms and conditions of employment (see Chapter 5, 'Changing terms and conditions') and information and consultation (see Chapter 8, 'Information and consultation') will not generally arise in such circumstances. Of course, the affected employees will still be protected to an extent by standard unfair dismissal and contract law.

1.10 **Transfer of undertaking's ownership not required.** It is well established that the Acquired Rights Directive and TUPE can apply even where the absolute ownership of the undertaking in question does not change hands. In fact, Reg 3(6)(b) expressly states that there may be a relevant transfer whether or not any property is transferred from the transferor to the transferee.

The ECJ's decision in Landsorganisationen i Danmark v Ny Mølle Kro 1989 ICR 330, ECJ, illustrates this point well. The events leading to this case began in 1980 when H, the owner of a tavern business, leased one of its taverns to L. Later that year, L, which had begun to run the tavern, concluded a membership agreement with the Association of Hotel and Restaurant Employees, under which it was required to comply with collective agreements entered into by the Association. In January 1981 H rescinded L's lease owing to L's breaching its terms, and took over the management of the business once more. An employee argued that the reversion of the lease to H constituted a transfer of an undertaking and that, consequently, L's obligations to comply with the terms of collective agreements negotiated with the Association passed to H. The Danish Labour Court referred the matter to the ECJ, in order for that court to consider whether the words 'transfer… to another employer, as a result of a legal transfer or merger' contained in Article 1(1)(a) of the Directive could cover a situation where the owner of an undertaking that has been leased takes back the running of the undertaking as a result of the breach of the lease by the managing lessee.

1.11 The ECJ emphasised that the purpose of the Directive is to safeguard, so far as possible, the rights of workers in the event of a change of employer, by allowing them to remain in employment on the same conditions as those agreed with the transferor. With this in mind, the Court felt that the Directive should apply whenever as a result of a legal transfer or merger there is a change in the natural or legal person responsible for the running of the undertaking and who because of this enters into contractual obligations as an employer towards the employees working in the undertaking. This is so, the ECJ continued, regardless of whether ownership of the undertaking has been transferred. In reaching this decision, it noted that the employees of an undertaking which changes its employers without a transfer of ownership are in a comparable situation to that of the employees of an undertaking which has been sold and therefore need equivalent protection. In the instant case, the managing lessee, L, acquired under the lease the capacity of employer, meaning that the transfer of the lease constituted a transfer of an undertaking falling within Article 1(1)(a) of the Directive. When the owner of the undertaking, H, took back the running of the undertaking, that resumption also constituted a transfer, in so far as L lost the capacity of employer and that capacity was reacquired by H.

It follows from this reasoning that the Directive – and hence TUPE – can apply to the granting, terminating, surrendering or assigning of a lease of land or property, where a business is intrinsically linked to such land or property and where, as a result of the transaction, the business changes hands and continues to be run as essentially the same business. So, if the tenant of, say, a petrol station, pub, farm or factory is replaced by the landlord (or indeed, by another tenant) following the transfer of the leasehold premises, those employed in the undertaking will be able to claim the protection of TUPE. This is subject to the usual rule that the undertaking in question retain its identity following the transfer – see 'When does an economic entity retain its identity?' below.

Similarly, the Directive and TUPE can apply to the conferring of a franchise, **1.12** licence or concession. Where, for example, a licensee enters into a contractual arrangement to carry out a business activity, the fact that certain key tangible and intangible assets of the business (e.g. intellectual property, premises and goodwill) continue to be owned by the person conferring the licence will not necessarily prevent the operation of the transfer rules.

Series of transactions can amount to a relevant transfer. Regulation 3(6)(a) **1.13** provides that a relevant transfer may be effected by a series of two or more transactions. This reflects a number of decisions of the ECJ, such as that in Foreningen af Arbejdsledere i Danmark v Daddy's Dance Hall A/S 1988 IRLR 315, ECJ.

In that case T was employed as a manager by IC, which had taken out a non-transferable lease of a restaurant/bar belonging to another company, PT. When IC learned that its lease was to be terminated, it gave its employees notice of dismissal. A new lease was concluded between PT and DDH, as a result of which the latter immediately re-employed the ex-IC staff (including T), albeit on different terms and conditions. Shortly afterwards, T was dismissed. He brought a claim arguing that the transfer rules had applied to transfer his employment from IC to DDH, meaning that he had been entitled to a greater period of notice than that which DDH had given him. The Danish Supreme Court referred the matter to the ECJ, asking whether the Acquired Rights Directive applies where a non-transferable lease is terminated and thereafter the owner, without interruption in the activities of the business, leases it to a new lessee who re-employs the staff of the former lessee.

The ECJ concluded that the Directive did apply in such circumstances. First, it **1.14** repeated the reasoning from Landsorganisationen i Danmark v Ny Mølle Kro (above), stating that the Directive 'applies as soon as there is a change... of the natural or legal person responsible for operating the undertaking who, consequently, enters into obligations as an employer towards the employees working in the undertaking, and it is of no importance to know whether the ownership of the undertaking has been transferred'. But it also went one step further. In the ECJ's view, 'the fact that... the transfer takes place in two phases, in the sense that as a first step the undertaking is transferred back from the original lessee to the owner who then transfers it to the new lessee, does not exclude the applicability of the Directive as long as the economic unit retains its identity'. This view was affirmed by the ECJ in the later case of P Bork International A/S (in liquidation) v Foreningen af Arbejdsledere i Danmark and ors 1989 IRLR 41, ECJ.

Regulation 3(6)(a) – which, to recap, reflects the above ECJ case law in providing that a relevant transfer may be effected by a series of transactions – is potentially wide-ranging. For instance, it can bring the transfer of a business by way of a number of apparently discrete though connected sales (a possible TUPE-avoidance tactic) within the auspices of the Regulations. In Longden and anor v Ferrari Ltd and anor 1994 ICR 443, EAT, Mr Justice Mummery, as he then was, made the point that Reg 3(6)(a) aims to ensure that TUPE applies where 'the parties... arrange for the transfer to be effected in a series of two or more transactions... for no sensible commercial purpose, other than to avoid the consequence of the application of Regulations enacted for the protection of employees'.

1.15 Note that although it is clear that a relevant transfer can be effected by a series of transactions, the decision in Celtec Ltd v Astley and ors 2005 ICR 1409, ECJ, established that it is necessary to identify one specific transfer date. Later in this chapter, in 'When does transfer occur?', we discuss some of the difficulties that the Celtec decision has given rise to in this regard.

1.16 **No contract required between transferor and transferee.** On their face, the words 'legal transfer or merger' in Article 1(1)(a) of the Acquired Rights Directive seem to suggest that a direct relationship between the transferor (the original employer) and the transferee (the new employer) is required in order for the Directive to apply. Case law, however, has shown that this is not so. Take Foreningen af Arbejdsledere i Danmark v Daddy's Dance Hall (above) as an example. There, IC's lease of a restaurant/bar came to an end and the landlord concluded a new lease with DDH. As a result, DDH took over the business previously run by IC. The ECJ held that those employed by IC at the restaurant/bar transferred under the Directive to DDH, rendering IC the 'transferor' and DDH the 'transferee', even though there was no direct relationship between them.

The concept of 'legal transfer' was considered further by the ECJ in Dr Sophie Redmond Stichting v Bartol and ors 1992 IRLR 366, ECJ. The transferor in that case was the Dr Sophie Redmond Foundation, which was funded by a local authority to provide assistance to drug addicts in the Netherlands. The local authority decided to terminate this funding and switch it to the Sigma Foundation (the transferee), which did similar work. Again, although there was no direct relationship between the Dr Sophie Redmond Foundation (which lost the funding) and the Sigma Foundation (which continued the work), the ECJ decided that the Directive applied, meaning that the employees working on the project transferred from one to the other. Having examined the previous case law, such as Daddy's Dance Hall and Bork (above), the Court accepted that the concept of a 'legal transfer' in Article 1(1) of the Directive must be broadly interpreted. It concluded that a legal transfer can be said to occur where 'a public body decides to terminate a subsidy paid to one legal person, as a result of which the activities of that legal person are fully and definitively terminated, and to transfer it to another legal person with similar aims', so long as the undertaking in question retains its identity. This is so whether the decision leading to the transfer was taken unilaterally by the public body or with the agreement of the body subsidised. The Court noted that 'there is equally a unilateral decision where an owner decides to change a lessee, a situation which the Court has held may fall within the scope of the Directive'.

Service provision changes. As the 1980s progressed, more and more bodies **1.17** began to outsource services such as cleaning and catering. The question soon arose as to whether the 'transfer' of such activities to an external service provider could attract the application of the Acquired Rights Directive. Unsurprisingly – given the principles set out in the cases outlined above – the ECJ in Rask and anor v ISS Kantineservice A/S 1993 IRLR 133, ECJ, answered this question in the affirmative. The Court decided that the Directive can apply to outsourcing where the owner of an undertaking entrusts to another, by means of contract, the responsibility for providing a service. This was so regardless of the fact that the activity transferred was only ancillary to the transferor's business.

It is now clear that the Directive and TUPE are capable of applying not only to outsourcing exercises but also to insourcing exercises and changes of service provider. However, the question of whether they actually do apply to a given set of facts has often proved difficult to answer. The problems that courts and tribunals have faced over the years in this regard are rehearsed at length under 'What is an "economic entity"?' and 'When does an economic entity retain its identity?' below. To remove the uncertainty, the 2006 Regulations included a second definition of 'relevant transfer' – Reg 3(1)(b) – to make it clear that the majority of service provision changes are now covered by TUPE. We discuss this rule later in this chapter under 'Service provision changes'.

Reorganisation within group of companies. In Allen and ors v Amalgamated **1.18** Construction Co Ltd 2000 ICR 436, ECJ, the European Court held that the Acquired Rights Directive, and hence TUPE, can apply to a business transfer between two companies within a group. This is so even where the companies have the same ownership, management and premises, and are engaged in the same activity. Simply put, this is because there is a change of employer in such circumstances – the two group companies in the Allen case were distinct legal persons, each having specific relationships with their employees. It followed, held the ECJ, that the Directive would apply where a group company decided to subcontract to another company in the same group work and labour for driveage work in mines, provided that the transaction involved the transfer of an economic entity, the identity of which was retained after the transfer.

A similar approach was taken by the ECJ in Ferreira da Silva e Brito and ors v Estado Português Case C-160/14, ECJ. In that case an airline, TAP, had wound up its charter subsidiary, AIA. TAP replaced AIA in contracts with tour operators, took over some of the charter routes previously flown by AIA and the lease of four of its aircraft, and employed some of its staff, who had previously been seconded to AIA in roles which were effectively identical. The ECJ considered that these facts brought the situation within the scope of Article 1(1) of the Directive. The fact that AIA's business had not retained an autonomous organisational structure, and had instead been integrated into TAP's existing structure, did not prevent the application of the Directive. This was because a link had been preserved between the assets and staff transferred to TAP on the one hand and the pursuit of activities previously carried on by AIA on the other. Given that link, it was immaterial that the assets and staff taken on by TAP had also been used to carry out scheduled flights.

1.19 **Court orders.** The transfer rules can apply where a court orders the transfer of a business. In Berg and anor v Besselsen 1990 ICR 396, ECJ, the European Court held that there was a transfer of an undertaking to which the Acquired Rights Directive applied when a lease/purchase agreement recognised under the law of the Netherlands was terminated by judicial decision. In that case, the business – a bar/discotheque – was owned and run by B, which transferred its operation, along with its employees, to S under a lease/purchase agreement. Under this type of agreement, the ownership of the business did not pass to S at this point. In time, the Dutch Court set aside the lease/purchase agreement before ownership had transferred, and ordered the business to be returned to B. The ECJ decided that there had been a transfer covered by the Directive when the business passed to S, and that there had also been a transfer covered by the Directive when the business returned by court order to B. Thus, B was responsible for all the arrears of pay due to employees for the period when S ran the business.

1.20 **Regulatory interventions.** A regulatory intervention may also lead to a TUPE transfer. In Rose v Dodd 2005 ICR 1776, CA, the Law Society, using its statutory powers under the Solicitors Act 1974, intervened in the practice of Reynolds and Dodd when the principal of the firm was suspected of dishonesty. The Law Society appointed as its agents another firm of solicitors to carry out the intervention and take full control of Reynolds and Dodd. A couple of months after the intervention, the firm's business was transferred, with court approval, to another firm of solicitors. The Court of Appeal held that employment of R, an employee of Reynolds and Dodd, had transferred under TUPE to the new firm.

Companies struck off Register. In Charlton and anor v Charlton **1.21** Thermosystems (Romsey) Ltd and anor 1995 ICR 56, EAT, Mr and Mrs Charlton were the sole directors and shareholders of a heating company. The company was struck off the Register of Companies for failing to file annual accounts, and was dissolved. Thereafter, however, Mr and Mrs Charlton continued to run the business. The EAT upheld an employment tribunal's finding that a relevant transfer had occurred, stating: 'Although the company was dissolved on 30 October 1990, the business retained its identity in the hands of Mr and Mrs Charlton, formerly directors of the company, who continued the operation, using the same assets and employees as the company had.'

Similarly, in Karalia Ltd v Eracli EAT 453/97, the EAT held that a TUPE transfer had occurred where the transferor, E Ltd, had been struck off the Register, and its business had continued immediately in the hands of a newly created company, A Ltd.

Unlawful activities and unlawful purposes. In Ejiofor t/a Mitchell and Co **1.22** Solicitors v Sullivan and ors EAT 0268/13 the EAT accepted that an undertaking must be lawful to fall within the scope of TUPE and that if it was for an inherently unlawful purpose, such as money laundering or drug dealing, TUPE would not apply. In the case before it, an employment tribunal had found that there was a relevant transfer when a small solicitors' firm changed hands. On appeal, it was argued that the business carried on before the notional transfer was unlawful because one of the firm's solicitors had been struck off the Roll of Solicitors. Upholding the tribunal's decision, the EAT stressed that TUPE does not require that all of the activities being transferred be entirely lawful. In this case, it was possible that the lack of certain qualifications held by certain people would have made some of the firm's activities unlawful at certain times, but the business was not carried on for an unlawful purpose – it was perfectly lawful to provide legal advice.

Public and private sector. Regulation 3(4)(a) stipulates that TUPE applies 'to **1.23** public and private undertakings'. It is clear that transfers both to and from the public sector can be covered by the rules. See 'The public sector' below for further details.

Insolvency. If a business gets into extreme financial difficulties, an insolvency **1.24** practitioner can be appointed either to keep the business running with a view to the sale of the whole or part of it as a going concern, or to wind it up and sell off its assets. Put extremely simply, the Acquired Rights Directive and Reg 3(1)(a) will apply to a transfer instigated by an insolvency practitioner in the former set of circumstances, but not the latter. We discuss this issue more fully in 'Insolvency' below.

1.25 What is an 'economic entity'?

Under Reg 3(1)(a) there is a 'relevant transfer' of an undertaking or part of an undertaking only where 'there is the transfer of an *economic entity which retains its identity*' (our stress). The italicised wording, which mirrors that of Article 1(1)(b) of the Acquired Rights Directive, is derived from the ECJ's decision in Spijkers v Gebroeders Benedik Abattoir CV and anor 1986 2 CMLR 296, ECJ, and was incorporated into the Directive when an updated version was issued in 2003.

In Whitewater Leisure Management Ltd v Barnes and ors 2000 ICR 1049, EAT, the Appeal Tribunal advised that 'it will normally be best and clearest for an employment tribunal to deal first with the question of whether there was a relevant and sufficiently identifiable economic entity, and then proceed, whatever be the answer to that question, to ask and answer whether there was... a relevant transfer of any such entity'. The EAT in Cheesman and ors v R Brewer Contracts Ltd 2001 IRLR 144, EAT, agreed, adding that 'whilst we do not say that it is invariably an error of law not to raise those two questions as separate questions or to fail to deal with them in that order, a tribunal which so fails runs a real risk of error'. Thus, when distilling UK and ECJ case law into guidance as to what amounts to a relevant transfer (which we set out below), the EAT in Cheesman attempted 'to divide considerations between those going to whether there is an undertaking and those, if there is an undertaking, going to whether it has been transferred'. In this chapter, we adopt the EAT's approach, focusing in this section on what might constitute an economic entity, before turning to the circumstances in which such an entity can be said to have retained its identity.

1.26 'Economic entity' is defined by Reg 3(2) (and indeed by Article 1(1)(b) of the Directive) as 'an organised grouping of resources which has the objective of pursuing an economic activity, whether or not that activity is central or ancillary'. Without more, this rather abstract definition is not particularly helpful. Thankfully, however, its meaning can be teased out by examining the case law.

Before we examine Reg 3(2) in detail, it should first be noted that, in essence, the question of whether an economic entity exists is a question of fact for the employment tribunal to decide. Since appeals from a tribunal to the EAT lie only on questions of law and not on questions of fact, decisions in this area are in theory difficult to challenge. Nevertheless, an error of law can arise if a tribunal, carrying out its assessment of the facts, fails to take into account a relevant factor, takes into account an irrelevant factor, or reaches an unsustainable conclusion on the facts found. Given that the definition of 'economic entity' in Reg 3(2) and the case law giving rise to it is fairly complicated, arguments as to which factors are relevant and which are irrelevant have become commonplace.

12

The Cheesman guidelines. Having trawled through decisions of both the UK 1.27 courts and the ECJ, the EAT in Cheesman and ors v R Brewer Contracts Ltd 2001 IRLR 144, EAT, set out the following principles with regard to the question of whether there is an 'economic entity' in existence:

- there needs to be a stable economic entity, which is an organised grouping of persons and of assets enabling (or facilitating) the exercise of an economic activity that pursues a specific objective. There will not be such an entity if its activity is limited to performing one specific works contract. It has been held that the reference to 'one specific works contract' is to be restricted to a contract for building works

- in order to be such an undertaking it must be sufficiently structured and autonomous but will not necessarily have significant tangible or intangible assets

- in certain sectors such as cleaning and surveillance the assets are often reduced to their most basic and the activity is essentially based on manpower

- an organised grouping of wage-earners who are specifically and permanently assigned to a common task may, in the absence of other factors of production, amount to an economic entity; and

- an activity is not of itself an entity; the identity of an entity emerges from other factors, such as its workforce, management staff, the way in which its work is organised, its operating methods and, where appropriate, the operational resources available to it.

As with the Reg 3(2) definition of 'economic entity', which is set out under 'What is an "economic entity"?' above, the Cheesman guidance is unlikely to leave non-TUPE experts much the wiser unless it is unpicked. Below, we explain the key principles in more detail and examine the cases in which they were laid down.

Organised grouping of resources. The expression 'organised grouping of 1.28 resources' found in Reg 3(2) derives from the case of Süzen v Zehnacker Gebäudereinigung GmbH Krankenhausservice 1997 ICR 662, ECJ, in which the ECJ ruled that the term 'economic entity' refers to 'an organised grouping of persons and assets facilitating the exercise of an economic activity which pursues a specific objective'. The ECJ also pronounced that an economic activity, in itself, is not sufficient to amount to an economic entity, stating that 'an entity cannot be reduced to the activity entrusted to it. Its identity also emerges from other factors, such as its workforce, its management staff, the way in which its work is organised, its operating methods or indeed, where appropriate, the operational resources available to it'.

In many 'business transfer' situations it will be self-evident that there is an organised grouping of resources – comprising, for example, physical and intangible assets (the latter including goodwill and intellectual property rights), the workforce, premises, customers, operating systems, etc. However, where this is unclear – perhaps where there is a transfer of part of a business only, or a service provision change – the following principles should be applied.

1.29 *Entity must be sufficiently structured and autonomous.* In Francisco Hernández Vidal SA v Gómez Pérez and ors 1999 IRLR 132 and Sánchez Hidalgo and ors v Asociación de Servicios Aser and ors 1999 IRLR 136, ECJ, the European Court explained that a group of resources pursuing an economic activity must be 'sufficiently structured and autonomous' in order to constitute an economic entity. In the following two cases the EAT suggested that, on the facts, no such structure and autonomy existed:

- **Wynnwith Engineering Co Ltd v Bennett and ors** 2002 IRLR 170, EAT: the claimants in this case took early retirement from British Aerospace, and were thereafter provided as agency workers to British Aerospace by W Ltd. When they were dismissed, they brought tribunal claims, in the course of which the question arose as to whether there had been a 'relevant transfer' from British Aerospace to W Ltd. An employment tribunal held that there had been such a transfer, but this decision was overturned by the EAT. The EAT noted that, in considering whether there had been an economic entity, the function of the employees had to be taken into account. In this case the employees carried out different functions across various parts of the employer's business. The fact that they shared the same employment status because they had taken early retirement and worked on short-term contracts was not sufficient to establish the existence of an economic entity that retained its identity after a transfer

- **Whitewater Leisure Management Ltd v Barnes and ors** 2000 ICR 1049, EAT: a leisure centre was managed by W Ltd under a management contract. W Ltd also managed other operations. Six employees of W Ltd's senior management team were involved with the centre, but the majority of their time was spent managing other aspects of W Ltd's business. A second group of W Ltd's employees at the centre – the core team – consisted of a manager, two assistant managers and 11 other full-time employees. A third group of employees included a general mix of part-time, casual and seasonal staff. W Ltd ran the Centre for six years, but then lost the contract to do so to the in-house team of the East Riding Yorkshire Council. None of the six senior managers moved to the Council, instead remaining employed by W Ltd. Of the 'core' team, seven of the 14 employees were taken on by the Council and seven stayed with W Ltd. The majority of the third group remained with W Ltd. The employees who did move across claimed that their continuity of employment had been preserved owing to the operation of TUPE. An employment tribunal disagreed, and the EAT upheld the tribunal's decision. In doing so, the EAT stated that, in this case, it was arguable that there had not been a stable and discrete entity, or a sufficiently structured and autonomous entity, because of the fact that the leisure centre was so intricately bound up with the rest of the outgoing contractor's operations. The senior management was plainly not discrete in so far as it spent the majority of its time working in other areas; and even if the management team was left out of account, it remained highly arguable that the entity in question was not autonomous.

Entity need not be 'separate' in hands of transferor. The above cases emphasised **1.30** that, in order for a business transfer to take place, a structured and autonomous economic entity must exist. In Fairhurst Ward Abbotts Ltd v Botes Building Ltd and ors 2004 ICR 919, CA, however, the Court of Appeal held that, where a transfer of a part of an undertaking takes place, the part in question need not itself exist as a discrete economic entity prior to its transfer.

The facts of the Fairhurst case were as follows. In April 1996 the London Borough of Southwark awarded B Ltd a three-year contract for the maintenance and alteration of its void domestic dwellings ('the Major Voids Contract'). A number of the Borough's employees, including the eight individuals involved in this case, transferred to B Ltd under TUPE. Towards the end of B Ltd's contract, the Borough decided to divide in two the geographical area covered by the original Major Voids Contract and invited separate tenders in respect of the two areas. FWA Ltd won the contract for Area 2. In B Ltd's opinion, TUPE applied to transfer the eight employees in question from it to FWA Ltd. FWA Ltd, however, refused to take the employees on. Consequently, from April 1999 the eight found themselves without an employer, and they launched proceedings in the employment tribunal claiming that they had been unfairly dismissed by either FWA Ltd or B Ltd. Naturally, the question arose as to whether a relevant transfer had occurred. When the case reached the Court of Appeal, FWA Ltd argued that the contract relating to Area 2 could not have transferred under TUPE because it had not existed as an identifiable economic entity before the alleged transfer took place.

The Court of Appeal accepted that, in order for TUPE to apply to a transfer, a **1.31** stable economic entity – being an organised grouping of persons and assets enabling or facilitating the exercise of an economic activity that pursues a specific objective – must be identifiable as existing in the hands of the transferor before the transfer takes place. However, neither legislation nor case law requires, in order for TUPE to apply to the transfer of part of an undertaking, that the part in question itself exists as an identifiable, stable, economic entity prior to its transfer. It is sufficient that part of an economic entity becomes identifiable as a separate economic entity on the occasion of the transfer separating the part from the whole. The Court noted that the aim of the Acquired Rights Directive and of TUPE is to preserve the continuity of employment relationships within an undertaking. In its view, this aim does not require a distinction to be drawn between a case where the part of an undertaking transferred was identifiable as a discrete part before the transfer on the one hand, and a case where the part transferred became identifiable as a separate entity only at the time of the transfer on the other. In the circumstances, the Court upheld an employment tribunal's decision that TUPE applied in this case.

1.32 **Significant assets not required.** It is established that although an 'economic entity' must be 'sufficiently structured and autonomous', it will not necessarily have significant tangible or intangible assets. As the ECJ noted in Francisco Hernández Vidal SA v Gómez Pérez and ors (above), in certain labour-intensive sectors of the economy (such as cleaning and surveillance) those elements are often minimal. With this in mind, the Court concluded that 'an organised grouping of wage earners who are specifically and permanently assigned to a common task may, in the absence of other factors of production, amount to an economic entity'.

A similar line was taken in Jouini v Princess Personal Service GmbH 2008 ICR 128, ECJ, when the European Court considered whether the Acquired Rights Directive applied to the situation where workers of a temporary employment business transferred to another temporary employment business in order to carry out the same activities for the same client. Finding that the Directive did indeed apply, the ECJ held that the fact that the workers assigned on a temporary basis were integrated in the organisational structure of the client to whom they are assigned was not capable, as such, of precluding a finding that an economic entity has been transferred. Those workers were nonetheless essential assets, without which the temporary employment business would, by definition, not be capable of performing its economic activity. A single grouping, consisting of management personnel, temporary workers and know-how, can pursue the objective of supplying temporary workers to businesses in return for remuneration, and such a grouping can constitute an economic entity which can operate without recourse to other significant assets or to other parts of the transferor.

1.33 **An 'economic entity' may have only one employee.** In Schmidt v Spar- und Leihkasse der früheren Ämter Bordesholm, Kiel und Cronshagen 1995 ICR 237, ECJ, the ECJ held that the fact that an economic activity is performed by a single employee is not sufficient, in itself, to preclude the application of the Acquired Rights Directive. The Court concluded that the Directive covers a situation 'in which an undertaking entrusts by contract to another undertaking the responsibility for carrying out cleaning operations which it previously performed itself, even though, prior to the transfer, such work was carried out by a single employee'. The Schmidt decision was expressly approved by the ECJ in Süzen v Zehnacker Gebäudereinigung GmbH Krankenhausservice (above). Yet, as we have seen, the ECJ in Süzen went on to define the term 'economic

16

entity' as 'an organised grouping of *persons* and assets' (our stress). Does this suggest that more than one employee is actually required?

The EAT had the opportunity to ponder this matter in Dudley Bower Building Services Ltd v Lowe and ors EAT 856/01. It was called upon to consider an employer's appeal against a tribunal's finding that a set of maintenance duties performed essentially by a single employee had amounted to an economic entity capable of being transferred under TUPE. The employee in question was L, who was employed by WSA Ltd to perform 'response maintenance' of various pieces of electrical equipment at RAF Cosford. This work comprised 'package six' of WSA Ltd's building management duties at the site. In time, WSA Ltd lost its contract and the MoD accepted a tender from S Ltd. S Ltd then subcontracted the 'package six' duties to WB, which did not take L on. L brought claims against WSA Ltd, S Ltd and WB, arguing that his employment had been protected by TUPE. The employment tribunal upheld his claims, and DBBS Ltd, which in the meantime had acquired WB, appealed against the tribunal's decision. It argued that, in the light of the ECJ's comments in cases such as Süzen, the performance of contractual duties by a single employee was not, in itself, sufficient to amount to an economic entity. In this case, 'package six' had consisted of nothing more than the performance of a number of duties by L, in respect of which there had been no management role, and which could not be described as sufficiently structured or autonomous to attract the application of the transfer rules.

Like the tribunal before it, however, the EAT accepted that there is no reason in principle why work performed by a single person cannot amount to an economic entity. It noted that the Schmidt decision had not been overruled or disapproved and stated that, in its view, the words 'grouping of persons' contained in Süzen and other cases did not suggest that more than one employee is required for such an entity to exist. The EAT noted, however, that the ECJ in Schmidt did not decide that the performance of contractual duties by a single employee is in itself sufficient to indicate the existence of a stable economic entity. Whether an entity is sufficiently structured and autonomous for the Acquired Rights Directive (and thus Reg 3(1)(a)) to apply to its transfer will depend on the facts of the case. The EAT pointed out that 'at one extreme, if the activity consists of no more than one cleaning lady and her mop, an economic entity may not exist, whereas if the task to be performed is complex and sophisticated and requires careful planning, specification and costings, it may be that an entity exists even though the work is performed by a single employee'. **1.34**

Turning to the facts of the case in question, the EAT held that there had been material upon which the tribunal had been entitled to decide that a transferable economic entity had been in existence. Although the 'package six' duties had been performed essentially by one employee, the facts 'demonstrated a well established, sophisticated operation'. A complex pricing structure had been laid down; each task had needed to be authorised and prioritised; and the performance of the duties had taken place within a disciplined and technical framework. Accordingly, the EAT dismissed DBBS Ltd's appeal.

1.35 **Requirement of stability – single specific works contracts not covered.** In the aforementioned cases, reference to the term 'stable economic entity' was often made by the courts when describing that which is capable of being transferred under the Acquired Rights Directive. Although the word 'stable' does not appear in the Directive's definition of an economic entity (and nor, for that matter, is it found in the TUPE Regulations), the ECJ, in Ledernes Hovedorganisation, acting for Rygaard v Dansk Arbejdsgiverforening, acting for Strø Mølle Akustik A/S 1996 ICR 333, ECJ, emphasised that 'stability' of an entity is a prerequisite of the Directive's application. This is reflected in the Cheesman guidance, set out under 'The Cheesman guidelines' above.

In the Rygaard case, R was employed by a firm of carpenters, SP, which was contracted by SAS to build a canteen. SP told SAS that they wanted another company, SM, to complete the final stages of the work. SM subsequently entered into a contract with SAS, agreeing to do so. The question arose as to whether SP's employees who had been working on the building project were protected by the Directive, meaning that their employment transferred to SM. When this matter was referred to the ECJ, that court explained that a distinction must be drawn between the mere loss of a contract and the transfer of a stable entity. To be stable, the entity has to have an expectation of continuing or future work, with its activity not limited to the performance of one specific works contract. The ECJ went on to hold that the Directive did not apply where there was a transfer from one undertaking to another of building works with a view to the completion of those works in circumstances where the transferor merely made available to the new contractor certain workers and materials for carrying out the works in question. Such a transfer could come within the terms of the Directive only if it included the transfer of a body of assets enabling the activities or certain activities of the transferor undertaking to be carried on in a stable way.

1.36 The UK courts and tribunals have, in general, downplayed the significance of the Rygaard case, deciding that it limits the Acquired Rights Directive's application only in narrowly defined circumstances. Three case illustrations:

- **Balfour Beatty Power Networks Ltd and anor v Wilcox and ors** 2007 IRLR 63, CA: H plc provided street lighting services, under a number of different contracts, for WPB. In time, it lost two of these contracts – a jointing contract and an aerial supply contract – one of which was awarded to BB Ltd and the other to Interserve. The new contractors did not take on all the employees dedicated to the contracts in question, and some of the spurned employees brought tribunal claims, arguing that TUPE applied. An employment tribunal held, for various reasons, that no relevant transfer had occurred from H plc to BB Ltd, but that such a transfer had taken place from H plc to Interserve. Interserve appealed to the EAT and then to the Court of Appeal, which held that the tribunal had not erred in finding that the aerial supply contract had amounted to a stable economic entity capable of transferring under TUPE from H plc to Interserve, even though there was no guarantee that the contract would continue and where, in fact, the contract was lost shortly after the transfer. Lord Justice Buxton stated that 'an enterprise may be stable as a matter of practical and industrial reality, even though its long-term future is not secured'

- **Argyll Training Ltd v Sinclair and anor** 2000 IRLR 630, EAT: AIE was set up to provide training to enterprise companies in Scotland. It subcontracted the provision of training services in the Argyll area to another company, BEST, which was responsible for, among other things, the placement of trainees with employers. S was employed by BEST as a training adviser. Her work was directed exclusively to the contract with AIE and she had sole responsibility for organising placements in Argyll. In May 1998, having learned that it had lost its contract with AIE, BEST terminated all training placements and made S redundant. A few weeks later another contractor, ATL, took over the arrangements for the former BEST trainees with retrospective effect. Of the 42 trainees who had been on BEST's books, 21 transferred to ATL's. S succeeded with a tribunal claim that she had been dismissed in connection with a transfer of an undertaking from BEST to ATL, and ATL appealed to the EAT. It argued, with reference to the ECJ's decision in Rygaard, that TUPE had not applied in this case, as the activity in question had been limited to one specific contract. The EAT, however, was not persuaded by ATL's argument. Having examined the cases of Spijkers and Schmidt (above), both of which were referred to in the Rygaard decision, the EAT stated that there was no basis for automatically excluding all single-contract undertakings from the possibility of transferring under the Directive. The EAT felt supported in this regard by the Süzen case (above), in which a school's contracted-out cleaning services transferred from one contractor to another. If the relevant undertaking in Süzen was the cleaning of the particular school, that could be described as an activity limited to one specific contract. However, the ECJ in Süzen had clearly not regarded the entity as being insufficiently stable to attract the Directive's application. The EAT concluded that the proposition derived from Rygaard – that the Directive does not apply to an activity 'limited to performing one specific works contract' – must 'be taken to be restricted to single specific contracts for building works'. Thus restricted, the Rygaard principle could not assist ATL, whose appeal was dismissed

- **BSG Property Services v Tuck and ors** 1996 IRLR 134, EAT: T and 13 others were employed by Mid-Bedfordshire District Council in the Housing Maintenance Direct Services Organisation (DSO) to carry out maintenance on council houses. In 1992 the Council decided that the DSO could no longer carry out the maintenance services economically. It gave the DSO employees notice of dismissal, and signed a contract with BSG under which that organisation agreed to provide the services. BSG did not take on the DSO employees, instead using a pool of self-employed workers to carry out the work. The DSO employees brought tribunal claims arguing that TUPE had applied, meaning that they had been unfairly dismissed by BSG, the transferee employer. The employment tribunal upheld their claims and BSG appealed to the EAT. It argued that TUPE had not applied in this case as there had been no 'stable economic entity' as required by the ECJ's ruling in Rygaard. In its view, the 'entity' in question had 'lacked organisational stability'. At best, the 'activity' amounted to 'the opportunity to carry out response maintenance work essentially under a series of works contracts, as and when required'. The EAT, however, dismissed BSG's appeal, stating that 'the requirement of "the stable economic entity" has to be read in the context of [the Rygaard] case and is apt to exclude activities under a short-term, one-off contract'. In the EAT's view, the 'continued and recurrent maintenance activities in this case' did not fall within this description, and were capable of transferring under the transfer rules.

1.37 The most restrictive approach seen in the above cases was that of the EAT in Argyll, which decided that the 'Rygaard principle' – that the Directive does not apply to an activity 'limited to performing one specific works contract' – is relevant only to single, specific contracts for building works. The EAT's decision in Argyll was referred to specifically in the Cheesman guidelines as to what amounts to an economic entity (see 'The Cheesman guidelines' above). It is worth bearing in mind, however, that the Cheesman guidelines appeared hot on the heels of the Argyll decision, meaning that Argyll was fresh in the EAT's mind at that time. In the years following the Cheesman guidelines, courts and tribunals have at times moved away from restricting Rygaard to the building arena.

In Mackie v Aberdeen City Council 2006 All ER 297, Ct Sess (Inner House), for example, the Court of Session decided that Rygaard applied to prevent the application of TUPE, even though the 'entity' under scrutiny was not concerned with building works. In that case, M was employed by S Ltd, which agreed to provide to the Council an 'operational smart card system' to be used for the cash-free payment of meals by schoolchildren and as a bus pass for senior citizens. The contract was for a fixed price and for a fixed task. Towards the end of the contract, M was offered employment with the Council. Though her new post involved some tasks related to the card scheme, she was primarily involved in work which went beyond anything she had undertaken at S Ltd. In time, she brought a number of claims before an employment tribunal, and the issue arose as to whether her move from S Ltd to the Council had been covered by TUPE. The matter eventually came before the Court of Session (Inner

House), which held that the tribunal had been correct to conclude that this case had involved the performance of a single contract of limited duration which, on the authority of Rygaard, could not amount to a stable economic entity capable of transferring under Reg 3(1)(a). It was clear that S Ltd had a contract to perform a particular and clearly defined task – the production of the smart card. The running of the smart-card system was always intended to be a matter for the Council. The Court stated: 'It is evident from the authorities that where the work in which the employee of the alleged transferor employer is involved is that of a single, one-off contract, there cannot be said to be an undertaking to which TUPE applies and it is in that context that the term "stable economic entity" is used.'

'Economic activity' does not require pursuit of profit. Regulation 3(4)(a) **1.38** stipulates that 'these Regulations apply to public and private undertakings engaged in economic activities *whether or not they are operating for gain*' (our stress). This implements Article 1(1)(c) of the Acquired Rights Directive, which in turn codifies the principle set out in the ECJ's decision in Dr Sophie Redmond Stichting v Bartol and ors 1992 IRLR 366, ECJ, which we discussed under 'Transfer "to another person"' above. To recap, the Dr Sophie Redmond Foundation was funded by grants from the local authority to provide assistance to drug addicts in the Netherlands. In time, the local authority decided to terminate its subsidy to the Redmond Foundation and switch it to the Sigma Foundation, which did similar work. Considering whether the Directive could apply to transfer employees from Redmond to Sigma, the ECJ stated: 'In accordance with the approach of the Court to give a sufficiently broad interpretation to the concept of "legal transfer" in Article 1.1 of the [Directive] there is a legal transfer where a public body decides to terminate a subsidy paid to one legal person as a result of which the activities of that person are terminated and transferred to another legal person with similar aims.'

Activities may be 'central or ancillary'. The last part of Reg 3(2) states that an **1.39** economic activity can amount to an economic entity capable of transferring under TUPE 'whether or not that activity is central or ancillary'. This wording makes the simple point – pertinent in particular to service provision changes – that the fact that a transferred activity is unconnected to the transferor's central activity does not exclude that operation from the scope of the Regulations.

The language of Reg 3(2) in this regard is taken from the ECJ's decision in Rask and anor v ISS Kantineservice A/S 1993 IRLR 133, ECJ. There, R was employed by Philips in a company canteen until 1 January 1989 when, following the contracting-out of the canteen services, she was taken on by the contractor, ISS. ISS attempted to change some of R's terms and conditions, but R refused to accept the changes and, as a result, was dismissed. R sought compensation before the national court in Copenhagen, which referred questions to the ECJ as to whether the Acquired Rights Directive had applied. The ECJ held that the situation where a company entrusts the responsibility for operating part of its business, such as a canteen, to another company, which thereby assumes responsibility as employer with regard to the employees working in that part, is capable of attracting the transfer rules. It went on to state: 'The fact that, in such a case, the activity transferred is only an ancillary activity of the transferor undertaking not necessarily related to its objects cannot have the effect of excluding that transaction from the scope of the Directive.'

1.40 **Seagoing vessels excluded.** Article 1.3 of the Acquired Rights Directive states that 'this Directive shall not apply to seagoing vessels'. Thus, the sale of a ship (with its crew) will not amount to a transfer within the meaning of Reg 3(1)(a). Note however, that in Castle View Services Ltd v Howes and ors 2000 SLT 696, Ct Sess (Inner House), the Court of Session set out its obiter (i.e. non-binding) view that TUPE would apply where the whole of a shipping business, including its ships, is sold.

1.41 **Public administration.** Regulation 3(4)(a) TUPE states that 'these Regulations apply to public and private undertakings engaged in economic activities'. However, Reg 3(5), reflecting ECJ case law, then provides that 'an administrative reorganisation of public administrative authorities or the transfer of administrative functions between public administrative authorities is not a relevant transfer'. We examine Reg 3(5), together with other matters to consider when a public sector employer is involved in a potential transfer situation, under 'The public sector' below.

1.42 **When does an economic entity retain its identity?**
It is one thing to identify an 'economic entity', but another thing altogether to conclude that such an entity 'retains its identity' following a transfer. Nevertheless, if the entity in question does not retain its identity, the transaction will fall outside both the Acquired Rights Directive and Reg 3(1)(a). The retention of identity issue has presented UK courts and tribunals with all manner of problems over the years, owing to the confusing messages from the European Court of Justice.

As with the question of whether an economic entity exists, the question of whether such an entity retains its identity is, at its heart, a question of fact for the employment tribunal. As we have noted, appeals from a tribunal to the EAT lie only on questions of law, and not on questions of fact. However, owing to the conflicting nature of the ECJ's decisions as to which factors should be taken into account in different sets of circumstances, it has regularly been possible for parties to appeal to the EAT, arguing that tribunals have failed to apply the law emanating from the European Court correctly.

1.43 **Introduction – the Spijkers test.** We start our examination of this somewhat tricky issue by focusing on the seminal case of Spijkers v Gebroeders Benedik Abattoir CV and anor 1986 2 CMLR 296, ECJ, from which the phrase 'retains its identity' is derived. In that case the ECJ stated: 'The decisive criterion for establishing the existence of a transfer within the meaning of the Directive is whether the entity in question retains its identity.' In its view, 'it is necessary to consider whether, having regard to all the facts characterising the transaction, the business was disposed of as a going concern'. This 'will be apparent from the fact that its operation is actually being continued or has been taken over by the new employer with the same economic or similar activity'. Furthermore, in order to decide whether such retention of identity has occurred, 'it is necessary to take account of all the factual circumstances of the transaction in question', including:

- the type of business or undertaking

- the transfer or otherwise of tangible assets such as buildings and stocks

- the value of intangible assets at the date of transfer

- whether the majority of the staff are taken over by the new employer

- the transfer or otherwise of customers

- the degree of similarity of activities before and after the transfer, and

- the duration of any interruption in these activities.

However, the ECJ continued, the above are merely factors in the overall assessment and 'cannot therefore be considered in isolation'. This suggests that no single factor is decisive, and that not all the 'criteria' need to be satisfied in order for the Acquired Rights Directive – and thus Reg 3(1)(a) – to apply. This 'multi-factorial' approach did not provide the formulaic certainty that the business community might have wished for.

1.44 Things became even more unclear in the mid-to-late 1990s, when the ECJ reached a series of arguably conflicting decisions as to when it could be said that an economic entity retains its identity following a service provision change (SPC). The uncertainty in this regard gave rise to a plethora of case law at both European and domestic level.

Below, we set out the main principles with regard to retention of identity as established by the EAT in Cheesman and ors v R Brewer Contracts Ltd 2001 IRLR 144, EAT. We then go on to examine some of the aspects of the 'Spijkers test' in more detail, before turning to the problems that have arisen in the SPC arena.

1.45 **The Cheesman guidelines.** The EAT's main guidance on the 'retention of identity' issue was laid down in 2000, in the case of Cheesman and ors v R Brewer Contracts Ltd (above). This guidance simply summarises the extensive case law, which we explore in more detail below, and does not provide a great deal of enlightenment in itself. Having said that, it highlights the pertinent

23

issues and acts as a useful reference point. Moreover, the principles set out in Cheesman have held much sway in UK courts and tribunals. In Project 90 Ltd v Oswald and anor EAT 0388/05, for example, the EAT remitted a matter to the employment tribunal with an express direction to consider the Cheesman guidance while determining whether a relevant transfer under Reg 3(1)(a) had taken place.

1.46 In Cheesman, the EAT examined the convoluted ECJ case law before stating that the following principles apply:

- the decisive criterion for establishing the existence of a transfer is whether the entity in question retains its identity, as indicated, among other things, by the fact that its operation is actually continued or resumed

- in a labour-intensive sector it is to be recognised that an entity is capable of maintaining its identity after it has been transferred where the new employer does not merely pursue the activity in question but also takes over a major part, in terms of their numbers and skills, of the employees specially assigned by his predecessors to that task. That follows from the fact that in certain labour-intensive sectors a group of workers engaged in the joint activity on a permanent basis may constitute an economic entity

- in considering whether the conditions for existence of a transfer are met it is necessary to consider all the factors characterising the transaction in question, but each is a single factor and none is to be considered in isolation

- among the matters thus falling for consideration are the type of undertaking, whether or not its tangible assets are transferred, the value of its intangible assets at the time of transfer, whether or not the majority of its employees are taken over by the new company, whether or not its customers are transferred, the degree of similarity between the activities carried on before and after the transfer, and the period, if any, in which they were suspended

- in determining whether or not there has been a transfer, account has to be taken, among other things, of the type of undertaking or business in issue, and the degree of importance to be attached to the several criteria will necessarily vary according to the activity carried on

- where an economic entity is able to function without any significant tangible or intangible assets, the maintenance of its identity following the transaction being examined cannot logically depend on the transfer of such assets

- even where assets are owned and are required to run the undertaking the fact that they do not pass does not preclude a transfer

- where maintenance work is first carried out by a cleaning firm and then by the owner of the premises concerned, the mere fact does not justify the conclusion that there has been a transfer

- more broadly, the mere fact that the service provided by the old and new undertaking providing a contracted-out service or the old and new contract-holder are similar does not justify the conclusion that there has been a transfer of an economic entity between predecessor and successor

- the absence of any contractual link between transferor and transferee may be evidence that there has been no relevant transfer but is certainly not conclusive as there is no need for any such direct contractual relationship

- when no employees are transferred, the reasons why that is the case can be relevant as to whether or not there was a transfer; and

- the fact that the work is performed continuously with no interruption or change in the manner or performance is a normal feature of transfers of undertakings but there is no particular importance to be attached to a gap between the end of the work by one subcontractor and the start by the successor.

Focus on transferring entity's identity. In applying the Spijkers v Gebroeders **1.47** Benedik Abattoir CV and anor test, courts and tribunals must focus on the identity of the entity transferred rather than on the nature of the transferor's and the transferee's businesses as a whole. The EAT made this point in Playle and ors v Churchill Insurance Group Ltd and ors EAT 570/98. There, C Ltd, an insurance company which marketed and sold its own policies, acquired the business of CGA Direct, which was not licensed to trade as an insurance firm in its own right, from CGA Group. An employment tribunal, considering whether this transaction gave rise to a TUPE transfer, pointed out that the nature of the two businesses – CGA Group and C Ltd – was inherently different, and that what C Ltd had essentially been concerned with was the acquisition of CGA's customer lists. It went on to find that TUPE had not applied in this case. The EAT, however, overturned the tribunal's decision. The mere fact that the transferee's business was different in nature to the business which it had acquired was immaterial. By concentrating on the similarity (or lack of it) between the transferor and the transferee, the tribunal had missed the main issue, which was whether the transferring entity had retained its identity post-transfer.

Since the focus must be on the transferring entity's identity, the question of how that entity is defined is clearly an important one. In Camden Primary Care Trust and University College London v Skittrall and ors EAT 0078/05 the Appeal Tribunal concluded that a tribunal had erred in defining an economic entity too narrowly, and consequently in finding that no TUPE transfer had taken place. In that case the degree-level education in podiatry offered by University College London (UCL) was taken over by the University of East London (UEL). The parties agreed that TUPE applied and all relevant staff were offered employment with UEL. Six staff objected to the transfer and an employment tribunal was asked to decide, by way of preliminary issue, whether there had been a relevant transfer. The tribunal found that no transfer had resulted, as the economic entity in question – 'the provision of a University of London BSc Honours degree in podiatry by UCL' – had not retained its identity after the changeover. The tribunal stated that the economic entity which came into being following the changeover – 'the provision of podiatric education in the form of a UEL BSc Honours degree in podiatry' – was a distinct undertaking. The EAT, however, overturned this decision. If the economic entity was the provision of a UCL degree in podiatry, its identity could not have been retained unless UCL had been successful on retender. In other words, the tribunal had defined the economic entity in such a way that no relevant transfer could occur. The EAT noted that a purposive approach to the application of TUPE is necessary in order that employees might be protected when a change of employer occurs, before concluding that the tribunal's decision could not stand.

1.48 **Type of entity.** One of the relevant factors identified by the ECJ in Spijkers was 'the type of business or undertaking'. As the ECJ pointed out in Süzen v Zehnacker Gebäudereinigung GmbH Krankenhausservice 1997 ICR 662, ECJ, 'it follows that the degree of importance to be attached to each criterion for determining whether or not there has been a transfer within the meaning of the Acquired Rights Directive will necessarily vary according to the activity carried on'.

1.49 **Similarity of activities.** In Spijkers, the ECJ stated that 'the degree of similarity of activities before and after the transfer' was a relevant factor going to the issue of whether an economic entity has retained its identity.

Where the nature of a business changes significantly upon its acquisition – for example, where X buys a café and thereafter runs it as a jewellery shop – there is little difficulty in concluding that the economic entity has not retained its identity. Some cases, however, are not as clear-cut – an example being Mathieson and anor v United News Shops Ltd EAT 554/94. There, a hospital shop operating from a Portakabin was redeveloped, and the hospital invited people to tender to run the new shop. The old shop had sold newspapers, magazines, confectionery and flowers. The new one sold the same goods, with the exception of flowers, as well as other items such as clothes, electrical equipment, cards and toys; opened for longer hours; and was run on a commercial basis. Applying Spijkers, a tribunal held that there had not been a relevant transfer as differences in stock, hours and commercial attitude meant that the new shop was a different business. This decision was upheld by the EAT.

1.50 On the other hand, minor changes in the way in which activities are carried out might not change the essential identity of the entity being transferred. This point is neatly illustrated by the case of Porter and anor v Queen's Medical Centre (Nottingham University Hospital) 1993 IRLR 486, QBD. There, the High Court held that a relevant transfer occurred where the supply of paediatric and neonatal services moved from two District Health Authorities to an NHS

Trust. The Court said that the fact that the business was carried out in a different way following the transfer did not preclude the application of TUPE. It went on to say that the provision of medical services is a type of undertaking in which it is particularly likely that different ways of carrying on the undertaking may be adopted without destroying its identity. The Court emphasised that while the methods of caring will be modified and improved as medical science advances, the object of the undertaking will not change.

Similarity of activities before and after the transfer is not necessarily the be-all and end-all. It is simply one element of the Spijkers test. As we highlighted in 'What is an "economic entity"?' above, the ECJ in Süzen v Zehnacker Gebäudereinigung GmbH Krankenhausservice 1997 ICR 662, ECJ, stated that 'an entity cannot be reduced to the activity entrusted to it. Its identity also emerges from other factors, such as its workforce, its management staff, the way in which its work is organised, its operating methods or indeed, where appropriate, the operational resources available to it.' We discuss the Süzen case and the impact it had on service provision changes later in this section under 'Service provision changes under Reg 3(1)(a)'.

Interruption of activities. Another relevant factor with regard to retention of **1.51** identity mentioned by the ECJ in Spijkers was 'the duration of any interruption in [the] activities'. In Landsorganisationen i Danmark v Ny Mølle Kro 1989 ICR 330, ECJ, the European Court considered whether a transfer of an undertaking under the Acquired Rights Directive could have occurred where the 'change of employer' took place while the business in question was not functioning. In that case H, the owner of a tavern business, leased one of its taverns to L. However, in January 1981 H rescinded L's lease owing to L's breaching its terms. The tavern – which was operated on a regular basis only during the summer – was closed until March 1981, when H began to manage it herself. The national court referred a number of questions to the ECJ, which stated that 'the fact that the undertaking in question was temporarily closed at the time of the transfer... certainly constitutes one factor to be taken into account in determining whether a business was transferred as a going concern'. The Court continued, however, to state that such a closure does not in itself preclude the application of the Directive. That was true in particular 'in the case of a seasonal business, especially where, as in this case, the transfer takes place during the season when it is closed. As a general rule, such closure does not mean that the undertaking has ceased to be a going concern.'

The ECJ repeated much of this reasoning in the later case of P Bork International A/S (in liquidation) v Foreningen af Arbejdsledere i Danmark and ors 1989 IRLR 41, ECJ. There, Bork leased a beechwood veneer factory from OTF. The lease terminated on 22 December 1981, and during that month Bork dismissed all the factory's employees. On 31 December JI purchased the factory from OTF and brought it back into operation on 4 January 1982, taking on more

27

than half of the staff previously employed by Bork. When some of the affected employees brought claims, the national court referred questions relating to the Directive's application to the ECJ. Referring to the Ny Mølle Kro case, the ECJ noted that a temporary closure was a relevant factor when considering whether a business was transferred as a going concern. It pointed out, however, that such a closure and the consequential absence of staff at the time of the transfer were not in themselves sufficient to preclude the existence of a transfer of an undertaking within the meaning of the Directive. Furthermore, the Court stated: 'That is true, in particular, in circumstances such as those of this case, where the undertaking ceased to operate only for a short period which coincided, moreover, with the Christmas and New Year holidays.'

1.52   As the EAT pointed out in Gardner Merchant Ltd v Ryan and ors EAT 1337/95, however, if a transfer of an undertaking is to occur despite a temporary cessation of activity, it is paramount that the business carried on after such cessation is the same as that which was carried on before. In that case, GM Ltd had a contract to provide canteen and related services to COI. When the operation of the contract became unprofitable, GM Ltd gave notice to terminate the contract, which it was legally entitled to do. The response of COI was to shut the restaurant. GM Ltd, seeking to avoid making redundancy payments to the employees assigned to the contract, argued that there had been a relevant transfer of the canteen services back to COI. This argument was rejected by both the employment tribunal and the EAT. Here, there had not been a temporary cessation of the canteen services, only for those services to be resumed by COI at a later date. Rather, the undertaking had ceased to be when GM Ltd terminated its contract.

1.53   **Entity subsumed post-transfer.** In 'What is an "economic entity"?' above, we examined the case of Fairhurst Ward Abbotts Ltd v Botes Building Ltd and ors 2004 ICR 919, CA. There, the Court of Appeal emphasised that where there is a transfer of a part of a business, the part in question need not exist as an identifiable, stable, economic entity prior to its transfer in order for TUPE to apply. It is sufficient that part of such an entity becomes identifiable as a separate economic entity on the occasion of the transfer separating the part from the whole.

But what happens when an entity that is identifiable prior to a transfer becomes subsumed or fragmented in the transferee's business? The Acquired Rights Directive does not require that, for an economic entity to retain its identity post-transfer, it must continue to be operated as an organisationally autonomous part of the business – Klarenberg v Ferrotron Technologies GmbH 2009 ICR 1263, ECJ. There K had worked as the head of a unit in a company in Germany which developed and manufactured certain products for the steel industry. The company sold the rights to a number of products that had been developed by the unit headed by the claimant, together with the production hardware and inventory of materials for the relevant products to FT GmbH. The products sold were incorporated into the range offered by FT GmbH and some employees who had worked in the relevant unit were engaged by FT GmbH and integrated into its organisational structure, carrying out work in relation not only to the products that had been sold but also to FT GmbH's other products. K, who had not been so engaged, sought a declaration that there was a relevant transfer of his employment to FT GmbH. On a reference by the national court, the ECJ ruled that for an entity to retain its identity after the transfer required the retention not of the specific organisation of the elements of production but of such a functional link of interdependence and complementarity between those elements as enabled the transferee to use them to pursue an identical or analogous economic activity, even if after the transfer they were integrated in a new and different organisational structure. The ECJ's decision accords with common sense, since if an economic entity did need to retain organisational autonomy post-transfer, then subsuming a purchased business into an existing structure would become an obvious means of avoiding the effect of the Directive (and hence TUPE). However, somewhat unhelpfully the ECJ did not decide whether there was 'functional link of interdependence and complementarity' in K's case – this potentially baffling question was left for the national court to determine.

1.54 The issue of a business being subsumed into the structure of a purchaser has also been considered by the EAT. In Farmer v Danzas (UK) Ltd EAT 858/93 F was employed by his own transport business, F Ltd. In essence, his business was to supply D Ltd with lorries and drivers so that D Ltd could provide a transport service called Eurapid to its customers. For this purpose, F leased and maintained the lorries and had accommodation in D Ltd's offices. In time, D Ltd decided to move the Eurapid service to its main site. It took the view that it needed to employ a manager to look after the Eurapid business and offered F the position on condition that F Ltd ceased trading. F accepted the post and started working for D Ltd on 1 October 1991. F Ltd's drivers were also taken on by D Ltd, and at first they continued to operate the Eurapid service as they had before – the only difference being that F Ltd's name had been taken off the lorries. By January of the following year, most of the drivers had been fully integrated into D Ltd's business. Thereafter, the leases on the lorries that had been taken out by F Ltd were allowed to lapse, and most of the vehicles were replaced by the end of 1992.

F was dismissed in early 1992 and brought a complaint of unfair dismissal. The preliminary issue for the tribunal was whether F had the two years' continuous employment then required to bring such a claim. This depended on whether there had been a TUPE transfer of the business of F Ltd to D Ltd, preserving his continuity of service. The tribunal was satisfied that F Ltd had a business or an undertaking which was capable of being transferred and that D Ltd had acquired an identifiable part of that business. Moreover, D Ltd had been able to carry on substantially the same activities as F Ltd without interruption. The tribunal concluded, however, that because D Ltd had always intended to integrate F Ltd's business into its own, the business transferred had not retained its identity, meaning that no TUPE transfer had occurred. F appealed to the EAT, which overturned the tribunal's decision. The EAT held that there is no rule that an economic entity ceases to retain its identity merely because its economic activity is subsumed into the transferee's business. Such a rule would emasculate the working of the Directive and the Regulations, since all businesses are likely to want to integrate the activities of a newly acquired entity into their own. In order for TUPE to apply, it is sufficient that the transferred undertaking retain its identity immediately after the moment of transfer. In the instant case, F Ltd's drivers did exactly the same work immediately following the transfer as they had done before, using the same equipment and serving the same customers, and the transferee was able to carry on the activities of F Ltd without interruption. What happened subsequently was neither here nor there. F's appeal was therefore allowed.

1.55 Contrast the situation in the Farmer case with that in AEEU and ors v Lyndon Scaffolding plc EAT 1242/99. The claimants in that case were employed by L plc at Ferrybridge power station, in order to fulfil L plc's contract with Powergen to provide scaffolding services at the site. When L plc's contract came to an end, Powergen invited tenders not simply for the scaffolding work but for a combination of scaffolding, insulation and cleaning services. L plc – a specialist scaffolding firm – was not invited to tender. The contract was won by Cape, which did not accept that a relevant transfer from L plc had occurred with regard to the scaffolding work. The claimants lost their jobs and brought unfair dismissal claims before an employment tribunal. An employment tribunal decided, as a preliminary issue, that no transfer of an undertaking had occurred. One factor it took into account was that the nature of Cape's contract with Powergen was fundamentally different from that made earlier between L plc and Powergen. The L plc contract was for the supply of scaffolding services only. On the other hand, although the Cape contract included scaffolding services, it also covered cleaning and insulation services, with all three under one management. On appeal, the employees argued that the tribunal had erred in elevating this factor into one determinative of the transfer question. They relied on the words of Morison J in the Farmer case (above) that there is nothing to suggest that an economic entity ceases to retain its identity merely because the economic activity is subsumed into the transferee's business. Moreover, they argued that the fact that the scaffolding service provided by L plc was subsumed into a wider contract entered into by Cape was actually irrelevant to the question of whether TUPE applied. The EAT, however, upheld the tribunal's decision. Unlike in the Farmer case, the tribunal here had not isolated one factor as being determinative of the transfer question, but had weighed up all the relevant factors. Furthermore, the EAT continued, if the nature of the service formerly provided differs materially from that provided by the incoming contractor, this is a factor which a tribunal is entitled to take into account in considering whether the former economic entity has retained its identity. Accordingly, the employees' appeal was dismissed.

Entity fragmented post-transfer. An example of a case concerning 1.56 fragmentation upon a transfer is Astle and ors v Cheshire County Council and anor 2005 IRLR 12, EAT. There, the Council outsourced certain architectural services to SGI, but thereafter became concerned about SGI's performance. The Council decided to terminate SGI's contract and to adopt what it referred to as a 'market economy' approach, under which a panel of consultants would be engaged to provide the services instead of a single contractor. Owing to this fragmentation upon the transfer, both an employment tribunal and the EAT concluded that the economic entity prior to the transfer had not retained its identity, meaning that TUPE did not apply.

Transfer of assets. It is well established that a transfer under the Acquired 1.57 Rights Directive and Reg 3(1)(a) can take place even though no assets transfer from the transferor to the transferee. The case of Merckx and anor v Ford Motors Co (Belgium) SA 1997 ICR 352, ECJ, involved Anfo Motors, a Ford dealer selling motor vehicles in several areas of Brussels. Ford decided to cease using Anfo, of which it was the majority shareholder, and instead began working with an independent dealer, Novarobel. The question arose as to whether a transfer of an undertaking had occurred between Anfo and Novarobel, and a number of issues were referred to the ECJ. That court concluded that the fact that neither tangible nor intangible assets were transferred from Anfo to Novarobel was not conclusive of the question of whether an undertaking retained its economic identity. In fact, the ECJ continued, the purpose of an exclusive dealership for the sale of motor cars of a particular make in a particular sector remains the same even if it is carried on under a different name, from different premises with different facilities.

Shortly after the Merckx decision, the ECJ noted in Süzen v Zehnacker Gebäudereinigung GmbH Krankenhausservice (above) that the importance of asset transfer will fluctuate depending on the type of entity transferred. The Court stated that 'where in particular an economic entity is able, in certain sectors, to function without any significant tangible or intangible assets, the maintenance of its identity following the transaction affecting it cannot, logically, depend on the transfer of such assets'. However, similar logic suggested that the transfer of assets would be an extremely important factor in asset-reliant sectors – a point thereafter emphasised in Oy Liikenne Ab v Liskojärvi and anor 2002 ICR 155, ECJ. We discuss the issues arising from the Süzen and Oy Liikenne decisions, which were concerned with service provision changes, at length under 'Service provision changes under Reg 3(1)(a)' below.

1.58   The following two cases emphasise that a transfer of assets can occur whether or not the actual ownership of such assets changes hands:

- **Abler and ors v Sodexho MM Catering GmbH and anor** 2004 IRLR 168, ECJ: the management authority responsible for an Austrian orthopaedic hospital contracted out its catering services for patients and staff to Sanrest. Under the outsourcing agreement, Sanrest prepared meals on the hospital premises, using water, energy and all necessary small and large equipment provided by the hospital. Some years later, the management authority terminated its agreement with Sanrest and awarded the contract to Sodexho, which proceeded to perform the catering operation using the hospital's facilities. Sodexho denied Sanrest's contention that what had occurred amounted to a transfer of an undertaking under the Directive, and refused to take any of Sanrest's employees on. Sanrest dismissed the employees, who brought claims arguing that their employment had transferred to Sodexho. The Supreme Court of Austria referred the matter to the ECJ, which, in ruling that there had been a transfer of an undertaking in the circumstances, confirmed that there had been a transfer of assets from Sanrest to Sodexho, despite the fact that the assets in question were owned by the hospital throughout. The ECJ stated: 'The tangible assets needed for the activity in question – namely, the premises, water and energy and small and large equipment ([including] the appliances needed for preparing the meals and the dishwashers) – were taken over by [the new contractor]'

- **Güney-Görres and anor v Securicor Aviation and anor** 2006 IRLR 305, ECJ: SA employed 295 workers to carry out airport security under a contract it had with the German Government. In 2003 the Government terminated this contract and awarded it to KAV, which took on 167 of SA's employees and used the aviation security equipment owned by the Government. Some of the employees who found themselves without work brought claims arguing that their employment had transferred from SA to KAV under the national transfer rules implementing the Directive. The German court hearing the claims noted that, under ECJ case law, an asset transfer is one of the criteria characterising a transfer of an undertaking. However, that court was unsure what the phrase 'asset transfer' actually meant. It decided to ask the ECJ whether, as German case law suggested, an asset transfer only takes place if the assets are used by the incoming contractor for its own purposes on an independent commercial basis. In this case, there was absolutely no scope for KAV to use the aviation security equipment – which was the property and the responsibility of the German state – for its own purposes. It could neither obtain any additional economic benefit from that equipment nor determine the manner or extent of its use. The ECJ held that 'the transfer of the assets for independent commercial use is not an essential criterion for a finding that there was a transfer of those assets from the original contractor to the new contractor'.

In Law Society of England and Wales v Secretary of State for Justice and Office **1.59** for Legal Complaints 2010 IRLR 407, QBD, the High Court was asked to make a declaration on the applicability of TUPE in the context of the imminent cessation of the Law Society's Legal Complaints Service (LCS) and its replacement with a new independent Office for Legal Complaints (OLC). In finding that there would be no business transfer within the scope of Reg 3(1)(a), the Court stressed that none of the tangible or indeed intangible assets of LCS were set to transfer. None of the buildings would be transferred to or used by OLC. None of the complaints being processed by LCS would be transferred over to be finished off by OLC. The only thing that was to transfer was the processing of future complaints about solicitors.

Change of location. In Merckx and anor v Ford Motors Co (Belgium) SA, **1.60** discussed under 'Transfer of assets' above, the ECJ confirmed that the fact that an economic entity, post-transfer, operates at a different location does not necessarily mean that its identity has not been retained. The Court stated: 'The purpose of an exclusive dealership for the sale of motor vehicles of a particular make in a certain sector remains the same even if it is carried on under a different name, from different premises and with different facilities. It is also irrelevant that the principal place of business is situated in a different area of the same conurbation, provided that the contract territory remains the same.'

Of course, when it comes to the contracting-out of services, a change of location might well mean that there is no transfer of the assets required to carry out the activity from the outgoing contractor to the incoming contractor. The absence of such a transfer might go a long way towards a finding that no business transfer under Reg 3(1)(a) has taken place, as we discuss under 'Service provision changes under Reg 3(1)(a)' below.

Intention of parties. Generally, the Acquired Rights Directive and TUPE apply **1.61** automatically if there is a relevant transfer, whether or not the parties want them to. However, the parties' views as to whether the Regulations apply may be taken into account by an employment tribunal in some circumstances.

In Lightways (Contractors) Ltd v Associated Holdings Ltd 2000 IRLR 247, Ct Sess (Inner House), L Ltd tendered for a contract to provide street lighting maintenance for Renfrewshire Council, bidding on the express basis that TUPE applied. L Ltd won the contract, but then proceeded on the basis that TUPE did not apply. Litigation ensued, and eventually the Court of Session held that an employment tribunal, in finding against L Ltd, had been entitled to take into account its expressed intention prior to the transfer. The Court said that it was legitimate, in determining whether or not a relevant transfer had taken place, to have regard not only to the events directly constituting the transaction, but

33

also to the surrounding circumstances. Therefore, a serious statement prior to the transfer that TUPE applied could throw light on the true nature of the transaction.

1.62 Service provision changes under Reg 3(1)(a). Earlier in this chapter we saw that cases such as Rask and anor v ISS Kantineservice A/S 1993 IRLR 133, ECJ, demonstrated that the Acquired Rights Directive, and hence Reg 3(1)(a) TUPE, can apply to service provision changes (SPCs) arising from outsourcing, insourcing or retendering exercises.

However, the question of when an entity can be said to have retained its identity following an SPC has caused much gnashing of teeth in UK courts and tribunals, which have struggled over the years to derive coherence from the ECJ case law on this point. Below, we analyse the main issues that have arisen, many of which can be traced back to the ECJ's decision in Süzen v Zehnacker Gebäudereinigung GmbH Krankenhausservice 1997 ICR 662, ECJ.

1.63 We reiterate that under the 2006 Regulations the vast majority of SPCs will fall within the scope of TUPE in any event, owing to Reg 3(1)(b), which we examine in the section on 'Service provision changes' below. It follows that the vexed issue of whether an economic entity has retained its identity following an SPC is no longer as central to the TUPE regime as it once was. Nevertheless, the case law in this regard is worthy of examination for two reasons: first, it enhances our understanding of the Reg 3(1)(a) test that is still conclusive to all transfers other than SPCs; and, secondly, owing to some of the exceptions to Reg 3(1)(b), some SPCs will still have to satisfy the traditional Reg 3(1)(a) 'retention of identity' if they are to be covered by TUPE.

1.64 *Inclusive approach in Schmidt.* The case of Schmidt v Spar- und Leihkasse der früheren Ämter Bordesholm, Kiel und Cronshagen 1995 ICR 237, ECJ, concerned S, who had been employed by a bank to clean its branch office. In February 1992 the bank decided to outsource this cleaning work to Speigelblank, the firm already responsible for cleaning most of the bank's other premises. The bank dismissed S, who was offered re-engagement by Speigelblank on new terms, which she rejected. S brought a claim in respect of her dismissal to the German Labour Court, and the question arose as to whether the Acquired Rights Directive had applied, meaning that S's employment had transferred to Speigelblank under the national transfer provisions. Unsure as to the answer to this question, the Court referred the matter to the ECJ.

The ECJ rejected the argument put forward by the German and UK governments that the Directive could not apply in a case such as this owing to the absence of a transfer of any tangible assets. Referring to the Spijkers case, the ECJ stated that 'the safeguarding of employees' rights, which constitutes the subject-matter of the Directive… cannot depend exclusively on consideration of a factor which the Court has in any event already held not to be decisive on its own'. The ECJ went on to proffer the view that 'the similarity in the cleaning work performed before and after the transfer, which is reflected, moreover, in the offer to re-engage the employee in question, is typical of an operation which comes within the scope of the Directive and which gives the employee whose activity has been transferred the protection afforded to him by that Directive'.

The EAT, when interpreting the Schmidt decision in cases such as Isles of Scilly **1.65** Council v Brintel Helicopters Ltd and ors 1995 ICR 249, EAT, seemed to reduce the 'retention of identity' issue in the SPC arena to a single question: are the activities being carried out after the transfer broadly similar to those which were carried out before? If the answer to this question was yes, then TUPE applied. This was a simplistic approach, which involved the EAT's essentially ignoring a number of factors identified as relevant by the ECJ in Spijkers. Nevertheless, it brought with it the advantage of certainty, in that almost all SPCs would be covered by the TUPE Regulations (as they now are by Reg 3(1)(b)). This certainty was dismantled, however, by the ECJ's decision in Süzen v Zehnacker Gebäudereinigung GmbH Krankenhausservice (above).

Süzen – transfer of assets or employees required. In the Süzen case S, a cleaner, **1.66** worked for ZG, a company that had a contract to carry out cleaning in a school in Bonn-Bad-Godesberg, Germany. ZG's contract was terminated with effect from 30 June 1994 and S was dismissed along with seven of her colleagues. The school then entered into a cleaning contract with another company with effect from 1 August 1994. That company did not employ S, and S instituted proceedings before the German Labour Court. That court sought a preliminary ruling from the ECJ as to whether the Acquired Rights Directive applied in these circumstances, meaning that S's employment had transferred to the new cleaning contractor.

The ECJ began by highlighting the established key criterion for determining whether there has been a transfer of an undertaking – namely, whether there is an identifiable economic entity that had retained its identity after the alleged transfer. Furthermore, the Court purported to affirm the list of relevant factors set out in the Spijkers case, stating that 'it is necessary to consider all the facts characterising the transaction in question, including in particular the type of undertaking or business; whether or not its tangible assets, such as buildings and moveable property, are transferred; the value of its intangible assets at the time of the transfer; whether or not the majority of its employees are taken over by the new employer; whether or not its customers are transferred; the degree of similarity between the activities carried on before and after the transfer, and the period, if any, for which those activities were suspended'.

Having set out this list of factors, the ECJ went on to resile from the Schmidt **1.67** decision set out above. The Court stated that it does not automatically follow that there is a transfer of an economic entity merely because the service provided by the old and the new contractors is similar, since an entity cannot be reduced

35

to the activity entrusted to it. Rather, 'its identity also emerges from other factors, such as its workforce; its management staff; the way in which its work is organised; its operating methods, or indeed, where appropriate, the operational resources available to it'. Consequently, the ECJ continued, the mere loss of a service contract to a competitor cannot in itself indicate the existence of a transfer of an undertaking covered by the Directive.

The ECJ then pointed out that 'the degree of importance to be attached to each criterion for determining whether or not there has been a transfer within the meaning of the Directive will necessarily vary according to the activity carried on'. So while accepting that in labour-intensive sectors such as cleaning, an economic entity – amounting to a group of workers engaged in a joint activity on a permanent basis – is able to function without any significant tangible or intangible assets, the ECJ put the cat among the pigeons by suggesting that such an entity is only capable of retaining its identity following a transfer when the new contractor 'does not merely pursue the activity in question but also takes over a major part, in terms of their numbers and skills, of the employees specially assigned by his predecessor to that task'. It went on to conclude that 'the Directive does not apply to a situation in which a person who had entrusted the cleaning of his premises to a first undertaking terminates his contract with the latter and, for the performance of similar work, enters into a new contract with a second undertaking, if there is no concomitant transfer from one undertaking to the other of significant tangible or intangible assets or taking over by the new employer of a major part of the workforce, in terms of their numbers and skills, assigned by his predecessor to the performance of the contract'.

1.68 This was controversial. On the one hand, the ECJ seemed to affirm the 'multi-factorial' Spijkers test with regard to retention of identity. On the other hand, it stated that, in order for the Acquired Rights Directive to apply to an SPC, a transfer of either assets or employees is essential. Furthermore, where the entity in question has no significant assets, the ECJ suggested that a single factor – the transfer or otherwise of the majority of the workforce in terms of numbers and skills – would be determinative of the retention of identity issue.

In the light of this, the Court of Appeal, in Betts and ors v (1) Brintel Helicopters Ltd (2) KLM ERA Helicopters (UK) Ltd 1997 ICR 792, CA, took the view that the Süzen case represented 'a shift in emphasis, or at least a clarification of the law, and that some of the reasoning of earlier decisions... may have to be reconsidered'. In Betts, the Court felt obliged by Süzen to reverse a High Court decision that a relevant transfer had taken place when Shell changed the supplier of its helicopter transport contract from Brintel to KLM. The Court of Appeal noted that the activity carried out before and after the change of contractor was very similar. Crucially, however, no staff or other significant assets were transferred. The incoming contractor had simply obtained a fresh contract for supplying helicopter services to the oil rigs, which it carried out from a different land base using different helicopters and different crews. In those circumstances, no transfer of an undertaking had occurred.

Labour-intensive entities – why was workforce not taken on? It was not long, **1.69** however, before the UK courts and tribunals became aware of some of the difficulties of the Süzen ruling, particularly with regard to SPCs in labour-intensive sectors. The thrust of Süzen was that, since the workers themselves comprise the principal assets of a labour-intensive undertaking such as cleaning, the transfer of the 'major part of the workforce in terms of their numbers and skills' is necessary in order for the undertaking to retain its identity and thus in order for the Acquired Rights Directive to apply. Accordingly, a strict interpretation of Süzen suggested that a prospective transferee in a labour-intensive sector could avoid the operation of the Directive (and hence fall outside what is now Reg 3(1)(a) of the 2006 Regulations) by the simple expedient of not taking on a major part of the outgoing contractor's workforce.

To many, it seemed both bizarre and unsatisfactory that the operation of a measure specifically designed to protect employees from being dismissed in the context of a transfer would be made entirely dependent on whether the incoming contractor voluntarily takes on the employees who are affected. At the very least, the test appeared to be circular in its reasoning. In order to avoid this outcome, UK courts and tribunals strived to avoid interpreting Süzen strictly with regard to labour-intensive transfers. They did this in two ways. First, they emphasised that the ECJ in Süzen had affirmed the multi-factorial test laid down in Spijkers v Gebroeders Benedik Abattoir CV and anor (above), meaning that all relevant factors – and not just the transfer or otherwise of the employees – needed to be considered. Secondly, they suggested that one such relevant factor was a prospective transferee's motive for refusing to take the relevant employees on. If the motive was simply to avoid the application of TUPE, the case would be assessed as if the employees had, in fact, transferred.

Below, we set out three important cases in which this approach of the UK **1.70** courts manifested itself:

- **ECM (Vehicle Delivery Service) Ltd v Cox and ors** 1999 ICR 1162, CA: A Ltd lost a contract with VAG to deliver cars from Grimsby to local car dealerships and delivery centres. The majority of A Ltd's work was thereafter performed by a different company, ECM Ltd. None of A Ltd's employees who had worked on the VAG contract were taken on by ECM Ltd and they claimed that they had been unfairly dismissed. An employment tribunal decided that there had been a relevant transfer from A Ltd to ECM Ltd, meaning that the employees had been protected by TUPE. When the case reached the Court of Appeal, ECM Ltd argued with reference to the Süzen case that, since it had not taken A Ltd's employees on, no relevant transfer could have occurred. The Court of Appeal rejected this argument. In Lord

37

Justice Mummery's view, 'the importance of Süzen has... been overstated' and 'the ruling... should be seen in its proper context'. Because Süzen did not claim to mark a departure from previous case law, such as Spijkers, it remained the case that it is for the national court to assess all the facts characterising a transaction in order to determine whether a transfer of an undertaking had taken place. This is what the tribunal in this case had done. It had noted the differences in the way the new contractor carried out the contract – for example, unlike A Ltd, ECM Ltd had no administrative staff in Grimsby and did not deliver to local delivery centres – but had pointed out, on the other hand, that the customers and the work carried out remained essentially the same. Moreover, Mummery LJ continued, 'the tribunal was entitled to have regard, as a relevant circumstance, to the reason why those employees were not appointed by [ECM Ltd]. The Court of Justice has not decided in Süzen or in any other case that this is an irrelevant circumstance or that the failure of the transferee to appoint any of the former employees of the transferor points conclusively against a transfer.' Accordingly, the Court upheld the tribunal's decision, concluding that it had made no error of law

- **ADI (UK) Ltd v Willer and ors** 2001 IRLR 542, CA: ADI Ltd provided security services at a shopping centre. Its contract came to an end and the incoming contractor, FSG Ltd, refused to take on the nine security officers who had been performing the work. ADI Ltd dismissed the officers, some of whom brought unfair dismissal claims before an employment tribunal. Both the tribunal and the EAT concluded that no TUPE transfer had taken place, meaning that the employees had not transferred from ADI Ltd to FSG Ltd. ADI Ltd appealed against this decision to the Court of Appeal. Having noted that this case concerned a labour-intensive entity, and having considered the Süzen decision, the Court accepted that there would clearly have been a relevant transfer for the purposes of TUPE had FSG Ltd taken on the security officers who were dedicated to the relevant contract. But since FSG Ltd had not, in fact, taken the employees on, the Süzen case suggested that no relevant transfer had occurred. Despite this, however, the majority of the Court found a way of upholding ADI Ltd's appeal. Referring to the ECM case (above), the majority noted that it was necessary to have regard, as a relevant circumstance, to the reason why FSG Ltd did not employ the security officers in question. The majority then went one step further, holding that if the reason for FSG Ltd's declining to employ the officers was that it wished to avoid the operation of TUPE, the tribunal should have assessed the case as if the officers had, in fact, been taken on by that company. So, if the reason or principal reason for FSG Ltd's not taking on the employees was to avoid the application of TUPE, a relevant transfer had occurred in this case. Otherwise, there had been no such transfer. The Court remitted the case for the tribunal to consider FSG Ltd's motive for declining to take on ADI Ltd's security officers. Note, however, that Lord Justice Simon Brown, in his minority judgment, was adamant that the ECJ jurisprudence did not support the approach taken by the majority. He concluded, interpreting Süzen strictly, that the decisive factor was that FSG Ltd had not taken on ADI Ltd's workforce. In his view, the reason for the incoming contractor's refusal to take the workforce on was 'immaterial'

- **RCO Support Services Ltd and anor v UNISON and ors** 2002 ICR 751, CA: the Aintree Hospitals NHS Trust (the Trust) administered two hospitals in Liverpool – Walton Hospital and Fazakerley Hospital. Over a four-year period, the Trust phased out all its in-patient wards and operating theatres at Walton and reopened them at Fazakerley. The cleaning services at Walton, which had been contracted out to IHS Ltd, and the catering services at Walton, which had been provided by the Trust, 'transferred' to RCO Ltd, which ran both cleaning and catering at Fazakerley. RCO Ltd denied that TUPE applied. However, it was prepared to employ some of the relevant staff on its own terms and conditions. In the event, none of the cleaners or caterers applied to work for RCO Ltd, and some of them brought unfair dismissal claims before an employment tribunal. The tribunal decided that there had been relevant transfers from IHS Ltd to RCO Ltd in respect of the cleaning staff, and from the Trust to RCO Ltd in respect of the catering staff. When the case reached the Court of Appeal, the Court upheld the tribunal's decision. It did so notwithstanding that none of the relevant workforces had been taken on by RCO Ltd and that there had been no significant transfer of assets. In the Court's view, the limits set out in Süzen did not mean that the Directive can never apply in a contracting-out case if neither assets nor workforce are transferred. Furthermore, the Süzen decision should not be read as singling out, to the exclusion of all other circumstances, the particular circumstance of none of the workforce being taken on and treating that as determinative of the transfer issue in every labour-intensive case. Such an interpretation would run counter to the retention of identity test in the Spijkers decision, which warned against considering single factors in isolation. The tribunal in the instant case had correctly followed the Spijkers approach. Moreover, the tribunal had not erred in treating RCO Ltd's willingness to take on the existing staff as a factor supporting the retention of the identity of the cleaning and catering undertakings – the Süzen decision did not require the tribunal to exclude from its consideration of all the facts characterising the transaction the circumstances of the decision by the putative transferee not to take on the workforce.

The EAT examined a prospective transferee's motive for failing to take on an **1.71** outgoing contractor's workforce in the case of Astle and ors v Cheshire County Council and anor 2005 IRLR 12, EAT. Cheshire County Council had for many years provided its own architectural services. In 1994 it contracted these services out to KD, and the relevant Council employees transferred under TUPE. In 1999 the Council awarded the contract to another contractor, SGI. Again TUPE applied, and the staff of KD, including 65 ex-Council employees, transferred to SGI. In time, the Council became concerned about SGI's performance, and felt that some of the staff who had originally been employed by the Council were part of the problem. The Council decided to terminate SGI's contract and to adopt what it referred to as a 'market economy' approach, under which a panel of consultants would be engaged to provide the services instead of a single contractor. The Council temporarily took over some of the responsibilities until the new arrangements were put in place. However, none of the relevant employees were taken on by the Council, and they brought tribunal claims arguing that they had transferred to the Council under TUPE.

The employment tribunal found that the Council did not want the SGI staff to continue to carry out the architectural services, and that 'the Council was therefore most concerned to avoid a TUPE transfer'. It also noted, however, that the Council had genuinely decided that the best way to deliver the services was by a panel of consultants rather than a workforce. The tribunal went on to conclude that the reason the Council did not accept the workforce back 'was not to defeat TUPE, but because it had given the responsibility of carrying out the provision of architectural services to a panel of consultants; thus the Council did not require a workforce to operate the business. In these circumstances the question of whether, had the workforce been transferred, [there would] have been a [TUPE] transfer, does not arise.' The fact was, the workforce did not transfer. Applying the multi-factorial test in Spijkers, the tribunal concluded that no relevant transfer had taken place. On appeal, the EAT upheld the tribunal's decision. There were no grounds for overturning the conclusion that, although the Council had wished to avoid the consequences of TUPE, its reason for not taking on the contractor's workforce was not to thwart the operation of the Regulations as such, but to implement the new structure as the best method of delivering the services in question. Far from being a case in which the new scheme or structure that the employer had put in place was without commercial or economic justification, the Council's new way of operating was plainly sensible. While another tribunal might have reached a different conclusion on the facts, the tribunal in the instant case had heard all the evidence and had made no error of law.

1.72 Often a client decides to change the contractor performing a service owing to concerns about the performance of the staff dedicated to the contract. In the following two cases clients did precisely this. Moreover, they instructed the incoming contractors not to take on the outgoing contractors' workforces. The new contractors obeyed these instructions and the employees concerned brought tribunal claims invoking TUPE. It fell to the EAT to grapple with the question of whether relevant transfers had occurred. In both cases, the EAT decided that the reason the employees were not taken on was the client's instruction, and not the transferee's wish to avoid TUPE. Accordingly, no relevant transfers had taken place:

- **Williams v Lockhart Security Services Ltd** EAT 1395/01: W worked as a security guard for L Ltd at the Darlington Retail Park (DRP). When L Ltd lost the guarding contract, DRP awarded a new contract to A Ltd. In doing so, it stipulated that it wanted none of the former L Ltd employees to continue working at its site. A Ltd thus declined to take W on, and he brought claims before an employment tribunal which gave rise to the question of whether a relevant transfer had occurred from L Ltd to A Ltd. The tribunal held that there had been such a transfer, but the EAT overturned its decision. The EAT concluded that where no physical assets or employees were transferred from L Ltd to A Ltd, and where the reason A Ltd had not taken on the employees dedicated to the contract was that they were prevented from doing so due to objection by the client, DRP, the economic entity had not retained its identity, meaning that no relevant transfer had occurred

- **Carlisle Facilities Group v Matrix Events and Security Services and ors** EAT 0380/04: CFG employed 32 security officers for Sea France on its cross-channel ferries. Sea France became dissatisfied by the general level of performance of the CFG staff, terminated the contract, and awarded it to MES, telling MES that it did not want any of CFG's staff to carry out the work. MES did not take the employees on, and some of them brought tribunal claims. The question arose as to whether there had been a relevant transfer from CFG to MES. An employment tribunal examined the reason why MES did not take the CFG security guards on, and decided that its decision not to do so could not be categorised as a ploy to avoid the Regulations. Rather, the reason why MES did not take the employees on was that Sea France had been dissatisfied with their performance. In so finding, the employment tribunal noted that it would have been easier for MES to have employed some of CFG's employees than to advertise for new labour. The tribunal went on to conclude that, since there were no relevant assets and none of the relevant employees had been taken on by MES, TUPE did not apply. On appeal, the EAT found no fault with the tribunal's decision.

The above two decisions are not without their difficulties. Essentially, they **1.73** return us to the much-criticised 'circular' situation discussed above – namely, that if the transferee, for whatever reason, chooses not to voluntarily take on the transferor's workforce, then a relevant transfer of a labour-intensive entity will not occur for the purposes of the Acquired Rights Directive or Reg 3(1)(a) TUPE. Moreover, the decisions chime with the radical approach recommended by the Advocate General in his Opinion in Süzen v Zehnacker Gebäudereinigung GmbH Krankenhausservice (above). He took the view that if the client does not want the incoming contractor to take on the relevant employees in an SPC situation, that should be sufficient to preclude the Directive from applying.

This approach (which was not, in fact, adopted by the ECJ in its final decision in the Süzen case) does not sit easily with the principal purpose of the Directive, which is to protect employees' rights.

Having said all that, cases such as Williams and Carlisle Facilities Group would now almost certainly fall within the TUPE regime, owing to the new SPC rules contained in Reg 3(1)(b) – see 'Service provision changes' below.

1.74 *Oy Liikenne – asset-reliant entities require asset transfer.* We have seen how the UK courts and tribunals attempted to downplay the importance of Süzen v Zehnacker Gebäudereinigung GmbH Krankenhausservice (above), preferring to believe that it fitted harmoniously into the body of previous ECJ case law. However, a spanner was thrown into the works by the ECJ in Oy Liikenne Ab v Liskojärvi and anor 2002 ICR 155, ECJ. Not content with upholding Süzen, the ECJ in Oy Liikenne went one stage further. It concluded that the absence of the transfer of a substantial body of physical assets in a case where the undertaking in question is heavily asset-dependent leads inexorably to the conclusion that the Acquired Rights Directive does not apply.

The facts in Oy Liikenne were thus. Following a tender procedure, the Greater Helsinki Joint Board awarded the operation of a number of the city's bus routes to OL. The outgoing contractor, HL, dismissed the 45 drivers who had worked on the routes. 33 of the drivers (including L and J) applied to be taken on by OL. All were successful, but were engaged on less favourable conditions than those which they had enjoyed under HL. No vehicles or significant assets connected with the operation of the bus routes were transferred to OL from HL, although OL leased two buses from HL for a few months while waiting for the delivery of 22 new buses. L and J brought actions against OL claiming that, owing to the operation of the Directive, they were entitled to terms and conditions no less favourable than those that they had enjoyed prior to the transfer. A Finnish court referred the matter to the ECJ.

1.75 Referring to its previous decision in Süzen, the ECJ noted that a labour-intensive entity, based essentially on manpower, is capable of maintaining its identity after a transfer where the new employer takes over a major part, in terms of their numbers and skills, of the employees employed by its predecessor. However, it continued, bus transport cannot be regarded as an activity based essentially on manpower. It requires substantial plant and equipment. The ECJ held that in a sector such as scheduled public transport by bus, where the tangible assets contribute significantly to the performance of the activity, the absence of a transfer to a significant extent from the old to the new contractor of such assets must lead to the conclusion that the entity does not retain its identity. In such circumstances, the Directive will not apply. So, on the facts of Oy Liikenne, in the context of a change in the contractor responsible for operating scheduled bus services, the absence of a transfer of the actual buses used by the previous operator meant that there could be no transfer to which the Directive applied.

This decision was surprising on several counts. First, many of the traditional 'Spijkers' factors pointing to a business transfer were present. For instance, there was a transfer of the customer base – albeit that the customer base in question took the form of bus passengers and therefore comprised a 'captive audience'. Secondly, a majority of the employees employed by the outgoing contractor to operate the bus routes were, in fact, taken on by the incoming contractor, without any break in their employment. Had this been a case of the transfer of a labour-intensive activity, the employees themselves would have been viewed as assets of the business, and as principal assets at that. And thirdly, one of the consistent propositions laid down by the ECJ in the pre-Süzen jurisprudence is that the transfer of physical assets is not a prerequisite for the transfer of an undertaking – see, for example, Merckx and anor v Ford Motors Co (Belgium) SA 1997 ICR 352, ECJ. In Oy Liikenne, however, far from downplaying the importance of physical assets, the ECJ conferred upon them such importance as to make them decisive of the question of whether or not the Acquired Rights Directive applied – at least in a case of an asset-dependent undertaking such as municipal transport services.

1.76 The ECJ adopted a similar approach to the importance of asset transfer in Abler and ors v Sodexho MM Catering GmbH 2004 IRLR 168, ECJ, but strangely enough reached the diametrically opposite outcome. The Abler case concerned a change of contractor responsible for providing catering services for an orthopaedic hospital in Austria. The old contractor, Sanrest, had prepared meals on the hospital premises, using water, energy and all necessary small and large equipment provided by the hospital. When management authority responsible for the hospital terminated its agreement with Sanrest, the new contractor, Sodexho, used the same equipment. However, it denied Sanrest's contention that what had occurred amounted to a transfer of an undertaking under the Directive, and refused to take any of Sanrest's employees on. Sanrest dismissed the employees, who brought claims arguing that their employment had transferred to Sodexho. When the Supreme Court of Austria referred the matter to the ECJ, the European Court stated that the catering activities in this case were based essentially on equipment – namely, the premises, water and energy, and small and large equipment, including the appliances needed for preparing the meals and the dishwashers. This equipment was used both before and after the transfer – in fact, a defining feature of the situation was the express and fundamental obligation to prepare the meals in the hospital kitchen and thus to take over those tangible assets. The ECJ concluded: 'The transfer of the premises and the equipment provided by the hospital, which is indispensable for the preparation and distribution of meals to the hospital patients and staff, is sufficient, in the circumstances, to make this a transfer of an economic entity.'

1.77 *UK courts downplay the importance of Oy Liikenne.* Despite the Oy Liikenne decision, the UK courts have stuck to their guns and continued to emphasise the multi-factorial approach advocated in Spijkers v Gebroeders Benedik Abattoir CV and anor (above). In downplaying the importance of Oy Liikenne, their message has been twofold. First, the ECJ did not mean to lay down a principle that an asset transfer must occur if an asset-reliant entity is to retain its identity following a transfer. Secondly, even if the ECJ did lay down such a principle, it will not necessarily affect a great number of cases. This is because tribunals are not obliged to decide that economic entities are either labour-intensive or asset-reliant. Many entities will fall somewhere in between these extremes. The following cases illustrate these points:

- **P&O Trans European Ltd v Initial Transport Services Ltd and ors** 2003 IRLR 128, EAT: Shell UK Ltd had a substantial fleet of in-house vehicles, used to transport the majority of its fuel products. Some of the transporting work, however, was carried out by contractors. Under an arrangement with Shell, both P&O and ITS provided backup petroleum delivery services. In late 1998 Shell decided to contract out the whole of its delivery function and P&O won the national contract as from 1 August 1999. As a result, Shell terminated its existing arrangement with ITS. P&O took on all of Shell's drivers and a large part of its fleet of vehicles. P&O also took on ITS's drivers, but none of its vehicles. The question arose of whether a relevant transfer had occurred from ITS to P&O. An employment tribunal found that the business carried on by P&O was essentially the same as that carried on by ITS. However, no tangible assets had been transferred, in that P&O had not taken on any of ITS's vehicles. The tribunal considered this an important factor, as a delivery service was dependent upon the use of such vehicles. However, it also noted that all ITS's drivers had been transferred; Shell remained the customer; and there was no suspension of activity when P&O took on the contract. Having weighed up all these factors, the tribunal concluded that ITS's activity of providing a backup delivery service had retained its identity having been taken over by P&O, and that there had thus been a relevant transfer. P&O appealed to the EAT, relying on the ECJ's decision in Oy Liikenne to argue that, in an asset-intensive industry such as the delivery of petroleum products by tanker, the absence of a transfer of tangible assets or a significant part of them must lead to the conclusion that there is no relevant transfer. The EAT, however, upheld the tribunal's decision, stating that the Oy Liikenne case did not lay down a principle that in all cases of asset-intensive industries the absence, to a significant extent, of a transfer of such assets would always lead to the conclusion that no transfer had taken place. Rather, the ECJ had made it clear that the approach in deciding whether a transfer of undertaking has occurred remains multi-factorial

44

- **Scottish Coal Co Ltd v McCormick and ors** 2005 All ER 104, Ct Sess (Inner House): from 1988 onwards C Ltd carried out mining activities at an opencast mining site in Ayrshire, pursuant to contracts with S Ltd. C Ltd possessed the necessary heavy excavating plant, dumper trucks and ancillary equipment to carry out these activities. It also erected workshops and office buildings on site. In April 2001 S Ltd took over C Ltd's activities at the site. S Ltd did not acquire C Ltd's plant or equipment as part of this transaction, since C Ltd did not wish to sell it. The majority of C Ltd's former employees returned to the site to work for S Ltd, resuming the same mining activities they had performed prior to the transaction. Some of the workforce brought claims before an employment tribunal, contending that the transaction between the two companies had been a transfer of an undertaking for the purposes of TUPE. The tribunal, feeling that this was a complicated case in which no single factor proved decisive, eventually concluded that the economic entity in question retained its identity after the transfer, meaning that TUPE applied. When the EAT upheld the tribunal's decision, S Ltd appealed to the Court of Session, contending that both the tribunal and the EAT had failed to follow the guidance set down by the ECJ in Oy Liikenne. In S Ltd's view, that case illustrated that the primary step in determining whether there has been a transfer of an undertaking is to characterise the undertaking as either 'asset-reliant' or 'labour-intensive'. It stated that C Ltd's mining operation had clearly been an 'asset-reliant' undertaking, unable to operate without the use of its plant and equipment. Since no plant had been transferred, no relevant TUPE transfer could have taken place. The Court of Session rejected this argument. It did not read either Oy Liikenne or Abler as 'laying down an invariable requirement that, in the context of a claimed TUPE transfer, a given business must necessarily be characterised as either "asset-reliant" or "labour-intensive", as if those were mutually exclusive categories that defined exhaustively the range of possibilities that could arise'. Rather, there would appear to be an unlimited 'range of intermediate possibilities'. The Oy Liikenne and Abler rulings illustrated 'the position at one end of the spectrum when a transfer must include the production assets of the entity. In intermediate cases, it must always be an issue for the fact-finding tribunal whether, on an appreciation of all relevant facts and circumstances, the undertaking in question can be said to have been transferred for the purposes of the 1981 Regulations'

- **Balfour Beatty Power Networks Ltd and anor v Wilcox and ors** 2007 IRLR 63, CA: H plc provided street lighting services for WPD under a number of different contracts. One such contract related to the maintenance of overhead lines and the replacement of poles. H plc leased the vehicles and specialist equipment required to carry out these activities. When H plc lost this contract to Interserve, these leased items did not transfer and Interserve made alternative arrangements. However, the new contractor did take on the majority (although not all) of the dedicated workforce. The employees who were not taken on brought tribunal claims, and argued successfully that their employment had transferred to Interserve owing to the operation of TUPE. When the case reached the Court of Appeal, Interserve argued that, in the present case, assets such as vehicles and tools were important to the performance of the contract and that, in light of the Oy Liikenne decision, the fact that they had not been transferred prevented the Directive and hence Reg 3(1)(a) TUPE from applying. The Court, however, upheld the tribunal's decision. Lord Justice Buxton approved the comments of the Court of Session in the Scottish Coal case above, expressing considerable doubts as to whether the ECJ had intended to lay down a rule as stark as that which Interserve suggested. In any event, he continued, this case presented an issue not yet addressed by the ECJ – namely, the relevance of the fact that the assets in question were leased by the transferor. He stated: 'They can... be better characterised as tools and equipment, rather than assets in the technical sense, and it is difficult to see them as an integral part of the former business... It is in this case difficult to see how exactly "transfer" of the leased assets would operate, or how the existence of those assets can override the general obligation to approach the case on a multi-factorial basis.'

1.78 **Conclusion.** After a long period of uncertainty following the ECJ's decisions in Süzen v Zehnacker Gebäudereinigung GmbH Krankenhausservice (above) and Oy Liikenne Ab v Liskojärvi and anor (above), the approach of the UK Courts and tribunals has essentially come full circle. When answering the question of whether an economic entity has retained its identity following a service provision change, meaning that a relevant transfer has occurred under Reg 3(1)(a) TUPE, an employment tribunal should take all the relevant factors into account. However, although this situation is clearer than it once was, the multi-factorial test still does not provide contractors with the certainty they would wish for. There will still be many sets of circumstances in which the retention of identity question will prove extremely difficult to answer.

Thankfully, most SPCs will in any event now be covered by the transfer rules owing to Reg 3(1)(b) of the 2006 Regulations, which, in order to put an end to the prevailing uncertainty and the inevitability of litigation that resulted, was specifically designed to ensure that such 'transfers' fall within TUPE's scope. However, the ECJ's decision in CLECE SA v Martín Valor and anor 2011 ICR 1319, ECJ, demonstrates that this uncertainty in terms of ECJ decisions still subsists today. In that case, a local authority contracted out the cleaning of schools and premises under its control. Eventually, the contract was terminated and the service brought back in house, but the local authority declined to employ the contractor's staff. Instead, it hired new employees to do the work. Also, no assets transferred from the outgoing contractor to the local authority. The ECJ held that the Acquired Rights Directive did not apply, as in the absence of the transfer of any assets associated with the undertaking, all that had been taken back in-house was the activity of cleaning. This – applying the Süzen test – was insufficient to amount to a transfer of an economic entity. Here, the entity in question was essentially based on manpower, and the identity of that entity could not therefore be retained where the majority of employees were not taken on by the alleged transferee. This is a clear example of a factual scenario which, had it occurred in the UK, would indisputably have constituted a relevant transfer under Reg 3(1) (b). We discuss Reg 3(1)(b) under 'Service provision changes' below.

Entity situated in UK immediately prior to transfer   1.79
Regulation 3(1)(a) states that a 'relevant transfer' under that provision only occurs where the transferring undertaking or business or part of undertaking or business is 'situated immediately before the transfer in the United Kingdom'.

Thus, on its face, Reg 3(1)(a) applies to business transfers taking place within the UK, and to business transfers from the UK outwards (presuming that the entity in question manages to retain its identity despite an arguably significant change of circumstances). It will not apply to transfers into the UK from elsewhere. However, if the transfer is from another country subject to the Acquired Rights Directive, it would seem that some sort of transfer regime should take effect based on the national law equivalent to TUPE of the country concerned. We focus on issues surrounding transfers from the UK to elsewhere, and from elsewhere to the UK, in Chapter 9, 'Transnational issues'.

The EAT examined the meaning of 'the United Kingdom' for the purposes of **1.80** Reg 3(1)(a) in Addison and ors v Denholm Ship Management (UK) Ltd and ors 1997 ICR 770, EAT. It decided that the territorial scope of the UK is confined to its land and territorial waters and does not extend to the UK sector of the Continental Shelf of the North Sea. It followed that the transfer of a contract for the supply of crew to a 'flotel' adjoining an oil installation in the UK sector of the Continental Shelf was not covered by TUPE.

Note that Reg 3(4)(b) clarifies that TUPE can apply to a business transfer notwithstanding that:

- the transfer is governed or affected by the law of another country, or

- the employment of the employees in the undertaking transferred is governed by the law of another country.

Furthermore, Reg 3(4)(c) provides that a relevant transfer can occur even where **1.81** persons employed in the undertaking, business or part transferred ordinarily work outside the UK. The BIS Guide explains: 'For example, if there is a transfer of a UK exporting business, the fact that the sales force spends the majority of its working week outside the UK will not prevent the Regulations applying to the transfer, so long as the undertaking itself (comprising, amongst other things, premises, assets, fixtures & fittings, goodwill as well as employees) is situated in the UK.'

1.82 Service provision changes

In 'Business transfers' above we saw that the circumstances in which the Acquired Rights Directive – and hence Reg 3(1)(a) TUPE – will apply to service provision changes (SPCs) have proved difficult to pin down. The decisions of the ECJ have been inconsistent in this regard, giving rise to much litigation and commercial uncertainty. The Labour Government which introduced the 2006 Regulations decided to respond to the difficulties created by ECJ case law by including a second definition of 'relevant transfer' in Reg 3(1)(b). Made under an enabling power in S.38 of the Employment Relations Act 1999, this second definition effectively brings most SPCs within the scope of TUPE.

The fact that Reg 3(1)(b) is a creation of domestic law rather than being EU-derived has two significant consequences. First, it means that its interpretation has largely been a matter for the EAT. In one of the first appellate cases under the new provision, Metropolitan Resources Ltd v Churchill Dulwich Ltd and ors 2009 ICR 1380, EAT, His Honour Judge Burke QC set out his view that since 'service provision change' is a wholly new statutory concept, it is not defined in terms of economic entity or any of the other EU law concepts considered above under 'Business transfers'. The circumstances in which service provision change is established are, in HHJ Burke QC's view, 'comprehensively and clearly' set out in Reg 3(1)(b) and 3(3).

1.83 The lack of an EU dimension to Reg 3(1)(b) also means that the provision can be repealed without infringing the UK's obligations under the Directive. Repeal was proposed by the Coalition Government in 2013, but eventually dropped after consultation responses persuaded it that the SPC provision was an example of where 'good regulation', additional to that required by a Directive, can deliver benefits for both business and individuals. As a result of that decision, there remain two methods by which a 'relevant transfer' can be taken to have occurred – a 'business transfer' as defined in Reg 3(1)(a), and an SPC as defined in Reg 3(1)(b). In Kimberley Group Housing Ltd v Hambley and ors and another case 2008 ICR 1030, EAT, the Appeal Tribunal stressed that the two definitions are not mutually exclusive – there will be circumstances which satisfy both. Nonetheless, as we will see below, it is the latter provision which, in most cases, is substantially wider in scope.

In the following sections we examine each of the components of a transfer under Reg 3(1)(b), beginning with the three types of service provision change.

1.84 The three types of SPC

Regulation 3(1)(b) states that the TUPE Regulations apply to 'a service provision change' where the conditions set out in Reg 3(3) are satisfied (see 'The Reg 3(3) conditions' below). Reg 3(1)(b) goes on to define three types of service provision change, as follows:

- where 'activities cease to be carried out by a person ("a client") on his own behalf and are carried out instead by another person on the client's behalf ("a contractor")' – Reg 3(1)(b)(i). This is the exercise commonly known as 'contracting out' or 'outsourcing'

- where 'activities cease to be carried out by a contractor on a client's behalf (whether or not those activities had previously been carried out by the client on his own behalf) and are carried out instead by another person ("a subsequent contractor") on the client's behalf' – Reg 3(1)(b)(ii). This concerns a change of contractor, usually following a retendering process, and is sometimes referred to as 'second generation contracting out'

- where 'activities cease to be carried out by a contractor or subsequent contractor on a client's behalf (whether or not those activities had previously been carried out by the client on his own behalf) and are carried out by the client on his own behalf' – Reg 3(1)(b)(iii). This is called 'contracting in' or 'insourcing'.

What are 'activities'? Each of the three SPC scenarios set out above involve **1.85** 'activities' ceasing to be carried out by one person and subsequently being carried out by another. However, although the word 'activities' is clearly crucial to the workings of the new SPC regime, it is not defined anywhere in the TUPE Regulations. That said, the lack of a statutory definition does not appear to have particularly troubled tribunals and the EAT. The greater focus of case law has been on the question of whether activities remain the same in the hands of the new contractor – a point we explore below under 'Transferor and transferee must carry out the same activities'.

The first appellate decision to consider 'activities' in the context of Reg 3(1)(b) was Kimberley Group Housing Ltd v Hambley and ors and another case 2008 ICR 1030, EAT, where the EAT suggested that an employment tribunal's first step in assessing whether there has been an SPC should be to identify the relevant activity or activities. On the facts of the case before it, the EAT held that the tribunal had not erred when finding that there had been an SPC when LH Ltd lost its Home Office contract to provide accommodation and related services for asylum seekers in Middlesbrough and Stockton, and was replaced by a two separate companies, KGH Ltd and AS Ltd. The EAT considered that the tribunal had been entitled to define the relevant activities as 'the provision of suitable accommodation and related support services to asylum seekers in Middlesbrough and separately in Stockton' and to find that they had ceased to be carried out by LH Ltd and were thereafter carried out by KGH Ltd and AS Ltd on behalf of the same client.

This was followed by Johnson Controls Ltd v Campbell and anor EAT 0041/12. **1.86** There, C was employed as a taxi administrator by JC Ltd. The role involved some element of organisation: combining jobs and pick-ups to ensure the best use of available transport; allocating work to subcontractor taxi companies; and entering the costs of subcontractors onto a database. C's assessment was that he spent 80 per cent of his time working on behalf of one of JC Ltd's clients, UKAEA. When UKAEA dispensed with JC Ltd's services and enabled UKAEA staff to book taxis directly, C claimed unfair dismissal, asserting that an SPC had taken place, with the effect that his contract of employment continued with UKAEA. An employment judge found that an important feature of the service provided by C when at JC Ltd was the fact that it was central and coordinated. As that feature was not retained by UKAEA, it was no longer performing the same activity. The EAT upheld this decision. In so doing, Mr Justice Langstaff (President of the EAT) noted that identifying an 'activity' is a question of fact and degree, and involves a holistic assessment by the tribunal. The matter is not decided simply by enumerating tasks and asking whether, quantitatively speaking, most of those same tasks are done both before and after the putative transfer. The judge had decided that the centralisation and coordination of the taxi-booking service made it more than the sum of its parts, and so was entitled to find that several people booking taxis individually within UKAEA was not the same activity.

1.87 **Definition of 'transferor' and 'transferee'.** One peculiarity of a TUPE transfer in a second-generation contracting-out scenario is that there is no direct relationship between the outgoing and incoming contractor. In effect, the contract is always transferred via the client for whom the service is being performed.

Regulation 2(1) states that 'in the case of a service provision change falling within regulation 3(1)(b), "the transferor" means the person who carried out the activities prior to the service provision change and "the transferee" means the person who carries out the activities as a result of the service provision change'. This clarifies that the client will effectively be left out of the equation in a second-generation case, and fits well with Reg 3(6)(a), which provides that a relevant transfer 'may be effected by a series of two or more transactions'.

1.88 **Definition of 'contractor'.** The term 'contractor', according to Reg 2(1), also includes sub-contractor. Accordingly, Reg 3(1)(b) can cover sub-contracting by a client's contractor and changes of sub-contractor.

1.89 **Client must remain the same.** Each of the three types of SPC defined in Reg 3(1)(b) refers to 'a client' who is then referred to as 'the client'. This wording has been held to mean that for an SPC to take place, the activities must continue to be carried out on behalf of the *same* client – Hunter v McCarrick 2013 ICR 235, CA. The facts of the Hunter case were as follows. WG Ltd, a property management company, held a number of commercial properties. On 3 February 2009, it contracted to transfer these properties to WCPM Ltd. However, on the same day, HM Revenue and Customs launched a petition to wind up WG Ltd, which had the effect of invalidating the sale until after a lengthy process of judicial approval. In the meantime, the commercial property remained in WG Ltd's ownership, but M and two other employees of WG Ltd, who managed the property, were treated as employees of WCPM Ltd and continued to provide the same property management services. Then, on 14 August, ACF Ltd, the mortgage lender on the commercial properties, appointed receivers to take control of the properties. This meant that there was no more property management work for M to do. However, H, the managing director of WG Ltd, continued to pay the salaries of M and the two other employees for some months, hoping to use their expertise to rescue the transaction and realise the sale of the commercial properties.

The question of M's continuity of employment came before an employment tribunal. It decided (and this was not challenged on appeal) that the transaction on 3 February gave rise to an SPC, by which M's employment transferred from WG Ltd to WCPM Ltd. It also decided that the change of property ownership on 14 August was also an SPC, by virtue of which M became employed by H. However, H successfully challenged this part of the decision on appeal. The EAT held that, for the purpose of Reg 3(1)(b)(ii), the 'client' on whose behalf activities are carried out must be the same before and after the transfer. The same conclusion would apply in respect of Reg 3(1)(b)(i) (outsourcing) and Reg 3(1)(b)(iii) (insourcing) because all three definitions cover situations where activities done on behalf of 'a client' change hands and are then carried out by another person or group of persons on 'the client's' behalf.

On further appeal, the Court of Appeal held that the EAT was correct to hold **1.90** that Reg 3(1)(b)(ii) requires the client to be the same before and after the putative transfer. Like the EAT, it considered that the wording of the provision was only consistent with a situation where the client remains the same. Moreover, it rejected the argument that a purposive construction was required. Lord Justice Elias, giving the leading judgment, accepted that there may be issues where a purposive interpretation is appropriate in respect of matters similar to those that fall to be analysed under Reg 3(1)(a). For example, it may be necessary not to be too pedantic with respect to the question of whether the activities carried on before and after the transfer are sufficiently similar, or to take a broad approach to the question of whether an employee is employed in the service transferred. However, there is no room for a purposive interpretation of the scope of Reg 3(1)(b), since there is no conflict between a straightforward construction and a purposive one: the natural construction gives effect to the draftsman's purpose. The concept of a change of service provision is not complex and there is no reason to think that the language does not accurately define the range of situations which the draftsman intended to fall within the scope of this purely domestic protection. Unlike the EAT, the Court of Appeal did not address the question of whether the client must also remain the same for an SPC to occur under Reg 3(1)(b)(i) and Reg 3(1)(b)(iii). However, the lack of any material difference in the wording leads to the conclusion that the three definitions of SPC must be interpreted consistently.

The EAT's decision in the Hunter case was relied upon in SNR Denton UK LLP v Kirwan and anor 2013 ICR 101, EAT. There, K was an in-house lawyer at J plc, which held contracts for facilities management services at premises it had built under PFI schemes. J plc was in financial difficulties and K spent 90 per cent of her time disposing of these contracts to outside purchasers. Administrators were appointed in March 2010. The administrators' solicitors, DWS, dismissed the majority of the employees in J plc's company secretarial department, including K, and took over some of the legal work, including that previously done by K. She argued that, since DWS was disposing of the service maintenance contracts, there had been a service provision change of that 'activity' within the meaning of Reg 3(1)(b)(i) and her contract of employment transferred to DWS. An employment tribunal accepted this argument but, on appeal, the EAT held that it had misapplied Reg 3.

1.91 It was clear to the EAT – following Hunter – that the 'client' had to be the same person or entity before and after the putative transfer. The tribunal's analysis was to the effect that DWS, as solicitors to the administrators, was acting on behalf of J plc, such that the activities previously done by K 'in house' had transferred to DWS to be done on J plc's behalf, as Reg 3(1)(b)(i) requires. But the EAT held that this was not the true legal position. The High Court's decision in Edenwest Ltd v CMS Cameron McKenna 2012 EWHC 1258, Ch, showed that it is not the case that, whenever a solicitor's firm is instructed by an administrative receiver who is appointed, in the ordinary way, as the company's agent, the firm is to be treated as retained by the company. The form of agency provided for by the Insolvency Act 1986 is of a particular kind, and the tribunal was wrong to assume that, because the administrator could act as agent for the company, the solicitors retained by the administrator were acting on behalf of the company when they acted in the administration. They might have been, but it could not be assumed that they necessarily were. Accordingly, the tribunal's analysis was flawed, and it was not entitled to proceed to the conclusion that, in effect, the activities done by K before the purported transfer were being done after it by DWS for the same client, i.e. J plc. Accordingly, there was no service provision change under the TUPE Regulations.

In Horizon Security Services Ltd v Ndeze and anor EAT 0071/14 the EAT held that 'the assessment of who is the client in a service provision change case will generally be a matter for the employment tribunal as a finding of fact'. Despite that pronouncement, it still went on to overturn the employment tribunal's conclusion on this point. N had been employed by PCS as a security guard at the Alpha Business Centre, which was managed by Workspace and owned by the London Borough of Waltham Forest ('the Council'). On 7 January 2013 PCS was informed that Workspace's contract with the Council would end on

25 January and that Workspace would accordingly no longer require PCS's security services after that date. The Council invited PCS to tender for the security services at the Alpha Business Centre, but the contract was ultimately won by HSS Ltd. PCS took the view that N's employment had transferred to HSS Ltd, and when it was confronted with a tribunal claim for unfair dismissal, it successfully applied to have HSS Ltd added as a respondent. The tribunal found that although PCS's contract was with Workspace and HSS Ltd's was with the Council, they had both carried out security services 'on behalf of' the Council, which was the owner of the building. However, on appeal the EAT considered that the tribunal had made an inference that was not supported by its findings of fact. PCS had never contracted with the Council. Rather, it had contracted with Workspace, which had been managing, and renting out office space within, the Alpha Business Centre. The security guards employed by PCS had taken calls on behalf of Workspace, interacted with its customers, and taken direction from it as to how to carry out their duties. There was no indication that PCS had any relationship with the Council prior to 25 January, so the tribunal had not been entitled to reach the conclusion that PCS was carrying out activities on behalf of the Council.

Another case entailing similar circumstances was Jinks v London Borough of **1.92** Havering EAT 0157/14. The London Borough of Havering ('the Council') owned a site comprising an ice rink and a car park. It contracted out the management of the whole site to S Ltd, which in mid-April 2013 sub-contracted the management of the car park to R Ltd. Around the same time the ice rink closed. The car park remained open for a few weeks but S Ltd gave up occupation of the whole site at the end of April. The Council took control of the site and closed the car park. It subsequently granted a licence to an NHS Trust to use it before finally converting it into a public car park. J was employed by S Ltd until mid-April, when his employment transferred to R Ltd. He contended that there had been a further transfer, by way of an SPC, when the Council took the management of the car park back in-house. When the Council refused to accept him as an employee, he brought a claim of unfair dismissal.

On the basis of pleadings alone (i.e. without making any findings of fact) an employment judge struck out J's claim as having no reasonable prospect of success: the judge considered that R Ltd's client for the purposes of Reg 3(1)(b)(iii) was S Ltd, not the Council. Overturning that decision and remitting the strike-out application for reconsideration, the EAT held that the employment judge had wrongly directed himself in law. He had overlooked Reg 2(1), which enables the word 'contractor' to be treated as including the word 'sub-contractor'. As a result, Reg 3(1)(b)(iii) could apply where activities cease to be carried out by a sub-contractor on a client's behalf and are carried out instead by the client on its own behalf. The instant case gave rise to an important factual question: on whose behalf was R Ltd carrying out the activities? In answering that question, the employment judge had taken an impermissible shortcut by treating the client of a sub-contractor as necessarily being, and only being, the contractor to which it was contractually bound to provide a service. The decision in Horizon Security Services Ltd v Ndeze and anor (above) made it clear that the strict legal or contractual relationships of the sub-contractor do not necessarily determine who is its client for the purposes of Reg 3(1)(b)(iii).

1.93 **No bar to more than one client.** While Reg 3(1)(b) refers to 'client' in the singular, there is no need to restrict its interpretation to one client. This was confirmed by the EAT in Ottimo Property Services Ltd v Duncan and anor 2015 ICR 859, EAT, where it held that an employment tribunal was wrong to conclude that because there were a number of different clients, each with a separate contract, there could be no SPC when those contracts were acquired by a different company following a retendering exercise. Her Honour Judge Eady QC, sitting alone, observed that there was nothing in either the TUPE Regulations or the case law to suggest that the ordinary rule of statutory interpretation, under which the singular includes the plural and vice versa, should not apply here. HHJ Eady QC could see no reason in principle why an SPC might not, for example, involve a contract for the provision of services to a group of persons collectively defined as 'the client' under that contract, provided they retain the same identity before and after the SPC, and provided they have a common intention with regard to the manner in which the activities are to be carried out for the purpose of Reg 3(3)(a)(ii) (see 'Single specific events or tasks of short duration excluded – "the client intends"' below). Furthermore, the fact that there are separate contracts for each client does not necessarily mean that there can be no SPC. It would be harder to demonstrate the necessary commonality of intention where there is no umbrella contract defining 'the client' but that does not prevent common intent being demonstrated in some other way.

1.94 **Public and private sector.** According to Reg 3(4)(a) the SPC rules apply to public and private undertakings engaged in economic activities, whether or not they are operating for gain. So, for example, privatisations, and outsourcing by central or local government of ancillary services to the private sector, can be covered. However, as with business transfers (discussed under 'Business transfers' above), there will be no relevant transfer under Reg 3(1)(b) where there is an administrative reorganisation of public administrative authorities or a transfer of administrative functions between public administrative authorities – Reg 3(5). We discuss what this means under 'The public sector' below.

1.95 **Professional business services not excluded.** The possibility of excluding 'professional business services' from Reg 3(1)(b) has been floated on two occasions. In the 2005 Consultation Document which preceded the introduction of the 2006 Regulations, the Labour Government suggested that 'service provision changes involving "white collar" services such as chartered accountancy, business consultancy, legal advice and computer software design rarely give rise to difficulties in practice' and 'the professionally qualified employees who are key to providing such services are – by virtue of having skills that are generally highly sought-after by employers – less in need of additional legal protection'. In the event, however, the proposal that professional business services be excluded from Reg 3(1)(b) was dropped.

In 2013 the Coalition Government's response to a consultation on amending TUPE noted calls from respondents for professional services to be excluded from the SPC rules. In reply, it stated this: 'The Government has considered whether it would be possible to provide an exception from SPCs for professional businesses based on a generic description of such services or by listing excluded services. The Government has concluded that it would not be possible to draft an exception precisely enough, while any list would be arbitrary and likely to lead to long-running disagreement. There is also an argument as to whether it would be fair to those employed in professional services to exclude them from TUPE.'

So, there is no reason why an SPC transfer under Reg 3(1)(b) could not take place **1.96** where a large professional services company, such as a law firm, has a team dedicated to meeting the needs of one important client, and where that client decides to change its adviser. Of course, the transferor law firm might not wish to lose some or all of the lawyers that were dedicated to the contract in question, and some of those lawyers might not wish to transfer. We examine the transferor's and the employees' options in such a situation in Chapter 2, 'Who transfers?', under 'Objecting to transfer' and 'Employees retained by transferor'.

Transferor and transferee must carry out same activities   1.97

In contrast to the definition of 'business transfer' in Reg 3(1)(a), the definition of SPC in Reg 3(1)(b) does not expressly require that there is an economic identity which retains its identity after the transfer. However, as we saw above under 'The three types of SPC', Reg 3(1)(b)(i), (ii) and (iii) all involve activities ceasing to be carried out by one person (either the client, or a contractor) and thereafter being carried out by another person (a second contractor, or the client). It follows, then, that it is the 'activities' that must be identifiable as 'the same' pre- and post-transfer if an SPC transfer is to occur. Indeed, following an amendment made on 31 January 2014, the TUPE Regulations now state explicitly what had previously been made clear in case law: that the activities carried out before and after the purported transfer must be 'fundamentally the same' if the SPC provisions are to apply – Reg 3(2A).

The leading case on this matter is Metropolitan Resources Ltd v Churchill Dulwich Ltd and ors 2009 ICR 1380, EAT. MH was a charity contracted by the Home Office to provide accommodation to asylum seekers. MH in turn had contracted CD Ltd to provide these services at its premises in Dulwich. However, MH decided not to renew its contract, and instead engaged MR Ltd to house asylum seekers at its premises in Croydon. From 26 January 2007 all new asylum seekers went to Croydon; a few asylum seekers stayed on at Dulwich for a further few weeks due to ill health, and ten of CD Ltd's employees remained there until the contract expired on 31 March 2007. CD Ltd wrote to MR Ltd, stating that it believed those ten had transferred to MR Ltd. This was disputed, and an employment tribunal claim followed. At a pre-hearing review to determine whether an SPC had taken place, the tribunal found that the relevant activities were the 'provision of good quality accommodation to asylum seekers together with associated administration and reporting services on behalf of MH'. When asylum seekers were sent to Croydon instead of Dulwich, MR Ltd provided essentially the same service or activity as CD Ltd had done. The tribunal specifically rejected MR Ltd's argument that differences in the way in which it provided the service – such as the new location at Croydon and the shorter length of time asylum seekers were accommodated – meant that it was not carrying out the same activities. On appeal, MR Ltd argued that the tribunal should have applied the 'multi-factorial' approach set out by the EAT in Cheesman and ors v R Brewer Contracts Ltd 2001 IRLR 144, EAT (see 'Business transfers – when does an economic entity retain its identity?' above), which required the consideration of a formal list of factors before deciding whether a stable economic entity had transferred. Had the tribunal adopted this approach, argued MR Ltd, it would have found essential differences between the services provided by the two companies.

1.98 Upholding the tribunal's decision on appeal, the EAT (His Honour Judge Burke QC sitting alone) held that Cheesman was essentially irrelevant to a claim under Reg 3(1)(b), as it concerned the Directive-led definition of 'business transfer' in Reg 3(1)(a). HHJ Burke QC explained that the definition of SPC in Reg 3(1)(b) stands on its own – it is not defined in terms of economic entity or any other concepts which have arisen under EU law. The question of whether Reg 3(1)(b) applies to a particular case is essentially a question of fact, to be determined on the basis of the straightforward language used in the provision. Those statutory words require the tribunal to concentrate upon the relevant activities. Tribunals will inevitably be faced with arguments that the activities carried on by the alleged transferee are not identical to the activities carried on by the alleged transferor because there are detailed differences between what the former does and what the latter did or in the manner in which the former performs and the latter performed the relevant tasks. However, it cannot have been the intention of the introduction of the new concept of service provision change that the concept should not apply because of some minor difference or differences in the nature of the tasks carried out, or in the way in which they are performed. A commonsense and pragmatic approach is required to enable a case in which problems of this nature arise to be appropriately decided. The tribunal needs to ask itself whether the activities carried on by the alleged transferee are *fundamentally or essentially the same* as those carried on by the alleged transferor. The answer to that question will be one of fact and degree, to be assessed by the tribunal on the evidence before it. In the instant case, the tribunal adopted the correct test when it looked for the essential service or activity provided by the initial contractor. The tribunal found that the activities carried on by both contractors amounted essentially to the provision of good quality accommodation to asylum seekers, together with associated services. None of the differences between the services were such as to make it impossible for the essential service provided by the two contractors to be regarded as the same.

HHJ Burke QC's analysis in Metropolitan Resources Ltd v Churchill Dulwich **1.99** Ltd (above) suggests that, since the question of whether the activities have remained fundamentally or essentially the same is one of fact and degree, the circumstances in which the EAT will be willing to interfere with a tribunal's finding on this point will be rare. Indeed, in all of the following appellate cases, the tribunal's finding was upheld:

- **OCS Group v Jones and anor** EAT 0038/09: OCS, a catering contractor, managed the catering operation at BMW's car plant at Cowley. Under the contract, OCS operated a centrally located restaurant serving cooked breakfast and hot and cold lunches and a bar facility supported by four satellite catering stations and a general shop. However, following the take-over of the contract by MIS, the catering service was substantially reduced to the provision of five dry goods kiosks (offering sandwiches and salads). An employment tribunal concluded that there was no SPC. On appeal, OCS contended that the tribunal should have found that the general activity – the provision of food – was the same under both contracts. However, the EAT held that the tribunal had adopted the correct approach, which is to concentrate on the relevant activities. Having analysed and heard from the employees and studied the different requirements as to food provision in the contracts of the two contractors, the tribunal had been entitled to identify the activity carried out by the outgoing contractor as being not merely the provision of food for staff but a full canteen service. Once it had defined the activity in that way, it was entitled to conclude that the incoming contractor was providing a wholly different operation that did not require the preparation of cooked food. These were not merely changes of menu or style of food, or changes in the way the activities were carried out, but substantial differences in the activities themselves. The tribunal's decision that there was no SPC was accordingly upheld

- **Ward Hadaway Solicitors v Love and ors** EAT 0471/09: WH had been a member of a panel that provided legal services to the Nursing and Midwifery Council (NMC). The NMC decided to tender out its work to a single provider, C, with effect from the date of expiry of its contract with WH on 1 October 2007. However, all work in progress as at that date, which was expected to last for at least six months, remained with, and was completed by, WH. A question arose whether TUPE applied. The employment tribunal accepted that there was an organised grouping of employees whose principal purpose had been the carrying out of activities on behalf of the NMC. However, it concluded that the 'activities' in question comprised the work in progress that WH was dealing with as at 1 October 2007, all of which remained with WH itself. There was therefore no change in the identity of the firm carrying out those activities. The tribunal also concluded that the activities carried out by C were sufficiently different from those carried out by WH not to amount to the same activities. On appeal, the EAT held that the tribunal had been entitled to conclude that the relevant 'activities' were simply those comprising the work in progress and not the expectation of future work which was awarded to C

- **Nottinghamshire Healthcare NHS Trust v Hamshaw and ors** EAT 0037/11: the Trust decided to change the way it provided care to vulnerable adults requiring long-term welfare and medical support. Until April 2010, care was provided at a residential institution, staffed by healthcare assistants and qualified nursing staff providing 24-hour care. From April 2010 the provision of care services was taken up by two private sector contractors. The vulnerable adults were moved out of the residential facility and given individual accommodation. Although they continued to be assisted by care workers, who slept over, the cared-for adults were expected to develop greater independence in the cleaning, care and management of their own homes. The EAT, having endorsed the analysis set out in the Metropolitan Resources case (above), held that an employment tribunal had been entitled to find that there was a material shift in the 'ethos' of the care service and the manner of its provision, which meant that the activities were not essentially the same before and after April 2010 and that there had therefore been no SPC.

1.100 The decision in the Nottinghamshire Healthcare NHS Trust case above raised a few eyebrows given that the essentials of the service were much the same – many of the same staff were providing similar levels of care to the same residents. Moreover, an 'ethos' could be interpreted as an intangible difference in the policy or manner of the service provision. Could, therefore, a service provider simply avoid the operation of TUPE by claiming that although it is carrying out much the same activities, it has done so with a different ethos? A closer examination of the judgment reveals that the word 'ethos' is something of a red herring. The tribunal found a difference in the activities that was much more concrete than a mere change of ethos. The service had gone from institutional, managed care to support in the individual's own home. Thus, it involved real, practical changes in the nature of the work that would be done by the carers.

Minor differences can be properly disregarded. The activities do not need to **1.101** remain identical post-transfer. The test of 'fundamentally or essentially the same' means that a tribunal can disregard those differences it considers to be minor. An example:

- **Gumbley and ors v Exel Europe Ltd and anor** ET Case No.1306658/07: Land Rover (LR) had contracted with JC to manufacture and supply seats for its Range Rover 2006 model. JC in turn sub-contracted with EE Ltd to transport the seats to LR's premises in Solihull from JC's site in Redditch. LR decided to terminate its contract with JC and instead contract with a different company, LC, to manufacture and supply seats for its Range Rover 2007 model. LC then subcontracted with BL Ltd to transport the seats to Solihull from LC's site in Coventry. The question arose as to whether, following this change, the employees employed by EE Ltd were transferred under TUPE to BL Ltd. An employment tribunal held that there had been a relevant transfer by virtue of Reg 3(1)(b) since the activity of transporting seats to LR in accordance with LR's requirements remained broadly unchanged when carried out by BL Ltd as it had under EE Ltd. The seats were being delivered to LR using the same trailers and stillages (i.e. pallets) albeit that they were transported from a different address. Changes to the seats were merely cosmetic in nature and were made in the context of the fact that LR updated its models from time to time.

Contractual documents not determinative. In deciding whether the activities **1.102** are fundamentally or essentially the same pre- and post transfer, an employment tribunal is not restricted to looking at what the parties actually contracted for. It is entitled to look at what actually happened 'on the ground' to test whether there has been some change in relation to what would be expected of the new contractor. In ALHCO Group Ltd v Griffin and anor EAT 0007/14 the question of whether there had been an SPC focused on one aspect of the activities previously carried out by MJT on behalf of a client and now carried out by ALHCO. The employment judge found that although the activities were not technically guaranteed under the contract, they were nonetheless an integral part of the services delivered by MJT and they continued to be provided by ALHCO after the transfer, such that there was an SPC. On appeal against that decision, ALHCO argued, among other things, that the contractual documents themselves should be taken to answer the 'activities' question. The EAT disagreed and upheld this aspect of the judge's decision, noting that the same argument had been run before the EAT in Lorne Stewart plc v Hyde and ors EAT 0408/12 and was rejected by His Honour Judge Burke QC. In the instant case, the EAT accepted that the reasoning of HHJ Burke was sound. Moreover, there was nothing in Reg 3(1)(b) that expressly limits the approach to 'activities' to such description as is given in contractual documents and, indeed, the TUPE Regulations could potentially operate in relation to the transfer of activities that are not the subject of any written agreement at all.

1.103 **Different mode of carrying out activities.** In Qlog Ltd v O'Brien and ors EAT 0301/13 the EAT held that a different mode of carrying out the activities in question did not preclude there being an SPC. MH Ltd, a haulage company, organised, loaded and delivered goods on the client's behalf. MH Ltd then lost the contract to Q Ltd which, instead of making the deliveries itself, subcontracted them to other hauliers on a job-by-job basis. Q Ltd refused to take on MH Ltd's drivers, arguing that only the warehousing and not the distribution service transferred to it. The EAT upheld an employment tribunal's decision that there was an SPC that included delivery, stating that the 'activities' concerned were 'the transfer of goods from the client's premises to its customers'. It did not matter that Q Ltd carried out the deliveries in a different way. Furthermore, the tribunal had been entitled to rely on contractual documentation that stated that the client wished to transfer the provision of its 'transportation, delivery and distribution services' to Q Ltd, and the fact that the risk in the goods to be transported passed to Q Ltd until the point of delivery. While the EAT acknowledged that the facts were 'somewhat unusual' and that another tribunal might have reached a different conclusion, it nevertheless affirmed the tribunal's decision in this case.

1.104 **Change in quantity of work.** In Department for Education v Huke and anor EAT 0080/12 the Appeal Tribunal stressed that, apart from considering the character and types of activities carried out pre- and post-transfer, it is also necessary to look at quantity. A substantial change (e.g. a reduction) in the amount of the particular activity that the client requires may lead to the conclusion that the activities after the supposed transfer are not 'essentially the same' as before.

That said, any change in quantity (or nature) of activities must be seen in context. In London Borough of Islington v Bannon and anor EAT 0221/12 a Council had outsourced its responsibility under the Children Act 1989 to provide 'independent visitors' to children in care. The contracting company, CSV, provided a 'proactive' service, actively advertising for volunteers to become independent visitors, providing training and promoting its activities. When CSV's contract came to an end and the Council's arrangements for a different organisation to take over fell apart, the Council reluctantly took the service back in-house, whereupon it temporarily managed the service itself on a 'reactive' basis, i.e. doing the required administrative work but dropping other activities such as active recruitment. An employment tribunal found that this was still an SPC and, on appeal, the EAT agreed. Although the Council had admitted that its performance of the service was unsatisfactory and unresourced, it was nonetheless doing the same essential activities, even if it was unable to do all of them. In His Honour Judge McMullen QC's view, such a situation is not uncommon on a TUPE transfer. When, for example, a canteen changes hands, the work may decline because people may not want to go to the new provider, but there is no change to the character of the activities being done just because, on accepting the change, not all of the activities can be carried out.

Change in scope of activities. If a change in service provider is accompanied **1.105** by a change in the scope of the activities, this may lead a tribunal to conclude that the activities have not remained the same. An example:

- **Williams and anor v Solo Services Group and anor** ET Case No.1605833/09: RCS was contracted to carry out industrial and domestic cleaning at D Ltd's factory. In March 2007, RCS lost the contract to SSG, which continued to employ two of RCS's employees. Towards the end of 2008, D Ltd decided to close the factory and sold some of its machines along with the factory itself. However, it continued to be permitted to use the premises under a leaseback arrangement. In March 2009, D Ltd informed SSG that its own operatives would do any necessary cleaning when the contract with SSG came to an end. By that stage, production had almost ceased, machines were no longer cleaned and the only cleaning was to clear up any spillages. When the two employees issued claims for redundancy pay and breach of contract, SSG argued that D Ltd was liable to pay these as there had been an SPC when D Ltd took the cleaning services back in-house. The employment tribunal held that there was no relevant transfer under Reg 3(1)(b)(iii) as the activities had changed from around 70 per cent industrial cleaning to cleaning of spillages on an ad hoc basis with no industrial element.

It is interesting to contrast the Williams case above with Aziz and anor v CPS Security Ltd and anor ET Case No.2301878/07. In that case an employment tribunal held that there was an SPC when services provided by CPS Ltd comprising 24 hour-a-day security, seven days a week, was taken over by R Ltd, which then provided security services from Mondays to Fridays during day-time only, six hours' security on Saturdays and a mobile patrol twice in the evenings. The services were deemed to be essentially the same before and after the service provision change.

Activities subsumed into wider operation. There will inevitably be **1.106** circumstances where a new contractor takes over a service contract and subsumes the activities to be performed under that contract into its existing operation. As ever, the question of whether this changes the activities on a fundamental level is one of fact and degree for the tribunal. In Snowley and ors v Lawson Distribution Ltd and anor ET Case No.1802321/13 LD Ltd had held an exclusive contract to supply haulage services to B Ltd. This involved transporting goods directly from B Ltd's warehouse to its customers, using LD Ltd's vehicles. In 2012, the contract for haulage services was awarded to NRD Ltd, which was a member of a national pallet distribution network. Under the new contract, B Ltd's goods were delivered by NRD Ltd to one of two central hubs, before being sorted by postcode along with goods belonging to other companies. All deliveries for a particular postcode, whether or not they were B Ltd's goods, would be delivered by a single driver. An employment tribunal recognised that there were differences between the way in which the activities were carried out, but concluded that the activities had remained essentially the same: the contract, as before, was concerned with 'transporting goods from A to B'. It therefore concluded that a transfer by way of an SPC had taken place.

1.107 **Fragmentation of 'activities'.** The BIS Guide recognises that the definition of SPC in Reg 3(1)(b) is capable of applying when some of the activities in a service contract are 'retendered and awarded to a new contractor, or where the original service contract is split up into two or more components, each of which is assigned to a different contractor'. However, it goes on to state that 'the activities might be divided up so much that there is no service provision change'. There are no hard and fast rules to determine when activities have become too fragmented for an SPC to have taken place – it is a question of fact and degree for the tribunal, as the following decisions of the EAT demonstrate:

* **Kimberley Group Housing Ltd v Hambley** 2008 ICR 1030, EAT: L Ltd contracted with the Home Office to provide accommodation and support services for the Teesside area from offices in Middlesbrough and Stockton. The Home Office then retendered the contract and ended up splitting the Teesside area between two new contractors, K Ltd and A Ltd. In Stockton, K Ltd won 97 per cent of the work. In Middlesbrough, K Ltd won 71 per cent of the work and A Ltd won 29 per cent. Three ex-employees of L Ltd based in Middlesbrough and another three from Stockton brought proceedings against both of the new contractors for redundancy payments and unfair dismissal. An employment tribunal decided, as a preliminary issue, that there had been a service provision change from L Ltd to the two new contractors. On appeal the EAT considered that there may be circumstances in which a service that is being provided by one contractor to a client is in the event so fragmented that nothing which one can properly determine as being a service provision change has taken place. The tribunal concluded that that had not happened in the instant case and that there was a service provision change. Since there were two overlapping contracts now providing for activities which were previously provided by one provider, the tribunal was entitled to come to that view. (Note that the EAT also allowed A Ltd's appeal against the tribunal's decision to apportion to it a percentage of the liability for redundancy payments and unfair dismissal – this is considered separately under 'Rights and liabilities can only pass to single transferee' below)

* **Clearsprings Management Ltd v Ankers and ors** EAT/0054/08: C Ltd was one of four private contractors who were awarded one of the contracts to provide an accommodation and support service to asylum seekers in the North West. Those contracts came to an end in October 2005 and

the various contractors (including C Ltd) each entered into a further short-term contract until 30 June 2006 so that the service continued to be provided during the process of contractual retender. Once this process was completed, new contracts were awarded to three of the existing contractors but C Ltd was unsuccessful. There was then a transition period from 20 March to 30 June 2006 when C Ltd and the new contractors each continued to provide the asylum service in the North West, and during that period responsibility for asylum seekers was gradually taken over solely by the new contractors. The EAT held that the employment tribunal had been entitled to find that the activity carried on by C Ltd was so fragmented following the transfer that no relevant transfer took place. None of the claimants (all former employees of C Ltd) were dedicated to a service transferred to any one of the new service providers and the allocation of responsibility for asylum seekers to individual claimants showed 'no discernible pattern'. The EAT contrasted the position in this case with that in the Kimberley Group Housing case, where a much larger percentage of the activities was taken over by a single putative transferee in both of the geographical regions affected by the transfer

- **Enterprise Management Services Ltd v Connect-Up Ltd and ors** 2012 IRLR 190, EAT: EMS Ltd had a contract to provide IT services to schools in the Leeds area. When the contract came up for renewal, the Council decided to remove the requirement for support for curriculum software, which had constituted 15 per cent of the workload. EMS Ltd did not bid, and the work was eventually split among five providers, including C Ltd. An employment judge found that there had been no transfer to C Ltd on the basis that: (i) the activities had not remained essentially or fundamentally the same; and (ii) the activities had become too fragmented after the change in service provider. The EAT had no hesitation in upholding these findings, stressing that it would only be able to interfere with them if they were legally perverse.

1.108 The issue of fragmentation in the context of an alleged SPC from a single transferor to a single transferee has also arisen. In Johnson Controls Ltd v Campbell and anor EAT 0041/12 Mr Justice Langstaff (President of the EAT) upheld an employment judge's decision that there was no SPC when a client dispensed with the services of an outsourced taxi administrator and allowed its staff, individually, to book taxis directly. C, who worked as the outsourced taxi administrator and claimed that he spent 80 per cent of his time on this particular client's account, argued that the taxi-booking activities he performed before the change were still the same when the client took them in-house. The only difference was that they were split up among several people. The EAT recognised that if an activity performed by a given employee is, after an SPC, to be performed by several employees in the transferee, it may be that the same activity is being carried on, but noted that this is a question of fact and degree.

Here, the judge was entitled to find that the crucial features of centralisation and coordination in the service provided by the administrator were no longer present when the client stopped using him, meaning that the same activity was not being performed before and after the alleged transfer. However, in so deciding, the EAT made it clear that it was not giving tribunals the green light to regard a fragmentation situation as being generally incapable of constituting an SPC.

1.109 *Rights and liabilities can only pass to single transferee.* In Kimberley Group Housing Ltd v Hambley (above) the work of L Ltd in Middlesbrough and Stockton had been divided between two new contractors, K Ltd and A Ltd. In Stockton, K Ltd won 97 per cent of the work. In Middlesbrough, K Ltd won 71 per cent of the work and A Ltd won 29 per cent. Having found that an SPC had taken place, the employment tribunal divided liability for redundancy payments and unfair dismissal between K Ltd and A Ltd by reference to the percentage of work that each company had taken on. The EAT, after holding that the tribunal had been entitled to find that an SPC had taken place, went on to allow A Ltd's appeal against the decision to apportion liability. It rejected the possibility that there could be any splitting of liability as between transferees, whether this reflected the proportional split of work between the new contractors or otherwise. Contrary to the tribunal's approach, it was not permissible to divorce a contract from the rights and liabilities under it. Therefore, although the activities could be split between more than one transferee, the rights and liabilities in respect of each affected employee could only transfer to one of those transferees. In determining to whom the rights and liabilities transferred, the EAT held that the factors set out in Duncan Web Offset (Maidstone) Ltd v Cooper and ors 1995 IRLR 633, EAT – a case concerning the assignment of employees in a 'business transfer' under what is now Reg 3(1)(a) – should be followed. These included but were not limited to the amount of time spent and the amount of value given by the employee; the terms of the employment contracts showing what the employee could be required to do; and how the cost of employing the employee was apportioned. The EAT stated that the 'overall principle' is to focus upon the 'link between the employee and the work or activities which are performed'. On this basis, and with regard to the Stockton-based claimants (where K Ltd had won 97 per cent of the work), the EAT held that their employment had transferred to K Ltd. Regarding the Middlesbrough-based claimants (where the split was 71 per cent to K Ltd to 29 per cent to A Ltd), the EAT determined the case solely on the basis of the work-split, and accordingly held that all rights, duties and liabilities under those employees' contracts should also pass to K Ltd.

1.110 **Is statutory test same as that set down in case law?** In Metropolitan Resources Ltd v Churchill Dulwich Ltd and ors (above) the EAT stated that the relevant activities must be *fundamentally or essentially* the same pre- and post-transfer. Reg 3(2A), which was inserted into TUPE with effect from 31 January 2014 by the Collective Redundancies and Transfer of Undertakings (Protection of Employment) (Amendment) Regulations 2014 SI 2014/16, states that the activities must be 'fundamentally the same'. Despite the difference in wording, it does not appear to be the case that there is any difference of substance between the two tests. The rationale for Reg 3(2A) was set out in the Government's response to its 2013 Consultation on its TUPE reform proposals: namely, that 'it may not be generally appreciated that case law has established that part of the test of whether a TUPE service provision change occurs is whether the activities carried on after the alleged transfer are "fundamentally or essentially the same" as those carried on before it'. The Government explained its intention 'to amend TUPE to set out expressly this test on the degree of similarity of the activities' but stated 'it may not necessarily refer to both "fundamentally" and "essentially"'. The intention behind Reg 3(2A) is therefore to codify the Metropolitan Resources decision and subsequent case law, rather than to introduce a new, narrower test.

The Reg 3(3) conditions   1.111
For an SPC as defined in Reg 3(1)(b)(i), (ii) or (iii) to amount to a 'relevant transfer', each of the conditions set out in Reg 3(3) must be met. These are :

- 'immediately before the service provision change there is an organised grouping of employees situated in Great Britain which has as its principal purpose the carrying out of the activities concerned on behalf of the client' – Reg 3(3)(a)(i)

- 'immediately before the service provision change the client intends that the activities will, following the service provision change, be carried out by the transferee other than in connection with a single specific event or task of short-term duration' – Reg 3(3)(a)(ii), and

- 'the activities concerned do not consist wholly or mainly of the supply of goods for the client's use' – Reg 3(3)(b).

Each of these conditions is examined in detail below.

Organised grouping of employees carrying out activities   1.112
The first of the conditions that must be satisfied in order for a 'service provision change' covered by Reg 3(1)(b) to occur is that 'immediately before the service provision change there is an organised grouping of employees situated in Great Britain which has as its principal purpose the carrying out of the activities concerned on behalf of a client' – Reg 3(3)(a)(i). As we shall explain further below, this condition has been interpreted in such a way as to mean that a significant number of SPCs will not amount to a relevant transfer.

The BIS Guide states that this requirement is intended 'to confine the Regulations' coverage to cases where the old service provider (i.e. the transferor) has in place a team of employees to carry out the service activities, and that team is essentially dedicated to carrying out the activities that are to transfer'. The Guide goes on to give an example where this requirement would not be met: 'If a contractor was engaged by a client to provide, say, a courier service, but the collections and deliveries were carried out each day by various different couriers on an ad hoc basis, rather than by an identifiable team of employees, there would be no "service provision change" and the Regulations would not apply.'

1.113 **Organisation must be intentional.** In Eddie Stobart Ltd v Moreman and ors 2012 ICR 919, EAT, the EAT held that, for Reg 3(3)(a) purposes, the organisation of the grouping must be more than merely circumstantial – the employees must have been organised *intentionally*. The 35 claimants in that case were employed by ES Ltd, a logistics business, at a depot that, by the time it closed in 2009, served only two clients. Work at the depot operated by way of a shift system, with the result that the nightshift employees worked principally on F's contract, while the dayshift focused on V's contract. When the depot closed, the claimants asserted that V's contract was taken over by FJGL Ltd and that they transferred by way of an SPC. An employment tribunal found that no SPC had occurred and the EAT upheld this decision on appeal. Mr Justice Underhill – then President of the EAT, who sat alone – held that Reg 3(3)(a)(i) does not require merely that a grouping of employees in fact carried out the activities in question; they must have been organised with that principal purpose in mind. In other words, the employees had to be organised in some way by reference to the requirements of the client. The statutory language did not naturally apply to a situation like this, where a combination of circumstances – essentially, shift patterns and working practices on the ground – meant that a group of employees were in practice, but without any deliberate planning or intent, found to be working mostly on tasks which benefited a particular client. The paradigm of an 'organised grouping' would indeed occur where employees were organised as 'the [Client A] team', although the definition could in principle be satisfied in cases where the identification was less precise.

Underhill P rejected the contention that his conclusion was objectionable on policy grounds in that, because it is rare in the logistics industry to have identified teams of employees, few in that industry would have the protection of TUPE. While the broad purpose of TUPE is to protect the interests of employees by ensuring that in specified circumstances they 'go with the work', it remains necessary to define the circumstances in which a relevant transfer will occur, and there is no rule that the natural meaning of the language of the Regulations has to be stretched in order to achieve a transfer in as many situations as possible. If anything, the policy considerations point the other way. It is important that, on a transfer, employees should, as far as possible, know where they stand, but if the putative 'grouping' does not reflect any existing organisational unit, there are liable to be real practical difficulties in identifying which employees belong to it.

The approach to the 'organised grouping of employees' requirement taken by **1.114** Underhill P in the Eddie Stobart case chimed with the obiter views of Lady Smith in a case handed down in the same week – Argyll Coastal Services Ltd v Stirling and ors EATS 0012/11. There, an employment tribunal had decided that the crew of a cargo ship along with two administrative workers transferred to another company under the SPC rules when the Ministry of Defence changed contractors for the delivery of cargo in and around the Falkland Islands. The EAT held that the tribunal had not undertaken the analysis that was necessary in order to reach this conclusion and remitted the case. Lady Smith observed that the phrase 'organised grouping of employees' seemed to connote a number of employees that is 'less than the whole of the transferor's entire workforce, deliberately organised for the purpose of carrying out the activities required by the particular client contract and who work together as a team'.

The Court of Session approved and applied the analysis in the above cases in Ceva Freight (UK) Ltd v Seawell Ltd 2013 IRLR 726, Ct Sess (Inner House), confirming that some element of conscious organisation is required by Reg 3(3)(a). In that case, M was employed by CF Ltd and spent 100 per cent of his time supervising work for one client, S Ltd. Indeed, his job description stated that the purpose of his employment was to enable the contract with S Ltd to be performed. However, he was not the only employee of CF Ltd who did work on that contract – several other employees spent up to 30 per cent of their time on it. The Court of Session (Inner House) held that M did not transfer via a service provision change when S Ltd took the work back in-house. Although Reg 2(1) makes it clear that an 'organised grouping' can be composed of a single employee, the Court considered that this definition is directed to the case where a client has need for the services of only one employee. Where the activities are in fact carried out by a plurality of employees, it is not legitimate to isolate one of that number on the basis that the employee in question devoted all, or virtually all, of his or her working time to assisting in the collaborative effort.

The requirement that the organisation of employees for the purposes of **1.115** Reg 3(3)(a)(i) be intentional, rather than arising through happenstance, means that tribunals must undertake a factual inquiry into how the work was organised. Two examples:

- **Dovaston and ors v Norbert Dentressangle Ltd and anor** ET Case No.1307117/12: D and his fellow claimants were employees of ND Ltd, whose business involved providing blast freezing and warehousing services to a number of clients, the largest of which was ABPE. When ABPE moved its contract for these services from ND Ltd to G Ltd, the claimants lost their jobs and brought claims for unfair dismissal, breach of contract and redundancy payments. A preliminary issue arose as to whether there had been a transfer by way of an SPC from ND Ltd to G Ltd. An employment judge, referring to the Eddie Stobart case (above), considered that, for an SPC to have taken place, the claimants would need to have been organised as a team dedicated to ABPE. However, the evidence showed that they were organised by job function rather than by client: 'as in Eddie Stobart, the claimants carried out the work which was presented to them'

- **Edwards and ors v RS Gormanley Ltd and anor** ET Case No.3300955/13: RSG Ltd was a family company which provided multi-skilled tradesmen to carry out repair and maintenance of void and occupied properties owned by the London Borough of Hillingdon (the Council). On 21 November 2012 the Council summarily terminated the contract with RSG Ltd and brought the maintenance work back in-house. It refused to employ the employees who had carried out the maintenance and repair work for RSG Ltd, and when they subsequently brought claims arising out of the termination of their employment, a preliminary question arose as to whether there had been a transfer by way of SPC to the Council. An employment judge found that the Council was effectively RSG Ltd's only client. The employees spent either the vast majority or the entirety of their working time on work for the Council – the only other activities to occupy them were administration or looking for more work. Since the entire business was geared to the needs of one client, RSG Ltd's workforce was an organised grouping of employees deliberately, and almost entirely, focused on one client. (Note that the result of this pre-hearing review was not appealed. The Council did, however, successfully appeal the tribunal's later decision that three members of the family which owned RSG Ltd had been assigned to the organised grouping – London Borough of Hillingdon v Gormanley and ors EAT 0169/14).

1.116 **Organised grouping can consist of single employee.** Regulation 2(1) explains that 'references to "organised grouping of employees" shall include a single employee'. This linguistically awkward statement doffs its hat to the case of Schmidt v Spar-und Leihkasse der früheren Ämter Bordesholm, Kiel und Cronshagen 1995 ICR 237, ECJ (see 'Business transfers – what is an "economic entity"?' above), in which the ECJ held that the fact that an economic activity is performed by a single employee is not in itself sufficient to preclude the application of the transfer rules. In Ceva Freight (UK) Ltd v Seawell Ltd 2013 IRLR 726, Ct Sess (Inner House), the Court of Session provided two hypothetical examples of an organised grouping consisting of a single employee: a single cleaner provided by a cleaning firm to a client; and a single solicitor within a firm working full time for an insurance client.

An actual, rather than hypothetical, example of a single employee constituting an organised grouping can be seen in the facts of Rynda (UK) Ltd v Rhijnsburger 2015 IRLR 394, CA. R was employed by DJD and was responsible for managing the Dutch properties of the R Group, which owned a large portfolio of properties across Europe. When DJD withdrew its services, R Group allocated the management of its property portfolio to one of its subsidiary companies, R Ltd. R was immediately employed by R Ltd, where she carried on her duties as before. She was the only employee who managed the Dutch properties and, other than a short period during which she assisted with the management of some properties in Germany, all of her time was devoted to that work. In R's subsequent unfair dismissal claim, an employment judge held that R had transferred by way of an SPC from DJD to R Ltd. The judge reached that conclusion on the basis that R was the only employee responsible for managing the Dutch properties; she was thus 'an organised grouping of employees', which had as its principal purpose the carrying out of that property management activity. The EAT upheld that conclusion, and R Ltd appealed to the Court of Appeal.

Dismissing the appeal, the Court observed that in Eddie Stobart Ltd v Moreman **1.117** (above), the employees were not specifically an 'organised grouping of employees', as they just happened to be a group which worked on tasks for a particular client because of the shift to which they were allocated. There was no deliberate planning or intent in the way that they were organised in relation to that client. Here, however, there was no similar external circumstance that caused R to spend all her time working for the Dutch properties, but rather it was due to a positive decision of the employer to assign her to those properties. Similarly, the instant case could be distinguished from Ceva Freight (UK) Ltd v Seawell (above), given that R was working exclusively on the Dutch properties and was neither part of a team that delivered services to other clients, nor was assisted by any other employees in managing those properties.

Principal purpose. In order for Reg 3(1)(b) to apply, the principal purpose of **1.118** the organised grouping of employees must be the carrying out of the activities on behalf of a client. The term 'principal purpose' is not given further definition in the TUPE Regulations, but by analogy with the law relating to unfair dismissal – where a tribunal must consider what was the reason, or principal reason, for dismissal – we can conclude that carrying out the activities on behalf of the client need not be the sole purpose of the group. It must, however, be dominant over any other purpose(s).

Deciding whether the 'principal purpose' requirement is satisfied where there are multiple clients will not always be straightforward. Take, for example, a group of staff at Contractor Ltd, who devote Monday to Wednesday each week to providing a service to one client (A), and spend the rest of each week providing the same service to a number of other clients (B, C, D, E and F). What will be the position if client A decides to end its contract with Contractor Ltd, and engage a different company, Cheaper Ltd, to provide the service? Will there be an SPC within Reg 3(1)(b) from Contractor Ltd to Cheaper Ltd? In one sense, the principal purpose of the relevant group of employees is to carry out the 'activities' on behalf of client A. That is what the employees spend 60 per cent of their time doing, and, as the BIS Guide states, a team of employees does not need to work exclusively on the activities that are to transfer for Reg 3(1)(b) to apply. In another sense, however, the group's principal purpose is to carry out the activities in question for a number of different clients. Such a conclusion would be reinforced if the employees were spending a lot of time working for client A simply because of a recent influx of work from that client, whereas the more normal pattern has been to carry out less work for client A and much more work, say, for clients B and C.

1.119 The decision in Eddie Stobart Ltd v Moreman and ors (above) established that it is necessary to examine whether the split of work has come about deliberately: in our example, a tribunal would need to consider whether the employees were organised into a 'Client A team', or whether they were organised more generally. This is a question of fact and degree for the tribunal – for the EAT to overturn an employment tribunal's findings on this point, it would need to be satisfied that the tribunal had either misdirected itself in law or reached a decision which met the high threshold for perversity.

Two examples of employment tribunals addressing the question of whether there was an organised grouping whose principal purpose was carrying out the activities on behalf of the client:

- **Murray and ors v Salvation Army and anor** ET Case No.2505640/10: the Salvation Army ran a hostel for homeless people in Darlington, at which all of the 18 claimants worked. TSC Ltd ran two similar hostels. Funding for all three hostels was supplied by the Borough Council, which decided to put the contracts out to tender. TSC Ltd won the contracts, but denied that the claimants had transferred to its employment. Considering complaints of unfair dismissal and a failure to inform and consult, an employment tribunal found that the claimants worked as a team – although there were differences in their roles, they were clearly an organised grouping. The activities they carried out included the provision of accommodation, clothing, food, education and housing – i.e. a total package of care and support for homeless people. Each of the claimants contributed to the common purpose. It was therefore clear to the tribunal that the Reg 3(3)(a)(i) test had been satisfied

- **Wilson and ors v Ferris Garage Ltd and anor** ET Case No.1700402/11: FG Ltd carried out breakdown and recovery work. It had a number of clients, of whom one, the RAC, took up about 30 per cent of the workload. In 2011 FG Ltd lost the RAC contract to FW Ltd. When, following the change of provider, the three employees who had been working for FG Ltd on the contract were dismissed and brought claims of unfair dismissal, a preliminary question arose as to whether there had been a transfer to FW Ltd. An employment tribunal concluded that the claimants had been part of an organised grouping of employees, but that its principal purpose was to render assistance to distressed motorists. None of the claimants had been specifically told, either in their contracts or verbally, that they would be predominantly working on the RAC contract, and the tribunal rejected the contention that the principal purpose of the organised grouping had been carrying out work for the RAC. It followed that there had been no transfer, and that liability for the dismissals lay with FG Ltd.

Fragmentation. When the 2006 Regulations were introduced, the accompanying **1.120** DTI Guide took the view that Reg 3(1)(b) would 'potentially cover situations where just some of those activities in the original service contract are retendered and awarded to a new contractor, or where the original service contract is split up into two or more components, each of which is assigned to a different contractor. In each of these cases, the key test is whether an organised grouping of employees has as its principal purpose the carrying out of the activities that are transferred.'

The above passage has not been included in the BIS Guide, reflecting case law under Reg 3(1)(b), which indicated that the Reg 3(3) organised grouping test has little bearing on the question of whether activities have become too fragmented for there to be an SPC. Instead, this question arises as part of the tribunal's consideration of whether the activities formerly carried out by the purported transferor are now carried out by the purported transferee. This case law is considered under 'Transferor and transferee must carry out same activities – fragmentation of "activities"' above.

Organised grouping must exist 'immediately before' SPC. The Reg 3(3)(a)(i) **1.121** condition will only be satisfied if the organised grouping of employees, which had as its principal purpose the carrying out of activities on behalf of the client, existed *immediately before* the SPC. However, the statutory language does not indicate whether or not the employees who constitute that grouping must actually be carrying out the activities immediately before the transfer. This is a potentially important point where an SPC takes place following a temporary cessation in work.

In Inex Home Improvements Ltd v Hodgkins and ors EAT 0329/14 the EAT held that an employment judge had erred when he treated the fact that the claimant employees had been temporarily laid off at the time of the transfer as determinative of the question of whether there had been an organised grouping. The judge had concluded that, since the employees had not been working immediately before the transfer owing to their being laid off, there was no organised grouping and accordingly no TUPE transfer. On appeal, the EAT recognised that there was a degree of ambiguity in Reg 3(3)(a)(i) and therefore considered it appropriate to adopt an interpretation that was in line with the purpose of the Regulations – the protection of employment. If a temporary cessation of work would automatically take employment outside the scope of

TUPE, it would undermine that protection. Remitting the matter to the employment judge to consider afresh, the EAT observed that the question to be asked was whether the organised grouping, despite the temporary cessation in work, had retained its identity. Answering this question would include a consideration of the purpose, nature and length of the cessation.

1.122   **Organised grouping must be 'situated in Great Britain'.** In respect of service provision changes, the TUPE Regulations only apply where there is an organised grouping of employees situated in Great Britain immediately before the service provision change. It follows that Reg 3(1)(b) only applies to SPCs within Great Britain or from Great Britain outwards – not to transfers into Great Britain from elsewhere.

For the purposes of Reg 3(1)(b) it is the 'organised grouping of employees' that must be within Great Britain. Nevertheless, Reg 3(4)(c) provides that a relevant transfer can occur even where some employees ordinarily work outside the UK. The BIS Guide gives an example of how Reg 3(4)(c) works in the context of SPC transfers. That example is of a contract to provide website maintenance, which comes to an end and is taken over by another contractor. If, of the organised grouping of employees that has performed the contract, one of the IT technicians works from home, which is outside the UK, that should not prevent TUPE from applying. On the other hand, if the whole team of IT technicians worked from home outside Great Britain, then a transfer of the business for which they work would not fall within the Regulations as there would be no organised grouping of employees situated in Great Britain.

1.123   **Northern Ireland.** The reference to 'Great Britain' in Reg 3(1)(b) might at first seem surprising. As we saw in 'Business transfers' above, Reg 3(1)(a) covers the transfer of undertakings 'situated immediately before the transfer in the United Kingdom' – that is, Great Britain and Northern Ireland. However, Schedule 1 to the Regulations – which deals with the extent to which the Regulations apply to Northern Ireland – expressly provides in para 2 that '[Reg 3(1)(b)] and any other provision of these Regulations insofar as it relates to that sub-paragraph shall not apply to Northern Ireland'. The reason for the exclusion of Northern Ireland from the Reg 3(1)(b) SPC provision is that S.38 of the Employment Relations Act 1999, which contains the power of the Secretary of State to extend TUPE protection to 'circumstances in which there is no transfer, or no transfer to which the Community obligation applies', does not apply to that Province. However, protection equivalent to that afforded by Reg 3(1)(b) of the TUPE Regulations has been extended to Northern Ireland by Reg 3 of the Service Provision Change (Protection of Employment) Regulations (Northern Ireland) 2006 SI 2006/177.

1.124   **Cross-border transfers.** With increasing globalisation and the expansion of outsourcing across international borders, the issue of how and when the TUPE Regulations apply to cases with an international element is clearly of importance.

Under Reg 3(1)(b), the main requirement is simply that of an organised grouping of employees situated in Great Britain immediately before the SPC. Thus, it seems at least arguable that an SPC involving, for example, a call centre that moves from the UK to India could be covered by the Regulations. This possibility was discussed by the EAT in Holis Metal Industries Ltd v GMB and anor 2008 ICR 464, EAT. We explore this issue in Chapter 9, 'Transnational issues', under 'Transfers from and to the United Kingdom'.

Single specific events or tasks of short duration 1.125

The second of the three conditions required for a transfer by way of an SPC to occur is that it must be shown that 'immediately before the service provision change... the client intends that the activities will, following the service provision change, be carried out by the transferee other than in connection with a single specific event or task of short-term duration' – Reg 3(3)(a)(ii).

Short-term duration. The Reg 3(3)(a)(ii) wording is not without its 1.126 difficulties. One possible interpretation is that the provision excludes from TUPE activities carried out in connection with (i) all single specific events, and (ii) all tasks of short-term duration. This would suggest, for example, that the award of a contract relating to a single specific event would be excluded, no matter how long that event is intended to take. An alternative reading is that an event or task must be both 'single specific' and 'of short-term duration' if the Reg 3(3)(a)(ii) exclusion is to apply.

The BIS Guide favours the latter interpretation. It provides two examples that would be caught by the Reg 3(3)(a)(ii) exclusion. The first is where a client engages a contractor to organise a single conference on its behalf – this is held up as an example of a 'one-off service' (i.e. a single specific event). The Guide goes on to state that 'to qualify under this exemption, the one-off service must also be "of short-term duration"'. To illustrate that point, it provides the example of two different contracts for the provision of security to the Olympic Games. The first contract, providing security advice to the event organisers over a period of years up to the Games, would relate to a single specific event, but its longevity would mean that it would not be excluded by Reg 3(3)(a)(ii). The second contract, to protect the athletes' security during the Games itself, would be a single specific event that was of a sufficiently short duration to come within the exclusion and thus fall outside the scope of the SPC rules.

The view expressed in the BIS Guide is, however, muddied by conflicting 1.127 opinions in the EAT. The first case to be considered is SNR Denton UK LLP v Kirwan and anor 2013 ICR 101, EAT. There, as we have seen under 'The three types of SPC – client must remain the same' above, the EAT held that there had not been a transfer by way of an SPC, because the identity of the client had changed. Although it was not necessary for the disposal of the appeal, Mr Justice Langstaff (President of the EAT) nevertheless set out his tentative view that

Reg 3(3)(a)(ii) only applies to events or tasks that are both 'single specific' and of 'short-term duration'. As for what would amount to 'short-term' in this context, Langstaff P noted that duration is not to be judged from a historical perspective but in the broader context of employment relationships as a whole. Langstaff P thought it relevant that, at the time that the 2006 Regulations were made, it would take a year for an employee to obtain many employment rights. An employee might expect to receive at most 12 weeks' notice from the employer and could in some circumstances give as little as one week, and would have three months within which to bring a claim of unfair dismissal. These considerations, plus the circumstance of the particular employment, all create a context within which 'short-term' must be judged. Accordingly, the question will be one of fact and degree for the tribunal.

The next case in the sequence was Liddell's Coaches v Cook and ors 2013 ICR 547, EAT, where a division of the Appeal Tribunal presided over by Lady Smith agreed with Langstaff P's observations on the meaning of 'short-term', but disagreed with his conclusion on the statutory wording. Here, the EAT interpreted Reg 3(3)(a)(ii) disjunctively – i.e. such that 'single specific events' stand apart from 'tasks of short-term duration' as distinct categories of excluded transfers. In the EAT's view, a single specific event is, by definition, of short duration, and so it would be tautologous if the words 'of short-term duration' were intended to qualify 'single specific event' as well as 'task'. It considered that the DTI Guide (since replaced by the BIS Guide, but without changes to the passages on Reg 3(3)(a)(ii)) was wrong to suggest that a single specific event could be of long-term duration. To take the DTI's example, a contract to provide security advice over a number of years to the organisers of the Olympic Games could still be regarded as connected to an event of short-term duration. There was a flaw in the DTI's thinking, which was to conflate 'activities' with an 'event' – the Olympic Games are a single specific event, and so activities done *in connection* with it – even those done over a period of years – may be excluded from TUPE. Applying this reasoning to the facts of the case, the EAT held that the employment tribunal had been entitled to find that a one-year contract between a local authority and a coach operator to transport schoolchildren to other schools while their school was being rebuilt was excluded from TUPE under Reg 3(3)(a)(ii). Although there were flaws in the tribunal's reasoning – for instance, the EAT did not agree that the construction of a school could properly be categorised as an 'event' – its conclusion that, viewed in context, the contract was 'short-term', given that local authority transport contracts were usually awarded for three years or more, was sufficient for the Reg 3(3)(a)(ii) exclusion to be engaged.

1.128 Demurring from Lady Smith's analysis in Liddell's Coaches, the EAT in Swanbridge Hire and Sales Ltd v Butler and ors EAT 0056/13 took the view that the words 'of short-term duration' in Reg 3(3)(a)(ii) qualify 'event' as well as 'task'. Mrs Justice Slade opined that a 'single specific event' is not self-evidently short-lived. She gave the example of a leak in an oil pipeline, which would be an 'event' capable of continuing for a considerable period of time. Slade J also indicated that, unlike the employment tribunal in the instant case, she would not consider an 18-month project to insulate and lag five industrial boilers at a power plant an 'event'. In her view, this was clearly a 'task'.

Slade J's analysis in Swanbridge was endorsed by the EAT in Horizon Security Services Ltd v Ndeze and anor EAT 0071/14, and given that it tallies with that of the President in SNR Denton UK LLP v Kirwan and anor (above), would appear to be the preferred approach. However, all of the above EAT views on the meaning of Reg 3(3)(a)(ii) are technically obiter (i.e. non-binding), since none of the cases turned on the point – Langstaff P observed that the distinction between the two interpretations of the provision gave rise to a 'somewhat theological question'. It is, perhaps, telling that we have yet to see a case involving a single specific event that is not of short-term duration.

However, the following cases are examples of two employment tribunal **1.129** decisions in which it was concluded that no SPC transfer had occurred because the *task* in question was of a short-term duration:

- **Gillard v Catercare Solutions Ltd and ors** ET Case No.2701897/12: G was employed by CS Ltd as a kitchen assistant, working in a residential care home owned by SRH. In April 2012, environmental health inspectors twice visited the home and raised serious concerns about the cleanliness of the kitchen and the food hygiene qualifications of those working in it. CS Ltd was given a short time frame in which to put matters right, and when it failed to do so, its contract was terminated. SRH then engaged an employment agency to provide temporary kitchen staff for a period of three months while the tendering process for the catering contract ran its course. When G subsequently claimed that she had been unfairly dismissed, an employment tribunal rejected the contention that there had been a transfer to SRH. It accepted the submission that SRH needed to take emergency action to ensure the residents continued to be fed. This clearly fell within the meaning of a specific event or task of short-term duration, with the result that TUPE did not apply

- **Mahdi and ors v ICTS UK Ltd and anor** ET Case No.3300116/14: ICTS Ltd had a contract with Middlesex University to provide security services at a number of sites. One such site was closed in 2012, and the claimants were assigned by ICTS to guard these vacant but valuable premises. In July 2013 the site was purchased by AUCMS, a Malaysian university. ICTS offered to enter into a new contract with AUCMS, but in the meantime continued to provide its security services. In November AUCMS informed ICTS that it would be appointing a new security company, FCS Group, with effect from 11 November. FCS Group denied that ICTS's employees had transferred to it: ICTS had continued to supply security to an empty site, whereas

FCS Group's role would be to provide security to a multi-million pound construction and renovation scheme. The employment tribunal agreed that AUCMS had engaged FCS Group to perform activities in connection with a task of short-term duration.

1.130 **'The client intends'.** The Reg 3(3)(a)(ii) exclusion will only apply if, immediately before the transfer, the client *intends* that the activities will be carried out by the transferee in connection with a single specific event or task of short-term duration. The 2005 Consultation Document concerning the draft 2006 Regulations explained that the wording of Reg 3(3)(a)(ii) is 'designed to avoid creating a loophole that would enable the application of the extended provision [that is, Reg 3(1)(b)] to be avoided simply by the client and the contractor entering into a succession of short-term, one-off contracts (e.g. to take an extreme case, a succession of daily contracts for the cleaning of an office building) for what was in truth always intended to be an ongoing service provision arrangement. It is for this reason that the client's intention has been made part of the test.' Nevertheless, Reg 3(3)(a)(ii) will operate to exclude an SPC from TUPE 'even if the client happens to engage a particular contractor on a number of separate occasions to provide one-off services on its behalf... if this is simply coincidental or fortuitous and, on each occasion, the client has no intention that this arrangement should become an ongoing, "preferred supplier" one'.

The Consultation Document went on to explain that 'if a dispute arises over this issue, the court or employment tribunal hearing the case will have to decide what the client's intention was based on the evidence before it'. This view is borne out by the few EAT cases to have considered the point. In SNR Denton UK LLP v Kirwan and anor 2013 ICR 101, EAT, Langstaff P commented (obiter) that, when considering the Reg 3(3)(a)(ii) exclusion, tribunals are dealing with the anticipation or intention of the client, not with an objective standard. The employment tribunal in that particular case had appeared to suggest (although this was unclear) that a continuation of activities for three months following a putative transfer might be excluded by Reg 3(3)(a)(ii). In Langstaff P's view, the actual time did not matter, since the tribunal's focus should have been on the intention of the client.

1.131 In Swanbridge Hire and Sales Ltd v Butler and ors EAT 0056/13 the EAT allowed an appeal against an employment tribunal's finding of an SPC where the tribunal had failed to make a primary finding of fact as to the client's intention. The tribunal also erred in its analysis of whether the work was 'short-term' when it took into account the length of time that the outgoing contractor had already spent on the project. The tribunal was required to assess the client's intention as to the duration of the work at the time of the putative SPC transfer. Thus, it should not have relied on the time it had taken for the outgoing contractor to complete work as an indicator of how long the client intended the incoming contractor to spend on it.

A client's 'hope or wish' that the contractor's activities would be of short-term duration was held to be insufficient to engage the Reg 3(3)(a)(ii) exclusion in Robert Sage Ltd t/a Prestige Nursing Care Ltd v O'Connell and ors and another case 2014 IRLR 428, EAT. There, A terminated its contract with the Council to provide care services for X, who had severe learning difficulties. The Council subsequently contracted with P to take over X's care until the Court of Protection approved its request to move X to a new location. An issue arose as to whether A's employees assigned to X's care transferred to P. The employment tribunal found that an SPC had taken place. In its view, the Reg 3(3)(a) exclusion did not apply because the Council merely 'hoped or wished' that P's involvement would be short term – it had no control over whether the Court of Protection would grant approval or how long such approval would take. On appeal, the EAT held that the tribunal had correctly found that the Council's 'hope or wish' could not be equated with an 'intention' for the purpose of Reg 3(3)(a). A transferee cannot 'intend' to do something which is not reasonably achievable.

Where there is more than one client, it will be necessary to establish a common **1.132** intention with regard to the manner in which the activities are to be carried out for the purpose of Reg 3(3)(a)(ii) – Ottimo Property Services Ltd v Duncan and anor 2015 ICR 859, EAT. The EAT there held that there is no reason in principle why an SPC might not, for example, involve a contract for the provision of services to a group of persons collectively defined as 'the client' under that contract, provided they retain the same identity before and after the SPC (see 'The three types of SPC – client must remain the same' above), and provided they have the requisite common intention for the purpose of Reg 3(3)(a)(ii). Furthermore, the fact that there are separate contracts for each client does not necessarily mean that there can be no SPC. It will be harder to demonstrate the necessary commonality of intention where there is no umbrella contract defining 'the client' but that does not prevent common intent being demonstrated in some other way.

Activities wholly or mainly for supply of goods excluded 1.133

The third condition that must be satisfied for a relevant SPC transfer to occur under Reg 3(1)(b) is set out in Reg 3(3)(b). This provides that the activities in question must 'not consist wholly or mainly of the supply of goods for the client's use'.

The BIS Guide sets out the following example to explain the intended scope of this condition: 'The Regulations are not expected to apply where a client engages a contractor to supply, for example, sandwiches and drinks to its canteen every day, for the client to sell on to its own staff. If, on the other hand, the contract was for the contractor to run the client's staff canteen, then this exclusion would not come into play and the Regulations might therefore apply.' In the 2005 Consultation Document, where the canteen example first appeared, the Government added: 'Even if the contractor, as part and parcel of the latter arrangement... supplies the food and drink to be served in the canteen, it is likely that this will be ancillary to those main activities; and the goods – the food and drink – will in any event be for direct sale to and consumption by the canteen's customers, not for the use of the client, so the circumstances will not fall within [Reg 3(3)(b)].'

1.134 The EAT referred to the above example when it considered the meaning of the Reg 3(3)(b) exclusion for the first (and, so far, only) time in Pannu and ors v Geo W King Ltd 2012 IRLR 193, EAT. In that case the claimants worked for GWK Ltd on a production line, assembling axles and related vehicle parts. GWK Ltd supplied these parts under contract to IBCV Ltd, which manufactured commercial vehicles. GWK Ltd went into liquidation and IBCV Ltd thereafter bought the parts under a contract with another company, P. The claimants asserted that there had been an SPC and that they were entitled to transfer either to LBCV Ltd or to P. An employment tribunal rejected their claims on the basis of Reg 3(3)(b) and the EAT dismissed an appeal against that decision. It noted that the fact that the claimants provided a service to their employer, the contractor, did not mean that the relevant activities were a service rather than the supply of goods. The EAT considered that the claimants' situation was analogous to that of the workers making sandwiches and drinks in the example given by the BIS Guide. Although GWK Ltd employed an organised group of employees on the assembly line dedicated to producing axles for use in IBCV Ltd's van manufacturing process, GWK Ltd's relevant activity as a contractor was the supply of those finished goods to IBCV Ltd. Since that was the activity which changed hands, there was no SPC transfer by virtue of Reg 3(3)(b).

The fact that only one appellate decision has considered the Reg 3(3)(b) exclusion suggests that its interpretation has not particularly troubled tribunals. However, problems could arise where the activities under a contract consist partially of the supply of goods for the client's use. Consider the following example. Supplier Ltd has a contract to supply specialist machinery to Big plc, its one major client. The contract also provides that Supplier Ltd will be responsible for servicing and repairing the machinery provided. If Big plc terminates this contract and enters into a similar contract with Goods Ltd, will the Reg 3(3)(b) exclusion take effect to prevent an SPC transfer from Supplier Ltd to Goods Ltd?

1.135 Here, it would seem that the main purpose of the *contract as a whole* is the supply of goods, with the service provision aspect – the service and repair of the machinery supplied – appearing to be merely ancillary to that purpose. So, at first glance, one might think that the transfer of the contract to Goods Ltd would fall within the Reg 3(3)(b) exclusion, and that no SPC transfer under

Reg 3(1)(b) would occur. However, it is important to note that Reg 3(3)(b) does not talk about the contract consisting wholly or mainly of the supply of goods. Rather, it is the *activities* concerned that must consist wholly or mainly of the supply of goods if the exclusion is to apply. Arguably, there are two sets of 'activities' transferring from Supplier Ltd to Goods Ltd in our example: first, the activities concerning the supply of goods, to which the Reg 3(3)(b) exclusion would apply; and secondly, the service and repair activities, to which the exclusion would not apply. In other words, the goods activities might be severable from the service activities for the purposes of the SPC transfer rules.

The question of whether activities are severable for the purposes of Reg 3(1)(b) has not been tested in case law – in Enterprise Management Services Ltd v Connect-Up Ltd and ors 2012 IRLR 190, EAT, HHJ Peter Clark observed that it was 'an interesting point' but declined to consider it as it had not been raised before the employment tribunal. However, presuming for the moment that activities are severable, and that Supplier Ltd had a dedicated team of staff whose principal purpose had been carrying out Big plc's ongoing service and repair needs, this team would be protected by Reg 3(1)(b) and would thus transfer to Goods Ltd. If this were the case, what would become of Supplier Ltd's other team of staff, who were dedicated to making and supplying the machinery to Big plc? They would not transfer to Goods Ltd under the new SPC rules owing to the Reg 3(3)(b) supply of goods exclusion. However, they would still be protected by the 2006 Regulations, and hence transfer, if they could show that a relevant transfer under Reg 3(1)(a) occurred – see 'Business transfers' above.

Guidance for tribunals

1.136

In the sections above we examined each of the components of an SPC transfer under Reg 3(1)(b). Given that the statutory words can be taken at face value, the straightforward approach to determining whether such a transfer has taken place is to first consider if an SPC within one of Reg 3(1)(b)(i), (ii) or (iii) has taken place, and then consider each of the Reg 3(3) conditions in turn. Although the guidance handed down by the EAT and the Court of Appeal has been a little more detailed than this, it does conform to the same basic structure.

Most recently, in Rynda (UK) Ltd v Rhijnsburger 2015 IRLR 394, CA, the Court of Appeal explained that there is a four-stage test that emerges from the authorities when considering whether there has been a service provision change within the terms of Reg 3 TUPE from company B to company A. The first step is to identify the service that company B was providing to the client. The next step is to list the activities that the staff of company B performed in order to provide that service. The third step is to identify the employee or employees of company B who ordinarily carried out those activities. And the fourth step is to consider whether company B organised that employee or those employees into a 'grouping' for the principal purpose of carrying out the listed activities.

1.137 While we would not dispute the order in which the Court of Appeal advises that a tribunal tackle the above four questions, this guidance does not appear to take into account the other Reg 3(3) conditions. A more rigorous step-by-step approach can be gleaned from His Honour Judge Peter Clark's summary of the authorities in Enterprise Management Services Ltd v Connect-Up Ltd and ors 2012 IRLR 190, EAT:

- an employment tribunal's first task is to identify the activities performed by the in-house employees (in an outsourcing situation) or the original contractor (in a retendering or insourcing situation)

- next the tribunal should consider the question of whether these activities are fundamentally the same as those carried out by the new contractor (outsourcing or retendering) or in-house employees (insourcing). Cases may arise where the activities have become so fragmented that they fall outside the SPC regime

- if the activities have remained fundamentally the same, the tribunal should ask itself whether, before the transfer, there was an organised grouping of employees which had as its principal purpose the carrying out of the activities on behalf of the client

- following this, a tribunal should consider whether the exceptions in Reg 3(3)(b) and (c) apply: namely, whether the client intends that the transferee, post-SPC, will carry out the activities in connection with a single specific event or task of short-term duration; and whether the contract is wholly or mainly for the supply of goods for the client's use

- finally, if the tribunal is satisfied that a transfer by way of an SPC has taken place, it should consider whether each individual claimant is assigned to the organised grouping of employees (a point we consider at length in Chapter 2, 'Who transfers?').

1.138 ### Have SPC rules increased certainty?
As outlined above, the decision to enact Reg 3(1)(b) was a response to the ECJ case law on the meaning of a 'relevant transfer', which had led to a large degree of uncertainty over whether TUPE would apply to a change of service provision. The rationale behind Reg 3(1)(b) was set out in the 2005 Consultation document that proceeded the 2006 Regulations: namely, that everyone involved in an outsourcing, retendering, or insourcing exercise 'should know where they stand... so that employers can plan effectively in a climate of fair competition and affected employees are protected as a matter of course'. At that time, it was assumed that Reg 3(1)(b) would bring the *vast majority* of SPCs within TUPE's scope.

80

Reality has not exactly tallied up with that expectation. While many more SPCs have been brought within TUPE's scope, case law has identified the following significant factors which can prevent this happening:

- the activities not remaining 'fundamentally the same' after the SPC, or becoming too fragmented as a result of passing to multiple service providers

- a change in the identity of the client, and

- an absence, immediately before the transfer, of a deliberately organised grouping of employees which had as its principal purpose the carrying out of activities on behalf of the client.

Since all these matters are questions of fact for the tribunal, it becomes difficult **1.139** to draw a clear dividing line between cases where an SPC gives rise to a transfer and those where it does not. In that sense, then, the 2006 Regulations have replaced the uncertainty over whether an SPC will fall within the Directive-led definition of relevant transfer now found in Reg 3(1)(a) with another type of uncertainty – that of whether the SPC rules apply.

It should not, however, be forgotten that when the Coalition Government proposed repealing the SPC rules and returning to a single Directive-led definition of a relevant transfer, 67 per cent of respondents to the Consultation opposed the move. Among the reasons cited was that repealing the SPC rules would increase uncertainty. It seems, therefore, that the SPC rules have made things clearer for business and employees, but the ultimate goal of crystal clear clarity – of knowing for sure in advance whether TUPE will apply – remains frustratingly elusive.

Insolvency

1.140

If a business gets into extreme financial difficulties, an insolvency practitioner can be appointed either to wind up the business or to keep it running with a view to the sale of the whole or part of it as a going concern. In assessing whether the Acquired Rights Directive, and hence Reg 3(1)(a) TUPE, applies to a transfer in an insolvency context, it is crucial to have an understanding of the purpose of the insolvency proceedings in question. This has been made clear by the European Court of Justice in the following cases:

- **Abels v Administrative Board of the Bedrijfsvereniging voor de Metaalindustrie en de Electrotechnische Industrie** 1987 2 CMLR 406, ECJ: the Dutch company for which A worked experienced financial difficulties and was given judicial leave to suspend debt payments. Thereafter, the company was placed into liquidation, and the liquidator transferred its business to another company. A was taken on by the new company, but became embroiled in a salary dispute. When he brought a claim before the national court, the question arose as to whether the transfer of A's employment had been covered by the Directive. The national court referred this matter to the ECJ, which held that the Directive does not apply to a transfer where the 'transferor' has been declared insolvent with a view to the realisation and distribution of the undertaking's assets on behalf of its creditors. The ECJ stated, however, that the Directive could apply to a transfer from an insolvent company where the main aim of the insolvency procedure in place was to protect the assets of the business and to ensure that the business continued to trade by means of an agreement to suspend payment of the transferor's debts

- **D'Urso and ors v Ercole Marelli Elettromeccanica Generale SpA (in special administration) and ors** 1992 IRLR 136, ECJ: in 1981 the Italian Minister of Industry issued a decree commencing 'special administration proceedings for large undertakings in difficulties' in respect of EMG, the company for which the claimants worked. At the same time the organisation was authorised to continue trading under that procedure. In September 1985 the whole undertaking was transferred to another company called Nuova EMG, which had been specially formed for this purpose. Many employees were taken on by the new company, but the claimants were not. They sought a declaration that their contracts of employment had continued with Nuova EMG under the provisions of the Italian Civil Code, which implemented the Directive into Italian law. The national court referred the matter to the ECJ, which made the point that the application of the Directive in an insolvency context depends on the purpose of the insolvency procedure in question. As the Abels case made clear, the Directive applies to the transfer of an insolvent business where the purpose of the insolvency procedure is to enable the undertaking to continue trading, but does not apply in the context of compulsory liquidation proceedings designed to dispose of an insolvent company's assets

- **Jules Dethier Équipement SA v Dassy and anor** 1998 ICR 541, ECJ: on 15 May 1991 the Belgian Commercial Court in Huy made an order putting SPRL – which employed D – into liquidation. On 5 June 1991 the liquidator dismissed D, and on 27 June transferred SPRL's assets to JDE under an agreement approved by the Commercial Court. When D brought an action, the question arose of whether his employment had transferred from SPRL to JDE. The national court referred to the ECJ the question of whether the Directive applied in such circumstances. In the ECJ's view, it was clear from its previous case law that the crucial question to be asked in determining whether the Directive applies to the transfer of an undertaking that is subject to an administrative or judicial procedure is: 'What is the purpose of the procedure in question?' If the answer is not immediately conclusive, then account should also be taken of the form of the procedure – in particular, whether the undertaking continues or ceases trading – and also of the Directive's objectives. The facts of the instant case disclosed that the undertaking continued to trade while it was being wound up by the court. In such circumstances, continuity of the business was assured when the undertaking was transferred. There was accordingly no justification for depriving the employees of the rights guaranteed under the Directive.

So, it appears that, so long as an insolvency practitioner runs the business and **1.141** retains its goodwill in order to make it viable for sale, the Acquired Rights Directive, and hence the TUPE Regulations, will apply to any eventual transfer to an outside purchaser. On the other hand, where an insolvent business has been broken up and the assets sold off, it would appear that neither the Directive nor Reg 3(1)(a) TUPE takes effect.

The EAT had the opportunity to examine the above case law in Perth and Kinross Council v Donaldson and ors 2004 ICR 667, EAT. There, Perth and Kinross Council contracted out its housing maintenance work to NCS Ltd. That company later ran into financial difficulties and a liquidator was appointed. On 16 January 2001 a court made an order for NCS Ltd to be wound up. The Council and NCS Ltd then entered into an informal arrangement, on terms accepted by the liquidator, whereby the company continued to carry out maintenance as and when required. The Council placed orders for work on a day-to-day basis on the understanding that the arrangement could be terminated at any time without notice. It became dissatisfied with the company's deteriorating performance, and terminated the arrangement with effect from 31 May 2001. As from that date the Council undertook the maintenance work itself. NCS Ltd ceased trading because the liquidator was unable to find any more work for it to carry out. A dispute arose as to whether there had been a transfer of an undertaking from NCS Ltd to the Council within the meaning of TUPE when the latter resumed the work in-house. An employment tribunal held that a transfer had taken place, and the Council appealed to the EAT.

Before the Appeal Tribunal, the Council relied on the ECJ's decision in Abels v **1.142** Administrative Board of the Bedrijfsvereniging voor de Metaalindustrie en de Electrotechnische Industrie (above) to argue that no TUPE transfer had occurred. In Abels, the ECJ had held that the Directive does not apply to the transfer of an undertaking where the transferor has been declared insolvent and the purpose of the transfer is the realisation and distribution of the undertaking's assets on behalf of its creditors. The Council argued that it followed that complete insolvency, as in the instant case, excluded the application of TUPE. The EAT agreed with the Council's submissions. Since the ECJ had made it clear that the Directive did not apply in a case of irretrievable insolvency and cessation of business, it followed that the TUPE Regulations – which as secondary legislation made under the European Communities Act 1972 could not go beyond the scope of the protection provided by the Directive – did not apply in this case either. Thus, there had been no relevant transfer when the Council took back work that it had contracted out to a company that had become insolvent and ceased to trade. In any event, the EAT continued, the ad hoc arrangements that had operated between the Council and NCS Ltd following the company's liquidation could not be regarded as establishing a stable economic entity (for which, see 'Business transfers – what is an "economic entity"?' above). By the time of the cessation of business brought about by the Council's declining to offer any more work, there was simply nothing left to transfer. Nothing passed between the parties, therefore, and the liquidator had simply brought the business to an end because there was no more work for it to do.

Note that it is entirely possible that situations such as that in the Perth and Kinross case would, if decided now, amount to an SPC transfer under Reg 3(1)(b). As discussed under 'Service provision changes' above, this provision offers TUPE protection over and above that required by the Acquired Rights Directive in the SPC arena. Essentially, it would have been sufficient for the purposes of Reg 3(1)(b) if the maintenance activities in question were carried out by an organised grouping of NCS Ltd's employees prior to the transfer, and by the Council thereafter.

1.143 We discuss the issue of insolvency at length in Chapter 6, 'Transfer of insolvent companies'. There, we focus in particular on the provisions (Regs 8 and 9) that were introduced by the 2006 Regulations with a view to assisting the rescue of failing businesses. The main substantive differences that apply in that context concern the ability of the purchaser of an insolvent business to effect changes to employees' contractual terms and conditions and the degree to which the purchaser inherits the transferor's pre-transfer liabilities.

1.144 ## The public sector

Regulation 3(4)(a) provides that TUPE applies to public and private undertakings engaged in economic activities whether or not they are operating for gain. This mirrors the wording of Article 1(1)(c) of the Acquired Rights Directive, which in turn reflects established case law. Thus, it is clear that transfers from public to private sector (and vice versa) can be covered by the Directive and hence Reg 3(1)(a). Two examples:

- **Sánchez Hidalgo and ors v Asociación de Servicios Aser and Sociedad Cooperativa Minerva and another case** 1999 IRLR 136, ECJ: a Spanish municipality had entrusted the provision of its home-help services to an outside contractor. That contract came to an end and a new contract was awarded to a different undertaking. The ECJ held that the Directive could apply to the change of contractor – the fact that the service contract was awarded by a public body did not preclude the Directive's application

- **Mayeur v Association Promotion de l'Information Messine (APIM)** 2002 ICR 1316, ECJ: M was employed as a publicity manager by APIM, a private non-profit-making association which aimed to promote the French

City of Metz. In time, APIM was dissolved and the municipality took over its activities. The ECJ held that the Directive applies where a municipality – i.e. a legal person governed by public law operating within the framework of specific rules of administrative law – takes over activities relating to publicity and information concerning the services which it offers to the public, where such activities were previously carried out, in the interests of that municipality, by a non-profit-making association which was a legal person governed by private law.

It is also clear that a transfer by way of an SPC can take place to or from the **1.145** public sector. For example, in Edwards and ors v RS Gormanley Ltd and anor ET Case No.3300955/13 there was a transfer within the meaning of Reg 3(1)(b)(iii) when the London Borough of Hillingdon took the maintenance of its housing estate back in-house.

The question of whether TUPE applies to transfers *within* the public sector is, however, more complicated. Nevertheless, as we shall see, a combination of specific legislation and the Cabinet Office's Statement of Practice, 'Staff Transfers in the Public Sector' (2000), aims to ensure that TUPE-style protection is afforded to employees in such circumstances.

Exclusion of public administrative functions   1.146
While Reg 3(4)(a) provides that TUPE will apply to public and private undertakings, Reg 3(5), which also mirrors Article 1(1)(c) of the Acquired Rights Directive, states that 'an administrative reorganisation of public administrative authorities or the transfer of administrative functions between public administrative authorities is not a relevant transfer'.

Neither the Directive nor TUPE define 'public administrative authorities' or 'administrative functions', so it is instead necessary to refer to the case law to determine the scope of the exclusion in Reg 3(5). The starting point is the ECJ's decision in Henke v Gemeinde Schierke and anor 1997 ICR 746, ECJ. That case involved H, who was employed as secretary to the Mayor of the municipality of Schierke, Germany. In July 1994 Schierke and other municipalities were reorganised, as permitted by the local government law for the Land of Saxony-Anhalt. As a result, all the tasks of the municipality of Schierke were transferred to a new local government body covering a number of municipalities, and the municipal administration of Schierke was dissolved. H lost her job and brought a claim that her contract of employment had been transferred to the new local government body. The ECJ held that there was no transfer of an undertaking in these circumstances. It stated that 'the concept of a "transfer of an undertaking, business or part of a business" does not apply to the transfer of administrative functions from a municipality to an administrative collectivity such as the one in question in the main proceedings'. It pointed out that the transfer 'related only to activities involving the exercise of public authority.

Even if it is assumed that those activities had aspects of an economic nature, they could only be ancillary.'

1.147 The ECJ's emphasis in Henke on the importance of activities being of 'an economic nature' does not sit easily with its earlier comments in Dr Sophie Redmond Stichting v Bartol and ors 1992 IRLR 366, ECJ (see 'Business transfers – what is an "economic entity"?' above) that the application of the Acquired Rights Directive is not restricted to 'commercial ventures'. Perhaps unsurprisingly, then, the Henke public administration exclusion has been interpreted narrowly. Two case examples:

- **Collino and anor v Telecom Italia SpA** 2002 ICR 38, ECJ: the Italian Minister for Posts and Telecommunications dissolved ASST, the state body responsible for operating certain public telecommunications services, and granted the exclusive concession in respect of those services to a state-owned company, Iritel. The question arose as to whether this could amount to a transfer of an undertaking within the meaning of the Directive. The ECJ held that the Directive applies where a public body transfers, by means of an administrative concession, the operation of a non-profit-making public telecommunications service to a state-owned company. It was settled case law that the Directive applies to all transfers of entities which are engaged in economic activities, whether or not they operate with a view to profit. Furthermore, the fact that the service transferred in the instant case was the subject of a concession by a public body did not exclude application of the Directive, since the activity in question was a business activity and not merely the exercise of public authority

- **Dundee City Council v Arshad** EAT 1204/98: a local government reorganisation took place in Scotland. As a result, a residential home 'transferred' from an abolished regional council to new unitary authorities. The EAT held that the 'Henke exclusion' did not take effect in these circumstances, and that the Directive and TUPE were capable of applying.

1.148 The limited scope of the administrative functions exclusion was re-emphasised in Scattolon v Ministero dell'Istruzione, dell'Università e della Ricerca 2012 ICR 740, ECJ, where the ECJ held that it did not apply to the transfer of a group of school cleaners from the employ of a local authority to that of the state. The ECJ noted that the fact that an economic entity is 'integrated within the public administration' cannot, on its own, take that entity outside the scope of the Directive. Although the transfer of administrative functions between public administrative authorities is expressly excluded by Article 1(1)(c), that exemption applies only where the transfer concerns activities falling within the exercise of public powers. The ECJ thought that case law such as Collino (above), far from establishing that any transfer connected with or falling within the context of a reorganisation of public administration must be excluded from the scope of the Directive, merely indicates that the reorganisation of public administration structures or the transfer of administrative functions between public administrative authorities does not, in and of itself, constitute a relevant transfer. The transfer of staff carrying out activities of an economic nature, albeit within a public administration, can indeed amount to a relevant transfer.

In Law Society of England and Wales v Secretary of State for Justice and Office for Legal Complaints 2010 IRLR 407, QBD, the High Court was asked by the Law Society to make declarations about the applicability of TUPE in the context of the imminent cessation of the Law Society's Legal Complaints Service (LCS) and its replacement with a new independent Office for Legal Complaints (OLC). In particular, the Law Society sought declarations on whether the cessation of the function of the LCS and the start of the function of the OLC would amount to a transfer under Reg 3(1)(a) and whether the exclusion in Reg 3(5) would apply. The Court found that the LCS was an 'undertaking' as it had a relatively autonomous identity separate from the Law Society. Furthermore, it was an 'economic entity', since it pursued an ancillary economic activity (providing redress or compensation for complainants). However, the High Court ultimately concluded that there would be no TUPE transfer. The mere similarity between the services being carried out by LCS and OLC was insufficient to bring the change within the scope of TUPE. None of the tangible or intangible assets of the LCS or its existing case load were to be transferred to the OLC. Thus, the LCS would not retain its identity within the OLC. The OLC's independence, wider range of powers and obligations meant that its culture and approach would be very different from that of the LCS. Although not strictly necessary, given his conclusion that the change from the LCS to the OLC would not be a TUPE transfer, the High Court judge did go on to to set out his obiter view that the change would be a transfer of an administrative function within the meaning of Reg 3(5) and so would be excluded from the application of the Regulations on that basis.

Although EU law has interpreted the underlying basis for the Reg 3(5) exclusion **1.149** narrowly, the BIS Guide nevertheless advises that 'transfers with central government are not covered'. Employees caught up in such transfers are, however, given a degree of TUPE-equivalent protection, as explained under 'TUPE-equivalent protection' below.

TUPE-equivalent protection **1.150**

As stated under 'Exclusion of public administrative functions' above, both the Acquired Rights Directive and the TUPE Regulations provide that neither a reorganisation of a public administration nor the transfer of administrative functions between public administrations will amount to a 'relevant transfer'. As the BIS Guides notes, however, 'intra-governmental transfers and reorganisations of administrative function/administrative authorities are covered by the Cabinet Office's Statement of Practice, "Staff Transfers in the Public Sector"' ('the Statement of Practice').

The Statement of Practice, which was first issued in 2000 and most recently revised in October 2013, applies directly to central government departments, the NHS, local government (where adopted by the relevant local authority) and public/private partnerships. It provides that contracting-out exercises to the private sector and voluntary organisations (including second-generation contracting out), and transfers between different parts of the public sector, will be conducted on the basis that staff will transfer and the principles of TUPE should be followed, unless there are exceptional circumstances. Furthermore, there should be appropriate arrangements to protect the occupational pensions, redundancy and severance terms of staff in all these types of transfer. In this regard, the Statement of Practice cross refers to another document, 'Fair Deal for Staff Pensions: staff transfers from Central Government', which was issued in October 2013. The 'fair deal' referred to there is that employees who are compulsorily transferred out of the public sector are to continue to have access to the public service pension scheme they enjoyed, rather than being offered a broadly comparable private pension scheme.

1.151 A second relevant Cabinet Office document, most recently issued in December 2010, is 'Principles of Good Employment Practice – a statement of principles that reflect good employment practice for Government, contracting authorities and suppliers'. This sets out six core principles dealing with, inter alia, a commitment to fair and reasonable terms and conditions, equality, dispute resolution and employee engagement. These apply on a non-mandatory basis to public sector organisations (other than local authorities) in their contractual arrangements with service providers.

The Statement of Practice and Principles of Good Employment Practice used to be augmented by a third document, the Code of Practice on Workforce Matters in Local Authority Service Contracts 2003, which applied where a local authority or best value authority (such as a police or fire authority) transferred employees to a private or voluntary sector contractor under a contract to provide services. However, this Code was revoked with immediate effect on 23 March 2011, and now only applies to employment contracts commencing before that date.

A more detailed discussion of these extra-TUPE protections can be found in Chapter 3, 'What transfers?', under 'Special protections for public sector transfers'.

1.152 **Section 38 of the Employment Relations Act 1999.** Earlier in this chapter, under 'Service provision changes', we explained that the enabling power for the SPC provisions in TUPE was S.38 of the Employment Relations Act 1999. This provides the Secretary of State with the power to make 'the same or similar provision' to TUPE, 'in circumstances other than those to which the EU obligation applies (including circumstances in which there is no transfer or no transfer to which the EU obligation applies)'. S.38 ERelA has also been used to create a series of Regulations providing TUPE-equivalent protection to employees caught up in specific public sector transfers.

As at October 2013, this power has been exercised in situations relating to rent officers (see the Transfer of Undertakings (Protection of Employment) (Rent Officer Service) Regulations 1999 SI 1999/2511); OFCOM (see the Transfer of Undertakings (Protection of Employment) (Transfer to OFCOM) Regulations 2003 SI 2003/2715); employees of the Department for Business, Innovation and Skills who transferred to RCUK Shared Services Centre Ltd on 1 November 2012 (the Transfer of Undertakings (Protection of Employment) (RCUK Shared Services Centre Limited) Regulations 2012 SI 2012/2413); and persons employed by various public bodies in public health activity whose employment transferred to the Department of Health as a consequence of new functions relating to public health conferred under the Health and Social Care Act 2012 to be performed by an executive agency, Public Health England (the Transfer of Undertakings (Protection of Employment) (Transfers of Public Health Staff) Regulations 2013 SI 2013/278).

When does transfer occur?   1.153

Presuming that the TUPE Regulations do apply to a given set of circumstances, the next crucial question is when the relevant transfer takes place. As explained in Chapter 2, 'Who transfers?', under 'Employed "immediately before" transfer', only those employees employed and assigned to the transferring undertaking 'immediately before' the transfer will transfer automatically to the transferee under Reg 4.

In most cases, the question of when a transfer occurs will be extremely simple to answer. The EAT's decision in Wheeler v Patel and anor 1987 ICR 631, EAT, is authority for the proposition that, where a transfer is effected by a contractual agreement, the date of the transfer is that on which the relevant contract was completed. However, this is subject to the qualification that in Wheeler, the transfer of the business and completion occurred on the same day. In other cases, the business may be transferred before the contract is formally completed. In Commercial Motors (Wales) Ltd v Howley EAT 0491/11, for example, the parties entered into a conditional sale agreement on 24 December 2008. Completion did not occur until 6 March 2009 after both the conditions precedent specified in the agreement had been satisfied. However, the transferee took over running the business on its own behalf, including taking responsibility for paying staff, with effect from 2 February 2009. The EAT upheld an employment tribunal's finding that that was the date of the relevant transfer. This was in accordance with the crucial test for determining whether there has been a transfer under the Acquired Rights Directive, which is 'where there is a change in the legal or natural person who is responsible for carrying on the business regardless of whether or not ownership of the business is transferred' – Celtec Ltd v Astley and ors 2005 ICR 1409, ECJ (discussed under '"Date of a transfer" must be identified' below). The EAT concluded that the mere fact that completion has not occurred is irrelevant to the issue of whether there has been a TUPE transfer when, as in that case, the transferee has taken on the responsibility of running the business.

1.154 In Housing Maintenance Solutions Ltd v McAteer and ors 2015 ICR 87, EAT, the EAT held that an employment tribunal was wrong to conclude that a transfer had occurred on the day when the transferee had assumed responsibility for the transferring employees. The fact that the transferee employer had consulted and informed transferring employees during a period of suspension of activities before they carried out any work for it did not mean that it had, as the employment tribunal had found, 'assumed responsibility' for those employees within the meaning outlined in the Celtec case. It is the date of the transfer of the undertaking that determines when responsibility of the transferee for employees employed in the undertaking transfers, not vice versa.

1.155 ## Series of transactions

Regulation 3(6) provides that 'a relevant transfer may be effected by a series of two or more transactions'. As we saw in 'Business transfers – transfer "to another person"' above, this reflects a number of decisions of the ECJ, such as that in Foreningen af Arbejdsledere i Danmark v Daddy's Dance Hall A/S 1988 IRLR 315, ECJ. That case saw IC's lease of a restaurant/bar terminated by the landlord, PT, which thereafter concluded a new lease with DDH. The ECJ held that the fact that the transfer of the restaurant from IC to DDH took place in two phases – first from IC to PT, and then from PT to DDH – did not exclude the applicability of the Acquired Rights Directive.

Often, where a transfer is effected by a series of two or more transactions, the transfer process happens over a period of time. In such circumstances, it might be difficult to identify a particular transfer date, and hence identify the group of employees assigned to the undertaking 'immediately before the transfer'. Recognising this, Reg 4(3) provides that where a transfer is effected by a series of transactions, an employee will transfer to the transferee if he or she was assigned to the transferring entity 'immediately before any of those transactions'. To an extent an anti-avoidance provision, it suggests that there need not always be one all-important cut-off point, but that there might be a series of dates immediately before which an employee can be employed in the undertaking if he or she is to be caught by the transfer rules.

1.156 The Directive, however, places a fairly large spanner in the works. Article 3(1), which states that 'the transferor's rights and obligations arising from a contract of employment or from an employment relationship existing *on the date of a transfer*... shall... be transferred to the transferee' (our stress), suggests that a specific transfer date must be identified. Indeed, this is the conclusion that the ECJ arrived at in Celtec Ltd v Astley and ors (discussed under '"Date of a transfer" must be identified' below).

'Date of a transfer' must be identified 1.157

In Celtec Ltd v Astley and ors 2005 ICR 1409, ECJ, the European Court ruled that the 'date of a transfer' in Article 3(1) of the Acquired Rights Directive is a particular point in time that cannot be postponed to another date at the will of the transferor or transferee. Both the choice of the word 'date' and the requirement for legal certainty indicated that the transferring must be identified at a particular point in the transfer process and not in relation to the length of time over which that process extends. The date in question, the Court continued, is that on which responsibility as employer for carrying on the business of the undertaking moves from the transferor to the transferee. With the ECJ having reached its decision, the case returned to the House of Lords. The task for their Lordships in Celtec Ltd v Astley and ors 2006 ICR 992, HL, was to examine the convoluted facts of the case in order to determine the 'date of the transfer'.

The facts of the Celtec case were as follows. In 1989 the Government decided to set up a number of Training and Enterprise Councils (TECs) in England and Wales to take over the training and enterprise responsibilities carried out by the Department of Employment (DoE). To assist with the transition, it was agreed that civil servants working in training and enterprise roles in the DoE's area offices would be invited to volunteer for three-year secondments to the newly created TECs. The first secondment began in 1990, with the last ending in 1996. The North East Wales TEC commenced business in 1990, and in September of that year A, H and O – three civil servants with responsibility for vocational training in North Wales – started three-year secondments there. In December 1991 the Secretary of State for Education and Employment, with the agreement of the TECs, announced that secondments would be phased out at the end of each of the TEC's fifth year of operation. As part of this move, seconded civil servants were free to choose whether to take up any offer of employment with the TECs or to return to the Civil Service after their secondments for redeployment. In 1993 H, O and A resigned from the Civil Service to take up employment with North East Wales TEC, which later became C Ltd. In 1998 C Ltd decided to effect redundancies, and, in the context of the calculation of redundancy payments, the question arose as to whether the claimants' continuous service with C Ltd should be aggregated with their service as civil servants with the DoE. They contended that it should, since their continuity had been protected by TUPE.

An employment tribunal found that there had been a transfer of an undertaking 1.158 from the DoE to what became C Ltd. It noted, however, that in order for the claimants' continuity to be preserved by TUPE, they had to show that they had been employed by the DoE 'immediately before the transfer'. Thus, a preliminary

91

issue arose as to when the undertaking in question transferred. Addressing this matter, the tribunal held that the transfer took place over several years – from the time the first secondment began in 1990 until the last one ended in 1996. It further held that each time a secondee became directly employed by C Ltd, this constituted one in a series of transactions by which the transfer was effected. As the secondees in question had been employed by the DoE immediately before the transaction that brought about their direct employment by the TEC, the tribunal held that the employees' continuous employment with the DoE had been preserved after the transfer. In time, this issue progressed to the House of Lords, which, as we saw above, learned from the ECJ that a specific date of transfer had to be identified. It followed that if the claimants had not been employed by the DoE immediately before that specific date, they had not, in fact, transferred under TUPE, and thus had lost their continuity of service when the identity of their employer changed.

The majority of the House of Lords (Lords Bingham, Hope and Carswell) held that, on these facts, the relevant transfer had occurred in September 1990, when the claimants were first seconded to the TEC, even though this was contrary to what all the parties understood to be the case at the time. In Lord Bingham's words: 'It is plain from the findings made below that Celtec set up in business in September 1990 and the employees seconded from the Department were the core of the business: without them there could have been no effective transfer. It is scarcely an exaggeration to say that they were the business.' Accordingly, their employment transferred from the DoE to the TEC/C Ltd under TUPE at that time – with their continuity preserved – notwithstanding that they had not resigned from the Civil Service in order to accept direct employment with the TEC until three years later.

1.159 **Difficulties arising from Celtec.** As Lord Mance pointed out in his dissenting judgment in Celtec Ltd v Astley and ors (above), the decision of the majority is problematic in that it suggests that employees – whom the transfer rules are meant to protect – could find themselves employed by the transferee without even realising it and without their informed consent. This will be of particular concern to organisations such as the NHS, which frequently use 'partnership agreements' and other similar secondment arrangements when conducting outsourcing of services to the private sector. We examine the impact of Celtec on such arrangements in detail in Chapter 2, 'Who transfers?', under 'Problems of secondment arrangements'. Also in Chapter 2, under 'Employed "immediately before" transfer – transfers effected by series of transactions', we shall discuss what Celtec specifically means for Reg 4(3) TUPE. As set out under 'Series of transactions' above, this provides that where a transfer is effected by a series of transactions, an employee will transfer to the transferee if he or she was assigned to the transferring entity 'immediately before any of those transactions'. In other words, it suggests that a wider group of employees than that employed in the undertaking immediately before the 'date of the transfer' might receive TUPE protection. Frustratingly, neither the ECJ nor the House of Lords in Celtec turned their minds to Reg 4(3), despite its clear relevance to the issue at hand.

2 Who transfers?

General effect of transfer on employees

Who is an 'employee' for TUPE purposes?

Contracts 'otherwise terminated by' transfer

Employed 'immediately before' transfer

'Assigned' to undertaking transferred

Objecting to transfer

Employees retained by transferor

Problems of secondment arrangements

Under UK common law, the relationship of an individual employee and his or **2.1** her employer is governed primarily by the contract of employment between them. It is, in theory, an entirely personal relationship. Therefore, on general common law principles, that particular employee is taken to contract with that particular employer and neither party can arrange unilaterally for another party to fulfil his or her contractual obligations. But what is the effect of this rule when the employer wants to sell the business in which the employee works? At common law, the application of the rule meant that an employer could not, without the consent of the employee concerned, arrange for the purchaser of the business to take over the employee's employment contract – Nokes v Doncaster Amalgamated Collieries Ltd 1940 AC 1014, HL. The House of Lords in that case said that the freedom of an employee to choose the employer for whom he or she wanted to work constituted 'the main difference between a servant and a serf'.

As a consequence of the common law position, the transfer of an undertaking constituted a repudiatory breach of an employment contract – i.e. a breach entitling the employee to treat the contract as terminated. This is because, while the employee was still ready and willing to perform his or her duties under the contract, the employer was no longer able to continue employing the employee in accordance with the terms of that contract. The virtue of the common law position was that employees were free to terminate their contracts with the transferor on the occurrence of such an event. The main disadvantage, however, was that any subsequent employment with the purchaser of the business (the transferee) involved a fresh contract, which might have been on less favourable terms. Another disadvantage was that the vendor of the business (the transferor) could take the opportunity of terminating some of his employees' contracts if that best suited his needs – where, for example, he wished to reduce his overheads to secure a better price for the business.

2.2 In 1977 the UK became subject to EC obligations designed to protect employees involved in the transfer of an undertaking (see the introduction to this Handbook). These obligations were set out in the EU Acquired Rights Directive, which, following subsequent amendments, was reissued in its entirety as Council Directive No.2001/23 of 12 March 2001 'on the approximation of the laws of the Member States relating to the safeguarding of employees' rights in the event of transfers of undertakings, businesses or parts of undertakings or businesses' ('the Acquired Rights Directive'). One of the aims of the Directive, in both its original and its amended form (the amendments essentially codifying interpretation by the European Court of Justice), is to ensure that employees of a transferred business should continue to be employed by its purchaser. To this end, Article 3(1) of the Directive states: 'The transferor's rights and obligations arising from a contract of employment or from an employment relationship existing on the date of a transfer shall, by reason of such transfer, be transferred to the transferee.' This sets out the principle of automatic transfer of employment contracts. Thus, Article 3(1) involves what may be regarded as a radical departure from UK common law principles on contracts of employment. In Rotsart de Hertaing v J Benoidt SA (in liquidation) and anor 1997 IRLR 127, ECJ, the European Court ruled that the contracts of employment and employment relationships existing on the date of the transfer between the transferor and the workers employed in the undertaking automatically pass to the transferee by the mere fact of the transfer. Moreover, by reason of the mandatory nature of the Directive, and in order not to deprive workers of the protection afforded by the Directive, the transfer of employment contracts automatically takes place regardless of the intentions of the transferor or the transferee and cannot be obstructed by the transferee's refusal to fulfil its obligations towards the transferred employees. The mandatory nature of Article 3(1) was confirmed by the European Court in Celtec Ltd v Astley 2005 ICR 1409, ECJ (see 'The Celtec decision' below).

Article 3(1) of the Acquired Rights Directive is transposed into domestic law by Reg 4 of the Transfer of Undertakings (Protection of Employment) Regulations 2006 SI 2006/246 (TUPE), which replace the 1981 Regulations of the same title.

2.3 In this chapter we discuss the issue of how to identify which members of the transferor's workforce have their contracts (and thus employment) automatically transferred by virtue of Reg 4. In Chapter 3, 'What transfers?', we address the related issue of which rights, powers, duties and liabilities transfer – along with the employment of transferred employees – to the transferee.

General effect of transfer on employees

Regulation 4(1) TUPE states: 'Except where objection is made under paragraph (7), a relevant transfer shall not operate so as to terminate the contract of employment of any person employed by the transferor and assigned to the organised grouping of resources or employees that is subject to the relevant transfer, which would otherwise be terminated by the transfer, but any such contract shall have effect after the transfer as if originally made between the person so employed and the transferee.'

The wording of the provision differs only slightly from that used in the 1981 Regulations. Such changes as have been made are designed to incorporate well-established developments in case law and to reflect more closely what the Government considers to be the correct interpretation of the Acquired Rights Directive. The reference to 'the organised grouping of resources or employees that is subject to a relevant transfer' is intended to encompass both types of relevant transfer provided for under the 2006 Regulations – i.e. a 'standard' transfer and a service provision change (see Chapter 1, 'Identifying a "relevant transfer"', for details). This concept derives from the ECJ's test of what amounts to an 'economic entity' capable of transferring under the Acquired Rights Directive, and replaces the definition of 'undertaking' as used in the 1981 Regulations, although no change of substance has been effected by the different definition. Whenever references are made in this chapter to 'transfer of an undertaking', these should be taken as being shorthand for a transfer of the organised grouping of resources or employees comprising the economic entity in question.

The basic rule – 'novation' of contract

Regulation 4(1) is central to the operation of the Regulations in that it establishes that the employment of employees who are subject to it transfers to the transferee. As Lord Justice Balcombe said in Secretary of State for Employment v Spence and ors 1986 ICR 651, CA: 'The paragraph has two effects: first, that a relevant transfer does not terminate a contract of employment; and the second effect, commencing with the word "but", is that there is a statutory novation of the contract.' The first effect is intended to override the common law contractual position (discussed in the introduction to this chapter). The second ensures continuity of the employment relationship with the undertaking in which the transferred employee is employed.

Statutory novation. The crucial part of Reg 4(1) so far as effecting the transfer **2.6** of employment is concerned is the final clause – 'but any such contract shall have effect after the transfer as if originally made between the person so employed and the transferee'. The stipulation that employment contracts shall have effect after the transfer as if originally made between the person so employed and the transferee is an example of a *statutory novation*. This is simply legal terminology for the substitution of a third party for one of the original parties to a contract. Under general contractual principles, any contract of whatever kind may be novated, but this normally happens by the consent of all the parties concerned and not by the intervention of statute. However, it should be noted that the effect of the particular novation or substitution provided for by Reg 4(1) is not to assign or transfer the contract but rather to extinguish the original contract and replace it by another. As a result, the transferee 'steps into the shoes' of the transferor and takes over all rights and obligations of the transferor under the contract as if the transferee had contracted with the employees concerned from the date on which they were originally employed by the transferor.

2.7 **Effect of novation.** The fact that this consequence flows from the provision of Reg 4(1) might, on the face of it, appear to make most of Reg 4(2)(a) – discussed in detail in Chapter 3, 'What transfers?' – otiose. That provision specifically stipulates that 'without prejudice to [Reg 4(1)]... all the transferor's rights, powers, duties and liabilities under or in connection with any [contract transferred by virtue of Reg 4(1)] shall be transferred by virtue of this regulation to the transferee'. Reg 4(2)(b) further provides that any act or omission done by the transferor prior to the transfer in respect of the contract transferred or a person assigned to the transferred undertaking is deemed to have been done by the transferee. The express provision for the 'transfer' of contractual rights and duties in Reg 4(2) is arguably unnecessary in view of the statutory novation effected by Reg 4(1). That said, Reg 4(2) serves to spell out in the plainest terms the full effect and logic of what follows once a contract is transferred to the transferee as a result of its novation.

The power of Reg 4(1), when it applies, is that it in effect reverses the position under UK common law as described at the start of this chapter. Rather than the transfer operating to bring about the termination of the contract (and with it the employment) of all employees employed by the transferor, the statutory provision operates to preserve the contract (and the employment under it) with the transferee as a successor to the original employer.

2.8 **Limitations on 'automatic transfer of employment' rule.** However, it is important to note that Reg 4(1) does not necessarily apply to every member of the transferor's workforce. Various limitations on the transfer of contracts are contained within the wording of Reg 4(1) itself, and for this reason the language of the regulation has to be carefully analysed. Were it not for these limitations, it would be possible to speak accurately of Reg 4 effecting the 'automatic' novation of contracts of employment and the employment regulated under such contracts. But the fact that there are limitations means that it is perhaps better to paraphrase Reg 4 as effecting the *quasi automatic transfer* of employment, especially since – as we shall see – employees are entitled to object to their employment transferring.

Scrutiny of Reg 4(1) shows that there are five limitations or 'caveats' to its operation. The first is gleaned from its opening words, which are 'Except where objection is made under paragraph (7)'. This is a reference to the right of anyone whose employment would otherwise be transferred by virtue of Reg 4(1) to object to the transfer, with the consequence of preventing Reg 4(1) and (2) from operating to transfer either the contract of employment or the rights, powers, duties and liabilities thereunder to the transferee. If a valid objection is made, Reg 4(1) will not apply. This is a crucial protection of the rights of employees caught up in a transfer situation and it – along with the other caveats – is discussed in detail under 'Objecting to the transfer' below.

Secondly, Reg 4(1) speaks of the transfer not operating 'so as to terminate the **2.9** *contract of employment* of any person *employed* by the transferor' (our stress). This shows that the statutory novation and the rights associated with it only apply to members of the transferor's workforce who are 'employees' employed under a 'contract of employment' as defined by the Regulations. As we shall see later in this chapter, the definition of 'employee' appears to go somewhat wider than the equivalent definition for statutory rights purposes (including unfair dismissal) under the Employment Rights Act 1996 (ERA). But anyone who does not fall within this extended definition will not have their employment transferred by virtue of Reg 4 to the transferee.

Thirdly, and immediately following on from the wording discussed above, Reg 4(1) states that it is directed only to employees '*assigned* to the organised grouping of resources or employees that is subject to the relevant transfer' (our stress). This means that any employee who is not actually 'assigned' to the undertaking being transferred will not be subject to the transfer of employment provisions of Reg 4. What is meant by 'assigned' is fully discussed under 'Assigned to undertaking transferred' below. It should be noted that this wording was introduced for the first time by the 2006 Regulations, but reflects the position that had already become established under the earlier TUPE Regulations as a result of decisions of the European Court of Justice determining to whom the principle of automatic transfer applies.

Fourthly, and straying for a moment outside the actual wording of Reg 4(1), **2.10** Reg 4(3) provides that the reference to 'a person employed by the transferor and assigned to the organised grouping of resources or employees' in Reg 4(1) is a reference 'to a person so *employed immediately before the transfer*, or would have been so employed if he had not been dismissed in the circumstances described in regulation 7(1)' (our stress). Thus, Reg 4 will not bite in respect of an employee who is not employed by the transferor and assigned to the transferred undertaking 'immediately before' its transfer to the transferee. As we shall see, the identification of precisely when the transfer takes place is therefore crucial. We shall also see that the reference in Reg 4(3) to Reg 7(1) essentially means that an employee will be 'deemed' to have been employed 'immediately before the transfer' if he or she has been unfairly dismissed prior to the transfer and the sole or principal reason for the dismissal is not an 'economic, technical or organisational reason entailing a change in the workforce'. (For a detailed discussion of unfair dismissal protection in the context of TUPE transfers, see Chapter 4, 'Unfair dismissal'.)

Fifthly, Reg 4(1) contains one last potential limitation on the operation of the automatic transfer principle that it enshrines. This centres on the words 'which would otherwise be terminated by the transfer'. Putting these words within the general context of the regulation, Reg 4(1) provides that 'a relevant transfer shall not operate so as to terminate the contract of employment of any person employed by the transferor... which would otherwise be terminated by the transfer'. Applying strict logic, we can deduce from this that only contracts of employment that would otherwise automatically terminate as a result of the transfer are caught by Reg 4(1). This raises the question: Which contracts are these? It is no use pretending that there is a simple or obvious answer to this. Indeed, the words 'which would otherwise be terminated by the transfer' – which also appeared in the antecedent provisions of Reg 5(1) of the 1981 Regulations – have given rise to a large amount of academic debate. Even though there has never been general agreement among TUPE experts as to whether, and to what extent, the words actually limit the application of the principle of automatic transfer, it is interesting that, despite this, the same wording was retained in the 2006 Regulations without any attempt to illuminate its opaque meaning. As we shall see, the provision is unlikely to represent a major limitation on the operation of Reg 4, although it may have some bearing in a case where an employee agrees to be retained in the service of the transferor following a relevant transfer.

2.11 Summary of principle of novation

Summarising, then, the basic rule of novation enshrined in Reg 4 in the order in which each of the individual elements of the rule are discussed below: the contract of employment of anyone employed by the transferor will be automatically transferred to the transferee, as well as all rights, powers, duties and liabilities under it, *unless*:

- the person concerned is not an 'employee' as defined by the Regulations

- he or she is regarded as being employed on a contract that would not otherwise be terminated by the transfer

- he or she is not employed by the transferor 'immediately before' the transfer

- he or she is not 'assigned' to the undertaking being transferred, or

- he or she makes a valid objection to the transfer.

Each of these caveats or qualifications is considered separately below. However, it is worth pointing out that although these limitations are highly technical and the discussion around them involves complex legal analysis, the vast majority of transfers will be unaffected by them. In most cases, it will be self-evident which of the transferor's workers are 'employees' for the purposes of the Regulations and which of these are employed by the transferor immediately before the transfer. Similarly, it will be clear whether or not an employee is assigned to the relevant undertaking at the time of the transfer.

Who is an 'employee' for TUPE purposes? 2.12

Not every member of a transferor's workforce is necessarily covered by the protections accorded by the Regulations. In common with most of the statutory rights conferred by the ERA – including the right to claim unfair dismissal and entitlement to a statutory redundancy payment – the TUPE protections in respect of the transfer of contracts (Reg 4) and the specific protection against unfair dismissal (Reg 7) apply to 'employees' employed by the transferor under a contract of employment.

It would have been helpful when ascertaining exactly who is and who is not an 'employee' for this purpose if the definition of 'employee' under the Regulations were exactly the same as that for unfair dismissal and redundancy purposes under the ERA. Unfortunately, this is not the case. For reasons explained below, it is arguable that the definition of 'employee' under the Regulations is wider than that under the ERA and that its unique formulation means that there is no exact equivalent in any other legislation. So while it is true that anyone who is an employee for the purposes of the ERA will fall within the TUPE definition of 'employee', it is also true that a further 'subset' of workers – to use a neutral term – may come within the protections of TUPE. The big problem lies in identifying this subset – a task made difficult by the lack of precision in the TUPE definition combined with the paucity of cases in which that definition has been scrutinised by the appellate courts.

Definition of 'employee' and 'contract of employment' 2.13
'Employee' is defined for the purposes of the Regulations in Reg 2(1) as: 'any individual who works for another person whether under a contract of service or apprenticeship *or otherwise* but does not include anyone who provides services under a contract for services' (our stress).

'Contract of employment' is defined in Reg 2(1) as '*any agreement* between an employee and his employer *determining the terms and conditions of his employment*' (our stress). This definition is crucial because the entire thrust of Reg 4 is to effect the transfer of the contract of employment of any employee who is employed by the transferor and assigned to the undertaking being transferred immediately before the transfer. It will be immediately observed

101

that the Regulations provide for a wide-reaching definition of 'contract of employment' in that the definition embraces any agreement devised in the context of an employment relationship that determines the terms and conditions applicable to that relationship.

2.14 Three certainties emerge from these definitions:

- any person employed under a contract of service will be covered by TUPE

- any apprentice employed under a contract of apprenticeship will similarly be covered

- anyone who merely provides services under a contract for services (i.e. someone in business on their own account or an independent contractor) will not be covered.

Apart from the above, nothing else is spelt out about who does and who does not come within the definition of 'employee' for TUPE purposes, other than that the scope of the definitions appears to embrace a wider group of persons than merely those employed under a contract of service. The uncertainty is almost entirely caused by the two words 'or otherwise' within the definition, since these raise the crucial question: what is meant by a person who works for another under 'a contract of service... or otherwise'? Case law helps in establishing the parameters, but not a lot.

2.15 The insertion of the vague words 'or otherwise' into the Reg 2(1) definition of 'employee' and the broad scope given to the definition of 'contract of employment' are explicable in terms of the Acquired Rights Directive. Article 3(1) of the Directive provides that: 'The transferor's rights and obligations arising from a contract of employment *or from an employment relationship* existing on the date of a transfer shall, by reason of such transfer, be transferred to the transferee' (our stress). The substance of this provision is implemented into UK law by Reg 4 of the 2006 Regulations. In enacting the original version of TUPE, the then Conservative Government felt it had to give full cognisance to the words emphasised by italics above because those words clearly envisaged that rights arising not just from a contract of employment but from an employment relationship had to be transferred. Hence, the words 'or otherwise' were added into the definition of 'employee'. All of this was explained in the Court of Appeal's decision in Governing Body of Clifton Middle School and ors v Askew 2000 ICR 286, CA. In that case, Lord Justice Peter Gibson referred to the Parliamentary debates on the initial TUPE Regulations, where Lord Lyell, on behalf of the then Government, noted that '[the] wider definitions of "employee" and "contract of employment" are to embrace the wider concept of what appears in the Directive as "employment relationship"' (Hansard 10.12.81, HL Debates, col 1496).

The relationship between the definitions of 'employee' and 'contract of employment' was analysed by the Court of Appeal in the Askew case. It was pointed out that the TUPE definition of 'employee' includes but goes beyond how an employee is defined for the purposes of the ERA. The TUPE definition of 'contract of employment' is likewise given an extended meaning to include any agreement between an 'employee' (as defined by Reg 2(1)) and an employer determining the terms and conditions of the employee's employment. Hence, 'contract of employment' is defined in TUPE to include not only contracts of service and apprenticeship – i.e. to cover contracts that would be 'contracts of employment' as under the ERA – but also any other agreement that records or evidences 'an employment relationship' as required by the Directive.

However, the Court's decision preceded the updating of the Directive in 2001. **2.16** Article 2(1)(d) of the current version states that an 'employee' shall mean any person who, in the Member State concerned, is protected as an employee under national employment law. But then, perhaps somewhat confusingly, Article 2(2) states that 'this Directive shall be without prejudice to national law as regards the definition of employment or employment relationship'. The definition of employee is therefore left to each Member State to determine, although it is arguable that this still requires some acknowledgement in national law that the Directive's protection must extend to those who are in an 'employment relationship' in the European sense.

The Directive also makes it clear that Member States cannot exclude those who are employed on a part-time or fixed-term basis from the scope of the Directive.

Employment within corporate group structure   2.17
The Court of Appeal in Governing Body of Clifton Middle School and ors v Askew (above) held that the relevant definitions of 'employee' and 'contract of employment' in Reg 2(1) cannot be extended so widely as to include an employment relationship in which there is no contractual agreement whatsoever between the putative employee and the employer determining the terms and conditions of employment – see under 'Limits on scope of extended definitions' below. This aspect of the Court's ruling has, however, been put into some doubt by the European Court's decision in Albron Catering BV v FNV Bondgenoten and anor 2011 ICR 373, ECJ. In that case R was employed by HNB BV, a subsidiary owned by Heineken International (HI), the group of Dutch beer producers. HNB BV performed the role of 'central employer' within the HI group, entering into a contract of employment with every employee and then assigning him or her to work for the various operating companies within the group. R was assigned to work for HN BV, another subsidiary of HI, which supplied catering for Heineken employees at their various company locations. In March 2005, the catering activities carried out by HN BV were transferred to AC BV, a company outside the HI group. When his terms and conditions were diminished, R brought an action against AC BV, seeking a declaration

103

that the transfer of the catering business from HN BV to AC BV constituted a 'transfer of an undertaking' within the meaning of the Acquired Rights Directive, and that employees of HNB BV who were assigned to HN BV automatically became employees of AC BV as from the date of the transfer. In addition, R sought an order that AC BV be required to comply with the terms and conditions of the contract that had applied between HNB BV and R.

The ECJ held that the wording of Article 3(1) – which refers to the transferor's rights and obligations arising from a contract of employment or from an employment relationship – suggested that there was no need for a contractual link between the transferor and the employees concerned in order for those employees to be able to benefit from the Directive's protection. The ECJ also reasoned that Article 1(1)(b) – which defines a transfer for the purposes of the Directive as 'a transfer of an economic entity which retains its identity' – presupposes a change in the person responsible for the economic entity transferred and who, in that capacity, establishes working relations as employer with the staff of that entity. It followed that a 'contractual employer', such as HNB BV – which is not responsible for the economic activity of the entity – is not necessarily to be determined to be the transferor in preference to a 'non-contractual employer', such as HN BV, which is responsible for the running of that entity. The ECJ therefore concluded that in the event of a transfer of an undertaking from within a group of companies, it is possible for the 'transferor' to be the company to which the employees were assigned on a permanent basis and which has established working relations with those employees, despite not being linked to them by a contract of employment and even though another subsidiary company within the group does have a contract of employment with those employees.

2.18 It is apparent that the ECJ in Albron has shown a preparedness to 'pierce the corporate veil' to ascertain the true employment situation. The transferor can be found to be the undertaking to which an employee is permanently assigned notwithstanding that he or she is actually (i.e. contractually) employed by another company within the same group. This may well increase the likelihood that arrangements operating within complex group structures by which employees are employed by service or holding companies will be ineffective as a means of evading the protections deriving from the Directive and, by extension, TUPE – see 'Assigned to undertaking transferred – employees engaged by service/holding companies' below. That said, it is unclear whether the wording of the TUPE Regulations is currently wide enough to cover the ECJ's interpretation. 'Employee' is defined as any individual who works for another person 'whether *under a contract* of service or apprenticeship *or otherwise*' (our stress) – Reg 2(1). According to Lord Justice Gibson in Askew (decided under the old TUPE Regulations), this wording requires a contractual relationship between the transferor and the employees. Furthermore, Reg 4 talks in terms of the transfer of rights, powers, duties and liabilities arising under or in connection with a contract of employment. What happens if the employee is contractually employed by a different group company from the one to which he or she is assigned and which is the subject of the transfer? A further question that could arise is how a transfer-related claim would be pursued against the transferor (e.g. unfair dismissal) if the transferor is not the contractual employer for the purpose of the right to claim unfair dismissal under the ERA. These are difficulties that will need to be ironed out in due course.

Suffice to say that employers will need to be alert to the implications of the Albron decision and to the possibility that employment tribunals may interpret TUPE in accordance with it. In this regard, private sector workers will be able to rely on the principle recently confirmed in EBR Attridge LLP (formerly Attridge Law) and anor v Coleman 2010 ICR 242, EAT, that national courts (including employment tribunals) must interpret provisions of domestic law that are intended to implement a Directive in order to achieve, 'so far as possible', an outcome consistent with the objective pursued by the Directive. To discharge this duty, courts have the flexibility to insert additional wording into domestic legislation. So far as public sector workers are concerned, they can simply rely directly on the relevant provisions of a Directive (assuming these are sufficiently clear and precise) to support their claim.

Limits on scope of extended definitions   2.19
As explained under 'Definition of "employee" and "contract of employment"' above, the addition of the words 'or otherwise' to the definition of employee given in Reg 2(1) clearly contemplates an extension of the definition of employee beyond merely those employed under contracts of service or apprenticeship. But this extension has its limits based on the wording of the TUPE Regulations as they are currently drafted. These are outlined below.

Requirement for contractual relations. TUPE protection can only extend to   2.20
individuals who work for another under some kind of contract. In other words, for Reg 4 to apply, there must be a contractual relationship between the individual and the transferor. This was made clear by Peter Gibson LJ in Governing Body of Clifton Middle School and ors v Askew (above), when he stated: 'In my judgment, it is clear that TUPE proceeds on the basis that there must be a contract. One gets that from the application of the *eiusdem generis* rule to "contract of service or apprenticeship or otherwise" in the definition of "employee", from the definition of "contract of employment" as meaning any agreement between an employee and his employer determining the terms and conditions of his employment, and from [what is now Reg 4(1)], which proceeds on the footing that there will be a contract of employment by the transferor in the undertaking or part transferred.' However, note that following the ECJ's decision in Albron Catering BV v FNV Bondgenoten and anor 2011 ICR 373, ECJ (discussed under 'Employment within corporate group structure' above), it is now possible for employees within a group structure to gain the protection

105

of the Acquired Rights Directive when the business for which they work is transferred, even if they were formally employed under a contract of employment not by the company actually running the business but by another company within the same group.

2.21 **Contract must be with transferor.** The second limitation to the expansive definition of 'employee' in Reg 2(1) is related to the first limitation discussed above – see 'Requirement for contractual relations'. Not only must the basis on which work undertaken by the individual on behalf of the other be underpinned by a contractual agreement, but that other has to be the actual or legal person who is the 'transferor' of the undertaking being transferred. However, again, this limitation must now be looked at in the light of the ECJ's decision in Albron (above), where it was held that, in the context of a group company structure, a 'non-contractual employer' was the transferor.

2.22 **Contract must provide for personal service.** A further limiting factor is that the TUPE definition of 'employee' explicitly requires the employment relationship to be one whereby the individual *works for another person* under one of the relevant types of contract. Essentially, this boils down to the relationship needing to be one of employment rather than some other arrangement. This was made clear by the Court of Appeal in Cowell v Quilter Goodison Co Ltd and anor 1989 IRLR 392, CA, where it was held that the TUPE Regulations did not apply to an equity partner of a firm that, following incorporation, was transferred as a limited company, which then employed the former partner under a contract of employment. In the judgment of Lord Donaldson MR (with whom the other members of the Court of Appeal agreed), an equity partner was someone who provides services under a contract for services and was not therefore an 'individual who works for another person whether under a contract of service or apprenticeship *or otherwise*' at the time of the transfer. Rather, the relationship, which was between the claimant partner and the other partners of the firm, was predicated on people carrying on business in common with a view to profit as governed by the Partnership Act 1890. That relationship was not one of employment; nor did the partnership agreement constitute a contract of employment or any kind of contract under which the individual worked for another person.

2.23 **Exclusion of those engaged under contracts for services**
The definition of employee in Reg 2(1) expressly excludes 'anyone who provides services under a contract for services'. This phrase is generally used to describe any contract under which services are provided that is not a contract of employment or apprenticeship. Occasionally, however, the phrase has a more specific and limited meaning, intended to be confined to contracts entered into by independent contractors. In that case, a contract with someone who is held not to be an employee, an apprentice or an independent contractor can properly be described as a 'contract sui generis' rather than a contract for

services – see Construction Industry Training Board v Labour Force Ltd 1970 3 All ER 220, Div Ct, where the Divisional Court held that the contracts of workmen who were neither independent contractors nor engaged under a contract of service should be described as 'contracts sui generis' (i.e. of a unique kind). If this is applied to Reg 2(1), then an individual employed under a contract sui generis would presumably be an 'individual who works for another person whether under a contract of service or apprenticeship or otherwise' and thus fall within the definition of 'employee'.

There is a compelling reason why the phrase 'contract for services' as used in Reg 2(1) should bear its restrictive rather than its more general meaning. Were it simply to mean any contract that is not a contract of employment or apprenticeship, then it would be difficult to see how anyone who is potentially brought within the definition of 'employee' by the words 'or otherwise' would not be immediately excluded by the qualification 'does not include anyone who provides services under a contract for services'. A better reading of the phrase 'provides services under a contract for services' would be 'provides services as an independent contractor under a contract for services'.

Workers
2.24

Having dissected the components of the definitions of 'employee' and 'contract of employment' in Reg 2(1), and the limitations that apply to the extended meaning of both terms, we now turn to particular types of individual or atypical worker. In each case the question is the same: Would the employment of such an individual by the transferor be subject to Reg 4, with the result that his or her 'contract of employment' is transferred to the transferee?

Certain statutory protection rights in the UK extend to individuals who do not technically work under a contract of service. This is sometimes signalled by use of the term 'worker' in place of the term 'employee' in the relevant legislation, in which case 'worker' is defined as one who either works under a contract of employment or works under 'any other contract, whether express or implied and (if it is express) whether oral or in writing, whereby the individual undertakes to do or perform personally any work or services for another party to the contract whose status is not by virtue of the contract that of a client or customer of any profession or business undertaking carried on by the individual'. This formula currently appears in the Working Time Regulations 1998 SI 1998/1833, the National Minimum Wage Act 1998, the Employment Relations Act 1999 in respect of the right to be accompanied at a grievance or disciplinary hearing, and the Part-time Workers (Prevention of Less Favourable Treatment) Regulations 2000 SI 2000/1551.

Distilling the definition into its constituent elements, the following are shown to be necessary for an individual to come within the definition of 'worker': 2.25

107

- there must be a contract, whether express or implied, and, if express, whether written or oral

- that contract must provide for the individual to carry out personal services; and

- those services must be for the benefit of another party to the contract who must not be a client or customer of the individual's profession or business undertaking.

In Byrne Brothers (Formwork) Ltd v Baird and ors 2002 ICR 667, EAT, the Appeal Tribunal laid down a helpful test to identify who is a 'worker' under the above definition. It held that the effect of the definition was to create an intermediate category of protected workers, who on the one hand are not employees but who on the other hand cannot be regarded as merely carrying on a business on their own account. The EAT said that to draw a distinction in a particular case would involve all or most of the same considerations that arise when deciding if somebody is an employee (e.g. degree of control, method of payment, provision of equipment, level of risk, etc). The effect of the definition of 'worker', however, is to lower the 'pass mark' so that persons who fail to reach the high mark necessary to qualify as employees may still qualify as workers. Adopting very similar reasoning, the EAT in JNJ Bricklaying Ltd v Stacey and ors EAT 0088/03 ruled that the relevant distinction is between workers whose degree of dependence is essentially the same as that of employees, and contractors who have more of an arm's-length and independent position and can therefore be regarded as being able to look after themselves.

2.26 It is relevant to note that, where the question of whether particular European employment measures apply to particular types of worker has arisen for consideration by the European Court of Justice, the Court has attached some importance to the issue of 'subordination'. So, for example, in the context of the application of equal pay to workers, the ECJ in Allonby v Accrington and Rossendale College and ors 2004 ICR 1328, ECJ, accepted that the concept of 'worker' should not be extended to include independent providers of services who are not in a relationship of subordination with the person who receives the services. However, the significance of the criterion of subordination has been rather downplayed by the UK courts when interpreting domestic law provisions. For example, in Bates van Winkelhof v Clyde and Co LLP and anor 2014 ICR 730, SC, the Supreme Court pointed out that, while subordination may sometimes be an aid to distinguishing workers from other self-employed people, it is not a free-standing and universal characteristic of being a worker. It may also be relevant to consider whether the individual has an ability to market their services to third parties and the degree to which the putative worker is integrated into the business as well as the other factors referred to by the EAT in Byrne Bros (Formwork) Ltd v Baird and ors (above). So in the Bates van

Winkelhof case itself the claimant was found to be a worker essentially because she could not market her services as an 'equity member' of a limited liability partnership to anyone other than the LLP. While there is no single key that applies in every case (as acknowledged by Lord Justice Maurice Kay in Hospital Medical Group Ltd v Westwood 2013 ICR 415, CA), it is also interesting to note that the absence of direction and control was considered critical by the Supreme Court in concluding that an 'arbitrator' was not a 'worker' in Hashwani v Jivraj (London Court of International Arbitration and ors intervening) 2011 ICR 1004, SC.

In Bacica v Muir 2006 IRLR 35, EAT, the Appeal Tribunal also cautioned that the mere rendering of a service personally is not sufficient to make a person a 'worker' under the statutory definition of worker in the employment protection provisions mentioned above. It is crucial not to ignore the last clause in the definition, which makes it clear that if a person renders services or performs work on the basis that the person to or for whom he or she does so is a customer of his or her business, he or she is not then to be regarded as a worker. Such work or service may well be rendered on a personal basis – for instance, it is well within the competence of many self-employed sole traders to do so and many secure business on the basis of selling their personal skills. In that case the EAT ruled that a claimant who carried out painting work for a company under the Construction Industry Scheme Regulations and whose accounts were submitted to the Inland Revenue on a self-employed basis was not a worker within the meaning of the Working Time Regulations 1998. (For further guidance, see IDS Employment Law Handbook, 'Contracts of Employment' (2014), Chapter 1, 'Employment status').

2.27 In the light of the above, the following are examples of those who have been held to be 'workers' engaged under a contract to provide personal service:

- a joiner working as a labour-only subcontractor. (Note that a contractual prohibition on substitution of the individual worker by another joiner without prior written consent was found not to prevent the contract being one to provide personal services) – Cavil v Barratt Homes Ltd EAT 0208/03

- a self-employed joiner who worked a 39-hour week exclusively for a firm of building contractors (notwithstanding that the worker completed his own tax return, paid his own tax and national insurance and provided his own hand tools) – Torith Ltd v Flynn EAT 0017/02

- bricklayers engaged under a building company's standard terms and conditions containing clauses that were inconsistent with a requirement to perform the work personally. (The Court of Appeal accepted that the factual background of the case, including the company's method of payment to each individual bricklayer, pointed strongly to the conclusion that, in

109

reality, the contracts with individual workers required them to perform the work personally) – Redrow Homes (Yorkshire) Ltd v Wright and another case 2004 ICR 1126, CA.

Would workers of this kind come within the extended definition of 'employee' in Reg 2(1) of the 2006 Regulations? Although there is no direct case authority on the point, it is arguable that they would. This is because such workers would appear, for the purposes of Reg 2(1), to be individuals who work for another person whether under a contract of service or otherwise. Provided that the requirement of personal service is met and that the putative worker is not exclusively providing his or her services as an independent contractor, then the only remaining requirement – as established by the Court of Appeal in Governing Body of Clifton Middle School and ors v Askew 2000 ICR 286, CA (discussed under 'Limits on scope of extended definitions' above) – is that the employment relationship be regulated by a contract of some kind. In the absence of such a contract, the individual would not, in any event, be regarded as a worker for the purposes of the relevant employment legislation where that definition applies. So long as such a contract exists, then, in our view, it is arguable that the individual could be regarded as someone who works for another whether under 'a contract of employment… or otherwise' and therefore comes within the extended definition of 'employee' under Reg 2(1).

2.28 Assuming that such workers would qualify for TUPE protection, a question as to the precise ambit of that protection might well arise. If such workers are not employees for the purposes of claiming, say, unfair dismissal, then they do not suddenly become entitled to such rights merely because their employment transfers following a transfer of an undertaking. Reg 7(6) in this regard expressly ensures that an individual who is otherwise excluded from claiming unfair dismissal cannot rely upon the provisions in the Regulations for deeming a dismissal by reason of the transfer to be unfair – see further Chapter 4, 'Unfair dismissal', under 'The TUPE unfair dismissal regime – which employees are protected?'.

More generally, it is well established that the objective of both the Acquired Rights Directive and TUPE is to preserve existing rights rather than to augment or create new ones. This was made clear by the ECJ in Viggósdóttir v Íslandspóstur HF 2002 IRLR 425, ECJ, when it stated that 'the objective of the Directive… is not to improve the situation of an employee following a transfer, but merely to preserve his acquired rights'. Taking its cue from this, the EAT (His Honour Judge McMullen QC presiding) in Computershare Investor Services plc v Jackson EAT 0503/06 has stated: 'We accept that one cannot use TUPE to advance upon a position which was not there on the date of the transfer.' This means that if individuals who are not employees employed under a contract of service nonetheless fall within the extended definition of 'employee' for the purposes of Reg 2(1), then, following the transfer, they will be entitled to enforce the same – but only the same – statutory rights against the transferee as they had with the transferor. For further discussion of this point, see Chapter 3, 'What transfers?', under '"Automatic transfer" principle – overview', and also under 'Individual statutory rights – TUPE does not augment statutory rights'.

Those in 'employment' for the purposes of discrimination law

The same reasoning can, subject to one further qualification, be applied in the case of those who come within the scope of UK anti-discrimination legislation. This, now codified in the Equality Act 2010 (EqA), uses neither the term 'worker' nor the term 'employee' to determine who is covered, but instead extends coverage to those in 'employment'. This is defined in S.83(2) EqA as 'employment under a contract of service or of apprenticeship or a contract personally to do any work or labour'. The definition is thus similar to, but wider than, that of 'worker' discussed under 'Workers' above.

The protection against discrimination thus extends not only to those employed under contracts of employment or apprenticeship but also to those employed under 'a contract personally to do any work or labour'. Two elements are necessary to fall within this type of contract:

- a requirement for a contract to exist; and

- a requirement that such contract provides for the work or labour under it to be executed personally.

The first of these requirements is, as we have seen, common to the definition of both 'worker' in employment protection legislation where that concept is used and 'employee' in Reg 2(1) of the TUPE Regulations. Without a contract of some kind – be it express or implied – neither of the relevant definitions will be satisfied.

The second requirement – that the contract, if not one of employment or apprenticeship, must nonetheless provide for personal execution of work or labour – has been interpreted to mean that it must have as its dominant purpose the execution of work or labour – Mirror Group Newspapers Ltd v Gunning 1986 ICR 145, CA. This means that the contracting party must perform the essential part of the work personally, although he or she is free to assign or delegate other aspects to another person without falling outside the definition of 'employment'. However in Hashwani v Jivraj (London Court of International Arbitration and ors intervening) 2011 ICR 1004, SC, the Supreme Court recognised that, in the light of European case law, 'dominant purpose' cannot be the sole test, although it may be relevant in arriving at the correct conclusion on the facts of a particular case. The focus is on the contract and relationship between the parties rather than exclusively on the purpose. If the dominant purpose of the contract is the execution of work, it is likely that the relationship

2.29

2.30

will be a case in which the person concerned performs services for and under the direction of the other party to the contract in return for remuneration as opposed to an independent provider of services who is not in a relationship of subordination with him.

2.31 With this in mind, would an individual employed on a contract personally to perform work or labour as defined above come within the definition of 'employee' under Reg 2(1) TUPE? Lord Justice Chadwick in Governing Body of Clifton Middle School and ors v Askew 2000 ICR 286, CA, certainly seemed to think so when he observed: '"Employee" includes a person who is not employed under a contract of employment in the sense that that phrase is used in the [ERA]; the definition in Reg 2(1) is at least as wide as that adopted by the legislature for the purposes of the Sex Discrimination Act 1975.' Although his Lordship did not go on to amplify his reasoning in this regard, it seems fairly clear that an individual who has an agreement the dominant purpose of which is to provide for him or her to personally do work for another would be an 'employee' for the purposes of Reg 2(1), since he or she would be an 'individual who works for another person under a contract of service... or otherwise'. Furthermore, that contract would comprise a 'contract of employment' as defined in Reg 2(1) in that it is 'an agreement between an employee and his employer determining the terms and conditions of his employment'.

An important caveat applies here. This concerns the fact that, unlike the definition of 'worker' previously discussed (see 'Workers' above), the definition of 'employment' in the anti-discrimination legislation does not contain an express exclusion for independent contractors. Such persons would include those who provide personal services for a client or customer in the course of practising a profession or running a business on their own account. For the most part, contractors of this kind receive protection from discrimination by virtue of specific provisions contained within the anti-discrimination legislation dealing with contract workers. However, in exceptional circumstances, such workers might also be able to bring themselves within the definition of 'employment' – see, for example, Kelly and anor v Northern Ireland Housing Executive 1998 ICR 828, HL, where the majority of the House of Lords held that a contract between a solicitor and a client for the retention of that solicitor's legal services could fall within the definition of 'employment' provided that the contract is one personally to execute work, one of the partners of the firm bringing the claim is a contracting party, and it is envisaged that that partner would be the individual who would have undertaken to provide the services personally. This is in line with the general approach of the Supreme Court subsequently adopted and applied in Bates van Winkelhof v Clyde and Co LLP and anor 2014 ICR 730, SC. In any case where these conditions are met by a contractor, the individual concerned would be shut out of TUPE protection on account of the exclusion in the definition of 'employee' in Reg 2(1) of 'anyone who provides services under a contract for services'. As we have seen, however, there is a strong case for giving a restrictive meaning to the concept of 'contract for services' in this particular context – see 'Exclusion of those engaged under contracts for services' above.

Agency workers   2.32

'Agency workers' are individuals engaged by an employment business who are assigned to work for clients of the business, usually under temporary worker agreements. The legal rights of such workers is an area fraught with difficulties since, even in the context of basic statutory rights such as unfair dismissal and redundancy entitlement, it is often unclear whether such workers are employees of the employment business, the client (i.e. end-user), or neither.

In the context of TUPE, the question often arises as to whether the employment of an agency worker assigned by an employment business to work for an end-user transfers following a transfer of the end-user's undertaking. In the absence of a direct contractual relationship between worker and end-user, recent case law suggests that the worker is highly likely to fall outside the relevant definition of 'employee' in Reg 2(1). This is because the only express agreement that he or she is likely to have is with the employment business. Rarely will there be any kind of written contractual agreement with the end-user. Thus, applying the Court of Appeal's decision in James v Greenwich London Borough Council 2008 ICR 545, CA, the worker would not be an 'employee' employed under a 'contract of employment' with the transferor. Quite apart from this, the Court of Appeal has held in Tilson v Alstom Transport 2011 IRLR 169, EAT, and Smith v Carillion (JM) Ltd 2015 IRLR 467, CA, that even if the agency worker is integrated into the business of the end-user and is subject to the end-user's direction and control, this will not justify the 'necessary' implication of an employment contract. In the words of Lord Justice Elias in the Smith case: 'Just because a claimant looked like an employee, acted like an employee and was treated like an employee, it does not mean that he was an employee.' The same reasoning may well apply to agency workers who 'work' for an end-user. It is therefore unlikely that such workers are covered by Reg 2(1), although there is, as yet, no reported authority specifically on the point.

A further obstacle that agency workers would need to overcome is that the **2.33** TUPE Regulations have been interpreted by the UK courts as requiring that any relevant contract has to be one to which the transferor is a party – see Governing Body of Clifton Middle School and ors v Askew 2000 ICR 286, CA, discussed in detail under 'Definition of "employee" and "contract of employment"' above. It should be noted that in Albron Catering BV v FNV Bondgenoten and anor 2011 ICR 373, ECJ, the European Court held that the wording of Article 3(1) of the Acquired Rights Directive – which refers to the transferor's rights and obligations arising from a contract of employment or from an employment relationship – suggests that there is no need for there to be a contractual link between the transferor and the employees concerned for those employees to be able to benefit from the Directive's protection. However, this decision was made in the context of an employee employed under a contract of employment with one company in a group who was permanently assigned to work for another company within the same group. When the latter company's business was transferred, the employee was found to be in an 'employment relationship' with the transferor company notwithstanding that his contract of employment was with a different company. In our view, it is unlikely that the Albron case will be interpreted by UK courts and tribunals as authority for the proposition that agency workers who lack any contract of employment either with the transferring company or another company within the same group should nevertheless be regarded as in an 'employment relationship' with the transferor to whom they are assigned by the agency to work.

2.34 **Non-employees who are 'protected' as employees**

Although, as we have seen, the Acquired Rights Directive applies to transfer the rights of those employed under an 'employment relationship' as well as under a contract of employment, the scope of 'employment relationship' in this regard has been held to extend only to 'persons who, in one way or another, are protected as employees under the rules of law of the Member State concerned' – see Mikkelsen v Danmols Inventar A/S (in liquidation) 1986 1 CMLR 316, ECJ. On one interpretation of this, the ECJ is saying no more than that the Directive applies only to those who are defined as 'employees' under national law. In that case, the definition of 'employee' for TUPE purposes would begin and end with the definition given in Reg 2(1). However, on a broader interpretation of the ECJ's ruling, the Court might be taken to be saying that the Directive must be construed as extending not only to those who are employees but also to those who, under national legislation, are treated as employees for the purposes of employment protection rights. Potentially, this would mean that the definition of 'employee' in Reg 2(1) would need to be interpreted as embracing a small but significant group of individuals who, though they are technically not 'employees' who work under a contract of employment, nevertheless receive the same or similar protections against unfair dismissal and redundancy as if they were.

Apart from the ECJ's observations in Mikkelsen, no other case appears to have tackled this issue, so uncertainty remains. But were it the case that the Directive (and therefore TUPE) does extend to individuals who are treated as employees for employment protection purposes, then with specific regard to the UK the following groups of individuals are protected against unfair dismissal as 'honorary' employees:

- *Crown servants*: although such workers are said to be 'appointed' rather than 'employed', and their appointment is 'at will and terminable by the Crown without notice', they receive the same protection against unfair dismissal as do ordinary employees by virtue of S.191(1) ERA. The same applies in respect of most other statutory employment rights

- *House of Commons and House of Lords staff*: Ss.194 and 195 ERA provide that unfair dismissal rights apply to 'relevant members' of staff of the two Houses of Parliament

- *persons employed in the police service*: although generally excluded from unfair dismissal rights, some members of the police service – i.e. those who hold the office of constable or are appointed as police cadets – are entitled to bring unfair dismissal claims on limited grounds, namely health and safety and protected disclosure (i.e. whistleblowing) – Ss.43KA and 134A ERA

- *mariners*: those employed on a ship registered in Great Britain, who are ordinarily resident in Great Britain and who do not ordinarily work outside Great Britain are entitled to unfair dismissal protection – S.199 ERA.

Of course, in practice, most of the categories of individual mentioned above are **2.35** unlikely to be caught up in a transfer of an undertaking to which TUPE applies. Of those that are listed, the most likely affected group are Crown servants, but it is improbable that the 'Mikkelsen question' will arise in respect of them since for many years it has been standard practice for TUPE to be faithfully applied to transfers (such as outsourcing) affecting the Civil Service and government departments – for further details, see Chapter 3, 'What transfers?', under 'Special protections for public sector transfers'.

Employees employed abroad   2.36

The TUPE Regulations apply to the transfer of an undertaking situated in the UK immediately before the transfer, and, in the case of a service provision change, where there is an organised grouping of employees situated in the UK immediately before the service provision change. However, neither Reg 4 nor any other provision deals specifically with the position of employees who, though employed in the undertaking (or part) transferred, ordinarily work abroad. The question arises as to whether the employment of such employees is transferred under Reg 4.

By virtue of Reg 3(4)(c), the Regulations expressly apply to a transfer of an undertaking, business or part of an undertaking or business situated in the UK, even where persons employed in the undertaking or part transferred ordinarily work outside the UK. It will be noted that this provision deals with the definition of a relevant transfer rather than the effect that such a relevant transfer has on employees employed in the undertaking who ordinarily work abroad. But the implication is – and there is nothing to contradict this – that such employees would be covered by Reg 4 provided they are actually 'assigned' to the undertaking (or part) being transferred at the time of the transfer. The issue of assignment is covered under '"Assigned" to undertaking transferred' below.

2.37 ## Contracts 'otherwise terminated by' transfer

Regulation 4(1) (set out at the beginning of this chapter) establishes the basic premise that a relevant transfer will not operate to terminate the 'the contract of employment of any person... *which would otherwise be terminated by the transfer*' (our stress). This implies that the 'automatic transfer of employment' rule applies to contracts of employment that would be terminated by the transfer and is inapplicable to those contracts of employment that would not be so terminated. However, this aspect of the wording of Reg 4(1) – which is identical in this regard to the previous wording in Reg 5(1) of the 1981 Regulations – has caused some difficulty because it is not at all clear which employment contracts would 'otherwise' be terminated by the transfer.

2.38 **Are employment contracts 'otherwise' terminated by transfer?**
The assumption that appears to underlie this provision is that, in the absence of the TUPE Regulations, transfers of an undertaking may, in and of themselves, cause the automatic termination of contracts of employment. In so implying, it is probable that the Parliamentary draftsman was seeking simply to reflect the common law position that the Regulations are intended to reverse. This, as we have seen in the introduction to this chapter, is based on two legal principles: (1) that employment contracts cannot be transferred unilaterally; and (2) that a transfer is likely to constitute a repudiatory breach of such contracts. However, for reasons explained below, the notion that such a repudiatory breach would according to the common law have the effect of automatically bringing about the termination of a contract of employment may well be technically erroneous, particularly in the light of the Supreme Court's ruling in Geys v Société Générale, London Branch 2013 ICR 117, SC. If that is the case, then the Regulations appear to have been based on a misapprehension as to the true common law effect of a transfer on contracts of employment.

Under general contract law, a breach by a party that goes to the root of a contract entitles the other party either to accept the repudiation (in which case the contract is terminated and the innocent party has the right to sue for damages), or to refuse to accept the repudiation (in which case the contract is not terminated and the innocent party may stand and sue for specific performance of the original contract). An unaccepted repudiation is 'a thing writ in water' – Howard v Pickford Tool Co Ltd 1951 1 KB 417, CA. In other words, a repudiatory breach in and of itself does not have the effect of automatically terminating the contract – the innocent party chooses whether or not to bring it to an end. This is known as the 'elective' theory of termination. So far as employment contracts are concerned, it has been a matter of some controversy whether the elective theory applies. On one view, it governs repudiatory breaches of contracts of employment just as much as any other kind of contract – see, for example, Gunton v Richmond-upon-Thames London

116

Borough Council 1980 ICR 755, CA. On an alternative view, employment contracts are an exception to the general need for acceptance of the repudiatory breach, and hence such contracts terminate automatically by the unilateral actions of one party – see Stapp v Shaftesbury Society 1982 IRLR 326, CA. This is known as the 'automatic' theory of termination – i.e. the contract automatically terminates without the innocent party electing to accept the repudiation as ending the contract. The Supreme Court in Geys v Société Générale, London Branch (above) – a non-TUPE case – has now come down firmly in favour of the 'elective' theory of termination, although it is hard to see how an employee could elect to keep the contract alive in a TUPE context given the personal nature of the employment relationship and the fact that employees do not, as a rule, have the power to prevent a transfer of a business or other undertaking from occurring.

Until the clarification made in the Geys case, the difference between these two **2.39** approaches may have been of some significance when considering the meaning of the phrase 'the contract of employment of any person employed by the transferor and assigned to the organised grouping of resources or employees that is subject to the relevant transfer, which would otherwise be terminated by the transfer' in Reg 4(1). It had previously been suggested that if the elective theory applied, then Reg 4(1) proceeds on a misconception about the effect of a transfer on a contract of employment at common law because, on a strict interpretation, a transfer would not, in itself, terminate such a contract. Actual termination would only occur if the employee accepted the repudiatory breach brought about by the transfer as terminating the contract. Thus, if the 'elective' theory of repudiation is correct, it would follow that contracts of employment subsisting at the time of the transfer would not fall into the category of those which would 'otherwise be terminated by the transfer' for the purposes of Reg 4(1), and so would not be subject to the novation rule which that regulation goes on to provide. Clearly, such an interpretation would make the Regulations circular in operation, as no contract of employment would be novated under them on the occurrence of a transfer.

It seems certain, therefore, that in the specific context of TUPE, the phrase '[contract] which would otherwise be terminated by the transfer' in Reg 4(1) must be interpreted as resting on the assumption that the transfer itself automatically terminates employment contracts either automatically or by reason of the employees' implied acceptance of the transferor's repudiatory breach. That is the only way that the key provision of the Regulations – the automatic transfer of employment to the transferee – could be made to work.

Authority for so construing Reg 4(1) can, to some extent, be gleaned from the **2.40** decision of the House of Lords in Litster and ors v Forth Dry Dock and Engineering Co Ltd (in receivership) and anor 1989 ICR 341, HL. In that case Lord Oliver considered what was meant by the reference in what is now

117

Reg 4(1) to a contract being terminated 'by' a transfer. His Lordship accepted that the phrase could embrace a number of different possibilities. He stated: 'If nothing at all occurs to disturb the relationship of master and servant apart from the simple unannounced fact of the transfer of business by the employer, it is the transfer itself which constitutes the repudiatory breach which, apart from Reg 4(1), "terminates" the contract. If, however, the employer, contemporaneously with the transfer, announces to his workforce that he is transferring the business and that they are therefore dismissed without notice, it is, strictly, the oral notification which terminates the contract; yet it could not, as a matter of common sense, be denied that the contract has been "terminated by the transfer" of the business... Similarly, if the employer, a week, or it may be a day, before the actual transfer, hands to each employee a letter announcing that he is proposing to transfer his undertaking at the close of business on the transfer date, at which time the employees are to consider themselves as forthwith dismissed, it could hardly be contended under the Regulations that their employment had not been terminated by the transfer, even though, at the date of the notice, the dismissal might be capable of taking effect independently; in the event, for instance, of the actual transfer of the business being postponed to a date or time later than the expiry of the notice. In each hypothetical case the employer's repudiation of the contract of service is differently communicated but its essential quality of a repudiation by the transfer of the undertaking remains the same and the contract can quite properly be described as having been terminated by the transfer.'

Clearly, Lord Oliver's construction of what is now Reg 4(1) means that, for the purposes of that regulation, contracts of employment subsisting at the time the transfer takes place will be automatically transferred on the basis that, apart from the Regulations, they would have been terminated 'by' the transfer. This approach is certainly in keeping with the obligations imposed upon Member States by the Acquired Rights Directive: Article 3(1) (which is set out at the beginning of this chapter) does not contain any wording equivalent to 'contracts which would otherwise be terminated by the transfer', and any detraction from the automatic transfer principle in Article 3(1) caused by a restrictive interpretation of these words in Reg 4(1) would clearly be in breach of the Directive.

2.41 It is interesting to note that in the original draft of the current Regulations published by the Department of Trade and Industry (DTI) in 2005, the reference to employment contracts that 'would otherwise have been terminated by the transfer' was omitted altogether. The explanation for this, according to the Public Consultation Document accompanying publication of the draft regulations, was that 'the Government considers these words add nothing of value to the meaning of the provision, and risk creating an unintended loophole in the Regulations' coverage – in that it has been argued by some commentators that they might have the effect of allowing the transferor to retain employees who would otherwise automatically transfer, on the basis that if they were to be retained, their employment would not be terminated by the transfer. This is contrary to the policy intention underlying the provision.' Why, then, was the original wording reinstated in the final version of the new TUPE Regulations? The explanation – as given by the DTI in its published response to the public consultation in February 2006 – was that the Government was persuaded by some respondents to the consultation that the original wording offered valuable scope for transferors to retain the services of employees who would otherwise transfer. The precise reasoning for this view is not further explained. Presumably, however, it was thought that the contracts of employees who agree with the transferor to be retained or who are permanently reassigned to a different part of the transferor's business before the transfer would not be contracts that would 'otherwise be terminated by the transfer'. This possibility is further explored below.

Contracts to which Reg 4(1) might not apply   2.42

If, then, ordinary contracts of employment are to be interpreted as comprising contracts that would otherwise be terminated by the transfer, the question arises: Which (if any) contracts of employment would not so terminate, with the result that employment under them would not automatically transfer under Reg 4(1)?

There is little case authority to assist in answering this question. But it is arguable that not every case of a transfer will amount to a repudiatory breach, even assuming that in the ordinary case such a transfer does indeed bring about the automatic termination of employment contracts. The following are scenarios where an employee's contract with the transferor might, at common law, be regarded as surviving the transfer intact.

Contracts containing wide-ranging mobility/flexibility clauses. Where the 2.43
terms of an employee's contract of employment include a wide job description, the employee may be contractually required to work in any part of the employer's business to do work which corresponds to that description. If, then, part of the business in which the employee is currently employed is to be sold, the transferor may be in a position to employ the employee in another part of the business under the terms of the contract between them. In this situation the transfer would not constitute a repudiatory breach of contract and therefore would not, apart from the Regulations, have resulted in the termination of the employment contract at common law. In consequence, Reg 4(1) would not operate to transfer that employee's contract to the transferee.

A similar outcome might result where an express flexibility contractual clause exists allowing the employer to require the employee to work in different parts of the business and/or at a different location and/or doing different types of work. If such a contractual term enables the transferor to ensure that the employee is, at the time of the transfer, employed in a part of the business that is not to be transferred, then once again Reg 4(1) will not operate to novate the employee's contract with the transferee. In this scenario, the question would also arise as to whether the employee is 'assigned to the organised grouping of resources or employees' (i.e. the undertaking) immediately before the transfer. The issue of 'assignment' is discussed in detail under '"Assigned" to undertaking transferred' below.

2.44 However, it may be open to the employee to argue that the employer's exercise of its contractual rights in these circumstances would fall foul of the anti-avoidance provisions in Reg 18. Some support for this view is to be found in the EAT's ruling in Jones and anor v Darlows Estate Agency EAT 1038/96 and comments made by Mr Justice Elias (as he then was) in Royal Mail Group Ltd v Communication Workers Union 2009 ICR 357, EAT, to the effect that, where a mobility clause is used for the very purpose of ensuring that employees who would otherwise transfer do not, this is inconsistent with the policy underlying the Acquired Rights Directive.

2.45 **Agreement that employee will be retained by transferor.** Sometimes, without making any formal objection to the transfer, the transferor and the employee enter into some kind of agreement whereby the former retains the services of the latter following the transfer. Such agreements may come about by the parties giving express consideration to the matter and reaching a position that reflects their mutual self-interest. However, they sometimes take a more passive form – whereby the parties simply carry on without reference to the transfer as if it has never happened.

Such retention of employees potentially causes considerable headaches from a legal point of view because, strictly speaking, the only way in which Reg 4(1) can be prevented from applying to an employee employed in the undertaking and assigned to it immediately before the transfer is for him or her to exercise the right to object conferred by Reg 4(7). This, as we shall see under 'Objecting to transfer' below, entails the employee adopting a proactive rather than a passive approach to voicing his or her objection to the transfer, and any such objection brings with it a particular set of legal consequences.

2.46 One way of 'accommodating' retention of the employee by the transferor within the scheme of the Regulations would be to regard the contract of employment between employee and transferor as not otherwise terminating by reason of the transfer. Such a proposition was accepted by the EAT in Direct Radiators Ltd v Howse and anor EAT 130/86, although it is fair to say that in other cases – for example, Visionhire Consumer Electronics Ltd t/a Visionhire v Easton EAT 20/87 – the courts have expressed disquiet about this way of dealing with the situation, preferring to analyse the matter in terms of the employee entering into a new or at least varied contract with the transferor. In view of this difference of opinion, it is interesting to bear in mind the

120

Government's view when enacting the 2006 Regulations. As we pointed out earlier, the original draft left out the phrase '[contract]... otherwise terminated by the transfer', but this was reinserted into the final version of Reg 4(1) on the ground that it might be of practical advantage to transferors wishing to retain the services of employees who would otherwise transfer. In the absence of employees' consent and cooperation, the same objection could be made as was raised by Elias J in the Royal Mail Group case (referred to above). The issue of the retention of employees following relevant transfers is discussed in more detail under 'Employees retained by transferor' below.

Agreed contractual variations. In a case where the contract of employment **2.47** would otherwise be terminated by the transfer, it is possible that an employee might consent to vary his or her contract in time to avoid the application of the automatic transfer of employment rule in Reg 4(1). So, for example, if, just prior to the transfer occurring, the employee agreed to be reassigned to another part of the transferor's business and so ceased to be assigned to the undertaking being transferred, his or her contract of employment might remain unaffected by Reg 4(1) as it would not 'otherwise be terminated by the transfer'. In such a case, there is a further reason why Reg 4(1) would not apply: the employee would not have been 'assigned to the undertaking immediately before the transfer' as now required by the wording of Reg 4(1). Similar reasoning would apply if the consensual variation concerned the introduction into the contract of a wide-ranging mobility or flexibility clause, or to an arrangement whereby the employee agreed to be seconded outside the part of the business being transferred.

Employed 'immediately before' transfer **2.48**

Once it has been established who, among the transferor's workforce, are 'employees' employed under 'contracts of employment' for the purposes of Reg 2(1), the next logical step in determining to whom the automatic transfer of employment rule in Reg 4(1) applies is to decide whether such employees are employed by the transferor and assigned to the transferred undertaking at the time of the transfer. Three separate issues may be relevant to this:

- when does the transfer take place?

- which of the transferor's employees are employed '*immediately* before the transfer'? (This is because Reg 4(1) only bites in respect of those employed by the transferor and who are, it would seem, also assigned to the transferred undertaking 'immediately before the transfer')

- in a case where the transfer is effected by two or more transactions, is the employee to be regarded as having been employed in the undertaking and assigned to it immediately before the first of those transactions? If so, then

Reg 4(1) will apply to transfer his or her employment even if he or she has ceased to be employed/assigned by the end of the transfer process.

Although these issues are very much interrelated, we examine each of them in turn below.

2.49 When does transfer occur?

Fixing the time of the relevant transfer is crucial because it is that point in time that is used to determine whether employees were in the employment of the transferor and assigned to the transferred undertaking for the purposes of the application of Reg 4. Only the contracts of employment of those employees (and not employees who are no longer employed as at the relevant date) automatically transfer to the transferee under Reg 4(1) – subject to the right of individual employees to object to the transfer. The time of the transfer also fixes the terms of the contracts of employment – i.e. the rights, powers, duties and liabilities – that are inherited by the transferee in accordance with Reg 4(2).

2.50 The Celtec decision. In view of these important consequences, the European Court of Justice and the UK courts have ruled that all relevant transfers must be regarded as taking place at a particular point in time rather than across a period of time. (However, this does not preclude a transfer from being effected by a series of separate steps – see 'Transfers effected by a series of transactions' below.) In Celtec Ltd v Astley and ors 2005 ICR 1409, ECJ, the European Court scrutinised the meaning of the words 'the date of a transfer' in the context of Article 3(1) of the old EU Acquired Rights Directive (No.77/187), which stipulated that 'the transferor's rights and obligations arising from a contract of employment or from an employment relationship *existing on the date of a transfer* within the meaning of Article 1(1) shall, by reason of such transfer, be transferred to the transferee' (our stress). This provision – which is now to be found in Article 3(1) of the current Directive – forms the foundation on which Reg 4(1) and (2) TUPE is based. The ECJ ruled that the 'date of a transfer' is the date on which the responsibility as employer for carrying on the business of the undertaking moves from the transferor to the transferee. That date, the Court emphasised, is a particular point in time that cannot be postponed to another date at the will of the transferor or transferee. Thus, contracts of employment or employment relationships existing on the date of the transfer between the transferor and the workers assigned to the undertaking transferred are deemed to be handed over on that date to the transferee, regardless of any alternative date that might have been agreed between the parties.

In coming to this conclusion, the ECJ reasoned that the reference to the 'date of a transfer' in Article 3(1) is designed to identify the workers who may rely on the protection established by that provision. Both the choice of the word 'date' and the requirement for legal certainty indicated that the workers in

122

question must be identified at a particular point in the transfer process and not in relation to the length of time over which that process extends.

The Celtec case had originally been referred to the ECJ by the House of Lords, **2.51** and it was therefore returned to the Lords to enable the ECJ's ruling to be applied to its particular facts (reported as North Wales Training and Enterprise Council Ltd (trading as Celtec Ltd) v Astley and ors 2006 ICR 992, HL). In the light of the ECJ's ruling, the crucial matter to be determined by their Lordships was the date of the transfer – i.e. the date on which responsibility as employer for carrying on the business of the transferred unit moved from the transferor to the transferee. This proved to be no easy task, given the complex factual matrix involved.

The case arose in the context of the setting up of Training and Enterprise Councils (TECs) in the early 1990s, which operated as private limited companies. In September 1990 the claimants, who were civil servants employed by the Department of Employment, were seconded on a voluntary basis to the North-East Wales TEC (Newtec) – which later became C Ltd – for a three-year period, during which all parties assumed they remained employed by the DoE. In November 1991, just over a year after Newtec was set up, the Government announced that secondments to the TECs would be phased out at the end of the fifth year of each TEC's operations and that, as part of this process, the civil servants involved would be given the choice of returning to the Civil Service or taking up employment with C Ltd. At the end of their three-year period of secondment (i.e. in 1993), the claimants all chose the latter option. In 1998, C Ltd decided to effect redundancies and the question arose as to whether, in the claimants' case, their redundancy entitlements should be calculated on the basis that their continuous service with C Ltd should be aggregated with their service as civil servants with the DoE. They contended that it should, on the basis that the TUPE Regulations applied to transfer their employment to C Ltd. However, to make good that claim, they had to show that they continued to be employed by the transferor – the DoE – at the 'date of the transfer'. If, at any time prior to that date, they had already become employed by C Ltd, they would be unable to rely on Article 3(1) of the Directive to transfer their accrued service because that provision only applies to contracts or employment relationships in existence as at the date of the transfer.

The majority of the House of Lords (Lords Bingham, Hope and Carswell) held **2.52** that, on these facts, the transfer had occurred in September 1990 when the claimants were first seconded to the TEC, even though this was contrary to what all the parties understood to be the case at the time. It was even contrary to what the claimants themselves had contended at all points prior to the House of Lords hearing. In Lord Bingham's words: 'It is plain from the findings made below that Celtec set up in business in September 1990 and the employees seconded from the Department were the core of the business: without them

123

there could have been no effective transfer. It is scarcely an exaggeration to say that they were the business.' Accordingly, their employment transferred from the DoE to the TEC/C Ltd at that time, notwithstanding that they did not resign from the Civil Service in order to accept direct employment with the TEC until three years later.

Lord Rodger, on the other hand, was concerned that this conclusion might have the effect of 'obliterating what had actually happened and of putting in its place an entirely fictitious version of events' whereby the claimants were in effect never seconded to the TEC. He therefore took the view that the date of the transfer did not coincide with the commencement of the employees' secondment from the Civil Service to the TEC in 1990 but occurred three years later when they resigned to take up direct employment with the TEC. In his judgment, that was the date on which the responsibility as employer for carrying on the business of the undertaking moved from the DoE to the TEC. On this basis, his Lordship agreed that the claimants remained in the employment of the DoE at the date of the transfer, with the consequence that their period of continuous employment as civil servants transferred at this point to C Ltd.

2.53 Lord Mance delivered a dissenting judgment. He highlighted the fact that the claimants had submitted at every stage of the case that they were seconded by the Department of Employment to TEC Ltd during the period September 1990 to 1993. At no point had they claimed that the transfer took place in September 1990, with the result that their employment with the transferee had started on that date. His Lordship thought that the case ought to be remitted to the employment tribunal for it to consider the new point and to make necessary additional factual findings. In so concluding, he drew attention to some of the problems associated with the conclusion that the transfer had occurred in September 1990. In particular, he observed that if the claimants unwittingly became employees of C Ltd at that date, the larger number of DoE employees who thought they were choosing to remain civil servants and volunteering to be seconded to C Ltd or another TEC must, in law, have also ceased to be civil servants in 1990. This would mean that, when given the choice between employment in the civil service or employment with the TEC in 1993, those who had elected to 'revert' to the Civil Service at this point would sustain a break in their continuity of employment.

2.54 **Practical difficulties caused by Celtec.** In most cases, the date of the transfer will be self-evident. Where the transfer is effected by a contractual agreement, the EAT's decision in Wheeler v Patel and anor 1987 ICR 631, EAT, is authority for the proposition that, when deciding when a TUPE transfer took place, the relevant date is the date when the contract for the transfer was completed. But this may take place at an earlier date if the employer assumes responsibility for running the business before completion. In Commercial Motors (Wales) Ltd v Howley EAT 0491/11 the EAT upheld an employment tribunal's conclusion that CM Ltd (the transferee) had assumed responsibility as employer 'by going to possession of [the transferor's] premises', 'running the business' and 'paying the wages of the staff working at [the transferor's] premises on 2 February 2009', even though completion of the business sale did not take place until 6 March 2009. The EAT considered that the tribunal's conclusion was consistent with Celtec and also with the ECJ's earlier ruling in Berg and anor v Besselsen 1990 ICR 396, ECJ. In the latter case, the European Court ruled that a purchaser of an undertaking under a lease-purchase agreement had assumed responsibility for carrying on the business that was the subject of the lease and that undertaking was to be treated as having transferred to the purchaser notwithstanding that legal ownership was only transferred at a later date on the final payment of the purchase price.

On the other hand, in Housing Maintenance Solutions Ltd v McAteer and ors 2015 ICR 87, EAT, the Appeal Tribunal ruled that an employment tribunal was wrong to conclude that an employing organisation had assumed responsibility for carrying on the business on the date when it was set up and had stated in the course of consultation with the trade unions that it intended to re-employ staff who had been made redundant following the insolvency of the transferor. Such a statement of intention was not a sufficient basis for it to be assumed that the transfer had been effected on that date. The claimants in the case were former employees of K Ltd who had entered into a contract with a housing association for the repair and maintenance of social housing stock. When K Ltd got into financial difficulties, the housing association set up HMS to take over the services provided by K Ltd with a start date of 1 July 2011. On 9 June 2011, K Ltd went into administration and the employees were made redundant with immediate effect. However, HMS needed to retain the workforce in order to provide the services and, in the course of consultation with the trade unions on 9 June gave the claimants 'reasurance' about their continued employment. HMS subsequently took over responsibility for the services previously carried out by K Ltd in phases, starting with the cleaning work on 20 June 2011 and then the maintenance and repair work on 1 July 2011.

The claimants brought claims under Part II ERA to recover their wages from **2.55** 9 June to 1 July. Initially, their claim was upheld by the employment tribunal but, on appeal, the EAT held that the tribunal's rationale for its decision was flawed. Although the Appeal Tribunal noted that in Landsorganisationen i Danmark v Ny Mølle Cro 1989 ICR 330, ECJ, the European Court had recognised that a transfer could take place when the business was temporarily closed or suspended and that, in principle, it might therefore have been open to the tribunal to conclude that HMS had assumed responsibility for the service on 9 June, the assurance given by it to the trade on that date was insufficient, in and of itself, to support the conclusion that there was a transfer of an undertaking from the transferor to the transferee on 9 June 2011. The EAT remitted the case to the employment tribunal to consider whether the transfer had taken place at the date on which HMS was set up and became operational (9 June), the date on which it began to carry out cleaning services (20 June), or the date when it commenced the maintenance and repair work (1 July).

The cases outlined above illustrate the particular problems sometimes involved in identifying the precise date of the transfer in accordance with the Celtec ruling in the context of complex transfers that take place in 'instalments'. This is often the case in outsourcing transactions or where, as in the Housing Maintenance Solutions case (above), the business is temporarily closed or the service temporarily suspended, or where a transfer occurs within a complex corporate structure in which employees are employed by a subsidiary to provide services to another subsidiary whose business is transferred.

2.56 Prior to Celtec, employment tribunals tended to get round these problems mainly by relying on provisions in the Regulations stipulating that a relevant transfer can be effected by a series of two or more transactions, and ensuring that employees will be regarded as having been employed immediately before the transfer so long as they are employed immediately before any of those transactions. It is a deeply frustrating aspect of Celtec that neither the ECJ nor the House of Lords dealt with these provisions and explained their impact on the requirement to pinpoint the actual date of the transfer. This is an issue to which we shall return in the discussion on 'Transfers effected by series of transactions' below.

The Celtec case also demonstrates that, in the absence of an explicit objection by employees to the transfer of their employment, Reg 4 can sometimes operate to transfer employment even though the parties may be completely ignorant that this has happened. This particular problem is further considered under 'Objecting to transfer' below.

2.57 On a related matter, there is finally the question of what impact the House of Lords' decision will have on secondment arrangements when these become embroiled in a TUPE transfer. This is of particular concern to organisations such as the NHS, which frequently use 'partnership agreements' and other similar secondment arrangements when outsourcing services to the private sector. We examine this issue in detail under 'Problems of secondment arrangements' at the end of this chapter.

2.58 Meaning of 'immediately before the transfer'

Returning to Reg 4(1), it will be recalled that this provides that the contract of employment of any employee 'employed by the transferor and assigned to the organised grouping of resources or employees that is subject to the relevant transfer' will, unless the employee formally objects, be transferred to the transferee. The first part of Reg 4(3) elucidates this. It says: 'Any reference in [Reg 4(1)] to a person employed by the transferor and assigned to the organised grouping of resources or employees that is subject to a relevant transfer, is a reference to a person *so employed immediately before the transfer*, or who would have been so employed if he had not been dismissed in the circumstances described in regulation 7(1)' (our stress). This wording differs somewhat from the equivalent provision in the 1981 Regulations – Reg 5(3) – in respect of the description of the transferred entity: in place of 'organised grouping of resources or employees' in Reg 4(3), old Reg 5(3) used the phrase 'undertaking or part of one'. However, for present purposes, what is material are the words 'employed immediately before the transfer', and these remain unchanged from the wording used in the original provision.

In practice, clarity as to the date of the transfer will suffice in most cases to determine whether an employee was employed by the transferor at the relevant time. Although, as we have seen above, it can sometimes be difficult to ascertain the precise date of the transfer, in the vast majority of cases this will not be so. Occasionally, however, the mere fact that an employee is employed in, and assigned to, the undertaking transferred on the date of transfer will not be enough. In such cases, the question of whether Reg 4(1) applies comes down to whether the employee was employed (or deemed to be so) at the precise moment of the transfer. This issue only arises where members of the transferor's workforce have been dismissed prior to the transfer, leaving them vulnerable to the argument that, as they were not employed by the transferor and assigned to the undertaking 'immediately before the transfer', neither their employment nor any liability for their dismissal transfers to the transferee.

2.59 The term 'immediately before' has, as we shall see below, been strictly and literally interpreted by the courts, with the consequence that the protection of Reg 4(1) applies only to employees still employed by the transferor at the very moment of the transfer. On the other hand, the courts have also taken steps to ensure that this interpretation does not lead to the application of the 'automatic transfer of employment' principle being thwarted where the sole or principal reason for pre-transfer dismissals is the transfer itself.

2.60 **'Immediately before' means at moment of transfer.** Prior to the Court of Appeal's decision in Secretary of State for Employment v Spence and ors 1986 ICR 651, CA, it was widely thought that the phrase 'immediately before the transfer' could properly be construed as spanning a period of time. Thus a person dismissed on a Friday could nevertheless be regarded as employed immediately before a transfer even if this did not occur until the following Monday. This 'liberal interpretation' was sought to be justified by reference to the aims of the Acquired Rights Directive, which was to protect employees' rights. The concern was that if transferors could simply dismiss employees shortly before the transfer as a means of ensuring that they were not employed 'immediately before the transfer', the consequence would be that what is now Reg 4 would not apply to transfer their contracts of employment to the transferee.

127

However, in Spence the Court of Appeal unequivocally rejected this approach in favour of a strict and literal construction of what is now Reg 4(3). In that case, S and Sons went into receivership on 16 November 1983. Since there was no guarantee of a successful outcome to the receiver's negotiations for the sale of the business, the receiver decided to cease trading and dismiss all the employees. As a result the workforce was dismissed with immediate effect at 11 am on November 28. At 2 pm on the same day the agreement for the sale of the business was concluded. The workforce was re-employed by the new owners the following morning. S and 20 others applied for redundancy payments in respect of their dismissal by S and Sons. Both the tribunal and the EAT upheld their claims, and the Court of Appeal took the same view. It unanimously held that Reg 4(1) only applied to contracts subsisting at the very moment of transfer and that the words 'employed immediately before the transfer' in Reg 4(3) had to be interpreted in that sense. Since the new owners had not acquired the contracts of employment from the transferor, the employees were entitled to redundancy payments by the receiver of S and Sons.

The general effect of the Court of Appeal's decision was that an employee could be dismissed just a matter of hours or even minutes before the transfer and yet be left unprotected by Reg 4(1) and (2), with the consequence that any liability for the dismissal would not cross to the transferee. This left employees at the mercy of the transferor's solvency. If the transferor was insolvent, an employee would have little hope of financial redress against his or her former employer.

2.61 **Employees deemed to be employed 'immediately before' transfer.** After the Spence decision, it became increasingly clear that the dismissal of employees before a transfer in order to avoid the TUPE Regulations was likely to be in breach of the Acquired Rights Directive. The European Court of Justice put the matter beyond doubt in P Bork International A/S (in liquidation) v Foreningen af Arbejdsledere i Danmark and ors 1989 IRLR 41, ECJ, when it held that the requirements of Article 4(1) of the Directive (which corresponds to the protection against unfair dismissal contained in what is now Reg 7) were mandatory. That Article provides that the transfer of an undertaking 'shall not in itself constitute grounds for dismissal by the transferor or the transferee' (although dismissals for 'economic, technical or organisational reasons entailing changes in the workforce' are permissible). The ECJ held that where an employee is dismissed in breach of Article 4(1) with effect from a date before the transfer, he or she must 'be considered as still employed by the undertaking on the date of the transfer'. Thus, the obligations of the employer towards the employee concerned would be fully transferred from the transferor to the transferee under Article 3(1) (which corresponds to Reg 4 TUPE).

Small wonder that, in the light of the Bork ruling, the Spence decision came under close scrutiny by the House of Lords as soon as it was given the opportunity to consider the matter. This came in the seminal case of Litster and ors v Forth Dry Dock and Engineering Co Ltd (in receivership) and anor 1989 ICR 341, HL. The facts were somewhat similar to those in Spence. FDD went into receivership in September 1983. Another company, FEE, was set up to acquire the business of FDD. All the employees of FDD were dismissed with immediate effect at 3.30 pm on 6 February 1984. The transfer of the business occurred at 4.30 pm. Only a few of the former employees of FDD were subsequently engaged by FEE, which ended up with a similar sized workforce to FDD, although it paid them lower wages than FDD had paid to its employees. The House of Lords held that it was necessary to give a purposive construction to what was then Reg 5(3) in order to give effect to the meaning of the Directive. What this actually involved was reading words into Reg 5(3) so that, after referring to a person employed immediately before a transfer, the provision read as if there were inserted '*or would have been so employed if he had not been unfairly dismissed in the circumstances described in Reg 8(1)*'. Their Lordships felt that the employees of FDD were unfairly dismissed under Reg 8(1) (now Reg 7(1)) for a reason solely connected to the transfer, and so must be deemed to have their contracts of employment 'statutorily continued' up to the point of transfer. In that way, the protection of Reg 5 would be triggered and the transferee automatically then took over the employment contracts and liability arising from their termination.

Following Litster, and particularly in light of the House of Lords' addendum to **2.62** the wording of Reg 5(3), the legal position can be summarised as follows. A dismissal that takes effect before a transfer where the sole or principal reason for it is the transfer is automatically unfair under what was then Reg 8(1) (now Reg 7(1)) unless it is for an economic, technical or organisational reason (ETO), and for the purposes of the operation of what was then Reg 5 (now Reg 4), the dismissed employees are therefore deemed to have been employed 'immediately before the transfer'. Liability for the dismissals will as a result be passed on to the transferee.

This position has now been consolidated into the express wording of Reg 4(3) through the addition of the words 'or would have been so employed if [the employee] had not been dismissed in the circumstances described in regulation 7(1)'. There is no doubt that this promotes the protection of employees' rights following transfer of the businesses in which they are employed and ensures that the Regulations are seen to be compliant with the requirements of the Directive as established by the ECJ in the Bork case.

It is important to note that none of this means that the interpretation given to **2.63** the words 'employed immediately before the transfer' by the Court of Appeal in Spence is wrong. Indeed, the House of Lords in Litster did not overrule the Spence decision. And nor does anything in the 2006 Regulations require a less strict interpretation to be given to the notion of 'immediately before'. In Litster, their Lordships noted that, unlike the facts of the case before them, there had

129

been no collusion in Spence between the transferor and transferee aimed at effecting pre-transfer dismissals as a means of evading the operation of the 'automatic transfer of employment' rule. The employees had been dismissed before an actual transfer deal had even been agreed at a time when the receiver was under pressure by the creditor bank to stop paying wages. In these circumstances, their dismissals were not rendered unfair by what is now Reg 7(1) since they were genuinely for an ETO reason. Given that the dismissals had taken place before the transfer – albeit only by a matter of hours – the upshot was that the employees were not employed (or deemed to be employed) 'immediately before' (i.e. at the moment of) the transfer, and the employment tribunal's decision that liability for their dismissals did not cross to the transferee was, therefore, correct on the facts.

In view of this, it is clear that Spence still applies for the purpose of interpreting the phrase 'immediately before the transfer'. The position is that, in order for Reg 4 to operate, the employee must in every case be employed at the moment of the transfer. But in view of the 'deeming' provision introduced by judicial interpretation in Litster and now codified in the wording of the 2006 Regulations themselves, most employees dismissed prior to a transfer will find themselves reaping the benefit of a fiction by which they are treated as having been employed at the moment of the transfer even though, in actual fact, they were not.

2.64 Outside of an insolvency context – for which specific provision is now made in the 2006 Regulations (see Chapter 6, 'Transfer of insolvent companies') – it will be rare that pre-transfer dismissals will not be rendered automatically unfair by Reg 7(1). Only dismissals for reasons unrelated to the transfer (dismissals on grounds of capability or misconduct, for example), or dismissals that are nonetheless for genuine 'economic, technical or organisational reasons entailing a change in the workforce', fall outside Reg 7(1). (ETO dismissals are explained in detail in Chapter 4, 'Unfair dismissal', under 'Dismissals potentially fair for an "ETO reason"'.) Only in respect of these dismissals, therefore, will it be possible to say that an employee was not employed at the moment of the transfer or deemed to be so.

Whenever a genuine ETO reason for a pre-transfer dismissal is made out, or where the reason for dismissal is patently unconnected to the transfer, then – subject to two caveats mentioned under 'Notice dismissals and appeals against dismissal' below – the employee will be shut out of the protection of Reg 4(1). This is because, in the light of Spence, he or she will not actually have been employed 'immediately before the transfer' and cannot claim, within the terms of Reg 4(3), that he or she 'would have been so employed if he [or she] had not been dismissed in the circumstances described in regulation 7(1)'. Even if the dismissal is found to be unfair applying the test for unfair dismissal, liability for such a dismissal will not be transferred to the transferee. For example, liability for dismissal of an employee who was dismissed in advance of the transfer on health grounds would not transfer to the transferee even if the illness was the result of an accident at work.

Notice dismissals and appeals against dismissal. The two caveats mentioned **2.65** above are, first, that if an employee is on notice of dismissal and the notice does not expire until after the transfer has occurred, he or she will still be employed 'immediately before the transfer', so that his or her employment will transfer to the transferee and, along with it, any liability for the dismissal.

Secondly, in a case where an employee is dismissed prior to the transfer but pursues an internal appeal, if the appeal is successful the original dismissal effectively 'vanishes'. This means that the employee will be regarded as continuing to have been employed by the transferor 'immediately before the transfer'. The EAT confirmed that this is so in G4S Justice Services (UK) Ltd v Anstey and ors 2006 IRLR 588, EAT, when it held that the contracts of employment of employees who had been summarily dismissed by the transferor, but whose internal appeals against those dismissals were still pending at the date of the transfer, were transferred to the transferee under what is now Reg 4(1). Although the contractual obligation to hear and determine the appeals lay, notwithstanding the transfer, with the transferor, once those appeals had been determined in favour of reinstatement, the original dismissals were expunged and the claimants were to be treated as having been employed by the transferor up until the transfer date.

Note, however, that this does not apply if the appeal is unsuccessful or has yet **2.66** to be determined by the transferor. It only applies if, following the transfer, the appeal is actually upheld. This was made clear by the EAT in Bangura v Southern Cross Healthcare Group plc and anor EAT 0432/12. B, who worked at a care home, was summarily dismissed on the ground of misconduct by SCHG plc on 12 August 2011. The following month, while her appeal against dismissal was pending, the care home service was transferred to FSH. Relying on the EAT's decision in the G4S case, B argued that her pending appeal meant that she ought to have been treated as 'suspended' at the time of the transfer and that her employment should have transferred to FSH. The EAT disagreed. Crucial to the EAT's decision in G4S was the fact that, following the transfer, the transferor had upheld the claimants' appeals and overturned their dismissals. In the instant case, by contrast, the transferor had not to date determined B's appeal, still less directed her reinstatement. Citing the Court of Appeal's decision in J Sainsbury Ltd v Savage 1981 ICR 1, CA, the EAT observed that, if an appeal is successful, it will retrospectively have the effect that an employee is no longer to be treated as dismissed. However, if the appeal is not successful, then the dismissal takes effect on the original date. 'The fundamental point is that when a notice of immediate dismissal is given that dismissal takes immediate effect.' Therefore, so far as things stood on the date

131

of the EAT's decision, B's effective date of termination was 12 August 2011, i.e. before the date of the transfer. Note that this case is discussed further under '"Assigned" to undertaking transferred – employees subject to pending disciplinary processes' below.

2.67 Transfers effected by series of transactions

As we saw in Chapter 1, 'Identifying a "relevant transfer"', in the section 'Business transfers', under 'Transfer "to another person" – series of transactions can amount to a relevant transfer', the definition of 'relevant transfer' includes a transfer that is 'effected by a series of two or more transactions' – Reg 3(6)(a). The issue of what potentially comprises such 'transactions' was also explored in that chapter. The second part of Reg 4(3) addresses the problem of identifying whether employees who were employed at some point during a transfer process that occurs in stages are to be regarded as being employed 'immediately before the transfer'. This, as we have seen, is crucial since only employees employed immediately before the transfer (or deemed to be so) are subject to the 'automatic transfer of employment' principle in Reg 4(1).

The wording of the second part of Reg 4(3) can only really be understood in the context of the entire regulation. This states that: 'Any reference in [Reg 4(1)] to a person employed by the transferor and assigned to the organised grouping of resources or employees that is subject to a relevant transfer, is a reference to a person so employed immediately before the transfer, or who would have been so employed if he had not been dismissed in the circumstances described in regulation 7(1), including, *where the transfer is effected by a series of two or more transactions, a person so employed and assigned or who would have been so employed and assigned immediately before any of those transactions*' (our stress).

2.68
An analysis of the italicised part of Reg 4(3) above shows that an employee will be regarded as being employed 'immediately before the transfer' in any case where the transfer has been effected by a series of transactions, provided that he or she either:

- was employed immediately before (i.e. at the moment of) any one of the transactions in question, or

- would have been so employed had he or she not been unfairly dismissed in the circumstances described in Reg 7(1) – i.e. dismissal by reason of the transfer itself.

The employee will be viewed in the former scenario as having actually been employed at the time of the transfer. In the latter scenario, he or she will be deemed to have been so employed.

2.69
It seems clear from this that Reg 4(3) effectively provides that an employee who has been dismissed for a reason entirely unrelated to the transfer (e.g. misconduct

132

or incapability) will nonetheless be regarded as having been employed immediately before the transfer provided that he or she can show that he or she was actually employed immediately before 'any' of the transactions in the series. In such a case, Reg 4(1) and (2) will apply to transfer any liability for the dismissal to the transferee. Equally, if all that precludes the employee from being employed immediately before any one of the transactions is that he or she was unfairly dismissed by the transferor in the circumstances described in Reg 7(1), then he or she will be deemed to have been employed immediately before the transfer.

The rationale underpinning this appears to be that, once the transfer process has begun, employees should receive the full protection of Reg 4 and that it should be the transferee who becomes responsible on the completion of the transfer for any liabilities for dismissals made by the transferor during that process. Where the transfer process is straightforward – i.e. comprises a single transaction – then, as we have seen under 'Meaning of "immediately before the transfer"' above, protection will only be conferred if the employee is actually employed at the moment of the transfer or deemed to be so as a result of having been unfairly dismissed for a reason falling within Reg 7(1). Unlike the employee dismissed during an extended transfer process, an employee whose contract is terminated prior to a single transaction transfer for a reason entirely unrelated to the transfer will not benefit from Reg 4 because he or she will not actually have been employed at the moment of the transfer, and nor will he or she be deemed to have been so.

Is the 'series of transactions' provision compatible with EU law? Since the **2.70** Acquired Rights Directive contains no equivalent provision for dealing with transfers effected by two or more interrelated transactions, it is clear that Reg 4(3) extends by some margin the protection conferred on employees in this situation. In view of this, are the Regulations incompatible with the Directive? The mere fact that the Regulations enlarge on the protection guaranteed by the Directive does not mean that they are incompatible. S.38 of the Employment Relations Act 1999 confers powers on the Secretary of State to make provision for implementing any EU obligation relating to the treatment of employees on the transfer of an undertaking. In particular, S.38(2) empowers the Secretary of State to 'make the same or similar provision in relation to the treatment of employees in circumstances other than those to which the Community obligation applies'. Therefore, provided that the national rule or law in question expands rather than diminishes the scope of protection accorded by the relevant Directive, it will not be ultra vires (i.e. beyond the legal scope of) the Directive.

A more thorny issue as to compatibility arises in relation to recent decisions of the ECJ and the House of Lords interpreting Article 3(1) of the Directive. These decisions – in Celtec Ltd v Astley and ors 2005 ICR 1409, ECJ, and North Wales Training and Enterprise Council Ltd (trading as Celtec Ltd) v Astley and

133

ors 2006 ICR 992, HL – have been discussed in detail under 'When does transfer occur?' above. To recap, it was established by the ECJ that, for the purposes of determining which employees were subject to the 'automatic transfer of employment' rule in Article 3(1), it was necessary to identify the precise date of the transfer. Given that the Celtec case was a UK case brought under the 1981 TUPE Regulations, one might have thought that the 'series of transactions' provision in what was then Reg 5(3) would have received considerable attention, especially from the House of Lords. Unfortunately, and rather bizarrely, it did not.

2.71 It will be recalled that the facts of the case entailed a number of transactions by which the claimants were transferred from the Department of Employment to a private Training and Enterprise Council (TEC). Initially, the employees were seconded to the TEC but remained employed by the DoE. Three years later, they elected to become employed by the TEC; and three years after that, the DoE terminated all remaining secondment arrangements. An employment tribunal concluded that there had been a relevant transfer, which had commenced in September 1990 when the claimants were first seconded to the TEC and which was only completed in 1996 when the final secondments ended. Since the claimants had been employed immediately before the first of the transactions, this was sufficient in the tribunal's view to establish that TUPE applied to transfer the period of continuous employment built up with the transferor (the DoE) to the transferee (the TEC).

The tribunal's decision was appealed, and during all stages up to and including the Court of Appeal, the legal arguments centred on the tribunal's findings and conclusion that the employees were employed immediately before the transfer in accordance with Reg 5(3). However, when the matter reached the House of Lords, their Lordships decided that the case should be referred to the ECJ. At this stage, the focus shifted away from the wording of the TUPE Regulations and onto the Directive. The question became whether, for the purposes of the 'automatic transfer of employment' provision in Article 3(1) of the Directive, it was necessary to establish a single specific 'date' for the transfer. The ECJ ruled that it was. And from that point onwards, the 'series of transactions' provision in the TUPE Regulations was lost sight of. On the case being returned to the House of Lords, the sole question that their Lordships addressed was 'when was the date of the transfer for the purposes of Article 3(1)?' A 3:2 majority concluded that the crucial date was the date the claimants had first been seconded to the TEC.

2.72 So where does this leave Reg 4(3)? Unfortunately, there have been few subsequent appellate decisions to clarify the matter. In Metropolitan Resources Ltd v Churchill Dulwich Ltd 2009 ICR 1380, EAT – the sole case that seems to have considered how the series of transactions provision in Reg 3(6)(a) interacts with the ruling in Celtec – His Honour Judge Burke QC, sitting alone

134

in the EAT, observed that the ability to effect a transfer via a series of transactions applies to both possible types of relevant transfer – i.e. a standard transfer and a service provision change. Regarding the latter, HHJ Burke accepted that the change pursuant to which the transferee performs the relevant activity instead of the transferor may well be achieved by a series of steps or transactions over a period of time, and that it was unlikely that a service provision change would in practice always be entirely achieved on a single day. Nor did the law require that it should be. He cited the House of Lords decision in Celtec as authority for requiring the tribunal to determine the precise date on which any relevant transfer occurred, but he did not think that that case required that all the steps constituting such a transfer had to take place on the same day. The issue in Celtec was not whether there had been a TUPE transfer but when it took place and in particular whether it had taken place over a period. Where the date of the alleged transfer was in issue, the tribunal had to determine the date at which the essential nature of the activity carried on by the putative transferor ceased to be carried on by it and instead was carried on by the transferee. That was a question of fact for the tribunal to determine. On the facts of the particular case, the EAT held that the employment tribunal had been entitled to conclude that, even before the expiry of a time-limited service contract to provide accommodation to asylum seekers, a service provision change TUPE transfer had occurred when the client had entered into a virtually identical contract with another service provider, which then took over the responsibility of providing accommodation for asylum seekers, albeit from a new location.

It is submitted that all that Celtec establishes is that it is necessary, in the context of a transfer effected by a number of separate transactions, to identify a specific date by which the transfer is regarded as having taken place. At that point, employees who are employed (or deemed to be so) in the transferor's undertaking are entitled to have their employment transferred to the transferee under Reg 4(1) (or its equivalent – Article 3(1)). On this view, the fact that the UK Government has chosen to extend such protection to any employee employed immediately before at least one of the transactions does not pose a problem. The effect of Reg 4(3) is to regard such an employee as having been employed at the date of the transfer whatever date that occurs. This does not mean that it is not necessary – as the Celtec case requires – for the 'date' of the transfer to be identified. For one thing, it will be that date which determines the cut-off point for establishing, in accordance with national law, which employees are actually employed by the transferor and assigned to the undertaking on the relevant date and which are not. And for another, it will be from that date that the transferee legally acquires the rights, powers, duties and liabilities in respect of any contracts of employment inherited from the transferor by virtue of Reg 4(2).

Arguably, in light of the above, the most useful lesson to be gleaned from the **2.73** House of Lords' decision in Celtec is that the actual date of the transfer may come much earlier in the transfer process than the parties anticipated or understood to be the case. Certainly, it came as a surprise to many legal commentators that the House of Lords found that the date of the transfer was the earliest possible date that it could have occurred – i.e. the date when the claimants were first seconded to the transferee on a voluntary basis. It is difficult to avoid the impression that what lay behind their Lordships' conclusion was their determination to provide an equitable outcome for the employees in that particular case. In most instances when something takes place by stages, the outcome is not finalised until the last of those stages. Nothing in Celtec precludes the same common sense applying in the context of TUPE. So, for this reason, when faced with cases entailing a complicated transfer process, most tribunals are likely to conclude that the transfer has been effected by the last (or certainly one of the later) transactions in the series.

The virtue of Reg 4(3) is that it enables protection to be accorded to employees right from the start of the transfer process. As we have seen, this may include an employee who was employed immediately before one of the transactions in question but who was dismissed before the last of these for a reason entirely unrelated to the transfer. Although the Regulations do not spell out precisely what happens to the employee's employment between the date of dismissal and the date of the transfer, it would make sense for Reg 4(3) to be interpreted so that the employment is deemed to continue during the interim period. Then, as from the date of the transfer (probably at the end of the series of transactions), Reg 4(1) and (2) operates to transfer the employment (and any liability for the pre-transfer dismissal) to the transferee.

2.74 Must employee be assigned to undertaking 'immediately before' transfer?

It is generally assumed from the wording of Reg 4(3) that, for the automatic transfer principle in Reg 4(1) to operate, an employee must show not only that he or she is employed by the transferor 'immediately before the transfer' but also that he or she is, at that time, assigned to the organised grouping of resources or employees that is the subject of the transfer. However, the actual wording of Reg 4(3) is ambiguous in this respect, since there is an argument that, given a strict and literal reading, the 'immediately before' condition applies only to the employment by the transferor and not to assignment to the organised grouping of resources. This argument is set out in detail under '"Assigned" to undertaking transferred – assignment "immediately before" transfer' below.

Suffice it to say here that it is unlikely that a literal reading accords with the Parliamentary intention behind Reg 4(3). And although the argument outlined above does not yet appear to have been considered by the courts, there are cases in which the EAT, when considering the issue of assignment, has decided the matter by determining the position of employees immediately before the

136

transfer – see, for example, WGC Services Ltd v Oladele and ors EAT 0091/14 and Jakowlew v Nestor Primecare Services Ltd (t/a Saga Care) and anor EAT 0431/14. In the latter case the EAT characterised the sole issue for decision as being 'whether the claimant was assigned to [the] organised grouping immediately before the transfer'. In the light of the above, the assumption is made in the remainder of this chapter that an employee must be assigned to the transferred undertaking or part transferred at the moment of the transfer in order for Reg 4(1) to bite.

'Assigned' to undertaking transferred 2.75

Regulation 4(1) preserves the contract of any employee who, on the occurrence of a relevant transfer, is 'employed by the transferor *and assigned to the organised grouping of resources or employees* that is subject to the relevant transfer' (our stress). The italicised phrase expands on the equivalent provision in the predecessor Regulations, which simply used the words 'employed by the transferor in the undertaking or part transferred'. The change in wording reflects the substantial body of case law that had already evolved prior to enactment of the 2006 Regulations on the scope of the 'automatic transfer of employment' provisions in the Acquired Rights Directive and the 1981 TUPE Regulations. For this reason, although most of the UK cases referred to in this section were decided on the basis of the old wording, it is likely that they will continue to provide valid guidance for interpreting the current wording of Reg 4(1).

Except for the fact that Reg 2(1) stipulates that assigned means 'assigned other than on a temporary basis', the Regulations offer scant guidance as to when an employee will be regarded as being assigned to an undertaking or business (or part business) transferred. This is unfortunate, since the issue is sometimes surprisingly difficult to determine, especially where, for complex commercial reasons, a number of subsidiary companies are spun off by a parent company and employees end up being engaged by one subsidiary company to service the employment needs of other subsidiaries. Usually, this difficulty presents itself within the context of intra-group transfers, but a similar problem can arise where the transfer is to an outside purchaser – particularly if only one part of the transferor's undertaking is sold off or where the transfer comprises a service provision change. In such a case, if the employee has performed many duties across different parts of the business as a whole, it can be hard to say whether he or she was employed in and assigned to the organised grouping of resources or employees transferred. Directors and group managers are classic examples of people who often have a global or group-wide remit. But any employee with wide-ranging responsibilities or a multi-faceted job description might also be caught up in this conundrum.

2.76 **General test for determining 'assignment'**
As already mentioned, the Regulations provide little help in ascertaining whether an employee is 'assigned' to the undertaking or part transferred. However, in Botzen and ors v Rotterdamsche Droogdok Maatschappij BV 1986 2 CMLR 50, ECJ, the European Court considered the matter within the context of the EC Acquired Rights Directive (the precursor to the current Directive). Indeed, it was the ECJ's decision in that case which first established that the basic test for working out whether the 'automatic transfer of employment' rule applied should be whether an employee is assigned to the part of the undertaking transferred.

2.77 **The ECJ's ruling in Botzen.** The Botzen case involved a company that had got into financial difficulties, as a result of which a new company was set up to acquire that company's activities. The old company's marine, general engineering, heavy machinery and turbine departments were all sold to the new company, but the general administrative, personnel, ship repair or offshore parts of its business were not. The question arose as to whether the claimants, who were mainly employed in the non-transferred parts of the transferor's business but who performed some duties for the transferred parts, were entitled to have their employment transferred to the new company in accordance with Article 3(1) of the Directive. The Dutch national court decided to refer the matter to the ECJ for a preliminary ruling.

To appreciate fully the ECJ's decision, it is useful first to consider how the Advocate General, Sir Gordon Slynn, proposed that the question should be answered. He observed: 'The only exception I would admit to the requirement that an employee must be "wholly" engaged in that part of the business [which transfers] would be where an employee was required to perform other duties to an extent which could fairly be described as de minimis [which means so minor or trivial as to be legally insignificant]. On the other hand, if a worker in fact is engaged in the activities of the whole business or in several parts then he cannot be regarded for the purposes of the Directive as an employee "of" the part of the business transferred.' Although the Advocate General's test was a strict one, it had the virtue of precision and certainty. According to his test, unless an employee was wholly employed in carrying out duties for and on behalf of the part of the undertaking transferred, then, subject to de minimis, the Directive would not apply to transfer his or her employment to the transferee.

2.78 However, the ECJ's judgment sidestepped the Advocate General's formulation and offered something far less clear-cut. The Court ruled that: 'An employment relationship is essentially characterised by the link existing between the employee and the part of the undertaking or business to which he is assigned to carry out his duties. In order to decide whether the rights and obligations under an employment relationship are transferred under Directive 77/187 by reason of a transfer within the meaning of Article 1(1) thereof, it is therefore sufficient

138

to establish to which part of the undertaking or business the employee was assigned.' No further elucidation was given as to what the ECJ meant by 'assignment'. It simply left it to national courts to determine as a question of fact to which part of a business employees are assigned.

UK case law interpreting Botzen. It is therefore necessary to see how courts **2.79** and tribunals in the UK have approached the matter in the light of the Botzen ruling. The first thing that is clear is that it will be an error of law for an employment tribunal to direct itself in accordance with the Advocate General's opinion in that case. In Kavanagh v Coral Racing Ltd and anor EAT 231/97 the EAT overturned a tribunal's decision that, on the basis of Sir Gordon Slynn's test, it was necessary for an employee to be wholly (or very substantially) engaged in the business or part of the business transferred. In that case, a tribunal had held that the claimant, who was a managerial supervisor, was not assigned to the undertaking transferred even though around 80 per cent of her time was spent doing tasks connected to the part of the undertaking that was transferred. Since she was also expected to perform other tasks and responsibilities that were not transferred and it was those responsibilities that justified the managerial role and commanded the commensurate salary, the tribunal concluded that she was not actually employed in the transferred undertaking. Allowing the employee's appeal, the EAT held that it was not necessary for an employee to be employed full time or substantially full time in the part transferred so long as he or she can properly be regarded as assigned to that part.

The same point concerning Botzen was made even more forcibly in OCO Mechanical Engineers Ltd v Bissett and ors EAT 06/98, where the EAT's then President Mr Justice Morison observed that: 'It is wrong for parties to cite the opinion of the Advocate General in Botzen without drawing attention to the fact, as it unquestionably is a fact, that the European Court of Justice itself did not accept the opinion as laying down the correct test to be applied... Accordingly, in future, we would not expect in the light of that decision, parties to rely on what was said by the Advocate General in that case, on this point.'

A question of fact. In the light of Botzen, and given that the concept of **2.80** 'assignment to the undertaking or part transferred' has not been statutorily defined, the UK courts have sought in a number of cases to set out a general conceptual framework for dealing with the issue. A point habitually stressed is that the issue of assignment is a question of fact to be determined by a tribunal considering all the relevant circumstances of the particular case – see Buchanan-Smith v Schleicher and Co International Ltd EAT 1105/94, as endorsed by the Court of Appeal in Jones and anor v Darlows Estate Agency 1998 EWCA Civ 1157, CA.

Botzen and service provision change. The Botzen test applies not only to cases **2.81** entailing standard business transfers but also to determining whether an employee is assigned to the grouping of employees that transfers to the new

139

service provider following a service provision change type of relevant transfer. This question is analytically distinct from whether there is an organised grouping of employees dedicated to the client for the purpose of Reg 3(3)(a)(ii) such as to constitute a transferrable entity – see Eddie Stobart Ltd v Moreman and ors 2012 ICR 919, EAT, and Seawell Ltd v Ceva Freight (UK) Ltd 2012 IRLR 802, EAT (as approved by the Court of Session in Ceva Freight (UK) Ltd v Seawell Ltd 2013 IRLR 726, Ct Sess (Inner House)). So, for example, an employment tribunal may find that, although there was an organised group of employees, a particular employee was not assigned to that grouping. It is therefore of particular importance to consider whether the particular employee is assigned to the service provided by the transferor. This was emphasised by the EAT in Edinburgh Home-Link Partnership and ors v City of Edinburgh Council and ors EATS 0061/11, which made the point that, in a 'service provision change' case under Reg 3(1)(b), it is not to be assumed that every employee carrying out work for the relevant client is 'assigned' to the organised grouping. An employee might only be helping out on a temporary basis, or might have a strategic role directed towards the survival and maintenance of the transferor rather than towards the provision of services to the client. Other cases illustrating this point are referred to under 'Employees who form part of organisational structure' below.

2.82 **Typical scenarios where problems of assignment arise.** The problem of determining who is assigned to the undertaking being transferred tends to be particularly acute in the context of certain fairly common factual situations. Three such situations were identified by Mr Justice Morison in Duncan Web Offset (Maidstone) Ltd v Cooper and ors 1995 IRLR 633, EAT, as follows:

- X has a business in which it employs a number of persons. X transfers part of that business to Y

- a person is employed by X to work in Y's business and Y transfers that business to Z

- X, which is part of a group of companies, employs a number of people on X's sole business. The whole of X's undertaking is transferred by X to Y. Some of X's employees worked partly for X and partly for other parts of the group.

Helpfully, Morison J offered the following observations in respect of each of these scenarios.

2.83 *Scenario one.* Regarding the first (i.e. a 'part-only transfer'), in order to determine which employees were employed in the part transferred it is necessary simply to ask which employees were assigned to the part transferred. Another way of putting the same question is to ask, as the Court of Appeal did in Gale v Northern General Hospital NHS Trust 1994 ICR 426, CA, whether a particular employee was 'part of the... human stock or resources' of the part transferred. Morison J in Duncan Web Offset acknowledged that difficult questions of fact often have to be determined by a tribunal to establish who was and was not 'assigned' to the part of the business that has been transferred; and, for this reason, it declined to give general guidance on the matter. However, he accepted that some of the factors that may be relevant included:

- the amount of time spent on one part of the business or the other

- the amount of value given to each part by the employee

- the terms of the contract of employment showing what the employee could be required to do (although subsequent cases such as Sunley Turriff Holdings Ltd v Thomson and ors 1995 IRLR 184, EAT, have stressed that the terms of the contract are not conclusive), and

- how the cost to the transferor of the employee's services was allocated between different parts of the business.

In addition, tribunals may take account of an agreement reached between the parties provided that this is not to the disadvantage of the employees – OCO Mechanical Engineers Ltd v Bissett and ors EAT 6/98.

2.84 Time spent in other parts of the business is not conclusive regarding the issue of assignment. This point was highlighted by Mr Justice Mummery in Buchanan-Smith v Schleicher and Co International Ltd EAT 1105/94 when observing that an employee may be regarded as being assigned to the transferor's business or undertaking even if he or she spends time looking after other parts of the employer's business. In the case of an employer carrying on two undertakings, an employee may be assigned to one of those undertakings even though engaged in the activities of the other. This proposition flows directly from the ECJ's ruling in Botzen and ors v Rotterdamsche Droogdok Maatschappij BV 1986 2 CMLR 50, ECJ (discussed under 'General test for determining "assignment"' above), to the effect that a person does not have to be engaged exclusively in the business or part transferred to be regarded as being 'assigned' to it. In this regard, Mummery J warned that the discharge by an employee of duties involving the use of assets or the discharge of beneficial administrative duties for the part transferred are insufficient to constitute 'assignment' to the undertaking.

The case law also demonstrates that the issue of assignment cannot necessarily be determined simply by establishing the relative percentages of time spent by the employee on activities associated with the part of the undertaking that is transferred compared with any part that is not. We shall examine the relevance of time spent in the part of the business transferred in more detail under 'Assignment to part of business only' below.

2.85 *Scenario two.* With regard to the second (i.e. 'the service company') scenario outlined in Duncan Web Offset (Maidstone) Ltd v Cooper (above), the EAT observed that, on its face, TUPE would not apply so as to transfer the

141

employment of the employee to the transferee, since the employee must actually be employed by the transferor in order for what is now Reg 4 to apply. However, Morison J emphasised that tribunals will be astute to ensure that the Regulations are not circumvented by the use of devices such as service companies, or by complicated group structures that conceal the true position. Thus, it might be possible to say that if the person always and exclusively worked on Y's business, then X was employing him on behalf of and as agent for Y. Alternatively, there may be circumstances in which X might be regarded as a party to the transfer, even if not expressly named in the contract of sale. Or it may be that the employee remained employed by X, who had other work for him or her to do. These would be matters for the tribunal to decide on the particular facts.

2.86 *Scenario three.* Finally, with regard to the third ('transfer of subsidiaries within a group') scenario, Morison J thought that in most cases where the transferor's entire business is sold to a purchaser, X's employees would be regarded as having been assigned to the undertaking transferred. However, in the case of a part-transfer only, he acknowledged there may be cases where it could be said that, despite being employed by X, some employees might in reality be assigned to the business of another part of the group that was not transferred. This recognises that the contract of employment test – i.e. what the employee is required to do according to his or her contract – is not the only matter for consideration, and that an employee might be employed by one company within the group but assigned to the business of another. The EAT again observed that it expected that tribunals would keep in mind the purposes of the Acquired Rights Directive and the need to avoid complicated corporate structures from getting in the way of a result that gives effect to that purpose.

Having set out the general guidance on 'assignment', it is useful to examine the three scenarios identified by the EAT in the Duncan Web Offset case to see how tribunals have resolved the question of assignment in practice.

2.87 **Assignment to part of business transferred**

As was recognised by the first of the three factual situations outlined by Morison J in Duncan Web Offset (Maidstone) Ltd v Cooper and ors 1995 IRLR 633, EAT (discussed under 'General test for determining "assignment"' above), one of the more common situations in which issues of assignment arise is where X transfers a part of his business or undertaking to Y. This may appear to be a simple scenario, but it masks the very difficult questions of fact that will often need to be determined before a tribunal is in a position to decide whether an employee was assigned to the particular part of the business/undertaking transferred. The cases below demonstrate this point well:

- **Buchanan-Smith v Schleicher and Co International Ltd** EAT 1105/94: B-S was one of only five employees of T Ltd, whose business was divided between the selling and the servicing of shredding machines. B-S dealt with the organisation and running of the service side, but was also involved in aspects of the sales side. Following financial difficulties the sales side was closed down and the service side transferred to S Ltd. On the question of whether B-S was assigned to the part of the business transferred (i.e. service of the shredding machines), an employment tribunal ruled that the fact that she had worked in both the sales and the service sides of the business meant that she was not 'assigned' to the service side. On appeal, the EAT held that the tribunal had adopted the wrong approach. It noted that the tribunal had itself found that it was B-S who ran and organised that part of the undertaking. It was also significant that the transfer of the sales side was accompanied by the closure of the rest of the company. There was therefore no longer any sales part to which B-S or any other employee of T Ltd could be regarded as assigned or allocated. The correct view was that B-S had been assigned to that part of T Ltd's business transferred to S Ltd

- **MRS Environmental Services Ltd v Dyke and anor** EAT 93/96: D worked for St Albans District Council on what was known as the Harpenden Town Council Work, looking after the village greens, the war memorial, the churchyard, the public hall and the council offices in that town. In 1994, the Council contracted out the Harpenden Town Council Work to MRS Ltd under a TUPE transfer. W duly became employed by MRS Ltd, carrying out the same duties, which took up 75 per cent of his time, and spending the remaining 25 per cent of his time working for the Council on services that remained their responsibility. When the Harpenden contract came up for renewal, MRS Ltd lost the contract to another bidder, M, who disputed that D was assigned to the transferred part of the undertaking. An employment tribunal came to the conclusion that D 'worked for a significant amount of time in the part of the undertaking transferred and that he was therefore allocated to that part'. On appeal, the EAT found no error of law in the tribunal determining the question of assignment in this case solely by reference to the amount of time D worked in the part transferred. The EAT noted that, in certain circumstances, the measure of time might be the only relevant factor and that, as M could not point to any other factor which the tribunal ought to have taken into account, the tribunal's findings of fact could not be disturbed

- **Moseley v Service Direct (UK) plc** EAT 0482/01: M was employed by ST Ltd as a telesales executive in the telesales department. His role entailed selling telecommunications equipment to, and furthering marketing projects with, dealers, as well as selling further products to existing customers who had service contracts, using the customer database operated by the service and maintenance department to do this. ST Ltd decided to sell off its service and maintenance department to SD plc. 50 or so employees went to work for that company but M was not one of them. Initially, he remained with ST Ltd, but, after being made redundant only two months later, he accepted new employment with SD plc as a telesales executive. However, a short while later, SD plc also decided to close its telemarketing department and M was made redundant once again. When M sought to claim for unfair dismissal, the tribunal had to decide, as a preliminary issue, whether M's employment had been transferred from ST Ltd to SD plc so as to give him sufficient continuity of employment to bring the claim. The tribunal found that M had not been subject to a relevant transfer as the telemarketing department in which he worked was not an 'integral part' of the service and maintenance operation that transferred; only those employees who were 'wholly and exclusively' concerned with the service and maintenance operation transferred to SD plc. The EAT dismissed M's appeal, rejecting his argument that the tribunal had not approached the matter of assignment correctly in that it had not referred to the term 'assignment' but instead focused on whether M was 'integral' to the part transferred. The EAT also declined to attach any significance to the fact that ST Ltd's telemarketing department closed soon after the transfer, which M argued implied that the department had 'little life left' without the service and maintenance department

- **Birmingham City Council v Gaston and ors** EAT 0508/03: between 1975 and 1979, G worked as a plumber in the Council's Housing Department, during which time he was allocated to Contract B, one of four housing repair contracts, each of which related to a different geographical zone within the Council's remit. In 1979, G was elected Chief Federation Steward for the recognised trade union, a position he held up until the relevant transfer in 2001. During this time, he was a full-time shop steward and did no work as a plumber, except for his inclusion on an out-of-hours rota covering all four zones. In April 2001, Contracts A and B were transferred to the second respondent, and Contracts C and D to a different transferee. For the purpose of G's unfair dismissal claim, an employment tribunal was asked to address the question of whether G was assigned, at the time of the transfer, to the part of the undertaking transferred to the second respondent. The tribunal found that he was not. For the last 20 years, plumbing had formed no part of G's day-to-day activities; instead, he had undertaken duties as a shop steward in relation to employees assigned to all four contracts, as well as employees who remained with the Council after the transfer. The Council appealed to the EAT contending that the tribunal had failed to attach weight to G's contractual position and had failed to make sufficient findings of fact. The EAT rejected these arguments, and also rejected the contention that G's position was analogous to that of a seconded employee. While a seconded employee might remain assigned to the particular part of the undertaking in which he or she normally worked, in the same way as might someone on extended sick leave or a sabbatical, it was highly improbable that this was so in the case of an employee absent for 22 years, particularly one who had in that time performed work extraneously to the part of the undertaking to which he had originally been assigned

- **CPL Distribution Ltd v Todd** 2003 IRLR 28, CA: T was employed by CPL as personal assistant to B, who was the manager of the company's concessionary coal business and later took on the additional role of CPL's business acquisitions manager. CPL subsequently sold the concessionary coal business to GF and a question arose as to whether T was employed in that particular part of CPL's business. She had kept a log of the correspondence she had dealt with which showed that most of her work related to the concessionary coal business. After the sale of the contract for that business, B continued to be employed by CPL solely in respect of the acquisitions management part of its business. An employment tribunal held that, on these facts, T was 'effectively assigned' to B, but not to the concessionary coal business that had been transferred. In the tribunal's view, the correct analysis was that T's post as personal assistant to B was potentially redundant after the transfer and that the employer should have dealt with the situation as a redundancy rather than treat T as being assigned to the contract that had transferred. CPL's appeals to the EAT and subsequently to the Court of Appeal were dismissed. In the Court of Appeal's view, the tribunal had been entitled on the facts to find that, since the concessionary coal business was but one area of B's responsibility and that a substantial part of his time was taken up with carrying out other duties for CPL, he could not be said to have been assigned to the transferred part of the business. Equally, as B's personal assistant, T was also involved in those other duties and was likewise not assigned to the concessionary coal business at the time that it transferred. The fact that the majority of the typing carried out by T was in relation to the concessionary coal business was not of itself conclusive evidence of assignment since a personal assistant's duties would normally be broader than just typing

- **Mowlem Technical Services (Scotland) Ltd v King and anor** 2005 CSIH 46, Ct Sess (Inner House): K was a branch manager for a private company in charge of running a council's housing maintenance contract. He was responsible for all of the contracts run by the company (including those with bodies other than the council) but the council contract represented 80 per cent of the company's work. In 2001 the council decided to terminate the housing maintenance contract and to bring the work back in-house but K was not on the list of employees to be transferred back to the council. On his claim for unfair dismissal by reason of a relevant transfer, an employment tribunal found that, although the contract was an 'undertaking' and it had been transferred, K was not wholly or predominantly assigned to that undertaking. He had had periodic meetings with the council, but the contract was managed on a day-to-day basis by an assistant, G. Two other employees who were found to have transferred spent around 80 per cent of their time actually working on the contract. The EAT dismissed K's appeal, as did the Court of Session (Inner House) on further appeal. The Court held, applying the test in Duncan Web (above), that time spent working on a particular project was only one factor to consider in determining whether an employee was assigned to that project when it transferred under TUPE. On this basis, it accepted that the employment tribunal had come to a perfectly proper conclusion on the evidence – particularly in relation to the differences between the jobs done by K and G. Whereas G's duties were intimately related to the performance of the contract in question, K's were of a much more general nature relating to the conduct, supervision and financial arrangements of the branch as a whole.

2.88　Perhaps the most significant and generally applicable point to emerge from these cases is that the problem of ascertaining assignment will rarely be simply a matter of making a mathematical calculation as to the proportionate amounts of time an employee spends working for different parts of a business. Only in one of the above cases – MRS Environmental Services Ltd v Dyke – was this approach found to be appropriate, and it may be no coincidence that the employee in that case was a manual worker rather than a manager or executive. The amount of time actually spent working for a particular part of a business is arguably a more reliable guide to the issue of assignment in the case of manual work than it is in the case of so-called 'white collar' work (see Costain Ltd v Armitage and anor EAT 0048/14 – discussed in detail under 'Employees who form part of organisational structure' below – as an illustration of this point).

2.89　Employees engaged by service/holding companies

Mr Justice Morison in Duncan Web Offset (Maidstone) Ltd v Cooper and ors 1995 IRLR 633, EAT (discussed under 'General test for determining "assignment"' above) thought that, on its face, the 'automatic transfer of employment' rule in what is now Reg 4 would not apply in the case of an employee employed by X to work in Y's business where Y transfers that business to Z. Typically, 'X' in this scenario comprises a service (or labour-supply) company or a holding company operating within a corporate group, and Y is either the parent or a trading subsidiary within that group. Reg 4 was not thought to apply because the employee in this example is not employed by the transferor and so the 'automatic transfer of employment' rule did not operate – Governing Body of Clifton Middle School and ors v Askew 2000 ICR 286, CA.

However, this view has now been called into question following the decision in Albron Catering BV v FNV Bondgenoten and anor 2011 ICR 373, ECJ. In that case, the ECJ observed that Article 1(1)(b) of the Acquired Rights Directive – which defines a transfer as 'a transfer of an economic entity which retains its identity' – presupposes a change in the person responsible for the economic entity transferred and who, in that capacity, establishes working relations as

146

employer with the staff of that entity. It followed that a 'contractual employer' not actually responsible for the economic activity associated with the transferred entity does not necessarily have to be found to be the transferor in preference to a 'non-contractual employer' responsible for the running of that entity. The ECJ therefore concluded that in the event of a transfer of an undertaking from within a group of companies, it is possible for the 'transferor' to be the company to which the employees were assigned on a permanent basis and which has established working relations with those employees, despite not being linked to them by a contract of employment and even though another subsidiary company within the group does have a contract of employment with those employees. For further discussion of the ECJ's ruling on this issue, see 'Who is an "employee" for TUPE purposes? – definition of "employee" and "contract of employment"' above.

Piercing 'corporate veil'. In Albron Catering BV v FNV Bondgenoten and anor **2.90** 2011 ICR 373, ECJ (above), the ECJ was prepared to lift the corporate veil to ascertain the true employment situation. The ruling would seem to make it more difficult for employers to use devices such as service or holding companies, or, for that matter, complex corporate structures, as a means of deliberately avoiding the protection that the TUPE Regulations are intended to provide. Indeed, in Duncan Web Offset (Maidstone) Ltd v Cooper and ors 1995 IRLR 633, EAT (above), Morison J hinted that where there is a legitimate suspicion that such devices are being used for this purpose, tribunals will lift the corporate veil or else use the law of agency to establish that the employee was effectively assigned to the organised grouping of resources/employees being transferred.

In practice, there is little evidence that tribunals are as willing as Morison J thought they would be to lift the corporate veil to determine the reality of the relationship between subsidiaries within a complex corporate structure. This is primarily because fundamental principles of company law are at stake. Each company within a group of companies is regarded as a separate legal entity possessed of separate legal rights and liabilities – see Solomon v A Solomon and Co Ltd 1897 AC 22, HL. Any liabilities that one of the subsidiaries incurs will rarely be passed on to the parent or other subsidiary companies within the group or on to associated companies over whom the parent has control, even if these remain solvent while the liable subsidiary does not. A 'corporate veil' effectively shields one company from the liabilities of another, and the courts are reluctant to pierce the veil except where it is being relied on as a device or façade to conceal impropriety or the true facts of the situation – see Ord and anor v Belhaven Pubs Ltd 1998 BCC 607, CA, and, specifically in relation to a TUPE transfer case, Print Factory (London) 1991 Ltd v Millam 2007 ICR 1331, CA.

There have been few cases decided within the context of TUPE where employees **2.91** are (or have become) employed by a service company supplying the labour needs of a transferred subsidiary. In Brookes and ors v Borough Care Services Ltd and anor 1998 ICR 1198, EAT, the Appeal Tribunal rejected the argument that the TUPE Regulations or the Acquired Rights Directive required, as a matter of 'purposive interpretation', the corporate veil to be pierced to enable two separate companies to be treated as a single entity.

2.92 In that case BCS, a company limited by guarantee, ran a number of care homes. In 1995 it decided to transfer the care homes to the voluntary sector. CLS, an industrial and provident society, made a successful bid for the homes and set up a company to which the homes would be transferred. Originally CLS's intention was to acquire BSC's business in the form of a TUPE transfer, but it changed track after becoming concerned that it might not lawfully be able to alter the acquired employees' terms and conditions after the transfer. So instead, CLS acquired the homes by taking control of BCS: it became the sole member of BCS and CLS's members became the directors of BCS. Even though it was conceded that this method of acquisition was specifically intended to avoid the TUPE Regulations coming into play, the EAT rejected all the bases upon which the employees contended that a relevant transfer had nevertheless occurred. It affirmed that there can be no relevant transfer for the purposes of TUPE where a limited liability company is acquired via a change in the identity of the company's members or shareholding as there is no change in the legal personality of the company concerned and therefore no transfer from one legal person to another – see Chapter 1, 'Identifying a "relevant transfer"', under 'Business transfers – transfer "to another person"'.

2.93 In another case – Banking Insurance and Finance Union v Barclays Bank plc and ors 1987 ICR 495, EAT ('the BIFU case') – the EAT showed itself to be equally reluctant, in the absence of suspected impropriety, to look behind such an arrangement to conclude that employees had, de facto, been employed by the transferred company. In the BIFU case, Barclays Bank plc decided to set up a new investment bank, Barclays de Zoete Wedd Ltd (BZW), to be formed by a merger between Barclays Merchant Bank subsidiary (BMB) and associated firms of stockbrokers and jobbers in which Barclays had a controlling interest. The staff who worked for BMB were seconded from and employed by Barclays itself. However, instead of transferring them along with BMB's enterprise directly to BZW, Barclays set up a further subsidiary, Barclays de Zoete Wedd Services Ltd (BZW/S), to which the employment of those members of staff was transferred. Barclays then planned to transfer BMB's business, unencumbered by the staff, direct to BZW and 'transfer' the staff from BZW/S to BZW under a labour supply agreement. The employees' trade union, BIFU, complained to a tribunal that Barclays was in breach of its duty under the 1981 Regulations to inform and consult the union about the transfers. Barclays contended that there had been no relevant transfer, denying that the transfers between Barclays, BMB, BZW and BZW/S constituted a series of transactions forming a single transfer.

148

Although the employment tribunal expressed unease about the position, accepting that 'unscrupulous employers can adopt these sorts of procedures to evade their responsibilities under the Regulations', it found that no such ulterior motive lay behind the corporate manoeuvres in this case. The tribunal concluded that, as no goodwill or assets had been transferred, there had been no relevant transfer. In upholding that conclusion, the EAT rejected the claimants' argument that assets had been transferred in the sense of a pool of available employees, and that goodwill had likewise been transferred in the form of the customer lists acquired by BZW from Barclays. Finally, the EAT rejected the argument that the decision as to whether there had been a transfer was affected by the fact that the tribunal had found that 'moral pressure' had been asserted on the employees to force them to agree to becoming employed by the newly created service subsidiary, BMZ/S. About this, the EAT simply observed: 'There may well be cases where something more than moral pressure is exercised where a tribunal would be entitled to say that that constituted a transfer. In the present case the effect of the moral pressure in our judgment is of no legal consequence. As was pointed out in argument, if no staff had elected to transfer there could have been no transfer.'

Although the BIFU case was decided early on in the history of TUPE and was **2.94** concerned with whether there had been a relevant transfer rather than whether the claimants were assigned to the undertaking transferred, the facts and decision of the case demonstrate how difficult it is for employees employed by service companies to show that they have been assigned to a trading subsidiary that is sold off. However, following the ECJ's decision in Albron Catering BV v FNV Bondgenoten and anor (above), it is likely to be a lot easier for employees to argue that the corporate veil should be lifted so as to focus on the realities of the situation regarding to whom the employees were assigned to work as opposed to by whom they were legally employed.

Two of the decisions discussed under 'Employees with global or group-wide responsibilities' (below) provide further instances of where, in the context of TUPE, the question of piercing the corporate veil arose. In Michael Peters Ltd v Farnfield and anor 1995 IRLR 190, EAT, the Appeal Tribunal declined to lift the veil so as to conclude that a director with global responsibilities across a large corporate group was, de facto, employed in and assigned to the particular subsidiaries transferred for TUPE purposes. However, by way of contrast, in Sunley Turriff Holdings Ltd v Thomson and ors 1995 IRLR 184, EAT, the Appeal Tribunal in Scotland upheld an employment tribunal's decision to lift the veil in circumstances where the employee was employed by one subsidiary but the transferee had acquired a different subsidiary – comprising a shell company without employees or physical assets – for whom the employee worked prior to the transfer. By choosing to lift the veil, the tribunal was able to establish to its satisfaction that, in reality, the transferred undertaking had acquired a large part of the business of the subsidiary by whom the employee was legally employed, and that he had therefore been assigned to the part of the undertaking transferred.

2.95 **One company acting as agent for the other.** A different possibility contemplated by the EAT in Duncan Web Offset (Maidstone) Ltd v Cooper (above) is that, in an appropriate case, employees employed by a service or holding company might be regarded as being employed and assigned to a sister company through the process of agency. Take, for example, the situation where employees are employed by company X, which supplies its services to another subsidiary company, Y, and it is Y that is bought by an outside purchaser. Is it possible to argue that in employing the employees X was acting as agent for Y, with the result that the employees' employment transfers to the new owner of Y?

This argument was unsuccessfully advanced in Brookes and ors v Borough Care Services Ltd and anor 1998 ICR 1198, EAT, as a basis for contending that two separate companies, BCS and CLS, should be treated as a single entity in circumstances where CLS obtained the control of BCS by effectively acquiring BCS's shares and members with the intention of circumventing the application of TUPE. The facts of the case have already been discussed above. Suffice it to say here that the EAT rejected the argument that BCS should be treated as acting as agent for CLS and as employing the employees as agents of CLS rather than on its own behalf. That argument was doomed to failure because, as a mere share acquisition, no change occurred in the legal personality of the acquired company, BCS. The Brookes decision is not therefore a very reliable guide as to the prospect of the agency argument succeeding in a different situation where a trading subsidiary is sold off to an outside purchaser but the subsidiary employing the staff who carry out the work on behalf of the trading subsidiary is not sold.

2.96 Perhaps more telling is Zabaxe Ltd v Nicklin and ors EAT 123/89, in which a relationship of agency was found to have arisen in a TUPE context between two subsidiary companies. In that case, one of the subsidiaries employed employees and the other was responsible for paying them. The EAT characterised the latter as an 'invoicing company' acting as an agent for the former. Admittedly, this was largely on the basis of concessions made by the principal company during the tribunal hearing and, unfortunately, the EAT was not called upon to analyse the matter further because the TUPE issues were overtaken by a procedural matter concerning adjournment of the proceedings. Even so, the Zabaxe case lends some support to the notion of agency operating within a service company set-up.

2.97 **Employees with global or group-wide responsibilities**
As previously pointed out, a TUPE transfer involving associated companies within the same corporate group can often give rise to the problem of identifying to which of the subsidiaries an employee is assigned. This is particularly so

where the employee has overarching or 'group-wide' responsibilities. This comes within the third scenario canvassed by the EAT in Duncan Web Offset (Maidstone) Ltd v Cooper and ors 1995 IRLR 633, EAT (outlined under 'General test for determining "assignment"' above).

The following are examples of this: 2.98

- **Michael Peters Ltd v Farnfield and anor** 1995 IRLR 190, EAT: MPG plc ('the Group') was the holding company for 25 subsidiary companies in the UK and abroad. The Group and four of the subsidiaries were based at the same premises in London and between them carried on the business of design consultancy. F was employed by the Group as Chief Executive and was responsible for overseeing the financial management and running of all the subsidiary companies. In August 1990, following the appointment of receivers, the business of four of the subsidiary companies was sold to an outside purchaser, CLK. One of the subsidiaries was MP Ltd (the transferee), which continued to trade under the same name after the transfer. F, who had been made redundant before the sale, complained that he had been unfairly dismissed for a reason connected with the transfer. Although an employment tribunal upheld his claim, the question of whether he had been employed in and assigned to the undertaking transferred only emerged as a result of the transferee's appeal to the EAT. In allowing the appeal, the EAT noted that the tribunal had made the crucial finding of fact that F was responsible for the running of the Group as a whole and was therefore to be taken to be assigned to the Group and not to any of the individual subsidiaries. In the EAT's view, this was not a case where it was appropriate to 'pierce the corporate veil' and to say that the business of the four companies was, in reality, the business of the Group. This was so notwithstanding that it was a Group company that owned the goodwill of the business; that only it was empowered to recover debts; and that it was that company which owned and transferred certain assets, including the premises, to CLK

- **Sunley Turriff Holdings Ltd v Thomson and ors** 1995 IRLR 184, EAT: T was employed as company secretary and chief accountant of both LC and LC(S), two subsidiaries of the L Group, although his contract of employment was with LC. In January 1993 receivers were appointed to the group. They sold the business of LC(S) to STH, but T was told that he was not one of the employees who were to be transferred to STH. He remained working for the receivers until they made him redundant a couple of months later. T brought unfair dismissal proceedings against STH, claiming that he was employed in the part of the undertaking that had been transferred and that his contract of employment had therefore passed to the transferee. In deciding this issue, the employment tribunal took the unusual step of lifting the 'corporate veil' in order to see precisely what had been transferred. It found that LC(S) was a shell company with no employees, no separate accounting records and no

151

proper bank account. What STH had really purchased was all contracts in the name of LC and LC(S), together with employees engaged in that part of the business transferred. On the evidence, the tribunal held that T was one of these employees. On appeal, the EAT upheld the tribunal's finding, stating that it was entitled to find as it did in the light of the Botzen case on the basis that T had been 'assigned' to the part transferred

- **Jones and anor v Darlows Estate Agency** 1998 EWCA Civ 1157, CA: J, a Regional Operations Director for a chain of estate agents based in Cardiff, had responsibility for a regional office comprising 20 branches in Wales and 11 branches in Devon. X – J's secretary and PA – carried out administrative and clerical functions associated with J's work. Following a TUPE transfer, the Welsh branches were sold to a new owner, but J and X were not taken on. An employment tribunal found that neither had been assigned to the undertaking transferred. The matter went to the Court of Appeal, which agreed with the tribunal that J's managerial and administrative responsibilities covered the business of the Wales and West of England region as a whole without assignment to one part of that business as opposed to the other. The fact that a greater proportion of both J's and X's recent time was spent on dealing with the branches in Wales did not alter this conclusion

- **Prosperis Ltd and anor v Spencer and anor** EAT 0988/03: S was engaged in July 2000 as an Executive Consultant by WEFS Ltd under an employment contract. This stated that he may at any time be 'transferred to work for another company within the same Group of companies as the employer, whether on a temporary or permanent basis'. The Group was a non-trading holding company with three subsidiaries: WEFS Ltd, Ward Evans Corporate ('Corporate') and One Direct Solutions Ltd ('One Direct'). There was also an independent costs centre, One Life, which was a trading name for WEFS Ltd's mortgage business and was part of its corporate structure. Throughout his time with WEFS Ltd, S was effectively the 'right-hand man' to D, who at all material times was a director of WEFS Ltd, and was also at various times Managing Director of WEFS Ltd, One Life and One Direct. For about the first 18 months of his employment, S worked on WEFS Ltd business; in early 2002 he was asked to focus his attentions on the mortgage business of One Life; in July 2002 he took on the role of Management Training Coordinator for the whole Group; and in September 2002 he began dealing with training issues in the customer service department of One Direct. When the companies went into administration in December 2002, the business and assets of WEFS Ltd were sold by receivers to HLW, which denied liability for S's employment, claiming that he was not assigned to WEFS Ltd at the time of the relevant transfer. An employment tribunal found that he was so assigned, and HLW appealed. The EAT dismissed the appeal. The tribunal had correctly characterised the situation as belonging to the third category identified by the EAT in Duncan Web Offset – S was one of WEFS Ltd's employees who worked partly for WEFS Ltd and partly for other parts of the Group. The tribunal had found, in essence, that S was employed by WEFS Ltd as a troubleshooter to be moved from job to job as required. He was not assigned to any other part of the Group because none of the tasks he undertook were intended to lead to a permanent transfer away from WEFS Ltd.

Finally, in (1) Tibbitt v Wagon plc and ors; (2) McNabb v Wagon plc and ors EAT **2.99** 0121–2/02 both claimants were employed in senior positions within the group of companies comprising HW Holdings Ltd ('Holdings'), HW Engineering Ltd ('Engineering') and HW Environmental Ltd ('Environmental'). Environmental had been created specifically to develop a particular product, the Environmental Vehicle Emission Control ('EVEC'), whose inventor took a 40 per cent holding in the company. Environmental had no employees, although it did have expenses by way of salaries and travel which were met by Engineering. At the relevant time, T was Managing Director of Environmental and M was Manager of Business Development and Marketing in Holdings, with responsibility for Environmental. Both concentrated their efforts on the EVEC project. In October 2000, Holdings and Engineering went into receivership, and W plc bought Engineering and certain assets belonging to Holdings. It was accepted that the purchase engaged TUPE, and most of the employees employed by Engineering went over. The claimants, however, did not, although four other employees who spent substantial amounts of their time on EVEC did. W plc asserted that the claimants were not assigned to the part of the undertaking that transferred. Deciding the issue of assignment, an employment tribunal weighed, on the one hand, the facts that T had been employed on paper by Engineering throughout; that the whole of that business transferred; and that all three companies were closely connected. Furthermore, T still spent a considerable amount of time on duties relating to Engineering, and both claimants used Engineering's assets in the performance of their duties. On the other hand, Environmental had been deliberately set up as a separate company and T was its Managing Director; the claimants were expected to spend a majority of their time on the EVEC project, which was the preserve of Environmental; and Environmental was not a wholly owned subsidiary. On balance, the tribunal concluded that as there was no transfer of Environmental, nor was there a transfer of the claimants' contracts of employment. The EAT dismissed their appeal. There was ample evidence on which the tribunal could conclude that Environmental had sufficient organisational structure to meet the criteria of the third category identified by the EAT in Duncan Web Offset (Maidstone) Ltd v Cooper (above), which structure included the claimants. The tribunal had therefore been entitled to find that the claimants were assigned to the work of Environmental, which did not transfer, rather than to Engineering or to the part of Holdings that did.

Some might feel that it is hardly in keeping with the purpose of the TUPE Regulations or the Acquired Rights Directive that an employee can be dismissed

153

on account of the transfer of the major and most viable part of a business – as occurred in Michael Peters Ltd v Farnfield and anor (above) – and yet be denied the protection of the Regulations because he or she is held not to have been assigned to work in the particular parts of the undertaking transferred. Indeed, it was probably considerations of this kind that prompted the tribunal and the EAT in the Sunley Turriff case to pierce the corporate veil in order to reach the conclusion that the employee was assigned to the particular associated company comprising the transferred undertaking in that case. But, as has already been made clear under 'Employees engaged by service/holding companies' above, the courts have repeatedly stressed that only in very limited circumstances is it appropriate to adopt this device for achieving 'justice' in a particular case.

2.100 **Employees who form part of organisational structure**
By analogy to the situation where employees have group-wide responsibilities (discussed under 'Employees with global or group-wide responsibilities' above), it may be important to determine in service provision change cases whether those who are employed in 'support services' are assigned to the group of employees who provide the service to the client. The cases referred to below illustrate this point.

In Edinburgh Home-Link Partnership and ors v City of Edinburgh Council and ors EATS 0061/11 the EAT observed – with regard to a 'service provision change' under Reg 3(1)(b) – that it is not the case that every employee who can be linked in some way to the relevant client activity is to be regarded as assigned to the organised grouping of resources or employees responsible for undertaking that activity. Otherwise, a person employed, for example, as a handyman at the transferor's head office keeping the building in a suitable condition for client work, or as a cook to feed the employees working for the client, would fall to be regarded as being assigned to the service following a change of service provider, even though he or she may be wholly unaware of the identity of the client or the transferring activities.

2.101 In the Edinburgh Home-Link case itself the respondent Council entered into contracts in the provision of care services to homeless people with two organisations: HOP, an unincorporated voluntary association and a charity, and H-L, an incorporated body. C and M had been co-directors of H-L and C was also the sole director of HOP. C's job description for each organisation was almost identical: his days were not divided up between the two jobs, and his role was described as 'strategic' for the purposes of delivering the contracted services in accordance with the Council's own service level agreements, with particular focus on an arduous retendering process. His employment contract with H-L came to an end prior to April 2008, after which he returned as H-L's director on a temporary basis. On 27 April 2009 the local authority decided to bring the services previously provided by H-L under the annual service level agreements back in-house. It was accepted by an employment tribunal that this constituted a TUPE transfer but, regarding the issue of whether M and C had been assigned to an organised group of employees immediately before the transfer, it held that they had not been. On appeal, the EAT took the view that it had not been established that the strategic work carried out by M and C was directed towards the delivery of the particular activities for which the Council had contracted. The mainstay of M and C's jobs had not been frontline work concerning homeless care provision at all; rather, the substance of their jobs had required them to carry out other activities not contracted for. The employment tribunal had therefore been entitled to conclude that the claimants were not assigned to the particular undertaking transferred.

The following cases also illustrate the approach that should be taken by tribunals to determine whether employees who operate support services across a wide organisational structure are assigned to the particular organised grouping of resources or employees that become the subject of a TUPE transfer: **2.102**

- **London Borough of Hillingdon v Gormanley and ors** EAT 0169/14: the claimants were employed by RG Ltd, which carried out repair and maintenance work for the housing stock owned by the London Borough of Hillingdon. Hillingdon decided to take the work back in-house. At this time, the Hillingdon contract was the only contract RG Ltd had. At a pre-hearing review, an employment judge held that TUPE applied to the service provision change that took place between RG Ltd and Hillingdon. At a further hearing, a second employment judge held that the claimants were assigned to the contract because they were assigned to an organised grouping of employees whose principal purpose was to carry out work under the Hillingdon contract, and were therefore subject to the TUPE transfer. However, on appeal, the EAT held that the judge had erred in failing to treat the issue of assignment separately from the issue of service provision change. He had also failed to consider the organisational structure of RG Ltd and the role of the claimants within that structure, including their contractual obligations, as required by the ECJ's ruling in Botzen and ors v Rotterdamsche Droogdok Maatschappij BV 1986 2 CMLR 50, ECJ (discussed in detail under 'General test for determining "assignment"' above). The EAT pointed out that the job description or statement of duties is likely to inform a decision as to whether their duties are confined to certain activities or whether they include more general duties. In this case, two of the three claimants continued to be employed by RG Ltd for more than six months after the Hillingdon contract was lost and it was contended that if they had found work for RG Ltd during this period they would have continued in employment. This showed the importance of considering what duties the claimants could be called upon to perform under the terms of their contracts as well as those which they were actually performing at

155

a particular moment in time. The case was remitted to the employment tribunal for further consideration of the assignment point in the light of this

• **WGC Services Ltd v Oladele and ors** EAT 0091/14: the two claimants, O and S, were both employed by J-K Ltd as area managers and were responsible for the supervision of housekeeping and cleaning services at 19 Premier Inn hotels under a contract between W plc and J-K Ltd. Between June and October 2010, W plc served termination notices in respect of each hotel site and entered into new contracts with other contractors in respect of those sites, including with WGC Ltd, which obtained a contract for six hotels. The final group of hotels transferred between November and December 2010. A pre-hearing review was subsequently held by an employment tribunal to determine whether the claimants' employment had transferred to WGC. O's evidence was that he had last worked specifically at the Euston hotel whereas S said that she had worked in the period immediately before the transfer at Euston and County Hall but not at King's Cross – all of which were included in the six hotel sites for which J-K Ltd had assumed responsibility. On this basis, the tribunal found that in the period immediately before the transfer the majority of the claimants' duties were required at J-K Ltd's larger sites of Euston, County Hall and King's Cross and that they were therefore assigned to the organised grouping of employees who were the subject of the relevant TUPE transfer. However, on appeal, the EAT found the tribunal's decision to be inadequately reasoned. It accepted that if WGC Ltd had won all the contracts under a single commercial contract, it would be easy to infer that both area managers transferred along with the contract, but that was not what happened here. This was a case where a number of contracts had been separately cancelled, yet the tribunal had not established to which hotel(s) the two claimants were specifically assigned immediately preceding the transfer, no doubt because it treated the six hotels covered by the new contract won by WCG Ltd as a group. It had in effect aggregated the individual contracts into a single whole rather than look at the hotels individually and consider whether the claimants had been assigned to the organised grouping of employees in respect of each of those hotels. The crucial issue was whether, taking into account the relevant contractual provisions in relation to the claimants' roles and responsibilities, they were assigned to the requisite group of employees and whether this comprised a group of hotels or hotels individually. Underlying this, it was important to identify what the activities, the relevant group of workers, and the transfer actually comprised. The case was accordingly remitted to a fresh tribunal to determine these matters.

2.103 Similar issues can arise where an employee in the course of performing a specific organisational role works on a specific contract. In these circumstances it is necessary to determine whether the employee is assigned to the specific contract or is merely carrying out his organisational role. The two cases below illustrate this point.

- **Williams v Advance Cleaning Services Ltd and anor** EAT 0838/04: W was employed as a project leader within the Train Care Division of ERS Ltd, which held three contracts for cleaning services on trains operating out of London train stations and at the stations themselves. W had extensive experience in project and personnel management, and it was for that reason that he was appointed to the Train Care Division in the first place, in the hope that he could improve performance on one of the three contracts – the 'London terminals contract' – which was proving particularly difficult to administer. In August 2003, ERS Ltd lost the London terminals contract to the respondent, ACS Ltd, and soon after went into liquidation. W brought a claim for unfair dismissal against both ERS Ltd and ACS Ltd, and it fell to be decided as a preliminary issue whether his employment had been transferred from the former to the latter. It was common ground that the change of contractor involved a transfer of a part of ERS Ltd's undertaking. It was also accepted that W spent most of his time on the London terminals contract (i.e. more than 50 per cent of his time and possibly as high as 70 per cent). The tribunal found that W was at all times a project manager in the employ of ERS Ltd. Historically, he had moved from one project to another and, had work been available, he would have moved on to the next project after the London terminals contract had been lost. He never became an integral part of the London terminals contract, and so was not assigned at the time of the transfer in the part of the undertaking transferred. On appeal, the EAT reminded itself that the question of assignment is one of fact and accordingly refused to interfere with the tribunal's conclusion

- **Costain Ltd v Armitage and anor** EAT 0048/14: A, a project manager, was found by the tribunal to have spent 67 per cent of his time working on the road maintenance contract that covered the organised grouping of resources that comprised a relevant transfer. The tribunal therefore concluded that A's employment had transferred under Reg 4. However, the EAT held that the tribunal had erred by focusing solely on the amount of time the employee spent on the particular project. In particular, it had failed to address the argument that A's role as project manager meant that he was engaged on projects in a troubleshooting capacity. Thus, the fact that he might have been more heavily involved in a particular road maintenance contract just before it transferred did not necessarily mean that he had been assigned to it in the required sense. The case was remitted to a fresh tribunal for reconsideration of the matter.

Assignment 'immediately before the transfer'   2.104

In this chapter we have seen that if an employee is to transfer from transferor to transferee under Reg 4, he or she must be employed by the transferor 'immediately before the transfer' within the meaning of Reg 4(3). Furthermore, the employee must be 'assigned to the organised grouping of resources or employees' transferred, within the meaning of Reg 4(1). But must the employee be *assigned to the organised grouping of resources or employees immediately before the transfer?*

Legal commentary on the 2006 Regulations has generally assumed so. But a closer analysis of the actual wording of Reg 4(3) suggests that the position may be more complex.

The problem can best be identified by dissecting the elements of Reg 4(3) into three parts, and italicising the words of significance for these purposes:

- part 1: 'Any reference in [Reg 4(1)] to a person *employed* by the transferor and *assigned* to the organised grouping of resources or employees that is subject to a relevant transfer,

- part 2: is a reference to a person so *employed* immediately before the transfer, or who would have been so *employed* if he had not been dismissed in the circumstances described in regulation 7(1),

- part 3: including, where the transfer is effected by a series of two or more transactions, a person so *employed and assigned* or who would have been so *employed and assigned* immediately before any of those transactions.'

2.105 The first thing to note is that the words 'and assigned' do not appear anywhere in the second part of Reg 4(3), in marked contrast to the third part dealing with transfers effected by a series of transactions. The regulation thus does *not* include the words in square brackets: 'Any reference ... to a person employed by the transferor and assigned to the organised grouping of resources... is a reference to a person so employed [and assigned] immediately before the transfer.' Nor does it go on to say 'or who would have been so employed [and assigned]'. Therefore, a literal reading of the actual wording of the second part of Reg 4(3) would more naturally lead to the conclusion that the requirement to be employed 'immediately before the transfer' relates only to being employed by the transferor and not to being assigned to the organised grouping of resources.

On its face, this is surprising, since nowhere in the DTI's Response to the Public Consultation on the initial draft of the 2006 Regulations published in February 2006 was any suggestion made by the Government that it intended such a result. In view of this, it is tempting to look past the drafting peculiarities of Reg 4(3) to construe it as requiring that, for Reg 4(1) to operate, the employee must be employed in and assigned to the undertaking immediately before the transfer. That outcome could be achieved by construing the first mention of the phrase '*so employed*' in the second part of Reg 4(3) as being shorthand for the reference to 'a person *employed by the transferor and assigned to the organised grouping of resources or employees*' in part one. But what is odd is that the Parliamentary draftsman appeared to make a deliberate decision to add the words 'and assigned' twice in the third part of Reg 4(3). This makes it absolutely expressly clear, in the context of a relevant transfer that is effected by a series of transactions, that the employee will be deemed to have been employed 'immediately before the transfer' provided that he or she is employed by the transferor and assigned to the undertaking immediately before any of the relevant transactions.

Applying normal rules of statutory interpretation, the draftsman is usually **2.106** assumed to have chosen his or her words deliberately. In which case, why did he or she choose to use the phrase 'so employed and assigned' twice in the third part and not at all in the second part of Reg 4(3), where the phrase is limited to the words 'so employed'? If it was thought that the words 'and assigned' were useful for the sake of clarity in part 3, why were they thought unnecessary in part 2?

The lack of any case law focusing on this issue means that any explanation is necessarily speculative. One possibility is that the particular wording of Reg 4(3), if given a strict and literal reading, helps guard against the transferor being able to 'cherry-pick' which employees go across to the transferee by preventing the issue of assignment being entirely dependent on whoever happens to be assigned to the transferred undertaking at the time of the transfer. Certainly, as the Response to the public consultation on the draft regulations made clear, this was a matter of concern for the Government. But if that is the mischief to which the drafting of Reg 4(3) was addressed, a different problem emerges: if the employee only has to be employed by the transferor, and not necessarily assigned to the undertaking, immediately before the transfer, what would stop him or her claiming the protection of Reg 4(1) if he or she had ceased to be assigned to the undertaking weeks, months or even years before the transfer?

The practical difficulties that result from a literal reading of Reg 4(3) drive one **2.107** to conclude that, despite the drafting uncertainties, a straightforward reading of the first and second parts of that regulation produces a more sensible outcome. This view can to some extent be supported by the stipulation in Reg 2(1) that '"assigned" means other than on a temporary basis'. Arguably, the determination of whether the employee's assignment to the transferred undertaking was permanent or temporary requires (or at least implies) that a specific date and time is identified by which to make that assessment. How else would it be possible to say whether a change in the pattern of an employee's assignment sometime before the transfer was permanent or merely temporary?

The remainder of this section therefore proceeds on the assumption that Reg 4(3) provides that the automatic transfer of employment rule in Reg 4(1) bites only if the employee is employed by the transferor and assigned to the organised grouping of resources or employees '*immediately before the transfer*'.

2.108 **How Reg 4(3) applies.** The precise meaning of the phrase 'immediately before the transfer' has been examined under 'Employed "immediately before" transfer' above. Essentially, the phrase has been interpreted to mean that an employee must be actually employed and assigned *at the moment of the transfer* or be *deemed* to be so. The deeming provision comes into play if, prior to when the transfer occurs, an employee is unfairly dismissed in the circumstances described in Reg 7(1) – that is to say, dismissed by reason of the transfer. In the event of such an unfair dismissal, the employee will be 'deemed' to have been employed at the moment of the transfer. And provided that the employee can also show at the time of dismissal that he or she was assigned to the undertaking, business or part transferred in accordance with the test for assignment as discussed in this section, Reg 4(1) will operate to transfer his or her employment to the transferee.

Regulation 4(3) also deals with the situation where a transfer is effected by a series of two or more transactions. Again, this has been discussed under 'Employed "immediately before" transfer' above. Essentially, if the employee can show that he or she is both employed by the transferor and assigned to the undertaking transferred immediately before any of the transactions in the series, then he or she is regarded as having been so employed and assigned 'immediately before' the transfer. Furthermore, the employee will be deemed to have been employed immediately before a relevant transaction if he or she would have been so assigned had he or she not been unfairly dismissed for the purposes of Reg 7(1).

2.109 **Relevant case law.** There is not much case law that considers the issue of the 'immediately before' stipulation in Reg 4(3) specifically in the context of assignment. The point is, however, taken up in the two cases outlined below:

- **J Murphy and Sons Ltd v Fox and anor** EAT 1222/96: F had been employed since 1986 by JM Ltd as a general operative. Although his work had taken him to various parts of the country, prior to October 1995 he had never worked at JM Ltd's main depot, from which a major maintenance contract with British Gas was serviced. However, from that date F was allocated work at the depot and carried out general duties in relation to the British Gas contract until mid-December 1995, when he was informed that JM Ltd had lost the contract to another company, N Ltd. F was told that, as from 8 January 1996, his employment would automatically be transferred to N Ltd under TUPE. He brought a claim of unfair dismissal against M Ltd, relying on the contention that, as he had never been assigned to the relevant undertaking (the British Gas contract), his employment had not transferred. An employment tribunal agreed. It asked itself the question: To which part of M Ltd's undertaking was F assigned at the date of the transfer? The tribunal answered this by looking at the 'reasonable expectations of the parties' as at October 1995 when F was first assigned to work at the main depot, and concluded, in the light of his previous employment history, that the expectation was that his assignment there was not permanent. M Ltd appealed, contending that the approach adopted by the tribunal had been erroneous. The EAT agreed. It held that, in determining the question of assignment, the tribunal had wrongly considered F's employment history and whether the British Gas work was temporary or permanent. The EAT observed: '[What is now Reg 4] provides that the employee need only be employed immediately before [the] transfer. There is no requirement for a long-term view of the previous employment.' Since he was assigned to the transferred work at the relevant time, F's employment was automatically transferred to H Ltd, and accordingly M Ltd was not liable to him for unfair dismissal

- **United Guarding Services Ltd v St James Security Group Ltd and anor** EAT 0770/03: H was employed by S Ltd as a security officer. Clause 4 of her contract provided that she would normally be based at 50 Broadway, Westminster, where S Ltd had a commercial contract to supply security services – although she could also be required to work at different sites within reasonable travelling distance if given a written direction to that effect. In practice, she worked exclusively at 50 Broadway until September 2002. At that point, a dispute arose between H and her manager, P, after which she worked at other sites for S Ltd over a three-week period. She then commenced employment tribunal proceedings alleging, among other things, that she had been unfairly dismissed and requesting that she be reinstated to her 'permanent' site from which she claimed to have been unfairly removed as a result of P's harassment and bullying. S Ltd's ET3 asserted that H had not actually been dismissed, and that, following an investigation into her allegations against P, it had found the allegations to be unfounded. As a result, it was prepared to continue employing her at a different site to avoid her coming into contact with P. Prior to the tribunal hearing, S Ltd lost the service contract in respect of 50 Broadway, and its operation was taken over by a different company, U Ltd, from 29 April 2003. In view of this, H amended her ET1 to claim that the change of contractor comprised a TUPE transfer and that, as she was assigned to the security undertaking at 50 Broadway, her employment had transferred to U Ltd. The tribunal found that H's position was 'analogous to "suspension" or something of that kind', in that, pending the resolution of her claims, her employment was continuing even though she was not actively working for the employer. The tribunal further held that she had been assigned to 50 Broadway at the time of the transfer and that her employment had accordingly transferred to U Ltd. On U Ltd's appeal, the EAT ruled that the tribunal had asked itself the right question – whether H was 'assigned' to 50 Broadway 'immediately before the transfer' – but had erred in concluding on the facts that she was so assigned. The proper approach was to apply a two-stage test by asking:

(a) what was the employee's contractual place of work? and (b) would she have been required to work there immediately before the transfer? If that test had been applied, there could only have been one answer: that H's contractual place of work, in the absence of a direction under clause 4 of her contract, was 50 Broadway, but that she would not have been required to work there immediately before the transfer on 29 April 2003. Since she was not allowed to work at those premises 'at all', she could not be said to be assigned to the contract to supply security services at the relevant time.

2.110 In both these cases, the EAT effectively decided that taking a 'snapshot' of the position at the date of the transfer determined whether the employees concerned were to be regarded as 'assigned' to the business or part transferred.

But the 'snapshot' approach has not been applied in all cases. In Argyll Coastal Services Ltd v Stirling and ors EATS 0012/11 the EAT observed that an employment tribunal 'needs to take care to consider the whole facts and circumstances in which a particular employee worked in order to answer the assignment question. It is not a question that will be answered simply by reference to the percentage of time worked by the employee on a particular contract unless the factual context demonstrates why that would be the relevant test in the particular circumstances. Simply stating that an employee spent 100 per cent of their time on the contract in question would not be sufficient. That might simply have represented a snapshot of the position at a particular moment in time, not an assignment to the organised group.' Referring to this principle the EAT in Costain Ltd v Armitage and anor EAT 0048/14 appeared to depart from the 'snapshot' approach: the fact that at the time of transfer, the claimant, a project manager, was spending 67 per cent of his time on the particular contractual services that transferred did not mean that he was assigned to the grouping of employees who worked on that contract because, as a project worker, this reflected his pattern of work. This is similar to the approach adopted and conclusion reached by the employment tribunal in Williams v Advance Cleaning Services Ltd and anor EAT 0838/04 (see 'Employees who form part of organisational structure' above). Similarly, in WGC Services Ltd v Oladele and ors EAT 0091/14 it was argued that it was necessary to take account of all the relevant circumstances rather than simply take a 'snapshot' of the position immediately before the transfer. It would therefore seem that in appropriate cases a tribunal may take into account the recent history of the employee's employment to determine the reality of whether he or she was assigned to the organised group of resources or employees that comprise the economic entity being transferred.

2.111 A concern about the 'snapshot' approach is that the position can be artificially engineered by the use of temporary assignments to shift employees in and out of certain parts of an undertaking in order to allow the transferor to retain those employees who are highly valued or 'dump' onto the incoming employer those who are regarded as a problem. It is likely, however, that this concern about cherry-picking is dealt with to some degree by the stipulation in Reg 2(1) of the 2006 Regulations that the word 'assigned' means 'assigned other than on a temporary basis'. This is considered in more detail immediately below. It suffices to say here that, had a similar provision been contained in the 1981 Regulations, the cases above might have been decided differently on their facts – especially J Murphy and Sons Ltd v Fox (above). There, the EAT rejected the view that, even if F's assignment to work on the British Gas contract was temporary, this could not affect the conclusion that he was assigned to the contract at the point when responsibility for operating it transferred. In the light of Reg 2(1), such a view could no longer be sustained. Admittedly, in that case, the employee was contending that his employment had not been automatically transferred because he had not been assigned to the relevant undertaking at the time of its transfer, whereas in more typical TUPE cases employees argue the exact opposite. But this does not alter the fact that any employee who would now wish to challenge the pattern of assignment that just happened to exist at the time of the transfer will find Reg 2(1) a useful tool in his or her armoury.

Temporary assignment
2.112

As mentioned under '"Assigned" to undertaking transferred' above, Reg 2(1) defines 'assigned' as meaning 'assigned other than on a temporary basis'. The BIS Guide – 'Employment rights on the transfer of an undertaking' ('the BIS Guide') (January 2014) – explains that this means that 'the new employer does not take over the contracts of any employees who are only temporarily assigned to the "organised grouping". Whether an assignment is "temporary" will depend on a number of factors, such as the length of time the employee has been there and whether a date has been set by the transferor for his return or re-assignment to another part of the business or undertaking.'

Although there was no equivalent to Reg 2(1) in the 1981 Regulations, case law had already established that an employee who was only temporarily assigned to the undertaking being transferred at the time of the transfer would not have his or her employment automatically transferred to the transferee – see Securiplan v Bademosi EAT 1128/02. In that case the claimant had worked for 21 years as a security officer at a Cable and Wireless (C&W) site for which his employer, S, provided security services. The claimant sustained an accident at work in July 2000 and when he was fit enough to return to duties there was no longer a vacancy for him at the C&W site. So, in January 2001, S placed the claimant at Marylebone magistrates' court, where he continued to work all year. S knew that the claimant was unhappy at the new site and on 3 December 2001 told him that he could return to work at the C&W site in January 2002. However, on 6 December, S's contract to provide security at the court was abruptly terminated and the contract awarded to C Ltd. S declined to continue employing the claimant, as a result of which he brought a number of tribunal

163

claims against the company. Upholding these, an employment tribunal rejected S's argument that the claimant was assigned to the magistrates' court contract on the date when S lost that contract, and that his employment had therefore automatically transferred to C Ltd.

2.113 On appeal, the EAT upheld the tribunal's decision. His Honour Judge McMullen QC, giving the EAT's judgment, observed that: 'We are not able to interfere with the express finding, that upon his return from industrial injury the vacancy at Cable and Wireless no longer existed, but the [claimant] was assigned on a temporary basis elsewhere. The judgment as to what is temporary and what is permanent is a matter for the employment tribunal.' Accordingly, the claimant's employment had not transferred. Instead, he was to be taken to have reverted to his duties either at the C&W site straight away or to other temporary assignments pending his return to that site at the beginning of January 2002.

An assignment may be found to be temporary even if it lasts longer than expected. For example, in Snowdon v Manufacturing Support Staff Ltd and anor ET Case No.2508907/08 S was employed by DHL as a sequencer, a job that involved picking car parts from stock and delivering them to the Nissan Production line. She was disabled in an industrial accident in December 2005 and as a result of her disability was given office work to do from September 2007. When Nissan subsequently transferred the contract for the provision of sequencing work from DHL to MSS Ltd, C was dismissed on the ground of medical capability because she was unable to do the work of a sequencer. She argued that she had been wrongly assigned to the group of employees who transferred because she was no longer a sequencer at the time of transfer. The employment tribunal disagreed: the medical prognosis was never clear and was not so bleak to suggest that she would never be able to work again as a sequencer. The office work she had been given had been a temporary adjustment even though it had lasted longer than anyone anticipated.

2.114 Furthermore, in Marcroft v Heartland (Midlands) Ltd 2011 IRLR 599, CA, the Court of Appeal rejected the proposition that an employee becomes assigned to an undertaking 'on a temporary basis' simply as a result of giving notice of resignation. M had been employed predominantly in the commercial insurance department at PMI since July 2008. On 15 September 2009 he handed in his notice to take effect on 26 October 2009. In the meantime, on 25 September, he was told that PMI's commercial insurance business was going to be sold to H Ltd. From then until 2 October 2009, when the transfer took place, M was not required to attend the office and did only a small amount of work from home, although he remained 'on call' if needed. The Court of Appeal held that M had continued to be assigned to the relevant part of PMI's business until the date of the transfer and, accordingly, that his employment contract had transferred to H Ltd under TUPE. It follows that in so-called 'garden leave' cases, the employee will remain assigned to the part of the business he was working in prior to going on garden leave.

Just as employees who are temporarily assigned to other work will normally remain assigned to the contract or undertaking that transfers, so, conversely, those who are assigned to the contract or undertaking on a temporary basis will not normally be regarded as assigned to the contract or undertaking itself. In Webster and anor v Liberty Gas Group and ors ET Case No.2416830/12, the claimants, W and S, were employed by LG Group, which operated a business to deliver specialist gas and maintenance services across the UK, including the North West. It had a contract with OVH Ltd to provide gas servicing over a four-year period. In April 2012, OVH Ltd served notice on LG Group that it was going to take the contract back in-house from 1 October. In May, W started working on the OVH Ltd contract occasionally and by the end of that month this work was taking up the majority of his time. The second claimant, S, worked as an auditor and his work for the gas servicing contract took up the majority of his time. At the point where the service was brought back in-house, OVH Ltd refused to accept that the claimants were protected by TUPE. An employment tribunal concluded that neither W nor S had transferred because, in W's case, he was only working on the gas servicing contract for OVH Ltd as a temporary assignment by way of alternative to redundancy and, in S's case, his primary role was to carry out audit works under individual contracts and he was not therefore part of the organised grouping of employees specifically assigned to the relevant contract.

Secondment. It is submitted that a similar approach to that adopted in **2.115** Securiplan v Bademosi (above) should be taken in most cases where, at the time of the transfer, an employee is seconded from outside into the transferred undertaking, or vice versa. However, it is true that particular difficulties concerning the application of TUPE can arise if the secondment arrangement is a transaction in a series of transactions leading to the transfer, as happened in Celtec Ltd v Astley and ors 2006 ICR 992, HL. As a result of the House of Lords' decision in that case, employees may find themselves regarded as having been 'assigned' to the undertaking to which they are seconded and thus transferred automatically to the transferee. This is a problem that may especially affect the public sector, where secondment arrangements (such as those that underpin the NHS Retention of Employment Model) are fairly commonplace. The issues that may arise are discussed in detail under 'Problems of secondment arrangements' at the end of this chapter.

Employees subject to mobility or flexibility clauses   2.116

Can an employee be said to be 'assigned' to a particular part of the business transferred if, under his or her contract of employment, he or she can be assigned to another part of the business under a mobility or flexibility clause? The answer is 'Yes' if, at the time of the transfer, the transferor has not sought

165

to exercise the right to reassign under the contractual clause in question; and 'No' if the employee has genuinely been reassigned under the clause at some point before the transfer or, in the case of an employee who was absent at that time, would have been reassigned had he or she returned to work before the transfer.

In Securicor Guarding Ltd v Fraser Security Services Ltd and ors EAT 350/95 S Ltd had a contract to supply security services to D Ltd at its site in Caerphilly. Two of S Ltd's employees were employed on a permanent basis as security guards at that site, although one of them did overtime work at other sites. However, a term of their contracts headed 'Mobility of employment' stipulated that, 'should the interests of the company demand it, you may be required to serve at [S Ltd's] head office in London or at one of the company's branches'. Following a competitive tendering exercise, D Ltd decided to terminate S Ltd's contract and award it to another company, FS Ltd, which then declined to take on the two employees. S Ltd had no other work available at any of its other sites, so the employees were dismissed. They claimed unfair dismissal against both S Ltd and FS Ltd. On the preliminary question of whether TUPE applied to transfer their employment to FS Ltd, a tribunal ruled, among other things, that the employees had not been 'assigned' to the activities carried on at the Caerphilly site because under the mobility clause they could be required by S Ltd to work elsewhere.

2.117 The EAT allowed S Ltd's appeal, giving short shrift to the tribunal's reasoning. The employees had been the permanent staff assigned solely to D Ltd's Caerphilly site unless and until transferred to another site. The fact that one of them performed additional overtime duties elsewhere was immaterial. In the words of His Honour Judge Peter Clark: 'It would be standing TUPE on its head to hold that because the transferee will not honour a relevant employee's existing terms and conditions of employment, and because the contract between the employee and the transferor contains a mobility clause, that has the effect of compelling the *transferor* to retain the employee on his existing terms.'

In a case where the evidence is that a mobility clause option has been validly exercised by the transferor so as to assign an employee to a part of its undertaking that is not the subject of the relevant transfer, then the employee will not be regarded as being 'assigned' to the undertaking transferred. This, in effect, is what happened in United Guarding Services Ltd v St James Security Group Ltd and anor EAT 0770/03 – discussed in detail under 'Assignment "immediately before the transfer"' above.

2.118 Employees absent at time of transfer

Where the employee was absent before the transfer, whether by reason of long-term sickness, maternity or paternity leave, suspension, strike action, lay-off, sabbatical leave or any other legitimate absence from the workplace, the question is always whether, upon returning to work, he or she would have been assigned to the undertaking or part transferred. That question should be answered by looking at the position as it obtained immediately before the transfer.

In Fairhurst Ward Abbotts Ltd v Botes Building Ltd and ors 2004 ICR 919, CA, the Court of Appeal confirmed that the issue of whether an employee on sick leave at the time of a transfer is employed in the undertaking or part of an undertaking transferred is a factual matter, which will be determined by reference to where he or she would be required to work if fit to do so. On this basis, an employment tribunal had erred in holding that the claimant, owing to his sickness absence from the part of the undertaking to which TUPE applied, had not been transferred. Although the Court, by a majority, ordered that the case be remitted to the tribunal for determination of where the employee would have been required to work had he not been on sick leave, Lord Justice May dissented on the basis that there was no need for the matter to be remitted as the tribunal had already found that the claimant had, some months before the transfer, been 'assigned' by the outgoing contractor to the part transferred. Therefore, in reality, he was in the same position as six other employees whom the tribunal had found had transferred under TUPE.

An employment tribunal made a similar finding in Nethercoat v Firm Security **2.119** Group Ltd ET Case No.33642/95. That case involved N, who worked at Sheerness for a security firm. In November he was sent on an assignment to another location, and a month later had an accident causing him to be absent until the end of March. In the meantime, his firm's contract with the Sheerness operation was transferred to another company. When the claimant returned to work at Sheerness, the new contractor disputed that his contract had been transferred to it, but an employment tribunal found that he had been employed in and assigned to the undertaking immediately before the transfer.

As stated by the EAT in Fairhurst Ward Abbotts Ltd v Botes Building Ltd and ors EAT 1007/00, the same principle applies to employees who are absent for other reasons such as holiday, study leave or maternity leave.

However, more recently the EAT has reached the conclusion that, in the context **2.120** of a service provision change (SPC), an employee who was permanently incapacitated with no prospect of ever returning to work was not to be regarded as 'assigned' to the organised grouping of resources that was the subject of the transfer. In BT Managed Services Ltd v Edwards and anor EAT 0241/14 E was employed as a Field Operations Engineer, initially by Orange, working within a team dedicated to a domestic network outsource (DNO) contract providing operational maintenance for mobile phone networks. In May 2006 he fell ill and began a long period of sick leave. Unsuccessful attempts were made to provide him with alternative work and he was thereafter regarded as being permanently incapacitated. In 2009 the DNO contract was transferred – along

167

with the employees servicing that contract – to BTMS Ltd, which thereafter continued to provide network maintenance services to Orange. Under BTMS Ltd, the team working on the DNO had its own separate and dedicated structure comprising its own managers, operatives, administrative and other staff, budget and cost centre. E last worked in January 2008 but remained an employee of BTMS Ltd so that he could continue to enjoy payments under a permanent health insurance scheme. After the liability of the insurers was extinguished, BTMS Ltd continued to make payments to E, who remained on the books of the DNO grouping. Such contact as he had with BTMS Ltd was conducted through the managers of the grouping and payments to him by BTMS were treated as an expense of the DNO team. Had he been able to return to work it would have been as part of the DNO team and he was never assigned to any other part of BTMS Ltd. In December 2012, following a process of competitive tender, the DNO contract was transferred to another service provider and an SPC formally took place in June 2013.

The question arose whether E was assigned to the grouping affected by the SPC. It was accepted by all parties that E's team constituted an organised grouping of employees the principal purpose of which was the carrying-out of the DNO contract on behalf of the client (Orange) within the meaning of Reg 3 TUPE. An employment tribunal held, however, that, in view of the fact that E had not worked since 2008 and there was no prospect of his ever returning to work, he had not contributed to the economic activity of the relevant grouping of resources/employees that was the subject of the SPC and he was not therefore assigned to that grouping within the meaning of Reg 4(1).

2.121 On appeal to the EAT, BTMS Ltd contended that, in determining whether E was assigned to the DNO grouping at the time of the transfer, the answer to that question was decisively determined by the fact that, as he would have been required to work in the DNO team had he been able to do so, he was necessarily assigned to that team. Actual participation in the economic activities of the grouping was an irrelevant consideration. In rejecting this argument, His Honour Judge Serota QC (sitting alone) held that assignment to the grouping of resources/employees that is the subject of a transfer will generally entail some level of participation by the employee in the activities which are the principal purpose of the organised grouping or, if the employee is temporarily absent, an expectation that the employee will at some point in the future carry out those activities. In this regard a distinction between temporary and permanent incapacity should be drawn. It was not the case – contrary to the submissions of BTMS Ltd – that in Botzen and ors v Rotterdamsche Droogdok Maatschappij BV 1986 2 CMLR 50, ECJ (discussed under 'General test for determining "assignment"' above) the ECJ had recognised that employees who were permanently unable to work could nonetheless be assigned to the entity subject to the service provision change. HHJ Serota reasoned that, since the organised grouping that is subject to the SPC is defined by Reg 3(2) by reference

168

to the economic activities pursued, an employee who has played no part in those activities and will never do so cannot be regarded as being assigned to that grouping. Mere administrative connection to the grouping is insufficient in the absence of some actual participation in the grouping's economic activity.

In many ways the facts of the Edwards case are most unusual – as was recognised by both the employment tribunal and the EAT. Not only had the claimant been on long-term sick leave for more than five years by the time of the transfer, but when payouts under his permanent health insurance had ended after four years, his employer – the transferor – had agreed to carry on making equivalent payments even though it was conceded by all concerned that the claimant would never be in a position to return to work. It is in these rather extreme circumstances – virtually amounting to retirement on the employee's part – that the EAT concluded that the claimant was not assigned to the undertaking transferred. However, absence from work of a more temporary nature (or which in any event had not been accepted by the parties as being permanent) does not necessarily preclude a finding that the claimant is assigned to the SPC grouping. This was recognised by HHJ Serota himself when he observed: 'Assignment will be a question of fact and degree and persons on long-term leave, say for sickness or maternity, may continue to be assigned to a grouping provided the absence is temporary, and in the case of long-term leave for sickness or maternity or temporary cessation of activity (for example, where there is a short-term lay-off caused by absence of work) employees in those conditions would not, in my opinion, be severed from the organised grouping.'

Employees subject to pending disciplinary processes

2.122

Are employees subject to pending disciplinary processes at the time of the transfer assigned to the organised grouping of employees who transfer within the meaning of Reg 4(3)? The answer to this is normally 'yes', particularly if the disciplinary hearing has been held before the transfer and the employee has not been dismissed. Two cases:

* **Jakowlew v Nestor Primecare Services Ltd t/a Saga Care and anor** EAT 0431/14: J was employed by NPS Ltd as a care manager working principally on a contract with the London Borough of Enfield. On 26 February 2013 she was suspended from work on full pay owing to an allegation of misconduct. A disciplinary hearing was held on 27 June 2013, following which J received a written warning and the suspension was lifted. Prior to this on 19 June, Enfield had instructed NPS Ltd, as it was empowered to do under the terms of the service contract, to remove J from the organised grouping of employees associated with that contract in view of the fact that a new service provider, WH Ltd, was due to take over the contract from 1 July. NPS Ltd, however, considered that instruction to be 'unreasonable' and refused to implement it. An employment judge ruled that J had not been assigned to the organised grouping on the date of the transfer of the

169

contract and that her employment had therefore remained with NPS Ltd. On appeal, however, the EAT held that the judge had erred: the suspension of J did not have the effect of removing her from the organised grouping of employees to which she belonged. As she had not been dismissed, demoted or transferred after her disciplinary hearing, the expectation of the parties would have been that she would return from suspension to work in the group to which she had belonged. Moreover, where a third party client – Enfield in this case – instructed a contractor to remove an employee from working on particular activities, the employee did not immediately cease to be assigned to the organised grouping irrespective of the contractor's stance. It was the contractor who decides to which grouping an employee is assigned. In this case, the employment judge erred in ruling that J had been removed from her service provision by virtue of Enfield's instruction. Rather, he should have concentrated on NPS Ltd's action and asked whether it required the employee to continue working in the organised grouping or would have done so but for her being excused from attendance by reason of the suspension immediately before the transfer. As it was clear that NPS had done nothing to remove J from her assignation to the organised group of workers to which she had belonged, she had remained assigned to that grouping and her employment had accordingly transferred to WH Ltd on 1 July 2013

- **Russell v First Security Guards** ET Case No.2700189/09: R was employed as a team manager supervising a team of security personnel at Credit Suisse premises. He was suspended on 22 August 2008 pending investigations into allegations of misconduct. During the period of suspension, his employer proposed to transfer the security contract on which he worked to the transferee. The employee was excluded from the list of transferring employees and he only became aware of this on the day of the transfer. The transferee refused to employ the employee as the transferor had previously excluded him as a transferring employee. An employment tribunal held that the employee was assigned to the contract that was transferred to the transferee and his dismissal on the date of the transfer by the transferee was automatically unfair.

2.123 The position may be different if, prior to the date of the TUPE transfer, the transferor has taken steps to actually remove an employee who is suspended from work pending a disciplinary inquiry from the organised grouping of resources of employees. The case of United Guarding Services Ltd v St James Security Group Ltd and anor EAT 0770/03 (summarised under 'Assignment "immediately before the transfer"' above) is an example of a situation where the employer had exercised rights analogous to suspension prior to removing the claimant from the part of the undertaking that was subsequently transferred, with the consequence that the claimant's employment was held not to have transferred.

Similarly in Robert Sage Ltd t/a Prestige Nursing Care Ltd v O'Connell and ors and another case 2014 IRLR 428, EAT, the Appeal Tribunal held that, on the particular facts of the case, a suspended employee did not transfer to a new service provider. T was one of a number of A's employees who looked after X, a woman with severe learning difficulties. In October 2011 T was suspended from work and later issued with a written warning. In January 2012 A informed her that, following the Council's request, she would not return to work with X but would be placed elsewhere. On 1 March 2012 P took over the provision of X's care and an employment tribunal found that all of A's employees, including T, transferred to P under TUPE. On appeal, the EAT held that a transfer had taken place but that this did not include T. While the terms of the contract under which an employee is employed at the material time are relevant to determining whether he or she is assigned to a part of the business transferred, the EAT held that, having regard to the Court of Appeal's decision in Fairhurst Ward Abbotts Ltd v Botes Building Ltd and ors 2004 ICR 919, CA, the question was to be answered by determining where the employee would be required to work immediately before the transfer. In this case, it was clear that the contractual place of work (i.e. X's home) was superseded by a prohibition on working there – A could not place T with X because the Council considered that it would be inappropriate for her to return to work there. Accordingly, the only possible conclusion was that T would not have been required to care for X immediately before the transfer, and she was not therefore assigned to the organised grouping of employees subject to the relevant transfer from A to P.

It is noteworthy that in Jakowlew v Nestor Primecare Services Ltd (above) the **2.124** EAT distinguished the claimant's position from that of the employee in O'Connell on the basis that the former's employer (the transferor) disputed the instruction issued by the client to remove the employee from the contract that was the subject of the TUPE transfer, whereas in the latter case the employer acceded to and acted upon the client's instruction.

A distinct but related question is what happens to those who have been dismissed but whose appeal is outstanding at the time of dismissal? Are they also deemed to be employed immediately before the transfer within the meaning of Reg 4(3)? This issue was considered by the EAT in G4S Justice Services (UK) Ltd v Anstey and ors 2006 IRLR 588, EAT. At the date of the transfer of the business, two employees were awaiting the outcome of internal appeals against their dismissals for gross misconduct. However, the transferee refused to reinstate them as they were not regarded as having been employed by the transferor immediately before the transfer. The EAT held that the successful appeal hearing had the effect of expunging the original dismissals and so the employees should be treated as having been employed by the transferor up to the date of the transfer. The EAT later confirmed in Salmon v Castlebeck Care (Teesdale) Ltd (in administration) and ors 2015 IRLR 189, EAT, that, in such a case, the expunging of the dismissal takes place without need for any clear statement by the employer that the employee has been reinstated. The tribunal had read Anstey as requiring the employer to make an express decision on reinstatement before the contract can be said to have been revived. However, the EAT considered that this would be contrary to the general principle set down by the Court of Appeal in Roberts v West Coast Trains Ltd 2005 ICR 254, CA. There is no reason in principle why an express revival or reinstatement should be necessary, since it must be implicit in any system of appeal, unless otherwise stated, that the appeal panel has the right to reverse or vary the decision made below. However, it was made clear by the EAT in Bangura v Southern Cross Healthcare Group plc and anor EAT 0432/12, that this principle does not apply if the appeal is unsuccessful or if it is yet to be determined. In both instances, the dismissal takes effect on the original date of termination, meaning that the employee will not be treated as having been employed by the transferor immediately before the transfer. The EAT noted that in J Sainsbury Ltd v Savage 1981 ICR 1, CA, the Court of Appeal had affirmed that if an appeal against dismissal is entered, the dismissed employee is to be treated as being 'suspended' without pay during the determination of his or her appeal – in the sense that if the appeal is successful he or she will receive full back pay for the period of the suspension. But this did not mean that the employee should be treated as being 'suspended' in the sense of continuing to be employed by the transferor immediately before the transfer. (Note that this case is discussed further under 'Employed "immediately before" transfer – meaning of "immediately before the transfer"' above).

2.125 Bogus or 'fraudulent' assignments

In Carisway Cleaning Consultants Ltd v Richards and anor EAT 629/97 the transferor's ruse to dump an unwanted employee into the part of the undertaking to be transferred was characterised by the EAT as 'fraudulent'. The claimant in that case, R, had worked for 19 years for C Ltd, a cleaning company with contracts to clean several of Sainsbury's stores. In October 1995, while based at the Ladbroke Grove store, the claimant was suspended pending an investigation into poor performance and alleged falsification of clock cards. The following day C Ltd offered him the choice of working at the store in Chesham, which he accepted and for which he received a significant pay increase. But unbeknown to him, C Ltd already knew that it had lost the contract to supply cleaning services at that store, and only two days after the claimant starting work at Chesham, it wrote to inform him that his employment was to be transferred to the new contractor, CCS. The claimant's name had not been included on any list of employees supplied by C Ltd to CCS. Following the transfer, R worked for a few weeks for CCS, but it did not work out and his employment was terminated.

The claimant brought tribunal proceedings against both C Ltd and CCS for unfair dismissal. An employment tribunal upheld the claim against C Ltd on the basis that the claimant had never been assigned to the part of C Ltd's undertaking that had transferred to CCS. It found that C Ltd had been attempting, by sleight of hand, to use the TUPE Regulations to offload a long-serving employee against whom there had been complaints and who enjoyed the employment protection rights that went with a lengthy period of continuous employment. In its view, the claimant could not be considered as part of the undertaking that was transferred, since he had been gulled into working for that undertaking.

The EAT's judgment rejecting C Ltd's appeal is notable not so much for the **2.126** fact that it upheld the employment tribunal's decision but for the trenchant words it used to describe the employer's actions in this case. His Honour Judge Hull QC, who gave the EAT's judgment, observed that in the wholly exceptional circumstances of the instant case, the employee had been 'defrauded' into moving to the undertaking that was about to be transferred. The transferor's action might well have been a fraud not only against the employee but also against the transferee, especially since the transferor had increased the employee's salary to such a degree that the cleaning contract that the transferee was to take over would have been totally profitless. The tribunal had correctly concluded that the transferor had acted fraudulently, and, as HHJ Hull found, what is fraudulent is void. Accordingly, the claimant was not employed in the part of the undertaking that was transferred, with the result that what is now Reg 4 did not apply to cause his contract to be transferred automatically to the transferee.

The EAT also dealt with the transferor's argument that the tribunal should have gone on to consider whether the claimant, having continued to work at the Chesham store once he knew that a transfer was imminent, had thereby waived the fraud. In its view this contention was unsound as there was nothing in the evidence to suggest that the claimant had decided to take that course and, in any event, the full extent of the transferor's fraud upon him did not come to light until the tribunal hearing.

The Carisway decision is intriguing given that the employee in question was **2.127** indisputably working in the relevant part of the undertaking both immediately before and after it was transferred, and, on their face, there was nothing in the Regulations to prevent the transfer of his employment to the transferee. It may be that the stipulation that 'assigned' in the context of the 2006 Regulations means 'assigned other than on a temporary basis' (see Reg 2(1)) would be a matter that would be considered by a tribunal were similar facts to arise in a future case. Ostensibly, however, the claimant in Carisway had been permanently reassigned to the undertaking at the time of its transfer in the sense that his removal to the Chesham store was not intended to be merely a temporary arrangement. It would seem that the EAT's reasoning, without expressly saying so, was really based on considerations of public policy. Given its comment that

173

the fraud arguably operated against the transferee as well as the employee, it is interesting to consider whether, in a case where a fraudulently assigned employee nonetheless wishes to become employed by the transferee, the latter could argue that he was not bound to take on the employee in the light of the transferor's conduct. Applying the assertion that what is a fraud is void, the transferee might well succeed in avoiding the application of Reg 4(1).

2.128 **Difficult issues arising from assignment to part of business**
When only a part of a business is transferred, and employees are judged to be assigned to the part transferred, logistical and practical problems can arise in respect of the employee's job under the transferee. Two such problems are discussed below.

2.129 **Position where employee's post-transfer role is reduced.** It is clear from the discussion above of the requirement to be assigned to the undertaking that the most common scenario in which difficult questions arise is where the employee concerned works some of the time for one part of the transferor's business and the remainder of his or her time for another part of the business. Assuming that the employee is found to have been assigned to the transferred part and is taken on by the transferee, what happens if he or she is left without a full-time job? Assume, for example, that prior to the transfer Y worked full time for Z Ltd, but that 70 per cent of his time was spent working in part A of the transferor's business, and 30 per cent in part B. If only part A is subject to a TUPE transfer, that would mean that, under the transferee, Y may lose 30 per cent of his role. What are the legal consequences of this?

Obviously, if the transferee is in a position to offer sufficient work of the kind that Y was doing for the majority of his time so that the 30 per cent difference can be made up, there should be no difficulty. Alternatively, it might be that some new aspect could be added to Y's transferred role to enable him to continue working full time. Or he might simply accept employment on a part-time basis. However, if none of these options are viable, the transferee might well have to consider making Y redundant. Technically, the situation would appear to meet the statutory definition of redundancy in S.139(1)(b) ERA – i.e. that there has been a diminishment in the requirement for employees to carry out work of a particular kind. The definition of redundancy is discussed in IDS Employment Law Handbook, 'Redundancy' (2008), Chapter 2, 'Redundancy'. It is worth pointing out that although the dismissal in this context would almost certainly be transfer-connected, it would probably be for an 'economic, technical or organisational reason entailing a change in the workforce' and thus potentially fair – see Chapter 4, 'Unfair dismissal', for details.

2.130 **Different parts of business subject to different transfers.** One scenario that, though far from common, may throw up even more difficult issues so far as TUPE is concerned would be if separate purchasers bought different parts of a transferor's business in circumstances where, prior to the transfer, the employee worked in both parts. Assuming the separate sales each constituted a relevant transfer, the question would arise of whether it is possible for an employee to be 'assigned' to two or more parts of the transferor's business at the same time. If so, would this mean that following the transfer of the separate parts, the employee becomes employed by the two different transferees?

The scenario outlined above occurred in Hassard v McGrath and ors 1996 NILR 586, NICA. The facts of that case were somewhat involved but centred upon the decision of the Northern Ireland Housing Executive to outsource its business of maintaining and repairing its housing stock, which was being administered through the direct labour organisation (DLO) which the Executive had previously set up. The claimant worked as a joiner in the Fermanagh district of the DLO's operation, and that district was divided into four modules, 010, 020, 030 and 040. Each module comprised a particular housing estate or set of estates. The claimant's recent pattern of working showed that he worked in varying amounts for all four modules. One of the bidding contractors, D, was appointed by the Executive to service the maintenance work of modules 010 and 030 (for which, when amalgamated, the claimant had spent 25 per cent of his time working). A separate bidder, M, was appointed to deal with modules 020 and 040 (for which the claimant worked 73.39 per cent of his time). The issue arose as to whether the change of contractors comprised separate relevant transfers and whether the claimant had been assigned, at the time of the transfers, to one or both or neither of the transferred parts of the DLO's undertaking.

2.131 An industrial tribunal in Northern Ireland held that the appointments of the bidders amounted to separate relevant transfers; that the claimant was assigned equally to the two parts of the undertaking that were the subject of those transfers; and that he thereupon became employed by two different employers, D and M. On appeal, the Northern Ireland Court of Appeal overturned that decision. It pointed out that if the tribunal's conclusion was correct, the claimant's contract of employment with the Executive became two contracts of employment and that, following the transfer, he became employed by the two contractors in differing proportions. The Court thought that was not a palatable conclusion. In its view, 'an employee is only protected by the [Acquired Rights] Directive or the TUPE Regulations if before the transfer he was assigned solely to one part of the undertaking transferred to a transferee'.

Although decisions of the Northern Ireland Court of Appeal are not, strictly speaking, binding on tribunals or the EAT in Great Britain, its decisions are of highly persuasive value, particularly in a context like TUPE where the relevant legislation does not materially differ. In any case, the NICA's decision is, it is submitted, a sensible one.

2.132 Objecting to transfer

As discussed at the start of this chapter, the TUPE Regulations oust the common law rule that an employer may not transfer a contract of employment to a third party without the express consent of the employee. By virtue of Reg 4(1), an employee who is employed, or is deemed to be employed, in the organised grouping of resources or employees being transferred at the time of the transfer has his or her contract automatically transferred to the transferee. This reflects the position – as it has been found to be by the European Court of Justice – under the Acquired Rights Directive. In Rotsart de Hertaing v J Benoidt SA (in liquidation) and anor 1997 IRLR 127, ECJ, the European Court ruled that the contracts of employment and employment relationships existing on the date of the transfer between the transferor and the workers employed in the undertaking automatically pass to the transferee by the mere fact of the transfer. Moreover, by reason of the mandatory nature of the Directive, and in order not to deprive workers of the protection afforded by the Directive, the transfer of employment contracts automatically takes place regardless of the intentions of the transferor or the transferee and cannot be obstructed by the transferee's refusal to fulfil his obligations towards the transferred employees.

2.133 Position under Acquired Rights Directive

Apart from causing the employee's contract to be transferred to the transferee, the TUPE Regulations also ensure that all the transferor's rights, powers, duties and liabilities under that contract pass to the transferee – Reg 4(2). The priority attached to the automatic transfer of the transferor's rights and duties over any objections that the employees concerned may have about it was confirmed by the ECJ in the Dutch case of Berg and anor v Besselsen 1990 ICR 396, ECJ. There, the question put to the European Court was whether the employment obligations of a transferor are transferred automatically to the transferee on the transfer of an undertaking. If so, did it then follow that an employee's consent to such a discharge of the transferor's obligations was unnecessary and that any objections by him or her could not prevent it? The claimant argued that his consent was required. The ECJ decided that Article 3(1) of what is now Directive No.2001/23 – upon which Reg 4(1) is based – must be interpreted as meaning that the transferor is discharged from all contractual employment obligations owed to transferred employees following a relevant transfer, and that this legal consequence was neither conditional on the consent of the employees concerned nor affected by any objections they might have.

The judgment in the Berg case was thought to be clear authority for the principle that the automatic transfer of employment contracts was a legal consequence of a relevant transfer, which was unaffected by any objections employees might have. However, the relevance of an employee's objections to the automatic transfer of his or her employment contract came under the ECJ's scrutiny in

176

Katsikas v Konstantinidis 1993 IRLR 179, ECJ, a case concerning the rights of an employee who had been dismissed because of his objection to working for the transferee to whom his employer's business was transferred. The ECJ considered the principle established in the Berg case but decided that it had no bearing on the issue in the case before it. Berg concerned an employee's objection to the transfer of his employer's obligations entered into prior to the transfer, not to the transfer of his own contract of employment. The Court pointed out that, if the Acquired Rights Directive were to be interpreted as obliging employees to work for the transferee rather than simply permitting them to do so on the terms and conditions agreed with the transferor, this would call into question the fundamental right of employees to select their employer. The ECJ concluded, therefore, that Article 3(1) did not prevent employees from opposing the automatic transfer of their contract of employment. On the other hand, neither did Article 3(1) oblige Member States to provide for the continuance of the contract with the transferor. The fate of the employment contract was left to the discretion of individual Member States.

2.134 However, the right to 'object' to the transfer, as recognised by the ECJ in Katsikas, was qualified by the ECJ in Merckx and anor v Ford Motors Co (Belgium) SA 1997 ICR 352, ECJ. In that case the issue under consideration was what happened where the reason for the employee's objection to the transfer is that he or she will incur a substantial and detrimental change to his or her terms and conditions as a result of the transfer. The Court ruled that where the contract of employment or employment relationship is terminated because the transfer involves a substantial change in working conditions to the detriment of the employee, the employer is to be regarded, by virtue of Article 4(2) of the Directive, as responsible for the termination. A change in the level of remuneration awarded to the employee constitutes a substantial change in working conditions, so that where the contract or employment relationship is terminated by the employee because the transfer involves such a change, the employer will be liable to pay compensation on the ground that he has dismissed the employee.

Position under TUPE Regulations

2.135 In so far as the ruling in Katsikas v Konstantinidis (above) left it to Member States to determine the effect on an employee's existing contract where he or she objects to the transfer, the UK Government addressed the position by implementing specific amendments to Reg 5 of the 1981 Regulations. These provided that, in the event of an objection being voiced to the transferor or transferee, the Regulations would not operate to transfer the employee's contract (or any rights, duties or liabilities in respect of it) to the transferee – old Reg 5(4A). However, in that situation, the employee's contract of employment would be terminated on the date of the transfer, but he or she would not be treated as having been dismissed for any purpose – old Reg 5(4B).

Following these changes, there was some confusion as to the interplay between these new provisions and the pre-existing right of an employee, by virtue of old Reg 5(5), to terminate his or her contract of employment without notice if a substantial change is made in his working conditions to his detriment. The question was whether such a right was compatible with, and survived, the new stipulation in old Reg 5(4B) that where the employee exerts his or her right to object to the transfer, that causes the termination of his or her employment with the transferor but the termination will not be treated as a dismissal for any purpose. How, then, could the employee bring any claim (such as unfair constructive dismissal) based on the termination?

2.136 **The Humphreys decision.** The position was rapidly made clear by the Court of Appeal in Humphreys v University of Oxford and anor 2000 ICR 405, CA. In that case the Court ruled that where an employee, prior to a proposed transfer, objected to the transfer under old Reg 5(4A) and the objection was based on an anticipated detrimental change in his or her working conditions, the contract with the transferor terminated as soon as the transfer took place. And despite the stipulation in old Reg 5(4B) that termination in these circumstances does not constitute a dismissal for any purpose, the employee retained the right to sue the transferor for constructive dismissal under Reg 5(5). That is because old Reg 5(4B) had to be read, in order to give effect to the purpose of the Acquired Rights Directive, as being subject to Reg 5(5), which preserves the employee's right to claim that he has been constructively dismissed in a case where the employee anticipates that the transfer will lead to a substantial and detrimental change in his working conditions.

The facts of the Humphreys case concerned an employee who worked for the University setting and marking GCSE and A-level exam papers. Under his existing terms, he had life tenure up to the age of 67. On being informed that his post was to be transferred to a separate examining body, he objected in writing, stating his reason to be that the transfer involved a significant change in his working conditions that was to his detriment. His concern was that the transferee would only be in a position to guarantee three years of employment up to the age of 65. Following his objection, he brought a claim against Oxford University in the High Court for damages for wrongful dismissal covering the unexpired period of his tenure. The University applied to have the employee's action struck out on the ground that it was misconceived. The High Court judge rejected that application and, on appeal by the University, the Court of Appeal ruled that he had been right to do so. The judge had properly interpreted the provisions of Reg 5 of the 1981 Regulations as entitling the employee to argue that, having objected to becoming employed by the transferee and thereby bringing his employment with the transferor to an end as soon as the transfer occurred, he could nevertheless claim that he had been constructively dismissed by the transferor on the ground that any transfer of his employment to the transferee would have caused a substantial change in his working conditions to his detriment.

Prior to the Humphreys case, the EAT in Sita (GB) Ltd v Burton and ors 1998 **2.137** ICR 17, EAT, expressed the opinion that any anticipation by employees that the transferee will fail to meet his obligations cannot found a claim of unfair constructive dismissal against the transferor because what is at risk is the preservation after the transfer of the employee's current terms in his contract with the transferor. The EAT's reasoning was that the TUPE Regulations provide an absolute answer by way of remedy to any attempt by the transferee to alter those terms unlawfully after the transfer. The EAT did not consider that the conduct of an employer could be regarded as sufficiently drastic with regard to the obligation of mutual trust and goodwill if it did nothing to alter the remedies available to the employee upon transfer. However, the Court of Appeal in the Humphreys case decided that the employee's right to claim constructive dismissal under what was then Reg 5(5) survived his objection to the proposed transfer and that the transferor was the appropriate defendant.

Outline of 'objection' provisions. The provisions dealing with the right of **2.138** objection and its effect on the employee's contract of employment are now to be found in Reg 4(7)–(11) of TUPE 2006. These largely mirror the right of objection that was contained in the old Regulations as amended, but with some important changes of wording discussed under 'Objection on basis of "substantial change to working conditions"' below. The Regulations provide as follows:

- Reg 4(7) states that the rules in Reg 4(1) and (2) providing for the automatic transfer of employment and of contractual rights and liabilities, etc 'shall not operate to transfer the contract of employment and the rights, powers, duties and liabilities under or in connection with it of an employee who informs the transferor or the transferee that he objects to becoming employed by the transferee'

- Reg 4(8) states that 'subject to paragraphs (9) and (11), where an employee so objects, the relevant transfer shall operate so as to terminate his contract of employment with the transferor but he shall not be treated, for any purpose, as having been dismissed by the transferor'

- Reg 4(9) states that 'where a relevant transfer involves or would involve a substantial change in working conditions to the material detriment of a person whose contract of employment is or would be transferred under [Reg 4(1)]', then, except in the specific context of insolvency, 'such an employee may treat the contract of employment as having been terminated, and the employee shall be treated for any purpose as having been dismissed by the employer'

179

- Reg 4(11) states that all the above provisions as well as the automatic transfer of employment rule in Reg 4(1) 'are without prejudice to any right of an employee arising apart from these Regulations to terminate his contract of employment without notice in acceptance of a repudiatory breach of contract by his employer'.

2.139 Putting all of these provisions together, the position is that, where an employee objects to the transfer, (a) the automatic transfer of employment rule will not operate, but (b) the transfer will have the effect of terminating the employee's contract with the transferor, and (c) he or she will not, for any purpose, be considered to have been dismissed by the transferor, *except* (d) where the transfer involves or would involve a substantial change in the employee's working conditions to his or her material detriment. In that case the employee is entitled to treat the contract as having been terminated and that termination will constitute a dismissal for any purpose. Finally, (e) none of the above affects the employee's general legal right to resign without notice in response to a repudiatory breach of contract by the employer – whether the employee is employed by the transferor at the time of resignation or has become employed by the transferee after a relevant transfer.

It will be seen that Reg 4(7)–(11) codifies and makes explicit the position under the previous Regulations as interpreted by the Court of Appeal in Humphreys v University of Oxford and anor (above). In particular, Reg 4(9) spells out that where the employee's objection to the transfer results in him or her resigning because the transfer involves (or is anticipated to involve) a substantial change to his or her working conditions, then this is an exception to the rule that such objection will not be regarded as a dismissal for any purpose. And Reg 4(11) contains a separate provision that now makes it explicit that the specific provisions under TUPE are without prejudice to the employee's right 'apart from these Regulations' to resign in the face of a repudiatory breach of contract by the employer. Again, this codifies the position as decided by the Court of Appeal in Humphreys, when it rejected the view taken by the EAT in Sita (GB) Ltd v Burton and ors (above) that any anticipation by an employee that the transferee will fail to meet its obligations under TUPE cannot found a claim of unfair constructive dismissal against the transferor (see 'The Humphreys decision' above).

2.140 It is thought that these provisions do not affect the reasoning or the conclusion of the Humphreys case on the point that a valid objection before the transfer prevents any liability for the employee transferring to the transferee. So, if the employee's resignation before the transfer amounts to a constructive dismissal or a Reg 4(9) dismissal, then any liability for the dismissal will remain with the transferor. The point was raised but left unresolved by the EAT in Centrewest London Buses v Musse 2012 IRLR 360, EAT, where the Appeal Tribunal remitted the question to the employment tribunal to determine whether the transferor or transferee was liable for the claimant's constructive dismissal following a change in work location. Although the ruling in Humphreys v University of Oxford and anor (above) does not appear to have been referred to, it is clear from the EAT's ruling that this kind of objection can be raised either before or after the transfer (see 'Dismissal by employer' below). It is only where the objection is raised before the transfer that the issue raised by the Humphreys case arises.

Timing of objection   2.141

On the face of it, the wording of Reg 4(7) implies that any objection to a transfer has to be made by the employee before (or at the latest, at the time of) the relevant transfer. That is because the provision stipulates that the rules providing for the automatic transfer of the contract of employment and the rights, duties and liabilities under the contract do not apply to an employee 'who informs the transferor or the transferee that he objects to *becoming* employed by the transferor'. If, therefore, the employee remains silent, and simply goes across to the transferee without demur, it is difficult to see how he or she can later claim to have objected to becoming employed by the transferee within the terms of Reg 4(7).

However, does this literal interpretation have to give way in circumstances where the employee did not know about the imminent change of employer? This was the question that faced the High Court in New ISG Ltd v Vernon 2008 ICR 319, ChD. There, the employee was kept in the dark about the identity of his new employer and the date of transfer prior to the transfer by the joint administrators. There was no attempt to inform, let alone consult, with appropriate representatives. When, two days after the transfer, he learned of the identity of the transferee, he resigned and subsequently went to work for a competitor. The new transferee immediately sought to enforce restrictive covenants in the employee's contract, contending that this had been transferred automatically in accordance with Reg 4 TUPE. Initially, the transferee was successful in obtaining a temporary injunction restraining the employee from working for the competitor. However, on review, a High Court judge lifted this on the basis that the employee, by resigning as soon as he found out about the transfer, had in effect objected to the transfer within the meaning of Reg 4(7). This had the consequence that his contract of employment had not transferred, so the transferee was not in a position to enforce the restrictive covenants contained within it. The judge rejected the transferee's argument that the employee's objection was ineffective because it was made after the transfer had occurred. The employee had not known of the identity of the transferee before the date of the transfer and had submitted a letter of resignation within two working days of the transfer. In those circumstances, while the wording of Reg 4(7) envisaged that an employee must object before or at the time of the transfer of the undertaking for the objection to be valid, the judge reasoned

181

that a purposive approach was necessary to give force to the principle behind the right to object.

2.142 The circumstances in the New ISG case were acknowledged to be 'exceptional' by the EAT in Capita Health Solutions Ltd v McLean and anor 2008 IRLR 595, EAT. In that case, an occupational health nurse raised a grievance in advance of the proposed transfer of the BBC's occupational health service to CHS Ltd. The grievance alleged that the change of employer entailed a significant change to the employee's role and pension benefits. However, in subsequent dealings, the employee and the BBC agreed that she would go to work for CHS Ltd for the six-week period (described as 'secondment') during which she was working out her notice of resignation, and that she would continue to be paid by the BBC during this period. At the end of the six weeks, the employee duly resigned and claimed unfair dismissal against both CHS Ltd and the BBC and the issue arose as to whether the transferor – i.e. the BBC – should be regarded as a proper respondent to the proceedings. This depended on whether the employee had validly objected to the transfer: if not, her employment would have transferred to CHS Ltd, making it the sole respondent potentially liable for the unfair dismissal.

The EAT ruled that the act of going to work for the transferee under a temporary secondment arrangement in circumstances where the employee was fully aware of the change in the identity of the employer was wholly inconsistent with having evinced an objection to the transfer. What, in fact, the employee's approach showed was that she was agreeable to working for CHS Ltd, albeit for only six weeks: this was wholly inconsistent with her claim that she had objected to the transfer. In the EAT's view, the intention of the parties, while a relevant consideration, was not determinative of the question of whether an objection within the meaning of Reg 4(7) had been made. This was wholly an objective matter to be decided on the facts and circumstances of the case at issue. Furthermore, the fact that the BBC had continued to pay the employee during the secondment period was irrelevant, as was the fact that the employee was working out notice given prior to the transfer. In Lady Smith's judgment, 'if... it had been intended that objecting employees be required or able to work out notice periods that ran on after the date of the transfer, it is more than reasonable to have expected that to be provided for in the Regulations... That is not to say that an objecting employee cannot be employed by the transferor employer after the transfer date, but the transferor is not obliged to retain such an employee in his employment. Any such employment would be under a new contract.' As a result the automatic transfer principle applied to the employee.

2.143 **Potentially draconian consequences of objecting**
It will be seen from the above that, if the exceptions contained in Reg 4(9) and (11) do not apply, the effect of an employee objecting to the transfer is draconian. Although the employee's employment with the transferor is not

transferred to the transferee according to his or her wishes, the employment automatically comes to an end at the point where the relevant transfer occurs, but that termination is not regarded as a 'dismissal' for any purpose whatsoever. This means that any remedy that the employee might ordinarily have sought as a result of being dismissed is unavailable. Furthermore, the normal protections in respect of contractual rights that the employee would have when his or her employment transfers under Reg 4(1) and (2) do not apply. Therefore, should the employee enter into a new contract after the transfer with the transferor (or, for that matter, the transferee), the employer can potentially insist on new and less favourable terms and conditions of employment without risking a finding that those terms have been varied by reason of the transfer and are accordingly void.

It might have been thought that in view of the legal consequences that flow from an objection to the transfer, the transferor would be under some obligation to explain the situation to the employee. But, as we see below, there is no such obligation. This means that the 'substantial change to working conditions' exception in Reg 4(9), which basically requires the employee to have good cause for objecting to the transfer, is of major importance in determining the employee's legal position if he or she chooses not to transfer to the transferee. The scope of this exception is discussed under 'Objection on basis of "substantial change to working conditions"' below.

Objection on basis of 'substantial change to working conditions' 2.144

As we have seen in the discussion under 'Position under Acquired Rights Directive' above, the ECJ in Merckx and anor v Ford Motors Co (Belgium) SA 1997 ICR 352, ECJ, required Article 3(1) of the Directive to be read as making the transferor responsible for termination of an employee's contract of employment if the latter has objected to the transfer by reason of the fact that it would entail a substantial and detrimental change being made to his or her working conditions. In Europièces SA v Sanders 2001 1 CMLR 25, ECJ, the European Court subsequently made it clear that it was for the national courts to decide whether the working conditions proposed by the transferee involved or would involve a substantial change for this purpose.

The Merckx ruling is transposed into UK national law by what is now Reg 4(9) and (11) of the 2006 Regulations. As explained under 'Position under TUPE Regulations – outline of "objection" provisions' above, these provide that where the relevant transfer involves or would involve a substantial change in working conditions to the material detriment of an employee employed by the transferor, the employee may treat the contract of employment as having been terminated, and the employee shall be treated for any purpose as having been dismissed by the transferor – Reg 4(9). This right is without prejudice to any right of an employee arising apart from the Regulations to terminate his contract of employment without notice in acceptance of a repudiatory breach of contract by his employer – Reg 4(11).

2.145 In enacting the 2006 Regulations, the Government took the view that the recasting of these provisions had made it clearer than under the previous Regulations that the substantial change to working conditions to the employee's material detriment does not necessarily have to be so serious as to amount to a repudiatory breach of contract such as to found a classic case of constructive dismissal. This point is discussed in greater detail in Chapter 4, 'Unfair dismissal', under 'Material detriment dismissals – scope of right under Reg 4(9)'.

The question of what amounts to a 'substantial change to working conditions' has been considered by the EAT in Tapere v South London and Maudsley NHS Trust 2009 ICR 1563, EAT, and Abellio London Ltd (formerly London Travel Ltd) v Musse and ors 2012 IRLR 360, EAT – both of which involved a change in an employee's place of work. The EAT ruled that the phrase 'working conditions' is wider than contractual conditions and is therefore capable of relating to both contractual and physical conditions and is thus wide enough to cover matters such as a change in the place of work. The EAT stated that whether the change was sufficiently substantial to justify the employee's resignation was a question of fact. In Tapere, it held that the transfer of the claimant, who was part of the hospital's procurement team based at Burgess Park, Camberwell, to Bethlem Hospital in Beckenham was a substantial change in working conditions. Similarly, in Musse, the EAT upheld the employment tribunal's conclusion that a transferee's requirement that bus drivers change their place of work from Westbourne Park to Battersea was sufficiently substantial as it added two hours to the claimants' working day in commuting time. By way of contrast, in Cetinsoy and ors v London United Busways Ltd EAT 0042/14, a change of work location from Westbourne Park to Stamford Brook some three and a half miles away, was found not to be so significant as to constitute a 'substantial' change.

2.146 In relocation cases or cases involving a change in role, it may be relevant to consider the terms of any express mobility or flexibility clause conferring on the employer the contractual right to transfer the employee to a different location or to change the job role. For different reasons, the mobility clauses in the Tapere and Musse cases were found not to give the employers the contractual right to transfer the employees to the new location, but in appropriate cases such as Centinsoy the existence of such a right may be relevant, though not conclusive. This is reflected in the BIS Guide on the TUPE Regulations, which says what might constitute a substantial change in working conditions 'will be a matter for the courts and the tribunals to determine in the light of the circumstances of each case. What might be a trivial change in one setting might constitute a substantial change in another. However, a major relocation of the workplace which makes it difficult or much more expensive for an employee to transfer, or the withdrawal of a right to a tenured post, is likely to fall within this definition.' This guidance is supported by the approach adopted in the cases referred to above.

Apart from the rulings in Tapere and Musse, the precise parameters of what is meant by 'substantial change to working conditions' is uncertain. Nonetheless, it is clear that the phrase potentially extends to changes to non-contractual terms and conditions. In Merckx and anor v Ford Motors Co (Belgium) SA (above) it will be recalled that this included a change in the employee's amount of remuneration (including a non-contractual bonus scheme). And in Nationwide Building Society v Benn and ors 2010 IRLR 922, EAT, the claimants successfully relied on Reg 4(9) when their job role and responsibilities were downgraded after the transfer as a result of their assimilation into the transferee's existing job role structure and the terms of their bonus scheme became less generous. The EAT confirmed that in these circumstances the tribunal had been entitled to conclude on the facts that the claimants had been either constructively dismissed under S.95(1)(c) ERA or dismissed by reason of a substantial change being made to their detriment within the meaning of Reg 4(9).

It is important to observe that Reg 4(9) includes the rider that a substantial **2.147** change to working conditions must be to the employee's *material* detriment. Although the employee may object to the transfer for any reason he or she wishes, he or she will only be entitled to rely on the free-standing right to terminate the contract of employment by reason of a substantial change to working conditions falling short of a repudiatory breach if it is shown not just that such a change has been or will be made but also that it is to the employee's material detriment. The equivalent provision under the 1981 Regulations merely spoke of 'where a substantial change is made in [the employee's] working conditions to his detriment'. The effect of the addition of the word 'material' was considered by the EAT in the Tapere and Musse cases (above). The EAT in both cases rejected the argument that the issue of 'material' detriment should be considered on an 'objective' basis, weighing up the employer's rights against those of the employee. Instead, the correct approach was to consider the matter from the employee's perspective and then for the tribunal to consider whether, objectively, the change was to the disadvantage of the employee. The EAT drew an analogy with the approach adopted in discrimination cases towards the issue of determining whether the claimant has suffered 'detriment' – see Shamoon v Chief Constable of the Royal Ulster Constabulary 2003 ICR 337, HL. Ultimately, the matter boils down to a question of fact for the tribunal to decide having regard to the relevant circumstances of the case. In Tapere, a relocation of just two and a half miles was found to be to the employee's detriment because she lived in Grays in Essex and the change would have materially increased her journey time and affected her childcare arrangements. Similarly, in Musse the relocation comprised a material detriment because it added two hours or more to the journey times of four of the five claimant bus drivers.

The circumstances in which it is fair to dismiss where there has been a substantial change within the meaning of Reg 4(9) are considered in Chapter 4, 'Unfair dismissal', under 'Material detriment dismissals – enforcing right to claim unfair dismissal'.

2.148 **Is change of employer's identity a 'substantive change'?** Another alteration made to the 'objection' provisions by the TUPE Regulations 2006 (compared to the position under the predecessor Regulations) concerns the provision dealing with a substantive change made to working conditions. The 1981 Regulations contained a stipulation at Reg 5(5) that a mere change in the identity of the employer could not constitute a substantial change in working conditions to the employee's detriment, unless the employee could show that it was a significant change and was to his detriment. This stipulation does not find its way into the 2006 Regulations. One view might be that the role of the words 'significant change' in Reg 5(5) of the 1981 Regulations is now taken up by the requirement for there to be a 'material' detriment in Reg 4(9) of the 2006 Regulations. It has been suggested that it may even cover the environmental or moral concerns of the employee, although there is no authority on this point.

It is likely to be highly exceptional that a simple change in the identity of the employer will amount to a substantial change in working conditions even if this is felt to be a material detriment by the employee. One such exception may be where a function of a large internationally recognised company is contracted out to a small unknown contractor: on the one hand, it might well be argued that an employee transferring in such circumstances would suffer a loss in status that could prejudice him or her in the job market in the future, and that this would constitute a substantial change in working conditions that is materially detrimental. On the other hand, it could be contended that a mere perception of a loss in status is not a 'material' detriment. The courts' view as to which approach is correct could have a significant impact on the ability of large companies to contract out in this manner, especially where labour-intensive functions are concerned: if all the employees concerned are able to object to the transfer and seek compensation, the transfer will not be able to go ahead because there will be no organised grouping of employees to transfer.

2.149 **Dismissal by 'employer'.** Regulation 4(9) states that where there is a substantial change in working conditions to the material detriment of the employee, 'such an employee may treat the contract of employment as having been terminated by the employer'. Similarly, the constructive dismissal provision of Reg 4(11) refers to a repudiatory breach of contract 'by the employer'. It is significant that neither regulation specifies whether the employer in question is the transferor or the transferee. This appears to be deliberate: it allows for the fact that the employee's decision to terminate the contract in either situation might occur before the transfer or after it. In other words, an employee can resign and claim that he or she has suffered a materially detrimental change to working conditions while still employed by the transferor or after the transfer has occurred when, technically, the employee has become employed by the transferee.

The same is true in the case of a resignation precipitated by a repudiatory breach of contract. If the breach and resignation occur before the transfer, then the relevant employer against whom the employee would bring a claim of constructive dismissal is the transferor. In some circumstances, however, liability for unfair dismissal will pass to the transferee even though the constructive dismissal was an act done by the transferor. If the reason for the constructive dismissal is the transfer itself within the meaning of Reg 7(1), then the employee will be deemed to have been employed immediately before the transfer, and liability for his or her unfair dismissal will pass to the transferee by virtue of Reg 4(2) – see 'Employed "immediately before" transfer' above. If the dismissal is not transfer-connected, or is for an economic, technical or organisational reason entailing changes in the workforce of the transferor or transferee within the meaning of Reg 7(2), then, provided the contract is terminated by the employee resigning prior to the transfer, liability will remain with the transferor. Where the repudiatory breach and resignation in response to it occurs after the transfer, then the 'employer' in question for the purposes of Reg 4(11) would be the transferee. For a detailed discussion of the transfer or otherwise of liability for unfair dismissal, see Chapter 3, 'What transfers?', under 'Unfair and wrongful dismissal liability'.

Meaning of 'objection' 2.150
Unfortunately there is no definition in the 2006 Regulations to clarify precisely what conduct will qualify as raising an objection. Reg 4(7) simply states that there will be no transfer of an employee's contract where that employee informs the transferor or the transferee that he objects to the transfer. Cases decided under the 1981 Regulations will continue to be applicable, however, and it has been held that there is a valid objection to the transfer where there is a refusal to give consent, and that refusal is communicated to either the transferor or the transferee in advance of the transfer – Hay v George Hanson (Building Contractors) Ltd 1996 IRLR 427, EAT.

In the Hay case the employee argued that he had not objected to the transfer, and that his employment had therefore automatically transferred to the transferee. An employment tribunal held otherwise. It found that the employee had taken all possible steps within his capacity to resist the transfer. For example, he had sought alternative employment with the transferor, without success, and after the transfer had continued to seek through his union a redundancy package from the transferor. At one stage the transferee had written to the employee informing him that in its opinion his behaviour meant that he was objecting to the transfer, but received no reply from either him or his union.

2.151 On appeal, the EAT upheld the tribunal's decision. It stated that the word 'object' in the context of what was then Reg 5(4A) of the 1981 Regulations means a refusal to consent to the transfer, and that such a state of mind does not amount to an effective objection unless and until it is conveyed to the transferor or the transferee. That said, objection could be imputed by either word or deed, or by both. In each case, it would be a question of fact whether the employee's state of mind amounted to a refusal to consent to the transfer and whether that state of mind was in fact brought to the attention of the transferor or transferee prior to the transfer.

The wording of old Reg 5(4A) (which remains unchanged in Reg 4(7) of the 2006 TUPE Regulations) was criticised by the EAT in Hay. It pointed out that, taken in its general context, the word 'object' could reflect a state of mind short of refusal, and that it was obvious that all manner of means might be used whereby information might be conveyed to the intended recipient. Furthermore, the regulation was silent as to the timing of the objection, and nor was there a requirement that any employee objecting to the transfer should be informed of the consequences of his objection by the transferor. Nevertheless, the EAT felt able to construe Reg 5(4A) in accordance with what it perceived to be the general scheme of the relevant provisions as a whole, which was to protect the right of an employee not to be transferred to another employer against his or her will. Thus, it concluded that the word 'object' effectively means a 'refusal to accept' the transfer, and that it is necessary for that refusal to be conveyed to the transferor or the transferee either by word or by deed.

2.152 Where an objection is clearly to the disadvantage of the employee – as it was in the Hay case – it might have been thought that it would take unequivocal evidence to persuade a tribunal that the employee had objected to being transferred. But the EAT's approach does not appear to be so exacting. Its method of ascertaining whether the employee has objected seems to be a matter of finding out whether his or her words or deeds revealed a withholding of consent, and then to determine whether or not that state of mind was in some way or other transmitted to either of the relevant parties. Yet what Reg 4(7) actually provides is that the employee's contract will not transfer if the employee 'informs the transferor or the transferee that he objects'. It might be contended that those words, on their plain and ordinary meaning, require some kind of formal and unambiguous notification to the existing employer or the transferee: they do not appear to leave room for an objection to be inferred solely from an employee's actions, which may be a reflection of genuine misgivings about a pending transfer – a state of affairs that arguably existed in the Hay case – even if those misgivings are communicated to the relevant parties.

A more generous approach, so far as employees' rights are concerned, was taken in Euro-Die (UK) Ltd v Skidmore and anor EAT 1158/98. In that case, the employee was anxious about his employment protection rights in the event that his employment was terminated by the transferee, and therefore refused to work for the new employer without first receiving assurances from the transferor that his continuity of employment would be protected. When these were not forthcoming, he decided not to present himself for work after the transfer and claimed unfair constructive dismissal, against both the transferor and the transferee. An employment tribunal found that the employee had been constructively dismissed by the transferor and that the transfer was the principal reason for his dismissal. The dismissal was therefore automatically unfair under what is now Reg 7(1). Liability for the dismissal, however, passed to the transferee by virtue of what is now Reg 4(1). On the transferee's appeal, the EAT ruled that the transferor's failure to give an assurance in respect of a matter as crucial as the protection of the employee's continuity of employment amounted to a fundamental breach of the implied term of trust and confidence and agreed with the tribunal that the resulting constructive dismissal was automatically unfair. Most interestingly, for present purposes, the EAT rejected the transferee's contention that, by raising his concerns about the preservation of his continuity of employment, the employee had objected to becoming employed by the transferee for the purposes of Reg 5(4A) (now Reg 4(7)) so as to prevent the automatic transfer of his contract. Since it was clear that the employee had no absolute objection to working for the new employer but had simply declined to do so unless he was given an assurance about his continuity, Reg 5(4A) did not apply to prevent the automatic transfer of his contract or to prevent the transferee being liable for the constructive dismissal of the employee under Reg 5(2) (now Reg 4(2)).

Similarly, in Senior Heat Treatment Ltd v Bell and ors 1997 IRLR 614, EAT, **2.153** employees were held not to have objected to becoming employed by the transferee in circumstances where they accepted the transferor's option of 'opting out' of the transfer of the business in return for receiving severance packages. Since the employees had, before the date of the transfer, entered into contracts of employment with the transferee to take effect immediately after the transfer, the EAT held that it had been open to the employment tribunal to find that, notwithstanding their agreement to 'opt out' of the transfer, they had not objected to it. In consequence, their contracts of employment were automatically transferred to the transferee and their continuity of employment remained unbroken for the purposes of claiming redundancy payments and compensation for unfair dismissal against the transferee. This case demonstrates that the operation of Reg 4(1) of the TUPE Regulations cannot be avoided by persuading an employee to opt out of the Regulations, unless the decision to opt out constitutes a genuine objection to becoming employed by the transferee within the meaning of Reg 4(7). The EAT sensibly pointed out that in the Senior Heat case the employees clearly had no objection to the transfer since they had in fact agreed to go and work for the transferee.

Likewise, in Capita Health Solutions Ltd v McLean and anor 2008 IRLR 595, EAT (discussed in detail under 'Timing of objection' above), the Appeal Tribunal (presided over by Lady Smith, sitting alone) held that an employee who had objected to her employment transferring to an outsourcing company, but who had subsequently agreed to work on a six-week secondment with the transferee, had not validly objected to the transfer. In the EAT's view, her acceptance of the secondment indicated that she was prepared to – and in fact did – work for the transferee and that this was inconsistent with a valid objection. The EAT reached this conclusion even though it was clear that the employee had marked objections to the change in the identity of the employer and voiced these by raising a grievance and giving notice of resignation. However, what scuppered her case that she had 'objected' to the transfer within the strict terms of Reg 4(7) was – according to the EAT – that she agreed to go to work for the transferee under a 'secondment' arrangement during the six weeks she was working out her notice. In the words of Lady Smith, 'when what was said and done is looked at as a whole, the only proper interpretation that can be put on it is that the claimant did not object to being employed by the [transferee]. She was, clearly, only prepared to work for them for a limited period of six weeks but that being so, she cannot, at the same time, insist that she objected. What her approach shows is that she was in fact agreeable to working for the [transferee] albeit only for a short period. That her preparedness was time limited does not mean that she objected to a transfer. Reg [4(7)] does not allow for post-transfer objection except perhaps in exceptional circumstances such as where employees are not made aware of the transfer in advance of it occurring, as happened in the New ISG Ltd case.' As a result, the automatic transfer principle applied to transfer the employee's employment to the transferee.

2.154 There is no requirement that an employee's refusal to consent to the transfer be informed: the only requirement is that the refusal be clearly communicated. In Ladies' Health and Fitness Club Ltd v Eastmond and ors EAT 0094/03 an employment tribunal had found that the employees' objection to the transfer had not been properly informed, and could not therefore amount to an effective objection for the purposes of the Regulations. The EAT disagreed. After considering a petition signed by the employees that had not been shown to the tribunal, it remitted the question of whether or not there had been an objection to the tribunal for reconsideration, saying: 'It appears to us clear that if there is an objection within the Regulation, the fact that it may be high-handed, ignorant, over-reactive or simply misconceived would not affect the position, although… it might be that on analysis what occurred did not amount to an objection if someone in fact does not know what they are doing.' This latter qualification may be crucial where an employee does not understand the effect of a formal objection in circumstances where the transfer does not involve any significant change in working conditions that is materially to his or her detriment. An employee may wish to voice opposition to a transfer while ultimately feeling powerless to resist it, and may make empty threats without realising that they may technically be resigning. Eastmond suggests that such employees may still transfer.

Options available to objecting employee 2.155
The options available to an employee who does not wish to transfer to the transferee on a relevant transfer are essentially these:

- to terminate the contract with notice on the ground that a substantial change has been (or will be) made to working conditions to his or her material detriment

- to resign (with or without notice) on the ground that the employer has repudiated the contract in circumstances entitling the employee to terminate the contract without notice by reason of the employer's conduct

- to otherwise object to the transfer.

Under the first option, the employee will be regarded as having been dismissed by the transferor – Reg 4(9). Under the second option, the employee – assuming a repudiatory breach has occurred – will be regarded as having been constructively dismissed – Reg 4(11). In both these cases, subject to what is said below, the employee will be entitled to claim unfair dismissal provided he or she has sufficient qualifying service to do so. Under the third option, although the Regulations provide that the contract will thus be terminated, the employee will not be treated as having been dismissed by the transferor for any purpose (including claiming unfair dismissal) – Reg 4(7) and (8).

While the provisions of Reg 4(7)–(9) and (11) clearly allow an employee to 2.156 elect to resign rather than transfer to the transferee, such a decision may prove to be a high-risk strategy. Unless the employee can be confident either that the transfer will involve a substantial change in working conditions that is materially to his or her detriment, or else that he or she has grounds for claiming constructive dismissal, then the termination of his or her contract will not be treated 'for any purpose' as a dismissal by the transferor. Thus, any claim for unfair dismissal, constructive dismissal or a contractual or statutory redundancy payment will be ruled out.

Where the transfer will only involve a change in identity of the employer, this change in itself will have to amount to a substantial change in working conditions that is materially detrimental (see 'Objection on basis of "substantial change to working conditions"' above) before any claim will be possible. In most cases, it seems, the choice will be to either work for the transferee or to resign and leave empty-handed or, where there is a potential change in working conditions within the meaning of Reg 4(9), to defer the decision until after the transfer.

191

2.157 **Unfair dismissal.** Assuming that the employee is able to show that the transfer involves (or will involve) a substantial change in working conditions to his or her material detriment, then he or she may terminate the contract. In that case, as made clear by Reg 4(9), the termination will be deemed to be a dismissal by the transferor. But what kind of 'dismissal' is it? In Humphreys v University of Oxford and anor 2000 ICR 405, CA (see 'Position under TUPE Regulations' above), the Court of Appeal assumed that it would be a constructive dismissal, thus conferring upon the employee the right to claim unfair dismissal against the transferor on that basis. However, this case was decided when the relevant provision as contained in the 1981 Regulations referred to 'the right of an employee arising apart from these Regulations to terminate his contract of employment without notice if a substantial change is made in his working conditions to his detriment'. It was therefore apparent that only changes amounting to a repudiatory breach of contract entitling the employee to resign without notice could comprise a 'substantial change to working conditions'. As we have seen, however, the Regulations have been reformulated to allow employees to terminate their contracts as a result of a change of this kind even if the change is not so fundamental as to amount to a repudiatory breach of contract.

The problem is that, in order to claim unfair dismissal, the employee has to show that he or she has been 'dismissed' within the meaning of S.95(1) ERA. The general assumption has been that a dismissal for the purposes of Reg 4(9) equates to a constructive dismissal under S.95(1)(c) ERA, which is defined as occurring where 'the employee terminates the contract under which he is employed... in circumstances in which he is entitled to terminate it without notice by reason of the employer's conduct'. The difficulty here is that the deemed dismissal of an employee who terminates the contract because the employer has substantially changed his or her working conditions within the meaning of Reg 4(9) will not fall within the S.95(1)(c) category of dismissal if the change in question falls short of being a repudiatory breach of contract. That is because anything less than a repudiatory breach will not comprise a circumstance in which the employee 'is entitled to terminate [the contract] without notice'. For rather complex reasons – fully set out in Chapter 4, 'Unfair dismissal', under 'Material detriment dismissals' – we submit that the better view is that dismissal in the circumstances described in Reg 4(9) should be regarded as an express dismissal by the employer as defined by S.95(1)(a) ERA. If correct, this at least establishes a cogent basis for a 'dismissal' upon which a claim of unfair dismissal can be founded.

2.158 Whether the dismissal is express or constructive, it is of course insufficient simply to establish that there is a dismissal to succeed in a claim of unfair dismissal: the dismissal in question must also be shown to have been unfair. It may be that a Reg 4(9) dismissal is potentially fair as being for an 'economic, technical or organisational reason entailing a change in the workforce' (ETO) within the meaning of Reg 7(2), Reg 7(3) and Reg 7(3A), though there are dangers here if the transferor seeks to rely on or anticipate a potential ETO reason that the transferee might have for dismissal once the transfer has occurred – see Chapter 4. In any event, the employee would still need to show that dismissal was not reasonable in all the circumstances for the purposes of S.98(4) ERA. Relevant factors in that determination would include, for example, an absence of proper consultation, or a failure to offer the employee suitable alternative employment that is available.

Constructive dismissal on other grounds. Regulation 4(11) states that **2.159** nothing in Reg 4(1), (7), (8) and (9) prejudices the employee's right, arising apart from the Regulations, simply to resign in response to his employer's repudiatory breach. This, as has previously been mentioned, preserves a right to claim constructive dismissal, and indicates that such a claim may be based on something other than where a substantial change in working conditions is made to the employee's material detriment. The test of constructive dismissal is well established. The focus is on the employer's conduct that has provoked the employee to resign, which must be shown either to constitute a significant breach going to the root of the contract or exhibit an intention no longer to be bound by an essential term of the contract, and in either case must be serious enough to entitle the employee to resign without notice – Western Excavating (ECC) Ltd v Sharp 1978 ICR 221, CA. Any employee who resigns by reason of such conduct will be regarded as having been dismissed within the meaning of S.95(1)(c) ERA. This will lay the foundation for a claim of unfair dismissal or, for that matter, breach of contract. In the case of an unfair dismissal claim, the dismissal will have to be shown to have been unfair for liability to arise.

Anticipatory breach of contract by transferee. An interesting question arises **2.160** as to whether an employee can rely on Reg 4(9) or Reg 4(11) to resign prior to the transfer in anticipation of a detrimental change being made to his or her working conditions or a repudiatory breach of contract by the transferee. If so, then it would appear from the Court of Appeal's decision in Humphreys v University of Oxford and anor 2000 ICR 405, CA, that the transferor will be left with residual liability for the dismissal regardless of whether the effective date of termination occurs before or after the transfer. In that case the Court accepted that, although the language of what was then Reg 5(5) was more appropriate to a case where an employee treats him or herself as dismissed after a transfer once a threatened change has become reality, Reg 5(5) had to be interpreted to apply also where the employee objects because a proposed transfer would result in such a change. The Court also ruled that an employee's objection to the transfer of his or her employment to the transferee had the effect of preventing his or her contract of employment from automatically passing to the transferee under what is now Reg 4(1). Instead, the employee's contract with the transferor terminated immediately upon the transfer. And since, in those circumstances, the transferee never becomes his or her employer,

193

the employee had no right to claim against the transferee in respect of the termination. Rather, it is the transferor who is left with residual liability for any unfair dismissal.

There is no reason to suppose that the Court of Appeal's reasoning with regard to the employee's ability to terminate the contract by reason of an anticipatory change to working conditions or a repudiatory breach by the employer would not continue to apply now that the two elements of Reg 5(5) have been separated into two different provisions (i.e. Reg 4(7) and (11)). However, there is greater ground for caution regarding the Court's position on whether it is the transferor or the transferee who is liable for any resulting unfair dismissal. These matters are considered in further detail in Chapter 4, 'Unfair dismissal', under 'Constructive dismissals'.

2.161 **Redundancy payment.** If an employee's objection and subsequent resignation on account of a substantive change being made to his or her contract constitutes an ETO reason that satisfies the statutory definition of 'redundancy', then provided that no suitable alternative employment is available with the transferor, the employee will be redundant and ought to be able to claim a statutory redundancy payment. This position was confirmed by the EAT in Gorictree Ltd v Jenkinson 1985 ICR 51, EAT, and by the wording of Reg 7(3A). In this regard, Reg 7(3)(b) stipulates that where an ETO reason for dismissal is made out, the dismissal will be regarded as having been by reason of redundancy if the statutory test for redundancy as set out in S.98(2)(c) ERA applies, or otherwise for a 'substantial reason of a kind such as to justify the dismissal of an employee holding the position which that employee held' within the meaning of S.98(1)(b) ERA.

2.162 **Limitation on claiming notice pay.** Regulation 4(10) adds a new provision not present in the 1981 Regulations. This specifies that 'no damages shall be payable by an employer as a result of a dismissal falling within paragraph (9) in respect of any failure by the employer to pay wages to an employee in respect of a notice period which the employee has failed to work'. This makes it clear that even where an employee objects to the transfer because it will involve a significant change in working conditions that is materially detrimental (thereby in most cases representing an anticipatory repudiatory breach of contract), no notice pay claim will be possible: the employee is required to work out his or her notice period even though under normal circumstances he or she would be entitled to resign immediately and obtain notice pay as part of any claim. However, since working for the transferor will have to cease on the date of the transfer, a question mark is raised over whether the transferor will be obliged to continue paying the employee for any period of notice that cannot actually be worked owing to the fact that the contract is terminated by the transfer before the notice period expires. What happens if the transferor stops paying the employee? For the same reason, it is also possible that notice pay will be available when a transferor dispenses with the employee's services immediately upon an objection being made, since the employee will again be unable to work out his or her notice period through no fault of his or her own.

Injunctions. The general rule on injunctions is that a court will not force the **2.163** parties to a contract of employment to work together once it has been breached. This is known as the rule against 'specific performance'. However, before the right to object to the automatic transfer of an employee's contract was accepted, the TUPE Regulations had precisely the same effect as an order for specific performance in that they compelled the employees concerned to work for a particular transferee. This naturally raised the question of whether employees could obtain an injunction to prevent the transfer from taking place and thus putting them in that position. In Newns v British Airways plc 1992 IRLR 575, CA, this issue was considered by the Court of Appeal. The Court began by noting that what is now Reg 4 changed the common law position whereby an employer could not transfer an employee to another employer without the employee's consent and instead provided for a statutory novation of the employee's contract. Thus, the effect of Reg 5 was that the transfer of an undertaking no longer constituted a repudiatory breach of contract. As there was no breach, the Court concluded that an employee was not entitled to an injunction to restrain the transfer. It should be noted that this position is subject to the qualification that where the transfer involves a significant change in the employee's working arrangements which is to his or her detriment – such as a change in location where there is no clause in the contract requiring mobility – the transfer will constitute a repudiatory breach enabling the employee to resign and claim constructive dismissal. Whether an injunction to restrain a transfer is available in such circumstances is not clear.

The Court did, however, leave open the possibility that an injunction might be granted where it was demonstrated that the employer had acted – or would act – in breach of the general duty of good faith in transferring the employee. As there are no authorities on the point, it remains to be seen what would constitute a breach of good faith in this context.

Is employee's knowledge of transfer necessary? **2.164**
Regulation 4(1) makes no reference to an employee's knowledge (or otherwise) of a transfer and contains no requirement that notice of the transfer be given to employees. In view of this, there remains some uncertainty as to the interesting question of whether an employee's contract of employment may be transferred along with his or her employer's business without his or her knowledge. Does a lack of knowledge fatally undermine the employee's right to be able to object to the transfer?

This question was first raised in Photostatic Copiers (Southern) Ltd v Okuda and anor 1995 IRLR 11, EAT. In that case the employee claimed not to have received a memorandum from his employer, the transferor, to the effect that a

TUPE transfer was about to occur and his employment would henceforth be transferred to the transferee. The EAT upheld an employment tribunal's decision that the automatic transfer of a contract of employment under what is now Reg 4(1) does not take effect unless the employee is given notice of the transfer and of the identity of the transferee. As a result, the employee remained employed by the transferor until he was dismissed by it after the transfer had occurred.

2.165 Two later decisions of the EAT took the opposite view and, in so doing, expressly declined to follow the Photostatic Copiers decision. In Secretary of State for Trade and Industry v Cook and ors 1997 ICR 288, EAT, the Appeal Tribunal held that the decision in Photostatic Copiers was inconsistent with the purpose of the Acquired Rights Directive and should not be followed in future by tribunals. There was no precondition that a TUPE transfer could only be effective if the employee knew of the transfer and the identity of the transferee. If there were such a requirement, unscrupulous employers would simply refuse to disclose what was happening, the EAT said. Therefore, if it were good law that the Regulations could only have effect if employees have the requisite knowledge, the very protection that the Directive and Regulations are designed to provide would be significantly undermined.

The EAT further took the view that there is no need to import such a precondition into the Regulations. An employee who is misled will not suffer any disadvantage, the EAT said. In relation to an employee dismissed immediately before the transfer, liabilities pass, as a matter of law, to the transferee. In relation to an employee who would have objected to being transferred had he known what was happening, he has lost nothing of value.

2.166 The accuracy of this latter proposition must be doubted. It is not necessarily true that an employee who is transferred without his knowledge, and who would have objected had he or she been aware of the transfer, has lost nothing of value. In many cases there will be a right to object to the transfer and claim compensation although, in the 'exceptional' circumstances where an employee has no knowledge of the transfer, it may well be that he or she retains the right to object for a period of time after the transfer until the new employer's identity does become known – see New ISG Ltd v Vernon 2008 ICR 319, ChD, discussed under 'Timing of objection' above. Nonetheless, a differently constituted EAT took the same view in MRS Environmental Services Ltd v Dyke and anor EAT 93/96. In that case a local authority employed a groundsman whose work was contracted out to a private company. That company later lost the contract, and told the groundsman that his employment would transfer to the new contractor, whose identity it did not know. The contractor, however, did not contact the groundsman, who claimed that he had been unfairly dismissed. The EAT held that, under the 1981 Regulations, statutory novation took effect regardless of whether the parties had consented or knew each other's identities. The earlier decision in Photostatic Copiers (Southern) Ltd v Okuda (above) could not be followed. The groundsman's contract of employment was therefore deemed by what is now Reg 4(1) to have transferred automatically to the new contractor, and he was, under what is now Reg 7(1), to be treated as having been unfairly dismissed. All obligations which the company had owed to him came to an end when the transfer was deemed to have taken place, and the transferor was not therefore liable, liability having passed to the transferee.

The question of the extent to which an employee has to be made aware of a transfer in order to be in a position to object to it arose for consideration in the House of Lords' decision in Celtec Ltd v Astley and ors 2006 ICR 992, HL. Other aspects of this case, including its particular facts, have been extensively discussed earlier in this chapter in the section on 'Requirement to be employed "immediately before" transfer'. In addressing the issue of knowledge of the transfer, their Lordships began by pointing out that the basic proposition that the right to automatic transfer of employment under Article 3(1) of the Directive may not be made subject to the consent of either the transferor or transferee nor of the employees themselves is subject to a single exception. This is that it is open to an employee, whose contract of employment would otherwise be transferred automatically on the date of the transfer, to withdraw from this arrangement by declining to enter the employment of the transferee. Application of that exception depends, first, on the employee being in a position to choose whether or not to enter the employment of the transferee after the date of the transfer and, secondly, on the employee in fact exercising that choice by deciding of his or her own free will not to do so.

2.167 The House of Lords proceeded to hold that the exception did not apply in the instant case because, although the employees were in a position on or after the date of the transfer to choose of their own free will not to work for the transferee, they did not do so. In 1990, the employees had agreed to be seconded from their positions as civil servants with the Department of Education to a newly created Training and Enterprise Council (TEC). In 1993, when given the choice, the particular claimants elected to become employed by the TEC rather than return to work for the DoE. A transfer was found to have occurred back in 1990 when the secondment arrangement was first put in place. On this basis, their Lordships concluded that the claimants' employment had transferred to the TEC at that time because they continued to do the same jobs after the transfer of the undertaking to the TEC, albeit in the belief that they remained in the employment of the Civil Service. In their Lordships' view, the exception to the automatic transfer rule did not work the other way round, so as to give effect to an employee's wish to remain in the employment of the transferor while continuing to be employed in the unit to which he has been assigned after its transfer to the transferee. The inevitable conclusion in the particular case, therefore, was that the claimants' contracts of employment had been transferred automatically to the transferee, with continuity of employment, on the date of the transfer.

There is no doubt that the House of Lords' decision is problematic in some ways, in that it suggests that employees, whom the transfer rules are meant to protect, could find themselves employed by the transferee without even realising it and possibly without their informed consent. In the Celtec case, it was very much in the employees' interests for the House of Lords to hold that they had in fact been transferred, as otherwise they would have lost their accrued employment rights with the transferor. But there could be cases in the future where the application of the principle set out by the House of Lords could work against an employee who in effect finds him or herself working for a new employer without realising that this is the case. It remains to be seen what, if anything, could be done to ameliorate the position of employees in this situation.

2.168 It should be remembered that the TUPE Regulations impose separate obligations to inform and consult about any proposed transfer. Reg 13(2) imposes an obligation to inform and consult representatives of any affected employees about any proposed transfer. Reg 13(10) and (11) provides that where there are no employee representatives to consult, there is a duty to invite elections, and where no such invitation is taken up within a reasonable time, the duty is to provide the relevant information to the affected employees individually. Failure to comply with consultation requirements will result in liability to pay compensation of up to 13 weeks' pay to each employee under Reg 15, and, by virtue of Reg 15(9), transferee and transferor will be jointly and severally liable for the payment of any such compensation (although the transferee may have a remedy against the transferor in respect of any failure to provide adequate 'employee liability information' in advance of the transfer). These provisions are discussed in detail in Chapter 8, 'Information and consultation'.

As a result of these duties, in most cases employees will be aware of an impending transfer, and the problem of some employees potentially losing their right to object will not therefore arise. It might be argued that a complete failure to inform and consult by the transferor amounts to a breach of mutual trust and confidence, which would entitle the employee who would otherwise have objected to resign and claim constructive dismissal against the transferee (the liability arguably created by the transferor's breach having been transferred by operation of Reg 4(2)). This situation would press transferees to require indemnities against any such liability, which in turn would effectively pass liability back to the transferor for its failure.

2.169 ## Employees retained by transferor

Subject to the right to object to the transfer (see 'Objecting to transfer' above), the contract of any person employed in and assigned to the undertaking at the moment of its transfer automatically passes over to the transferee under Reg 4(1). However, where the transferor and the transferee agree that certain

198

staff employed in the undertaking to be transferred are to remain in the employment of the transferor, the question arises as to whether Reg 4(1) still applies to transfer the contracts of those employees. The general view that has emerged from the cases (although they are not consistent) is that the application of Reg 4(1) can only be avoided where there is also a contractual arrangement to that effect between the transferor and the employees concerned before the transfer takes place.

The cases below (all of which were decided under the 1981 Regulations) **2.170** illustrate the different ways in which the courts have tackled the issue of whether the employment of an employee retained by the transferor after a relevant transfer is automatically transferred to the transferee:

- **Direct Radiators Ltd v Howse and anor** EAT 130/86: H was employed by S as a bookkeeper in S's business. That business was sold to D Ltd on 28 February 1985. Before the transfer, D Ltd had made it clear that it did not require H's services. S retained H from 28 February to 5 April 1985 to help with clerical and bookkeeping work relevant to the collection of outstanding business debts owed to him. She was then dismissed and claimed a redundancy payment from D Ltd. A tribunal upheld her claim, finding that the transferee, D Ltd, had become H's contractual employer liable in respect of her contract by virtue of Reg 5(1) TUPE 1981. As a result, it was liable to pay H a redundancy payment. On appeal to the EAT, D Ltd argued that Reg 5 could not apply because H had been retained after the transfer under a contract of employment with S and, therefore, she was not at the time of the transfer working under a contract that 'would otherwise have been terminated' by reason of the transfer for the purposes of Reg 5(1). The EAT accepted that if the relationship between S and H after February 28 was a contractual one, then D Ltd's argument was well founded. However, the tribunal had failed to make a clear finding as to whether H was still working for S under an employment contract after the transfer and so remitted the case for determination on that point

- **Visionhire Consumer Electronics Ltd t/a Visionhire v Easton** EAT 20/87: an employee was offered a new contract with the transferee which was to take effect a week after the transfer. In the meantime, the employee continued working for the transferor. The EAT rejected the transferee's argument that, because the employee had been retained by the transferor, Reg 5 did not effect the automatic transfer of his employment contract since it was not one which would 'otherwise have been terminated by the transfer'. Mr Justice Popplewell commented that: 'Apart from the fact that [the transferee's argument] would, in the view of the industrial members, cause immense difficulty as a matter of practice in industry and lead to grave disadvantages for the workforce, it does not in our view accord with what Reg 5 says...

199

If it is intended to retain part of the staff after a transfer then that would have to be done by a novation of contract between the transferor and the employee before the transfer'

- **A and G Tuck Ltd and anor v Bartlett** 1994 ICR 379, EAT: B had worked as a production manager for S since 1966. In 1983 S took over another company, H. From 1989 onwards, B worked for both companies but remained an employee of S throughout. On 10 August 1992, B discovered that S had been sold to C while he was on holiday. B's name was not on the list of employees who were transferred to C, but his employer asked him to assist C in the running of S for two weeks, which he did. On 12 August C invited B to work for him; an arrangement that S supported. C subsequently dismissed B and he complained that his dismissal was unfair. The EAT rejected the argument that Reg 5(1) applied to transfer B's contract to the transferee on the basis that, because B was kept on by the transferor, he was not in the position where his contract 'would otherwise have been terminated by the transfer'.

2.171 In reality, the claimant in the last-mentioned case did transfer to the transferee, even though he was not recognised as being formally employed by it until two weeks after the transfer. The ruling that the automatic transfer of employment rule did not apply in his case in fact made little difference given that his dismissal occurred within a sufficiently short period of the transfer date such that his continuity of employment remained intact. However, given that there was no express novation of the employee's contract with the transferor, that he did go to work for the transferee, and that the relevant transfer happened without his knowledge, one wonders whether the same conclusion that the employee's employment did not automatically transfer to the transferee would be reached were a case on similar facts to arise now. It could be argued that this is precisely the kind of situation in which the TUPE Regulations were intended to intervene and transfer the contract of employment automatically. In finding otherwise, the EAT's judgment would appear to be inconsistent with the House of Lords' decision in Celtec Ltd v Astley and ors 2006 ICR 992, HL (discussed under 'Objecting to transfer – is employee's knowledge of transfer necessary?' above) – and particularly the view expressed in that case that it is not open to an employee to go to work for the transferee and yet argue that he or she remains employed by the transferor once the transfer takes place.

It is submitted that, in general, the analysis of the EAT in Sunley Turriff Holdings Ltd v Thomson and ors 1995 IRLR 184, EAT, is the best way of approaching the operation of Reg 4(1) in a case where an employee is retained by the transferor after the transfer. The Appeal Tribunal concluded that the operation of the 'automatic transfer of employment' rule could only be avoided in such a situation by an express agreement with the employees concerned provided that at the time of such an agreement this was seen as being to the

200

employees' advantage (see 'Contracts "otherwise terminated by" transfer – contracts to which Reg 4(1) might not apply' above).

In the Sunley Turriff Holdings Ltd case, T was employed by LC to work as **2.172** company secretary and chief accountant of LC and LC(S), two subsidiaries of a group. Receivers were appointed to the group, who sold LC(S) to STH. T was not included in the list of employees to be transferred to STH; he was told that he was to remain employed by LC. T continued to work for the receivers until they made him redundant shortly after the transfer. T claimed a redundancy payment from STH, the transferee, on the basis that he was employed in the undertaking which had been transferred to it. The tribunal found that there had been a transfer to which the Regulations applied and that T was employed in the part transferred, but STH appealed to the EAT against that finding. STH argued that T's employment had not automatically transferred to it because his employment with LC had continued after the date of the transfer. The EAT decided that if an employee continues to work for a transferor after a transfer which, under the Regulations, legally has the effect of transferring his or her employment to the transferee, then that continued employment must be as a result of a new agreement, or a variation of the previous agreement, between the transferor and the employee. While there was a great deal of uncertainty about T's position, Reg 5, in the EAT's view, was imperative in its terms and must apply whatever misunderstandings there may have been. The EAT considered that it would be contrary to the objectives of the Regulations to allow uncertainty to prejudice the position of employees to whom they applied. The receivers had been mistaken in their view that T's contract continued with LC and the EAT upheld the tribunal's finding that T had done nothing which might suggest that he had agreed to continue in the employment of LC. T, therefore, succeeded in his claim against STH.

In reaching its conclusion, the EAT considered the decision in Direct Radiators Ltd v House and anor (above) and commented that that case must have been decided on the assumption that something had occurred following the transfer to terminate the employment with the transferee brought about by the Regulations and to bring into existence the new employment with the transferor. On this basis, the EAT reasoned that its decision in the instant case was not inconsistent with the decision in Direct Radiators.

The Sunley Turriff case makes it clear that a mistaken belief that the Regulations **2.173** do not apply to a particular employee cannot defeat the principle of the automatic transfer of contracts of employment under the Regulations. The EAT also stated that there may be circumstances in which it would be possible to infer that an employee who continues in the transferor's employment may be taken to have agreed to do so. However, it seems that when there is

201

confusion or misunderstanding, the employee who continues to work for the transferor is unlikely to jeopardise his or her position in relation to the application of the Regulations.

2.174 Problems of secondment arrangements

The decision of the House of Lords in Celtec Ltd v Astley and ors 2006 ICR 992, HL, has been extensively discussed elsewhere in this chapter. However, its implications for the continued use of secondment arrangements have yet to be analysed in any depth. Such arrangements are especially widely used by public sector employers as part of the Public Finance Initiative (PFI) under which public services are outsourced to private sector contractors. So, for example, under the 'Retention of Employment model' (RoE) deployed across the National Health Service following any outsourcing of cleaning, catering, laundry, portering and security services, NHS employees are seconded to incoming private contractor firms. This is to ensure that they retain their favourable terms, including membership of the NHS Pension Scheme and access to NHS pay scales. Indeed, it is the retention of public sector pay and pension rights that is usually the main driver behind such arrangements. Although the application of the RoE in theory only applies to the NHS, similar arrangements have been applied elsewhere in the public sector where PFI is used to effect the contracting out of public services. Although secondment is not as prevalent in the private sector, it is sometimes used – particularly with regard to professional and managerial staff.

The Celtec case concerned employees employed by the Civil Service who were seconded in September 1990 to work for a new enterprise council, which later became Celtec Ltd (C Ltd), in order to provide vocational training on behalf of the Department of Education. In July 1993, the claimants were given the choice between continuing to work for the DoE or becoming employed by C Ltd. They chose the latter option, although many of their colleagues chose the former. It was later accepted that a relevant transfer of the DoE's training service to C Ltd had occurred at some point but it was not clear precisely when. A majority of the House of Lords ruled that the relevant date was September 1990, when the claimants had first been seconded, and not, as the parties had assumed, 1 July 1993, when the claimants had elected to enter the employ of C Ltd. This meant that the employment of employees (including the claimant) had been transferred automatically to C Ltd back in September 1990 even though they, the DoE and C Ltd were all oblivious of this at the time.

2.175 The House of Lords' ruling creates considerable difficulties for all those who utilise secondment arrangements of the kind described above. This is because the entire strategy underpinning these arrangements is to prevent what is now Reg 4 from applying to transfer the contracts of employees to the recipient of the employees' services following the outsourcing of the service in question. As we have seen in Chapter 1, 'Identifying a "relevant transfer"', under 'Service provision changes', the 2006 Regulations introduced a new definition of 'relevant transfer' that makes it far more likely that a change of service provider will constitute a transfer to which the Regulations apply. And as the Celtec case makes clear, the 'automatic transfer of employment' is likely to apply to all employees who happen to be assigned to the 'organised grouping of employees' supplying the service on the date when the change of service provider occurs regardless of their expectations or wishes in the matter. This means that their employment with the transferor will cease and they will become employed by the transferee. If that happens in a secondment context, the seconded employees will no longer be eligible for membership of their former employer's pension scheme.

The objection route   2.176

The question arises whether it will be possible for arrangements such as the NHS RoE to survive the decision in Celtec Ltd v Astley and ors (discussed above). It might be thought that the most obvious way around the problem is that, just prior to a change of service provider, employees formally object to the transfer to ensure that Reg 4(1) does not operate to transfer their employment to the incoming contractor. Indeed, that is the tactic currently deployed by the RoE. The difficulty, however, is that the act of actually going to work for the transferee is, according to Lord Hope (one of the Lords who made up the majority decision in Celtec), completely incompatible with the suggestion that the employee has objected to the transfer. His Lordship emphasised that the sole reservation to the operation of the automatic transfer of employment rule is where the employee objects to the transfer. In this regard, 'it is a fundamental right of the employee to be free to choose his employer. So he cannot be obliged to work for an employer whom he has not freely chosen: Katsikas v Konstantinidis 1993 IRLR 179, ECJ, para 32. From this it follows that it is open to an employee whose contract of employment would otherwise be transferred automatically from the transferor to the transferee on the date of the transfer of his own free will to withdraw from this arrangement by declining to enter the employment of the transferee... That, then, is the extent of the sole reservation... It does not... work the other way round. It does not enable effect to be given to an employee's wish to continue to be employed by the transferor while continuing to be employed in the unit to which he has been assigned after its transfer to the transferee. But the application of the rule that he can withdraw from the arrangement depends on two things: first, that the employee is in a position to choose whether or not to enter the employment of the transferee after the date of the transfer; and second, that he in fact exercises that choice by deciding of his own free will not to do so.'

Assuming Lord Hope's analysis to be correct, it will be seen that the 'objection route' cannot therefore be relied upon in a secondment situation even if, unlike the claimants in the Celtec case, all the parties were fully cognisant of the fact

203

of the transfer and of the date it occurred. Effective objection to the transfer simply cannot go hand in hand with the subsequent act of working for the transferee (see also the recent case of Capita Health Solutions Ltd v McLean and anor 2008 IRLR 595, EAT – discussed under 'Objecting to transfer – timing of objection' above – which supports Lord Hope's view).

2.177 One of the major implications of this is that the seconded employee will risk incurring a break in his or her continuity of employment once the secondment arrangement is concluded and he or she returns to working for the transferor. This can be seen from the particular facts of the Celtec case. As it turned out, the majority's decision worked out well for the particular claimants in that case: they had argued that they had continuous employment with C Ltd dating back to at least 1993. In the event, they were handed a windfall when the House of Lords ruled that their continuity stretched as far back as September 1990 when the relevant transfer was found to have occurred on the basis that that was when the secondment agreement was first put in place. The problem, however, is that what was true of the claimants must, in all logic, have been equally true of the large number of employees who elected in July 1993 not to become employees of C Ltd and instead to return to work for the DoE. Since the transfer of their employment would presumably have likewise occurred in September 1990, they, like the claimants, would have ceased to be employed by the DoE from that date and instead have become employed by C Ltd. This meant that the legal effect of their election in July 1993 was not so much that they *continued working* for the DoE as that they *entered into new employment* with it three years after they had ceased to be employed as civil servants and had become employed by C Ltd. Since no relevant transfer was found to have occurred in July 1993 to transfer C Ltd's undertaking back to the DoE, the employees' continuity of employment with C Ltd must be judged to have broken and begun afresh with the DoE. This is so even though the employees in question were under the impression that they had remained employed by the DoE all along.

Perhaps the solution lies along the lines of the decision in New ISG Ltd v Vernon 2008 ICR 319, ChD, where the High Court adopted a pragmatic approach towards whether an employee had objected to the transfer within the terms of Reg 4(7). The Vernon case has been discussed in detail under 'Objecting to transfer – timing of objection' above. In that case the High Court held that an employee who had not been informed of the change in the identity of his employer had not been accorded a valid opportunity to object to the transfer. Accordingly, his action in working for the transferee for a couple of days until he was actually informed of the transfer did not preclude him making an objection at that point. While it is true that this scenario is very different from that in Celtec, it may well be that tribunals will be keen to adopt a similarly pragmatic approach to any case where an employee, through no fault of his or her own, would otherwise be denied the freedom of choice implicit in the 'objection provision' of Reg 4(7).

The Reg 4(1) route   2.178

Such are the practical and legal difficulties that the decision in Celtec Ltd v
Astley and ors (above) may cause when secondment arrangements are caught
up in a TUPE transfer. Is there anything that can help the parties to such
arrangements to ensure that seconded employees remain employed by the
transferor? A possible solution would be for the parties to rely heavily on the
words 'which would not otherwise have been terminated by the transfer' in
Reg 4(1). We have seen in the section on 'Contracts "otherwise terminated by"
transfer' above that this wording appears to preclude the application of the
automatic transfer of employment rule to any contract of employment that
would not, at common law, have been terminated automatically by reason of
the transfer. Although the precise scope of this qualification is not clear, it might
be that it would be found to extend to secondment arrangements based on the
rationale explained in the examples given below:

- *Example 1*: if the secondment is time-limited to achieve a particular objective,
it may be argued that such arrangements are not TUPE transfers within the
meaning of Reg 3(1) but are new and specific contractual arrangements that
lie outside the contract of employment. Since the intention of the parties
entering into such arrangements is for the employee to return to the seconder
in due course, it might be argued that the resulting contractual relations are
not caught by the automatic transfer of contracts of employees employed
immediately before the transfer under Reg 4(1)

- *Example 2*: If the parties to a relevant transfer have agreed in advance
that employees will continue to be employed by the transferor but will
be seconded to work for the transferee, then so long as the employees in
question enter into such an arrangement of their own free will, they might
arguably be taken to be employed on contracts that would not otherwise
terminate as a result of the transfer. So if, by way of example, employees of
a local authority are seconded to an NHS body, the local authority would
have to retain responsibility for all the services to which the employees are
assigned. If the authority retains overall managerial control and ensures
that the employees owe their duties to the seconder, rather than to the host
directly, the secondment is likely to be held to be genuine.

It is true – as we have seen in the discussion on 'Employees retained by   2.179
transferor' above – that this analysis has not tended to find much favour in the
few appellate cases where the words 'would not otherwise have terminated'
have come under scrutiny. But none of those have dealt with the situation where
there is a formal secondment agreement of the kind used in the public sector.
It may well have been considerations of this kind that induced the Government
to retain the wording in the new version of TUPE, having originally disclosed
its intention to remove it.

205

3 What transfers?

3.1 The primary value of any business often lies not in its tangible assets but in its goodwill, intellectual property and contacts with clients or customers. Most transfers of undertakings will entail the transfer of these intangible assets. But any purchase of an economic entity will also involve the acquisition by the transferee of 'hidden' rights and liabilities, particularly given that, by virtue of Reg 4 of the Transfer of Undertakings (Protection of Employment) Regulations 2006 SI 2006/246 (TUPE) the transferee will acquire not only the staff assigned to the entity transferred – as we discussed in Chapter 2, 'Who transfers?' – but various rights, powers, duties and liabilities that go with those employees and their contracts of employment.

'Automatic transfer' principle – overview

3.2 Regulation 4(2) of the TUPE Regulations states that on the completion of a relevant transfer:

207

- all the transferor's rights, powers, duties and liabilities under or in connection with any such contract shall be transferred to the transferee – Reg 4(2)(a), and

- any act or omission before the transfer is completed, of or in relation to the transferor in respect of that contract or a person assigned to that organised grouping of resources or employees, shall be deemed to have been an act or omission of or in relation to the transferee – Reg 4(2)(b).

These provisions are subject to a number of other regulations which qualify their impact – see 'Rights and liabilities that do not transfer' below.

3.3 It is important to note that the two limbs of Reg 4 are distinct. This was stressed by the EAT in Perry's Motor Sales Ltd and anor v Lindley EAT 0616/07 (discussed in detail under 'Individual statutory rights' below). In that case, the EAT held that liability for a dismissal rendered unfair by virtue of S.104 of the Employment Rights Act 1996 (enforcement of a statutory right) could crystallise on the transfer and become a liability transferred to the transferee by virtue of Reg 4(2)(b) even though it was not a liability that transferred under Reg 4(2)(a).

3.4 **Ignorance no excuse**
Ignorance of the duties or liabilities that attach to a contract, or of any relevant acts or omissions of the transferor, will not prevent Reg 4(2) applying. Article 3(2) of the EU Acquired Rights Directive (No.2001/23) ('the Acquired Rights Directive') makes this clear: 'A failure by the transferor to notify the transferee of any such right or obligation shall not affect the transfer of that right or obligation and the rights of any employees against the transferee and/or transferor in respect of that right or obligation.' Indeed, employment rights and obligations transfer irrespective of the wishes of the parties – Rotsart de Hertaing v J Benoidt SA (in liquidation) and anor 1997 IRLR 127, ECJ, and Celtec Ltd v Astley and ors 2005 ICR 1409, ECJ (and even if the employees themselves are unaware of the fact of the transfer or of the identity of the transferee – Secretary of State for Trade and Industry v Cook and ors 1997 ICR 288, EAT). It is therefore vital for transferees to carry out careful and comprehensive due diligence when acquiring an undertaking. Contracts of employment do not, as we shall see, contain a comprehensive list of the various employee-related duties and liabilities with which the transferee is likely to be encumbered.

It was in order to help address this issue that there is an obligation on the transferor to notify the transferee of certain 'employee liability information' – Reg 11. This limited statutory list includes basic information about the employees; the information contained in their particulars of employment; information about relevant collective agreements; and information about disciplinary action, grievances or legal action from the last two years before the

208

date of the transfer. This obligation is dicussed in detail in Chapter 8, 'Information and consultation', under 'Employee liability information'. What is important to note here is that the statutory obligation provides the transferee with basic protection only. Employees are likely to benefit from more extensive contractual benefits than would be contained in their statutory particulars of employment, and the fact that a right of action arose more than two years ago does not necessarily mean that it will not be actionable now. Therefore, irrespective of the statutory protections, transferees should conduct full due diligence and require relevant warranties and indemnities to be included in the acquisition documentation – see Chapter 11, 'Practical aspects of transfers', for practical advice in this regard.

Note that Reg 4(2)(a) refers to the rights, powers, duties and liabilities *of the* **3.5** *transferor* under the employment contract. In discussing the implications of employment contracts transferring to the transferee, it is common to think more in terms of the rights of *employees* under the contract, particularly given that the aim of the Regulations is to preserve employees' rights. The point is, to a degree, academic, as an employee's right is the counterpart to an employer's liability. But it is important, for the purposes of understanding how Reg 4(2)(a) applies, to be aware of the actual wording. For further discussion of this point, see 'Acts or omissions committed before transfer' below.

Transfer principle applies only to existing rights/liabilities   **3.6**
The effect of Reg 4(2) is to protect the rights of employees *as they exist at the time of the transfer.* (For discussion as to when a transfer is likely to have taken place, see Chapter 1, 'Identifying a "relevant transfer"', under 'When does transfer occur?') It does not create or augment rights. Two cases demonstrating this:

- **Computershare Investor Services plc v Jackson** 2008 ICR 341, CA: in 1999 J started work with a bank that did not have a severance pay scheme. She transferred to CIS plc in 2004. CIS plc had a severance pay scheme, the terms of which differed depending on whether the employee 'joined' before or after 2002. When J was made redundant in 2005 she was treated as having length of service extending back to 1999, but it was the terms of the post-2002 joiner scheme that were applied to her. An employment tribunal found that she should have been entitled to benefit from the pre-2002 joiner scheme but that decision was overturned by the EAT and, on further appeal, the Court of Appeal held that the EAT's decision was correct. Lord Justice Mummery noted that the object of the Acquired Rights Directive was to ensure that employees' rights are safeguarded in the event of a transfer rather than to improve on existing rights – Viggósdóttir v Íslandspóstur HF 2002 IRLR 425, ECJ. On this basis, the effect of what is now Reg 4(1) is not to give a transferred employee access to employment benefits other than those to which the employee was entitled before the transfer of the undertaking. In the instant case, the fact that the claimant's employer calculated her severance pay on the basis of her deemed continuity of service from 1999 was irrelevant to the question of whether she was a post-2002 entrant within the meaning of the employer's enhanced severance terms. That question was determined by the date when, as a fact, she joined the employer's employment. It was not possible to make artificial use of the TUPE Regulations for the purpose of interpreting the employer's contract for enhanced severance pay in a way which displaced the correct finding of fact that J began work for the transferee in 2004 or which miraculously transformed her from being a post-2002 new entrant into a pre-2002 entrant

- **Werhof v Freeway Traffic Systems GmbH and Co KG** 2006 IRLR 400, ECJ: W was employed by Siemens in Germany under a contract of employment that was governed by a collective agreement and wage agreement negotiated between the trade union for the industry and the employers' association of which Siemens was a member. On 1 October 1999 Siemens transferred the part of its business in which W worked to FTS. FTS was not a member of any employers' association that concluded collective agreements. In May 2003 the trade union and the employers' association concluded a new collective agreement that provided for an increase in the wage rate and an additional payment. W commenced proceedings against FTS claiming the difference between his basic salary and the sum provided for in the new collective agreement, plus the additional payment. The German court asked the ECJ whether a transferee who inherits a collective agreement but was not an original party to it is bound by collective agreements subsequent to the one in force at the time of the transfer. The ECJ noted that under the Directive the rights and obligations arising from the collective agreement are automatically transferred to the new employer even though the latter is not a party to it. However, the ECJ stated, the Directive's objective is merely to safeguard rights and obligations in force on the day of the transfer. Article 3(3) makes it clear that the terms and conditions of the collective agreement in force at the time of transfer are to continue to be observed only until the date of its termination or expiry, or the entry into force or application of another collective agreement. This wording does not indicate that the Community legislature intended the transferee to be bound by collective agreements other than the one in force at the time of the transfer. FTS was, therefore, not liable for the additional payments.

3.7 The principle established by the above cases was applied by the EAT in Small and ors v Boots Co plc 2009 IRLR 328, EAT, when rejecting the claimants' claim to be entitled to backdated payment of bonuses from the transferee relating to the period when they were employed by the transferor. The EAT upheld the employment judge's finding that as no such contractual entitlement to the bonus payments accrued pre-transfer, there could be no question of the transferee being or becoming liable to pay the bonuses claimed.

210

The principle was also confirmed in a case where employees were seeking payments out of the National Insurance Fund following the transferor's insolvency. In Secretary of State for Business, Innovation and Skills v Dobrucki and ors EAT 0505/13 the EAT ruled that only those debts that had accrued before or coincident with the transfer remained the liability of the transferor, and it was these and only these that were therefore abrogated to the Secretary of State in accordance with the statutory regime for payments out of the Fund under Part XII of the ERA. It followed that the Secretary of State, as he had acknowledged, was liable for the arrears of pay up to and until the date of the transfer but not thereafter. As for notice pay and statutory redundancy payments, the Secretary of State was not liable at all for these since they had not accrued by the date of the transfer. In so far as any such sums were payable to the employees, it was the transferee who was liable to pay them.

It is clear, therefore, that the TUPE Regulations cannot be used to improve upon existing rights; but neither may such rights be diluted as a consequence of a relevant transfer. It is ironic that, as a result of the 'non-dilution' principle, transferring employees seem to acquire an extra degree of protection – a quasi-statutory assurance that their contracts cannot be varied – which they would not have had in the absence of the transfer, or had the transfer fallen outside TUPE's protection: see Chapter 5, 'Changing terms and conditions', under 'Varying terms in a TUPE context', for further discussion.

Only parties to transfer caught by automatic transfer principle 3.8

As the cases above demonstrate (see 'Transfer principle applies only to existing rights and liabilities'), a broad range of rights and obligations are capable of being transferred upon a relevant transfer – including both those that attach to the individual employee and those that are collectively negotiated (although there is inevitably some crossover between the two). However, Article 3 of the Acquired Rights Directive has its limits. In Kirtruna SL and anor v Red Elite de Electrodomésticos SA and ors 2008 ECR I-7907, ECJ, the European Court held that Article 3 did not transfer the lease of commercial premises entered into by the transferor with a third party, even though the termination of the lease was likely to entail the termination of transferred contracts of employment. The Court read Article 3(1) as only applying to the relationship between employer and employee and held that the Directive could not be allowed to affect the rights of third parties unconnected with the transfer by imposing on them an obligation not clearly provided for in the Directive.

The ECJ's reluctance to encumber third parties with the legal effects of a transfer would appear to place an appropriate limitation on the scope of the Directive. However, in Martin v Lancashire County Council and another case 2001 ICR 197, CA – discussed under 'Tortious and other civil liabilities' below – the Court of Appeal held that not only did the transferor's liability for personal injury sustained by a transferred employee pass to the transferee, but so did the transferor's vested or contingent right to an indemnity under its employer's liability insurance policy. This meant that the insurer would be obliged to cover the transferee's liability for damages to the injured employee (subject to the policy's usual limitations). This aspect of the decision contrasts with the ECJ's unwillingness, in Kirtruna, to extend the effects of a TUPE transfer to third parties. The Court of Appeal reasoned that the transfer of the employer's right to an indemnity was within the purpose and wording of TUPE. Although the right to an indemnity arose under the contract of insurance, it was a right connected to or arising from the contract of employment. Lord Justice Clarke expressly declined to construe TUPE as being limited to the transfer of rights and liabilities as between the employee and the transferor.

3.9 Contractual rights and liabilities

The most obvious sets of rights and liabilities that transfer on the completion of the relevant transfer are those pertaining to the transferred employee's contract of employment. Indeed, express reference is made to the contract of employment in Reg 4(2) TUPE, which speaks of 'all the transferor's rights, powers, duties and liabilities under or in connection with any *such contract*' (our stress). 'Such contract' is a reference back to Reg 4(1), which stipulates that 'a relevant transfer shall not operate so as to terminate *the contract of employment* of any person employed by the transferor and assigned to the organised grouping of resources or employees that is subject to the... transfer'.

3.10 Express and implied terms

Although, as we shall see later in this chapter, Reg 4(2) is apt to transfer even non-contractual rights and benefits (such as statutory rights and tortious liabilities), the most immediately apparent rights and liabilities that transfer are those contained by way of *express* terms in an employee's contract of employment. These may include, for example:

- job title and function

- place of work

- hours of work

- salary

- holiday entitlement

- enhanced contractual sick leave and pay

- enhanced contractual maternity leave and pay

- length of contract (where it is fixed-term)

- notice provisions.

212

Note that express terms may have been agreed orally between the parties, although to some extent these should be recorded in the employee's statutory statement of particulars of employment. Orally agreed terms are no less valid than written terms and are capable of transfer in the same way. But even the most obvious contractual terms may have hidden implications for the recipient transferee. Take the following examples:

- *job title or description* – these may not always be contractual but are likely to be so, especially where an employee is relatively senior. Where an undertaking's day-to-day activities are little affected by the transfer and an employee is of lower-than-managerial status, there should be no difficulty in his or her retaining a pre-transfer title or description. However, employees of executive or managerial level may be required to slot into a new management structure upon transfer and thereby sacrifice their pre-transfer designation or function. This is permissible by virtue of Reg 4(5) if it is for an economic, technical or organisational reason entailing changes in the workforce or if the terms of the contract permit the variation in question, but not otherwise – see Chapter 5, 'Changing terms and conditions'

- *length of notice period* – senior employees will often seek to protect their position by insisting upon a substantial notice period. Where such rights have been renegotiated with the transfer in mind, they are likely to be void under Reg 4(4). This provides that any purported variation of a contract of employment that is to be transferred is void if the sole or principal reason for the variation is the relevant transfer or a reason connected with the transfer that is not an economic, technical or organisational reason entailing changes in the workforce. However, where this is not the case the notice period, however long, will continue to apply after the transfer. Transferees should therefore look out for onerous notice rights in the course of their pre-transfer due diligence.

Of course, a contract is not limited to its express terms. Other types of contractual term include: **3.11**

- *implied terms* – terms that are not spelt out in so many words but which parties are taken to have agreed either because they are too obvious to need recording, or because they are part of the custom and practice of the business or industry, or because they can be logically deduced from the conduct of the parties. Terms may also be implied if they are necessary to give 'business efficacy' to the agreement as a whole

- *incorporated terms* – terms that are incorporated into individual contracts from other sources such as collective agreements or works rules

- *statutory terms* – terms that are derived from provisions contained in statutes affecting the employment relationship, such as the insertion by the

Equality Act 2010 of a 'sex equality clause' into every individual contract of employment.

Terms falling within any of the above categories are, with certain caveats, capable of transferring to the transferee under Reg 4(2).

3.12 In CSC Computer Sciences Ltd v McAlinden 2013 EWCA Civ 1435, CA, the Court of Appeal accepted that, where an employer's words and conduct convey to employees that a benefit is a contractual right then that benefit may become contractual through 'custom and practice', and entitlement to that benefit may thus transfer under Reg 4(2). This is the case even where, on close analysis, the employer is mistaken that supply of the benefit is a contractual obligation. What matters is the effect of the employer's communication, viewed objectively – the employer's subjective understanding of the legal position is irrelevant. Thus, on the facts of the case, the fact that the transferee was mistaken in its belief that, in awarding inflation-linked pay increases for seven years following the transfer, it was acting in accordance with an existing legal obligation arising from custom and practice that pre-dated the transfer, did not prevent a right to such pay increases crystallising in the contract. The employer's consistent payment of RPI annual increases in prior years and, crucially, its consistent message to employees that they were contractually entitled to such increases, meant that, objectively viewed, it had given the impression of conforming with a legal obligation.

Normal contractual principles apply to determine the precise nature of what transfers. In Learning and Skills Council v Barfoot and ors EAT 0621/03, for example, the London East Technical and Enterprise Council (LETEC) established a contractual bonus scheme for some of its employees in September 1998. LETEC sent letters to the employees setting out the terms of the new scheme and stating that the 'bonus structure' would cease at the end of 2000. In June 2000, a further letter was sent indicating the level of bonuses for the period 1 April 2000 to 31 March 2001. On 26 March 2001, the Learning and Skills Council (LSC) acquired the employees upon a TUPE transfer. It decided not to reintroduce a contractual bonus scheme, and paid bonuses to the employees on a discretionary basis. The employees brought claims for unauthorised deductions from wages, alleging that they had not been paid the bonuses to which they were contractually entitled. On the evidence, the employment tribunal found that although the contractual bonus scheme ceased at the end of 2000, a contractual obligation to pay a bonus after that remained. The EAT, however, allowed LSC's appeal. It held that 'contractual documents should be given the meaning which the documents would convey to a reasonable man having all the background knowledge which would reasonably have been available to the parties in the situation in which they were at the time of the contract'. No such reasonable observer, having given the letter mature thought and having all the background knowledge available to the parties at the time, would have thought that it meant that, although the terms of the bonus scheme which was then being established would cease at the end of 2000, the employees' entitlement to a contractual bonus under some other bonus structure would continue indefinitely. The EAT remitted the claim to a fresh tribunal for reconsideration.

For a detailed discussion of contractual terms, see IDS Employment Law **3.13** Handbook, 'Contracts of Employment' (2014), Chapter 3, 'Contractual terms', and Chapter 5, 'Incorporated terms'.

Enhanced redundancy schemes **3.14**

There have been a number of decisions on the question of whether enhanced redundancy schemes transfer under TUPE. The answer largely depends upon whether the terms of such schemes are contractual in nature. If so, then they will transfer along with other contractual terms under Reg 4(2)(a). For a general discussion of whether, and to what extent, enhanced redundancy schemes have contractual status, see IDS Employment Law Handbook, 'Redundancy' (2011), Chapter 6, 'Redundancy payments', under 'Enhanced redundancy pay – entitlement to enhanced redundancy pay'.

The obligation to pay enhanced redundancy compensation was specifically held to transfer to the transferee in Bousted v Reliance Security Services Ltd ET Case No.1701352/07. There, B worked for a series of companies as a security and fire safety officer from 1983 and his employment was transferred under TUPE on a number of occasions. His previous employers had made several redundancies in the past and on each occasion the same enhanced redundancy payments were automatically made. The terms of these were published on company notice boards even though they were referred to as 'ex-gratia' payments in severance documents. However, in B's case, the transferee refused to honour the terms of the enhanced redundancy scheme that had been operated by his previous employer. An employment tribunal held that B was entitled to the enhanced terms of severance although they had not been expressly incorporated into his contract of employment or referred to in the staff handbook. The tribunal took account of the fact that the ex-gratia payments had been published by the transferor and had, without exception, been automatically paid to clerical staff made redundant in the past.

In contrast, in Jefferies v Powerhouse Retail Ltd EAT 1328/95 the claimant failed **3.15** in a claim brought against a transferee based on the contention that she was entitled to the same or similar redundancy pay-outs that had been made to other employees by the transferor on two previous occasions. The EAT accepted the employment tribunal's finding that the termination packages agreed had been formulated with the unions and had been tailored to the particular circumstances of the redundancy situations that had arisen on those two previous occasions. The claimant was not therefore contractually entitled to the same package.

215

Where an enhanced scheme does transfer, what happens if the transferee is forced to amend it because it is not legally compliant? This was the situation in Corrie v Exel Europe ET Case No.1202589/07, where the transferor's scheme provided that employees with at least ten years' service would receive redundancy compensation based solely on their age – 26 weeks' pay for those under 31, rising to 104 weeks for those aged 50 and then reducing by five weeks each year up to the age of 62. The transferee sought to amend these provisions to ensure compliance with age discrimination legislation and to harmonise all terms across its group of companies. The claimant's union protested against this purported variation, arguing that the scheme was protected by TUPE and could not be amended to the detriment of transferred employees. An employment tribunal held that the scheme was non-contractual but that, even if it had been, its original terms were unlawfully discriminatory. Accordingly, the employee's claim for enhanced redundancy compensation was dismissed.

3.16 Non-contractual working arrangements

It has sometimes been assumed that if there is no contractual basis to a particular term, then it will not transfer – unless it can be argued that a refusal to provide it constitutes a breach of an implied contractual term, such as the duty to maintain the employee's trust and confidence. For example, in London Borough of Newham v Smith and anor EAT 1345/00 the EAT had to consider whether working arrangements that the transferring employees had had with the London Borough of Waltham Forest passed to the London Borough of Newham upon a relevant transfer. The EAT said this: 'The tribunal firstly and primarily had to decide... whether the working arrangements operated by Waltham Forest which we have described were embodied into the contracts of employment of the employees at the time of the transfer. If they were, the effect of Reg 5 [now Reg 4] would have been to transfer the contractual obligations of the transferor, Waltham Forest, in respect of those arrangements to the transferee, Newham. If they were not, then no obligations in respect of those arrangements existed and there was nothing in respect of those arrangements which could be transferred by way of contractual obligation to Newham.' On the facts of the case, a system under which employees could be called out for emergency work outside normal working hours was found to be non-contractual, and therefore 'in respect of those arrangements, no obligations passed to Newham', but a system whereby employees were allowed free use of the employer's vans for travelling to and from work was a contractual arrangement, which Newham was, therefore, obliged to uphold.

Note, too, the decision of the EAT in Jefferies v Powerhouse Retail Ltd EAT 1328/95, upholding an employment tribunal's conclusion that, since certain enhanced redundancy terms were not incorporated into the claimant's contract, 'those terms cannot have transferred under [the 1981 Regulations] when the transfer took place'.

However, there are problems with this approach. The wording of Reg 4(2) is not **3.17** limited to matters arising from the contract of employment. Reg 4(2)(a) provides for the transfer of rights, powers, duties and liabilities not only 'under' the contract but also '*in connection with*' the contract and it is hard to see why this phrase was added unless it was to extend the scope of the rights, powers, duties and liabilities that are capable of transfer to those which are not themselves part of the contract but somehow assist in its performance. Furthermore, Reg 4(2)(b) attributes to the transferee any act or omission by the transferor, not only in respect of a novated contract but also in respect of a person assigned to the relevant undertaking. This wording – not limited to those matters that can be described as rights, powers, duties or liabilities – is, arguably, capable of covering the transferor's actions in maintaining for its employees a non-contractual emergency cover system, such as that under consideration in London Borough of Newham v Smith and anor (above), for example.

In Secretary of State for Employment v Spence and ors 1986 ICR 651, CA, the Court of Appeal concluded that the wording of Reg 5(2)(b) (now replaced by Reg 4(2)(b), but with slightly different phrasing), 'clearly can have the effect of transferring obligations other than contractual obligations'. And as Lord Justice Peter Gibson put it in the combined appeal of Martin v Lancashire County Council and another case 2001 ICR 197, CA (in relation to the question of whether or not tortious liability transferred – see 'Tortious and other civil liabilities' below): under sub-paragraph (a) 'rights etc are not limited to those under the contract but include those "in connection with" the contract. That prepositional phrase is far wider and it does not suggest that the rights etc need be contractual. That is supported by sub-paragraph (b) of Reg 5(2) [now Reg 4(2)(b)]. It is not just what is done by the transferor in respect of the contract that is deemed to have been done by the transferee but also anything done by the transferor in respect of the employee. That does not suggest that it is limited to what will result in contractual rights and liabilities.'

Although the above cases all concerned the 1981 version of the TUPE **3.18** Regulations, the position remains the same under the 2006 Regulations. Reg 5(2)(b) TUPE 1981 referred to 'anything done... in respect of... a person employed in that undertaking', and Reg 4(2)(b) TUPE 2006 refers to 'any act or omission... in respect of... a person assigned'. Indeed, if anything, the inclusion of the new concept of 'omission' in Reg 4(2)(b) makes the scope of the 2006 Regulations wider than that of its predecessor in this respect. Finally, note also that the existence of Reg 4(6), which excludes liability for criminal offences from the operation of Reg 4(2), suggests that Parliament felt that Reg 4(2) was potentially capable of transferring liabilities of a patently non-contractual nature.

Furthermore, the language of the Acquired Rights Directive also envisages that non-contractual rights and obligations transfer. Article 3(1) expressly applies to rights and obligations of the transferor arising from an 'employment relationship' and not just from an employment contract. In Albron Catering BV v FNV Bondgenoten and anor 2011 ICR 373, ECJ, the European Court observed that the term 'employment relationship' suggested that there was no need for a contractual link between the transferor and the employees concerned in order for those employees to be able to benefit from the Directive's protection – see Chapter 2, 'Who transfers?', under 'Who is an "employee" for TUPE purposes? – definition of "employee" and "contract of employment"' for a fuller discussion of the Albron ruling. Also, in the Martin case (above) Peter Gibson LJ observed: 'It would seem to me to be surprising if the rights and obligations were to be limited to contractual claims and to exclude claims in tort. Why should there be such a dividing line (in accordance with the distinction in English law between tort and contract) in a [European] Directive? It is the more surprising when the language used in the Directive is broad ("arising from") and when it is not only a contract of employment but also an employment relationship (which is plainly something different) from which the rights and obligations must arise.'

3.19 'Employment relationship' is not defined in the Directive but it seems doubtful whether the wording adopted by the UK ('in connection with' the employment contract) adequately implements the Directive in this regard, although – as we have discussed – Reg 4(2)(b) has a potentially broader extent, covering as it does acts and omissions in relation to the person assigned to the transferred entity. In any event, if Reg 4, when taken as a whole and construed literally, does not effect the transfer of all rights and obligations envisaged by the Directive, then following the ruling of Lord Templeman in Litster and ors v Forth Dry Dock and Engineering Co Ltd (in receivership) and anor 1989 ICR 341, HL, the courts must give it a purposive construction to ensure that it does so. Lord Oliver envisaged that such a construction would be applied even though it may involve some departure from the 'strict and literal application of the words which the legislature has elected to use'.

It is clear then that, in addition to contractual matters, statutory and civil rights and duties transfer and, for the purpose of determining what transfers, it should therefore be unnecessary (as Peter Gibson LJ implied in Martin v Lancashire County Council and another case (above)) to impose a strict delineation as to what is and what is not contractual. But what about non-contractual working practices of the kind at issue in both London Borough of Newham v Smith and anor (above) and Jefferies v Powerhouse Retail Ltd (above)? One can understand a reluctance to hold that non-contractual working conditions are capable of transfer in view of the difficulties of replicating the precise working environment of an organised grouping in the hands of the transferee. But it is, we submit, the entirely logical continuation of the above analysis. Thus, we would argue that non-contractual working arrangements and benefits *do* pass to the transferee, but that the same principles affect their application and enforcement in the transferee's hands as they did before the transfer. In other words, non-contractual working practices under the transferor remain non-contractual working practices under the transferee – and the transferee is at as much liberty to resile from them as the transferor would have been. (This is subject to any implied contractual obligation to exercise discretions in a non-capricious way and to the right of the employee to be treated as having been dismissed if he or she resigns on the ground that a substantial change has been made to working conditions that is to the employee's material detriment. This latter right – conferred by Reg 4(9) – is not dependent on the change amounting to a breach of contract – see Chapter 4, 'Unfair dismissal', under 'Material detriment dismissals', for full details.)

The question of whether a particular practice or procedure is contractual **3.20** therefore remains highly pertinent and the usual principles will apply. For further details, see IDS Employment Law Handbook, 'Contracts of Employment' (2014), Chapter 3, 'Contractual terms', and Chapter 5, 'Incorporated terms'.

If a disciplinary or redundancy procedure is of a contractual nature and a transferred employee is dismissed by the transferee in breach of it following the transfer, he or she is likely to have a contractual claim for wrongful dismissal against the transferee. If the transferor is responsible for the breach, the transferee will acquire liability for it if the employee would otherwise have transferred – see 'Unfair and wrongful dismissal' below. But even if such arrangements are of a non-contractual nature, thereby allowing the transferee to end or replace them at will, an affected employee may still have a claim. This is because a serious breach of a particular policy may amount to a breach of the implied term of trust and confidence, even if the policy itself is non-contractual (for example, imposing unreasonable disciplinary sanctions – short of dismissal – that are outside the range of sanctions provided by the relevant disciplinary procedure – Abbey National plc v Holmes EAT 406/91). In these circumstances, the employee would be able to resign and claim constructive dismissal. Furthermore, Reg 4(9) provides that if a relevant transfer involves or would involve a substantial change in working conditions to the material detriment of the transferring employee, then he or she can treat the contract as terminated and will be treated as having been dismissed by the employer. He or she may then be able to claim unfair dismissal, without the need to demonstrate a breach of contract – see Chapter 4, 'Unfair dismissal', under 'Material detriment dismissals', for further details.

Discretionary rights and benefits **3.21**
A discretionary right or benefit involves an element of uncertainty in that its application or value is unascertainable until the relevant discretion is exercised. We take the view that regardless of this element of uncertainty, discretionary

219

rights and benefits pass to the transferee under Reg 4(2)(a) as liabilities and powers under or in connection with the employment contract. What the transferee can then do is entirely dependent upon the terms of the relevant right or benefit, and the extent to which the discretion has already been exercised.

This was the approach taken by the High Court in Procter and Gamble Co v Svenska Cellulosa Aktiebolaget and anor 2012 IRLR 733, ChD. The Court held that the employees' expectation of being fairly treated in exercising their entitlement to be considered for early retirement benefits constituted a liability that transferred under TUPE, notwithstanding that the entitlement was discretionary. What transferred was the discretionary power to provide those early retirement benefits, which the transferee would have to exercise in good faith.

3.22 In Moir v First Security ET Case No.2204146/09 M's contract provided that company sick pay would be paid at her employer's discretion subject to the provision of a medical certificate and that payment would not be made if employees unreasonably refused to undergo a medical examination or to allow the employer to request a medical report from their GP. M was taken ill and was on sick leave for three months during which he was only paid statutory sick pay. When his employment transferred under TUPE, the transferee refused to award him contractual sick pay since its own employees were only entitled to SSP. An employment tribunal held that while the contract clearly provided a discretion, it was equally clear from the wording that company sick pay would be paid provided there was no reason to believe that employees were abusing the system or being uncooperative. M's claim for company sick pay was upheld as the transferee had wrongly exercised its discretion by giving consideration to its own circumstances rather than those that it acquired following the transfer.

A discretionary (i.e. non-contractual) benefit scheme – as opposed to discretionary benefits under a scheme – is also likely to transfer. As the High Court in Procter and Gamble Co v Svenska Cellulosa Aktiebolaget and anor (above) observed, TUPE is not confined to contractual liabilities – see further 'Non-contractual working arrangements' above. In Bousted v Reliance Security Services Ltd ET Case No.1701352/07 (discussed under 'Enhanced redundancy schemes' above), an enhanced redundancy compensation scheme was held to have been transferred following a transfer even though the benefits payable under it were referred to as 'ex gratia' payments and the terms of the scheme were not expressly incorporated into the employee's contract or staff handbook.

3.23 **Tribunal judgments made against transferor**
Where there is a relevant transfer, Reg 4(2)(a) transfers all accrued liabilities in respect of the transferred employees. Presumably these include tribunal and other court judgments made against the transferor prior to the date of the transfer, so that the employee would be entitled to enforce the terms of the

judgment against the transferee. There appear to be no cases confirming this, but it would seem to flow from the basic principle that the transferee steps into the shoes of the transferor following a TUPE transfer. Criminal liabilities are one of the few exceptions to this rule – see 'Rights and liabilities that do not transfer' below.

Acts and omissions   3.24

As we have seen, 'rights, powers, duties and liabilities under or in connection with' an employee's contract of employment are transferred on a TUPE transfer under Reg 4(2)(a). But that is not all. Reg 4(2)(b) provides that 'any act or omission before the transfer is completed, of or in relation to the transferor in respect of [the contract of employment] or a person assigned to [the] organised grouping of resources or employees' is deemed to have been an act or omission of or in relation to the transferee. In other words, any acts or omissions of the transferor before the transfer are treated as having been done by the transferee and any liability arising therefrom accordingly attaches to the transferee.

Thus, the transferee inherits liability under Reg 4(2)(b) for the transferor's past breaches of contract – such as arrears of wages – in addition to the responsibility to maintain ongoing rights and benefits. This liability for past breaches is not limited to obligations arising out of the contract existing on the date of the transfer, but also those arising from previous contracts with the transferor – DJM International Ltd v Nicholas 1996 ICR 214, EAT (which considered inherited liability for a discrimination claim – see 'Individual statutory rights' below) – although claims will be subject to length of service limitations and any statutory time limits.

The transferee may also inherit unfair dismissal liability not only where the **3.25** sole or principal reason for dismissal was the transfer itself but also for non-transfer-related dismissals in respect of employees assigned to the undertaking or organised grouping of resources at the time of its transfer. So if, for example, the transferor omits to carry out a proper dismissal procedure in respect of an assigned employee subsequently dismissed for capability or misconduct, the liability for unfair dismissal arising out of that omission will be passed on to the transferee by virtue of Reg 4(2)(b). For further discussion of this point, see 'Unfair and wrongful dismissal liability – dismissals unconnected with transfer' below.

Acts/omissions must be committed prior to transfer   3.26
It is important to note, however, that in Coutinho v Vision Information Services (UK) Ltd and anor EAT 0469/07 the EAT made it clear that Reg 4(2)(b) can only be relied upon to transfer liability for an act or omission on the part of the transferor if the act or omission took place *before* the transfer. In that case, the claimant contended that a transferor's failure to provide an accurate job

---

221

reference gave rise to victimisation liability that transferred to the transferee following a TUPE transfer. In upholding the employment tribunal's rejection of the claimant's contention, the EAT ruled that as the request for the reference had only been made once the transfer had taken place, the omission to provide an accurate reference was not an act or omission on the part of the transferor that had occurred before the transfer and accordingly any liability in respect of it was not acquired by the transferee.

3.27 **Pre-transfer misconduct by employee.** Normally, when considering what transfers on a TUPE transfer under Reg 4(2)(b), the focus is on the acts or omissions of the transferor. But it should be noted that Reg 4(2)(b) speaks of '*any* act or omission before the transfer is completed, of *or in relation to the transferor* in respect of the [transferred employee]' (our stress). It can be inferred from this that the transferee is entitled to rely upon acts or omissions *by an employee* committed while in the employment of the transferor as a basis for disciplining the employee or even in some cases for commencing legal action against him or her. In Balcome v Dye and anor t/a The Lane End Public House ET Case No.2400765/13, for example, an employment tribunal held that there is no reason in law why a transferee cannot take disciplinary action against a transferring employee in relation to conduct that is alleged to have occurred before the transfer. It reminded itself that the essence of the TUPE Regulations is to provide for the continuation of the employment relationship.

Similar reasoning would seem to apply where the claimant has participated in illegality so as to render the contract of employment unenforceable – see, for example, the Northern Ireland Court of Appeal's decision in McGlinchey v McGurk t/a McGurk and Moore 2014 NICA 3, NICA.

3.28 Contingent rights and 'golden parachutes'

As we discussed at the beginning of this chapter under '"Automatic transfer" principle – overview', TUPE protects only those employment rights that exist at the time of the transfer, not those which arise subsequently. It could be argued, therefore, that contingent rights – those that have not fully matured at the time of the transfer but are expressed to crystallise upon, for example, the employee's dismissal – are also excluded from the scope of the Regulations. However, this is not the case, as the European Court ruled in Martin and ors v South Bank University 2004 ICR 1234, ECJ.

In that case, M, D and W were lecturers at an NHS nursing college, employed under the General Whitley Council (GWC) conditions of service. Included in these conditions were the terms of the Collective Agreement on Premature Payment of Superannuation and Compensation Benefits. For employees aged between 50 and retirement age, who had at least five years' service within the NHS Superannuation Scheme, this provided for early retirement with immediate payment of a retirement pension and compensation in three circumstances: dismissal for redundancy; voluntary early retirement on organisational change; and early retirement in the interests of the efficiency of the service. In November 1994 the nursing college became part of SBU and the claimants' employment transferred under TUPE. The claimants chose to remain on their existing terms of employment but joined the Teachers' Superannuation Scheme, as they were unable to continue their membership of the NHS retirement scheme following the transfer. In January 1997 SBU wrote to all staff aged over 50 offering them early retirement in the interests of the efficiency of the service. M and D accepted. The terms offered for early retirement in the higher education sector differed from those provided to NHS employees by the GWC conditions of service. Under the applicable regulations, a teacher aged 50 or over who took early retirement because of redundancy or in the interests of the service was entitled to an early retirement pension based on actual years of pensionable service, and a lump sum. However, whereas NHS employers were obliged to pay an additional compensatory annual allowance and lump sum when an employee took early retirement, employers in the higher education sector had a discretion whether or not to do so. Furthermore, NHS employers were obliged to credit the employee with a prescribed number of additional years' service when calculating the compensatory benefits, but employers in the higher education sector had a discretion to determine how many years' service with which to credit the employee.

The claimants contended that they were entitled to the more favourable NHS **3.29** terms of early retirement. The employment tribunal referred a number of questions to the ECJ for a preliminary ruling, including whether rights that are contingent upon dismissal or early retirement by agreement with the employer are subject to Article 3(1) of the Acquired Rights Directive, and therefore transfer with the transfer of an undertaking, or whether they fall within the exclusion in Article 3(4) relating to pension schemes (for which, see 'Rights and liabilities that do not transfer – terms relating to pensions' below). The ECJ considered that it was clear from Article 3 that – except those specifically excluded by Article 3(4) – *all* the transferor's rights and obligations arising from the contract of employment or employment relationship are transferred to the transferee, even if their implementation is contingent on a particular event, the occurrence of which may depend on the will of the employer.

This case focused on contingent rights relating to early retirement and shows that if, following the transfer, the transferee exercises its power to grant early retirement, it becomes bound by the rights and obligations of early retirement established by the employee's contract of employment or employment relationship with the transferor. However, the principle is not limited to early retirement schemes and would apply equally to other contingent rights such as 'golden parachutes'.

3.30 So-called 'golden parachute' clauses may be included in the contracts of senior executives. These trigger the payment of a liquidated sum upon the occurrence of a specified event – typically dismissal, but also sometimes where the business is subject to a takeover. In principle, there is nothing to prevent liability under a golden parachute passing to the transferee under Reg 4(2)(a) TUPE as a liability of the transferor under the employment contract of an employee assigned to the relevant undertaking. Where the golden parachute is triggered to 'open' on the occasion of the transfer, the transferee will become immediately liable to the employee for payment. Even where the clause does not crystallise upon transfer, the latent liability will pass to the transferee as a contingent right. The liability in these circumstances may be substantial, as such payments – being structured as a debt as opposed to compensation – are not subject to mitigation by the executive and must be paid in full.

A transferee might possibly succeed in having a golden parachute clause set aside if it can argue that the executive negotiated the clause with the prospective transfer in mind. Reg 4(4) provides that, subject to an exception in the case of insolvency, any purported variation of a contract of employment that is to be transferred is void if the sole or principal reason for the variation is the relevant transfer or a reason connected with the transfer that is not an economic, technical or organisational reason entailing changes in the workforce – see further Chapter 5, 'Changing terms and conditions', under 'Varying terms in a TUPE context – changes prohibited by Reg 4(4)'.

3.31 ## Seniority rights and continuity of employment

Continuity of employment is preserved in the event of a relevant transfer, although it is not entirely clear whether the TUPE Regulations themselves have the effect of preserving continuity or whether this is governed by the Employment Rights Act 1996 (ERA). S.218 ERA specifically preserves continuity of employment following a change of employer in relation to the transfer of a business or undertaking and in relation to a change in the partners of a firm (provided, of course, that the employee remains in employment) – see Chapter 7, 'Continuity of employment', for more details. It is clear, certainly, from the underlying policy and objectives of the Acquired Rights Directive, and from relevant case law, that continuity must be preserved whenever the Directive (and the national law that implements it) applies. For example, in Collino and anor v Telecom Italia SpA 2002 ICR 38, ECJ, the European Court stated that, although transferred employees' length of service with their former employer does not as such constitute a right that can be asserted against the new employer, in calculating rights of a financial nature – such as a termination payment or salary increases – the transferee 'must take into account the entire length of service of the employees transferred, both in his employment and that of the transferor'.

As the Collino case demonstrates, the fact that a relevant transfer does not break continuity of employment for transferring employees may significantly affect the nature of the liabilities towards those employees that are preserved in the context of a relevant transfer. First, length of service may affect whether a particular employee qualifies for certain statutory rights. Secondly, length of service may have an impact on the calculation of certain statutory or contractual benefits. We examine these possibilities in turn.

Service qualification for statutory rights 3.32

In most cases, an employee must have at least two years' continuous service to claim unfair dismissal – S.108(1) ERA. Thus, a transferee who acquires an employee who was employed by the transferor for 21 months prior to the transfer will become liable to that employee for unfair dismissal three months following the transfer (not two years, as would be the case if it had taken on the new employee in a non-transfer-related context). However, the continuous service provisions are disapplied in most 'automatic unfair dismissal' cases. For our purposes, the most significant of these is a claim of unfair dismissal for asserting TUPE rights under S.104(4)(e) ERA (dismissal for asserting a statutory right). In such cases, continuity of employment ceases to be relevant. Somewhat surprisingly, two years' qualifying service *is* required for claims under Reg 7(1) TUPE (i.e. where the reason for dismissal was either the relevant transfer or a reason connected with the transfer that was not an 'ETO reason') – see MRS Environmental Services Ltd v Marsh and anor 1997 ICR 995, EAT, and Chapter 4, 'Unfair dismissal', under 'The TUPE unfair dismissal regime'.

The right to a statutory redundancy payment is also dependent on two years' continuous service – S.155 ERA. Thus, an employee with 18 months' service at the point of transfer will become entitled to claim statutory redundancy pay after six months' employment with the transferee.

Calculating benefits 3.33

It is common for employers to seek to encourage the loyalty or motivation, or reward the experience, of their workers by incorporating a service-related element into the calculation of contractual benefits. (The Equality Act 2010 permits this, within certain parameters.) Clearly, the fact that continuity is preserved on a transfer can greatly enhance the value of such benefits, and of service-related statutory benefits, to the employee. In Computershare Investor Services plc v Jackson 2008 ICR 341, CA (see below), in spite of the dispute over when the claimant *joined* the severance pay scheme, her employer never failed to take into account her pre-transfer employment for the purpose of calculating length of service under the scheme – to the employee's considerable financial advantage.

However, it may not be necessary for the transferee to recognise length of service in exactly the same way as the transferor. In Scattolon v Ministero

225

dell'Istruzione, dell'Università e della Ricerca 2012 ICR 740, ECJ, S had nearly 20 years of service, which entitled her to a certain level of service-related pay under the collective agreement that applied to the transferor. On the transfer, that collective agreement was replaced by an agreement concluded by the transferee, as permitted by Article 3(3) of the Acquired Rights Directive. The transferee calculated S's pay under the new agreement by reference to a notional period of service. S claimed that her entire period of service, including service with the transferor, should be recognised under the new agreement.

3.34 The ECJ noted that the ruling in Collino and anor v Telecom Italia SpA (above) established that, while transferred employees' length of service does not as such constitute a right enforceable against the transferee, in so far as it is used to determine financial rights those rights must, in principle, be maintained by the transferee in the same way as by the transferor. Thus, according to Collino, Article 3 requires that, when calculating rights of a financial nature, the transferee must take into account transferred employees' entire length of service, in so far as its obligation to do so derives from the employment relationship between those employees and the transferor and in accordance with the terms agreed in that relationship. But the ECJ noted a potentially significant difference between the present case and Collino – namely, that S's right to service-related pay derived from a collective agreement that had been lawfully replaced on the transfer, whereas in Collino the right to service-related pay arose out of the employment contract itself. However, the ECJ went on to hold that the replacement of the collective agreement, while lawful, could not have the aim or effect of imposing conditions on transferring employees that are, overall, less favourable than those applicable before the transfer. Thus, it would be contrary to the Directive for the transferee not to take account of length of service 'in so far as is necessary approximately to maintain the level of remuneration received by [the transferred employees] with the transferor'.

On a straight application of that principle, S would apparently be entitled to have her full 20 years' service recognised by the transferee, but the ECJ went on to make an important clarification. It noted that it would be for the national court to verify whether S had indeed suffered a loss of salary following the transfer. The court would need to take into account the transferee's argument that the calculation of pay by reference to a notional period of service did in fact ensure that transferred employees were not in an overall less favourable position compared with their situation immediately before the transfer. In other words, so long as S received (approximately) the same salary after the transfer as before, the fact that the calculation of that salary by reference to the new collective agreement did not take into account her full length of service would not necessarily be a breach of the Directive.

3.35 Although continuity of employment is preserved across a transfer, an employee cannot rely on his or her pre-transfer employment for all purposes.

In Computershare Investor Services plc v Jackson 2008 ICR 341, CA, J had worked for the transferor since 1999 under a contract of employment that contained no provision for enhanced redundancy pay. In June 2004 her employment transferred under TUPE to CIS plc, which operated a dual system of redundancy terms that offered more generous benefits to those who had joined it before 1 March 2002. When J was made redundant in 2005 she argued that since the operation of TUPE meant that she was to be treated as having continuity of employment with CIS plc dating back to 1999, she should be afforded the benefit of the pre-March 2002 redundancy terms. CIS plc disagreed and J brought claims of unfair dismissal and breach of contract for non-payment of enhanced contractual severance pay. The employment tribunal found as a matter of fact that J had joined CIS plc at the point of transfer in 2004. However, it held that since what is now Reg 4(1) required that a transferred employee's contract of employment shall be deemed to have originally been made with the transferee, it was appropriate to treat J as having joined CIS plc before 2002. As a result, she was entitled to the enhanced redundancy payment. CIS plc successfully appealed to the EAT and J further appealed to the Court of Appeal.

The Court of Appeal, agreeing with the EAT, held that it is not the purpose of the **3.36** TUPE Regulations to place transferred employees in a *better* position than they were in prior to the transfer. Thus, J, whose employment transferred in 2004, had no right to be treated as a pre-2002 entrant for the purposes of the transferee employer's enhanced redundancy scheme, notwithstanding that she was deemed to be continuously employed by the transferee from the date on which she started employment with the transferor. So far as the employer's redundancy scheme was concerned, the date of the employee's joining the company was an objective fact that was unaffected by the deeming provisions of TUPE.

It will be interesting to see whether the same approach is taken where an employer's redundancy provisions are based on length of service, rather than a specific joining date. If, for example, an employer's terms state that anyone with more than five years' service with the company is entitled to an enhanced redundancy package, then on one view it might be argued that the employee's pre-transfer service, which is deemed by virtue of Reg 4(1) and (2) to be with the transferee, should be included in the service calculation. But the employer might be able to argue that, on the basis of the Court of Appeal's decision in the Jackson case, it is only years of actual (as opposed to deemed) continuous employment with the company that counted for the purposes of the redundancy scheme.

Calculating period of continuous employment **3.37**
It is likely that an employee's continuity has to be calculated in accordance with the detailed rules contained in Ss.210–219 ERA. The date on which the period of continuous employment started is usually the date on which the employee

227

started work with the transferor. However, note that if the employee was subject to a previous TUPE transfer, the start date will be earlier.

Continuity of employment will have other, practical implications for the transferee that should not be overlooked. For example, employees who are transferred while absent on sick leave or maternity leave will not restart their leave at the point of transfer: the transferee will be credited with the length of leave such employees have taken and whatever pay they have received for the purposes of applying the relevant absence and pay policies. And, in another example, the reference period for assessing employees' average weekly working hours under the Working Time Regulations 1998 SI 1998/1833 will 'roll over' the transfer date, so the transferee will need to take account of hours worked by employees in the weeks leading up to the transfer in assessing whether they are averaging under the statutory limits.

3.38 Note that even if the acquired employees have no rights under TUPE – because, for example, the acquisition does not constitute a relevant transfer – their employment may nevertheless be deemed to be continuous under S.218 ERA – see Chapter 7, 'Continuity of employment', for details.

3.39 Unfair and wrongful dismissal liability

In Chapter 4, 'Unfair dismissal', we discuss at length the extent to which employers, whether transferors or transferees, can effect dismissals fairly in a transfer situation – and in what circumstances an employee's own decision to leave his or her employment can amount to a dismissal, giving rise to a potential unfair dismissal claim. Here, we consider who – transferor or transferee – shoulders the liability for unfair and wrongful dismissals that are carried out around the time of – or otherwise in connection with – a relevant transfer.

3.40 TUPE-related dismissals

Regulation 7(1) of the TUPE Regulations, which implements Article 4(1) of the Acquired Rights Directive, provides that (following amendments that came into effect in respect of TUPE transfers occurring on or after 31 January 2014) TUPE-related dismissals will be automatically unfair. In particular, it provides that where, either before or after a relevant transfer, any employee of the transferor or transferee is dismissed, the employee shall be treated for ERA purposes as unfairly dismissed if the sole or principal reason for dismissal is the transfer itself.

If the sole or principal reason for dismissal is an economic, technical or organisational reason entailing changes in the workforce ('an ETO reason'), then the dismissal will not be automatically unfair but may be so when judged in accordance with the normal reasonableness test set out in S.98(4) ERA. For a detailed discussion of what constitutes an ETO reason, see Chapter 4, 'Unfair dismissal', under 'Dismissals potentially fair for an "ETO reason"'.

As discussed in Chapter 2, 'Who transfers?', an employment contract and the **3.41** liabilities in respect of it will transfer if the employee in question is employed by the transferor and assigned to the transferring entity immediately before the transfer, *or would have been so employed if he or she had not been dismissed in the circumstances described in Reg 7(1)* – Reg 4(3). In other words, the transferee will (almost) always be liable for dismissals that are automatically unfair under Reg 7(1). If the sole or principal reason for the dismissal is the relevant transfer itself, then the dismissal will be automatically unfair under Reg 7(1) and, owing to Reg 4(3), liability for the dismissal will pass to the transferee. (Note that there is no obligation on the transferee to re-employ employees who were unfairly dismissed by the transferor in such circumstances, although the transferee is responsible for all liabilities relating to those employees. However, as the BIS Guide, 'Employment rights on the transfer of an undertaking' ('the BIS Guide') (January 2014), points out, an obligation to re-employ could, theoretically, arise were a tribunal to uphold a claim of unfair dismissal and order reinstatement or re-engagement.)

However, there are two exceptions to the principle that liability for such unfair dismissals transfers. First, Reg 7(1) protects '*any* employee of the transferor or transferee' (our stress) – not just those who have been assigned to the organised grouping to be transferred. This means that employees who are not so assigned and whose contracts of employment do not transfer in accordance with Reg 4(1) and (2) are none the less protected if they are dismissed by reason of the transfer. However, liability for those unfair dismissals will not pass to the transferee but will instead remain with the transferor. For the second, more limited, exception, see the discussion on anticipatory breach of contract under 'Constructive dismissals' below.

Wrongful dismissal
3.42

The effect of Reg 4(2) is that the transferee will inherit liability for any pre-transfer breach of employment contract by the transferor or, for that matter, any other act or omission in respect of relevant employees who are employed (or deemed to be employed) immediately before the transfer. For example, if an unfairly dismissed employee was given insufficient notice, or dismissed in breach of a contractual disciplinary or redundancy procedure, his or her claim of wrongful dismissal will also lie at the door of the transferee, who may thus be liable for damages for pay in lieu of notice. Note that this is not the case in respect of an employee who relies on Reg 4(9) (see 'Material detriment dismissals' below), because Reg 4(10) provides that 'no damages shall be payable by an employer as a result of a dismissal falling within paragraph (9) in respect of any failure by the employer to pay wages to an employee in respect of a notice period which the employee has failed to work'. There is no such

229

restriction where an employee claims unfair constructive dismissal under normal principles.

The question arises whether an employee who has been given no or insufficient contractual or statutory notice of dismissal by the transferor in circumstances where the reason for dismissal is not transfer-related would nonetheless be entitled to claim that any liability for wrongful dismissal lies with the transferee. Normally, as explained below, it would be the transferor who remains liable, since an employee whose dismissal for a non-transfer-related reason takes legal effect prior to the transfer is not regarded as employed immediately before the transfer, with the consequence that Reg 4(1) and (2) does not apply. However, an employee may seek to argue that had he or she been given proper notice, he or she would have still been employed at the point of the transfer and that liability for the breach of contract (i.e. wrongful dismissal) should therefore pass to the transferee by virtue of Reg 4(2). A similar point could be made by an employee who is summarily dismissed but receives a payment in lieu of notice in circumstances where the contract of employment does not provide for termination to be effected by payment in lieu. In either case, the employee's contention is emboldened by reliance on the so-called 'elective theory', which asserts that a repudiatory breach of contract requires the innocent party to accept the repudiation and that, until such acceptance is communicated by word or deed, the contract remains alive and ongoing. Years of dispute as to whether the elective theory applies in the context of the termination of contracts of employment finally came to an end when in Geys v Société Générale, London Branch 2013 ICR 117, SC, the Supreme Court held that the theory does indeed apply. On this basis, it would seem that provided the employee does nothing to accept the repudiatory breach entailed in the transferor's failure to give proper notice, and provided the length of notice entitlement is sufficient to cover the period between the date of dismissal and date of the transfer, the tab for any liability arising from the wrongful dismissal would be picked up by the transferee. The same argument could be run where the repudiatory breach entails a failure by the transferor to comply with the terms of a contractual termination procedure.

3.43 Dismissals unconnected with a relevant transfer

Where an employee is dismissed by the transferor before the transfer in circumstances that are entirely unconnected with the transfer – for example, for capability or misconduct – Reg 7(1) will not apply to make the dismissal automatically unfair. For this reason, the dismissed employee will not, subject to the point about repudiatory breach made under 'Wrongful dismissal' above, be 'employed by the transferor' immediately before the transfer within the meaning of Reg 4(1) and (3). Therefore, his or her contract of employment and associated rights, powers, duties and liabilities will not transfer to the transferee under Reg 4(2)(b) unless he or she was dismissed on notice and that notice expired only after the date on which the transfer occurred.

Clearly, if the dismissal is effected by the transferee after the transfer, the transferee will bear liability for it, even if the misconduct occurred before the transfer. The fairness or otherwise of the decision to dismiss will be assessed by applying the normal reasonableness test set out in S.98(4) ERA. It is possible that in such circumstances the dismissed employee's claim of unfair dismissal may relate to the way in which the disciplinary process that commenced before the transfer was conducted by the transferor. If that is the case, and assuming that the employee was assigned to the transferred undertaking, Reg 4(2)(b) ensures that whatever the fault of the transferor in relation to the initial conduct of the disciplinary procedure, this will be attributed to the transferee upon the relevant transfer as an 'act or omission' in respect of the employee. This will be the case even if the subsequent dismissal itself bears no relation to the transfer. Transferees should be careful in such circumstances to 'remedy' the pre-transfer failings of the disciplinary procedure by ensuring that any appeal conducted after the transfer amounts, in effect, to a rehearing – and, of course, by insisting upon appropriate warranties and indemnities against the transferor in respect of such risks – see Chapter 11, 'Practical aspects of transfers', for practical advice in this regard.

Constructive dismissals   3.44

A 'constructive dismissal' occurs where an employee resigns, with or without notice, in response to a repudiatory breach of contract on the part of his or her employer. In such circumstances the employee will be treated as having been 'dismissed' within the meaning of S.95(1)(c) ERA, and thus (provided he or she has the requisite qualifying service) will be able to bring an unfair dismissal claim under that Act. So, an employer that unilaterally seeks to make changes to the employment relationship or to the terms and conditions of employment, prompted by the transfer or a reason connected with it, risks provoking employees to resign and claim unfair constructive dismissal. Reg 4(11) specifically provides that other provisions in Reg 4 are 'without prejudice to any right of an employee arising apart from these Regulations to terminate his contract of employment without notice in acceptance of a repudiatory breach of contract by his employer'.

As a general rule, Reg 7(1) and (2) apply whether dismissals are express or constructive. So, with regard to a constructive dismissal that is shown to be by reason of a relevant transfer, the dismissal will be automatically unfair under Reg 7(1). Liability will (usually) pass to the transferee if the constructive dismissal occurs while the employee is employed by the transferor before the transfer, and will rest with the transferee if the dismissal occurs after the transfer.

231

Generally, where an employee does nothing in response to an employer's repudiatory breach of contract, he or she is likely to be regarded as having sanctioned it, thereby affirming the contract, and will lose the right to resign and claim that he or she has been constructively dismissed. Note, however, that where a detrimental change to terms and conditions occurs in connection with a relevant transfer under TUPE, case law suggests that such a change will be void, even where the employee in question purports to agree to it. Logically, therefore, an employee will be able to claim constructive dismissal years after the initial breach, notwithstanding his or her inaction at the time – despite the principle that the objective of the Acquired Rights Directive is not to improve on employees' existing rights. Transferees need to be aware of their extended potential liability in this regard.

3.45 **Anticipatory breach of contract.** Where an employer manifests a clear intention to commit a breach of contract at some date in the future, an employee can resign and claim constructive dismissal in anticipation of the breach of contract. Clearly, where a transferring employee resigns after the transfer, in anticipation of a breach of contract by his or her new employer, the transferee will be liable if the constructive dismissal is found to be unfair. But who will be liable if an employee, while still employed by the transferor, anticipates a change being made to his or her fundamental terms and conditions by the transferee and, in view of this, resigns and claims unfair constructive dismissal before the transfer?

It seems that the answer will depend on whether the employee is taken to have formally objected to the transfer. The rationale on which this proposition is based is complex and is explained in detail in Chapter 4, 'Unfair dismissal', under 'Constructive dismissals – resignation in anticipation of breach by transferee'. Suffice to say here that in Humphreys v University of Oxford and anor 2000 ICR 405, CA, the Court of Appeal considered the interrelationship between the right to object to the transfer under what is now Reg 4(8) and the right to claim constructive dismissal under what is now Reg 4(11). The Court ruled that, notwithstanding that the then equivalent of Reg 4(8) stipulated that, where an employee objects, the relevant transfer will operate to terminate his or her employment with the transferor but that termination shall not be regarded as constituting a dismissal for any purpose, the employee's right to claim unfair constructive dismissal against the transferor was nonetheless preserved. This was because what is now Reg 4(7) is, by virtue of Reg 4(11), subject to 'any right... arising apart from these Regulations' to claim constructive dismissal.

3.46 However, the Court made it clear that, in order for the transferor to be regarded as having constructively dismissed the employee, the employee's objection to the transfer would have to be one of substance (i.e. a fundamental change in working conditions). If, on the other hand, the employee's objection was merely based on the fact that the identity of his or her employer was about to change as a result of the imminent transfer, that would not be a repudiatory breach of contract. In these circumstances, the employee would simply be left with the legal consequences specified by Reg 4(8) when an objection to the transfer is made – i.e. the relevant transfer would serve automatically to terminate the employee's contract, but he or she would be unable to claim to have been 'dismissed' for any purpose whatsoever.

Although, in a case where the employee has both objected to the transfer and resigned on the basis of constructive dismissal, the Court of Appeal in Humphreys makes it clear that liability for the dismissal will remain with the transferor, it would appear that the position is different where the employee resigns in the face of a fundamental breach of contract by the transferor but does not formally object to the transfer. In Euro-Die (UK) Ltd v Skidmore and anor EAT 1158/98 the EAT ruled that any liability for constructive dismissal in these circumstances will pass to the transferee if the dismissal was automatically unfair as a result of what is now Reg 7(1) – i.e. if the dismissal is by reason of the transfer or for a reason connected to it that is not an ETO reason. If, however, there is an ETO reason for the constructive dismissal within the meaning of Reg 7(2), the liability for it would not transfer but would instead remain with the transferor. A full explanation of the rationale upon which the EAT reached this conclusion is given in Chapter 4, 'Unfair dismissal', under 'Constructive dismissals – resignation in anticipation of breach by transferee'.

3.47 There is no doubt that the rules regarding which employer – transferor or transferee – is liable with regard to a pre-transfer constructive dismissal can yield quirky results. On the one hand, where an employee, owing to his or her anticipating a repudiatory breach by the transferee, both objects to a relevant transfer and successfully claims constructive dismissal, the transferor will be liable for the dismissal through little or no fault of its own (see Humphreys v University of Oxford and anor (above)). On the other hand, where an employee does not formally object to the transfer but successfully claims unfair constructive dismissal on the back of a failure by the transferor, where such failure is connected with the relevant transfer, liability is likely to pass to the transferee under TUPE, through little or no fault of the transferee's (see Euro-Die (UK) Ltd v Skidmore and anor (above)). This analysis illustrates why it is extremely important that both transferor and transferee consider carefully the nature of the warranties and indemnities that are to be contained in the transfer agreement, under which the parties can essentially decide between themselves who is to bear the liabilities for transfer-connected dismissals – see Chapter 11, 'Practical aspects of transfers', for further details.

Material detriment dismissals

3.48 Where an action by the transferee – actual or anticipatory – is not sufficient to amount to a repudiatory breach of contract for the purposes of a constructive dismissal claim, the employee might nevertheless be entitled to 'resign' and treat him or herself as dismissed under Reg 4(9). This provides that, if a relevant transfer involves or would involve 'a substantial change in working conditions to the material detriment of a person' whose contract of employment is transferring, 'such an employee may treat the contract of employment as having been terminated, and the employee shall be treated for any purpose as having been dismissed by the employer'. This form of dismissal is discussed in detail in Chapter 4, 'Unfair dismissal', under 'Material detriment dismissals'.

It is important to note that the substantial change to working conditions that forms the basis of a Reg 4(9) dismissal need not amount to a repudiatory breach of contract, or even to a breach of contract at all, following the wording of Reg 4(9) (which statutorily reverses the Court of Appeal's decision in Rossiter v Pendragon plc and Crosby-Clarke v Air Foyle Ltd 2002 ICR 1063, CA). The circumstances in which Reg 4(9) can operate are therefore potentially much wider than the normal concept of constructive dismissal. There is nothing, however, to prevent an employee claiming unfair dismissal on the basis of both material detriment dismissal under Reg 4(9) and constructive dismissal under Reg 4(11).

3.49 Regulation 4(9) states that where a relevant transfer involves or would involve substantial changes to the employee's material detriment, the employee may treat the contract as having been terminated and the employee will be treated as having been dismissed 'by the employer'. The employer in question will, we suggest, be the transferor where the effective date of termination occurs before the transfer takes place, and the transferee if the relevant date falls after the transfer. Subject to what is said below, however, it is submitted that liability for a pre-transfer dismissal would pass to the transferee in any event under Reg 4(2) and (3) if, as is often likely to be the case, the dismissal is shown to be by reason of the transfer under Reg 7(1).

This is subject to the caveat discussed under 'Anticipatory breach of contract' above. If an employee formally objects to the transfer, then Reg 4(7) precludes the contract of employment and the rights, powers, duties and liabilities under or in connection with it from transferring to the transferee. Thus, where an employee objects to the transfer within the meaning of Reg 4(7) and successfully claims material detriment dismissal under Reg 4(9), liability in these circumstances would not be transferred but would remain with the transferor.

3.50 Obligations specifically tailored to transferor's identity

Although the vast majority of contractual terms do not give rise to particular difficulty in the context of their transfer under Reg 4(2) TUPE Regulations, certain terms may be couched very specifically by reference to the transferor's identity. If and in so far as the automatic transfer principle applies to these, the difficulty arises as to how, following the transfer, such terms can be interpreted to cover the substitution of a different employer altogether (i.e. the transferee), since clearly that party was not envisaged when the contract of employment was drafted.

Below, we consider some of the more usual instances of terms that are tailored to the transferor's specific identity and discuss the principles that the courts have devised for dealing with the application of Reg 4(2) to such terms.

Mobility clauses

3.51

Where transferred employees have mobility clauses in their contracts, the question may well arise after the transfer of whether the transferee will be entitled to enforce an equivalent mobility clause appropriate to its own place of business. This issue has been considered by the EAT in Tapere v South London and Maudsley NHS Trust 2009 ICR 1563, EAT. In that case, T's employment was transferred in April 2007 from Lewisham Primary Care Trust (LPCT) to South London and Maudsley NHS Trust (SLMT) following a TUPE transfer. After the transfer, SLMT attempted to relocate T to another hospital site in reliance upon the mobility clause in her contract with LPCT, which permitted relocation 'to similar locations within the Trust'. However, T did not wish to be relocated and brought a claim against SLMT under Reg 4(9) on the ground that she had been subjected to a substantial change to working conditions to her material detriment in respect of which she was entitled to claim unfair dismissal. An employment tribunal rejected that claim, ruling that the mobility clause was not in this case restricted, post-transfer, to the transferor's (LPCT's) geographical location, but that the benefit of it transferred, entitling SLMT to transfer T to any of the locations at which it operated. In so holding, the tribunal concluded that the words 'within the Trust' in the mobility clause did not add anything: an employer with a mobility clause would only transfer an employee to other locations which that employer itself owned or operated.

On appeal, the EAT was adamant that the phrasing of a contractual mobility clause fell to be construed in light of the facts and circumstances that appertained at the time the contract containing the clause was entered into. Where, in a TUPE context, there are practical impediments to permitting the clause to be implemented by the transferee with precisely the same benefits and obligations, then the equivalent of these can be substituted provided that neither benefit nor burden is increased or enlarged (the concept of 'substantial equivalence'). It was not necessary to consider substantial equivalence if the relevant contractual term can be continued, post-transfer, without practical difficulty. In the instant case, the words 'within the Trust' could not be regarded as surplus or meaningless. They were plainly words of definition, which restricted the intended geographical area to which the mobility clause applied. The interpretation adopted by the employment tribunal had increased the scope of the geographical area in which the employee could be required to relocate.

235

This resulted in the terms of her contract being altered to her disadvantage and in her employment being less protected after the transfer than it was before. The tribunal had erred in finding that there had been no dismissal within the terms of Reg 4(9).

3.52 The EAT's approach to the mobility clause in the Tapere case underlines the fact that the practical difficulties experienced by a transferee following a transfer cannot be invoked to override or modify an employee's contractual rights.

3.53 **Restrictive covenants and implied duty of fidelity**
Restrictive covenants preventing the solicitation of customers and working for competitors, along with clauses preventing the disclosure of confidential information, are often set out in the employment contract, or at least in an agreement that is collateral to the employment contract. Therefore, on a straightforward reading of Reg 4(2)(a), the benefit of these should pass to the transferee upon a relevant transfer. However, as the courts have identified, problems arise from attempting to transfer such employer-specific rights and obligations.

3.54 **Enforceability by transferee.** First, there is a question of enforceability. Restrictive covenants are strictly speaking contrary to public policy, so will be enforced by the courts only where the restraint can be shown to be no wider than is reasonably necessary to protect the legitimate business interests of the employer. For this reason, covenants are usually 'tailor-made' to suit the needs of that particular employer in relation to its products, customers and catchment area. Were it to be applied, literally, to a different employer, with possibly different products, customers and catchment area, a covenant may cease, as drafted, to be reasonable, and thus be unenforceable.

Related to this, the question arises as to whether Reg 4(2) can possibly have the effect of transferring the benefit of a restrictive covenant to a purchaser whose specific needs may be very different. The Court of Session in McCall v Initial Supplies Ltd 1992 SLT 67, Ct Sess (Outer House), doubted that it could. To hold otherwise, the Court reasoned, would mean that in certain situations the substitution of the transferee could radically alter the rights and duties of the parties to the contract of employment. To take an example, a restrictive covenant which prohibits the poaching of an employer's customers may be reasonable in the context of a small company. However, if that company is transferred to a large multinational, the group of customers to whom the restriction purportedly applies may increase substantially, in both numerical and geographical terms.

3.55 Another argument against the transfer of restrictive covenants could be that the whole purpose of the Acquired Rights Directive (and therefore the purpose of the national law that implements it) is to protect employees who are subjected

236

to a transfer. As restrictive covenants are in the interests of the employer, surely TUPE has no place in seeking to preserve them.

In Morris Angel and Son Ltd v Hollande and anor 1993 ICR 71, CA, however, the Court of Appeal confirmed that restrictive covenants *do* transfer under TUPE. The question is rather how the transferred covenant should be interpreted. The covenant in question, which was contained in H's service agreement, restrained him from dealing after his dismissal with persons who had done business with the employer or its subsidiaries in the previous year. H was dismissed when the company for which he worked was transferred to MA Ltd under TUPE. The Court found that what is now Reg 4(1) gave the purchasing employer standing to enforce the covenant to restrain the employee from dealing with former clients of the transferred undertaking. However, the covenant could not be read in a way that restricted H from dealing with those who had been customers of the transferee in the year leading up to the transfer, since that would be to radically alter the nature of the agreement (and H had not been seeking to deal with those customers in any event). As Dillon LJ put it: 'Such an obligation was not remotely in contemplation when the service agreement was entered into and I can see no reason why [Reg 4] should have sought to change the burden on the employee.' However, the Court went on to hold that Reg 4(1) required the covenant to be read, purposively and retrospectively, as though it had been agreed between H and the transferee as *owner* of the undertaking. This gave the transferee standing to enforce the covenant in respect of persons who had been clients of the transferred undertaking in the year prior to dismissal. This solution also deals with the problem of enforceability, discussed above, as the reinterpreted covenant was no wider than it had been before the transfer. In effect, the 're-interpretation' of the covenant to take on board the entrance of the transferee into the equation is to be filtered through the prism of the position as it pertained with the transferor with regard to the customer base, competitors, location, etc.

3.56 The Court of Appeal in Morris Angel also dealt with the issue of the protective purpose of TUPE: 'There is no doubt that the protection of employees' rights was the primary objective but any contract of employment is a complex of rights and obligations on each side, and in Litster and ors v Forth Dry Dock and Engineering Co Ltd (in receivership) and anor 1989 ICR 341, HL, Lord Templeman summed up the effect of the Acquired Rights Directive as being that upon the transfer of a business from one employer to another the benefit and burden of a contract of employment between the transferor and a worker in the business should devolve on the transferee.'

The distinguishing factor between the decisions in McCall v Initial Supplies Ltd (above) and Morris Angel and Son Ltd v Hollande and anor (above) is probably that in Morris Angel the employee was dismissed immediately after the transfer and so the transferred undertaking and its clients could still be seen as a separate entity from the rest of the transferee's business, while in McCall the employee remained with the company for a year after the transfer. Thus, it remains to be seen whether Morris Angel establishes a general rule or whether it turns to a large extent on its own facts. In particular, the Court did not have to consider what meaning the covenant might have had if the employee had been dismissed (or resigned) six or 12 months after the transfer. If Morris Angel does establish a general rule, its effect will be to freeze the scope of, for example, a non-dealing covenant as at the date of the transfer, and any dealings that the employee has after termination with persons who became customers of the transferee after the transfer will not be caught by it.

3.57 Even with the benefit of the Court of Appeal's approach in Morris Angel and Son Ltd v Hollande and anor (above), a restrictive covenant may cease to provide suitable protection for the new owner. If covenants are to receive a limited interpretation following transfer, it would be advisable for transferees to renegotiate more appropriate ones once the transfer has taken place so as to make them more relevant to the transferee's business, and thus more likely to be enforced by the courts. But considerable care needs to be taken in this regard. Any renegotiated covenants could be set aside under Reg 4(4) on the basis that the sole or principal reason for the variation was the transfer – see Crédit Suisse First Boston (Europe) Ltd v Lister 1999 ICR 794, CA. In order to ensure that any agreed variation is valid and enforceable, the transferee would have to show that the sole or principal reason for the variation is 'an economic, technical or organisational reason entailing changes in the workforce' or that the terms of the contract permit the employer to make the variation in question – Reg 4(5). For a further detailed discussion, see Chapter 5, 'Changing terms and conditions', under 'Varying terms in a TUPE context'.

3.58 **Continued enforceability by transferor.** The problem, however, does not end there. What are the consequences for the transferor? If it transfers only part of its business, it loses the benefit of the restrictive covenant for the retained part of the business. This issue may be best addressed by warranties or indemnities between the transferor and the transferee. The transferor will also lose the benefit of provisions as to confidential information, whether express or implied. Remember, too, the principle that an employer may not enforce the benefit of a contract where it has committed a repudiatory breach. As the transferee inherits any breaches of contract from the transferor by virtue of Reg 4(2)(b), its ability to enforce restrictive covenants may be jeopardised.

In New ISG Ltd v Vernon 2008 ICR 319, ChD, the identity of the transferee was withheld by the transferor. On learning of the identity of their new employer after the transfer had taken place, a number of employees objected to the TUPE transfer. The transferee sought interim injunctions to enforce restrictive covenant clauses in the employees' contracts of employment. It argued that the right to object to the TUPE transfer must be exercised before the transfer and, as the employees did not do so, they could not prevent Reg 4(2) from operating to transfer the benefit of the restrictive covenants to it. The High Court held that, in the circumstances, the employees' objection could be treated as if it had occurred before the transfer, since no valid opportunity had been accorded to the employees to object to the change of employer before then. The objection had retrospective effect and prevented the operation of TUPE from automatically transferring the employees' contracts of employment containing the restraint of trade clause to the transferee. Therefore, the transferee employer's application for injunctive relief was refused.

Implied contractual duty of fidelity. All contracts of employment contain an **3.59** implied duty on the part of the employee to provide faithful service to the employer. Essentially, this means that the employee is under an obligation not to act in a way that is contrary to the interests of the employer, and this can include an implied obligation not to compete with the employer's business and commercial interests without authorisation. Clearly, whenever the contract of an employee is transferred on a relevant TUPE transfer, the transferee inherits the benefit of this implied term by virtue of the application of Reg 4(2).

However, in rare cases, difficulties can arise. For example, what if the transferred employee worked part time with the transferor and part time for another employer which happens to be a commercial rival of the transferee? Can the transferee rely on and enforce the implied duty of fidelity to prevent the employee from continuing to work for the competitor? Although there do not appear to have been any decided cases addressing this issue, it is arguable that a distinction can be drawn between an express restraint clause on the one hand and on the implied duty of fidelity on the other. As discussed under 'Enforceability by transferee' above, in the former situation, although the transferee may inherit the benefit of a restrictive covenant, its ambit will be assessed by reference to the identity of the customers and competitors of the transferor, which may well mean that the scope of the clause would not necessarily preclude the worker continuing to work for a company that was not a competitor of the transferor even though it is a competitor of the transferee. In contrast, the implied duty of fidelity is not normally dependent on, or limited by, the express terms of the contract of employment. This makes it more likely that the transferee could simply argue that the duty of fidelity owed by the transferred employee extends to faithful service to it judged by reference to the transferee's prevailing interests, including the identify of its competitors, whether or not these are different from the transferor's.

Share option schemes   3.60

Employers generally seek to keep share incentive arrangements distinct and separate from the recipient's contract of employment in an attempt to limit the damages the employee might be able to claim for the loss of the share incentive if dismissed. However, in the context of TUPE the expectation that share schemes (especially all-employee share plans) lie outside the employment contract has to be adjusted, since the right to participate in a scheme is clearly either a term of the contract of employment or at least a right very closely connected with it, and as such falls within the scope of Reg 4(2)(a). Rights and liabilities under such a scheme would accordingly be transferred to the transferee. The same would appear to be the case with an employee's right to participate in a profit-sharing scheme (see below).

But a conclusion that liability to continue a share option scheme passes to the transferee upon a relevant transfer is likely to cause considerable practical difficulties. Where, for example, the business of a company is sold to a trading partnership it will be impossible for the partnership to provide the employees with the same rights to buy shares in the new, unincorporated, business. There may therefore be convincing commercial grounds for stopping employees from participating in share option schemes upon the occasion of a relevant transfer. The problem is that in that case the transferee could be in breach of contract and have to face claims for damages – which could be substantial – or even claims of constructive dismissal. Executive employees in particular may lose out on the chance to obtain future share options, as well as the opportunity to exercise existing rights.

3.61 The little case law on the subject that exists demonstrates, however, that it is by no means a given that rights under share option schemes may be enforced against the transferee following a relevant transfer. The precise terms of a scheme are likely to be decisive in determining whether it is capable of surviving the transfer of a business. In Chapman and anor v CPS Computer Group plc 1987 IRLR 462, CA, C and E were employed by a subsidiary of CPS and were entitled to participate in CPS's share option scheme. They could not exercise their rights in the scheme until a specific period of time had passed unless, at any time before the end of that period, one of a number of events intervened – for example, if they were dismissed for redundancy. CPS sold the subsidiary and C and E sought to exercise their options, claiming that they had become redundant because CPS had ceased to carry on the business in which they were employed, despite the fact that what is now Reg 4 applied to transfer their contracts to the purchaser. In the course of its decision, the Court of Appeal held that although Reg 4 transferred the claimants' employment, it did not affect their rights to exercise their options under the share option contract, which was a separate and discrete contract and so was not transferred by Reg 4(2). On the facts of the case, therefore, the sale of the business triggered the claimants' rights to exercise their options.

However, although the Chapman case has never been overruled or officially doubted in subsequent cases, we take the view that it is likely that this point would be decided differently today. Given the Court of Appeal's decision in Martin v Lancashire County Council and another case 2001 ICR 197, CA (see

'Tortious and other civil liabilities' below) – that Reg 4(2)(a) could extend even to a transferor's right against a third party insurer – so long as the right related to a liability 'under' or 'in connection with' the employment contract, it seems unlikely that a contract that contained benefits connected with the employment contract (or at the very least, with the employment relationship) would not be covered by Reg 4(2)(a), even if that contract was 'separate and discrete'. However, there is at least one scenario in which share option rights might not be capable of transfer. Reg 4(2)(a), as we have seen, operates to transfer the 'rights, powers, duties and liabilities' of the transferor under or in connection with the employment contract. Where an employee owns options over stock in a group company that is not the transferor, it is arguable that those options are incapable of transfer under Reg 4(2)(a). The same could apply to a profit-sharing scheme where an employee of a subsidiary receives benefits from another group company calculated on the basis of the profits of the group of companies as a whole.

3.62 Even if Chapman and anor v CPS Computer Group plc (above) was wrongly decided and share options contained in collateral contracts *are* capable of transfer under Reg 4(2)(a), it may well be the case that TUPE preserves rights in any share option scheme after the transfer only to the extent that the rules of the scheme allow. The employment contract itself may permit an employee to be a member of such a scheme, but the rules may provide employers with a unilateral right of termination and exclusion of liability.

The question of whether such rules are enforceable arose for consideration in Micklefield v SAC Technology Ltd 1990 IRLR 218, ChD, and Levett v Biotrace International plc 1999 ICR 815, CA. In Micklefield, a clause in a share option agreement stating that the option holder had to continue to be employed in order to exercise the option granted, and would be deemed to have waived his right to damages for loss of his option rights as part of any claim for compensation for loss of office, was held to exempt the employer from liability to pay compensation for loss of rights under the option scheme. In the circumstances, the plaintiff was not entitled to recover damages for loss of his option rights even if he could show that he had been wrongfully dismissed just before the date when the option became exercisable. In Levett, however, the Court of Appeal took a different line, holding that an employee who was summarily dismissed by a company in breach of his contract of employment was entitled to exercise an option to purchase shares that the company had previously granted him. Although the rules of the share option scheme provided that the option would lapse in the event of the employee being dismissed following disciplinary action, the unlawfulness of the dismissal prevented the employer from relying upon it to deprive the employee of his rights under the scheme. That was because the general rule of construction – that a party to a contract cannot take advantage of his or her own wrongdoing – applied in the absence of any clear wording to the contrary within the scheme's rules.

241

3.63 Thus, it seems that, while share option schemes are capable of transfer, the extent to which a transferee is bound by them will depend upon the rules of the scheme (including any condition excluding the employer's liability for damages for the cessation of share option rights) and the circumstances of the case. But even if a transferee inherits liability under a share option scheme, it will still find itself faced with the difficulties outlined above of applying that scheme in practice. In such circumstances, it is likely that the obligation on the transferee is to provide a 'substantially equivalent' scheme – see Mitie Managed Services Ltd v French and ors 2002 ICR 1395, EAT (a case concerning a profit-sharing scheme, discussed under 'Profit-sharing schemes and profit-related and performance-related pay' below). The transferee will need to take legal advice about this, especially as – for the reasons outlined above – it is likely to be difficult for a new employer to provide transferred employees with exactly the same benefits they would have received if they had stayed in their original employer's share plan. The new employer may not even be a company and so may not be able to offer any type of share incentive arrangement. Even if it is a company, it cannot issue employees with shares in the old employer. Indeed, in many cases, the employees might not benefit from such an arrangement – the TUPE transfer itself may have been prompted by the fact that the transferor company had been performing badly or has ceased or intends to cease to trade.

What a 'substantially equivalent' all-employee share scheme might comprise could be determined by negotiation between the transferor and the transferee or between the transferee and the employees or their union, or by application to an employment tribunal for a determination of the relevant particulars of employment under S.11 ERA – see Mitie Managed Services Ltd v French and ors (above). The replacement plan clearly need not be in precisely the same form as the transferor's original plan and might, for example, take the form of a phantom share plan. This typically provides a right to receive a cash bonus calculated by reference to a notional share option. The bonus paid equals the gain that could have been realised at the time the bonus is paid on the exercise of an option to acquire a certain number of shares at a certain exercise price (usually defined by the market value of the shares at the time the phantom option was granted). Other features of phantom option arrangements also closely replicate the operation of real share option arrangements. For example, phantom options will usually be subject to performance conditions, continued employment requirements and vesting periods, all of which – in order to satisfy the 'substantial equivalence' requirement – should match as closely as practicable the terms of the original scheme.

3.64 **Profit-sharing schemes and profit-related and performance-related pay**

Profit- or performance-related schemes usually provide for a payment to be made to an employee in respect of past performance, either of the business or the individual, calculated over a reference period. Problems may occur, therefore, where a profit-sharing scheme is based on the overall performance of a company that is selling only part of its business – in order to continue such a scheme, the purchaser of that part would have to have inside access to details of the transferor's overall performance. Or, where the payment date for a profit- or performance-related scheme falls after the date of a relevant TUPE transfer, the transferee will (assuming it inherits the transferor's liabilities under such a scheme) have to calculate payments due by reference to work done during a qualifying period with the transferor.

However, such potential logistical difficulties have not prevented the courts holding that liabilities under such schemes transfer under Reg 4(2). In Unicorn Consultancy Services Ltd v Westbrook and ors 2000 IRLR 80, EAT, W and others were employed by WSA Ltd, a company forming part of the Atkins Group. The employees belonged to a profit-related pay scheme and had all worked for the full profit year for the scheme, from 1 April 1996 to 31 March 1997. On 31 March 1997 the contract on which the employees were engaged came to an end and a new contract was awarded to UCS Ltd. The transfer – a 'relevant transfer' for the purposes of TUPE – took place on 1 April. The employees brought employment tribunal proceedings against UCS Ltd on the ground that the new employer had a continuing duty to pay them profit-related pay. The EAT held that under what is now Reg 4(2)(a) the transferor's liability to pay profit-related pay to its employees transferred to the transferee upon a relevant transfer. In addition, Reg 4(1) and (2)(b) meant that the rules of the scheme had to be interpreted on the basis that the employees' contracts were to have effect after the transfer as if they had been made between the employees and the transferee. So where the rules provided that 'only those employed' in a company in the Atkins Group at a particular date would receive payment, this was to be construed as merely requiring employment in the undertaking transferred, not as requiring continued employment by a company within the Atkins Group. The employees therefore qualified for payment of profit-related pay.

The Unicorn case makes it clear that if the performance period has expired, the **3.65** transferee is obliged to make payment. Where the period for calculating the payment spans the transfer, however, more difficult problems potentially arise. Following the transfer, how can profits continue to be calculated by reference to the profits of the transferor – which no longer has any control over the performance of the entity transferred and with which the relevant employees no longer have any connection? Or, where the name of the transferee is simply substituted for that of the transferor – to quote Lord Coulsfield's obiter observation in McCall v Initial Supplies Ltd 1992 SLT 67, Ct Sess (Outer House) – 'an employee whose remuneration included an annual bonus related to his employer's profits for the year would... be entitled to claim a bonus related to the acquirer of the undertaking, if the acquisition had taken place during the year'. This would have the effect of radically altering the rights and obligations of the parties, if the new owner was considerably more (or less) profitable than the old. Mr Justice Charles acknowledged these difficulties in the Unicorn case, when he expressed his obiter opinion that where a TUPE transfer takes place during the profit period, a transferee might be under an obligation to provide a replacement scheme, or make payments equivalent to those earned under the transferor's scheme – and that this would accord with the underlying purpose of TUPE.

The EAT has since had the opportunity to address this issue directly in Mitie Managed Services Ltd v French and ors 2002 ICR 1395, EAT, where F was employed by a company that was part of the Sainsbury's group, and was entitled under her contract to the benefits of an Inland Revenue-approved profit-sharing scheme ('the Sainsbury's Scheme'). Under the Sainsbury's Scheme, eligible employees received either cash payments or awards of shares in the parent company. The size of such payments or awards related to the annual consolidated profits of the group. On 17 May 1999 the part of the undertaking in which F was employed transferred to PBMS Ltd under TUPE. Following the transfer, F and six colleagues brought an application in an employment tribunal under S.11 ERA seeking a declaration as to their particulars of employment with PBMS Ltd. The employees argued that, by virtue of what is now Reg 4, they were entitled to continue to receive payments and awards of shares under the Sainsbury's Scheme, for which their new employer, PBMS Ltd, would be liable. The tribunal considered that all existing contractual terms had transferred under Reg 4 and had to be honoured or lawfully varied, however inconvenient that might be. It held, therefore, that the employees' contracts continued to contain a clause entitling them to payments and awards under the Sainsbury's Scheme. PBMS Ltd appealed to the EAT.

3.66 Before the appeal hearing, a further transfer of the undertaking took place, this time to MMS Ltd, which was substituted for PBMS Ltd as the appellant. MMS Ltd argued that it would be impossible for it to carry out obligations that the employment tribunal said had transferred, since it had no way of accessing the confidential information required to operate the Sainsbury's Scheme and no ability to issue shares in Sainsbury's. Furthermore, MMS Ltd argued that it would be odd if the employees' pay were to be determined by reference to the profits of a company for which they no longer worked. MMS Ltd stated that these problems could be avoided if the EAT were to take a broad approach to Reg 4 and argued, by reference to Unicorn Consultancy Services Ltd v Westbrook and ors (above), that the employees' rights could be safeguarded if they were entitled to participate in a different profit-sharing scheme, operated by reference to the performance of the employing entity. The employees argued for a strict interpretation of Reg 4 as set out by the tribunal – if the legislature had intended to create a special rule in respect of profit-sharing schemes then it would have been done so expressly, in the same way that it created an express rule to exclude pension schemes. They cited in support the decision of the ECJ in Abels v Administrative Board of the Bedrijfsvereniging voor de Metaalindustrie en de Electrotechnische Industrie 1987 2 CMLR 406, ECJ, in which the Court held that the existence of a specific exclusion for pension schemes led to the conclusion that all other rights of employees must transfer.

The EAT held that the employment tribunal had erred in finding that, following a transfer of an undertaking, contractual terms relating to profit-related pay had been preserved word-for-word under the transferring employees' contracts, thereby entitling the employees to continue to participate, at the transferee's expense, in a profit-sharing scheme operated by the transferor. Any interpretation of Reg 4(2) should avoid giving rise to absurdities or injustices. In this case, the transferee was unable to issue shares in the transferor company and was not entitled to confidential information belonging to the transferor. The entitlement found by the employment tribunal would be impossible for the transferee to perform and, accordingly, the tribunal's construction of Reg 4(2) produced a result that was absurd and unjust. In the light of the ECJ's decision in Abels, it would be difficult if not impossible to argue that a profit-related pay entitlement could not be the subject of a transfer, but that case is not conclusive as to precisely what transfers by way of contractual entitlement in relation to a particular scheme. The EAT concluded that, in a case such as this, the transferred employees were entitled to participate in a scheme of substantial equivalence but one that was free from unjust, absurd or impossible features. Such an approach was consistent with the purpose of the Regulations and of the Acquired Rights Directive to protect workers and, more particularly, to safeguard their rights upon a change of employer. The EAT therefore allowed the transferee's appeal and remitted the case to the employment tribunal to determine appropriate particulars substantially equivalent to the transferor's profit-sharing scheme.

3.67 This is not the first time that the courts have needed to take a broad view of Reg 4 in order to produce a workable result: see, for example, Morris Angel and Son Ltd v Hollande and anor 1993 ICR 71, CA (discussed under 'Restrictive covenants and non-compete obligations' above), where the Court of Appeal had to consider the effect of Reg 4 on a restrictive covenant restraining the employee from dealing with the transferor's clients following termination of employment. In Mitie Managed Services Ltd v French and ors (above), the EAT anticipated that in most cases a transferee company would be able to negotiate an equivalent scheme with the employees or their unions, but failing that an application could be made to an employment tribunal for a determination of the relevant particulars of employment under S.11 ERA. It is possible that the validity of a 'substantially equivalent' scheme might be open to challenge by a disgruntled employee in the light of the House of Lords' decision in (1) British Fuels Ltd v Baxendale and anor (2) Wilson and ors v St Helens Borough Council 1998 ICR 1141, HL, on the basis that an agreement to vary the terms of employment had been reached by reason of the transfer of an undertaking and

245

was therefore void by virtue of Reg 4(4) – see Chapter 5, 'Changing terms and conditions', under 'Varying terms in a TUPE context', for a detailed explanation of the effect of Reg 4(4). However, Mr Justice Maurice Kay in Mitie considered that the issue was not consensual variation of the profit-related pay entitlement, but 'what has been transferred in the absence of such consensual variation'. In any event, employees have the right, under Reg 4(9), to treat their employment as having been terminated if a relevant transfer involves a 'substantial change' in their working conditions to their material detriment – see Chapter 4, 'Unfair dismissal', under 'Material detriment dismissals'.

This issue was revisited by an employment tribunal in Tomlin v EDS Ltd ET Case No.2702211/07. T began working for Vodafone Ltd in October 1999 and his employment was transferred to EDS Ltd in January 2007. He claimed that EDS Ltd had breached his contract in that he had lost the opportunity to participate in a share save and incentive scheme operated by his previous employer. The tribunal dismissed his claim as the share scheme T had referred to was, in fact, provided by Vodafone Group plc, which was not the transferor. Furthermore, in order for the transferee to create a tax-free scheme similar to that operated by Vodafone, it would have been necessary for the EDS Group to create a scheme that was open to all of its employees, including those employed by EDS Ltd. However, EDS Group was not the transferee either. The tribunal held that the scheme fell outside the scope of TUPE as it would not be appropriate to expect third parties who have nothing to do with the TUPE transfer to create schemes of this nature.

3.68 Staff discounts

Similar issues may arise in relation to benefits that can only be provided by the transferor (for example, staff discounts on the employer's own products or services). Although this is not a matter that appears to have been tackled by the UK courts or tribunals, it has come up for consideration by the courts in Germany. In Endres v T-Systems International GmbH, unreported, Federal Labour Court Germany, the claimant was a former employee of DaimlerChrysler AG. Under the terms of its 'company member scheme', the employer granted employees favourable conditions for acquiring vehicles produced by the company, i.e. Mercedes-Benz cars. These benefits included the ability to purchase vehicles at a reduced purchase price, have them serviced free of charge, and sell them back to the company at a later date. In 2000 DaimlerChrysler AG sold the division in which the claimant worked to T-Systems International GmbH. In the course of this sale the claimant's employment relationship was transferred under the German legal equivalent to TUPE. The claimant, who had purchased Mercedes vehicles under the company member scheme on a number of occasions, ordered a new Mercedes after his employment relationship had passed to T-Systems International GmbH and requested a discount on the basis of the terms of the scheme. In dismissing his claim, the Federal Labour

Court held that the transferee was not under an obligation to grant staff whose contracts had been transferred the right to purchase products from their previous employer (i.e. Mercedes-Benz vehicles) with the same special staff conditions. The Court ruled that staff purchases could only be made for products that the employer actually produced itself and that the loss of this right with regard to the transferor's products did not constitute a breach of the business transfer provisions.

It has to be stressed that the Endres case concerned remunerative benefits applicable to the transferor's own products. Had the benefits applied to products and services offered by a third party (for example, gym membership or a discount scheme arranged with a national department store), then there would be no reason why the transferee should not be required to provide the equivalent benefit under the principle established by the EAT in Mitie Managed Services Ltd v French and ors 2002 ICR 1395, EAT (discussed under 'Profit-sharing schemes, profit-related pay and performance-related pay' above).

Equipment hire schemes   3.69

The benefit of cycle-to-work schemes are increasingly offered to employees who work in large cities. They typically entail the employer purchasing bicycles and related equipment and loaning these to employees, who pay for the 'hire' during the loan period through a salary sacrifice arrangement. Such schemes are tax-efficient because employees' payments come out of their gross rather than net pay. Usually, at the end of the loan period, the employees are eligible to purchase the bike or return it to the employer. The problem in a TUPE context is that, following a transfer, the transferor may have difficulty continuing to obtain repayment once the employee has ceased to be employed by it. Even if the bikes are returned at the time of transfer, the transferor will be left with a depreciating asset in the form of a stockpile of bicycles it no longer needs. This is likely to be the case even if the transferee has an existing cycle-to-work scheme in place which the transferred employees can join or sets up a new scheme in order to match the benefit previously provided by the transferor. Similar issues are likely to arise in respect of other equipment loaned to employees where the debt to the employer is reimbursed via a salary sacrifice arrangement (e.g. laptop loan schemes).

To deal with this problem, it may be possible for the transferor and transferee to agree between themselves that the hire agreements with the employees are transferred to the transferee; or alternatively, that the transferor's debts are recovered as part of the overall transfer deal.

Settlement agreements   3.70

It is common for employers to use settlement agreements to seek to protect themselves against potential claims from employees whom they have made redundant (or whose employment has otherwise been terminated) – all the

247

more so where an employee is dismissed in the context of a TUPE transfer, as the parties are likely to feel even more uncertain as to their position in law. We discuss the extent to which settlement agreements are effective to compromise an employee's rights under TUPE – and whether it is effective to use settlement agreements to manage the dismissal of employees for the purpose of re-engaging them post-transfer on different terms and conditions – in Chapter 5, 'Changing terms and conditions', under 'Alternative strategies for effecting changes', and Chapter 10, 'Contracting out of TUPE'. Here, we consider the extent to which the transferee can benefit from a settlement agreement that was made between the transferor and an employee who was (or would have been had he or she not been dismissed) assigned to the transferring entity.

There is little case law on the subject. But if a settlement agreement can be argued to contain benefits for the transferor 'in connection with' the employment contract, within the meaning of Reg 4(2)(a), then those benefits will pass to the transferee. It might be argued that while a settlement agreement may indeed seek to compromise an employee's contractual claims, it is likely to relate also to the settlement of statutory employment claims (given that employment-related statutory claims cannot, as a rule, be settled except through the means of a formal settlement agreement or an Acas-conciliated settlement). However, this would be an unduly restrictive objection. Following the ruling of Lord Templeman in Litster and ors v Forth Dry Dock and Engineering Co Ltd (in receivership) and anor 1989 ICR 341, HL, the courts must give the TUPE Regulations a purposive construction to ensure that they effect the transfer of all rights and obligations envisaged by the Acquired Rights Directive. And Article 3(1) of the Directive states that the transferor's rights and obligations transfer to the transferee upon a relevant transfer, where they arise from an employment contract 'or from an employment relationship'. It seems likely that a settlement agreement effected between the transferor and an employee will contain rights arising from their employment relationship.

3.71 Another objection might be that if the point of the Directive is to protect employees' rights upon a relevant transfer, why should it seek to impute to the transferee rights to enforce a settlement agreement as against the employee? A settlement agreement, though perhaps in the employee's financial interest, hardly protects his or her employment rights. However, the wording of Article 3(1) of the Directive is clear – the rights of the transferor, as well as its obligations, pass to the transferee. And, following Litster, 'upon the transfer of a business from one employer to another the benefit and burden of a contract of employment between the transferor and a worker in the business should devolve on the transferee'.

Sometimes the parties to a transfer will adopt a belt and braces approach and seek to enter into tripartite agreements – between the transferor, transferee and employee – compromising the employee's rights. Such an agreement, if entered into before the transfer, would have to be very clearly worded to enable the transferee to enforce it, as the employee would be compromising his or her rights against the transferee in respect of claims that do not yet exist – see Royal National Orthopaedic Hospital Trust v Howard 2002 IRLR 849, EAT, and University of East London v Hinton 2005 ICR 1260, CA. However, if for any reason settlement agreements are not concluded before the date of the transfer, the transferee must ensure that it is a party to them in order to benefit from their terms. In Thompson and ors v Walon Car Delivery and anor 1997 IRLR 343, EAT, BRS Automotive Ltd lost a contract for car distribution with Saab to WCD. WCD did not want to take on the relevant BRS employees, so BRS began to negotiate settlement terms with those employees. In the event, while settlement terms were reached in draft form by the date of the transfer, these were not formalised, through Acas conciliation, until a few days after the transfer. The EAT held that liability for the employees' unfair dismissals passed to the transferee at the moment of transfer and the transferee could not rely on a settlement agreement entered into between the transferor and the employee *after* the date of the transfer to avoid such liability. (Note that the situation might have been different had the employees attempted to make claims for breach of contract against the transferee instead of unfair dismissal, given the tribunal's finding that the terms of the settlement agreement, which included settlement of contractual claims, were 'in place' by the date of the transfer. In so far as a settlement fulfils the common law requirements for a binding legal contract, it will be effective to compromise contractual claims, even if it has not yet been formalised.)

If the benefit of a settlement agreement entered into between the transferor and **3.72** the employee before the transfer passes to the transferee, the transferee will be protected in respect of any claim made against it by the employee according to the settlement terms, to the extent that the agreement is valid. This will, however, leave the transferor without the benefit of the settlement agreement (see 'Continuing liability of transferor?' below). The transferor should therefore address this issue by negotiating indemnities against future liabilities with the transferee – see Chapter 11, 'Practical aspects of transfers', for practical advice in this respect. (In certain circumstances, however, a transferor may be able to benefit from a sum paid to an employee under a settlement agreement with the transferee after dismissal on the date of the transfer. In Steele v Boston Borough Council EAT 1083/01 the EAT held that an employee who was not assigned to the entity transferred had not made a valid compromise agreement (as settlement agreements were then called) with the transferee because he was not its employee. But the sum paid to him by the transferee as purported consideration for that agreement could be taken into account when calculating compensation in respect of his subsequent claim for unfair dismissal against the transferor. The same result was reached in Optimum Group Services plc v Muir 2013 IRLR 339, EATS, even though the employment tribunal in that case found that there was in fact no relevant transfer. The money that the claimant received from the putative transferee in settlement of his claim against it fell to be deducted from his compensation from the putative transferor for ordinary unfair dismissal.)

3.73 Occupational pensions

Occupational pension schemes are expressly excluded from the operation of the automatic transfer principles in Regs 4 and 5 of the TUPE Regulations (Reg 5 is concerned with the transfer of collective agreements and is discussed under 'Collective rights and liabilities – transfer of collective agreements' below). In this regard, Reg 10(1) provides that Regs 4 and 5 shall not apply:

- to so much of a contract of employment or collective agreement as relates to an occupational pension scheme – Reg 10(1)(a), or

- to any rights, powers, duties or liabilities under or in connection with any such agreement or otherwise arising in connection with that person's employment and relating to such a scheme – Reg 10(1)(b).

The exclusion of occupational pension schemes has the important consequence that employees' rights under such schemes do not automatically transfer to their employment with the transferee, even though their contracts are otherwise preserved by virtue of Reg 4(1). The Acquired Rights Directive allows Member States to exclude pension schemes in their implementing legislation, so the Regulations are not in breach of the Directive in this respect. Article 3(4)(a) states that, unless Member States provide otherwise, the automatic transfer provisions do not cover 'employees' rights to old-age, invalidity or survivors' benefits under supplementary company or inter-company pension schemes outside the statutory social security schemes in Member States'.

3.74 However, it is important to note that the ambit of the permissible exclusion is tightly defined. As a consequence, many aspects of modern occupational pension schemes and the benefits payable under or in association with them may fall outside the scope of the Reg 10 exclusion and will thus be transferred by virtue of Regs 4 and/or 5. Furthermore, all employers are now under a statutory duty to provide a basic floor of pension rights to employees, which means that a transferee will be required to continue a minimal level of pension provision to employees following the transfer. These matters are dealt with in more detail below.

3.75 Aspects of pension schemes that do transfer

Notwithstanding the general exclusion of occupational pension schemes from the automatic transfer principle by virtue of Reg 10, the transferee should not assume that it will escape any responsibility relating to pensions. Note the following:

250

- Reg 10 applies only to *occupational* pension schemes (as defined by S.1 of the Pensions Schemes Act 1993). Therefore Reg 4 will apply to transfer in full any rights, powers, duties and liabilities that relate to non-occupational pension schemes such as personal pension schemes. This includes private pension arrangements that are administered through the employer where a contribution is made by the employer into each employee's private pension plan – see Evans and ors v Television Versioning and Translation Ltd ET Case No.3302295/11

- Reg 10(2) provides that any provisions of an occupational pension scheme that do not relate to benefits for old age, invalidity or survivors shall not, for these purposes, be treated as being part of the scheme. In other words, Regs 4 and 5 will apply to transfer liability relating to rights and benefits under any part of an occupational pension scheme that does not relate to benefits for old age, invalidity or survivors: see discussion of Beckmann v Dynamco Whicheloe Macfarlane Ltd 2003 ICR 50, ECJ, and Martin and ors v South Bank University 2004 ICR 1234, ECJ, under 'Definition of "occupational pension scheme" – benefits for old age, invalidity or survivors' below

- under Reg 5, the transferee will inherit the terms of any collective agreement relating to a personal pension scheme – see 'Collective rights and liabilities – transfer of collective agreements' below

- although terms relating to occupational pension schemes do not transfer (subject to the exclusion in Reg 10(2) discussed above), UK law provides that the transferee must make available for eligible transferring employees, after the transfer, a minimum level of future pension benefits. The relevant provisions are set out in the Pensions Act 2004 and the Transfer of Employment (Pension Protection) Regulations 2005 SI 2005/649. For more detail, see 'Ongoing obligation to protect immediate and prospective rights – duty to provide future pension protections' below

- Reg 10(1) excludes the operation of Regs 4 and 5 only. In other words, the transferee will continue to bear responsibilities under other provisions in the TUPE Regulations relating to occupational pension schemes. For example, it will be obliged to include as a matter for information and consultation under Reg 13 any measure that it proposes to take in relation to affected employees' pension rights and benefits.

3.76 A transferee cannot rely upon the exclusion in Reg 10 TUPE if it has expressly or impliedly agreed to replicate employees' occupational pension entitlements. In such a case the transfer of pension rights then operates via a form of *contractual* novation entirely independently of TUPE – see Whitney v Monster Worldwide Ltd 2010 EWCA Civ 1312, CA. Contractual novation – whereby two parties to a contract agree that a third party, who also agrees, shall take the place of one of them – is by no means a new concept. However, the Whitney

251

case is a particularly striking example of the principle. The Court of Appeal held that an employer's assurances to an employee made over 20 years ago that he would be no worse off when his accrued occupational pension benefits were transferred from a final salary scheme to a money purchase scheme were contractually binding, despite the absence of any single formal document setting out the contractual arrangement. Furthermore, the employer's obligations under the arrangement passed to the employee's subsequent employer following a TUPE transfer, notwithstanding the fact that old age occupational benefits are exempt from TUPE. The Court held that, rather than a statutory novation under TUPE, there had been a form of contractual novation, whereby the transferee employer had agreed to replicate the transferred employee's pension entitlements following the transfer.

Later cases indicate that this agreement may be inferred if it is not explicit. In BT plc v Adamson and ors EAT 0282/12, for example, the EAT approved an employment tribunal's decision to award compensation for pension loss to transferred employees who had been unfairly dismissed in connection with the transfer. The tribunal had been entitled to accept evidence that BT plc customarily honoured transferring employees' pension rights. Thus, it was more likely than not that, absent the unfair dismissal, BT plc would have given the claimants a pension no less favourable than that which they enjoyed pre-transfer.

3.77 Definition of 'occupational pension scheme'

An 'occupational pension scheme' for the purposes of the Reg 10 exclusion is defined in S.1 of the Pension Schemes Act 1993. Broadly speaking, such a scheme aims to provide benefits to, or in respect of, people in a particular employment or employments, and is established by (or by persons who include) the employer, a relevant employee or an interested body. The administration of the scheme must fall within either the UK or another country outside the EU. Where a pension scheme fails to meet this description – as will be the case in respect of a personal pension scheme and, probably, a group personal pension scheme – the scheme will not fall within the exclusion in Reg 10 and will therefore pass to the transferee under Reg 4(2).

3.78 Benefits for old age, invalidity or survivors.

Regulation 10(2) states that any provisions of an occupational pension scheme that do not relate to benefits for old age, invalidity or survivors shall not, for the purposes of Reg 10, be treated as being part of the scheme. In other words, Regs 4 and 5 will apply to transfer rights under any part of an occupational pension scheme that does not relate to benefits for old age, invalidity or survivors. Predictably, this provision – or at least Article 3(4) of the Acquired Rights Directive, from which it derives – has spawned a number of cases on the meaning of 'old age, invalidity or survivors' benefits'. In each of the following cases the claimants were employed on the former General Whitley Council (GWC) conditions of service (now substituted by equivalent arrangements under the NHS 'Agenda for Change' initiative). The GWC was a system of establishing employment conditions in the public sector through joint negotiations between employers and employees. Section 45 of the GWC conditions of service provided for lump sum redundancy payments to be made to employees of various NHS bodies on dismissal by reason of redundancy, with such payments to be paid by the employer. Section 46 set out the terms of the Collective Agreement on Premature Payment of Superannuation and Compensation Benefits. For employees aged between 50 and normal retirement age who had at least five years' service within the NHS Superannuation Scheme, Section 46 provided for early retirement with immediate payment of a retirement pension and compensation in three circumstances: dismissal for redundancy; retirement in the interests of the efficiency of the service; or premature retirement following organisational change.

In Frankling and ors v BPS Public Sector Ltd 1999 ICR 347, EAT, the claimants were originally employed by the Eastbourne Hospitals NHS Trust. In September 1996 the Trust contracted out the claimants' department to BPS and their contracts of employment were transferred under TUPE. In 1997 BPS made the claimants redundant. Although it paid them redundancy payments in accordance with Section 45 of the GWC conditions, it did not make any payments under Section 46. The claimants brought tribunal claims to enforce what they claimed to be their entitlements under Section 46. The tribunal held that the accelerated and enhanced early retirement benefits in Section 46 fell within the exclusion in TUPE relating to occupational pension schemes, so the transferee was not obliged to provide these. In the course of rejecting the claimants' appeal, the EAT found that Section 46 'relates to an occupational pension scheme' within the meaning of what is now Reg 10(1) of the 2006 Regulations. The benefits guaranteed by Section 46 would accordingly be excluded from the operation of the automatic transfer of contract provisions in what is now Reg 4 unless it could be said that they 'do not relate to benefits for old age, invalidity or survivors' within the meaning of Reg 10(2). As to this, although the early retirement provisions of Section 46 were triggered by the fact that the claimants had been dismissed for redundancy, the provisions of a pension scheme did not cease to relate to benefits for old age merely because the employees had not taken retirement at the normal retirement age. 'Benefits for old age' are retirement benefits or benefits which come from retirement, whether compulsory or voluntary, and whether paid at normal retirement age or earlier. A benefit does not change its character or identity merely because it is enhanced or accelerated. The claimants' benefits were calculated by reference to age and years of service and were transmissible to survivors on death. It followed that the benefits falling due to redundant employees under Section 46 were 'old age' and 'survivors' benefits' within the meaning of Reg 10(2) and, as such, were excluded from the operation of TUPE by Reg 10(1). The transferee was therefore under no contractual obligation to provide the benefits under Section 46.

253

3.79 The correctness of the decision in Frankling was put in doubt, however, by two subsequent ECJ decisions: Beckmann v Dynamco Whicheloe Macfarlane Ltd 2003 ICR 50, ECJ, and Martin and ors v South Bank University 2004 ICR 1234, ECJ.

In Beckmann, B worked within the NHS for the North West Regional Health Authority (NWRHA). On 1 June 1995 the body for which she worked was TUPE-transferred to DWM. B worked for DWM until her dismissal for redundancy on 6 May 1997, when she was paid a lump sum redundancy payment in accordance with Section 45 of the GWC conditions of service. However, although B met the conditions for receipt of benefits under Section 46, DWM did not provide her with any benefits under that section. B brought legal proceedings seeking a declaration that she was entitled to the Section 46 early retirement benefits and an order that DWM pay them.

3.80 The High Court referred to the ECJ the question of whether B's entitlement to the early payment of a pension and a retirement lump sum constituted a right to an old-age, invalidity or survivor's benefit within the meaning of Article 3(4) of the Directive. On that point, the ECJ held that early retirement benefits paid in the event of dismissal for redundancy to employees who have reached a certain age are not old-age, invalidity or survivors' benefits within the meaning of Article 3(4), even if calculated by reference to the rules for calculating normal pension benefits. Since the general objective of the Directive is to safeguard the rights of employees in the event of transfers of undertakings, the exceptions specified in Article 3(4) to the rule that the transferor's rights and obligations arising from contracts of employment, employment relationships and collective agreements transfer to the transferee have to be interpreted strictly. Accordingly, the exceptions could only apply to benefits listed exhaustively in Article 3(4) – i.e. old-age, invalidity or survivors' benefits – and the excepted benefits had to be construed in a narrow sense. In the ECJ's view, benefits can be classified as 'old-age benefits' within the meaning of Article 3(4) only when they are benefits paid from the time when an employee reaches the end of his or her normal working life as laid down by the pension scheme in question. In the instant case, the particular payment made on dismissal for redundancy under Section 46 of the GWC conditions of service could not be classified as old-age benefits because they were not to be paid out when the employee had reached the end of her working life. This was so even though the benefits were determined by reference to the rules for calculating normal pension benefits. The respondent's argument that the early payment of benefits that are, by definition, old-age benefits does not alter their nature could not be accepted.

Similar logic was applied by the ECJ in Martin and ors v South Bank University 2004 ICR 1234, ECJ. In that case, M, D and W were lecturers at an NHS nursing college. In November 1994 the nursing college became part of SBU and the claimants' employment transferred under TUPE. The claimants chose to remain on their existing terms of employment but joined the Teachers' Superannuation Scheme, as they were unable to continue their membership of the NHS retirement scheme following the transfer. In January 1997 SBU wrote to all staff aged over 50 offering them early retirement in the interests of the efficiency of the service. M and D accepted. The terms offered for early retirement in the higher education sector differed from those provided to NHS employees by the GWC conditions of service. Under the applicable regulations, a teacher aged 50 or over who took early retirement because of redundancy or in the interests of the service was entitled to an early retirement pension based on actual years of pensionable service, together with a lump sum. However, whereas NHS employers were obliged to pay an additional compensatory annual allowance and lump sum when an employee took early retirement, employers in the higher education sector had a discretion whether or not to pay such additional benefits. Furthermore, NHS employers were obliged to credit the employee with a prescribed number of additional years' service when calculating the compensatory benefits, but employers in the higher education sector had a discretion to determine how many years' service with which to credit the employee. The claimants argued that they were entitled to the more favourable NHS terms of early retirement instead of SBU's terms. An employment tribunal referred a number of questions to the ECJ for a preliminary ruling, including whether rights that are contingent upon dismissal or early retirement by agreement with the employer are subject to Article 3(1) of the Directive, and therefore transfer with the transfer of an undertaking, or whether they fell within the exclusion in Article 3(4) relating to pension schemes. The ECJ considered that it was clear from Article 3 that – except where provided by Article 3(4) – all the transferor's rights and obligations arising from the contract of employment or employment relationship are transferred to the transferee.

In Procter and Gamble Co v Svenska Cellulosa Aktiebolaget and anor 2012 **3.81** IRLR 733, ChD, the High Court had a slightly different issue to decide: whether benefits paid after the normal retirement age (NRA), but first triggered as early retirement benefits before NRA, were 'old-age benefits'. The Court concluded that 'instalments of pension paid to someone after NRA, where the characteristic of the benefit and its obvious and only purpose has always been to support the recipient after retirement having attained a specified age and without any other trigger, fall to be characterised as old-age benefits, and none the less so simply because the pension had first come into payment before NRA'. The High Court distinguished Beckmann and Martin on the basis that neither case was concerned with benefits payable after NRA. (Note that the High Court did not need to decide whether early retirement benefits payable only after the attainment of a given minimum retirement age and without any other triggering event except the employer's agreement, might also be characterised as 'old-age benefits', in addition to those paid post-NRA, so this issue remains open.)

3.82 **Effect of pension exclusion**

Assuming that a pension scheme amounts to an 'occupational pension scheme' as defined above – and to the extent that it relates to benefits for old age, invalidity or survivors within the meaning of Reg 10(2) – what is the effect of the exclusion in Reg 10(1) from the transferee's perspective? The employee's right to be a member of the transferor's scheme, and his or her entitlement to benefits under it, do not pass to the transferee. This means that the transferee is not obliged to continue the transferor's scheme, and nor – as the High Court confirmed in Adams and ors v Lancashire County Council and anor 1996 ICR 935, ChD – is the transferee obliged (by the TUPE Regulations or the Acquired Rights Directive at least) to provide a replacement.

In the Adams case, Lancashire County Council operated its own school catering service until 1993. It employed over 3,000 people, most of whom were part-time workers employed at a low hourly rate. All workers, however, were entitled to join the Local Government Pension Scheme. In 1993, the Council put its school catering service out to tender and the bid put in by BET Ltd, a private catering company, was successful. While it was accepted by the parties that BET's acquisition of the contract was covered by the TUPE Regulations, BET made it clear that it would not be offering access to a pension scheme to any employee who earned less than £15,000 a year. In response, 11 employees who earned less than that sum commenced High Court proceedings against both BET and the Council, claiming that they were entitled to equivalent pension rights in their employment with BET. They argued that the purpose of the Directive was to protect the pay and conditions of workers when their employment was transferred to a new employer following the transfer of an undertaking. Since Community law recognised pensions as a form of deferred pay, the transferee's refusal to offer pensions rights at least equivalent to those that the employees had enjoyed with the transferor meant that the employees were worse off in terms of pay than they had been before the transfer. In the employees' view, such unfairness was contrary to the general purpose of the Directive, which was to protect the terms and conditions of employment following a transfer.

3.83 The High Court held that occupational pension schemes were excluded from the scope of TUPE by virtue of Reg 10, and this was clearly compatible with the wording of Article 3 of the Directive. Accordingly, under the TUPE Regulations, the transferee was not required, following a relevant transfer, to give the transferred employees rights to an occupational pension scheme that were comparable to those that they had enjoyed with the transferor prior to the transfer.

Note that there are obligations *outside* TUPE for ongoing pension benefits to be provided in appropriate circumstances (see 'Ongoing obligation to protect immediate and prospective rights' below). Note too that in practice, at least in public sector transfers, it is often a condition of acquisition that pension protection be given to the acquired employees, particularly in contracting out or second generation outsourcing situations.

An employee is precluded from claiming unfair constructive dismissal on the **3.84** ordinary basis in respect of loss or reduction in his or her rights under an occupational pension scheme in consequence of a relevant transfer by virtue of Reg 10(3). This provides that any employee 'whose contract of employment is transferred in the circumstances described in Reg 4(1) shall not be entitled to bring a claim against the transferor for (a) breach of contract; or (b) constructive unfair dismissal under S.95(1)(c) [ERA] arising out of a loss or reduction in his rights under an occupational pension scheme in consequence of the transfer'. (Note that this does not apply to alleged breaches or dismissals that occurred before 6 April 2006 when the 2006 Regulations came into force.) The reasoning behind the introduction of this provision was that, given that rights to occupational pension schemes do not pass to the transferee upon a relevant transfer, an employee who loses such rights on account of the transfer might, theoretically, be entitled to sue the transferor for breach of contract or for unfair constructive dismissal based upon the loss sustained. Whether this was actually the case, or whether such rights simply dissipated upon transfer, was never tested directly in the courts, although the comments of Lord Justice Pill in Powerhouse Retail Ltd and ors v Burroughs and ors 2005 ICR 222, CA, to the effect that 'the pension terms fall out of the contract of employment with the transferee and no further pension rights can be accrued against the transferor', suggested that the latter was the likely position. (Note that the case was further appealed to the House of Lords, where it became known as Preston and ors v Wolverhampton Healthcare NHS Trust and ors (No.3) 2006 ICR 606, HL. However, in upholding the Court of Appeal's decision, nothing in Lord Hope of Craighead's speech – with which the other Law Lords agreed – suggests a view differing from that taken by Pill LJ.)

The prohibition in Reg 10(3) in respect of claiming unfair constructive dismissal only relates to S.95(1)(c) ERA. Does this mean that an employee could make a claim for unfair constructive dismissal against the transferor under Reg 4(9) of the Regulations themselves, on the basis that the loss (or prospective loss) on the transfer of his or her occupational pension rights involves a substantial change in working conditions to his or her material detriment? Given that Reg 10(1)(b) excludes Reg 4 from applying to any rights, powers, duties and liabilities arising in connection with a person's employment which relate to an occupational pension scheme, this seems unlikely but not impossible.

It should be emphasised here that neither the Regulations nor the Directive **3.85** exclude pension rights from transferring in the sense that they *require* an existing arrangement to come to an end. There is nothing, bar logistical difficulties, to stop a transferee continuing arrangements voluntarily, and this may be desirable (if permitted by the rules of the scheme and by the Inland Revenue) if there is a prospect of the employees in a labour-intensive undertaking otherwise objecting to the transfer en masse, thereby preventing its execution. The transferor must carefully consider any promises it makes to the workforce in respect of post-transfer pension provision, however, as any misleading statements may give rise to liability for negligent misrepresentation (which will not pass to the transferee upon the transfer to the extent that it relates to an occupational pension scheme within the meaning of Reg 10(1) – see Hagen and ors v ICI Chemicals and Polymers Ltd 2002 IRLR 31, QBD, under 'Tortious and civil liabilities' below).

3.86 Ongoing obligation to protect immediate and prospective rights
Although the TUPE Regulations do not oblige a transferee to continue or replace a transferor's occupational pension scheme, Article 3(4)(b) of the Acquired Rights Directive provides that Member States shall 'adopt the measures necessary to protect the interests of employees and of persons no longer employed in the transferor's business at the time of the transfer in respect of rights conferring on them immediate or prospective entitlement to old age benefits, including survivors' benefits'. In Walden Engineering Co Ltd v Warrener 1993 ICR 967, EAT, the Appeal Tribunal concluded that this was clearly addressed to Member States and did not create any liability on a transferor or transferee in the private sector to protect interests under company pension schemes.

The obligations imposed on Member States by Article 3(4) are two-fold. First, they are required to protect rights conferring *immediate* entitlement to old age benefits. These are the rights that crystallise at the time of the transfer vis-à-vis the transferor's scheme – i.e. accrued pension rights. UK law seems fully to satisfy this requirement, since under Ss.69–82 of the Pension Schemes Act 1993 (as amended) occupational pension schemes must provide employees who have been in the scheme for at least two years with the right to a preserved pension upon leaving the scheme, whether or not a transfer has taken place.

3.87 Secondly, Member States are required to protect rights conferring *prospective* entitlement to old-age benefits. Although there is nothing in the TUPE Regulations themselves that requires transferees to provide ongoing pension benefits to incoming staff, such requirements do exist in separate legislation. Employees involved in transfers within or out of the public sector have benefited for some time from special pension protections conferred by the 'Fair Deal for Staff Pensions' and related practice – discussed under 'Special protections for public sector transfers' below. However, a set of statutory provisions that came into force in April 2005 now impose basic requirements on transferees in both public and private sector acquisitions to provide ongoing pension protection.

Duty to provide future pension protections. The Pensions Act 2004 (PA **3.88** 2004) – and in particular Ss.257 and 258 of that Act – together with the Transfer of Employment (Pension Protection) Regulations 2005 SI 2005/649 ('the 2005 Regulations') require transferees to ensure that ongoing pension protection is accorded to employees acquired following a relevant transfer.

These provisions apply where, immediately prior to the transfer, an occupational scheme is in force 'in relation to which the transferor is the employer' – S.257(1)(c)(i) PA 2004. Most occupational pension schemes will obviously satisfy this requirement. However, it should be noted that the definition of an occupational pension scheme in S.1 of the Pension Schemes Act 1993 also covers schemes that are established by persons other than the employer, such as interested bodies or indeed an employee in the relevant employment. This suggests that the members of such schemes could be left without any protection at all following a transfer. While their schemes will be excluded from transfer by virtue of Reg 10, since they fall within the definition of 'occupational pension schemes' in S.1 of the 1993 Act, they would not qualify for the basic protections guaranteed under the PA 2004 as their schemes would not satisfy the S.257(1)(c)(i) requirement.

Assuming that the transferor has an occupational pension scheme immediately **3.89** prior to the transfer that satisfies S.257(1)(c)(i), the minimal pension protections guaranteed under the 2004 Act and 2005 Regulations apply where the employee:

- is an active member of the scheme – S.257(2)

- is not an active member but is eligible to be one – S.257(3), or

- is not, and is not eligible to be, an active member but would have become eligible if his or her employment had not been curtailed – S.257(4) PA 2004.

The existing scheme may be a defined benefit scheme or money purchase scheme. If any of the benefits that may be provided by the scheme are money purchase benefits, then for the pension protections to apply the transferor must be required to, or actually have made, contributions to the scheme in respect of the employee (or would have been required to do so if the employee had been an active member). So if the scheme includes money purchase benefits but the employer has not and is not or would not be required to make contributions to it, the transferee will fall under no obligation to make any substitute pension provision for an employee who loses his or her rights under Regs 4 and 10.

Assuming the pension protections apply, S.258 PA 2004 puts the transferee **3.90** under an obligation to provide a replacement scheme for incoming employees. However, the transferee has a free choice as to what kind of pension scheme to implement. It may be:

259

- a defined benefit scheme in relation to which the level of benefits meets a statutory minimum standard, or

- a stakeholder or money purchase occupational pension scheme to which the employer contributes at a specific rate.

Where the transferee adopts a *money purchase* (i.e. defined contribution) scheme, the transferee must secure that the employee is, or is eligible to be, an active member of either an occupational money purchase scheme or a stakeholder scheme into which the transferee makes 'relevant contributions'. These must amount to contributions that either are not less than those that the transferor was required to pay in respect of the individual employee immediately before the transfer or match those of the employee, up to a maximum of 6 per cent of the employee's remuneration (i.e. gross basic salary, not including fluctuating emoluments), provided that these contributions were solely for the purpose of producing money purchase benefits – see S.258(2)(b) and Reg 3 of the 2005 Regulations.

3.91 With regard to defined benefit (final salary) scheme provision, where the transferee adopts a scheme that is *not a money purchase scheme*, the transferee must secure that the employee is or is eligible to be an active member of an occupational pension scheme which:

- satisfies the statutory reference scheme test defined in S.12A of the Pensions Schemes Act 1993 (the minimum benefit standard required for defined benefit schemes to be contracted out of the state pension)

- entitles the member to benefits of a value equal to at least 6 per cent of pensionable pay (as defined under the rules of the scheme) for each year of employment together with the total amount of contributions made by the member (contributions which, if required by the scheme, must not exceed a rate of 6 per cent of the member's pensionable pay), or

- provides for the transferee to make 'relevant contributions'. As above, these must amount to contributions that match those of the employee, of up to 6 per cent of the employee's gross basic salary (not including fluctuating emoluments) – see S.258(2)(c) PA 2004 and Reg 2 of the 2005 Regulations.

Note that there is no requirement that the transferee mirror any death or ill-health benefits that may have been included in the transferor's pension before the transfer.

By virtue of S.258(6) PA 2004, the employee can agree to contract out of the TUPE protection pension provisions outlined above.

3.92 **Auto-enrolment**
It is important to note that the statutory provisions mentioned above concerning a transferee's obligations to provide pension benefits run in parallel with new

'auto-enrolment' duties imposed on all employers under the Pensions Act 2008 (PA 2008) and related secondary legislation. These introduce, by progressive stages, the right of 'jobholders' to be automatically enrolled into an eligible pension scheme if they are not already active members of a qualifying occupational pension scheme or personal pension scheme. An auto-enrolment scheme for these purposes may comprise a defined contributions pension scheme, a hybrid scheme (i.e. one in which the risk of contributions being insufficient to fund specified benefits is jointly borne by the employer and the employee) or a personal pension plan. Employers are also required to make a minimum level of contributions into the auto-enrolment scheme. This new regime is being phased in over a period of five and a half years, ending in early 2018. Employers' obligations begin on different dates (termed 'staging dates') depending on the size of their PAYE workforce.

The current staging timetable began to run on 1 October 2012 (in respect of employers with more than 250 employees) and is envisaged to end on February 2018 (in respect of new employers set up between 1 April 2012 and 30 September 2017), with medium and small employers having staging dates between these two extremes. The regime is also subject to transitional arrangements providing for minimum levels of contributions payable by the employer where a defined contributions scheme has been chosen as the vehicle for complying with auto-enrolment. From July 2012 to September 2017, the minimum employer contribution will be 1 per cent of the employee's earnings, increasing to 2 per cent for the period between October 2017 and September 2018 and 3 per cent thereafter.

3.93 Prior to the amendments made to Reg 3 of the 2005 Regulations by the Occupational Pension Schemes (Miscellaneous Amendment) Regulations 2014 SI 2014/540 ('the 2014 Regulations') (which came into force on 6 April 2014), the pension protection accorded by a combination of the PA Act 2004 and the 2005 Regulations simply required a transferee to match the contribution rate paid by a transferring employee up to a ceiling of 6 per cent of the employee's remuneration. However, given that these protections are expected to run in parallel with the new auto-enrolment provisions, there was concern that transferring employees might become entitled to claim more generous pension contributions from the transferee than those available to them prior to the transfer from the transferor, particularly where the transferor paid contributions at the statutory minimum contribution levels applicable to automatic enrolment during the transitional periods mentioned above. What was previously a requirement on the transferor – by virtue of the PA 2008 – to pay 1 per cent of qualifying earnings during the first transitional period would have become an obligation on the transferee – by virtue of the PA 2004 and the unamended Reg 3 – to match contributions of up to 6 per cent of a transferring employee's remuneration. To address this discrepancy, Reg 3 was amended to make it crystal clear that, following a TUPE transfer, a transferee's obligation is simply

261

to make contributions at the same rate as that previously made by the transferor immediately prior to the transfer and to cap this – regardless of the actual rate paid – at 6 per cent.

Another tricky issue thrown up by auto-enrolment is the potential confusion over the different staging dates that apply to the transferor and transferee where the scale of their PAYE workforce differs significantly. For example, where the transferor has passed its applicable staging date for auto-enrolment because it has more than 250 jobholders but, owing to its much smaller workforce, the transferee has not, the question arises of whether the transferee has to comply with its auto-enrolment obligations sooner than originally envisaged in respect of transferred employees, or whether it is entitled to wait for its original staging date and then deal with both the transferred employees and its existing employees at the same time. Although not absolutely certain, it would seem that the transferee's original date still stands and that any transferred employees who are *not* already members of a qualifying scheme under the transferor can be dealt with along with the existing employees on the staging date that originally applied to the transferee. However, if the transferred employees are already enrolled into a qualifying scheme with the transferor, they would be entitled to be auto-enrolled into an appropriate scheme by the transferee immediately on the transfer.

3.94 **Public sector pension provision**

As previously mentioned, special pension protections apply where, in the context of outsourcing of public functions and services, employees of a public sector employer are transferred into the private sector under the TUPE Regulations. The same protections apply where employees are transferred under secondment arrangements to a private employer in the context of public finance initiative schemes. In both cases, employees ordinarily retain the right to access the appropriate public sector occupational pension scheme. For full details, see 'Special protections for public sector transfers' below.

3.95 ## Tortious and other civil liabilities

It is now well established that the transferee inherits liability in respect of the tortious acts of the transferor in so far as such acts are committed against a person employed in the transferred undertaking. Such liability is acquired not just under the 'acts and omissions' provision of Reg 4(2)(b) but also under the basic provision transferring all the transferor's rights, powers, duties and liabilities under or in connection with the employee's contract of employment in Reg 4(2)(a).

The point was tested in Taylor v Serviceteam Ltd and anor, Romford County Court, 24.10.97 (Case No:RM602374) where T was employed by the London Borough of Waltham Forest ('the Borough') as a refuse collector. In May 1994 he sustained an injury to his wrist while retrieving a bin that had slipped into a dustcart because it was the wrong size for the loading mechanism. T alleged that his employer was negligent and had breached the Manual Handling Operations Regulations 1992 SI 1992/2793, which obliged employers, so far as reasonably practicable, to avoid the need for employees to undertake manual handling operations that involved a risk of injury. In August 1994 the Borough's refuse collection service was contracted out, under TUPE, to S Ltd, which became T's new employer. T sought to recover compensation for his injury from S Ltd and the Romford County Court had to decide, as a preliminary issue, whether the Borough's potential liability for negligence or breach of statutory duty had passed to the transferee by virtue of Reg 4(2)(a). The Court considered that although liability for negligence or for breach of statutory duty was not a liability under an employment contract within the meaning of Reg 4(2)(a), an employer's duty to operate a safe system of work arose by virtue of the existence of a contract of employment. Accordingly, liability for failure to operate a safe system of work and for breach of an employer's statutory duty was a liability arising 'in connection with' an employment contract under Reg 4(2)(a). A tortious act or breach of statutory duty also amounted to an act 'done… in respect of' an employee within the meaning of old Reg 5(2)(b) (now Reg 4(2)(b) but with slightly different wording). It followed that the transferor's potential liability in tort and for breach of statutory duty in respect of the personal injury sustained by the employee passed to the transferee of the undertaking by virtue of Reg 4(2).

Personal injury/negligence

3.96

Tortious acts, in the employment context, can often be categorised in a number of different ways, as the Taylor v Serviceteam Ltd case (above) demonstrates. The common law tort of negligence may also interface with a breach of the implied contractual term to provide a safe system of work, or breaches of statutory duties contained in health and safety legislation. However, given that the question as to whether a liability passes is referable not just to the contract of employment but also to the wider concept of the 'employment relationship' – according to the Acquired Rights Directive – it does not normally matter in which way a claim is framed (other than the fact that the duty to mitigate loss applies to damages claims for breach of contract in a way that does not apply to claims in tort). In Martin v Lancashire County Council and another case 2001 ICR 197, CA, the Court of Appeal held that an employee's personal injury claim was capable of transfer whether the claim was pleaded in negligence, contract or breach of statutory duty. Indeed, the fact that the employees in the two combined cases that were the subject of the Court of Appeal's decision happened to sue in negligence but could alternatively have sued in contract for breach of an implied term to provide a safe system or place of work underlined the point that the employer's liability for negligent breach of its duty of care

263

could be said to be 'in connection with' the contract of employment within the meaning of Reg 4(2)(a).

Similarly, in Wilson and ors v West Cumbria Health Care NHS Trust 1995 PIQR P38, County Court, the county court, considering statutory provisions applicable to the NHS that closely mirrored those of TUPE, held that any liability established in connection with accidents at work would transfer from the transferor to the transferee. In that case, the claimants suffered personal injuries in 1992 while employed by the West Cumbria Health Authority. In 1993 the hospital at which the plaintiff worked became a part of the newly established West Cumbria Health Care NHS Trust, which thereupon became the claimants' employer under the provisions of the Community Care Act 1990. The claimants argued that tortious liability for their personal injuries was transferred to the defendant Trust, which sought to strike out their actions on the basis that the transferor Authority remained the appropriate defendant. The county court judge dismissed the strike-out application, holding that, on a proper construction of the 1990 Act, employers' liability transferred across from the transferor Health Authority to the defendant Trust. In the judge's view, liability for personal injury was the product of the contract of employment and if causes of action arose out of the contract of employment they were to be regarded as being based on the contract of employment and so would transfer under the provisions of S.6 of the 1990 Act (the equivalent to Reg 4(2) TUPE).

3.97 The cases discussed above dealt with circumstances in which an employee sustained an injury *before* the transfer and the issue was whether liability for that injury transferred to the transferee. What is the situation where a risk of injury is evident before the transfer, but the injury itself is not sustained until *after* the transfer? The result is likely to depend upon the extent to which the employer should have been aware of the risk to the employee – in other words, if the employee brought the issue to the employer's attention or if the risk was objectively obvious. In a transfer situation, if the transferor was or should have been aware of the risk, but did nothing about it, this omission will be imputed to the transferee under Reg 4(2)(b), so that when and if an injury occurs the transferee will not be able to hide behind the transfer to avoid liability. This drives home the need for the transferee to undertake probing due diligence – and to obtain appropriate indemnities and warranties in respect of information provided by the transferor – see Chapter 11, 'Practical aspects of transfers', for discussion on these matters.

3.98 Personal injury insurance cover
The decision in Martin v Lancashire County Council and another case (above) is also significant in that it addresses the problem of personal injury insurance. Prior to the Court of Appeal's decision, whenever an employee was injured before the transfer and liability for that injury passed to the transferee upon transfer, the transferee would not be able to take advantage of the transferor's

insurance under the Employers' Liability (Compulsory Insurance) Act 1969. This was because the transferor's insurer would only incur liability where the *transferor* was liable (the principle of secondary liability). Such liability would not, however, arise where the transferor offloaded its liability to the employee onto the transferee at the moment of transfer as a result of Reg 4(2). The problem was exacerbated by the fact that the transferee could not claim under its own employer's compulsory liability insurance policy, as this would not cover injuries to an employee that occurred before the employee entered the transferee's employment.

In Taylor v Serviceteam Ltd and anor (above), the county court registered its concern that 'although the [Acquired Rights] Directive is intended to safeguard employees' rights, one of the curious consequences of such transfer of such rights to the transferee is that whereas an employee would be certain to recover (all other things being equal) damages from the transferor or its insurance company because of compulsory employer's liability insurance, the transferee would probably not have such cover for an event occurring before the undertaking was transferred to it. The transferee might well not be able to meet the cost of a liability about which it knew nothing and for which it would not otherwise have been responsible. In that event the employee's rights would not have been safeguarded.' Given that the limitation period for commencing personal injury proceedings is three years, prior to the decision in the Martin case transferees could be faced with potentially substantial claims arising from acts that occurred some time before the transfer. Were such a transferee in financial difficulty and unable to meet such claims, the injured transferring employee would be severely prejudiced. The only solution was for the transferee to ensure that the transferor gave appropriate and comprehensive warranties and indemnities.

Fortunately, the Court of Appeal in Martin v Lancashire County Council and **3.99** another case (above) held that a transferor's right to an indemnity under an employer's liability insurance policy could be a transferable right within the meaning of Reg 4(2)(a). The employees in the joined appeals were a refuse collector and a catering assistant who had each been injured at work before their employments were transferred under TUPE and who sought damages from their new employers. Having found that tortious liabilities were capable of transfer under Reg 4(2) (see 'Personal injury/negligence' above), the Court went on to consider whether a transferor's right to be indemnified in respect of tortious liabilities under its employer's liability insurance passes to the transferee under Reg 4(2). S.1(1) of the Employers' Liability (Compulsory Insurance) Act 1969 obliges all employers who are not exempted to insure against liability in respect of personal injuries sustained by employees arising out of and in the course of their employment. The Court noted that although employees do not have a right of action under that Act, it was enacted for their benefit, ensuring that employers were able to meet any personal injury liability arising. Given the

— 265

Court's decision that the transferor's liability to an employee in tort was a liability 'in connection with' the contract of employment within the meaning of Reg 4(2)(a), the transferor's vested or contingent right to recover from its insurers in respect of that tortious liability therefore also amounted to a vested or contingent right in respect of a liability 'in connection with' the contract. Although the right to recover an indemnity was a right under the contract of insurance – and not 'under' the contract of employment within the wording of Reg 4(2)(a) – the Court of Appeal ruled that that right was nonetheless 'in connection with' and 'arising from' the contract of employment because the liability being insured was a liability for bodily injury or disease sustained by employees arising in the course of their employment. Accordingly, the Court concluded that Reg 4(2)(a) was not limited to the transfer of rights and liabilities only as between the employee and the transferor.

The main problem, even after the decision in Martin, was that not every employer is obliged to take out insurance covering possible personal injury claims by its employees. Public sector companies, for example, are exempted from the requirement to take out personal injury insurance by S.3 of the Employers' Liability (Compulsory Insurance) Act 1969. So a transferee buying an undertaking from a public sector company could inherit an uninsured claim that it might be unable to meet. The TUPE Regulations specifically address this point in Reg 17 by imposing on the transferor and transferee joint and several liability in respect of liability for personal injury sustained by employees – for further details, see 'Continuing liability of transferor' below. But the Martin case will still be relevant in cases regarding insurance that is affected by the Employers' Liability (Compulsory Insurance) Act 1969. It should be noted in this regard that the principle established by that case, while welcome, does not leave either transferees or transferred employees entirely protected. Where, for example, the transferor has failed in some respect to comply with the insurance policy – perhaps by not notifying the insurer of relevant information – the insurer may refuse to pay out, or the transferee may find that there is an excess to pay. The lesson to be drawn from this is that pre-transfer warranties and indemnities should never be dispensed with.

3.100 Transfer of other tortious liabilities

Most cases dealing with the transfer of tortious liability relate to personal injury claims, but other tortious claims (such as those based on misrepresentation or negligent misstatement) are also capable of transfer. In Hagen and ors v ICI Chemicals and Polymers Ltd and ors 2002 IRLR 31, QBD, for example, the claimants comprised some 439 employees who were originally employed in the Central Engineering Resource section of ICI Chemicals and Polymers Ltd until August 1994, when ICI divested that part of its business to Redpath Engineering Services (RES). It was common ground that TUPE applied and all of the employees' contracts of employment transferred to RES. The employees were very reluctant to transfer out of ICI because of, among other things, ICI's culture of job security and its favourable pension scheme. The case was unusual in that the managements of both ICI and RES accepted that the deal would not go ahead without the support of the workforce as a whole. Although the employees eventually agreed to the transfer, they later claimed that they had been persuaded to do so because of certain promises given and representations made to them by ICI and RES. The employees claimed that these representations were in fact false and as a consequence they had been misled and had suffered loss. They brought actions in the High Court seeking damages on the basis of, inter alia, negligent misrepresentation. The High Court found that ICI was in breach of an implied term in the employees' contracts of employment and an equivalent duty in tort to take reasonable care over the accuracy of the representations made to the employees. ICI had negligently misrepresented to the employees the extent to which the pensions on offer from RES were 'broadly comparable' to the pensions provided by the ICI scheme. The Court found that the employees had relied on those representations to their detriment when agreeing to the transfer going ahead, and that had the employees known the true position under the RES pension scheme they would, on the balance of probabilities, have successfully renegotiated so that no one was more than 2 per cent worse off. The question then arose as to whether Reg 4 operated so as to pass ICI's liability for negligent misrepresentation to RES. The High Court held that following the Court of Appeal's decision in Martin v Lancashire County Council (above), a transferor's liability to its employees in tort is, in principle, capable of passing to a transferee, particularly where it mirrors a contractual liability. It is a liability that arises 'in connection with' a contract of employment within the meaning of Reg 4(2)(a). However, Reg 10 provides that Reg 4 does not apply to liabilities arising under or in connection with so much of the contract as relates to an occupational pension scheme. Where, as on the facts in this case, the transferors had negligently misrepresented the benefits to be conferred under an occupational pension scheme, their liability was 'in connection with' that part of the contract relating to the scheme. Accordingly, the transferor's liability was caught by Reg 10 and did not pass to the transferee – see 'Occupational pensions – effect of pension exclusion' above.

Vicarious liability   3.101

Employers are also vicariously liable for the torts of their employees committed in the course of employment. So, where one employee commits a tortious act against another, it seems likely that the injured employee could claim against a transferee who has inherited the transferor's vicarious liability for the unlawful act. However, this may not extend to a transferor's vicarious liability to a third party for an employee's tort. Although there is no case law on the matter, it is probable that Reg 4(2) is best interpreted as transferring only liabilities of the transferor vis-à-vis its employees (as opposed to liabilities owed by the transferor to third parties as a result of its own employees' tortious acts, which is unlikely

267

to be regarded as coming within the protectionist aim of the Acquired Rights Directive). And it would surely be the case that occupier's liability to a third party visiting the premises would not be transferred, since it would arise wholly independently of employment contracts or an employment relationship, and thus not fall within the ambit of Reg 4(2).

3.102 ## Immigration status checks

Employers are liable to a civil fine of up to £20,000 (previously £10,000) in respect of each individual found to be illegally working, subject to a 'statutory excuse' defence based on the carrying out of certain prescribed steps prior to the commencement of employment (including the checking of original copies of an employee's immigration documentation, such as passports and visas). The steps to be followed in this regard are set out in full in Home Office guidance entitled 'An employer's guide to acceptable right to work documents' (May 2015).

In addition, employers who *knowingly* employ an individual who has no permission to work in the UK expose themselves to a criminal offence and on conviction are liable to a penalty of up to two years' imprisonment or an unlimited fine (or both) for each offence. This replaced the previous criminal offence, which – as with the civil penalty – had a statutory defence if the employer had checked certain documents before the employee started work.

3.103 The impact of the civil penalty scheme in a TUPE context is addressed in the Home Office guidance, 'An employer's guide to right to work checks' (May 2015). It states:

> '[The TUPE Regulations] provide that right to work checks carried out by the transferor (the seller) are deemed to have been carried out by the transferee (the buyer). As such, the buyer will obtain the benefit of any statutory excuse acquired by the seller. However, if the seller did not conduct the checks correctly, the buyer would be liable for a penalty if an employee is later found to be working illegally. Also, a check by the buyer would be necessary to determine when any follow-up check should be carried out. For these reasons, employers who acquire staff through TUPE regulations should undertake a right to work check on all new TUPE members of staff.

> We recognise that there may be practical problems in undertaking these checks before the employment commences for workers acquired as a result of a TUPE transfer and for this reason a period of grace has been provided during which you should undertake the check. Since 16 May 2014, this period is 60 days from the date of the transfer of the business to correctly carry out their first statutory document checks in respect of these new TUPE employees. There is no such grace period for any subsequent follow-up checks.'

This guidance accords with the 'automatic transfer' provisions of TUPE – and in particular with Reg 4(2)(b), which, it will be recalled, provides that 'any act or omission before the transfer is completed, of or in relation to the transferor... shall be deemed to have been an act or omission of or in relation to the transferee'. This means that the checks carried out by the transferor are deemed by virtue of that provision to have been carried out by the transferee. However, an employer can only avail itself of the statutory excuse for inadvertently employing an illegal worker if the necessary checks were made prior to employment commencing. This means that the transferee must, at the very least, be satisfied within the 60-day grace period that these checks were performed by the transferor at the right time. But if there is any doubt at all, clearly the transferee should conduct its own checks, as suggested by the guidance. And even if the required checks have been carried out by the transferor, the transferee will be responsible for carrying out any necessary follow-up checks, including, for example, conducting updated checks about an employee's immigration status where the original checks revealed limitations on the permission to remain or pending applications for asylum, etc. As the Guidance implies, a failure to do this exposes the transferee to a civil fine of up to £20,000 per individual.

3.104 In view of the risks, it is highly advisable that transferees seek warranties and indemnities from the transferor in relation to the potential civil liabilities and ensure that original document checks (in accordance with the current regime) are carried out in respect of each employee within 60 days of the transfer. A thorough pre-transfer due diligence process should help identify any potential problems in this regard.

Transfer of transferor's status as a 'sponsor'

3.105 Under the UK's points-based immigration system, employers who wish to employ migrants from outside the European Economic Area need to be registered as a 'sponsor' with the UKBA. This registration does not automatically pass to the transferee on a TUPE transfer. Where a transferee acquires 'sponsored' employees as a result of a transfer, both the transferor and transferee have an obligation to notify the Home Office of the change and the transferee must apply for a sponsor licence, if it does not already have one, within 20 working days of the transfer. If the transferee fails to do this, the Home Office is likely to curtail the permission of the sponsored migrants to remain in the UK to 60 days. If an application is made but is unsuccessful, all migrants who were due to transfer will have their permission to stay and work in the UK similarly curtailed.

Disclosure and Barring Service checks

3.106 The Disclosure and Barring Service (DBS), which was established under the Protection of Freedoms Act 2012, began operating on 1 December 2012 having merged functions previously carried out by the Criminal Records Bureau (CRB)

269

and the Independent Safeguarding Authority (ISA). It is the DBS that now maintains the lists of persons barred from working with children or vulnerable adults and provides disclosure of criminal records and other information about employees and job applicants. Employers have a duty to check whether an individual is on one of the barred lists if he or she is to engage in 'regulated activity' and must make a referral to the DBS if an employee is believed to have engaged in conduct that could endanger a child or vulnerable adult. If the person does appear on the relevant barred list, this will mean that the employment cannot be offered (or continue). Indeed, under S.7 of the Safeguarding Vulnerable Groups Act 2006 it is an offence for an individual to seek to participate in regulated activity from which he or she is barred. An employer commits an offence under S.9 of that Act if it knowingly allows such a person to participate in the activity.

In order to avoid liability, employers must carry out criminal record checks in respect of relevant employees. In a TUPE context, the question may arise as to whether checks carried out by the transferor prior to the transfer remain valid following the transfer so that the transferee is in a position to rely on such checks without having to undertake fresh ones. In this regard, guidance issued on the GovUK website entitled 'DBS checks: guidance for employers' (updated 14 July 2015) offers the following advice: 'Ultimately it is for the employer to determine whether to accept previously-issued CRB/DBS checks. You should consider the following before making a decision:

- the applicant's criminal record or other relevant information may have changed since its issue

- the decision made by a Chief Police Officer to disclose information on a CRB/DBS certificate was made based on the position for which the criminal record check was originally applied for; you cannot assume that no other intelligence would be disclosed for a different position

- the information revealed was based on the identity of the applicant, which was validated by another registered body, at the time that the original check was requested; you should ensure that the identity details on the certificate match those of the applicant.'

3.107 Although there is no official period by which a DBS check will become invalid or expire, many professional bodies, local authorities and public sector employers provide detailed guidance on the circumstances in which DBS certificates should be obtained or renewed in respect of staff and volunteers. In any event, it remains the employer's responsibility to satisfy itself of the suitability of employees working within sectors dealing with vulnerable persons whenever such employees are newly acquired or undergo role changes that result in their starting to work alongside vulnerable children or adults. So it is in the interests of transferees to ensure that relevant checks are up to date rather than simply rely on previously issued checks undertaken by the transferor. An online update service is available that should assist with this. Individual employees who are required to possess a valid DBS check are entitled to subscribe to the service for a small annual fee (free for volunteers) and to carry their check between jobs in respect of which the same type and level of check is required (referred to as moving within 'the same workforce'). Similarly, employers are entitled to a free online check to see if any new information has come to light about an employee since the date of the original check. This greater 'portability' means that it will not be necessary for a new check to be made every time an employee starts a new job or is transferred following a TUPE transfer, provided an existing check is in place and the type of check remains valid in respect of the job the employee is employed to do.

However, there are limitations on the extent to which a transferee may rely on the DBS update service. In particular, it should be borne in mind that:

- if information has changed since the original check was first made, an update check will only reveal that fact, not what the nature of the change is. A new DBS check will therefore be needed to ascertain those details and whether the employee is cleared to work within the relevant sector

- the availability of the update service does not herald any changes to the statutory obligations on employees to obtain the appropriate level of DBS certificate and on employers to undertake the requisite checking. It is more in the nature of a process change, making the task of verifying/rechecking an employee's DBS status a little easier than it was before, and

- the update service will not be appropriate to use in every case. It is likely to be most useful for people who undertake a similar role for different employers or who transfer in exactly the same role, or where the employer wishes to regularly check that a previously issued certificate remains current.

Individual statutory rights   3.108

Many rights of employees vis-à-vis their employers are derived not from the terms of their employment contracts but from statute. Some, such as the right to equal pay for men and woment, are inserted into the contract expressly by legislation, while others, such as rights under health and safety legislation, are not referable to the contract at all (with the proviso that breaches of such rights may also constitute breaches of implied contractual terms such as the obligation on the employer to provide a safe system of work and a safe workplace). Clearly, all employees benefit from such rights to the extent that they are covered by the relevant legislation, so the transferee will bear such responsibilities towards its 'new' employees simply by virtue of being their current employer. But to what extent is the transferee liable for the transferor's breaches, committed before the transfer, of the transferred employees' statutory rights?

The brief answer is that the transferee inherits liability for the statutory rights of transferred employees, with the exception of liability under a continuation order – see 'Continuation orders' below – and the partial exception of the duty to inform and consult in relation to a relevant transfer – see 'Collective rights and liabilities – duty to inform and consult' below. If a statutory right or liability of an employer can be said to have arisen under or in connection with an employment contract, then it will be transferred by Reg 4(2)(a).

3.109 **Equal pay.** Special considerations apply with respect to the transfer of the sex equality clause contained within all contracts of employment and the impact this may have on equal pay claims in the context of a relevant transfer. These are discussed under 'Equal pay claims' below.

3.110 Rights associated with employment relationship

Even if an employee's individual statutory right does not clearly arise from association with the employment contract, it is likely that the transferee will nevertheless acquire responsibility for it. The Acquired Rights Directive clearly intends liability for employees' statutory rights to be transferred. As discussed under 'Contractual rights and liabilities' above, Article 3(1) expressly applies to all rights and obligations of the transferor arising from an employment relationship, not just those relating to the employment contract. In Martin and ors v South Bank University 2004 ICR 1234, ECJ, the European Court considered that it was clear from Article 3 that – except where provided by Article 3(4) – all the transferor's rights and obligations arising from the contract of employment or employment relationship were transferred to the transferee, regardless of whether the rights and obligations in question derived from statutory provisions or were implemented by such provisions.

The EAT's decision in Alamo Group (Europe) Ltd v Tucker and anor 2003 ICR 829, EAT, concerned whether a transferee inherited the transferor's liability to pay employees compensation for failure to consult with employee representatives regarding a proposed transfer under what is now Reg 13 of the TUPE Regulations (for which, see 'Collective rights and liabilities – duty to inform and consult' below). The EAT took the view that as the employment relationship includes not only contractual rights but also rights and liabilities from statute and regulations that neither party can exclude, it would make no sense for the legislature to intend to exclude statutory or regulatory rights that it had introduced for the very purpose of protecting employees. Reg 4 therefore applied, the EAT said, to rights and obligations derived from statute and regulations, even if not expressly or impliedly incorporated in the contract of employment, provided these exist 'in connection with' the contract of employment or (following the wording in the Directive) 'the employment relationship'. After all, in the seminal cases of Litster and ors v Forth Dry Dock and Engineering Co Ltd (in receivership) and anor 1989 ICR 341, HL, and (1) British Fuels Ltd v Baxendale and anor (2) Wilson and ors v St Helens Borough

272

Council 1998 ICR 1141, HL, it was established that liability for unfair dismissal under Reg 7 is transferred in accordance with Reg 4, notwithstanding that protection against unfair dismissal is a statutory and not a contractual right.

Failure to fulfil statutory obligations

3.111

Regulation 4(2)(b) TUPE is capable in itself of effecting the transfer of statutory rights and liabilities, as it attributes to the transferee *any act or omission* of or in relation to the transferor in respect of the transferred employment contract or *in respect of the employee* assigned to the transferred undertaking. This includes an employer's omission to fulfil its statutory responsibilities towards its employees that are independent of the employment contract, as well as those that are implied or incorporated into the contract. Two examples:

- **DJM International Ltd v Nicholas** 1996 ICR 214, EAT: N transferred under TUPE to DJM. She had previously been employed full time but had been forced by her previous employer to retire at 60 and be re-employed by it on a part-time basis. When DJM later made her redundant, she brought several claims against it, including sex discrimination relating to her forced retirement. The EAT held that the issue was not whether the alleged act of sex discrimination was in respect of a particular contract, but whether it was in respect of a person employed in the undertaking transferred. Under Reg 5(2) of the 1981 Regulations (which Reg 4(2) of TUPE 2006 has since replaced), any 'things done' by a transferor were deemed to have been done by the transferee, so DJM was potentially liable for the alleged discrimination

- **Taylor v Serviceteam Ltd and anor**, Romford County Court, 24.10.97 (Case No.RM602374) (discussed under 'Tortious and other civil liabilities' above): the county court held that liability for failure to operate a safe system of work and for breach of an employer's statutory duty was a liability arising 'in connection with' an employment contract under what is now Reg 4(2)(a). A breach of statutory duty also amounted to an act 'done… in respect of' an employee within the meaning of Reg 4(2)(b). On the facts of the case, the transferor's potential liability for breach of statutory duty (and in tort) in respect of an employee's personal injury passed to the transferee by virtue of Reg 4(2).

In Perry's Motor Sales Ltd and anor v Lindley EAT 0616/07 the EAT held that liabilities that 'crystallise' on the transfer are capable of transferring to the transferee. In that case, L was dismissed by the transferor prior to the transfer on the instruction of the transferee. The unusual facts were that L had previously worked for the transferee and had brought claims against it. After the transfer, she brought tribunal proceedings against the transferee arguing that her dismissal had been automatically unfair under S.104 ERA on the ground that she had been dismissed for seeking to enforce a statutory right (i.e. the right to claim unfair dismissal when previously employed by the transferee). Both the employment tribunal and the EAT agreed that L's dismissal by the transferor should be treated as an act of the transferee by virtue of Reg 4(2)(b). The EAT specifically rejected the contention that, because the claimant was never in the position to bring S.104 dismissal proceedings against the *transferor* on the basis of a previous claim since she had never actually brought a previous claim against it, no such liability could pass to the transferee under Reg 4. Mr Justice Wilkie, giving the judgment of the Appeal Tribunal, stated: 'The transferor, by its actions prior to the transfer, can, by Reg 4(2)(b), cause to crystallise, on the transfer, a liability in the transferee, whose actions they are deemed to be, which was not a liability of the transferor prior to the transfer, which does not transfer under Reg 4(2)(a), but which, nonetheless, is a liability of the transferee as the employer of the claimant.'

3.112 However, in Coutinho v Vision Information Services (UK) Ltd and anor EAT 0469/07 the EAT held that liability for an act of victimisation committed by a transferor after a relevant transfer in relation to a former employee whose contract terminated prior to that transfer was not an existing liability of the transferor at the date of the transfer and thus could not pass to the transferee. The act did not fall within Reg 4(2)(a) or Reg 4(2)(b) as it took place after the transfer. The claimant's claim for victimisation against the transferee was therefore struck out by the tribunal.

3.113 Types of statutory right that transfer
In addition to those relating to discrimination, equal pay, unfair dismissal and redundancy, individual statutory rights and liabilities which pass to the transferee include rights and liabilities in respect of the minimum wage; the minimum notice period; annual leave and other working time provisions (for example, any opt-out entered into by the employee may continue to apply); trade union membership; part-time or fixed-term worker status; and family leave.

3.114 TUPE does not augment statutory rights
Just as the application of TUPE protection cannot create or increase contractual or collectively agreed rights upon a relevant transfer (see the section 'Automatic transfer principle – overview', under 'Transfer principle applies only to existing rights/liabilities' above), so neither can it artificially augment an employee's statutory rights. In Cross and anor v British Airways plc 2006 ICR 1239, CA, C and G worked for British Caledonian Airways Ltd (BCA) until 1988, when the company merged with British Airways plc (BA). Under their terms and conditions with BCA, C and G had a contractual retiring age (CRA) of 60. Following the merger, they became employed on BA's terms and conditions, which included an earlier CRA of 55 for all flight crew. When BA terminated their employment upon their reaching 55, C and G brought tribunal claims arguing that they had been unfairly dismissed. BA argued that the tribunal had no jurisdiction to hear

274

the unfair dismissal claims because C and G had reached the normal retiring age (NRA) for the job they were doing – 55 – and were therefore excluded, under S.109 ERA, from the right not to be unfairly dismissed. The main issue for determination was whether C and G's statutory NRA of 60 had transferred with them by operation of TUPE. The matter reached the Court of Appeal, which noted that, while there is a presumption that an employee's NRA is the same as his or her CRA, an NRA must in fact be determined by reference to the facts at the time of dismissal and not at the time the contract was entered into or at the time of the transfer. Furthermore, determining an NRA is an objective test – one concerned with how the facts affect all employees in the employee's position, and not merely the individual employee in question. The essential issue, as summarised by Lord Justice Peter Gibson in Barclays Bank plc v O'Brien and ors 1994 ICR 865, CA, is 'what, at the effective date of termination of the applicant's employment and on the basis of facts then known, was the age which employees of all ages in the group could reasonably regard as their NRA?'

Having made the above observations, the Court of Appeal agreed with BA that an NRA is subject to change, both pre- and post-transfer, depending on the facts at the time of dismissal. 'It is not something that is capable... of being frozen in perpetuity as at the moment of transfer.' This is because statute requires that it be determined according to the NRA of employees in the same position at the time of dismissal. Put another way, the Court of Appeal accepted that if an employee's NRA may vary, then 'there is nothing there to transfer or to preserve as at the time of transfer'. All that is transferred is a right not to be unfairly dismissed before reaching the NRA, whatever that may be at the time of dismissal. The Court of Appeal therefore dismissed the appeal and upheld the EAT's decision that C and G had an NRA of 55 (and were thus excluded from the right not to be unfairly dismissed).

Equal pay claims

3.115

The right to equal pay (or, more accurately, the right to equality of contractual terms) is given effect by S.66(1) of the Equality Act 2010 (EqA) (previously S.1(1) of the Equal Pay Act 1970 (EqPA)). This implies a 'sex equality clause' (previously simply called an 'equality clause' under the EqPA) into all contracts of employment. The effect of the clause is to modify any term of the claimant's contract of employment that is less favourable than the corresponding term of a comparator's contract (or to include such a term where the comparator benefits from a term that is not present in the claimant's contract) – see S.66(2). The comparator necessarily must be of the opposite sex and both the claimant and comparator must perform 'equal work' – i.e. like work, work rated as equivalent under a valid job evaluation study, or work of equal value. (For the purposes of the discussion below, it will be assumed that the claimant is female, which statistically is usually the case, and the comparator male.)

275

The interaction between TUPE and the right to equal pay enshrined in S.66 EqA can throw up a number of complex (interrelated) issues. These are discussed below.

3.116 Is transferee responsible for pre-transfer inequality?

Given that a sex equality clause is statutorily deemed to be incorporated into all contracts of employment, the question arises of whether its effect takes hold on a claimant's contract as soon as any less favourable term comes into being, or whether it requires a claim to enforce the clause to have been successfully brought in order for the right to equal pay to crystallise. This issue is of some importance in a TUPE context because, if the former is true, a claimant may have a potential claim under the EqA and may be able to prosecute that claim against the transferee, even if no prior steps have been taken during her employment with the transferor to enforce the sex equality clause. If, on the other hand, a less favourable term is modified only once she brings an action under the EqA to enforce her rights, this could affect her chances of securing equal pay against the transferee, given that, if her comparator did not transfer, it may be difficult to prosecute an equal pay claim where the comparator is no longer employed in the same employment.

This matter was first addressed by the EAT in Armstrong and ors v Newcastle upon Tyne NHS Hospital Trust EAT 0158/04. In that case, the Newcastle Health Authority was accustomed to making bonus payments to both its domestic ancillary workers (most of whom were female) and its porters (most of whom were male). In 1985, the domestic work was put out to tender and an in-house tender was accepted, which led to the domestic staff losing the right to bonuses, whereas bonus payments to porters continued. In 1991 a TUPE transfer occurred when responsibility for the Authority's four hospitals was divided between two new hospital trusts, the Royal Victoria Infirmary (RVI) and the Freeman. In 1998, a further TUPE transfer occurred when the RVI and the Freeman merged to become the Newcastle upon Tyne NHS Hospital Trust (the NHT). In 2001 a group of female domestic workers brought equal pay claims against the NHT. They argued that their work was of equal value to that of male porters working at the RVI, who continued to receive the bonus payments to which the domestic workers were no longer entitled. One of the issues before the EAT was: what were the effects on the sex equality clause of the two TUPE transfers, in 1991 and again in 1998? The EAT observed that the effect on the claimants' contracts was that they were deemed always to have been with the transferee (the NHT). From any date when a claimant's contract commenced, the sex equality clause operated to vary her contract of employment to include continued entitlement to a bonus even if she had ceased to be able to rely upon a comparator owing to the fact that she was no longer in the same employment as him as a result of the transfer. (It should be noted that the Armstrong case was subsequently appealed to the Court of Appeal but on entirely different issues – see Armstrong and ors v Newcastle upon Tyne NHS Hospital Trust 2006 IRLR 124, CA.)

The issue was revisited – this time by the Court of Appeal – in Sodexo Ltd and **3.117** anor v Gutridge and ors 2009 ICR 1486, CA. In that case, G was one of a number of cleaners and domestic staff employed by North Tees and Hartlepool NHS Foundation Trust until 1 July 2001, on which date they transferred in accordance with TUPE to S Ltd. Over five years later, in December 2006, G and several of her colleagues brought equal pay claims against S Ltd. They based their claims on a comparison not with any of S Ltd's current male employees but with maintenance workers who had been employed by the Trust at the same time as them but who had not transferred. The claimants argued that the sex equality clause in what is now S.66 EqA had taken effect prior to the transfer, thus conferring upon them the enhanced contractual rights that the male maintenance workers had enjoyed. Furthermore, given that under Reg 4(2) TUPE all the Trust's rights, powers, duties and liabilities under or in connection with the employees' contracts had been automatically transferred to S Ltd, that company had been obliged to honour the 'amended terms' – regardless of the fact that, in the absence of successful equal pay claims, it had no way of knowing that such terms existed.

The employment tribunal held a pre-hearing review to determine whether the claims were misconceived or out of time, the upshot of which was that the employment judge allowed them to proceed. He agreed with the claimants that (presuming that there had, in fact, been unequal pay contrary to the EqPA) the sex equality clause had the effect, prior to the transfer, of substituting more favourable terms and conditions of employment into the claimants' contracts; that these terms were protected following the TUPE transfer; and that S Ltd could be liable for its ongoing failure to adhere to them. On appeal, the EAT essentially upheld the tribunal's decision on this point, accepting the claimants' submission 'that the equality clause does not simply hover over the employment relationship between an employer and employee; it bites once the conditions for its application are met'. Thus, the sex equality clause could take effect without the need for a tribunal determination with regard to unequal pay. In the words of Mr Justice Elias, then President of the EAT: '[A] woman cannot continue to compare herself with the man once he ceases to be a comparator, but she does not lose such enhanced rights as have already been incorporated into her contract. Those rights are by then crystallised and she remains entitled to enforce them as a term of the contract. It would be wholly at odds with the purposes of the Equal Pay legislation if the woman could receive the male rate only whilst the male was employed on equal work.' So, the claimants could enforce their claims 'in so far as they relate to the failure by the transferee to honour their contracts'.

When the case reached the Court of Appeal, a split developed on the question **3.118** of when the time limit for G's claim began to run, which had an important effect on the ability of the claimants to recover back-pay in respect of the period, pre-transfer, during which the transferor had failed to comply with the sex equality clause – see 'Time limits applicable to backdated payments' below for full details. However, the Court was unanimous in rejecting S Ltd's argument that the claimants' right to equal pay had not survived the transfer because the sex equality clause operated only during the period when the claimants and comparators were in the same employment. Approving the reasoning of Elias P below, the Court held that the claimants were seeking to rely on a right that had crystallised while they were in the same employment as their male comparators and which continued to be their right until validly terminated or varied. That right, which was the counterpart of S Ltd's liability to pay the higher rate enjoyed by the male comparators, was not terminated on transfer; rather, it was transferred to the transferee under Reg 4.

So, the Sodexo case suggests that the sex equality clause, inserted into employment contracts by S.66 EqA, operates to amend an employee's contract regardless of whether an equal pay claim is actually brought. In consequence, a transferee may, as a matter of law, be held liable in respect of pay discrimination for which a transferor was responsible, even where that discrimination does not come to light until a long time after the transfer. This is clearly an issue for lawyers to consider when drawing up warranties and indemnities in a TUPE context – see further Chapter 11, 'Practical aspects of transfers'.

3.119 Reliance on comparators still employed by transferor

Equal pay claimants will be in difficulty if they seek to rely upon the current terms enjoyed by comparators with whom they had previously been employed on equal work under the same employment with the transferor, but who (unlike the claimants) were not transferred to the transferee following the relevant transfer. In King and anor v Tees Valley Leisure Ltd ET Case No.2500814/05, for example, K was employed by a council until her employment was transferred to TVS Ltd. She sought to claim that her right to equal pay with a comparator employed by the council was a right that transferred under what is now Reg 4(2). An employment tribunal dismissed K's claim. It pointed out that a comparator for equal pay purposes must be employed by the same or an associated employer. The right to equality with someone in the same employment does not equate to a right to be compared with someone who, because of a TUPE transfer, is no longer in the same employment at the time when the comparison is made.

This position was confirmed by Mr Justice Elias, then President of the EAT, in Sodexo Ltd v Gutridge and ors 2009 ICR 70, EAT. In fact, the claimants in that case, who had transferred under TUPE, did not seek to argue that they were entitled to make post-transfer, cross-employer comparisons. Nevertheless, Elias P's observations on this issue are of interest. He stated: 'It was conceded that [the claimants] could not, with respect to the period *after* the transfer, continue to receive the benefit of any improvements in the terms and conditions afforded to the [transferor's employees]. The equality clause could not continue to operate with respect to employees of the transferor once claimant and comparator were employed by a different employer. Comparison across employers is exceptionally possible... [but the] claimants concede that this is not the case here' (our stress).

Time limits applicable to backdated payments

3.120

Section 129(2) EqA stipulates that an equal pay complaint 'may not be brought in an employment tribunal after the end of the qualifying period'. The duration of the qualifying period depends on what type of equal pay case it is, as defined in S.130. This sets out four classifications of case: a 'standard case', a 'stable work case', a 'concealment case' and an 'incapacity case'. For full details of each of these types of case, see IDS Employment Law Handbook, 'Equal Pay' (2011), Chapter 9, 'Enforcement', under 'Time limits'. For present purposes, we concentrate solely on standard cases.

In a standard case, the qualifying period is 'the period of six months beginning with the last day of the employment or appointment' – S.129(3) EqA. (Unlike most other employment legislation, there is no provision allowing for an extension allowing equal pay claims to be heard out of time.) So, time starts running not on the date on which the equality clause is breached, but when the 'employment' (or 'appointment' in the case of office holders) in respect of which the breach occurred comes to an end. This raises the question: does 'the employment' for these purposes continue where an employee transfers automatically from one employer (the transferor) to another (the transferee) under TUPE? In particular, does TUPE have the effect of extending the 'employment' in which the woman is employed, with the consequence that the S.129(3) qualifying period in respect of a claim based on her employment with the transferor does not start to run until the end of her employment with the transferee?

The starting point is a consideration of the House of Lords' decision in Preston **3.121** and ors v Wolverhampton Healthcare NHS Trust and ors (No.3) and another case 2006 ICR 606, HL – a case also known as Powerhouse Retail Ltd and ors v Burroughs and ors (and which we shall refer to as 'Powerhouse' in order to distinguish it from other aspects of the Preston litigation). In Powerhouse, the claimants were employed for many years within the nationalised electricity industry. Until 1988, they were excluded from their occupational pension scheme on account of their being part-time workers. On 1 April 1988 the ban on part-time workers belonging to the pension scheme was removed and the claimants became members of the scheme. Following the privatisation of the electricity industry, the claimants' contracts of employment transferred under TUPE to PR Ltd. They brought equal pay claims against the transferor (i.e. their original employer) in relation to their exclusion from the occupational pension scheme. However, these claims were presented to the employment tribunal substantially more than six months after the date of the transfer of their employment to PR Ltd. The tribunal held that the claims were out of time under S.2(4) EqPA (now S.129(3) EqA). In the tribunal's view, S.2(4) meant that the claims needed to have been brought within six months of the date of the transfer. In other words, the transfer brought about the end of the 'employment' for equal pay purposes.

The case was eventually appealed to the House of Lords. In upholding the tribunal's decision, their Lordships thought that the plain and natural meaning of S.2(4) when read as a whole was that a claim must be brought within six months of the end of the employment to which the claim relates. In the instant case, since TUPE did not transfer liabilities connected with occupational pension schemes – see Reg 10 – the claim related only to the claimants' employment with the transferor.

3.122 At first glance it might be assumed that the principle in Powerhouse applies only to pensions cases. The fact that pension liabilities do not transfer under TUPE seemed central to their Lordships' reasoning, allowing them to arrive at the conclusion that 'the employment' to which old S.2(4) EqPA (now S.129(3) EqA) referred meant only that with the transferor employer. However, in Sodexo Ltd and anor v Gutridge and ors 2009 ICR 1486, CA, the majority of the Court of Appeal ruled that Powerhouse was not restricted to occupational pension cases but was of wider application, establishing a general principle that any equal pay claim relating to periods prior to a transfer has to be brought within six months of the transfer and not within six months of the termination of the employee's employment with the transferee. Two of the judges (Lord Justices Pill and Wall) reasoned that a transferred employee cannot have any greater rights against the transferee than she had against the transferor, and the employee's equal pay rights against the transferor are limited in time in that she is required to make a claim within six months of the termination of her employment with the transferor. It is that right which transfers. In other words, although the right to bring proceedings is against the transferee, the right is time-limited to six months after the termination of her employment with the transferor; that is, six months after the date of the transfer. Lady Justice Smith, however, delivered a powerful dissent, arguing that the ratio of Powerhouse was restricted to the transfer of occupational pension rights and did not provide authority for the general proposition that claims in respect of pre-transfer breaches had to be brought within six months of the date of the transfer. She thought that in standard equal pay cases, the employer is exposed to claims for as long as the claimant's employment continues, even though the comparator may have left the employment years ago and the reasons why they were paid differently may have been lost in the mists of time.

Although the Court of Appeal in Sodexo was split regarding the operation of the six-month limitation period so far as the transferee's *pre-transfer* equal pay liability was concerned, it was unanimous when it came to the application of the limitation period to the *post-transfer* liability of the transferee. The Court held that the time limit in respect of claims relating to the post-transfer failure of the transferee to honour the equality clause in transferred employees' contracts does not begin to run until the termination of the employees' contracts with the transferee. That was because, as we have already seen, such a claim seeks to rely on a right to equal pay that crystallised while the employees were in the same employment as their comparators and which continued to be the employees' right until validly terminated or varied. That right, which was the counterpart of the transferor's liability to pay the non-discriminatory rate, was not terminated upon the transfer but was transferred to the transferee under what is now Reg 4 TUPE – see 'Is the transferee responsible for pre-transfer inequality?' above. Therefore, the time limit does not begin to run until the termination of the employees' employment with the transferee.

Effect of Sodexo decision. The effect of Sodexo Ltd and anor v Gutridge and **3.123** ors (above) is complicated to say the least. In summary, the contractual rights and liabilities derived from the effect of the sex equality clause are transferred upon a TUPE transfer, and claimants will therefore be entitled to enforce those rights as if they had arisen under an equality clause with the transferee. This means claimants benefit from a continuing liability on the part of the transferee to honour the contractual terms they were entitled to at the date of the transfer, i.e. terms no less favourable than those enjoyed by their comparators when employed by the transferor. And they will have six months from the date of termination of their employment with the transferee to bring claims in this regard.

But the liability incurred by the transferor before the transfer has to be separately considered. This liability ceases at the time of the transfer and, although it is a liability that transfers to the transferee by virtue of Reg 4, the claimant must (subject to other possible options outlined below) present her equal pay claim in respect of this particular liability to the employment tribunal within six months of the date of the transfer. Otherwise, she will be out of time.

But this does not necessarily mean that a claimant cannot recover up to six **3.124** years' back-pay from the transferee in respect of the transferor's failure to honour the sex equality clause, even if an equal pay claim has not been made within six months of the date of the transfer. The options, in this regard, are explored below.

The first option is procedural: if the claimant has brought an equal pay claim against the transferor to recover payment, then in exceptional circumstances it may be possible to apply to the tribunal to amend the claim in order to join the transferee as a respondent. This is so even if the application for joinder is made more than six months after the date of the transfer. This is precisely what happened in Walsall MBC and anor v Birch and ors EAT 0376/10. In that case,

103 claimants sought equal pay in respect of the failure by the transferor (Walsall Metropolitan Borough Council) to pay them in accordance with the equality clause. The transfer took place on 2 April 2008 and the claims were presented on 29 April 2008, but at that time the claims named the transferor as the sole respondent. One year later, the claimants' solicitors applied to have the transferee (H Ltd) joined as a respondent. It was accepted by the parties, the employment tribunal and subsequently by the EAT that, in view of Reg 4(2) TUPE, all the Council's duties and liabilities under or in connection with the claimants' contracts of employment were transferred to H Ltd and that any act or omission committed by the Council before the transfer was completed was deemed to have been an act or omission by H Ltd. Accordingly, even if the Council was in breach of the equality clause prior to the transfer, that liability could not be enforced by the transferred employees against it after the transfer, but instead had to be enforced against H Ltd as the transferee. However, as the EAT pointed out – relying upon the majority decision of the Court of Appeal in Sodexo Ltd and anor v Gutridge and ors (above) – once the claimants had transferred to H Ltd, the six-month time limit specified in S.2(2) EqPA (now S.129(3) EqA) for bringing a standard equal pay claim began to run from the date of the transfer. This meant that by the time the application to amend the claim and join H Ltd to the proceedings was made, the six-month time limit for bringing a claim had well and truly expired.

3.125 Even so, the EAT upheld an employment judge's decision to grant the joinder. Applying the principles set out by the EAT in Selkent Bus Co Ltd v Moore 1996 ICR 836, EAT, the judge had concluded that the balance of hardship came down in favour of granting the claimants' application. On appeal, His Honour Judge Richardson presiding at the EAT accepted a concession made by H Ltd's counsel that, on the state of the authorities at present, an employment tribunal has discretion to allow an amendment which introduces a new claim out of time and that there is no rule of law that such an amendment cannot be allowed simply because it would, if presented as a fresh claim, be time-barred. The EAT further rejected H Ltd's contention that the employment judge's decision circumvented the decision in Sodexo to the effect that the limitation period for bringing an equal pay claim in respect of pre-transfer arrears of pay was six months from the date of the transfer. In HHJ Richardson's view, while it was an important consideration that the relevant limitation period had already expired prior to the joinder of a new party, equal pay claims were not in a special category simply because they are subject to immutable time limits, whether as to the commencement of the claim or to the period of time over which arrears may be claimed. It was clear that, in the instant case, the employment judge had taken into account that the limitation period had expired and had accorded considerable weight to that factor.

A second option – and one that is likely to be of far greater general application – is for claimants to bring a civil action for damages based on breach of the equality clause. Notwithstanding that they may be out of time for prosecuting a statutory claim against the transferee in an employment tribunal, it would seem that there is scope for bringing claims in the county court or High Court, where the applicable time limit is six years. Such claims rely on the fact that, since entitlement to equal pay for equal work is implemented through the mechanism of a contractual equality clause, there is nothing to prevent the claimant from accessing normal contractual remedies for enforcing this entitlement.

The availability of such claims was confirmed by a majority of the Supreme **3.126** Court in Abdulla and ors v Birmingham City Council 2012 ICR 1419, SC. Giving the judgment of the majority, Lord Wilson considered that the fact that Parliament had never made the time limit for claiming equal pay in a tribunal extendable indicated that it recognised the availability of claims in the alternative forum of the county courts or High Court. Furthermore, although S.2(3) EqPA (now S.128 EqA) allows equal pay claims brought in the civil courts to be struck out if they could more conveniently be disposed of by an employment tribunal, a claim can never 'more conveniently' be disposed of by a tribunal if it would be rejected for being out of time. In this regard, Lord Wilson confirmed – contrary to the High Court's decision in Ashby and ors v Birmingham City Council 2012 ICR 1, QBD – that the reasons why a claim was not brought within the six-month tribunal time limit are not relevant to the notion of convenience. Accordingly, a claimant does not need to satisfy the county court or High Court that it was reasonable for him or her not to have met the six-month deadline.

These cases are discussed in more detail in IDS Employment Law Handbook, 'Equal Pay' (2011), Chapter 9, 'Enforcement', under 'Jurisdiction of tribunals – choice of forum'.

Contrast with discrimination claims. It should be noted that the effect of the **3.127** time limit rules is very different in the context of discrimination and harassment claims. In Vernon v Azure Services Ltd EAT 0192/13 the EAT held that there was no reason why the transfer of an employee under the TUPE Regulations should bar that employee from bringing a claim against the transferee in respect of pre-transfer discriminatory treatment. In that case V had been employed by PV Ltd, the operator of a football club. On 4 July 2011, her employment was transferred under the TUPE Regulations to AS Ltd. V continued to work with PV Ltd until she was dismissed on 19 October 2011 after being accused of having a relationship with one of the club's footballers. V claimed that she had been sexually harassed by B – the club's sales manager – both before and after the transfer of her employment and that the failure of both PV Ltd and AS Ltd to take any action in respect of her complaint amounted to discrimination on the ground of sex from June 2011 until 1 October 2011. An employment tribunal found that B's harassment was a 'continuing act' and that since her

283

claim had been lodged on 29 December 2011, the claim in respect of the harassment *up to* the date of transfer was in time. However, as V and B had become employed by different employers from the date of the transfer – i.e. while V had become employed by AS Ltd, B remained employed by PV Ltd – PV Ltd could not be vicariously liable in respect of any continuing acts of harassment *after* that date.

On appeal, AS Ltd contended for the first time that, in view of the fact that V was no longer employed by PV Ltd, the acts of B that had previously constituted an actionable wrong such as to found vicarious liability on the part of VP Ltd could not be said to have continued after 4 July. Therefore the tribunal should not have found in favour of V's claim that the transferee – AS Ltd – was liable in respect of the pre-transfer harassment since that part of her harassment claim was out of time. In so contending AS Ltd relied on the Court of Appeal's decision in Sodexo Ltd and anor v Gutridge and ors (above) to draw a comparison with the tribunal's lack of jurisdiction to hear a claim under the equal pay provisions in respect of the post-transfer period. In particular, it contended that, as with equal pay claims, the three-month time limit for bringing discrimination and harassment claims from the date of the act of discrimination complained of – as set out in S.123(1) EqA – began to run when the claimant's employment with the transferor was terminated as a result of the transfer. On that basis, the time limit had commenced on 4 July and V's presentation of her claims on 29 December was accordingly out of time.

3.128 The EAT rejected that contention, holding that the Sodexo decision did not inform the relevant legal position in this case. The limitation regime for equal pay claims was very different from that which applied to discrimination and harassment claims and there was no reason why the transfer of an employee from one employer to another should bar a claimant from making a claim in respect of pre-transfer discrimination for which, but for limitation, the transferee would be liable. Whether V's employment by PV Ltd did or did not end on 4 July did not determine when the primary time limit started to run against her in the present case. That question fell to be decided by the application of the provisions of S.123 EqA. Applying these, it was clear that the primary time limit would have expired in respect of acts of harassment that preceded the transfer – and also in respect of acts of harassment which were subsequent to the transfer but before 30 September (i.e. three months before the lodging of the ET1 on 29 December) – unless the conduct was found to have been 'conduct extending over a period', as it was in this case. The tribunal's conclusion on that matter had not been challenged and had the effect that the primary time limit had not expired by the time V's claim was lodged, the last act being less than three months before that date. In any event, the tribunal would have been entitled in the circumstances to find that it was just and equitable to extend time pursuant to S.123(1) EqA.

Collective rights and liabilities

The capacity of the TUPE Regulations to automatically transfer collective rights, duties and liabilities is considerable. This is partly because many such rights and liabilities, etc, although contained in collective agreements made between employers and recognised trade unions, are often incorporated into employees' individual contracts of employment and so transfer by virtue of Reg 4(2) (as discussed in the previous sections of this chapter). But it is also because separate provisions in TUPE – namely, Regs 5 and 6 – provide respectively for collective agreements and trade union recognition agreements to be transferred to the transferee on the completion of a relevant transfer. It is these latter provisions that this section focuses upon.

Transfer of collective agreements

Collective agreements, although negotiated with the employer or employers' association by a trade union, seek to regulate the employment relationship and, as such, may be expressly incorporated, in whole or in part, into individual contracts of employment. However, whether or not their terms have contractual effect in this way, the TUPE Regulations provide that collective agreements continue to apply as soon as the transferee acquires the undertaking following a relevant transfer. Reg 5(a) stipulates that:

- any collective agreement made by or on behalf of the transferor with a trade union recognised by it in respect of any transferring employees, that is in force immediately before the transfer, shall have effect after the transfer in so far as it applies to any relevant employees, just as if it had been made by or on behalf of the transferee with the union

- anything done under or in connection with the collective agreement (as it applies to the employee), by or in relation to the transferor before the transfer, shall, after the transfer, be deemed to have been done by or in relation to the transferee.

This transposes into national law Article 3(3) of the Acquired Rights Directive, which stipulates that: 'Following the transfer, the transferee shall continue to observe the terms and conditions agreed in any collective agreement on the same terms applicable to the transferor under that agreement, until the date of termination or expiry of the collective agreement or the entry into force or application of another collective agreement.' Article 3(4) goes on to provide that 'Member States may limit the period for observing such terms and conditions with the proviso that it shall not be less than one year'. However, this option has never been adopted by the UK.

'Collective agreement' has the meaning given to it by S.178(1) of the Trade Union and Labour Relations (Consolidation) Act 1992 (TULR(C)A), which is 'any agreement or arrangement made by or on behalf of one or more trade unions and one or more employers or employers' associations and relating to one or more of the matters specified [in S.178(2)]'. Those matters are:

- terms and conditions of employment or physical working conditions

- engagement, non-engagement, dismissal or suspension of workers

- allocation of work

- matters of discipline

- union membership or non-membership

- facilities for trade union officials, and

- machinery and procedures for negotiation and consultation on any of the above matters and on trade union recognition.

The definition applies not only to formal written agreements but also to 'arrangements' – so any unwritten arrangements between the transferor and a union are nevertheless capable of transfer. However, a collective agreement that covers only matters outside the scope of S.178(2) – perhaps concerning the development of business strategy – will not be subject to Reg 5 and so will not continue to have post-transfer effect. If a collective agreement covers matters that fall within the scope of S.178(2) and matters that fall outside it, it will nevertheless constitute a 'collective agreement' within the meaning of S.178(1) and thus be transferred under Reg 5. Arguably, in such a case the non-S.178(2) matters covered by the agreement will have effect after the transfer, along with the rest of the agreement, to the extent that they apply to 'any relevant employees', according to the wording of Reg 5.

3.132 Regulation 5(a) also states that anything done by the transferor in respect of a collective agreement is treated as having been done by the transferee. Presumably matters such as commitments made by the transferor during pay negotiations would be covered by this phrase.

It has been argued that if a transferee is bound by the terms of an incorporated collective agreement because of the effect of Reg 4(2) – as opposed to Reg 5(a) – then this renders Reg 5(a) otiose. However, the significance of Reg 5 lies primarily in ensuring the continuity of a collective agreement unless and until it terminates or is replaced. Such continuity is particularly important, from a legal point of view, where legislation imposes a duty – say, on employment tribunals – to take account of the contents of collective agreements. For example, agreed procedures in collective agreements concerning time off for union matters for union officials and members will be significant when tribunals are deciding – in accordance with the Acas Code of Practice on Time Off for Trade Union Duties and Activities (2010) – whether an employer has unreasonably refused time off – see Ss.168–170 TULR(C)A. Additionally, a collective agreement covering redundancy procedure and selection criteria might be relevant to any claim by an employee covered by the collective agreement that his or her redundancy dismissal was procedurally unfair.

In Österreichischer Gewerkschaftsbund v Wirtschaftskammer Österreich, **3.133** Fachverband Autobus-, Luftfahrt- und Schifffahrtsunternehmungen 2014 ICR 1152, ECJ, the ECJ ruled that Article 3(3) of the Directive was not intended to maintain the application of a collective agreement as such but the 'terms and conditions' put into place by such an agreement, and thus required such terms and conditions to continue to be observed following the transfer unless and until a new collective agreement was duly agreed between the transferee and the employees concerned. The ECJ explained that this interpretation was consistent with the objective of the Directive, which was to prevent workers who are subject to a transfer from being placed in a less favourable position solely as a result of the transfer. Consequently, the terms and conditions laid down in a collective agreement continued to have effect with regard to the employment relationship despite the termination of that agreement so long as that employment was not subject to a new collective agreement or a new individual agreement was not concluded with the employees concerned.

And in Deveci v Scandinavian Airlines System Denmark-Norway-Sweden 2015 IRLR 138, EFTA Court, the European Free Trade Association Court of Justice ruled that rates of pay specified in a collective agreement were, in principle, 'terms and conditions' within the meaning of Article 3(3) and could continue to bind the transferee until such time as the agreement was validly replaced. However, the EFTA Court went on to state that the Directive did not prevent the terms of a collective agreement from ceasing to apply immediately after the transfer, provided that another collective agreement has entered into force or become applicable to the transferred employees. Whether this has occurred had to be determined in accordance with applicable national law. If national requirements governing the replacement of collective agreements are not met, then the transferor's collective agreement will continue to apply. The Court also made it clear that it is permissible for the transferee to apply the terms of its own collective agreement to transferred employees in place of the transferor's collective agreement, provided that the new collective agreement is made in accordance with applicable national law.

Returning to the impact of the TUPE Regulations, it should be emphasised that **3.134** Reg 5 transfers the effect of collective agreements only in respect of employees whose contracts of employment are transferred under the Regulations. So an employee engaged after the transfer by the transferee will not be covered automatically by a transferred collective agreement. This is illustrated, in relation to the application of the Directive, by Landsorganisationen i Danmark v Ny Mølle Kro 1989 ICR 330, ECJ. In that case, H owned a tavern, which she let to L. A few months later L concluded an agreement with the relevant

287

employees' association, under which she agreed to comply with a prior collective agreement that had been negotiated with the employers' association in so far as it applied to employees who were members of the association. At the beginning of 1981 L breached the lease and H took over operation of the tavern. In May 1983 H engaged a waitress to work over the summer. Subsequently, the Danish Trades Union Congress brought an action against H on the ground that the wage she paid to the waitress was not the same as that due under the collective agreement, which was binding on H due to the effect of the Danish equivalent of the TUPE Regulations. The Danish court referred several questions to the ECJ. In the course of its answer, the ECJ held that the obligation on the transferee to observe the terms and conditions of a collective agreement applied only in respect of employees employed at the time of the transfer, and not in respect of those engaged after the transfer.

Regulation 5(b) provides that as well as taking over a collective agreement, the transferee takes over 'any order made in respect of that agreement' in so far as it applies to the relevant employees. It is unclear what this is intended to cover. Perhaps Parliament envisages that the Central Arbitration Committee's remit will one day extend to making orders about the scope or application of specific collective agreements, which, currently, is a matter for negotiation between the parties (subject to the definition of 'collective agreement' in S.178(1) TULR(C)A, see above, and matters for collective bargaining that may be imposed by the compulsory recognition procedure – see 'Trade union recognition' below).

3.135 Note that Reg 10 expressly excludes any terms relating to occupational pension schemes from the operation of Reg 5 (just as it excludes any such terms in individual contracts from the operation of Reg 4 – see 'Occupational pensions' above). Terms in collective agreements relating to other sorts of pension schemes, or relating to terms within occupational pension schemes that do not relate to benefits for old age, invalidity or survivors, will transfer.

3.136 **Harmonisation of different collective terms.** A transferee is likely to experience problems where existing employees are covered by a collective agreement that is incompatible with an agreement covering transferred employees. However, unlike the harmonisation of contractual terms – as to which see Chapter 5, 'Changing terms and conditions', under 'Harmonising terms and conditions' – the harmonisation of collective agreements that are not legally binding will not be hindered by provisions of the TUPE Regulations. This, of course, is subject to the point made above that a transferee may be legally bound by the terms of a collective agreement to the extent that such terms are incorporated into the individual contracts of employment of the employees transferred. In that case, such rights will be automatically transferred by virtue of Reg 4(2), and any variation of those terms in order to harmonise them with the terms applicable to the transferee's existing workforce is likely to be rendered void by Reg 4(4) – see Chapter 5, 'Changing terms and conditions', under 'Varying terms in a TUPE context'.

Presumption that collective agreements legally unenforceable. Although **3.137** Reg 5 is clear that collective agreements transfer to the transferee on a relevant transfer, there are significant questions as to the effect this will have upon the transferee in practice. The main reason for this is the presumption in UK law that collective agreements are not legally enforceable. Initially, this presumption arose out of the common law – see, for example, Ford Motor Co Ltd v Amalgamated Union of Engineering and Foundry Workers and ors 1969 2 QB 303, QBD – but it is now codified on a statutory basis in S.179 TULR(C)A. (The presumption does not apply in respect of collective agreements made between 1971 and 1974. However, in practice, many such agreements, if still applicable today, expressly state that they are not intended to be legally enforceable.) The presumption as to non-enforceability is rebutted where the parties have expressly agreed in writing that the contrary intention applies – S.179(2), which they very rarely do. Thus, if a collective agreement was only binding 'in honour' on the transferor of an undertaking before the transfer, it will likewise only be binding in honour on the transferee following the transfer.

This position may not have been anticipated by the European legislators. The wording of Article 3(3) of the Acquired Rights Directive seems to indicate an assumption that collective agreements will be enforceable as against the transferee, since it states that: 'Following the transfer, the transferee shall continue to observe the terms and conditions agreed in any collective agreement on the same terms applicable to the transferor under that agreement, until the date of termination or expiry of the collective agreement or the entry into force or application of another collective agreement.' However, the position in UK law has not yet been challenged and it would be anomalous if collective agreements acquired enforceability in the UK only by virtue of a TUPE transfer.

Effect of incorporated terms. The legal unenforceability of collective agreements **3.138** does not mean, however, that they can necessarily be ignored by the transferee after a transfer takes place. As we noted above, the terms of a collective agreement can be incorporated into individual contracts of employment.

The EAT considered whether terms had been so incorporated in Glendale Grounds Management v Bradley EAT 484/97, where B, a maintenance worker originally employed by Nottinghamshire County Council, transferred to GGM after his work was contracted out. The TUPE Regulations 1981 applied to the transfer. A clause in B's contract provided that his terms and conditions of employment were subject to collective agreements negotiated nationally by the National Joint Council (NJC). They were incorporated into his contract of employment 'after approval by the County Council'. B claimed that he was entitled to a pay increase in accordance with the NJC agreement – a claim that the employment tribunal upheld. On appeal, the EAT ruled that the tribunal

289

had erred and that B's contract did not incorporate the NJC agreement. This was because it was plain as a matter of construction of the employee's contract as a whole that the expression 'County Council' was a reference to the employee's employer, which originally was Nottinghamshire County Council and, following the transfer, became GGM. Since, GGM had not approved the NJC agreement that contained the pay increase which B sought, the increase was not incorporated into B's contract of employment.

For further discussion on the incorporation of contractual terms from collective agreements, see IDS Employment Law Handbook, 'Contracts of Employment' (2014), Chapter 5, 'Incorporated terms'.

3.139 Pay bargaining arrangements

In Werhof v Freeway Traffic Systems GmbH and Co KG 2006 IRLR 400, ECJ, the European Court held that where a transferred employee's contract contains a clause referring to a collective agreement that binds the transferor, a transferee who is not a party to that agreement is nonetheless obliged to observe its terms and conditions since they are preserved by the Acquired Rights Directive. However, as explained under 'Are new collective agreements binding on transferee?' below, the ECJ made it clear that this does not extend to *new* collective agreements entered into by the transferor *after* the date of the transfer.

As previously noted, when terms of an unenforceable collective agreement have been incorporated into individual employees' contracts of employment, they take legal effect as contractual terms that are directly enforceable between the individual and the employer – Marley v Forward Trust Group Ltd 1986 ICR 891, CA, and Robertson and anor v British Gas Corporation 1983 ICR 351, CA. After a transfer, incorporated collective terms (which may well deal with crucial matters such as pay and so be 'apt' for incorporation) will be directly enforceable against the transferee as part of an individual employee's contract of employment – but this will be because of the operation of Reg 4(1) and (2) (automatic transfer of individual contracts of employment) and not because of Reg 5 (transfer of collective agreements). Thus any incorporated terms will be unaffected by any subsequent unilateral withdrawal by the transferee from the collective agreement from which those terms derive.

3.140 The contractual effect of incorporated terms may even survive the replacement of the negotiation machinery that produces the relevant collective agreement. In Visteon Engineering Services Ltd v Oliphant and ors EAT 0010/13 a group of employees were given a 'mirrored terms agreement' (MTA) when they transferred under TUPE from FMC Ltd to VUK Ltd. The MTA was incorporated into their contracts of employment and provided that, following the transfer, and 'for the duration of [their] employment with VUK Ltd', their terms and conditions would mirror those negotiated for FMC Ltd employees. The MTA also provided that, for six years following the transfer, the

290

employees would continue to be represented by the negotiation procedure and bargaining arrangements that applied to FMC Ltd employees. Thereafter the MTA provided that VUK Ltd would have to establish new bargaining arrangements for transferred employees, which it duly did. When a dispute arose over pay entitlement around ten years later, VES Ltd – which had by then taken on the relevant employees from VUK Ltd under a further TUPE transfer – argued that the employees were only entitled to mirrored terms and conditions for six years after the transfer from FMC Ltd (i.e. when the bargaining arrangements established by FMC Ltd were applicable). The tribunal and the EAT rejected that argument, holding that on a proper construction of the MTA the claimants were entitled to the same pay increases as the equivalent FMC Ltd employees for the lifetime of their employment with VUK Ltd. The EAT considered that there was no inconsistency between the employees' terms being determined by FMC Ltd settlements and VUK Ltd setting up replacement bargaining arrangements after six years, which had in fact occurred. The replacement negotiating forum would be able to agree changes to terms and conditions, which would be given contractual effect in the usual way and thereby supersede the MTA. However, no such agreement had been reached and so the pay terms of the transferred employees continued to mirror those of FMC Ltd employees.

It should be noted, however, that in Ralton and ors v Havering College of Further and Higher Education 2001 IRLR 738, EAT, the Appeal Tribunal ruled that, in the context of fixed-term contracts, an employment tribunal had correctly concluded that a transferee was not bound by the Directive to continue to employ the claimants on the terms contained in a collective agreement after the termination of their existing fixed-term contracts that incorporated those terms and their re-employment under new contracts that did not incorporate those terms. In that case the claimants were employed by the local education authority on contracts that expressly incorporated the terms of the 'Silver Book' collective agreement. In 1993 their employment was transferred, under TUPE, to Havering College. When their fixed-term contracts expired, they were re-employed on contracts for an indefinite term which did not incorporate the Silver Book terms. The EAT's reasoning for concluding that there had been no breach of the Directive (and therefore of TUPE) was that it was clear as a matter of UK law that, prior to the transfer, the transferor would have been at liberty to enter into new terms that did not incorporate the collective terms on the expiry of the fixed-term contracts. The claimants did not acquire a right to continued enjoyment of the incorporated terms merely because there had been a transfer to which the Directive applied. The purpose and effect of the Directive was not to alter the rights and obligations between employer and employee after a transfer but to safeguard and continue the existing rights and obligations for the protection of employees.

3.141 Are new collective agreements binding on transferee?

Even if collectively agreed terms are found to be incorporated into the contracts of transferring employees, their precise wording, and the way in which they are construed, will have a significant impact upon the transferee following the transfer. Particular problems can emerge where there has been a change of service provider in a contracting-out situation. In this scenario, the case law shows that the difficulty lies in determining to what extent the transferee continues to be bound by negotiating mechanisms referred to in collective agreements even though, as a private employer, it is not represented in those mechanisms and cannot influence the negotiations. This happens where the collective agreements refer, for example, to a national JNC or other body such as the Whitley Council for the purposes of setting terms and conditions.

One of the questions that arises in this situation is whether, where a transferred employee's contract incorporates the terms of a particular collective agreement, the transferee is bound, after the transfer, by a new replacement collective agreement negotiated by the same parties to the original agreement. The answer, according to the ECJ in Werhof v Freeway Traffic Systems GmbH and Co KG 2006 IRLR 400, ECJ, is to be found in the interpretation to be accorded to Article 3(3) of the Acquired Rights Directive, which makes it clear that the obligation on the transferee to observe the terms of the transferor's collective agreement lasts only 'until the date of termination or expiry of the collective agreement or the entry into force or application of another collective agreement'.

3.142 In the Werhof case the claimant was employed by Siemens in Germany under a contract of employment governed by the framework collective agreement and the wage agreement in force for the North Rhine-Westphalia iron and steel, metal and electrical industry. The collective agreement had been negotiated between the trade union for the metal industry and the Metal and Electrical Industry Federation (the Federation), of which Siemens was a member. On 1 October 1999 Siemens transferred the part of its business in which the claimant worked to FTS. FTS was not a member of any employers' association that concluded collective agreements. In May 2003 the Federation and the trade union concluded a new collective agreement, with effect from 1 June 2003, which provided for an increase in the wage rate and an additional payment. The claimant commenced proceedings against FTS claiming, from 1 June 2003, the difference between his basic salary and the sum provided for in the new collective agreement and the additional payment. The German court asked the ECJ whether a transferee who inherits a collective agreement but was not an original party to it is bound by collective agreements subsequent to the one in force at the time of the transfer.

The ECJ noted that the rights and obligations arising from the collective agreement were automatically transferred to the new employer even though the latter was not a party to it. However, the Court went on to observe that the

292

Directive's objective is merely to safeguard the rights and obligations of employees in force on the day of the transfer. Article 3(3) makes it clear that the terms and conditions of the collective agreement in force at the time of transfer are to continue to be observed only until the date of its termination or expiry, or the entry into force or application of another collective agreement. It further adds that Member States may limit the period for observing the terms and conditions of a collective agreement provided that that period is not less than one year (an option not adopted in the UK). The ECJ therefore concluded that the wording of the Directive does not indicate that the Community legislature intended the transferee to be bound by collective agreements other than the ones in force at the time of the transfer. Moreover, if future collective agreements were binding on a transferee who was not a party to the collective agreement, this would infringe its fundamental right not to join an association under Article 11 of the European Convention on Human Rights.

A year and a half before the ECJ's decision in Werhof, the EAT had similarly **3.143** ruled in Ackinclose and ors v Gateshead Metropolitan Borough Council 2005 IRLR 79, EAT, that employees could not benefit from terms negotiated under a new collective agreement for local authority workers which, two years after the transfer, had replaced the agreement incorporated into the transferred employees' contracts. Notwithstanding that other cases decided by the UK courts took a different line, the ruling in Werhof shows that the EAT's decision in Ackinclose was correct.

Is post-transfer pay bargaining by transferor binding on transferee? **3.144**

The scenario where employees are transferred on contracts of employment incorporating pay bargaining arrangements throws up another tricky question. Is the transferee bound, after the transfer, by further negotiations between (and agreed pay deals reached by) the parties to the collective agreement (i.e. the transferor and relevant trade union)? This is a particular issue in the context of outsourcing by local authorities and other public bodies that, even after a relevant transfer of a particular service to the private sector, continue to operate the same pay bargaining machinery in respect of its remaining workforce.

Until recently, the TUPE Regulations were silent on this matter and a considerable body of inconsistent case law emerged on the subject. As we shall see, the question was eventually resolved by the ECJ in Alemo-Herron and ors v Parkwood Leisure Ltd 2013 ICR 1116, ECJ, but prior to this a number of UK cases concluded that transferees were bound by subsequent decisions under pay bargaining arrangements in which they had no active role. Such cases included BET Catering Services Ltd v Ball and ors EAT 637/96 and Whent and ors v T Cartledge Ltd 1997 IRLR 153, EAT. The latter entailed claimants who originally worked for the London Borough of Brent's street lighting department under contracts of employment providing that their pay and conditions would be set

293

in accordance with the local authority's National Joint Council (NJC) collective agreement 'as amended from time to time'. The street lighting work was subsequently contracted out to an independent contractor, TC Ltd, which then derecognised the trade union that was represented on the NJC. TC Ltd wrote to the employees to inform them that the collective agreement would no longer have effect and that in future their pay would be determined on an individual basis. An employment tribunal dismissed the employees' claims that the failure to pay them the NJC-agreed rates constituted an unlawful deduction from wages contrary to Part 1 of the Employment Rights Act 1996. The EAT overturned that decision on appeal, holding that the transferee was bound by the NJC agreement, as it remained incorporated into individual contracts of employment even though the transferee had sought to terminate it. Therefore the employees retained the right to have the benefit of the terms negotiated by the NJC until the individual contracts of employment had been effectively varied by agreement or the employee had been dismissed and re-engaged on terms that did not include the NJC agreements.

3.145 The line of reasoning represented by the Whent decision was swept away as a result of a combination of two ECJ rulings: Werhof v Freeway Traffic Systems GmbH and Co KG 2006 IRLR 400, ECJ (discussed under 'Are new collective agreements binding on transferee?' above), and Alemo-Herron and ors v Parkwood Leisure Ltd (above). Before Alemo-Herron reached the ECJ, the Court of Appeal (in Alemo-Herron v Parkwood Leisure Ltd 2010 ICR 793, CA) had held that an employment tribunal did not err when finding that a transferee was no longer bound to pay transferred employees in accordance with a collective bargaining agreement that was incorporated into the employees' contracts of employment. In so holding, the Court cited the Werhof ruling as authority for the proposition that Article 3 of the Acquired Rights Directive required a *static* interpretation of the burden on transferees of employment contracts incorporating terms fixed from time to time by collective agreement. This was opposed to a *dynamic* interpretation allowing the terms of the collective agreement to continue to govern transferred employees' pay bargaining based on pay deals reached by the transferor when utilising the same pay bargaining arrangements after the date of the transfer. The Court of Appeal concluded that the ECJ in Werhof had inferred from Article 3(2) that the Directive did not intend a transferee to be bound by any collective agreement other than the one in force at the time of the transfer. This conclusion was consistent with the objective of the Directive, which is to safeguard the rights and obligations of employees in force on the day of the transfer, not to protect mere expectations to rights and hypothetical advantages flowing from future changes to collective agreements.

Although the Court of Appeal's decision in Alemo-Herron found that nothing in the language of Reg 5 of the TUPE Regulations indicated that the UK Parliament had intended to allow for a dynamic approach, it did accept that this would have been a permissible approach for the national legislature to have adopted had it chosen to do so. However, when the matter reached the ECJ – following referral by the Supreme Court – it became clear not only that the static approach was the correct one, but that Member States would be in effect acing ultra vires (outside their powers) if they legislated for or permitted the dynamic approach to be taken. In particular, the ECJ was adamant that the Directive does not simply aim to safeguard the interests of transferred employees but also seeks to ensure 'a fair balance' between the interests of those employees and the transferee. Specifically, the transferee must be in a position to make the adjustments and changes necessary to carry on its operations post-transfer. A transfer between the public and private sector will, in the ECJ's view, require significant adjustments and changes given the 'inevitable differences in working conditions' between the two sectors. A 'dynamic' clause referring to collective agreements intended to regulate changes in working conditions in the public sector is liable to limit the ability of a private sector transferee to make such changes. It is therefore liable to undermine the 'fair balance' of interests.

Furthermore, according to the ECJ, the Directive had to be read in a way that **3.146** was compatible with the Charter of Fundamental Rights of the European Union, Article 16 of which lays down the freedom to conduct a business, including the freedom of contract. This requires that a transferee be able to assert its interests effectively in a contractual process to which it is a party and to negotiate changes in the working conditions of its employees. On the facts of the particular case, the transferee (a private sector employer to whom a local authority had transferred its leisure services) was unable to participate in the relevant collective bargaining body (the NCJ) and thus could not assert its interests effectively. While Member States are entitled to take measures that are more favourable to employees than those set out in the Directive, they are not entitled to limit contractual freedom to the point that it is liable to adversely affect the 'very essence' of a transferee's freedom to conduct a business. Thus, the Court held that Member States are *precluded* from providing that 'dynamic' clauses referring to collective agreements negotiated and adopted after the date of a TUPE transfer are enforceable against the transferee where that transferee does not have the possibility of participating in the negotiation process of such collective agreements concluded after the transfer date.

Amendments to TUPE Regulations to reflect 'static interpretation'. In the **3.147** light of the ECJ's rulings in Werhof v Freeway Traffic Systems GmbH and Co KG (above), and Alemo-Herron and ors v Parkwood Leisure Ltd (above), the TUPE Regulations have now been amended to place the 'static interpretation' on a statutory footing. With effect from 31 January 2014, the Collective Redundancies and Transfer of Undertakings (Protection of Employment) (Amendment) Regulations 2014 SI 2014/16 inserted a new Reg 4A into the TUPE Regulations. This states that where a transferred contract incorporates such provisions of collective agreements 'as may be agreed from time to time',

295

Reg 4(2) does not transfer any rights, powers, duties and liabilities in relation to any provision of a collective agreement agreed after the date of the transfer if the transferee is not a participant in the collective bargaining for that provision.

In addition, Reg 4 has been amended to enable employers to make changes to transferred terms that derive from collective agreements. New Reg 4(5B) disapplies the Reg 4(4) prohibition on transfer-related variations of contract in respect of variations that apply to a term or condition incorporated from a collective agreement, provided that (a) the variation takes effect more than a year after the transfer, and (b) following the variation, the employee's contract is overall no less favourable to the employee than it was before. For further details, see Chapter 5, 'Changing terms and conditions', under 'Types of change permitted by TUPE'.

3.148 In practice, the change effected by Reg 4A is unlikely to have any significant impact over and above what has already been achieved by the ECJ's decision in Alemo-Herron and ors v Parkwood Leisure Ltd (above). However, it is possible that the amendment goes slightly wider than the scope of the ECJ's decision. Whereas the latter made it clear that a dynamic approach is precluded only where the transferee does not have the opportunity to participate in the relevant collective bargaining arrangements, the wording of Reg 4A might be interpreted as also covering the situation where the transferee has the opportunity to participate but chooses not to.

It is important to note that the new provision in Reg 4A only applies to changes to pay terms agreed by the transferor and unions under the relevant collective bargaining arrangements *after* the transfer has taken place. It does not affect any collective terms agreed before the date of the transfer but which come into effect afterwards. For example, any pay deal agreed before the transfer will still bind the transferee even if the pay increase itself doesn't take effect until after the transfer.

3.149 Trade union recognition
Regulation 6 of the TUPE Regulations provides that where an independent trade union is recognised to any extent by the transferor in respect of employees of any description who become employees of the transferee after a relevant transfer, then the union is deemed to be recognised by the transferee to the same extent in respect of employees of that description. However, this transfer of recognition applies only where the transferred organised grouping of resources or employees 'maintains an identity distinct from the remainder of the transferee's undertaking' – Reg 6(1). Therefore, if the transferred workforce becomes integrated into the new employer's workforce following the transfer, union recognition will not be deemed to have been transferred. There is no equivalent restriction, however, on the application of Reg 5 concerning the effect of collective agreements after the transfer (as to which see 'Transfer of

296

collective agreements' above). Therefore, even if the transferred workforce fails to maintain a distinct identity following the transfer and a particular union loses recognition as a result, any collective agreement made by it may still continue to have effect.

Meaning of 'maintains an identity distinct'. Questions will inevitably arise **3.150** as to what constitutes maintaining a 'distinct' identity. If the organised grouping of resources or employees fails to maintain a distinct identity, it is in theory arguable that there has not been 'a transfer of an economic entity which retains its identity' within the meaning of Reg 3(1)(a) for the purpose of determining whether there has been a relevant transfer at all (in cases not involving a service provision change). We assume that Reg 6 is intended to apply in Reg 3(1)(a) types of transfer, and not just to service provision changes (which are covered by Reg 3(1)(b)). If so, the two phrases 'retains its identity' (Reg 3(1)(a)) and 'maintains an identity distinct' (Reg 6(1)) cannot have exactly the same meaning, because Reg 6(1) is predicated on the fact that there has been a relevant transfer to start with. In other words, the internal logic of the Regulations must allow for the possibility that an economic entity can retain its identity and yet fail to 'maintain an identity' distinct from the remainder of the transferee's undertaking. So, in order for Reg 6 to apply, the economic entity must retain its identity a little bit more closely than it had to in order to give rise to a relevant transfer in the first place. The rather tortuous nature of this reasoning perhaps indicates that the legislators did not anticipate such a disjunction.

However, there are ways round this difficulty. First, the wording of Article 6 of the Acquired Rights Directive may be helpful. This provides that employee representation shall be preserved following a transfer so long as the relevant undertaking 'preserves its autonomy'. If Reg 6 is read in this light, it is easier to see that an economic entity may retain its identity following a transfer in terms of, for example, the activities it undertakes, and yet sacrifice to a new parent company its ability to make strategic decisions in respect of the administration and running of its business, in a way which would cause it to fall outside the scope of Reg 6 while still qualifying as a relevant transfer. Note, too, the EAT's decision in Farmer v Danzas (UK) Ltd EAT 858/93 that there is no rule that an economic entity ceases to retain its identity, for the purpose of identifying whether there has been a relevant transfer, merely because its economic activity is subsumed into the transferee's business, since all businesses are likely to want to integrate the activities of a newly acquired entity into their own. The EAT held that in order for the TUPE Regulations to apply, it is sufficient that the transferred undertaking retain its identity immediately after the moment of transfer. On this basis, we would suggest that the proper interpretation of Reg 6(1) is that it requires that the transferred entity maintains its identity distinct from the remainder of the transferee's undertaking on a slightly more permanent basis than is required by Reg 3(1)(a).

297

3.151 **Independent union.** Unlike Reg 5 – which provides for the continuation of a collective agreement regardless of the status of the trade union with which it is made, so long as it is 'recognised' – Reg 6 only applies to an *independent* union. It seems likely that the independence of trade unions for the purposes of Reg 6 will be determined according to the definition of 'independent trade union' provided in S.5 TULR(C)A. This states that an independent trade union is one that is not under the domination or control of an employer or group of employers or of one or more employers' associations, and is not liable to interference by an employer or group or association tending towards such control. In addition, S.8 TULR(C)A provides that if the Certification Officer has issued a certificate of independence to a trade union and the certificate is in force, then this is 'conclusive evidence for all purposes that a trade union is independent'. All of the main trade unions in the UK are listed with the Certification Officer with certificates of independence. (For a more detailed discussion on trade union independence, see IDS Employment Law Handbook, 'Trade Unions' (2013), Chapter 1, 'Trade unions', under 'Independence'.)

3.152 **Extent of recognition.** Regulation 6(2) provides for an independent trade union that is recognised 'to any extent' by the transferor in respect of the transferred employees to be recognised 'to the same extent' by the transferee after the transfer. This means that in each case the detail of the recognition arrangements needs to be examined in order to determine what precisely is transferred to the new employer. In practice, the bargaining issues in respect of which a union may be recognised can vary substantially. For example, under the statutory procedure for trade union recognition, the issues for collective bargaining are restricted to pay, hours and holidays, unless the parties have agreed to cover other matters – paras 3(3) and 54(3), Sch A1 TULR(C)A. In cases of voluntary recognition, the union may be recognised for only limited purposes, such as for representing union members who have individual grievance and disciplinary issues. (It is possible that in this type of case the union may not be recognised for the purposes of 'collective bargaining' at all, in which case Reg 6 will not apply.)

It should be noted that Reg 10 – which excludes the application of Regs 4 and 5 to the extent that the contracts of employment or collective agreements relate to an occupational pension scheme – does not affect the operation of Reg 6. Therefore if a union is recognised for bargaining in respect of pensions, it will continue to be recognised in this respect after the transfer.

3.153 What constitutes recognition is a mixed question of fact and law. Voluntary recognition is often established by a written collective agreement between the employer and trade union that sets out the details of the recognition that is being conferred, the procedures to be followed and what facilities will be provided to union representatives in respect of carrying out their duties. However, voluntary recognition can arise, without any express agreement, based on a clear and unequivocal course of dealings – see National Union of Gold, Silver and Allied Trades v Albury Brothers Ltd 1979 ICR 84, CA. Recognition can also arise from use of the statutory procedure for trade union recognition contained in Schedule A1 to the TULR(C)A, under which an employer may be compelled to recognise a union for collective bargaining purposes in certain circumstances.

Trade union recognition is dealt with in detail in IDS Employment Law Handbook, 'Trade Unions' (2013), Chapter 5, 'Trade union recognition', and Chapter 6, 'Statutory recognition'.

Voluntary and statutory recognition. Having made the distinction between **3.154** statutory and voluntary recognition, it is worth pausing to note that, until recently, Government guidance on the Regulations implied that Reg 6 applied to cases of voluntary recognition only. The original guidance issued in 2006 by the Department for Trade and Industry (DTI) observed that 'where at the time of the transfer a union is recognised by the transferor employer via the statutory recognition procedure, then different arrangements apply... Regulations are to be made, in due course, under paragraph 169B of Schedule A1 [TULR(C)A] to ensure that declarations made by the [Central Arbitration Committee (CAC)], and applications made to the CAC, are appropriately preserved in the event of a change in the identity of the employer.' This position was reiterated word-for-word in updated guidance issued by the Department for Business, Innovation and Skills (BIS) in June 2009. However, in the latest incarnation of the BIS Guide, 'Employment rights on the transfer of an undertaking' ('the BIS Guide') (January 2014), the quoted passage has been deleted altogether. Moreover, at no time have any regulations of the kind alluded to in the original DTI guidance ever been issued, even in draft form. This suggests that the Government no longer seeks to draw any distinction between voluntary and statutory recognition for the purposes of Reg 6.

The meaning of 'union recognition' for the purposes of Reg 6 is defined in Reg 2(1) as being the same as that in S.178(3) TULR(C)A, which defines this in terms of 'the recognition of the union by an employer, or two or more associated employers, to any extent, for the purpose of collective bargaining'. Reg 2(1) likewise refers to S.178(1) TULR(C)A for the meaning of 'Collective bargaining', which is defined as negotiations relating to or connected with one or more of the matters set out in S.178(2). These matters are listed under 'Transfer of collective agreements' above.

No distinction between statutory and voluntary recognition is actually made in **3.155** Reg 6 itself. It is true that the statutory recognition procedure disapplies the meaning of collective bargaining given by S.178(1) (which is precisely the definition adopted by Reg 2(1) of TUPE) – paras 3(2) and 54(2), Sch A1 TULR(C)A. However, Reg 6 itself simply provides that where, before the transfer, an independent union is 'recognised' in respect of transferred

— 299

employees, it shall be deemed to have been so 'recognised' by the transferee. Even if the statutory procedure does not use the definition of collective bargaining from S.178(1), it does not disapply the meaning of the term 'recognised' – from S.178(3) – which applies throughout the TULR(C)A. In practice a statutorily recognised trade union is likely to conduct negotiations relating to or connected with precisely those matters contained within S.178(1), even if the definition is not expressly used. For completeness we assume here that Reg 6 is apt to apply to statutory recognition, while noting the indications given in earlier versions of official guidance on the Regulations that the application of TUPE to declarations and applications under the statutory recognition procedure may, in time, be covered separately within the TULR(C)A itself.

3.156 **Effect of Reg 6.** While a trade union may be recognised to a greater or lesser extent for the purposes of collective bargaining, the fact that it is recognised at all has significant legal consequences, whether the recognition is voluntary or under the statutory procedure. The statutory legal consequences for the union include:

- the right for its representatives to be informed and consulted about a relevant transfer under Reg 13

- the right for its representatives to be informed and consulted about collective redundancies under S.188(1) TULR(C)A

- the right to information for the purposes of collective bargaining under S.181 TULR(C)A

- the right of the union's representatives and trade union learning representatives to time off under Ss.168 and 168A TULR(C)A.

These consequences will have effect after the transfer to the extent that Reg 6 applies.

3.157 **Is recognition legally binding?** Regulation 6(2)(b) provides that where a transferor before the transfer recognised an independent trade union in respect of transferring employees, then after the transfer 'any agreement for recognition may be varied or rescinded accordingly'. This implies that the same process for variation or rescission would apply after the transfer as applied before – and therefore perhaps states the obvious. In most cases, trade union recognition by an employer is voluntary. Voluntary recognition is not legally binding and so the employer may at any time, subject to the terms of the recognition agreement, derecognise the trade union. In other words, where a transferee is deemed by Reg 6 to have recognised a union in respect of transferred employees, the transferee can proceed to derecognise the union following the transfer. Unless the recognition agreement is stated to be legally binding, which is highly unlikely in practice, the union and union members

300

will have no legal remedy (see Associated Newspapers Ltd v Wilson and anor 1995 ICR 406, HL). However, derecognition may cause unrest among the affected employees and possibly provoke a statutory trade union recognition claim. Were such a claim to succeed and the CAC to grant statutory recognition, then it would be far harder for the employer to derecognise the union and remedies would become available for any failure by the employer to comply with the statutory recognition procedure. If the parties were unable to reach agreement between themselves within the required time frame, the CAC would be obliged to specify the method of collective bargaining and this would then become legally enforceable between the parties unless they then agreed that the specified method was not to be legally binding – see paras 31(3)–(5), Sch A1 TULR(C)A.

Does Reg 6 add anything to Reg 5? As previously discussed, Reg 5(a) provides **3.158** that collective agreements have effect after a relevant transfer as if made by or on behalf of the transferee – see 'Transfer of collective agreements' above. The meaning of a 'collective agreement' covers a broad range of agreements or arrangements relating to any matter or matters that are suitable for collective bargaining – including recognition procedures. A collective agreement is capable of transfer even if it is not made by the transferor itself, so long as it is made on its behalf – so could potentially cover 'arrangements' imposed under the compulsory recognition procedure contained in Schedule A1 to the TULR(C)A. Given all this, it is arguable that Reg 6 adds nothing, in terms of substantive legal effect, to Reg 5.

Duty to inform and consult
3.159

One issue that has vexed the courts has been whether liability in respect of the duty under Reg 13 TUPE to inform and consult representatives of affected employees – to the extent that it applies to the transferor – passes to the transferee upon a relevant transfer. (For full details of the Reg 13 duty, see Chapter 8, 'Information and consultation', under 'Informing and consulting appropriate representatives'.) The answer is a qualified 'yes'. Reg 15(9) provides that the transferee is jointly and severally liable with the transferor in respect of compensation payable to an employee for the transferor's failure to carry out any of various aspects of the Reg 13 duty.

Liability for failure to inform and consult. Regulation 15(9) was introduced **3.160** in response to conflicting case law on this issue under the 1981 Regulations. In the following two cases, the EAT reached different conclusions:

- **Transport and General Workers' Union v James McKinnon, JR (Haulage) Ltd and ors** 2001 ICR 1281, EAT: the EAT held that the transferor's liability to pay compensation for its failure to inform and consult representatives prior to a relevant transfer did not pass to the transferee under what is now Reg 4(2) of the 2006 Regulations. TUPE would be construed in a way that

301

ensures that a transferor has an incentive to comply with the information and consultation obligations imposed upon it during the transfer process. This required the conclusion that the transferor would retain the liability to pay compensation for its own failure to consult

- **Alamo Group (Europe) Ltd v Tucker and anor** 2003 ICR 829, EAT: the EAT reasoned that rights and obligations are subject to what is now Reg 4(2) if they arise under or in connection with the contract of employment or – in line with Article 3 of the Acquired Rights Directive – the employment relationship. Reg 4(2) applies to rights and obligations derived from statutory provisions, even if not expressly or impliedly incorporated in the contract of employment, provided the necessary 'connection' is made. The EAT thought that no distinction should be drawn between, on the one hand, statutory liability to inform and consult under TUPE itself, and general liability arising out of the contract of employment on the other. The modern employment relationship includes both contractual rights and rights and liabilities derived from statute and regulations which neither party can exclude and which give added protection to employees. Had the legislature intended to exclude from the scope of Reg 4 statutory or regulatory rights introduced for the very purpose of protecting employees – such as those contained in what is now Reg 13 – it would have expressly done so.

The legislature clearly took note. The Government's chosen solution, found in Reg 15(9) of the 2006 Regulations, was to make the transferor and transferee jointly and severally liable – that is, both collectively and individually liable – where a transferor has failed to inform or consult in respect of affected employees. In deciding upon this course of action, the Government, in the 2005 consultation document on the draft new Regulations, reiterated the EAT's concern in the TGWU case that if liability were to pass wholly to the transferee, there would be little or no statutory incentive for the transferor to comply with the information and consultation requirements.

3.161 The 2009 version of the BIS Guide on the 2006 Regulations explained how the system of joint and several liability works. It notes that it will be for the appropriate representatives or individual employees seeking redress to choose whether to take action against the transferor, the transferee or both. Furthermore, a party who is a sole respondent in such an action will be able to join others who are jointly liable in respect of the same liability. When this occurs, it will be for the employment tribunal to apportion the compensation between the two respondents fairly. Alternatively, if judgment is given against a sole respondent, that respondent might be able to recover a contribution from others who are jointly liable in respect of the same liability by suing them in the civil courts. In such a case, liability would then be apportioned fairly, in line with the provisions of the Civil Liability (Contribution) Act 1978. (Note that the current version of the BIS Guide (January 2014) omits all of the guidance

302

outlined above. With the exception of the point made immediately below, this should not be viewed as indicating that that guidance is no longer valid).

It should, however, be noted that the 2009 Guide was inaccurate in so far as it suggested that an employment tribunal is able to apportion compensation between two respondents. In Country Weddings Ltd v Crossman and ors EAT 0535/12 the EAT made it clear that the suggestion that tribunals may apportion liability themselves is incorrect. The terms of Reg 15(9) are unequivocal and the EAT's decision in Todd v Strain and ors 2011 IRLR 11, EAT, is clear authority requiring tribunals to order compensation for breach of Reg 13 on a joint and several basis. If liability is to be apportioned between the transferor and transferee(s), it must be done by the ordinary courts under the Civil Liability (Contribution) Act 1978.

Where a court is obliged to consider how liability should be apportioned, it **3.162** will focus on the extent of each respondent's responsibility for the damage in question. Since joint and several liability only arises in respect of the transferor's failure to inform and consult, and not the transferee's, one would imagine that the transferor will usually be required to pay most if not all of the compensation awarded.

In practice, although the Regulations ultimately empower the court or tribunal to conduct the apportionment exercise, the transferor and transferee may well have agreed between themselves, by way of indemnities, who will actually bear the cost for any failure on the part of the transferor to inform or consult.

Liability in respect of unassigned employees. The duty that arises in respect of **3.163** Reg 13 is a duty to inform and consult representatives of 'affected employees'. These are defined as 'any employees of the transferor or the transferee (*whether or not assigned to the organised grouping of resources or employees that is the subject of a relevant transfer*) who may be affected by the transfer or may be affected by measures taken in connection with it' (our stress) – Reg 13(1). Any affected employee may bring a claim that an employer has failed to comply with a requirement of Reg 13 (or of Reg 14, which relates to requirements governing the election of employee representatives). So transferees should be aware that they may inherit liability (albeit on a joint and several basis) in respect of employees who are not assigned to the transferred undertaking and who are thereby not covered by the provisions in Reg 4(1) and (2). It seems unlikely that this can have been the Government's intention, given that the transferee will never have an employment relationship with such employees. For further discussion of this apparent oversight, see Chapter 8, 'Information and consultation', under 'Informing and consulting appropriate representatives – claims for failure to inform or consult'.

Transferee's failure to provide information. There is one situation in which the **3.164** transferee will be solely liable for the transferor's failure to inform transferring

303

employees. Reg 15(8)(b) states that where the transferor (after giving notice to the transferee in accordance with Reg 15(5)) shows that its failure to inform was due to the transferee's own prior failure to provide it with the information specified in Reg 13(4), the tribunal may order the transferee to pay appropriate compensation to such descriptions of affected employees as may be specified in the award.

3.165 **Failure to comply with compensation order.** Thus far we have discussed the already rather complex issue of which of the commercial parties bears liability for a failure to inform and consult. The position is complicated yet further when one considers who bears liability for a failure to comply with a compensation order made by a tribunal in respect of an employer's failure to inform and consult.

If a tribunal makes an award of compensation under Reg 15 for failure to comply with a requirement of Reg 13 (or Reg 14), and the employer in question fails to pay it wholly or in part, the affected employee may complain to a tribunal – Reg 15(10). If the tribunal upholds such a complaint, it shall order the transferor or transferee as applicable to pay the complainant the amount owed – Reg 15(11). As we discussed above, Reg 15(9) provides that the transferee and transferor are jointly and severally liable in respect of an order for compensation made against the transferor. However, Reg 15(9) also provides that the parties are jointly and severally liable in respect of compensation payable under Reg 15(11). In other words, the transferee is jointly and severally liable with the transferor for a claim that either one of them has failed to comply with a compensation order.

3.166 This leads to an incongruous result. We saw above that where the transferor (after giving notice to the transferee in accordance with Reg 15(5)) shows that its failure to inform was due to the *transferee's* failure to provide the information specified in Reg 13(4), then the transferee is solely liable to pay compensation for the transferor's consequent failure to inform – Reg 15(8)(b). However, if the transferee then fails to pay up, and a tribunal upholds an employee's complaint about this, then under Reg 15(11) the *transferor* will bear joint and several liability with the transferee for the transferee's failure. (Under Reg 15(11) the transferor will also be jointly and severally liable with the transferee for the transferee's failure to comply with a compensation order made under Reg 15(7) in respect of the transferee's failure to comply with its obligations under Regs 13 or 14.) Clearly this spreading of liability is in the best interests of the affected employees, but seems rather tough on the transferor, who was not liable for the original failure that led to the relevant compensation order. All of these potential outcomes need to be addressed carefully in the warranties and indemnities covering the transfer – see further Chapter 11, 'Practical aspects of transfers'.

304

Protective awards   3.167

The statutory duty on employers to inform and consult workplace representatives about large-scale redundancies is imposed by S.188 TULR(C)A. This states that 'where an employer is proposing to dismiss as redundant 20 or more employees at one establishment within a period of 90 days or less, the employer shall consult about the dismissals all the persons who are appropriate representatives of any of the employees who may be affected by the proposed dismissals or may be affected by measures taken in connection with those dismissals'. Consultation must begin 'in good time' and must in any event begin:

- where 100 or more redundancies are proposed at one establishment within a 90-day period, at least 45 days before the first of the dismissals takes effect

- otherwise at least 30 days before the first dismissal takes effect – S.188(1A).

If an employment tribunal finds that an employer has acted in breach of S.188, the tribunal must make a declaration to that effect and may make a 'protective award' – S.189 TULR(C)A. This is an award of pay up to a maximum of 13 weeks (90 days) based on the statutory definition of a 'week's pay' but with no financial cap or ceiling being applied in respect of each week's pay. Protective awards are payable to those employees who have been dismissed as redundant, or whom it is proposed to dismiss as redundant, and in respect of whom the employer has failed to comply with the requirements of S.188 – S.189(3).

The duty to collectively consult commonly arises in the context of a relevant **3.168** transfer as redundancies are often a by-product of a change in ownership. As with the duty to inform and consult under Reg 13 prior to the amendments made in 2006 (see 'Duty to inform and consult' above), there has been conflicting case law as to whether a transferor's duty to collectively consult and liability to pay a protective award in respect of a failure to comply with the collective consultation requirements in the TULR(C)A passes to the transferee by virtue of Reg 4(2).

In Angus Jowett and Co Ltd v National Union of Tailors and Garment Workers 1985 ICR 646, EAT, the Appeal Tribunal held that an employer's duty to consult recognised unions over impending redundancies under S.188 TULR(C)A and liability for a protective award under that Act for failure to consult were not automatically transferred under what is now Reg 4(2). This was on the basis that such duties and liabilities were not 'under or in connection with any such contract' within the meaning of Reg 4(2)(a). In the words of Beldam J: 'It is true that the words "in connection with" are extremely wide; but it seems to us that the [transferor's] duties or liabilities which lead to the making of a declaration and protective award... arise in connection not with any contract with an individual employee but by reason of a failure to consult recognised unions.'

_____ **305**

3.169 The issue was revisited by the EAT 15 years later in Kerry Foods Ltd v Creber and ors 2000 ICR 556, EAT. WHL Ltd, which operated a sausage-making business near Plymouth, was in financial difficulties and on 24 January 1997 receivers were appointed. The receivers dismissed some of the employees on 27 January and a further ten employees were dismissed on 31 January, the day that production ceased. Soon afterwards the business was sold to KF Ltd as a going concern. It refused to take on any of WHL Ltd's staff and the remaining employees were dismissed on the day the business was sold. No trade union was recognised by WHL Ltd and none of the staff were consulted regarding the redundancies or the transfer of the business. The employees complained to an employment tribunal that they had been unfairly dismissed and that they had not been consulted about the redundancies or the transfer. The tribunal found that there had been a relevant transfer and that responsibility for the employees' contracts passed to KF Ltd. In the course of its decision, the tribunal held that the employees were entitled to a protective award of four weeks' pay as there had been no collective consultation with them about the impending redundancies. KF Ltd was ordered to pay compensation and it appealed. The EAT held that the duty to consult employee representatives, whether or not there is a recognised union, is a right 'in connection with' an individual's contract of employment and therefore falls within the meaning of liabilities 'under or in connection with any... contract' for the purposes of what is now Reg 4(2)(a) of the 2006 Regulations. What is now Reg 4(2)(b), which attributes to the transferee any act or omission of or in relation to the transferor in respect of the transferred employment contract or in respect of the assigned employee, was also held to be wide enough to cover the failure to consult.

The EAT in the Kerry Foods case felt able to distinguish Angus Jowett and Co Ltd v National Union of Tailors and Garment Workers (above) as that decision was reached at a time when the Employment Protection Act 1975 (and the 1981 TUPE Regulations) only required consultation with recognised trade unions. The European Court of Justice had since made it clear that the EC Collective Redundancies Directive (No.75/129) was intended to protect the rights of employees as individuals and as a result the TULR(C)A (and TUPE) now requires consultation with 'appropriate representatives', who may be either trade union representatives or elected representatives of the affected employees. In the light of this, the EAT felt that no valid distinction could any longer be drawn between liabilities arising in connection with individual contracts of employment on the one hand and liabilities arising in connection with a failure to consult on a collective basis on the other. The EAT therefore held that the transferor's liability for the failure by the receivers to consult passed to the transferee upon the completion of the transfer. It is highly likely that it would have reached the same conclusion had the issue been whether the transferor's liability to pay a protective award made against it passed to the transferee upon transfer.

306

It is therefore the case that an employer's liability for a failure to consult its **3.170** employees or their representatives will pass to a transferee following a transfer of the undertaking. Note that the provisions in Reg 15(9) providing for joint and several liability (discussed under 'Duty to inform and consult' above) apply only to the various obligations to inform and consult under the TUPE Regulations, and not to the collective consultation requirements in the TULR(C)A. However, the cases decided under the TUPE Regulations are likely to be relevant, by analogy, in any discussion as to the transfer or otherwise of liability for failure to collectively consult on redundancies and liability for protective awards in respect of such failure.

Special protections for public sector transfers   3.171

Great care must be taken where a transfer involves the transfer of an economic entity from, to or within the public sector. This is because there are extensive protections, over and above those provided by the TUPE Regulations, that apply to employees transferring within and out of the public sector. This is so whether or not the transfer in question is legally capable of protection under TUPE and EC Community law.

Rights under TUPE   3.172
First, a reminder of the extent to which public sector transfers are protected by TUPE itself. Reg 3(4)(a) provides that the Regulations apply to 'public and private undertakings engaged in economic activities whether or not they are operating for gain'. This confirms that TUPE applies, for example, to the outsourcing of ancillary services from central or local government and government agencies to the private sector; privatisations; and transfers and service provision changes by charitable or 'not for profit' organisations – see further Chapter 1, 'Identifying a "relevant transfer"', under 'Business transfers – what is an "economic entity"?'

However, there will be no relevant transfer in the case of 'an administrative reorganisation of public administrative authorities or the transfer of administrative functions between public administrative authorities' – Reg 3(5) – following the decision of the ECJ in Henke v Gemeinde Schierke and Verwaltungsgemeinschaft 'Brocken' 1997 ICR 746, ECJ (again, see Chapter 1, 'Identifying a "relevant transfer"', under 'The public sector – exclusion of public administrative functions'). The most recent BIS Guide states that:

'Both the Acquired Rights Directive and the TUPE Regulations make it clear that an administrative reorganisation of a public administrative authority, or the transfer of administrative functions between public administrative authorities, is not a relevant transfer within the meaning of the legislation. In addition, there needs to be a change of legal employer for the TUPE Regulations to apply, so transfers within central government are not covered. However,

307

such intra-governmental transfers and reorganisations of administrative function/administrative authorities are covered by the Cabinet Office's Statement of Practice "Staff Transfers in the Public Sector", which provides for TUPE-equivalent protection to be given to transferring employees. In the case of the transfer of administrative functions between public administrative authorities, this protection is often provided in the legislative mechanism by means of which the employees are transferred to the new employer.'

3.173 TUPE-equivalent protection

Special protections derived from a series of Statements, Guidance, legislative provisions and a Code of Practice (often referred to as the 'TUPE plus' arrangements) have accorded, save in exceptional circumstances, TUPE-style protections to employees transferring in and out of the public sector. The relevant provisions make the observance of these protections mandatory. All of the arrangements discussed below continue to hold sway in public sector transfers irrespective of the fact that TUPE protection has now been extended to cover most service provision changes (see Chapter 1, 'Identifying a "relevant transfer"', under 'Service provision changes'). Furthermore, the practical significance of the TUPE plus arrangements remains undiminished, as some of the protections offered – in particular in the context of pension provision (often a highly valuable benefit in public sector contracts) – exceed those conferred by the TUPE Regulations (and, in the context of pensions, by Ss.257 and 258 of the Pensions Act 2004 and the Transfer of Employment (Pension Protection) Regulations 2005 SI 2005/649 – see 'Occupational pensions' above).

3.174 Cabinet Office Statement of Practice. The Cabinet Office Statement of Practice on 'Staff Transfers in the Public Sector' (January 2000) is probably the most important of the public sector protections. It provides that where a transfer, such as a transfer under central government control, is excluded from TUPE by virtue of Reg 3(5) (see 'Rights under TUPE' above), it should nevertheless be treated as if TUPE applies to it, and that certain public sector bodies, such as the NHS, should treat TUPE as being applicable to almost all transfers in the public sector, whether or not it applies in fact. Accordingly, the Statement applies to transfers involving any of the following:

- central government departments and agencies
- local government (where adopted by the relevant local authority)
- the NHS
- public private partnerships (including contracting out and Public Finance Initiative (PFI) projects)
- internal transfers among public sector bodies generally
- second-generation and subsequent-generation outsourcing.

Although the Statement of Practice is not legally enforceable, it is generally followed in practice by private sector service providers, and compliance with it is usually stipulated in the outsourcing contract.

Section 38 Employment Relations Act 1999. Section 38 of the Employment **3.175** Relations Act 1999 gives the Secretary of State power to make statutory instruments providing TUPE-equivalent protections to cases or classes of cases falling outside the scope of the Acquired Rights Directive. This power has been exercised in situations relating to rent officers (see the Transfer of Undertakings (Protection of Employment) (Rent Officer Service) Regulations 1999 SI 1999/2511); OFCOM (see the Transfer of Undertakings (Protection of Employment) (Transfer to OFCOM) Regulations 2003 SI 2003/2715); employees of the Department for Business, Innovation and Skills who transferred to RCUK Shared Services Centre Ltd on 1 November 2012 (the Transfer of Undertakings (Protection of Employment) (RCUK Shared Services Centre Limited) Regulations 2012 SI 2012/2413); and persons employed by various public bodies in public health activity whose employment transferred to the Department of Health as a consequence of new functions relating to public health conferred under the Health and Social Care Act 2012 to be performed by an executive agency, Public Health England (the Transfer of Undertakings (Protection of Employment) (Transfers of Public Health Staff) Regulations 2013 SI 2013/278).

Fair Deal for staff pensions: staff transfer from central government. The **3.176** HM Treasury guidance, 'Fair Deal for staff pensions: staff transfer from central government' (October 2013), is a revised version of original guidance first published in June 1999 and deals with how pension issues are to be dealt with when staff are compulsorily transferred. It applies directly to central government departments, agencies, the NHS, maintained schools (including academies) and any other part of the public sector under the control of Government ministers where staff are eligible to be members of a public service pension scheme. However, it does not apply to local authorities or other best value authorities (as listed in S.1 of the Local Government Act 1999). Having said that, similar arrangements exist in respect of those bodies – see 'Protection for local authority employees' below.

The Fair Deal guidance is necessary to ensure continued occupational pension provision for affected employees given the general exclusion of pension rights from the ambit of TUPE. Under the previous version, where staff were compulsorily transferred from the public sector, their new employer was obliged to give them access to an occupational pension scheme that was broadly comparable to the public service pension scheme they were leaving. However, a policy review undertaken by the previous Coalition Government in 2012 concluded that the provision of final salary pension schemes within the public sector, combined with the requirements of the Fair Deal policy, operated as a barrier to plurality of public service provision. As a result, the revised version of the Fair Deal guidance issued in October 2013 provides that staff who are compulsorily transferred from the public sector will now simply be offered continued access to a public service pension scheme rather than being offered a broadly comparable private pension scheme.

3.177 The new guidance came into effect immediately upon its publication (3 October 2013) and its provisions had to be reflected in procurement practice as soon as was practicable, although allowance was made in respect of projects already at an advanced stage. In any event, the guidance made it clear that the revised Fair Deal policy must be followed in all cases from April 2015 onwards.

Under the revised guidance, staff who are members of a public service pension scheme and who are compulsorily transferred out of the public sector, and who remain continuously employed on the delivery of the outsourced service or function, remain eligible to be members of their public service pension scheme, i.e. their legacy scheme. Moreover, such staff continue to be eligible to be members of the legacy scheme following any subsequent transfer of the relevant function/service by the independent contractor. The Fair Deal policy provides that it is the duty of the public sector transferor to ensure that these rights are set out in the affected employees' contracts of employment with the independent contractor so that they can be contractually enforced, if necessary. It is expressly provided, however, that the provisions of policy do not apply to other employees of the contractor, including any staff employed to deliver the outsourced service or function who were not compulsorily transferred from the public sector.

3.178 With regard to transfers before October 2013, the old Fair Deal policy continues to apply, with some modifications. In essence, compulsorily transferred employees under the previous guidance are entitled to be offered a 'broadly comparable' scheme to the public sector pension scheme and the equivalent new scheme will be rigorously scrutinised by an appropriately qualified actuary to ensure that there is no material detriment overall in terms of future accrual of pension rights for the individuals affected. Moreover, with regard to pension benefits already accrued, the 1999 guidance (as updated by supplementary guidance, 'Fair Deal for Staff Pensions: Procurement of Bulk Transfer Agreements and Related Issues', issued in June 2004) provides that there must be a 'bulk transfer agreement' in place where staff become early leavers of the public sector pension scheme of which they were members prior to the transfer. Such an agreement effectively shields early leavers from suffering the normal disadvantages that apply when transferring out of a final salary (otherwise known as a defined benefit) pension scheme by attributing a higher transfer value for accrued benefits than would normally be the case. This can be a highly valuable benefit for affected staff and can increase the cost of bids by hundreds of millions of pounds in large-scale public procurement project transfers.

310

The revised Fair Deal guidance also sets out instructions for dealing with the situation where a procurement contract that entailed the compulsory transfer of employees under the old Fair Deal regime is subsequently retendered. In this case, the public sector transferor is expected – so long as this is compatible with its obligations under the Public Contracts Regulations 2015 SI 2015/102 – to require bidders for new contracts to provide employees with access to the appropriate public service scheme for so long as they continue to be employed on the contracted service or function. The appropriate scheme will normally be the scheme that staff would be in had they remained in the public sector and not been transferred out. The benefits in the relevant scheme are ordinarily those applicable at the date on which the new contract commences.

Protection for local authority employees. A problem with the Cabinet Office **3.179** Statement of Practice on 'Staff Transfers in the Public Sector' (see 'Cabinet Office Statement of Practice' above) was that it did not protect non-public sector employees recruited to the private sector following the transfer, and therefore could not prevent the rise of a 'two-tier workforce'. This phrase refers to the different terms and conditions that apply, following a transfer, to the transferee's existing workforce on the one hand and the employees whom it acquired as a result of the transfer on the other. In order to deal with this issue, the 'Code of Practice on Workforce Matters in Local Authority Service Contracts' – also variously known as the 'Best Value Code' and the 'Two Tier Workforce Code' – was introduced in March 2003. While operative, this Code was enforceable by contract and ensured that the terms and conditions applicable to employees within local authorities were protected when they were transferred to independent contractors. This extended to the right to continuing access to the Local Government Pension Scheme (LGPS) or an alternative scheme of good quality (subject to actuarial analysis). Although the Code did not require that new (as opposed to transferring) employees be given terms and conditions identical to those of transferred staff, their terms and conditions were required to be fair and reasonable and no less favourable overall, which included being offered reasonable pension provision.

However, the 2003 Code was revoked with immediate effect on 23 March 2011 and remains relevant only with regard to procurement contracts entered into before that date. Apart from specific provision in relation to pensions (see 'Pensions' below), nothing has been introduced to replace the Code and it would appear that the position of transferred local authority employees is now governed by a combination of the Cabinet Office Statement of Practice (see 'Cabinet Office Statement of Practice' above) and by the set of 'Best Value' principles that apply in general to the procurement of services by 'best value authorities' as defined by S.1(1) of the Local Government Act 1999. These include local authorities, police and fire authorities and certain other public sector bodies and agencies. A best value authority is under a statutory duty 'to make arrangements to secure continuous improvement in the way in which its

311

functions are exercised, having regard to a combination of economy, efficiency and effectiveness' – S.3(1) of the 1999 Act. In September 2011 the Government published Best Value Statutory Guidance aimed at reducing barriers that prevent voluntary organisations from competing for local authority contracts and promoting broad consultation about the decommissioning of services. Revised statutory guidance was subsequently issued in March 2015 requiring best value authorities to, among other things, avoid 'gold-plating' the Equality Act 2010 or imposing contractual requirements on private and voluntary sector contracts over and above the obligations in that Act.

3.180 *Pensions.* In addition to the above, the Best Value Authorities Staff Transfers (Pensions) Direction 2007 (issued pursuant to S.101 of the Local Government Act 2003) requires that best value authorities secure pension protection for employees whose employment is compulsorily transferred to a private sector employer following the transfer or decommissioning of services. The Direction applies only in cases where the best value authority enters into a service provision contract for the provision of services that are currently provided by the authority and carried out by its employees. The obligation is to secure 'pension protection' – defined as the right to acquire pension benefits that are the same as, or broadly comparable to or better than, those the employee had, or had a right to acquire, when employed by the authority. In practical terms, this means the contractor can either offer employees membership of a pension scheme that has been certified by the Government Actuary's Department as broadly comparable to the LGPS, or allow the employees to remain in the LGPS by becoming an 'admitted body' to the LGPS and paying the requisite pension contributions.

The 2007 Direction also applies to second generation outsourcings. In this regard, the service provision contract must stipulate that the subsequent contractor is obliged to secure pension protection for any transferring original employees and that the pension protection provided is enforceable by those employees.

3.181 It is evident, therefore, that transferred employees of local authorities and other best value authorities continue to enjoy a superior level of protection to that which the TUPE Regulations by themselves provide, at least so far as occupational pension rights are concerned. However, there is no longer any initiative of the kind previously set out in the 2003 Code of Practice, which, as we have seen, extended similar rights to members of the transferee's existing workforce in order to address the two-tier workforce concern.

3.182 **Principles of Good Employment Practice.** In addition to the 2003 Code of Practice (see 'Protection for local authority employees' above), a further Code of Practice – the 'Code of Practice on Workforce Matters in Public Sector Service Contracts' – was published in 2005 aimed at extending the reach of the 2003 Code beyond local authorities to cover most of the public sector. However, with effect from 13 December 2010, this Code was withdrawn on the grounds that the then Coalition Government believed it had increased the costs of public sector outsourcing and acted as a barrier to smaller companies, charities and social enterprises bidding for public sector contracts. In place of the 2005 Code, the Government published non-mandatory 'Principles of Good Employment Practice', described as 'A statement of principles that reflect good employment practice for Government, Contracting Authorities and Suppliers'. The six core principles cover: the Government as a good client; training and skills; a commitment to fair and reasonable terms and conditions; equality; dispute resolution; and employee engagement. They are voluntary and, among other things, require that contracting organisations ensure that supplier policies are consistent with the provisions of the Equality Act 2010.

It is important to note that all procurement contracts that were concluded under the 2005 Code will remain in force until retendered and that the provisions of the Code will therefore continue to apply in such cases. However, the Code will no longer apply if such contracts are, or have been, put out for retender at any time after the repeal of the Code. If the original contract was entered into before repeal of the Code but is extended by agreement between the parties, then the provisions of the Code will continue to apply provided that there is a term in the contract to this effect. Where no such term exists, or where a new service provider enters the picture following a retendering process, then the 2005 Code is no longer applicable.

Retention of Employment model. The Retention of Employment model 3.183 (RoE) was first developed by the Department of Health to limit the number of non-clinical staff employed in the NHS from having their employment automatically transferred under TUPE to private sector employers under private finance initiative (PFI) schemes. It was recognised that the operation of the TUPE Regulations can have particular disadvantages in these circumstances since, from the employees' point of view, transfer from a public to a private employer can be perceived as giving rise to a gradual erosion of rights and benefits – especially with regard to occupational pension provision. Employees stood to lose the benefit of membership of the NHS Superannuation Scheme, which, so far as this applies to non-clinical staff, is structured in such a way that private employers cannot obtain admitted body status to the scheme. And for the PFI companies and any sub-contractors, in the absence of special arrangements the application of TUPE would mean that they would have to meet the higher cost of employing ex-public sector employees on transferred levels of pay and other benefits.

It was in this context that the Government announced its intention in 2001 to pilot a 'new model for ancillary staff in PFI hospitals' – now known as the 'Retention of Employment model'. The basic principle behind RoE is that instead of TUPE applying to transfer the employment of front-line employees, they remain employed by the NHS and are seconded to and managed by the private sector partner on a long-term basis. As a result, they remain on their existing terms and conditions and subject to existing NHS policies and procedures. The private sector partner, however, retains responsibility for providing the outsourced services, and management-level and supervisory staff transfer to it under TUPE as normal.

3.184 In order to ensure that such arrangements do not fall foul of TUPE by amounting to agreements to contract out of the Regulations contrary to Reg 18 – see Chapter 10, 'Contracting out of TUPE' – the employees exercise their formal right to object to a transfer under Reg 4(7). They will then be treated as having resigned rather than having been dismissed. They are then immediately re-employed by the NHS Trust on the same terms and conditions as before but under long-term secondment to the private sector partner. This device preserves their continuity of employment and right to participate in the NHS Superannuation Scheme. Obviously, an employee is not compelled to exercise his or her right to object if he or she does not want to and is entitled to go across to the new employer under TUPE in the ordinary way, but in that case he or she would stand to lose the special entitlements conferred by the RoE agreement.

Since its creation, RoE has been developed as a model for use in a variety of non-PFI settings and has expanded beyond the NHS. However, prompted by governmental concern about the cost to the tax payer of the retention model, a general review was conducted in 2009. Following this, it was made clear that the use of RoE would henceforth be restricted to soft facilities management in PFI schemes (e.g. catering and cleaning) and staff working in independent sector treatment centres. In these settings, secondments tend to be shorter and management responsibility remains with the employing public sector organisation. This reflects case law that makes it clear that too much devolution of management responsibility to the private sector provider can create the risk of an employment relationship being inferred between a seconded employee and the private sector provider – see, for example, Fitton v City of Edinburgh Council EATS 0010/07, where the EAT upheld an employment tribunal's finding that the claimant was legally employed by the private sector party to a secondment arrangement with the local authority based on application of the ordinary contractual principles determining employment status, including the 'control' test. This potential flaw in the RoE model can be best addressed by ensuring that secondments are temporary so that they do not give the impression of having become permanent; that work remains available within the public sector organisation to which secondees can return once their secondment is terminated; and that secondees do not 'relinquish' their employment with the public sector employer – a fact that should be sufficiently evidenced by making the intention to re-employ clear at the time the election to opt out of TUPE is made.

314

In the absence of a clear legal decision sanctioning RoE, a degree of uncertainty **3.185** exists as to the model's legal effectiveness. The general consensus is that it is legally viable but not entirely risk free, since there remains a possibility that sometime in the future a court or tribunal may rule that employees to whom an RoE process was applied have in fact transferred to the relevant provider as a matter of law under TUPE. This is particularly so against the backdrop of cases such as the House of Lords' decision in Celtec Ltd v Astley 2006 ICR 992, HL, and the EAT's decision in Capita Health Solutions v McLean and anor 2008 IRLR 595, EAT – both discussed in detail in Chapter 2, 'Who transfers?', under 'Problems of secondment arrangements' and 'Objecting to transfer – timing of objection' respectively.

Rights and liabilities that do not transfer   3.186

Certain rights and liabilities are expressly excluded from the principle of automatic transfer in the Regulations, mainly for public policy reasons. These are:

- criminal liabilities

- terms relating to occupational pensions

- insolvency

- continuation orders.

Apart from pensions (discussed under 'Occupational pensions' above), these are considered below.

Criminal liabilities   3.187

Regulation 4(6) TUPE states: 'Paragraph (2) shall not transfer or otherwise affect the liability of any person to be prosecuted for, convicted of and sentenced for any offence.' Accordingly, liability for a criminal offence committed by a transferor will not be transferred with the business to the transferee.

Some legislative breaches give rise to both criminal and civil liabilities. In the employment context, where an employer commits certain breaches of health and safety legislation or of the Protection from Harassment Act 1997, for example, it may in appropriate circumstances be prosecuted for a criminal offence and be liable to be sued separately in a civil court. In such a case, following Reg 4(6), the transferee would not incur any criminal liability of the transferor on the occasion of a transfer. But would it become responsible for paying civil damages in respect of the breach – for example, for failing to provide a safe system of work? As discussed under 'Tortious and other civil liabilities' above, a transferor's civil liabilities are certainly capable of transferring to the transferee under Reg 4(2). Therefore, where a transferor has committed a tortious act before the transfer, and been prosecuted and sued for

315

the relevant breach, it is likely that civil liability for it would pass to the transferee. But what is the position where the transferor has committed an act before the transfer that *might* give rise to criminal and civil liability, but which has not yet prompted a prosecution or civil claim? Reg 4(6) makes it clear that Reg 4(2), in its entirety, is not to be read as either transferring criminal liability *or otherwise affecting* the criminal liability of a person. In other words, Reg 4(2)(b) – which provides that any act or omission of the transferor before the transfer shall be deemed to have been an act or omission of the transferee following the transfer – cannot have the effect of attributing to the transferee potentially criminal acts or omissions of the transferor as this would *affect the liability* of the transferee to be prosecuted for a criminal offence. Arguably, this is the case even if that act or omission may also give rise to civil liability.

3.188 If this interpretation is correct, it has potentially nonsensical consequences. An affected employee, following the transfer, could not sue the transferee, because the transferee would not have been deemed to have committed the breach – but neither could he or she sue the transferor, because under Reg 4(2)(a), to the extent that the breach gave rise to civil liability, this would have 'transferred' to the transferee.

Note that an employer who fails to notify the Secretary of State about collective redundancies under S.193 TULR(C)A commits a criminal offence – S.194. Where a transferor proposes to dismiss as redundant 20 or more employees within a 90-day period in the course of a TUPE transfer, it should note that it will not escape liability for failing to inform the Secretary of State in advance of the redundancies.

3.189 Terms relating to occupational pensions
We have previously seen that occupational pension schemes are expressly excluded from the operation of the automatic transfer principles in Regs 4 and 5 TUPE by virtue of Reg 10. However, this exclusion is tightly defined and does not cover personal pension plans into which the transferor makes contributions or any aspect of an occupational pension scheme unrelated to 'benefits for old age, invalidity or survivors'. Furthermore, a raft of statutory provisions outside of TUPE impose upon transferees ongoing duties to provide minimal levels of pension protection.

The scope of the Reg 10 exclusion and the wide caveats to it are discussed under 'Occupational pensions' above.

3.190 Insolvency
The TUPE Regulations 2006 introduced provisions not contained in the precursor Regulations aimed at promoting the 'rescue culture' in respect of businesses that are insolvent. It has always been the case that TUPE will apply where a business, or the underlying profitable part of it, is continued during the

course of the insolvency proceedings and subsequently sold as a going concern by the insolvency practitioner. What changed was that the normal TUPE rules regarding the transfer or rights, duties and liabilities were modified to encourage transferees to acquire businesses that have got themselves into financial or other trading difficulties by limiting the employment liabilities they take on.

The key provisions are contained in Regs 8 and 9 of the 2006 Regulations. These provide that:

- where the transferor is subject to bankruptcy or analogous insolvency proceedings instituted with a view to liquidating the transferor's assets under the supervision of an insolvency practitioner, both Regs 4 (dealing with the automatic transfer of contracts of employment) and 7 (unfair dismissal) are disapplied in their entirety – Reg 8(7). This means that the transferee will not have to take on any of the employees assigned to the undertaking that is the subject of any relevant transfer. It also means that if such employees are voluntarily re-engaged by the transferee, none of the rights, duties, powers and liabilities under or in connection with their contracts of employment are automatically transferred; nor are the employees protected in the usual way against detrimental variation of their contractual terms or unfair dismissal by reason of the transfer

- where the transferor is the subject of 'relevant insolvency proceedings', Reg 4 will continue to apply except that certain core debts (such as statutory redundancy payments, payments in lieu of notice and unpaid holiday pay of up to six weeks) will not transfer but will instead remain with the transferor – Reg 8(5). These will become payable by the Secretary of State for Trade and Industry out of the National Insurance Fund. 'Relevant insolvency proceedings' for these purposes are defined in Reg 8(6) as 'proceedings which have been opened in relation to the transferor not with a view to the liquidation of the assets of the transferor and which are under the supervision of an insolvency practitioner'. In practice, this will cover administrative receiverships and administrations

- in the context of 'relevant insolvency proceedings', the transferor, transferee or the insolvency practitioner may also agree 'permitted variations' with appropriate representatives of assigned employees, which will then take effect as a term or condition of the employees' contracts of employment – Reg 9(1) and (6). A 'permitted variation' is defined as a variation where the sole or principal reason for it is the transfer and it is designed to safeguard re-employment opportunities by ensuring the survival of the undertaking being transferred – Reg 9(7). (Outside of an insolvency context, the normal position under TUPE – as set out in Reg 4(5) – is that contractual variations are permissible only if the terms of the contract of employment permit the variation in question or the reason for it is an economic, technical or

317

organisational reason entailing changes in the workforce and the variation has been agreed between the parties.)

The provisions of Regs 8 and 9 are examined in detail in Chapter 6, 'Transfer of insolvent companies'.

3.191 Continuation orders

We have previously discussed the extent to which statutory rights are transferred on a relevant transfer – see 'Individual statutory rights' above. One such right that has been found not to transfer is the benefit of an interim relief order for continuation of contract (CCO) on the ground of trade union-related discrimination, pursuant to Ss.163 and 164 TULR(C)A – an admittedly limited but interesting exception.

In Dowling v ME Ilic Haulage and anor 2004 ICR 1176, EAT, D was employed by a haulage company, IH, as a driver's mate. He was dismissed for gross misconduct on 15 December 2002 and brought a claim under S.152 TULR(C)A, alleging that the real reason for the dismissal was his participation in trade union activities as a shop steward. He also applied for interim relief. That application was heard on 3 February 2003 and a CCO was granted. The hearing of D's unfair dismissal claim was listed to take place on 22 April 2003. Meanwhile, on 14 April, part of IH's business was acquired by another company, BL Ltd. The parties accepted that TUPE applied and BL Ltd was joined as a second respondent to the unfair dismissal claim. However, a tribunal chairman subsequently dismissed BL Ltd from the proceedings. Her reasoning was that, at the date of the transfer, D was not employed under a contract of employment for the purposes of Reg 4(1), and accordingly IH's obligations under the CCO did not pass to BL Ltd by virtue of Reg 4(2)(a). D appealed to the EAT.

3.192

The appeal was heard by the then President of the EAT, Mr Justice Burton. He agreed with the tribunal chairman that the relationship that is effected by a continuation order is not a 'contract of employment' for the purposes of TUPE because it is purely statutory and unilateral, in that the employee receives pay but has no corresponding obligation to provide services. He rejected the argument that D's position was similar to that of an employee absent on maternity leave or long-term sick leave. In his view, an individual who is the subject of a CCO is an ex-employee and there is no subsisting employment contract upon which Reg 4(1) can bite. D sought to counter that view by citing the case of Litster and ors v Forth Dry Dock and Engineering Co Ltd (in receivership) and anor 1989 ICR 341, HL, in which the House of Lords held that Reg 4(1) must be construed purposively so that an employee dismissed before a transfer for a reason connected with it is deemed to have been employed in the undertaking immediately before the transfer. He argued that a similar analysis applied in the context of continuation orders. However, Burton J did not accept this analogy. In his view, it was much more difficult to construe Reg 4(1) as effecting a statutory continuation of the employment contract in the present context than it was in Litster, where the aim was to prevent the parties from evading the application of TUPE.

Burton J also reasoned that, in any event, it was plain from the narrow wording of S.164 TULR(C)A that a continuation order was not intended to have this effect. S.164(1) prescribes two exclusive and limited purposes for which the contract of employment continues in force – pay and benefits, and calculation of the employee's period of continuous employment. He made the additional point that, for the duration of a continuation order, an employer can do nothing to terminate its obligations under S.164, short of applying to the tribunal for variation or revocation of the order under S.165. Even if a continuation order were capable of effecting a statutory continuation of the employment contract, the contract created or continued by the order would not – indeed, could not – be terminated in the event of a transfer of the business. Thus, it was not a 'contract which would otherwise [have been] terminated by the transfer' within the meaning of Reg 4(1). Burton J concluded that a continuation order does no more than create, on the part of the former employer, a financial liability which does not pass to a transferee of the undertaking. Accordingly, he dismissed D's appeal.

With respect to the EAT's reasoning in the Dowling case, it could be argued **3.193** that a CCO clearly envisages the continuation of the employment relationship and the effect of any such order is generally understood to be that the individual remains the employer's employee, albeit that he or she is suspended on full pay. Although Dowling remains the only case specifically on the point, support for the view that TUPE should be regarded as operating to transfer a CCO can be derived from the EAT's decision in Langton v Secretary of State for Health 2014 ICR D2, EAT. That case concerned a continuation of contract order made under Ss.129 and 130 ERA – which contain virtually identical provisions to Ss.163 and 164 TULR(C)A but apply to applications for interim relief made where the alleged reason for dismissal concerns whistleblowing. Although the Langton case did not deal with the question of whether TUPE operates to transfer obligations under a CCO to the transferee, the decision suggests that an employment tribunal's power to make such an Order should not be defeated by a transfer of liabilities under an employment contract.

The facts of the Langton case were as follows. L was employed by an NHS Trust and was dismissed on 31 March, the same day on which the Trust was dissolved under the Health and Social Care Act 2012. On 4 April she lodged a claim of automatically unfair dismissal under S.103A ERA, asserting that she had been dismissed for having made a protected disclosure. She named the Trust as respondent and sought interim relief under S.128 ERA. Before the tribunal dealt with the question of interim relief, it accepted an application

319

from the Secretary of State for Health to be substituted for the Trust as the respondent to the claim. The Secretary of State adopted the Trust's stated reasons for dismissal and sought to defend the S.103A claim. The tribunal decided that, in these circumstances, it could not make a CCO, given that the employer – the Trust – no longer existed. On appeal, the EAT rejected this analysis of the law. It held that the Secretary of State had stepped into the shoes of the Trust for the purpose of litigation, having regard to the fact that, under S.70 of the National Health Service Act 2006, the Secretary of State was statutorily required to ensure that all of the Trust's civil liabilities were dealt with. This included any potential liability for an order under Ss.128–130 ERA. Referring to Dowling v ME Ilic Haulage and anor (above), the EAT noted that the effect of a CCO would not be to create a new contract of employment, but simply to preserve L's right to pay and other benefits and to deal, if necessary, with the question of continuity of employment. It would not, therefore, be a case of ordering the Secretary of State to enter into a contract of employment with L.

3.194   In our opinion, this analysis would also apply, by close analogy, to a situation where the transfer of liabilities has been effected by TUPE. This view is supported by clear conclusions reached by His Honour Judge Peter Clark in Langton. When summing up his reasoning in that case he stated: 'There is nothing in my view in Ss.128–130 ERA that prevents the tribunal making a continuation order against a party who has chosen to substitute himself for the original respondent but is not the employer as defined in S.230(4) ERA.' Apart, perhaps, from the reference to 'choosing' to stand in the previous employer's shoes, this neatly describes the position of a transferee under TUPE.

If, and in so far as, CCOs are properly regarded as being excluded from the ambit of Reg 4(1), then the position can be contrasted with that in which employment is deemed to have continued following a successful appeal from a summary dismissal. In G4S Justice Services (UK) Ltd v Anstey and ors 2006 IRLR 588, EAT, A and S were summarily dismissed on 13 April 2005 for gross misconduct and lodged internal appeals against their dismissals. Their disciplinary procedure provided that, in the event of a successful appeal against dismissal, continuity of employment would be classed as unbroken service with full restitution of lost earnings. Before the employees' appeals were heard, however, their employer lost the contract on which they worked to another contractor, G4S, which took over on 1 May. Following the transfer G4S declined to hear the employees' appeals, claiming that it had never been their employer. As a result their appeals were heard by GSL, which allowed both and directed that they be reinstated. G4S refused to reinstate them on the basis that they had not been employed by GSL 'immediately before' the transfer within the meaning of Reg 4(3), with the result that their employment had not transferred to G4S under Reg 4(1) and (2). A and S subsequently brought claims of unfair dismissal against both GSL and G4S. The EAT upheld an employment tribunal's finding that the claimants' contracts of employment had transferred to the transferee under TUPE. Although the claimants had been summarily dismissed by the transferor, they had lodged appeals against those dismissals that were still pending at the time of the transfer. The EAT found that the contractual obligation to hear and determine the claimants' appeals against dismissal lay, notwithstanding the transfer, with the transferor. The transferor's subsequent decision to uphold those appeals and reinstate the claimants with full continuity of service had the retrospective effect that the dismissals were expunged and the claimants were employed 'immediately before the transfer'. Therefore, the obligation on the transferor to reinstate the claimants transferred to the transferee under the TUPE Regulations.

Continuing liability of transferor?

3.195

Once Reg 4(2) of the TUPE Regulations has operated to transfer rights and duties to a transferee, it is not possible for a transferring employee to bring a claim against the transferor in respect of them. Equally, however, a transferor will no longer be able to assert any right transferred to the transferee against the transferred employees – which may be of particular consequence in relation to, for example, the loss of the right to enforce restraint of trade clauses and clauses relating to confidential information, or settlement agreements – see 'Obligations specifically tailored to transferor's identity' above, under 'Restrictive covenants and non-compete clauses' and 'Settlement agreements'.

This reflects the position under the Acquired Rights Directive, as clarified by the ECJ in Berg and anor v Besselsen 1990 ICR 396, ECJ. Its analysis of Article 3(1) showed that a relevant transfer entails the automatic transfer from the transferor to the transferee of the employer's obligations arising from a contract of employment or an employment relationship – subject, however, to the right of EU Member States to provide for joint (now joint and several) liability of the transferor and transferee following the transfer (see 'Joint and several liability' below). Therefore, the ECJ held, unless the Member States provide otherwise, the transferor is released from its obligations as an employer solely by reason of the transfer. This legal consequence is not conditional on the consent of the employees concerned and cannot be prevented by their objection to the transfer.

The Court of Session confirmed in Stirling District Council v Allan and ors 1995 ICR 1082, Ct Sess (Inner House), that this is also the position under UK law. In that case Stirling District Council conducted a competitive tendering exercise under which the contract on which the claimants worked was awarded to B Ltd. A and seven of his colleagues were dismissed for redundancy and initiated employment tribunal proceedings against the Council. The tribunal held that their dismissals were automatically unfair under what is now Reg 7(1) of the Regulations. However, it refused to uphold the claims against the Council

3.196

321

on the basis that the employees had initiated proceedings against the wrong party, given that under Reg 4(2) rights and liabilities under contracts of employment are automatically assigned to the transferee where the employees were deemed to be employed immediately before the relevant transfer. The EAT allowed the employees' appeal. It took the view that it would be contrary to the Regulations' main purpose of protecting employees' rights if Reg 4(2) were to be regarded as transferring to the transferee exclusive responsibility for a dismissal carried out entirely by the transferor and taking effect before, or simultaneously with, the transfer. The Council appealed.

3.197 The Court of Session held that the tribunal had correctly held that liability to compensate the employees for the dismissals fell exclusively on the transferee. In concluding that the transferor was accordingly not liable for the unfair dismissals, the Court cited the following reasons:

- there was no ambiguity in Reg 4(2)(b)'s provision that, on completion of a relevant transfer, all the transferor's contractual liabilities towards the employees were transferred to the transferee. The word 'transferred' necessarily denotes that the transferor's liabilities, whether accrued or continuing, pass to the transferee and that the transferor is no longer subject to any such liabilities. Therefore, while it is true that the responsibility of an employer for the dismissal of an employee should not be excluded in the absence of express provision or necessary implication, Reg 4(2)(a) unambiguously and clearly provided such express provision

- it was a natural consequence of the subsequent provision in Reg 4(2)(b) – which states that anything done before the completion of the transfer by the transferor in relation to a contract of employment was deemed to have been done by the transferee – that the liability of the transferor for the act of unfair dismissal should be discharged. Again, this expressly and unambiguously excluded the transferor's responsibility for an employee's dismissal

- the employees' contention that the transferor remained liable was inconsistent with the terms of the Directive. The fact that Article 3 gave Member States the option of providing for the continued liability of the transferor, in addition to the transferee, clearly confirmed that the transferor did not remain liable unless provision to that effect had been made.

Although a decision of the Court of Session does not strictly bind the lower courts in England and Wales, the decision in the Allan case was followed by the EAT in Secretary of State for Employment v Mapstone and ors EAT 1060/94, which noted that the Court of Session's decision was 'manifestly right' and 'whether or not that is binding upon us we should not dream of departing from such authority unless we were satisfied that it is wrong'. Indeed, the Court of Session in Allan took into account the obiter dictum of the EAT in Ibex Trading

Co Ltd (in administration) v Walton and ors 1994 ICR 907, EAT, that 'use of the word "transfer" in its natural and ordinary meaning suggests a taking away from one and a handing over to another' – in holding that, in fact, 'the word cannot bear any other meaning in any circumstances'.

Joint and several liability 3.198

As the Court of Session in Stirling District Council v Allan and ors (above) noted, Article 3(1) of the Acquired Rights Directive contains an option for Member States to provide for joint and several liability of transferor and transferee after the transfer in respect of obligations which would otherwise fall exclusively on the transferee. The UK has opted to impose joint and several liability under TUPE in the following two areas only:

- liability to pay compensation for the transferor's failures to comply with its information and consultation requirements under Reg 13 or Reg 14, and liability for either party's failure to pay compensation awarded to an employee in respect of such failures under Reg 15(7) or (8) – Reg 15(9); and

- liability for personal injury claims (so far as this relates to the employee's period of employment with the transferor) in situations where the transferor is not required to take out personal injury insurance under S.3(1)(a)–(c) of the Employers' Liability (Compulsory Insurance) Act 1969 – Reg 17(2).

The effect of joint and several liability is that an employee may sue either the transferor or the transferee or both for compensation.

Joint and several liability in respect of failure to inform and consult. We 3.199 discussed the effect of the provisions as to joint and several liability in respect of failure to inform and consult under 'Collective rights and liabilities – duty to inform and consult' above. The provisions seek to address the problem raised by Alamo Group (Europe) Ltd v Tucker and anor 2003 ICR 829, EAT. In that case the EAT held that liability for a failure to inform and consult passed like any other liability to the transferee upon transfer – with the unjust effect that transferors could with impunity conduct perfunctory consultation exercises upon transfer.

Joint and several liability for personal injury. We discussed the effect of the 3.200 Court of Appeal's decision in Martin v Lancashire County Council and another case 2001 ICR 197, CA, under 'Tortious and other civil liabilities' above. The Court there held that a transferor's right to be indemnified in respect of tortious liability under compulsory employers' liability insurance passes to the transferee under Reg 4(2). This is because the liability against which employers are obliged to insure, by the Employers' Liability (Compulsory Insurance) Act 1969, is liability for bodily injury or disease sustained by their employees arising out of and in the course of their employment – and, therefore, any right

323

to be indemnified in respect of that liability is a right in respect of liability 'in connection with' and 'arising from' the contract within the meaning of Reg 4(2).

However, the Court's conclusion in Martin was not relevant where a transferor was not obliged to take out insurance covering possible personal injury claims by its employees. In this regard, S.3(1)(a)–(c) of the Employers' Liability (Compulsory Insurance) Act 1969 provides that the following authorities and bodies are *not* required to effect insurance under the Act:

- health service bodies; National Health Service Trusts; NHS Commissioning Board; NHS Foundation Trusts; Primary Care Trusts; Local Health Boards

- the Common Council of the City of London; London Borough Councils; councils of a county or county borough in Wales; councils constituted under S.2 of the Local Government etc (Scotland) Act 1994 in England and Wales or joint committees in Scotland which are so constituted as to include among their members representatives of any such council; joint authorities established by Part IV of the Local Government Act 1985; economic prosperity boards established under S.88 of the Local Democracy, Economic Development and Construction Act 2009

- the Broads Authority; the Strathclyde Passenger Transport Authority

- police authorities; any local policing body; any chief constable established under S.2 of the Police Reform and Social Responsibility Act 2011; the Commissioner of Police of the Metropolis

- the London Fire and Emergency Planning Authority; the Scottish Fire and Rescue Service

- the Commission for Equality and Human Rights, and

- employers that are exempted by regulations (as listed in Schedule 2 to the Employers' Liability (Compulsory Insurance) Regulations 1998 SI 1998/2573).

3.201 So a transferee acquiring a business from an NHS Trust, for example, could inherit an uninsured claim that it might be unable to meet. It was to address this loophole that the 2006 TUPE Regulations introduced Reg 17(2), which imposes joint and several liability on the transferor and the transferee in respect of claims for personal injury arising out of an employee's employment with a potentially uninsured transferor. This, however, has served to give rise to a disparity between cases in which a transferor is from the private sector and those in which the transferor falls within the list of exempted bodies above. In the former, following the decision in Martin v Lancashire County Council and another case (above), the transferee will inherit full liability for personal injury claims; in the latter, the transferee is jointly and severally liable with the transferor.

324

Possibility of dual employment

There remains one further hypothetical situation where the transferor may continue to bear liability in respect of individual transferred employees. We discuss in Chapter 2, 'Who transfers?', the possibility that, in the context of a relevant transfer arising out of a service provision change, the identifiable group of employees assigned to the transferring activity may only work on that activity for part of their weekly working time. Could it be the case that if, say, those employees work from Monday to Wednesday on the activity to be transferred, that part of their employment will transfer to the transferee but for the remaining two days the employees will continue to work for the transferor? If this were the case, the relevant employees would have dual employment following the transfer and the transferor would thus retain liability in respect of their employment to the extent that it was not transferred. It is probable, however, that whole-time dedication may be required on the part of employees to give rise to a relevant transfer in the first place – for a fuller discussion see Chapter 2, 'Who transfers?', under '"Assigned" to undertaking transferred – difficult issues arising from assignment to part of business'.

4 Unfair dismissal

Article 4(1) of the EU Acquired Rights Directive (No.2001/23) ('the Acquired **4.1** Rights Directive') states: 'The transfer of the undertaking, business or part of the undertaking or business shall not in itself constitute grounds for dismissal by the transferor or the transferee. This provision shall not stand in the way of dismissals that may take place for economic, technical or organisational reasons entailing changes in the workforce.'

This provision was initially transposed into domestic law by Reg 8 of the 1981 TUPE Regulations and then by Reg 7 of the Transfer of Undertakings (Protection of Employment) Regulations 2006 SI 2006/246 (TUPE). The wording of some parts of Reg 7 has been amended by the Collective Redundancies and Transfer of Undertakings (Protection of Employment) (Amendment) Regulations 2014 SI 2014/16 ('the 2014 Amendment Regulations'). This applies to all dismissals, whether effected with or without notice, which took place on or after 31 January 2014. (This chapter is therefore primarily based on the current wording of Reg 7, although there may be occasions where it is necessary to refer to the 1981 Regulations (i.e. pre- the 2014 amendments) and to the earlier version of the 2006 Regulations in order to understand the way the law has developed and to reflect the fact that many of the cases are based on the original wording of Reg 7.) The rules apply to both 'ordinary' TUPE transfers and transfers by way of service provision change.

In essence, the underlying purpose of Article 4(1) and Reg 7 is to restrict the **4.2** circumstances in which employers – transferors or transferees – can effect dismissals fairly in a transfer situation. The amendments introduced by the 2014 Amendment Regulations were intended to somewhat liberalise the previous law but, as will be explained, the extent to which this is possible within the framework of EU law is open to doubt. Furthermore, the essentials of the unfair dismissal regime as now set out in Reg 7 remain the same as under the 1981 Regulations: a dismissal because of the transfer is automatically unfair

327

unless it is for an economic, technical or organisational (ETO) reason which entails changes in the workforce of either the transferor or the transferee. If it is for an ETO reason, the dismissal must still be fair in accordance with ordinary principles of fairness under S.98(4) of the Employment Rights Act 1996.

Regulation 7 augments, and hence cannot be divorced from, the general unfair dismissal law contained in the Employment Rights Act 1996 (ERA). Accordingly, we begin this chapter by giving a brief overview of the relevant ERA provisions. We then explain how the Reg 7 TUPE unfair dismissal rules fit together, before examining in depth the two questions central to the Reg 7 regime: first, when will a dismissal be automatically unfair?; and secondly, what will amount to 'an economic, technical or organisational reason entailing changes in the workforce' (an ETO reason)?

4.3 Also in this chapter, we discuss at length the two routes by which an employee's decision to leave his or her employment, taken in response to the actions of a transferor or transferee, can amount to a 'dismissal' giving rise to a potential unfair dismissal claim. First, as Reg 4(11) acknowledges, a constructive dismissal might occur where an employee resigns in response to a repudiatory breach of contract by his or her employer. Secondly, Reg 4(9) states that 'where a relevant transfer involves or would involve a substantial change in working conditions to the material detriment of a person whose contract of employment is or would be transferred... such an employee may treat the contract of employment as having been terminated, and the employee shall be treated for any purpose as having been dismissed by the employer'. Having examined these provisions, we end the chapter by briefly considering which employer – transferor or transferee – will be liable for unfair dismissals carried out around the time of a relevant transfer.

Note that we presume, for the purposes of this discussion, that a relevant transfer within the meaning of Reg 3 of the TUPE Regulations has taken (or is about to take) place. For an examination of what amounts to a relevant transfer, see Chapter 1, 'Identifying a "relevant transfer"'.

4.4 Overview

This Handbook does not cover general unfair dismissal law in detail. In this section, however, we outline the main features of the unfair dismissal regime contained in the Employment Rights Act 1996 that can impact upon TUPE-connected dismissals. For a more detailed analysis of this area, see IDS Employment Law Handbooks, 'Unfair Dismissal' (2010) and 'Redundancy' (2011).

4.5 Who is eligible to claim unfair dismissal?
An individual must meet certain eligibility criteria in order to bring an unfair dismissal claim, whether or not such a claim is TUPE-connected. In summary:

- only 'employees' can claim – S.94(1) ERA. An employee is defined as 'an individual who has entered into or works under a contract of employment' – S.230(1). A 'contract of employment' is defined as 'a contract of service, whether express or implied and (if it is express) whether oral or in writing' – S.230(2)

- an employee must have been continuously employed by the employer for at least two years in order to claim – S.108(1) ERA, and

- only claims relating to 'employment in Great Britain' can be brought. However, expatriate employees working wholly outside Great Britain will be entitled to bring unfair dismissal claims in certain unusual circumstances – see Lawson v Serco Ltd and other cases 2006 ICR 250, HL.

Meaning of 'dismissal' 4.6
In order to succeed in an 'ordinary' unfair dismissal claim, an employee has to show that he or she has been 'dismissed' within the meaning of S.95(1) ERA. This provides that a dismissal occurs in each of the following three circumstances:

- the employer terminates the employee's contract with or without notice – S.95(1)(a)

- the employee is employed under a fixed-term contract which terminates upon its expiry without being renewed on the same terms – S.95(1)(b), and

- the employee terminates the employment contract, with or without notice, in circumstances where he or she is entitled to do so without notice owing to the employer's conduct (known as a constructive dismissal) – S.95(1)(c).

Section 95(1) ERA also applies in TUPE cases. The extent to which Reg 4(9) extends the right to bring a claim where there has been 'substantial change in working conditions to the material detriment of a person' is considered in the section on 'Material detriment dismissals' below.

Reason for dismissal 4.7
Once an employee has established that a dismissal has occurred, the onus is on the employer to show that the reason or principal reason for dismissal is one of the potentially fair reasons set out in S.98(1) and (2) ERA: the employee's capability or qualification, conduct, redundancy (see 'Redundancy' below), inability to work owing to a statutory requirement, or dismissal 'for some other substantial reason of a kind such as to justify the dismissal of an employee holding the position which the employee held'.

Certain reasons for dismissal are *automatically* unfair – for example, dismissals by reason of trade union membership; pregnancy; and, as this chapter explains, the transfer of an undertaking where there is no 'economic, technical or organisational reason entailing changes in the workforce'.

329

4.8 Reasonableness

In addition to showing a fair reason for dismissal, in order to escape unfair dismissal liability the employer must also have acted reasonably in all the circumstances, having regard to equity and the substantial merits of the case – S.98(4) ERA. In other words, the employer must have acted reasonably in treating the reason as a sufficient reason for dismissal and have acted fairly and in accordance with relevant procedures. This also applies in TUPE cases where a dismissal is found to be for an economic, technical or organisational reason entailing changes in the workforce – see McGrath v Rank Leisure Ltd 1985 ICR 527, EAT.

With regard to reasonableness, the tribunal should not simply consider whether it would have dismissed in the circumstances and substitute its view for that of the employer – Iceland Frozen Foods Ltd v Jones 1983 ICR 17, EAT. Rather, the test to be applied is whether the employer's decision to dismiss fell within the range of reasonable responses available to it – see (1) Post Office v Foley (2) HSBC Bank plc v Madden 2000 ICR 1283, CA.

4.9 Procedural requirements

The fairness of a dismissal also depends on the employer's compliance with any contractual and statutory procedural requirements – for example, proper redundancy consultation and selection procedures. In dismissing, employers have to be sure that they comply with the revised Acas Code of Practice on Disciplinary and Grievance Procedures issued under S.199 of the Trade Union and Labour Relations (Consolidation) Act 1992. Arguably, the Code does not sit easily with non-fault dismissals such as those usually associated with relevant transfers, and there is an express exclusion in the case of redundancy dismissals and the non-renewal of fixed-term contracts. However, as there is no such exclusion in the case of TUPE-related dismissals, it may be sensible for employers to err on the side of caution and familiarise themselves with the provisions of the Code, many of which are based on generally accepted standards of fairness and reasonableness. For a detailed discussion of the issue of ensuring fairness in the context of internal dismissal procedures, see IDS Employment Law Handbook, 'Unfair Dismissal' (2010), Chapter 3, 'Unfairness', under 'Fairness of internal procedure'.

4.10 Time limit

An unfair dismissal claim must be brought in an employment tribunal within three months of the effective date of termination or, if that is not reasonably practicable, within such further period as the tribunal considers reasonable – S.111(2) ERA. The time limit may also be extended to allow for early conciliation or cross-border mediation – S.111(2A) ERA.

4.11 Remedies

The remedies available to an unfairly dismissed employee are:

- reinstatement, i.e. an order that the employee be reinstated in his or her old job with no financial loss – S.114 ERA

- re-engagement, i.e. an order that the employee be re-engaged in a job comparable to that from which he or she was dismissed, or in other suitable employment – S.115, or

- compensation – Ss.118–124A ERA, which is the usual remedy. This is divided into a basic award calculated according to a set formula (subject to a current maximum (from 6 April 2015) of £14,250) and a compensatory award of such amount as the tribunal considers just and equitable in all the circumstances, having regard to the loss sustained by the employee as a consequence of the dismissal (subject to a current maximum (from 6 April 2015) of £78,335 or a year's pay, whichever is the lower).

Redundancy   4.12

Dismissals effected by a transferor or transferee will often be by reason of redundancy. As we saw under 'Reason for dismissal' above, redundancy is one of the potentially fair reasons for dismissal set out in S.98(2) ERA.

Definition of redundancy. In order for redundancy to be established as the 4.13
reason for dismissal, the statutory definition of redundancy set out in S.139 ERA must be satisfied. Under that provision, an employee is dismissed by reason of redundancy where the dismissal is wholly or mainly attributable to the fact that:

- the employer has ceased or intends to cease to carry on the business either for the purposes of which or in the place where the employee was employed, or

- the requirements of the business for employees to carry out work of a particular kind or to carry out work in the place where the employee was employed have ceased or diminished or are expected to cease or diminish.

Even if there is a genuine redundancy situation, however, a redundancy dismissal will still be unfair under the ERA if the employer has not acted reasonably in all the circumstances – S.98(4) (see 'Reasonableness' above).

Pool for selection. The first thing that an employer must do in order to carry 4.14
out a fair redundancy dismissal is to identify the group of employees from which those who are to be made redundant will be drawn. This group is known as the 'pool for selection'.

A employer generally has a good deal of flexibility in defining the pool – it need only show that it has applied its mind to the issue and acted rationally, from genuine motives. However, the following should be borne in mind:

- an employer will need to have justifiable reasons for excluding a particular group of employees from the selection pool where those in the excluded category do the same or similar work to those who are up for selection. In the context of redundancies made following a TUPE transfer, the selection pool should generally be from all employees of the transferee doing similar work, not just transferred staff

- a fair pool for selection is not necessarily limited to those employees doing the same or similar work. Employers might be expected to include in the pool those employees whose work is interchangeable.

4.15 **Selection criteria.** The next step is to apply reasonable selection criteria to the pool of employees up for selection. There are no legal requirements as to the precise criteria that should be used, but they should not depend solely upon subjective opinion, so some criteria at least should be capable of objective assessment.

Note that some reasons for redundancy selection will render a dismissal automatically unfair – for example, maternity, race, disability, trade union membership or the assertion of a statutory right.

As a general rule, where redundancy occurs specifically within a TUPE context, the transferee should take care to ensure that the agreed selection criteria are applied fairly and uniformly across all members of the relevant pool in circumstances where the pool comprises a mix of the transferee's own employees and those previously employed by the transferor. Where the criteria include subjective elements such as skill, attitude and performance quality, there may be a risk that the managers responsible for scoring the selection matrix will be more familiar with employees with whom they have previously worked, thus inadvertently leading to bias in favour of these employees compared with those acquired following the transfer.

4.16 There is a limit, however, to the extent to which transferees will be minutely scrutinised to ensure fairness in this regard. In First Scottish Searching Services Ltd v McDine and anor EATS 0051/10 the EAT held that an employment tribunal erred when it found that the claimants' dismissals were unfair because the transferee had failed to take steps to incorporate 'some system for moderating the scores' between the two sets of employees (i.e. the transferees' own employees and those previously employed by the transferor) in so far as those scores applied to the more subjective of the criteria used for selection. The tribunal had concluded that this failure 'risked unfairness'. On appeal, however, Lady Smith, presiding at the EAT, concluded that the tribunal had fallen into the trap of 'engaging in "microscopic" or "over-minute" examination' of the type against which the Court of Appeal had warned in British Aerospace plc v Green 1995 ICR 1006, CA. The tribunal had simply based its decision regarding the unfairness of dismissal on the fact that it had identified a risk, without assessing the extent of that risk and whether it had had any impact on the selection outcomes in the particular case. In Lady Smith's words: '[The tribunal] had sought perfection and... to look for perfection is to depart from what S.98(4) ERA requires.'

Consultation. After warning of the potential for redundancy, the employer is **4.17** obliged to consult individually with all employees provisionally selected for redundancy before any final decision to dismiss is taken. What constitutes a fair and proper consultation is a question of fact for the tribunal to determine, but clearly the consultation must be genuine. The employee should be provided with information regarding the reasons for the redundancy and for the employee's provisional selection for redundancy and, if applicable, his or her individual scores against the selection criteria. While the individual scores of other employees should not be disclosed, employees should be given an idea of how they scored comparatively. Discussions should also take place on the steps that have been or will be taken to avoid making the employee redundant, and in particular on the search for suitable alternative employment (see below). Notice of termination should not be served until consultation has concluded.

Suitable alternative employment. A dismissal may be considered unfair if no **4.18** consideration is given to finding the employee another suitable job within the organisation or group. Since the fairness of a dismissal for redundancy is judged not simply at the date on which notice is given but also with regard to events up to the date on which it takes effect, a suitable vacancy arising during the notice period should be offered to the otherwise redundant employee.

Redundancy payment. Employees with at least two years' continuous **4.19** employment will be eligible for a statutory redundancy payment, which is calculated according to a set formula in the same way as the basic award for unfair dismissal. However, an employee who refuses an offer of suitable alternative employment loses this right.

The TUPE unfair dismissal regime   **4.20**

Regulation 7(1) of the TUPE Regulations, which implements Article 4(1) of the Acquired Rights Directive, provides that certain TUPE-related dismissals will be automatically unfair.

Before 31 January 2014, the scheme of Reg 7 was as follows. Reg 7(1) stated: 'Where either before or after a relevant transfer, any employee of the transferor or transferee is dismissed, that employee shall be treated for the purposes of Part X of the 1996 Act (unfair dismissal) as unfairly dismissed if the sole or principal reason for his dismissal is (a) the transfer itself; or (b) a reason connected with the transfer that is not an economic, technical or organisational reason entailing changes in the workforce.'

333

4.21 Regulation 7(2) and (3) then provided that Reg 7(1) would not apply to render a TUPE-connected dismissal automatically unfair where there was an 'economic, technical or organisational reason entailing changes in the workforce' (an ETO reason) for it; and Reg 7(3) clarified that, for the purposes of the general unfair dismissal provisions of S.98 ERA (see 'Overview' above), a dismissal for an ETO reason would be potentially (not automatically) fair either by reason of redundancy or for 'some other substantial reason'. The fairness or otherwise of such an ETO dismissal would be determined in the normal way, with reference to the S.98(4) reasonableness test.

On 31 January 2014, the 2014 Amendment Regulations came into force. Among other things, they recast the protection from unfair dismissal in Reg 7. Now, Reg 7(1) states simply that a dismissal will be automatically unfair if 'the sole or principal reason for the dismissal is the transfer', thereby dropping all reference to reasons 'connected with the transfer'. Reg 7(2) and (3) goes on to provide that Reg 7(1) 'does not apply' where the sole or principal reason for dismissal is an ETO reason, as defined above. The intention behind this change of wording was to bring the Regulations more closely into line with the Directive but, unfortunately, the new drafting opens up the possibility that TUPE protection might have become weakened in comparison to the position prior to the amendments. The main area of uncertainty is summarised under 'Changes to Reg 7(1) made in January 2014' below.

4.22 Position under 2006 Regulations prior to 31 January 2014
Prior to amendments made with effect from 31 January 2014 (as to which see 'Changes to Reg 7(1) made in January 2014' below), Reg 7(1) provided that: 'Where either before or after a relevant transfer, any employee of the transferor or transferee is dismissed, that employee shall be treated for the purposes of Part X of the 1996 Act (unfair dismissal) as unfairly dismissed *if the sole or principal reason* for his dismissal is (a) the transfer itself; or (b) *a reason connected with the transfer that is not an economic, technical or organisational reason entailing changes in the workforce*' (our stress). This wording made it clear that not only was it automatically unfair to dismiss an employee if the sole or principal reason for dismissal was the transfer, but also if that reason was connected with the transfer but not for an ETO reason. By way of defence to a claim of automatic unfair dismissal, employers could seek to point to an 'economic, technical or organisational reason entailing changes in the workforce of the transferor or the transferee' within the terms of Reg 7(2) in respect of dismissals carried out for a reason that was connected with the transfer.

Regarding whether dismissal in a TUPE context was automatically unfair, a crucial word was first introduced by the 2006 TUPE Regulations – the word 'sole' in the context of the phrase 'sole or principal reason'. That word was absent from the 1981 Regulations, which meant that even if a relevant transfer or a reason connected with it was merely a minor reason for dismissal, with the principal reason being unconnected with the transfer, the dismissal could be automatically unfair. The introduction effected by the 2006 Regulations of the word 'sole' into Reg 7(1) ensured that this was no longer the case.

Changes to Reg 7(1) made in January 2014

4.23

With effect from 31 January 2014, the position under Reg 7(1) of the TUPE Regulations 2006 as described above was altered by an amendment introduced by the 2014 Amendment Regulations.

Following amendment, Reg 7(1) now provides that a dismissal is automatically unfair if 'the sole or principal reason for the dismissal is the transfer'. There is no longer any reference to a dismissal for a reason 'connected with the transfer'. Reg 7(2) and (3) goes on to provide that where 'the sole or principal reason for the dismissal is an economic, technical or organisational reason entailing changes in the workforce' (ETO), Reg 7(1) 'does not apply' and the fairness of dismissal is to be judged by reference to S.98(4) ERA, which sets out the standard 'reasonableness test' that applies to ordinary unfair dismissal. Reg 7(3)(b) specifically states that an ETO dismissal will be deemed to be either for 'redundancy' (assuming it meets the statutory definition of redundancy) or for 'a substantial reason of a kind justifying the dismissal of an employee holding the position which [the] employee held' (SOSR).

The obvious question arises: what is the practical effect of the amendment to **4.24** Reg 7(1)? Under the pre-amended version of that provision, tribunals were still required to scrutinise a dismissal occurring in the context of a TUPE transfer to establish whether the main reason for it was the transfer. The difference was that even if the transfer was not the sole or principal reason, Reg 7(1) could still apply to render the dismissal automatically unfair if it was prompted by a more tenuous (non-ETO) reason associated with the transfer. This led many tribunals to formulate their reasoning for upholding claims on the basis that the dismissal was 'by reason of the transfer or for a reason connected with it'. In other words, they were not forced to nail their colours to the mast by explicitly stating whether the reason for dismissal was the transfer itself or was merely a reason connected with the transfer. Now, following the amendment to Reg 7(1), this looser formulation for a finding of automatic unfair dismissal is no longer available.

In the absence to date of any case law on the subject, it is difficult to know for certain how much impact the change to Reg 7(1) will be. One line of thought is that some 'borderline' cases, which previously might have been found to be automatically unfair on the basis that the reason for dismissal was connected with the relevant transfer, will now be found to fall outside Reg 7(1) on the basis that the principal reason is not the transfer. If so, the amendment will effect some slight narrowing of the capacity of employees to succeed in claims of automatic unfair dismissal. This certainly appears to have been the

335

Government's intention when making the amendment, judging by the explanation given in its response to the public consultation on the proposed changes to the TUPE Regulations which eventually came to fruition in the form of the 2014 Amendment Regulations. In its response (BIS/13/1023) the Government observed that: 'The aim of amending Regulation 7 is to reduce the likelihood that the current regulation is interpreted more widely than the restriction in the [Acquired Rights] Directive, reducing legal risk, and giving some enhancement of clarity in relation to dismissals... The Government considers that the present wording of the Regulations ('connected with') is too wide. It is important to recognise that although these amendments might lead to a few cases where the dismissal of an employee may not be automatically unfair, dismissals where the reason is the transfer itself will remain automatically unfair. This will not mean that any dismissal, which might have been considered as being a reason "connected with" the transfer under the current provisions would not be automatically unfair under the new provision; rather it will be a new test. The Government will provide guidance on this. The Government acknowledges that there might be some short term uncertainty in adjusting to the changes, but over time it believes this will be more certain and currently there is, in any case, uncertainty as to the breadth of the words "connected with".'

4.25 Unfortunately, the promised guidance, when it arrived, failed to advance our understanding of the impact of the amendment to Reg 7(1) one jot. The Guidance issued by BIS entitled 'Employment rights on the transfer of an undertaking' ('the BIS Guide') (last updated in January 2014), simply states: 'Neither the new employer (the transferee) nor the previous one (the transferor) may fairly dismiss an employee if the sole or principal reason for the dismissal is the transfer. Such dismissals will be automatically unfair for the purposes of unfair dismissal law. Whether the transfer is the sole or principal reason for a dismissal will depend upon the circumstances. For cases to which the 2014 amendments do not apply, the test was whether the sole or principal reason for the dismissal is the transfer itself, or a reason connected with the transfer that is not an economic, technical or organisational reason entailing changes in the workforce. *This new test could cover cases where the sole or principal reason for the dismissal was, under the old test, considered to be connected with the transfer*' (our stress).

Far from suggesting a narrowing of the capacity for succeeding in automatic unfair dismissal claims, the italicised sentence can even be interpreted as encouraging tribunals to recast the way they express their reasoning for upholding claims based on Reg 7(1) by categorising any transfer-related reason for dismissal as being 'solely or principally by reason of the transfer'. If this is what happens, then the impact of the amendment to Reg 7(1) will be negligible. All that will happen is that the phrase 'the sole or principal reason for the dismissal is the transfer' in the amended version of Reg 7(1) will be expanded to cover reasons that previously would been regarded as connected with a relevant transfer. Indeed, case law concerning other provisions of TUPE provides indirect support for the argument that that is how the concept of the 'principal reason' for dismissal should be interpreted. The case of Wilson and ors v St Helens Borough Council 1998 ICR 1141, HL, concerned the extent to which a variation of contract can be said to be solely or principally by 'reason of the transfer' and hence void by virtue of Reg 4(4). In considering that matter, Lord Slynn (with whose judgment the other Law Lords agreed) treated the test for determining whether the sole or principal reason for the variation was the transfer as one of causation, stating: 'I do not accept the argument that the variation is only invalid if it is agreed on as a part of the transfer itself. The variation may still be due to the transfer and for no other reason even if it comes later. However, it seems that there must, or at least may, come a time when the link with the transfer is broken or can be treated as no longer effective.' These words were quoted with approval by Lord Justice Underhill in Manchester College v Hazel and anor 2014 ICR 989, CA. Applying this rationale and extending it to the phrase 'sole or principal reason for dismissal is the transfer' in Reg 7(1) (as amended), if an employment tribunal is satisfied that the dismissal has been caused by or substantially contributed to by the transfer itself it is surely viable for the principal (if not the sole) reason to be found to be 'the transfer', thus rendering the dismissal automatically unfair.

It also needs to be borne in mind that the amended Reg 7(1) will still fall to be **4.26** interpreted in accordance with the broad purpose of Article 4(1) of the Acquired Rights Directive. This was described as a 'mandatory rule' by the ECJ in P Bork International A/S (in liquidation) v Foreningen af Arbejdsledere i Danmark and ors 1989 IRLR 41, ECJ, and was applied as such by the House of Lords in Litster and ors v Forth Dry Dock and Engineering Co Ltd (in receivership) and anor 1989 ICR 341, HL (discussed in the section 'Automatically unfair dismissal' below, under 'Timing of dismissal – pre-transfer dismissals'). It follows that a literal and narrow interpretation of Reg 7(1) as amended may well be considered inconsistent with the protection conferred by Article 4(1) of the Directive.

The three categories of dismissal

4.27

It follows from the above that dismissals which take effect from 31 January 2014 – whether carried out by the transferor or the transferee – will fall into one of three categories, as follows:

- dismissals for which the sole or principal reason is the transfer. These will be automatically unfair under Reg 7(1)

- dismissals for which the sole or principal reason is not the transfer but an ETO reason. By virtue of Reg 7(2) and (3), these will be potentially fair by reason of redundancy or some other substantial reason. Thus, they will be actually fair if the reasonableness test of S.98(4) ERA is satisfied (see 'Overview' above), or

- dismissals for which the sole or principal reason is neither the transfer nor an ETO reason. The fact that these take place around the time of a relevant transfer is merely a coincidence and it will be left to the application of S.98(2) ERA (reason for dismissal) and S.98(4) (reasonableness) to determine the fairness or otherwise of such dismissals. Clear examples of dismissals falling within this category would be where an employee is dismissed for gross misconduct or poor performance. But the category might also include – depending on the way in which the wording of Reg 7(1) as amended is interpreted by courts (see 'Changes to Reg 7(1) made in January 2014' above) – dismissals which, though connected with the transfer, are not principally by reason of it and are also not for an ETO reason.

We discuss the first two of these categories – i.e. those with regard to which the TUPE Regulations have an impact – under 'Automatically unfair dismissal' and 'Dismissals potentially fair for an "ETO reason"' later in this chapter.

4.28 **Which employees are protected?**
We now consider who might benefit from the unfair dismissal protection afforded by Reg 7 of the TUPE Regulations. In this regard, two essential points need to be made:

- only those employees who are entitled to claim unfair dismissal under the ERA – for instance, those with a minimum of two years' qualifying service – will be entitled to claim automatically unfair dismissal under Reg 7, and

- Reg 7 protects not only those employees who are to move from the transferor to the transferee as a result of TUPE, but all employees of the transferor or the transferee eligible to claim unfair dismissal who are dismissed by reason of the transfer, whether or not they are assigned to the grouping of resources or employees that is or will be transferred – Reg 7(4).

Employees must be eligible to claim unfair dismissal under the ERA. As stated in the introduction to this chapter, the TUPE Regulations are intended to implement the protection against dismissal conferred by Article 4 of the Acquired Rights Directive. However, the second subparagraph of Article 4(1) states that 'Member States may provide that the first subparagraph shall not apply to certain specific categories of employees who are not covered by the laws or practice of the Member States in respect of protection against dismissal'. So, as the High Court put it in R v Secretary of State for Trade and Industry ex parte Unison 1996 ICR 1003, QBD, this 'permits or envisages derogation by Member States' from the principle that transfer-connected dismissals are not allowed. This fits in with the objective of the Directive, which, as the ECJ explained in Viggósdóttir v Íslandspóstur HF 2002 IRLR 425, ECJ, is 'not to improve the situation of an employee following a transfer, but merely to preserve his acquired rights'. In other words, if an individual has not already acquired the right to claim unfair dismissal, the Directive is not designed to step in to provide him or her with that right simply because he or she is dismissed in relation to a transfer.

4.29 Regulation 7(6) takes advantage of the opportunity for derogation provided by Article 4(1). It clarifies that Reg 7(1) – which, as we have seen, renders certain transfer-related dismissals automatically unfair – will not protect an employee who is excluded from the right to claim unfair dismissal under the ERA. For example, Reg 7 will not protect:

- anyone who is not an 'employee' as narrowly defined by S.230 ERA (see 'Overview – who is eligible to claim unfair dismissal?' above), or

- anyone who does not have the continuous service required by S.108(1) ERA in order to claim unfair dismissal (currently two years) – see MRS Environmental Services Ltd v Marsh and anor 1997 ICR 995, EAT.

Note that the definition of 'employee' contained in Reg 2 TUPE Regulations is considerably wider than that contained in S.230 ERA – see Chapter 2, 'Who transfers?', under 'Who is an "employee" for TUPE purposes?' for details. The upshot of this is that there will be certain groups of individuals who are protected by TUPE generally, but will gain no benefit from the Reg 7 unfair dismissal provisions.

4.30 As stated above, it is important to note that it is not just potentially transferring employees who are protected by Reg 7. The TUPE unfair dismissal rules cover 'any' employee of the transferor or the transferee – Reg 7(1). Reg 7(4) clarifies that 'the provisions of this regulation apply irrespective of whether the employee in question is assigned to the organised grouping of resources or employees that is, or will be, transferred'.

The practical effect of this is that the following employees may be eligible to claim automatically unfair dismissal via Reg 7 (assuming they meet the other qualifying requirements – see 'Overview' above):

- those dismissed by the transferor prior to the transfer, whether or not they are employed in the undertaking or part of the undertaking to be transferred

- those retained by the transferor after the transfer but dismissed subsequently

- those who transfer under TUPE from the transferor to the transferee and are thereafter dismissed by the transferee, and

- those in the transferee's existing workforce who are dismissed before or after the transfer – for example, as a result of redundancy or a reorganisation exercise triggered by the influx of transferring employees.

339

4.31 Automatically unfair dismissal

As we saw under 'The TUPE unfair dismissal regime – changes to Reg 7(1) made in January 2014' above, the wording of Reg 7(1) of the TUPE Regulations (as amended by the Amendment Regulations) provides that where, either before or after a relevant transfer, any employee of the transferor or transferee is dismissed, that employee shall be treated for ERA purposes as unfairly dismissed if the sole or principal reason for dismissal is 'the transfer'. In other words a dismissal in such circumstances is deemed to be automatically unfair.

So, if the sole or principal reason for the dismissal of an employee eligible to claim unfair dismissal is the transfer itself, that is the end of the matter: the dismissal will be automatically unfair under Reg 7(1). On the other hand, if the sole or principal reason for the dismissal is an economic, technical or organisational reason entailing changes in the workforce, then the dismissal will not be automatically unfair, but may be rendered unfair by virtue of the ordinary 'fairness' test set out in S.98(4) ERA – Regs 7(2) and (3). We consider what might amount to an ETO reason in 'Dismissals potentially fair for an "ETO reason"' below.

4.32 In the remainder of this section, we focus on the circumstances in which it might be said that a dismissal is by reason of the relevant transfer itself within the meaning of Reg 7(1). This, it should be noted, is a question of fact to be determined by the employment tribunal in the circumstances of the case.

4.33 Dismissals by reason of transfer itself

The question of whether a dismissal is rendered automatically unfair by reason of the transfer itself is primarily one of causation: 'Was the transfer itself the sole or principal reason for dismissal?' A number of issues may be relevant to ascertaining the answer to that question, depending on the circumstances of the particular case. These include:

- the timing of the dismissal
- the reason for dismissal, and
- whether the specific transferee had been identified by the time the dismissal took place.

Each of these matters is considered separately below.

4.34 Timing of dismissal

In P Bork International A/S (in liquidation) v Foreningen af Arbejdsledere i Danmark and ors 1989 IRLR 41, ECJ, the European Court held that it was for national courts to determine whether a dismissal was 'by reason of' a relevant transfer, by considering the objective circumstances in which the dismissal occurred. The ECJ stated that a court should take particular note of whether the dismissal in question took place at a time close to that of a relevant transfer, and whether the employee was subsequently re-engaged by the transferee.

So, in general, the closer in time a dismissal is to a relevant transfer, the more likely an employment tribunal will be to find that it is transfer-connected. In fact, where a dismissal takes place around the time of the transfer, there will be a strong presumption that it is so connected. However, as the case law discussed below demonstrates, timing is not everything. If an employer can show that the reason for a dismissal is genuinely conduct, capability, statutory bar or retirement, the dismissal will most likely not be transfer-connected regardless of its timing. Furthermore, even where a dismissal occurs owing to an employer's need to reduce the workforce, the fact that it takes place around the time of a relevant transfer may be merely coincidental – that is, it might well have occurred regardless of the transfer process. If that is the case, then the dismissal will not be automatically unfair under Reg 7(1).

4.35 We now consider some of the domestic case law – first, relating to pre-transfer dismissals, and then relating to post-transfer dismissals – in which courts and tribunals have considered whether the reason for dismissal was by reason of a relevant transfer.

4.36 **Pre-transfer dismissals.** An early, high-profile case in which pre-transfer dismissals were held to be connected with a relevant transfer was that of Litster and ors v Forth Dry Dock and Engineering Co Ltd (in receivership) and anor 1989 ICR 341, HL. There, Forth Dry Dock and Engineering Co Ltd went into receivership in September 1983. In November of that year a new company, Forth Estuary Engineering Ltd, was incorporated with the objective of taking over the business of Forth Dry Dock, and the actual transfer was executed at 4.30 pm on 6 February 1984. At around 3.30 pm on the same day the entire workforce of Forth Dry Dock – about 25 employees – were handed letters dismissing them with immediate effect. The letters stated that no further funds were available for paying wages, accrued holiday pay or statutory notice pay and that any claims would have to be made against the Department of Employment. Within 48 hours of the dismissals the ex-employees of Forth Dry Dock learned that Forth Estuary was recruiting labour. A group of them filled in application forms for employment, but none were successful, and only three ex-employees of Forth Dry Dock were ever taken on by Forth Estuary. Forth Estuary, however, very soon had a workforce of similar size to Forth Dry Dock, having recruited from a pool of similar unemployed tradesmen who were willing to accept lower rates of pay. L and 11 other ex-employees of Forth Dry Dock presented unfair dismissal complaints with reference to TUPE. A tribunal upheld their claims – a decision that was eventually endorsed by the House of Lords. Their Lordships recognised that it was clear on the facts that the dismissal of the existing workforce had been engineered by the receivers and

341

the purchaser specifically with a view to preventing liabilities transferring under TUPE. In the circumstances, the dismissals were by reason of the transfer and automatically unfair owing to what was then Reg 8(1) of the TUPE Regulations 1981, and what is now Reg 7(1) of the TUPE Regulations 2006.

More recently, the Court of Appeal in Spaceright Europe Ltd v Baillavoine and ors 2012 ICR 520, CA, accepted that an employment tribunal had correctly concluded that an employee had been automatically unfairly dismissed prior to a relevant transfer within the terms of Reg 7(1). In that case the administrators of the insolvent business by which the employee was employed decided to dismiss in order to make the business a more attractive proposition to prospective transferees as a going concern. The Court of Appeal held that such a reason could never constitute an 'ETO reason' and that, since the principal reason for dismissal was self-evidently connected to and thus caused by, the transfer, it fell within Reg 7(1).

4.37 It is clear, however, that dismissals can be carried out just before a relevant transfer without that being the sole or principal reason for the dismissals. For instance, a struggling business might need to dismiss employees owing to financial constraints, regardless of the impending transfer. Below we set out four case examples in which pre-transfer dismissals were held to be unconnected with the transfer, with the consequence that the TUPE unfair dismissal regime did not assist the employees concerned:

- **Secretary of State for Employment v Spence and ors** 1986 ICR 651, CA: S and Sons went into receivership on 16 November 1983. On Friday 25 November the receivers entered into negotiations with a company for the sale of the business. There was no guarantee of a successful outcome, and, when the deadline for the sale stipulated by S and Sons' principal customer passed, the receivers decided to cease trading and to dismiss all the employees. As a result, the assembled workforce was dismissed with immediate effect at 11 am on Monday 28 November. At 2 pm on the same day, the agreement for the sale of the business was concluded. The members of the workforce were told by the purchaser to report for work the following morning, at which point they were re-employed. S and 20 others applied for redundancy payments in respect of their dismissals by S and Sons. Before an employment tribunal their claims were resisted by the Secretary of State for Employment (on whom liability would have fallen because of S and Sons' insolvency) on the ground that the employees had not been redundant, but had transferred to a new employer under TUPE. The tribunal held, however, that the employees were entitled to redundancy payments, and the tribunal's decision was upheld by both the EAT and the Court of Appeal. On the facts, the dismissals were not transfer-connected within the meaning of what was Reg 8(1) of the 1981 TUPE Regulations.

Rather, the receivers dismissed the workforce because, at the time of the dismissals, there was no prospect of work for the business

- **Longden and anor v Ferrari Ltd and anor** 1994 ICR 443, EAT: on 14 March 1991 K Ltd contacted the receivers of F Ltd with a view to a possible purchase of some or all of F Ltd's undertaking. K Ltd made what it termed a 'budgetary offer' for a division of F Ltd, but did not have sufficient information about the business to enter into a binding agreement. When K Ltd refused to sign the relevant documentation, F Ltd's receivers, who were under pressure from the company's bank, decided to 'pull the plug' – that is, to close down the undertaking, auction off its assets and dismiss its staff. K Ltd, however, thought it crucial that F Ltd should continue to operate while negotiations were ongoing, and on 27 March agreed to pay the receivers £4,000 to enable the company to keep 'ticking over' for another week. Also on 27 March, K Ltd supplied the receivers with the names of the F Ltd employees whom it believed it was essential to retain. The next day, the receivers gave the non-essential staff – including L – notice of dismissal. In the event, a sale took place from the receivers to K Ltd on 10 April. An employment tribunal dismissed L's complaint of unfair dismissal against K Ltd since, in its view, L had not been dismissed for a transfer-connected reason. He had been dismissed by F Ltd's receivers because of financial constraints, and because of pressure from the bank which had appointed them, and not because of an instruction from K Ltd. In its view, K Ltd's identification of the employees whom it was essential to retain did not carry with it a request that the other employees be dismissed. On appeal, the EAT upheld the tribunal's finding. There had been evidence on which the tribunal could reasonably have concluded that financial constraints and pressure from the bank were the reasons for the dismissal of employees on 28 March, and that neither the transfer on 10 April nor a reason connected with it was the reason or principal reason for those dismissals

- **Honeycombe 78 Ltd v Cummins and ors** EAT 100/99: in January 1998 HW Ltd ran into financial difficulties. On 15 January H – an insolvency practitioner – reported to Mr and Mrs G – the directors and shareholders of the company – that the sale of the business should be pursued, but that the only likely purchaser was a legal vehicle set up by Mr and Mrs G themselves. On 26 January an administration order was made and H was appointed administrator. On 27 January he dismissed all of HW Ltd's employees, and on 30 January concluded an agreement between HW Ltd and a new 'shelf' company to be purchased by Mr and Mrs G for the sale to the new company of HW Ltd's assets. That agreement was conditional on the obtaining of a court order, which was forthcoming on 6 February. On 11 February Mr and Mrs G purchased a shelf company called H Ltd and the parties concluded the agreement on that date. H Ltd took on all but four of HW Ltd's former employees. These four lodged tribunal claims, arguing that they had been dismissed for a transfer-connected reason contrary to TUPE. The employment tribunal found that it had been evident all along that any sale effected by H would be in favour of some legal body set up by Mr and Mrs G, and noted that the time span from H's appointment on 27 January to the conclusion of the agreement on 11 February was a period of 15 days. In these circumstances, the tribunal concluded that the claimants had been dismissed by reason of the transfer; that their dismissals were automatically unfair; and that liability for the dismissals passed to the transferee, H Ltd, under TUPE. H Ltd appealed to the EAT, pointing in particular to the tribunal's finding of fact that H had 'made it clear immediately on his appointment that he would not allow [HW Ltd] to trade and would dismiss the staff because there were no assets to pay them at that stage and that is what he did on 27 January'. H Ltd argued that, in the light of this, it was clear that the principal reason for dismissal was economic, and not connected to the transfer. H did not make the decision to dismiss in order to trim down the business for a sale. In fact, he reached his decision despite the outline proposal by Mr and Mrs G to purchase the business and keep on the staff. As at 27 January there was no certainty that a sale would be effected, and the economic reason for dismissal was paramount. The EAT accepted H Ltd's argument, concluding that the tribunal's decision had been plainly and unarguably wrong

- **Kavanagh and ors v Crystal Palace FC Ltd and anor** 2014 ICR 251, CA: CP Ltd, a professional football club, went into administration in January 2010 as a result of not being able to pay a creditor, S Ltd (the owner of the club ground). The administrator wished to sell the club as a going concern to avoid liquidation but the negotiations proved complex. By May 2010 an agreement to purchase the club was reached with a consortium pending further negotiations to purchase the stadium from S Ltd (which was also now in administration). However, the administrator encountered severe cash flow difficulties and decided to 'mothball' the club over the 'closed season' at a time when no matches would be played in the hope that it might be possible to sell CP Ltd at a future date. He asked the managing director to produce a list of employees who could be made redundant while allowing the core operations of the club to continue during the closed season. As a result, on 28 May 2010 dismissal letters were given to K and 28 of her colleagues. Following further complex negotiations, sale formalities were eventually completed on 19 August 2010. K and some of her colleagues complained that their dismissals had been automatically unfair contrary to Reg 7(1). An employment tribunal concluded that, although the reason for dismissal was connected with the transfer, it was an ETO reason in view of the fact that, at the time of the dismissals, the administrator had run out of money and the club would have had to go into liquidation if it had not reduced staff costs by effecting dismissals. Although the tribunal's decision was overturned by the EAT on appeal, it was restored by the Court of Appeal on the basis that the tribunal had been entitled to conclude, on the facts, that the dismissal was for an ETO reason under Reg 7(2) rather than a dismissal by sole reason of the transfer under Reg 7(1). The Court reasoned that the tribunal had been entitled to distinguish between the administrator's ultimate objective (the sale of S Ltd as a going concern) and his reason for implementing the dismissals; namely, to reduce the wage bill in order to continue to run the business and thereby avoid liquidation.

All these cases were decided under either the 1981 TUPE Regulations or the **4.38** pre-amended version of Reg 7(1) of the 2006 Regulations – both of which provided that a dismissal was automatically unfair not only if the sole or principal reason for it was the transfer but also if the reason was 'connected with' the transfer. It is in view of this that the decisions in these cases frequently refer to 'transfer-connected' or 'transfer-related' dismissals when concluding that the respective dismissals were not automatically unfair because the sole or principal reason for them was neither the transfer nor a reason connected with it. However, as explained under 'The TUPE unfair dismissal regime – changes to Reg 7(1) made in 31 January 2014' above, following the amendment of Reg 7(1), 'transfer-connected dismissals' has now been deleted as a separate category of TUPE dismissal. Notwithstanding this, there is no reason to suppose that the outcome of the above cases would have been any different had they been decided under Reg 7(1) as amended.

Other examples of reasons unconnected with the transfer are provided in the section on 'Reason for dismissal' below.

Post-transfer dismissals. In the absence of any intervening change in **4.39** circumstances, the reason for a dismissal that takes place shortly after the transfer is likely to be found to be linked to the transfer itself. For example, in Vallance v Maes Corporation Ltd ET Case No.1101491/09, an employee who was employed as a chambermaid at a hotel was held to have been automatically and unfairly dismissed when she was dismissed by the transferee after it was awarded a contract to provide cleaning services to the hotel. The transferee had not checked the employee's previous employment history (including her length of service); nor was it aware of the latitude she had been given by the hotel regarding how she was permitted to carry out her duties. She was dismissed when she and a colleague left work without completing their allocation of rooms. On her claim of unfair dismissal, an employment tribunal held that the dismissal was substantively and procedurally unfair as well as being automatically unfair under Reg 7(1) in view of the fact that the transferee had failed to appreciate the employee's rights under the TUPE Regulations and the effect this had on the preservation of her contractual terms following the relevant transfer.

4.40   However, if the chain of causation between a relevant transfer and a dismissal is broken by some intervening event, the principal reason for dismissal may well be found not to have been the transfer. This can be so even if the dismissal takes place close to the time of transfer, as the following cases demonstrate:

- **Rickards v Shipperley** EAT 0019/93: S and his wife were joint shareholders of Y Ltd. He was managing director and she was company secretary. As an employee of the company, S was remunerated by way of salary. In time, Y Ltd ran into financial difficulties, and on 30 June 1992 its stock and assets were sold to R. There was an understanding that R, who intended to carry on the business, would retain the existing employees and premises, and would continue to deal with the same suppliers and the same customers. However, it became almost immediately apparent that the suppliers would not maintain a relationship with the business if S remained involved in it. Owing to this, R gave S a note on 3 July which stated: 'Following my takeover of [Y Ltd's] business your services are no longer required. Your employment is terminated forthwith.' S brought a tribunal claim that he had been unfairly dismissed for a transfer-connected reason, contrary to what is now Reg 7. The employment tribunal upheld his claim, but R appealed successfully to the EAT. The EAT bore in mind that there was a short period of time between the relevant transfer and the dismissal, and noted the unfortunate wording of the dismissal letter. Nevertheless, it felt unable to conclude that S's dismissal was for a transfer-connected reason. It stated: 'The transfer did not cause or contribute to the dismissal – what caused the dismissal was the attitude shown by the suppliers... The transfer may have resulted in the dismissal, in the sense that it highlighted and brought into focus one of the trading problems which faced this company, but it was not the reason for the dismissal... The reason for the dismissal was the continued participation in the business of a man with whom the suppliers of the business felt unable to deal'

- **Hayes v Concorde Interiors (Europe) Ltd** ET Case No.1202865/09: C was employed by C Ltd as a mobile maintenance engineer working on a contract to supply maintenance services to S Ltd, a national supermarket. C Ltd decided not to continue with the contract with effect from 31 July 2009 and a new contractor, CI Ltd, took over responsibility for supplying the maintenance services for 113 of S Ltd's stores in London and the southern region. During the due diligence process, CI Ltd discovered that C Ltd had employed twice as many engineers as CI Ltd believed were needed and had also been receiving an additional payment from S Ltd that was no longer going to be paid. Having identified this problem prior to the transfer, CI Ltd decided to review the position after the transfer. By mid-September it had established that the contract was running at a loss and some of the engineers, including C, were consequently made redundant. An employment tribunal concluded that the transfer was not the principal reason for the dismissals. The real reason related wholly to a redundancy situation that CI Ltd had inherited from CF Ltd but which the latter had not addressed. Accordingly, Reg 7(1) did not apply to render C's dismissal automatically unfair.

It is fair to say that the further the date of dismissal is from the date of the **4.41** relevant transfer, the more sympathetic an employment tribunal is likely to be towards the employer's argument that the sole or principal reason for the dismissal was not related to the transfer. Or to put it another way, that the chain of causation has been broken between the transfer and the dismissal. This thinking is likely to be reinforced by the amended wording of Reg 7(1), which now only renders automatically unfair a dismissal the sole or principal reason for which is the transfer rather than a 'reason connected with the transfer'. The following cases – based on the unamended version of Reg 7(1) – deal with the situation where there was a substantial gap between the transfer and dismissal:

- **Norris and ors v Brown and Root Ealing Technical Services Ltd** EAT 386/00: in 1994 the London Borough of Ealing contracted out its Technical Support Group (TSG) to B Ltd. On 1 April of that year B Ltd inherited the TSG workforce by operation of TUPE. B Ltd achieved the efficiency savings stipulated by its contract with the Borough for the first two years, but in 1996 started to experience problems owing to underfunding. Because of this, in October 1996 B Ltd offered the TSG employees cash sums payable upon their accepting new, less favourable, terms and conditions. In December 1996 B Ltd gave notice of termination to the employees who had not agreed to revised terms and conditions and, upon the expiry of that notice in February 1997, dismissed those employees and re-engaged them on the new terms. A number of those employees applied to an employment tribunal claiming that their dismissals had been automatically unfair, in that they had been carried out for a reason connected with the TUPE transfer. The employment tribunal, however, accepted that B Ltd had carried out the dismissals since it was experiencing serious cash-flow difficulties, and that those difficulties had been caused by the underfunding of the contract between the company and the Borough, arising from an error in the original pricing schedule. The tribunal went on to note that B Ltd's decision to dismiss the employees had not been made until August 1996, which was two years and four months into its five-year contract, and that there had been significant intervening events between the relevant transfer and the dismissals. The tribunal concluded that the dismissals had not been connected with the relevant transfer and had not, therefore, been automatically unfair under Reg 7(1). It went on to hold, with regard to the provisions of S.98 ERA, that the dismissals, which had been carried out for 'some other substantial reason', had been fair. The EAT upheld the tribunal's decision

347

- **Addison and ors v Community Integrated Care** ET Case No.2507729/11: the claimants were employed as support workers by CIC, which provided social care to vulnerable clients living in independent establishments under a contract with a county council. The claimants had been transferred to CIC in 1996 on protected NHS terms and conditions. On 7 January 2011 the county council informed CIC that its costs were too high and that the service would be put out to retender unless it could reduce its costs. CIC proposed that the claimants should be put onto the same terms and conditions as the rest of their employees but when it failed to secure the claimants' agreement to do this it decided to dismiss them and offer re-engagement on its standard terms and conditions. An employment tribunal concluded that although the transfer back in 1996 had provided the background to the dismissals, the principal reason for them was CIC's need to make financial savings as part of the 2001 retendering exercise in order to retain the contract. This was a supervening event that had taken place some 15 years after the original transfer and therefore the dismissals were not by reason of the transfer within the terms of Reg 7(1).

4.42 Having said that the passage of time makes it less likely that the principal reason for dismissal will be linked to the transfer, this will not always be so. It would be a mistake to think that there is a specific point in time after which a transferee has carte blanche to dismiss transferred employees. As the following cases show, a dismissal taking place a significant amount of time after a transfer might, once the surrounding circumstances are taken into account, still be held to contravene Reg 7(1):

- **Taylor v Connex South Eastern Ltd** EAT 1243/99: T refused to accept changes to his terms and conditions (in particular, to his redundancy terms), which were introduced, for harmonisation purposes, around two years after his employment transferred under TUPE from British Rail to CSE. Owing to his refusal, T was dismissed, and he brought an unfair dismissal claim, arguing that he had been dismissed for a reason connected with a relevant transfer. The employment tribunal hearing T's claim accepted that there is no particular time limit after which dismissals will not be transfer-connected. However, it was in no doubt that the chain of causation weakens with the passage of time, and that two years appeared to be a long time to maintain a connection. The tribunal went on to conclude that, at the time of T's dismissal, there had long ceased to be any possibility of his being dismissed for a transfer-connected reason. On appeal, however, the EAT overturned the tribunal's decision. In doing so, it noted that the reason why the chain of causation tends to weaken over time is that time provides greater opportunity for intervening events to break it. But if no such intervening events occur, the passage of time in itself will not weaken or break the chain. Turning to the facts of the case, the EAT found it 'abundantly clear' that it

348

was one of the important terms transferred under TUPE that was the subject of CSE's attempt to change T's contract. In the circumstances, the EAT felt able to conclude that T's dismissal by reason of his refusing to accept the change was carried out for a reason connected with the transfer

- **London Metropolitan University v Sackur and ors** EAT 0286/06: the claimants were members of the academic staff of London Guildhall University (LGU). In August 2002 LGU merged with the University of North London (UNL) to form the London Metropolitan University (LMU). The merger constituted a TUPE transfer. In April 2004 the claimants' employment was terminated and they were re-employed on the same terms as LMU academic staff, which were less favourable than LGU terms. An employment tribunal held that the sole reason for the claimants' dismissals was the transfer or a reason connected to it and that the claimants had therefore been automatically unfairly dismissed. In particular, it found that the decision to dismiss and offer new contracts was intended to effect a harmonisation of all the academic staff conditions, and that this was related to the transfer/merger. On appeal by LMU, the EAT held that the tribunal had been entitled to find that the principal reason for the dismissals was harmonisation. From the outset, the intention had been to place all of the academic staff on the same terms as UNL and the fact that this process had been implemented nearly two years after the merger did not mean that the dismissals were not for a reason connected with the transfer.

Reason for dismissal

4.43

A common theme running through the cases referred to under 'Timing of dismissal' above is the need to scrutinise in some detail the sole or principal reason for dismissal – i.e. 'the set of facts known to the employer or beliefs held by him, which causes him to dismiss the employee' (Abernethy v Mott, Hay and Anderson 1974 ICR 323, NIRC) – to see whether or not this is linked to the transfer itself. It should be stressed that what matters are the reason(s) that operated on the employer's mind at the time of dismissal so as to cause the employer to dismiss – Manchester College v Hazel and anor 2014 ICR 989, CA. This is likely to be even more important given the post-amendment wording of Reg 7(1) and the need to see whether the transfer itself is the sole or principal reason for dismissal.

The necessity to scrutinise the motive of the person who takes the decision to dismiss raises particular difficulties in TUPE cases involving the disposition of an insolvent business or part-business. This is illustrated by several of the cases discussed under 'Timing of dismissal' above and also by the further cases summarised below:

- **CAB Automotive Ltd v Blake and ors** EAT 0298/07: on 4 May 2005, following the insolvency of a major client, I Ltd (a car interior design

349

business) was put into administration. An administrator, M, was appointed to 'tidy up the business to sell to somebody else'. On 6 May, M told senior managers that the business needed to be 'cut back to the bone' and that all employees, except those involved in the operational needs of the sustainable business, were to be dismissed on the ground of redundancy. 72 employees were dismissed later that day. Six days later a new company, CAB Ltd, was formed from I Ltd and another company that had become insolvent with the purpose of servicing a commercial contract that had belonged to the other company, and the following day CAB Ltd agreed with M that it would acquire I Ltd's assets and residual workforce. The dismissed employees subsequently presented claims of unfair dismissal against I Ltd and, in the alternative, CAB Ltd, on the basis that they had been unfairly dismissed for a reason connected with the transfer of I Ltd's business to CAB Ltd. An employment tribunal, upholding their claims, ruled that M's intention to slim down the business and find a buyer meant that the dismissals were 'connected with the transfer' even though the identity of the eventual transferee was not at that time apparent. However, on appeal, the EAT held that the tribunal had failed to consider properly the central question under Reg 7(1): whether the transfer, or a reason connected with it, was the reason or principal reason for the claimants' dismissals. A conclusion of automatic unfair dismissal would have required in the instant case an explicit finding to the effect that M had felt that transfer was a realistic possibility and that he had made the dismissals to encourage the transfer. The EAT remitted the case to the tribunal to determine whether this was so

- **Kneesway and ors v Gam Realisations Ltd and anor** ET Case No.2700882/13: in 2012 the relationship between the founders of GR Ltd deteriorated as a result of which it was put into administration on 20 December. A day later, the administrators attended the company's site and an agent was appointed to find a buyer for the business. A buyer was identified and an offer of purchase made but the buyer subsequently withdrew owing to concerns about the impact of TUPE. GR Ltd ceased to trade on 3 January 2013 and the claimants were dismissed. However, a week later GS Ltd made an offer to the administrators to purchase the business and a purchase agreement was signed on 11 January. An employment tribunal held that the principal reason for the dismissals was the transfer and that there were two related reasons why this was so: first, the administrators had sought to encourage potential buyers to proceed by making them realise that if they delayed they would lose employees with the necessary expertise and reputation to prevent the dissipation of the business's goodwill; and secondly, the dismissals were effected in order to reduce the price of the sale. The dismissals were therefore automatically unfair under Reg 7(1).

4.44 Close scrutiny of the motives for dismissal was also undertaken in Dynamex Friction Ltd and anor v Amicus and ors 2009 ICR 511, CA – again in the context of the sale of an insolvent business. In that case, the Court of Appeal held (by a majority) that an employment tribunal had not erred in finding that the employees of an insolvent company had been dismissed by the administrator for the economic reason that he had no money to pay them, rather than for a reason connected with the transfer of the undertaking within the meaning of what is now Reg 7(1), notwithstanding the employees' allegations that the director of the insolvent company had stage-managed matters so that he might continue the business under a new name free of its liabilities to the employees. The employment tribunal had been wholly justified in taking the view that those matters could not have any relevance because they did not impinge upon the decision-making by the administrator.

In deciding whether a dismissal was for a reason connected with the transfer, Lord Justice Ward in the Dynamex case (with whose judgment Lord Justice Rimer agreed) stressed that it is the person who took the decision to dismiss whose thought processes must be the subject of analysis. Once it was established in the instant case that it was the administrator's decision to dismiss the employees, then nothing done by the director of the company before that decision was taken or after it could have any bearing on the reasons why the administrator acted as he did. Although it was clear that the company director cynically manipulated the insolvency of the company and placed the company in administration with every expectation that it would soon fall into his hands unburdened by any liabilities to his former employees, it was the administrator who dismissed the employees and his actions were unsullied by the company director's scheming.

It is interesting to note the reasoning of Lord Justice Lawrence Collins in his **4.45** dissenting judgment. He suggested that case law of the European Court of Justice supported a more liberal interpretation of the TUPE Regulations, under which it would be a relevant consideration that the director of the insolvent company 'stage-managed the administration and used the administrator as his unwitting tool to regain the business' without any liability to his former employees. In the view of Collins LJ, the ECJ cases 'do not shut out the argument which the respondents make in this case, namely that the national court should not look solely at the motives of the legal entity which in law effects the dismissal. I do not say that they are bound to win if they can show stage-management by [the director of the insolvent company]. What I do say is that this is not a proper case for their claim to be, in effect, struck out on a point which has not been raised below and which has not been the subject of adequate findings of fact. It is a point which is of sufficient general importance to justify the further findings of fact which the EAT thought necessary, perhaps followed, at the appropriate stage, by a reference to the European Court.'

Again, it should be noted that all of the decisions discussed above (including Dynamex) were made at the time when the TUPE Regulations rendered automatically unfair not only dismissals where the sole or principal reason was the transfer but also where the reason was 'connected with the transfer' but not an ETO reason. As explained under 'The TUPE unfair dismissal regime – changes to Reg 7(1) made in January 2014' above, this second category of automatically unfair dismissal has now been done away with following the amendment made to Reg 7(1) with effect from 31 January 2014. This leaves only the first category of dismissal in place in terms of automatic unfairness. A dismissal that is not solely or principally by reason of the transfer will be either a dismissal for an ETO reason within the terms of Reg 7(2), in which case the dismissal will only be unfair if it offends the ordinary reasonableness test set out in S.98(4) ERA, or else nothing whatsoever to do with the transfer, in which case the TUPE Regulations will be entirely irrelevant with regard to the issue of fairness (although the S.98(4) ERA reasonableness test will still apply). For the reasons discussed under 'The TUPE unfair dismissal regime – changes made to Reg 7(1) in January 2014', it is possible that the 2014 amendment may make a difference in borderline cases where, even though the reason for dismissal might be said to be connected to the transfer, the transfer itself is not the principal reason.

4.46 The approach adopted by the courts when determining the reason for dismissal in the context of insolvency cases as outlined above also applies to non-insolvency cases. This is illustrated by the EAT's decision in Enterprise Managed Services Ltd v Dance and ors EAT 0200/11. In that case EMS Ltd provided appliance maintenance services to MHS while an entirely different contractor, W, provided building maintenance services. From October 2008, MHS advised all of its contractors of the need to improve performance. Following this, in January 2009, EMS Ltd reviewed the terms of employment of its appliance maintenance engineers and introduced measures designed to produce improvements in service delivery that included performance-related pay and different hours. These changes were accepted by its employees in February and March 2009. W, however, made no such changes. In April 2009, MHS transferred the contract for building maintenance from W to EMS Ltd and W's employees transferred under TUPE to EMS Ltd, which then decided to harmonise the terms of the former W employees with its own employees. Most of W's employees accepted the changes but 20 did not, as a consequence of which they were dismissed and re-employed on the revised terms. The dismissed employees contended that their dismissals were automatically unfair contrary to Reg 7(1).

The majority of the tribunal (comprising the lay members) ruled in favour of the claimants, finding that the reason for dismissal was a reason connected with the transfer; namely, the harmonisation of terms. The employment judge, however, dissented: on the issue of causation he found that EMS Ltd had not sought to harmonise the contracts for a reason connected with the transfer but because it wanted its new employees to achieve the same standards of productivity and efficiency as had been achieved in relation to its existing workforce. The measures were taken in the belief that there was a serious risk that the contract would ultimately be lost if it failed to ensure that those standards were met by all of their employees.

On appeal, the EAT overturned the majority's decision on the basis that its **4.47** findings had been contradictory: on the one hand, it had accepted that the principal reason for the variation in terms was not the transfer itself but the need to improve performance and efficiency in order to retain the contract with MHS Ltd. On the other hand, it had still concluded that the changes were connected with the transfer. The EAT remitted the case to the tribunal to consider what was the reason in the minds of management for invoking proposals to change the terms and conditions.

Reasons for dismissal seemingly unconnected to the transfer. Where the sole **4.48** or principal reason for dismissal is some wholly unconnected reason – for example, capability or gross misconduct – it will normally be extremely difficult to show that the transfer itself was the sole or principal reason for dismissal. So, for example, in Bangura v Southern Cross Healthcare Group plc and anor EAT 0432/12 the EAT upheld an employment tribunal's decision that an employee who was dismissed for gross misconduct prior to a TUPE transfer (and whose appeal had not yet been heard) was not employed at the date of transfer. Given that there was no link between the dismissal and the transfer, Reg 7(1) did not come into play. It followed that liability for her dismissal did not transfer to the transferee and any liability which remained with the transferor was limited to 'ordinary' unfair dismissal.

However, exceptionally, even dismissals which appear to be conduct or capability-related, or for redundancy, may be found to be principally by reason of a TUPE transfer and thus automatically unfair. Two examples:

- **Vallance v Maes Corporation Ltd** ET Case No.1101491/09: V was employed as a chambermaid in a hotel. When MC Ltd was awarded the cleaning contract for the hotel, her employment was transferred to it by operation of TUPE. V's previous employer had given her a great deal of latitude in the way she carried out her duties and she had not been subject to close supervision. MC Ltd was determined to improve standards and V was dismissed because she failed to complete her allocation of rooms within an acceptable time frame. An employment tribunal concluded that the dismissal was unfair on procedural and substantive grounds but it also held that the dismissal was automatically unfair under Reg 7(1) as a result of MC Ltd's failure to appreciate V's employment rights and the effect of TUPE

- **Harmon and ors v Creative Support Ltd** ET Case No.2104780/09: the claimants were care workers. When, following a TUPE transfer, their contracts of employment were transferred to CS Ltd in March 2009, they

353

were informed that, as a result of a reduction in the number of care hours to be provided under the contract, a small number of job losses might be necessary. At a meeting in April CS Ltd announced that, as it had no quantifiable measure to assess the employees' competence in their roles, it would have to conduct an assessment exercise as the basis for making the selection for redundancies. Eight of the affected employees failed to reach the imposed benchmark and were made redundant. An employment tribunal rejected the contention that failing to meet the benchmark constituted an ETO reason for dismissal. It concluded that CW Ltd had taken the opportunity, under cover of a redundancy exercise, to dismiss those employees who had transferred to it under TUPE on the basis that they had not achieved the benchmark figure and were deemed unsuitable for continued employment. Their dismissals were thus by reason of the transfer and automatically unfair by virtue of Reg 7(1).

4.49 Need transferee be identified?

One factor that may be relevant to determining whether the sole or principal reason for dismissal is the transfer for the purposes of Reg 7(1) is the extent to which the identity of the transferee has already emerged by the time the decision to dismiss is taken. This is a particular issue in the context of insolvency. Receivers, administrators or liquidators will often feel the need to terminate the employment of some employees to increase the chance of a successful sale of an insolvent company's business and may carry out these dismissals whether or not they have a purchaser lined up. This raises the question of whether, if at the time of dismissal there is no specific purchaser with whom negotiations are ongoing, the sole or principal reason for the dismissal can be said to be by reason of the transfer itself.

Here the distinction between the pre-amended version of Reg 7(1), which referred to a dismissal being for a reason 'connected with the transfer', and the amended wording limiting automatic unfairness to where the 'sole or principal reason for the dismissal is the transfer', may be of significance. The general effect of the amendment is discussed under 'The TUPE unfair dismissal regime – changes to Reg 7(1) made in January 2014' above.

4.50 In the two cases decided under the 'old' law set out below the EAT reached conflicting conclusions on this matter:

- **Harrison Bowden Ltd v Bowden** 1994 ICR 186, EAT: NGS got into grave financial difficulties and in January 1991 went into receivership. The company was run on a day-to-day basis on behalf of the receivers by G. On 29 January 1991 G placed an advertisement in the *Financial Times* for the sale of the business as a going concern. The following day HB Ltd responded to the advert, showing interest in the business, but nothing more. On 31 January the majority of NGS's staff, including B, were dismissed by G, purportedly by reason of redundancy. A sale of the business to HB Ltd was completed on 8 February. When B claimed unfair dismissal, an employment tribunal decided that the 31 January dismissals were transfer-connected, as their object was to facilitate a proposed or possible transfer. HB Ltd appealed to the EAT, arguing that what is Reg 7 of the 2006 TUPE Regulations only has effect where there is an actual, or at least a prospective, transferee at the moment of dismissal – which there was not in the present case as it had done no more than make enquiries about the sale of the business. HB Ltd pointed to the fact that the old Reg 7 (as does the new) speaks of dismissals being connected with 'the' transfer – that is, the transfer to the specific transferee – as opposed to 'a' transfer that might occur sometime in the future. The EAT, however, held that the tribunal had not erred in holding that the dismissals by the receiver were for a reason connected with 'the' transfer (and indeed automatically unfair) even though no actual or prospective transferee had been identified when the dismissals were carried out, and even though the dismissals did not occur owing to collusion between the receivers and the eventual purchaser. The reason for the dismissals was the facilitation of a transfer and, in that sense, the dismissals were connected with the transfer that took place at a later date

- **Ibex Trading Co Ltd (in administration) v Walton and ors** 1994 ICR 907, EAT: W was employed by ITC Ltd when, in August 1991, administrators were appointed to preside over the company's affairs. The administrators decided to free the company of its debts and then sell it. To this end they sought to reduce the size of the workforce and lower the wages of those who remained. On 16 October 40 of the 94 employees were given notice of dismissal for redundancy, and the dismissals took effect on 4 November. On 11 November the administrators received an offer for the business, and the sale – which amounted to a relevant transfer – was completed in the following February. W and some of his ex-colleagues brought unfair dismissal claims against both the transferor and the transferee. A tribunal rejected the notion that the complainants had been dismissed in connection with the transfer, and the EAT upheld this decision. Accepting the linguistic argument that had been rejected in Harrison Bowden (above), the EAT ruled that, while it could be said that the employees were dismissed for a reason connected with 'a' possible transfer, they had not been dismissed for a reason connected with 'the' transfer. At the time the employees were dismissed, no offer had been made for the business and any transfer was 'a mere twinkle in the eye and might well never have occurred'.

Faced with these inconsistent decisions, the Appeal Tribunal in Morris v John **4.51** Grose Group Ltd 1998 ICR 655, EAT, again turned its mind to this issue and ended up following the Harrison Bowden approach in preference to that taken in the Ibex case. In Morris M was a service manager for a Ford motor dealership, MMC Ltd, in respect of which receivers were called in on 27 September 1996.

355

Almost immediately, the receivers decided that the workforce had to be slimmed down, in order that the business might keep trading with a view to its being sold as a going concern. At a staff meeting early on 30 September, M learned that he was one of those who were to be dismissed. Later that morning, the receivers held initial discussions with representatives of JGG Ltd, a potential purchaser, at a meeting arranged by Ford. The parties started formal negotiations in October and a deal was eventually struck on 5 November. M brought a tribunal claim, arguing that his dismissal had been automatically unfair under what was Reg 7(1) of the 2006 TUPE Regulations. The employment tribunal, following the approach of the EAT in the Ibex case, decided that 'the' transfer could not have been the reason for M's dismissal, because on 30 September 'the' transfer did not exist: the eventual transferee, JGG Ltd, had not even gone so far as to make an offer for the dealership. The most that could be said was that M had been dismissed by reason of 'a' transfer – an event that the receivers may have hoped for or expected, but which at the time of the dismissal was not near to happening.

On appeal, however, the EAT overturned the tribunal's decision. In its view, the words 'the transfer' appearing in Reg 7(1) do not necessarily have to refer to the particular transfer that has actually occurred. If the rule were interpreted otherwise, this would lead to unfair anomalies. For example, employees dismissed by reason of a particular anticipated transfer that did not, in the event, go through, but which was promptly replaced by another comparable transfer in circumstances where a transfer to someone was inevitable, would not have the benefit of Reg 7, even though they would have had such protection had the original transfer of an undertaking materialised. Accordingly, the EAT's statement in the Harrison Bowden case that no special significance should be attached to the use of the definite article 'the' in Reg 7 would be preferred to the alternative approach taken by the EAT in the Ibex case. In the light of this, the tribunal in the instant case should not have asked whether 'the' transfer to JGG Ltd, or a reason connected with 'the' transfer to JGG Ltd, was the reason for M's dismissal. Rather, it should have asked whether 'a' transfer to any transferee who might appear, or a reason connected with such a transfer, was the reason, or principal reason, for his dismissal.

4.52 In CAB Automotive Ltd v Blake and ors EAT 0298/07 the EAT endorsed the Morris approach, suggesting that Reg 7(1) can apply, for example, where a number of potential transferees are interested but, at the time of the dismissal, matters were at a very early stage.

The Morris approach was finally approved by the Court of Appeal in Spaceright Europe Ltd v Baillavoine and ors 2012 ICR 520, CA. The Court there endorsed an employment tribunal's decision that the dismissal of a chief executive officer by the administrators of his company was for a reason connected with its transfer one month later, even though no specific transferee had been identified

356

at the time of dismissal. The Court stated expressly that the Harrison Bowden and Morris cases are more consistent than the Ibex case with the broad purpose of the Acquired Rights Directive, which TUPE implements. The approach in Spaceright was subsequently followed by the Court of Appeal in Kavanagh and ors v Crystal Palace FC Ltd and anor 2014 ICR 251, CA (the facts of which have already been set out in the discussion of that case under 'Timing of dismissal' above).

Therefore, prior to the 2014 amendment to Reg 7(1), the case law clearly **4.53** established that it was not necessary to have a particular purchaser in mind for the dismissal to be connected with the transfer. However, this may have now been thrown into doubt by the removal of the words 'connected with the transfer'. The issue is whether the removal of these words affects the continued correctness of the Court of Appeal's rulings in the Spaceright and Kavanagh cases and the earlier case law referred to above. Some commentators have argued that, as a result of the amendment to Reg 7(1), in a situation where there is no identifiable transferee, even if the dismissal might previously have been said to be 'connected with the transfer', it is more difficult now to say that the transfer itself was the 'sole or principal reason' for dismissal. If this interpretation is correct, then Reg 7(1) would not apply where the transferee cannot be identified at the time of dismissal and a dismissal in such circumstances would not be automatically unfair. Nor would liability for such a dismissal transfer to the transferee pursuant to Reg 4(3).

On the other hand, it is arguable that the earlier cases did not turn on any distinction between 'the transfer' and a reason 'connected with the transfer', and that the reasoning in the Morris case (as approved in Spaceright) – namely, that the reference to 'the transfer' in Reg 7(1) should be interpreted to cover 'a transfer' – remains correct and thus capable of being applied to the current wording of Reg 7(1). The argument that the 2014 amendment has not made any difference is also bolstered by the fact that in some of the previous cases – including Spaceright – the courts specifically stated that their interpretation of Reg 7(1) was consistent with the broad purpose of the Directive as an employment protection measure.

At the time of writing, there is no case authority to establish whether or not the **4.54** position has changed in the light of the 2014 amendment to Reg 7(1). If the pre-2014 interpretation remains the correct one, then where it can be shown that the principal reason for a dismissal is simply to make a business a more attractive proposition to potential purchasers, the dismissal would be automatically unfair. But if, on the other hand, the amended version of Reg 7(1) is interpreted by the courts as not applying to a dismissal where the transferee cannot be identified at the time of dismissal, the question arises of whether a dismissal in these circumstances would fall within Reg 7(2) as being for an ETO reason (see 'Dismissals potentially fair for an "ETO" reason' below).

That is because Reg 7(2) applies where the sole or principal reason for the dismissal is 'an economic, technical or organisational reason entailing changes in the workforce of either the transferor or the transferee before or after *a* relevant transfer' (our stress). The use of the indefinite article ('a') – as opposed to the definite article ('the'), which is used in Reg 7(1) – is intriguing. It is arguable that even if an employee is not dismissed because of *the* transfer within the meaning of Reg 7(1), he or she should be regarded as having been dismissed for an ETO reason before *a* transfer, in which case, by virtue of Reg 7(2) and (3), the reason for dismissal will be regarded as either 'redundancy' or 'a substantial reason of a kind such as to justify the dismissal', and consequently the normal 'reasonableness test' applicable to such dismissals as set out in S.98(4) ERA would have to be applied to determine whether the dismissal was fair or unfair in the circumstances.

Whatever the position, it is definitely the case that, as explained under 'Reason for dismissal' above, it will be necessary for the tribunal carefully to scrutinise the motives of the person who carries out the dismissal or, in the case of an insolvency, the reason why the insolvency practitioner requires dismissals to be effected. In the context of insolvency, it should be noted that any ulterior motives of third party sellers or purchasers are irrelevant – see Dynamex Friction Ltd and anor v Amicus and ors 2009 ICR 511, CA (discussed under 'Reason for dismissal' above).

4.55 Validity of dismissals in breach of Reg 7(1)

Article 3(1) of the Acquired Rights Directive provides that all the rights and obligations of the transferor with regard to the transferring employees will transfer to the transferee (see Chapter 3, 'What transfers?'), and Article 4(1) provides that the transfer shall not in itself constitute grounds for dismissal unless there is an ETO reason entailing changes in the workforce.

These provisions once led to considerable debate as to whether transfer-connected dismissals should actually be invalid. In other words, if a dismissal occurs where the principal reason for it is the relevant transfer, is the dismissal rendered null and void? This matter was central to the case of (1) British Fuels Ltd v Baxendale and anor (2) Wilson and ors v St Helens Borough Council 1998 ICR 1141, HL, which concerned a joined appeal to the House of Lords from two separate decisions of the Court of Appeal, which had reached opposite conclusions on the question of whether, where an employee is dismissed by reason of a relevant transfer, the dismissal is ineffective such as to prevent re-employment on inferior terms. The House of Lords concluded that the effect of the automatic transfer of employment contracts provisions in what is now Reg 4, combined with the protection against unfair dismissal in what is now Reg 7, was that an actual dismissal before, on or after the transfer was effective and not a nullity and the employee could not compel the transferee to employ him on the same terms and conditions as he or she had previously enjoyed.

Rather than the terms of the original contracts themselves passing to the transferee, all that passed to the transferee was the potential liability to compensate the employees for their dismissals.

In reaching this decision, their Lordships noted that there is no right under **4.56** English law for a dismissed employee to insist that the employer continue to employ him or her. The nearest to such 'specific performance' countenanced by UK employment law is the ability of tribunals to order reinstatement under S.114 ERA. Note that ultimately, however, a transferee can refuse to comply with a reinstatement order, at the cost of an additional award of compensation as a penalty.

In Primark Stores Ltd v Beck and anor EAT 0209/06 the EAT (presided over by Mrs Justice Cox), after referring to the Wilson decision, helpfully explained how the TUPE regime deals with transfer-related dismissals. She stated: 'A dismissed employee cannot compel the transferee to employ him. Where the transferee does not take on the transferor's employees because they have already been dismissed by the transferor then the transferee is obliged to meet all the transferor's contractual and statutory obligations unless there is an economic, technical or organisational reason for the dismissal entailing changes in the workforce. The liability transferred by virtue of TUPE is a liability to pay damages for wrongful dismissal or to comply with an order under the relevant employment legislation for unfair dismissal.'

The issue of liability for unfair dismissal in a TUPE context is discussed in Chapter 3, 'What transfers?', under 'Unfair and wrongful dismissal liability'.

Dismissals potentially fair for an 'ETO reason'   4.57

We saw under 'The TUPE unfair dismissal regime' and 'Automatically unfair dismissal' above that a dismissal carried out solely or principally by reason of the relevant transfer itself will be rendered automatically unfair by Reg 7(1) of the TUPE Regulations (as amended by the Collective Redundancies and Transfer of Undertakings (Protection of Employment) (Amendment) Regulations 2014 SI 2014/16). However, Reg 7(2) and (3) provides that a dismissal will not be automatically unfair 'where the sole or principal reason for the dismissal is an economic, technical or organisational reason entailing changes in the workforce of either the transferor or the transferee before or after a relevant transfer'.

So, where an employer successfully shows that the sole or principal reason for dismissal was an 'ETO reason' the dismissal will not be automatically unfair under Reg 7(1). However, it might nevertheless be unfair under the general unfair dismissal provisions of the ERA – see McGrath v Rank Leisure Ltd 1985 ICR 527, EAT. In other words, an 'ETO dismissal' is only *potentially* fair. Where such a dismissal occurs, the employment tribunal must determine the

359

issue of fairness by applying the 'reasonableness test' contained in S.98(4) ERA, examining matters such as consultation, selection and dismissal procedures (see 'Overview' above).

4.58 The onus is upon the dismissing employer to establish that a reason that appears to be connected to the relevant transfer is in fact an ETO reason – see Litster and ors v Forth Dry Dock and Engineering Co Ltd (in receivership) and anor 1989 ICR 341, HL.

In this section we focus on the meaning of the phrase 'economic, technical or organisational reason entailing changes in the workforce' set out in Reg 7(2), in order to ascertain the types of situation in which an employer might establish an ETO defence. Unfortunately, this key phrase is defined neither by Article 4 of the Acquired Rights Directive, from which it was taken, nor by the Regulations themselves. As a result, the task of determining the scope of the Reg 7(2) exception to the Reg 7(1) automatic unfairness rule has been left to the courts and tribunals.

4.59 Note that there are essentially two limbs to the employer's Reg 7(2) 'ETO defence'. First, there must be an 'economic, technical or organisational reason for dismissal', and secondly, that reason must 'entail changes in the workforce'. We consider case law concerning both of these limbs below.

It should be also noted that some of the cases discussed below refer to the ETO reason being connected to the dismissal. However, as previously explained, Reg 7 has now been amended with effect from 31 January 2014 to specify just two types of TUPE dismissal: (i) dismissals where the sole or principal reason is the relevant transfer; and (ii) dismissals for an ETO reason. Prior to the amendment, Reg 7 used to envisage a third type of TUPE dismissal – where the reason was 'connected with the transfer that is not an [ETO] reason'. But the amendment did away with this, at least in respect of any dismissal where the effective date of termination falls on or after 31 January 2014. For full details of the effect of the amendment, see 'The TUPE unfair dismissal regime – changes to Reg 7(1) made in January 2014' above.

4.60 **Economic, technical or organisational reason**
The first thing that an employer must do in order to rely on the Reg 7(2) 'ETO defence', and hence to avoid a finding that a TUPE transfer dismissal is automatically unfair under Reg 7(1), is demonstrate that the sole or principal reason for the dismissal was an 'economic, technical or organisational' one. The BIS Guide on the TUPE Regulations is broadly speaking correct when it states that: 'The courts and tribunals have not generally sought to distinguish between each of the three ETO categories, but rather have treated them as a single concept.' But some cases have identified with a little more precision than that which of the three categories is relevant.

360

At first glance, one might consider that most TUPE-connected dismissals will be carried out for an 'economic, technical or organisational' reason of some sort. However, as we shall see, the courts have been keen to interpret the words 'economic', 'technical' and 'organisational' narrowly in order to give substance to the protection envisaged by Article 4(1) of the Acquired Rights Directive and thus Reg 7 of the TUPE Regulations, which serves to transpose that provision into UK law.

Economic reason. A case in which the EAT construed the word 'economic' **4.61** narrowly for the purposes of the Reg 7(2) ETO defence is Wheeler v Patel and anor 1987 ICR 631, EAT. That concerned the transfer of a shop from G to P. By a letter dated 12 December 1985 G told all the employees (including W) about the proposed sale, and said that the completion date would be 20 January 1986. The letter terminated their employment as from 17 January 1986. After completion, P engaged some of the dismissed employees, but he did not take on W. W claimed unfair dismissal, but a tribunal rejected her complaint. On appeal, the EAT established from the tribunal's findings that G's reason for dismissing W was either his concern to comply with the purchaser's wishes or his desire to make the sale proceed more easily. Either way, it was clear that the transfer of the business from G to P was the reason, or was connected with the reason, for the dismissal. Therefore, the dismissal would be declared unfair under what is now Reg 7(1), unless G could mount a successful ETO defence. Attempting to do so, he argued that his reason for dismissing W was 'economic' within the meaning of Reg 7(2). The EAT, however, rejected G's argument and upheld W's appeal. It held that an 'economic' reason for dismissal must relate to the conduct of the business concerned. Broader economic reasons were not relevant. It followed that G's desire to obtain an enhanced price for the business, or to achieve a sale by capitulating to demands by the purchaser to dismiss the workforce, did not constitute an 'economic' reason for dismissal. Accordingly, G's dismissal of W had been automatically unfair.

The approach adopted in the Wheeler case was affirmed by the EAT in Gateway Hotels Ltd v Stewart and ors 1988 IRLR 287, EAT. There, it was held that there was no 'economic' reason for dismissal for TUPE purposes where hotel employees were dismissed prior to a transfer in order to enhance the sale price of the business concerned. More recently, in Spaceright Europe Ltd v Baillavoine and ors 2012 ICR 520, CA, the Court of Appeal held that the dismissal of a struggling company's CEO by the administrators prior to sale was not for an ETO reason as it was simply designed to give the best prospect of the business being sold as a going concern to prospective purchasers rather than related to the conduct of the business. Lord Justice Mummery stated that, for the ETO defence to be available, '*there must be an intention to change the workforce and to continue to conduct the business,* as distinct from the purpose of selling it. It is not available in the case of dismissing an employee to enable the

361

administrators to make the business of the company a more attractive proposition to prospective transferees of a going concern' (our stress).

4.62 It follows that if employees of a failing business are dismissed solely in order to make the business a more attractive proposition for sale (especially if there is evidence of collusion between transferor and transferee) this is unlikely to be viewed as an ETO reason, meaning that such dismissals will almost certainly be automatically unfair under Reg 7(1). For further discussion of the relevant case law, see 'Automatically unfair dismissals – need transferee be identified?' above.

However, as the following cases demonstrate, the need to reduce a workforce in order to make a failing business viable as a going concern – an aim that might sometimes appear only subtly different to that of making a business more attractive for sale – is capable of amounting to an 'economic' reason for dismissal within the meaning of Reg 7(2):

• **Thompson v SCS Consulting Ltd and ors** EAT 0034/00: T was employed as a sales executive in the UK by SCS Ltd and subsequently by LS Ltd, both of which were wholly-owned subsidiaries of a Canadian company, LS Inc. In late 1998 the two subsidiary companies were in financial difficulty, and receivers were appointed. It was agreed that another company, OTUK Ltd, would acquire the assets of SCS Ltd and LS Ltd. On 23 December 1998 the receivers met with a representative of OTUK Ltd and informed him that, because of the lack of funds and the unsuccessful nature of the businesses to be sold, they proposed to dismiss the entire workforce immediately. However, OTUK Ltd wished some of the staff to remain. It was eventually agreed that those employees whom OTUK Ltd did not wish to retain would be dismissed prior to the transfer 'on the grounds that they are not required for the operation of the business and that it would not be economically viable for the business to continue if the dismissed employees remained in the employ of the vendors'. Some 25 employees, including T, were dismissed by the receivers on 29 December with immediate effect. The transfer to OTUK Ltd took place 11 hours later. T complained to an employment tribunal that he had been automatically unfairly dismissed for a reason connected with a relevant transfer. The tribunal found, however, that the businesses of SCS Ltd and LS Ltd had been overstaffed, inefficient and insolvent, and could only have been made viable as going concerns by reducing the workforce. It went on to hold that, in the circumstances, there had been an 'economic, technical or organisational reason' for the dismissals falling within Reg 7(2) and that, accordingly, T's dismissal was not automatically unfair under the Regulations. On appeal, the EAT upheld the tribunal's decision. Where, in order to make the businesses viable as going concerns, it was necessary for their workforces to be reduced, and where, left to their own devices, the receivers would have dismissed all of the employees, it had been open to an employment tribunal to find that there had been an 'economic' reason for dismissal, notwithstanding the fact that the subsequent transferee of the businesses had dictated which employees should be dismissed and which should be retained

- **Kavanagh and ors v Crystal Palace FC Ltd and anor** 2014 ICR 251, CA: the claimants were 'non-core' employees of a football club in administration who had been dismissed when the administrator decided to 'mothball' the club during the closed season. The administrator was at the time working towards achieving a sale of the club, which did eventually occur, and the claimants argued that their dismissals were unfair under Reg 7(1) because they were connected to the eventual transfer and there was no ETO reason. However, an employment tribunal found that the dismissals were for an economic reason; namely, keeping the club alive as a going concern. Although the administrator did have the longer-term aim of selling the club, this was not the reason for the dismissals. The EAT allowed an appeal against this decision but the Court of Appeal restored the tribunal's judgment. It held that the tribunal had been right to draw a distinction between the administrator's reason for these particular dismissals and his ultimate objective. The case could be distinguished from that of Spaceright Europe Ltd v Baillavoine and ors 2012 ICR 520, CA where the claimant in that case – the CEO of the insolvent company – was dismissed on day one of the administration as no purchaser would require his services. Thus, he was dismissed not because the money to continue the business had run out but to make the business more attractive to potential purchasers.

It is not just in insolvency situations that employees are dismissed for 'economic' **4.63** reasons. Often, transferees will decide that redundancies are necessary post-transfer and provided the reason for these is genuine this might be regarded as being the paradigm 'economic' reason for dismissal. In fact, the example of an economic reason contained in the BIS Guide is one relating to 'the profitability or market performance of the transferee's business'. Below, we set out two cases in which a transferee employer was able to rely on an economic reason for dismissal within the meaning of Reg 7(2):

- **Whitehouse v Charles A Blatchford and Sons Ltd** 2000 ICR 542, CA: W was employed by JS Ltd as one of 13 technicians working on the company's contract to supply prosthetic appliances to Sheffield's Northern General Hospital. In 1996 JS Ltd lost that contract to CAB Ltd. Owing to a reduction in annual funding from the health authority, the hospital required CAB Ltd to reduce the number of technicians from 13 to 12. On 1 April 1997 CAB Ltd began work on the contract, and took on all the relevant JS Ltd employees. After unsuccessfully seeking a volunteer for redundancy, CAB Ltd selected W as the employee to be dismissed. W claimed that he had been dismissed for a reason connected with the transfer contrary to what is now Reg 7(1) and that his dismissal was therefore automatically

363

unfair. The employer resisted the claim on the ground that there was an ETO reason for dismissal. An employment tribunal noted that it was a condition of the contract with the hospital that the new contractor should reduce the contract price by reducing the number of technicians. In those circumstances, said the tribunal, a redundancy was inevitable. The tribunal concluded that W's dismissal was for an economic or organisational reason which entailed a change in the workforce, and that CAB Ltd had therefore established an ETO defence. The tribunal further held that the employer had acted reasonably in treating the ETO reason as a sufficient reason for dismissal, and thus rejected W's claim. This decision was upheld by the EAT and the Court of Appeal. After the transferee was awarded the contract, noted the Court, there was a demand for the services of 12 rather than 13 technicians. That would have been the case even if the transferor had retained the contract. In those circumstances, the transfer of the undertaking was the occasion for the reduction in the hospital requirements from 13 to 12 technicians, but it was not the cause of or the reason for that reduction. The circumstances in this case were in no way analogous to the position of the vendor of a business who, for the sole purpose of achieving the best price for the business, dismisses employees. In the instant case, the reduction in employees was directly connected with the provision of services under the contract

- **Meikle v McPhail (Charleston Arms)** 1983 IRLR 351, EAT: M was employed as a bartender at a public house in Paisley. On 24 June 1982 McP took over the pub. One of the terms of his deal with the transferor was that he would take over most of the existing staff, including two full-time bartenders, one part-time bartender and a cleaner. After consultations with his accountant McP realised that he had over-committed himself and that substantial salary savings and economies would have to be made. On 28 June he dismissed all the staff, including M, except one full-time bartender. M brought an unfair dismissal claim before an employment tribunal, although it was not suggested that she should have been retained in preference to the other bartender. The tribunal held that M's dismissal had been connected with a relevant transfer, but accepted McP's argument that there had been an economic reason for the dismissal within the meaning of what is now Reg 7(2) since reductions in '[McP's] staff was an economic necessity and therefore redundancies were inevitable'. The tribunal went on to conclude that McP had made out an ETO defence and that, accordingly, M's dismissal had not been automatically unfair. Furthermore, McP had acted reasonably in carrying out the dismissal, meaning that it was fair for the purposes of the ERA. On appeal, the EAT upheld the tribunal's decision.

4.64 **Technical reason.** Assessing the scope of the phrase 'technical reason' is less problematic. The BIS Guide states that this includes 'a reason relating to the nature of the equipment or production processes which the [transferee] operates'. So, for example, where a transferee introduces new machinery that an employee does not have the necessary skills to operate, there might be a technical reason within the meaning of Reg 7(2) for the employee's dismissal.

Of course, in order to succeed with the ETO defence the employer would also have to show that the technical reason 'entailed changes in the workforce' (see 'Entailing changes in the workforce' below). Furthermore, in order for the employer to avoid unfair dismissal liability under the ordinary provisions of the ERA, the dismissal must have been within the 'range of reasonable responses' available to it (see 'Overview' above). In some cases – perhaps where the employer has considerable resources and/or the skills in question are not particularly difficult to attain – it would be unreasonable for the employer to dismiss rather than to provide the employee with the training that would enable him or her to continue in employment.

Organisational reason. The BIS Guide states that the phrase 'organisational **4.65** reason' includes 'a reason relating to the management or organisational structure of the [transferee's] business'. Two situations immediately spring to mind in which a transferee might be able to rely upon an organisational reason for dismissal. First, where the transferee simply does not require every member of the transferring workforce, as well as every member of his existing workforce, to carry out his needs. Secondly, where the transferee decides to reorganise job functions in order to carry on the transferring business, or provide the transferring service, in a different way. The following cases are illustrations of 'organisational' reasons:

* **Burstal v Compass Cleaning Ltd** ET Case No.1402457/02: a company lost the contract comprising 98 per cent of its work to R, and it was accepted that the company's employees transferred to R by the operation of TUPE. However, B, the assistant to the transferor company's managing director, was dismissed by R upon the transfer, and claimed unfair dismissal. In rejecting her claim, an employment tribunal noted that since the contract in question had been subsumed into R's operation, neither a managing director nor a managing director's assistant was required in respect of that contract. It followed that B's dismissal was for an ETO reason entailing changes in the workforce and hence was not automatically unfair

* **Porter and anor v Queen's Medical Centre (Nottingham University Hospital)** 1993 IRLR 486, QBD: a relevant transfer occurred where the supply of paediatric and neonatal services moved from two District Health Authorities to an NHS Trust. Following the transfer, the Trust decided to reorganise the way that the services would be performed, with a focus on the importance of highly developed specialisms. It did not re-engage P or N, two consultant paediatricians who had been dedicated to the services in question prior to the transfer, and instead carried out a recruitment process focusing on the desired specialisms – which included neonatology,

365

neurology and community health care. P and N brought a legal action in the High Court, but the Court accepted that, owing to the reorganisation of the way in which the service was to be performed, the Trust had dismissed the claimants for an ETO reason

- **Nationwide Building Society v Benn and ors 2010** IRLR 922, EAT: B and 20 other employees were employed by the Portman Building Society (PBS) until their employment was transferred to the Nationwide Building Society (NBS) in August 2007 under TUPE. The employees argued (and the employment tribunal accepted) that NBS had altered their terms and conditions to their detriment after the transfer in that their job roles and responsibilities were downgraded when they were assimilated into NBS roles; that there was a significant difference between their pre- and post-transfer roles; that the assimilation process transferring them was itself a breach of mutual trust and confidence; and that the NBS bonus scheme was less generous than the previous PBS scheme. The claimants resigned and brought unfair constructive dismissal and Reg 4(9) 'material detriment' dismissal claims. The tribunal dealt with two of the claimants' cases as a test case. It held that, while the claimants had been constructively dismissed and/ or suffered a material detriment for the purpose of Reg 4(9), their dismissals were not automatically unfair as there was an ETO reason: the new roles the employees were required to perform post-transfer represented a diminution in skills and responsibilities. Following the transfer, the claimants were unable to continue selling products for which they were licensed and were losing their qualifications in that respect. However, the principal reason for the change in the claimants' roles and thus their dismissal was that NBS did not have in place the range of products or funds which would have enabled the claimants to continue to function at their previous level. The tribunal concluded that this amounted to an 'organisational' reason within the meaning of Reg 7(2). Similarly, the change to the bonus scheme under the transferee had been connected with the claimants' job functions and was also made for an ETO reason

- **Ffoulkes v Danwood Group Ltd ET** Case No 3502523/10: F was employed by the transferor at its head office in a town six miles outside Leicester doing senior accounts work. The company's directors sold the company to DG Ltd, which told all the employees informally that their jobs were safe but that it would be necessary to change the location of the office. Eventually it was decided that F's job had to be performed at DG Ltd's head office in Lincoln. As she did not want to commute to Lincoln, she was made redundant. An employment tribunal concluded that although F was dismissed as a direct result of the transfer, there were sound economic and organisational reasons for the transfer. Accordingly, F's dismissal was for an ETO reason.

One example of where an employment tribunal rejected the contention that a **4.66** dismissal was for an 'organisational' reason is Radford v McKesson Information Solutions UK Ltd ET Case No.2405482/09. In that case R's employment transferred from Capita to MIS Ltd when it won the contract for the provision of payroll services to various NHS Trusts. R's role prior to the transfer was to manage teams in Blackburn and Cambridge, and she was based in Darwen. MIS Ltd made it clear prior to the TUPE consultation that the only vacancies it had were based in Bangor and that employees who did not wish to relocate there would be at risk of redundancy. R wrote to MIS Ltd asserting her right to transfer under TUPE, stating that she therefore expected the transferee to provide details of suitable roles for her. She was told that as she did not wish to move to Bangor and had not expressed an interest in any other post, redundancy consultation would begin. Her employment was subsequently terminated on the ground of redundancy. With regard to her claim that she had been automatically unfairly dismissed within the terms of Reg 7(1), MIS Ltd maintained that the activities for which she was employed ceased to continue at the location at which she was employed, and that this comprised an organisational reason for dismissal entailing changes in the workforce. An employment tribunal, however, held that R was unfairly dismissed following a TUPE transfer and that there was no ETO reason. The work to be carried out in Bangor was the same as that which had been carried out in Darwen. Looked at as a whole, the workforce remained substantially unchanged, so there was no organisational reason for the dismissal.

It should be noted in passing that in both the Radford and Ffoulkes cases above the tribunals did not appear specifically to address the issue of whether the change in location entailed 'a change in the workforce', which is a prerequisite to enabling the ETO defence to be made out. It is likely that, as the law stood at the time, a change of location would not have been regarded as entailing a change of the workforce, although the position has now altered following amendments brought into effect on 31 January 2014 and the consequent introduction of new Reg 7(3A). This expressly stipulates that a change in the place where employees are employed to work does come within the phrase 'changes in the workforce' for the purposes of the ETO defence. For further details, see the discussion of 'Change of work location' in the section on 'Entailing changes in the workforce' below.

Although it will usually be the transferee who will seek to rely on an organisational **4.67** reason for carrying out transfer-connected dismissals, there are circumstances in which the transferor will be able to do so. For example, if a transferor employer loses a major contract, it might need to reorganise the workforce that it retains – i.e. those employees who were not dedicated to the contract in question – and, as a result, might feel the need to carry out redundancy dismissals. In such circumstances, these dismissals could well be for an organisational (or indeed an economic) reason within the meaning of Reg 7(2).

367

Most, if not all, of the above examples have concerned genuine redundancy situations. But what else might amount to an organisational reason for dismissal? It seems that dismissals, express or constructive, as a result of a transferee's wish to fundamentally alter hours of work, or to harmonise terms and conditions, could potentially qualify. However, the major stumbling block for the employer in such circumstances will be establishing that such a reason 'entailed changes in the workforce' – the second limb of the Reg 7(2) test, to which we now turn our attention.

4.68 Entailing changes in the workforce

In order to avail itself of the Reg 7(2) ETO defence, an employer is not only required to point to an 'economic, technical or organisational reason' for dismissal, but must also demonstrate that such a reason 'entails changes in the workforce'. Below, we consider what both 'entailing' and 'changes in the workforce' mean in this context.

4.69 **Meaning of 'entailing'.** In the leading case of Berriman v Delabole Slate Ltd 1985 ICR 546, CA, Lord Justice Browne-Wilkinson (as he then was) said that, owing to the word 'entailing' in what is now Reg 7(2), 'the phrase "economic, technical or organisational reason entailing changes in the workforce"… requires that the change in the workforce is part of the economic, technical or organisational reason. The employers' plan must be to achieve changes in the workforce. It must be an objective of the plan, not just a possible consequence of it.'

This means that where an employer has an economic, technical or organisational reason for doing *something*, but that something does not necessarily entail 'changes in the workforce', any dismissals that happen to arise as a result of that reason will not fall within the Reg 7(2) 'ETO' exception. Put another way, 'changes in the workforce' must flow inexorably from, rather than be a possible end-result of, the employer's ETO reason.

4.70 The necessary link between an ETO reason and a 'change in the workforce' was lacking in the Berriman case. That involved B, a quarryman, who was paid £100 per week prior to transferring to DS Ltd under TUPE. Following the transfer, DS Ltd informed B that it intended to harmonise the terms and conditions of the transferring employees with those of its existing employees. Since this process was to involve a significant reduction in his pay, B resigned and claimed that he had been unfairly constructively dismissed for a reason connected with a relevant transfer, contrary to Reg 7(1). An employment tribunal rejected his claim on the basis that DS Ltd had established an ETO reason for dismissal under Reg 7(2). On appeal, however, the EAT and thereafter the Court of Appeal disagreed with the tribunal's decision. The Court of Appeal held that DS Ltd's 'organisational reason' for B's dismissal – the plan to harmonise terms and conditions – had not 'entailed' changes in the workforce (such changes being, as we shall see below, changes in either workforce numbers or workforce functions, or a change in employees' location). The harmonisation process was not one that necessarily led to changes in the workforce. The most that could be said was that it might (not must) lead to the dismissal of any employees who did not fall into line.

Meaning of 'changes in the workforce'. The meaning of 'changes in the **4.71** workforce' is mostly derived from case law but has recently been supplemented by legislation (as explained in the discussion on 'Change of work location' below). The position under the case law as it currently stands is that an employer must show one of two things in order to establish that an economic, technical or organisational reason for dismissal entailed (i.e. necessitated) 'changes in the workforce': either that the ETO reason entailed a change in the numbers of the workforce overall, or that it entailed a change in the functions of members of the workforce. So, for example, while a change in function may be wide enough to cover a restructuring in shift arrangements, it is unlikely to cover a change in working hours as such for the reasons explained below.

The case law position, like the meaning of the word 'entailing', discussed under 'Meaning of "entailing"' above, was established by the Court of Appeal in Berriman v Delabole Slate Ltd (above). To recap, that case concerned an attempt by a transferee employer, DS Ltd, to harmonise the terms and conditions of its inherited workforce with those of its pre-existing workforce. B, an employee who transferred to DS Ltd under TUPE, resigned and claimed that he had been unfairly constructively dismissed for a reason connected with a TUPE transfer. His claim was eventually upheld by the Court of Appeal, which rejected the employer's argument that the dismissal had occurred for an ETO reason 'entailing changes in the workforce'. In this case, DS Ltd's 'organisational reason' for acting – namely, its wish to produce standardisation of pay terms – had led to B's dismissal, but B's position had thereafter been filled by a new employee who was prepared to accept DS Ltd's conditions of service. Such a scenario did not, in the Court's view, involve 'changes in the workforce' as required by Reg 7(2). In this regard, Browne-Wilkinson LJ stated: 'To our minds, the word "workforce" connotes the whole body of employees as an entity: it corresponds to the "strength" or the "establishment". Changes in the identity of the individuals who make up the workforce do not constitute changes in the workforce itself so long as the overall numbers and functions of the employees looked at as a whole remain unchanged.'

The Berriman decision was clarified by the EAT in Crawford v Swinton **4.72** Insurance Brokers Ltd 1990 ICR 85, EAT. There, an employee argued that, in the absence of a reduction in workforce numbers, a change in the identity of at least one of the employees must occur if there are to be 'changes in the workforce'. The EAT rejected this submission. In determining whether changes in the workforce have occurred, it reiterated that it is the workforce as an

369

entity, rather than the identity of the individuals who make it up, that must be examined. With this in mind, the EAT was satisfied that there could be 'changes in a workforce' for the purposes of the ETO defence 'if the same people are kept on but they are given entirely different jobs to do'.

In Manchester College v Hazel and anor 2014 ICR 989, CA, Lord Justice Underhill summarised the effect of the Berriman interpretation of the phrase 'entailing changes in the workforce' by suggesting that it effectively required that dismissals be for 'redundancy or redeployment'. In other cases the EAT has suggested that a broader concept might apply. For example, in Meter U Ltd v Ackroyd and ors 2012 ICR 834, EAT – a case focusing on the specific meaning of the word 'workforce' in the context of the phrase 'entailing changes in the workforce' – the EAT, presided over by Mrs Justice Slade, thought (without having to decide the point) that changes in the number of employees or in their duties are not the only changes which may constitute 'changes in the workforce' within the meaning of Reg 7(2). In particular, Slade J thought that a change in status from 'employee' to 'independent contractor' might be capable of constituting such a change. The objection here is that a change of this kind, unaccompanied by any substantial change of job function, would amount to a change in neither the numbers nor the functions of the workforce and so would fail the Berriman test. We think that, while Underhill LJ's interpretation of an ETO may be unduly narrow given that some reorganisations involving a change in job functions may not necessarily amount to a 'redundancy or redeployment', Underhill LJ's overall approach is more consistent with the Court of Appeal's interpretation of an ETO reason for dismissal in Berriman. Furthermore, Underhill LJ's narrower interpretation compared with Slade J's suggested broader interpretation also fits more comfortably with the fact that the Acquired Rights Directive and the TUPE Regulations are envisaged to be employment protection measures aimed at facilitating the continuation of employment following a transfer.

4.73 *Standardisation of terms and conditions.* The issue in many cases since the Berriman case has been whether changes to transferred employees' terms and conditions of employment in order to bring these into line with those of the transferee's existing workforce amounts to an economic or organisational reason entailing a 'change in the workforce'. In view of the narrow interpretation accorded by the Court of Appeal, the dismissals of employees who refuse to accept such harmonisation initiatives have on the whole failed to avoid findings of automatic unfair dismissal because they typically entail changes in neither the numbers nor the functions of the workforce. The following cases illustrate this:

● **Bullard and anor v Marchant and anor** 1986 ICR 389, EAT: B was employed as a part-time assistant in a newsagents. He was dismissed by the owner, M, just prior to the sale of the business – a relevant transfer – to P.

P then offered B employment on the same number of working hours, but at different times of the day. B accepted the offer, but soon afterwards resigned and brought a tribunal claim with regard to his dismissal. An employment tribunal declined to find B's dismissal unfair, and B appealed to the EAT. The EAT held that B's dismissal had been automatically unfair because the dismissal was principally by reason of the transfer. With regard to the employer's ETO defence, there had been no 'changes in the workforce' within the meaning of Reg 7(2), but only changes in terms and conditions of employment falling outside the meaning of those words

- **Crawford v Swinton Insurance Brokers Ltd** 1990 ICR 85, EAT: following a relevant transfer to S Ltd, C had to change from typing and clerical work to selling insurance; had to work different, less flexible hours; and lost the use of her company car. She resigned and brought an unfair constructive dismissal claim, contending that the reason for dismissal was transfer-related and was automatically unfair under Reg 7(1). An employment tribunal rejected her claim, holding that the principal reason for dismissal was an 'organisational reason entailing changes in the workforce' within the meaning of Reg 7(2), and so was not automatically unfair. Unlike the Berriman case (above), where the employer had sought simply to harmonise contractual terms, S Ltd's objective in this case had been to change the content of C's job. On appeal, the EAT noted that where the same employees are kept on after a relevant transfer, but are engaged in a different occupation, there is a change in the workforce for the purposes of the ETO defence. However, the EAT was not satisfied that the tribunal in this case had ascertained whether bringing about a change in job functions was the principal reason motivating S Ltd in its decision to impose the contractual changes on C. The EAT thought that there were several potential reasons for the employer's plan, and that rationalisation of its organisation did not necessarily involve taking away C's car and taking away her right to flexible working hours. As a result, the case was remitted to the same tribunal for consideration of what was the principal reason for C's dismissal

- **Crown Leisure Ltd v Waldron** EAT 307/91: W was employed by the transferor as one of four service engineers who worked on fruit machines in clubs. Following a TUPE transfer, the new employer, CL Ltd, sought to impose detrimental changes to his hours, holiday and sick pay entitlement. W resigned and claimed constructive dismissal, arguing that his dismissal was automatically unfair under TUPE. An employment tribunal upheld his claim, and CL Ltd appealed to the EAT. It contended that W's dismissal was for an 'organisational reason entailing changes in the workforce', in that, instead of continuing to be general engineers who turned their hands to workshop repair, on-site servicing and installation, the claimant and his colleagues were required, after the transfer, to form part of a specialised corps separately comprising service engineers, installation engineers and workshop repair engineers. The EAT, however, upheld the tribunal's conclusion. In its view, there was no suggestion from the evidence that W was being asked to accept any significant change to his job description. The document containing the new terms and conditions was headed 'service engineers' – the exact same job title that had applied to W under the transferor. The EAT observed that 'the employers were... engaged in a perfectly understandable operation of trying to harmonise the terms and conditions of employment of the whole of their workforce... That may be perfectly understandable for commercial reasons, may be perfectly defensible in many ways, but it simply is not what Reg 8(2) [of the TUPE Regulations 1981, now Reg 7(2) of the 2006 Regulations] is talking about, because although the requirement that there shall be organisational reasons... may well be satisfied, there is no relevant change in the workforce entailed by those reasons'

- **Gibson v Ciro Cittero (Menswear) plc** EAT 1276/97: G was employed as a sales assistant at the Romford branch of a clothes store. In June 1996 the business was acquired by CCM plc, which already had more than 200 stores country-wide. Prior to the transfer, G had been a key holder for the branch and was paid an extra £20 a week (8 per cent of her total weekly earnings) for bearing that responsibility. Following the transfer, however, CCM plc decided that her key-holder duties should be transferred to a more senior manager, consistent with its general policy in other stores. G ended up resigning and claiming unfair constructive dismissal owing to the loss of her additional allowance. An employment tribunal found that, although she had been constructively dismissed, her dismissal was not unfair on account of the fact that the reason for dismissal comprised an ETO reason entailing changes in the workforce. In particular, the tribunal ruled that there had been a change in G's job function, as she no longer had the role of key holder, and that this change was far from being a mere 'standardisation' in pay. Rather, it constituted an organisational reason entailing a change in the functions of a member of CCM Ltd's workforce. On appeal, the EAT accepted the tribunal's reasoning with regard to the question of whether CCM plc had an ETO reason for G's dismissal. However, it held that the tribunal had failed to consider whether the dismissal was nonetheless unfair under S.98(4) ERA as being unreasonable in all the circumstances, and remitted the case to a different tribunal for determination of that matter

- **London Metropolitan University v Sackur and ors** EAT 0286/06: in August 2002 the University of North London (UNL) and the London Guildhall University (LGU) merged to form London Metropolitan University (LMU). The merger was effected by a transfer of UNL to LGU, which, immediately upon that transfer, changed its name to LMU. The parties accepted that TUPE applied. Staff originally employed by LGU enjoyed slightly better terms and conditions than those who had been employed by UNL. LMU took the decision that the UNL terms and conditions were to be the standard form of contract for all new and existing staff, and in September 2004 it imposed the new terms on staff originally employed by LGU, dismissing and offering to re-engage those who refused to accept. A group of former LGU employees brought claims based on Reg 7(1) TUPE, which were upheld by an employment tribunal. In its view, the dismissals were effected in order to harmonise terms and conditions, which, according to settled case law, was a transfer-connected reason. Furthermore, LMU had failed to establish an ETO reason entailing changes in the workforce. The Court of Appeal's decision in Berriman had established that 'changes in the workforce' means changes in the numbers or job functions of employees, neither of which was present here, as it was LMU's intention to retain all transferred staff in their existing roles. LMU appealed to the EAT, but the EAT upheld the tribunal's decision. In its view, Berriman remained good law, and was correctly applied by the tribunal.

Two cases where the outcome has been more favourable to employers: **4.74**

- **Lane v Dyno-Rod plc** ET Case No.17833/85: L was employed by R Ltd, which ran a drain cleaning business, as 'area manager'. When the business transferred to D-R plc, L's terms and conditions were substantially altered. His title became 'senior engineer', and his status and duties changed. Although his remuneration was initially substantially the same, L felt that his changed circumstances would reduce his earning capacity, so he resigned and claimed constructive dismissal. An employment tribunal held that D-R plc had constructively dismissed L in connection with a relevant transfer, but had made out an ETO reason for doing so which had entailed changes in its workforce. The fact that the company did not need an area manager – the reason which resulted in L's becoming employed as a senior engineer – showed that there had been a restructuring of the business, and that this had necessarily involved changes to the duties of at least one member of the workforce

- **Green v Elan Care Ltd** EAT 18/01: G was employed as the care manager at a residential home. The residential home business fell into financial difficulties and, in April 2001, was acquired by E Ltd. The acquisition amounted to a TUPE transfer. The principal shareholder of E Ltd – who had previously been employed in the care home as its financial manager – decided to implement a reorganisation of management, combining the functions previously performed by G and the care home's proprietor with his own functions. Thus, the jobs of three managers were to be merged into one. G was offered alternative employment as senior carer, but this meant that she would no longer be a manager and her annual salary would be reduced from £19,000 to £10,000. She declined the offer and was subsequently dismissed. G claimed that her dismissal was automatically unfair under what is now Reg 7(1). In her view, her dismissal had been connected with

373

the transfer, and had not been for an ETO reason entailing changes in the workforce within the meaning of Reg 7(2) since E Ltd had simply sought to change her terms and conditions. An employment tribunal rejected G's claim. It held that the proposal of alternative employment entailed a fundamental change to G's job functions, and hence that the reason for dismissal had been an ETO reason entailing changes in the workforce. On appeal, the EAT upheld the tribunal's conclusion. The EAT acknowledged that, under the proposed changes, the number of employees in the workforce was to remain the same. However, case law demonstrated that this did not prevent the tribunal from concluding that E Ltd's reason for dismissal fell within Reg 7(2). Furthermore, while a minor change in the functions of one employee or a small number of employees in a large workforce might not be sufficient for the purposes of that provision, where the steps taken by the employer involve a real change in functions in a substantial or key area of the workforce, it is open to a tribunal to find that changes in the workforce are entailed. In this case, had G accepted the proposal, she would have been retained in a wholly different and non-managerial position. The changes accordingly involved a wholesale reorganisation in the management structure and a reduction in the number of managers by at least one. In view of this, it was open to the tribunal to find that E Ltd's organisational reason for G's dismissal entailed changes in the workforce.

4.75 The following conclusions can be drawn with some certainty from the substantial body of case law discussed in this section. First, as the Berriman, Bullard and Sackur cases (above) illustrate, in order to amount to a 'change in the workforce' within the meaning of Reg 7(2), a change in 'job function' must involve, to some extent at least, a change to the actual *tasks* that employees are required to perform. So, neither a simple harmonisation of terms and conditions (for more on which, see Chapter 5, 'Changing terms and conditions', under 'Harmonising terms and conditions'), nor a simple change in working hours will, in themselves, suffice. Transfer-related dismissals arising from such changes are almost certain to be automatically unfair under Reg 7(1). This is so even when the harmonisation process occurs against a background of changes in the workforce. In Manchester College v Hazel and anor 2014 ICR 989, CA, the Court of Appeal upheld an employment tribunal's decision that employees dismissed post-transfer because they refused to accept less favourable terms and conditions were not dismissed for an ETO (organisational) reason entailing changes in the workforce. The transfer had set in train a number of redundancy dismissals as well as a renegotiation of contract terms. The transferee argued that the reason for the changes to the claimants' contracts was not, therefore, simple harmonisation, but harmonisation that also gave rise to a change in workforce numbers. The tribunal and the EAT rejected this argument and on further appeal the Court of Appeal endorsed their decisions. The Court accepted that the proposed harmonisation of terms was in a general sense related to the redundancies in that both were part of the same package of proposals intended to reduce costs. However, the important question for the purpose of Reg 7 was what factors operated on the employer's mind so as to cause it to dismiss the employees. In the instant case, it was clear that the principal reason for the claimants' dismissals was their refusal to agree to the new terms and conditions – the employer's need for redundancies played no part in the decision to dismiss.

The second general conclusion that can be drawn from the case law is that, as the EAT expressly decided in Crawford v Swinton Insurance Brokers Ltd (above), where workforce numbers are not reduced but employees are given *entirely different jobs* to do, this will be sufficient to amount to 'changes in the workforce' for the purposes of the Reg 7(2) ETO defence. This analysis concurs with the current BIS Guide, which states that 'a functional change could involve a new requirement on an employee who held a managerial position to enter into a non-managerial role, or to move from a secretarial to a sales position'. The cases of Lane and Green (also above) provide good examples of 'changes in the workforce' taking place post-transfer by reason of employees being required to perform different roles.

Minor job role changes. The above two scenarios – first, a simple harmonisation **4.76** process which does not alter an employee's job function at all and, secondly, a reorganisation leading to an employee doing a completely different job – represent two extremes. But what about a more nuanced situation where, for an organisational reason, an employee's duties do change, but only in a fairly minor way? Will this amount to a 'change in the workforce' enabling the employer to rely on the Reg 7(2) ETO defence? On the one hand, the message from Crown Leisure Ltd v Waldron (above) seems to be that where an employee's duties remain essentially the same after the transfer as before it, the transferee might find it difficult to convince a tribunal that any change to terms and conditions was prompted by an ETO reason entailing a change of job 'functions'. On the other hand, it is noteworthy that in Gibson v Giro Cittero (Menswear) plc (above) the EAT did not disturb a tribunal's finding that there had been a 'change in the workforce' where an employee lost a key-holding responsibility at a clothes store, even though she otherwise continued in the same role. This suggests that the wholesale changes to an employee's role envisaged by Crawford v Swinton Insurance Brokers Ltd (above) and the BIS Guide are not necessarily required for the employer's ETO defence to be invoked.

Indeed, in RR Donnelley Global Document Solutions Group Ltd v Besagni and ors 2014 ICR 1008, EAT, the Appeal Tribunal reasoned that, while in order to fall within Reg 7(2) the changes must be to a body of people constituting the workforce, a requirement that members of the workforce demonstrate additional skills or qualifications would amount to an ETO reason entailing changes in the workforce even if the basic jobs they do remain

375

the same. Similarly, in Nationwide Building Society v Benn and ors 2010 IRLR 922, EAT (the material facts of which are set out under 'Economic, technical or organisational reason – organisational reasons' above), the Appeal Tribunal held that the lack of an equivalent product range to that which the transferred employees had been able to offer customers pre-transfer entailed a change to the employees' job function. These decisions likewise suggest that there does not have to be a radical change in employee function for Reg 7(2) to apply.

4.77 Note also the EAT's decision in Miles v Insitu Cleaning Co Ltd EAT 0157/12, a case concerning a cleaner who was dismissed when she refused to accept changes to her working arrangements following a TUPE transfer. The EAT accepted in principle that the loss of key-holding responsibilities and the addition of window-cleaning duties were capable of 'entailing changes in the workforce'. But it also made clear that, in order to be defined as such, those changes have to be 'more than minor', citing the reasoning of the EAT in Green v Elan Care Ltd (above) as authority for this.

The EAT in the Miles case also observed that the change in job function must apply to the particular employee who is dismissed if the employer is to rely on it as an ETO reason for that employee's dismissal. If that were not so, an employer could make changes to the rest of the workforce but not to the individual claimant or claimants, and then argue that there was an ETO reason for dismissal.

4.78 *Change of work location.* A 'change in the workforce' now includes a change in the employees' place of work. This is the result of an amendment made to Reg 7 by the Collective Redundancies and Transfer of Undertakings (Protection of Employment) (Amendment) Regulations 2014 SI 2014/16, which came into force on 31 January 2014. The 2014 Regulations inserted a subsection (3A) into Reg 7, which provides that 'the expression "changes in the workforce" includes a change to the place where employees are employed by the employer to carry on the business of the employer or to carry out work of a particular kind for the employer'.

The consultation paper outlining the proposed amendments to the Regulations recognised that, up to that point, the interpretation accorded by the courts to the phrase 'entailing changes in the workforce' had not included a change in work location. It made clear that the Government's aim behind what became Reg 7(3A) was to align the scope of the ETO defence with the definition of 'redundancy' in S.139 ERA, which covers both the complete cessation (i.e. closure) of the business at the place where the employee was employed to work and a diminution in the requirements of the business for employees to carry out work of a particular kind in the place where the employee was employed. The BIS Guide explains that Reg 7(3A) is thus intended to cover 'a change to the place where employees are employed to carry on the business of the employer, or particular work for the employer' and that, accordingly, 'where a transfer involves the employer changing the location of its business or part of it, dismissal due to that change will not usually be automatically unfair, even if the employer still needs the same number of staff in the new location'.

Shortly before the 2014 amendment came into effect, the EAT in RR Donnelley **4.79** Global Document Solutions Group Ltd v Besagni and ors 2014 ICR 1008, EAT, had reached the unequivocal conclusion that a change of workplace did not entail 'changes in the workforce' within the meaning of Reg 7(2) as it then stood. Although this point is now academic in relation to transfers taking place on or after 31 January 2014 or to dismissals that take effect on or after that date, it clarifies the position in respect of earlier transfers.

Some commentators have suggested that the 2014 amendment may be in breach of Article 4(1) of the Acquired Rights Directive, since there is nothing in that provision indicating that Member States may provide in their national law that the ETO defence prevails in a situation where transfer-related dismissals are made for a reason that has no effect on the numbers or functions of the workforce. Although this contention was raised in the RR Donnelley case, the EAT did not come to any specific conclusion about it as the case fell to be decided solely on the basis of Reg 7 prior to the 2014 amendment.

Notwithstanding Reg 7(3A), it will still be necessary to determine whether the **4.80** change has been brought about by a change in location or for some other reason. In Kearney v Sceptre Leisure Solutions Ltd ET Case No 1401907/10 K's employment transferred to SLS Ltd on 15 December 2009 when the transferee acquired the transferor's gaming and leisure equipment business. She had previously been based in Wimborne, Dorset, and her job involved collecting money from gaming machines, counting the money, banking it and completing paperwork and computer records. Under her contract she was required to work within a 150-mile radius of her work base. Prior to the transfer she travelled 78 miles a day and this meant that sometimes she could complete her weekly work in less than the 37.5 hours on which her pay was based. Shortly after the transfer SLS Ltd asked K to transfer her base to Bristol. She initially agreed to this but subsequently realised that the change would result in a significant increase in both her mileage and working time with no corresponding increase in pay. K raised her concern with the employer but after it failed to address the matter she resigned and claimed unfair constructive dismissal. An employment tribunal held that, by allocating K a work route that she could not complete within her standard working day and causing her hourly rate of pay to be reduced to below the national minimum wage, SLS Ltd had breached her contract of employment; that that breach was connected to the transfer; and that she had been constructively dismissed. The principal reason for the dismissal was not an ETO one because there had been no change in the numbers or functions of the workforce. Accordingly, the dismissal was automatically unfair under Reg 7(1).

While it could now be argued that the change arose as a result of a change in location within the meaning of Reg 7(3A), that would not alter the fact that the fundamental cause of K's resignation was the impact this had on her working hours and rate of pay. It is difficult to see how the reason for dismissal would amount to an ETO reason even if the case had been decided at a time when Reg 7(3A) applied.

4.81 **Meaning of 'workforce'.** Regarding the meaning of the particular word 'workforce' in Reg 7(2), this came under judicial scrutiny in Meter U Ltd v Ackroyd and ors 2012 ICR 834, EAT. In that case the EAT held that the word does not embrace individuals providing their services as franchisees through their own independent limited companies. The issue arose when MU Ltd, a company providing meter reading services, took over contracts from companies that employed meter readers. MU Ltd's business model was to sub-contract the work to individuals who provided their services as franchisees, and so it did not actually employ any meter readers itself. When it sought to impose this model on the transferring employees, it dismissed as redundant those who refused to comply. Two employment tribunals, hearing claims from two different groups of transferred employees, decided that although redundancy was an ETO reason, it did not on these facts involve changes in workforce numbers. The 'workforce' included all those working in MU Ltd's business, whether as employees, franchisees or otherwise. On this analysis, there was no change in the size of the workforce following the transfer – MU Ltd required the same number of meter readers; they were just engaged under different contractual arrangements. On appeal, the EAT held that this approach was incorrect. Although neither TUPE nor the Acquired Rights Directive defines 'workforce', common sense suggested that the term refers to individual employees and does not include franchisees who operated as limited companies (unless the franchise arrangements were found to be a sham, which they were not in the present case). It followed that the dismissal of the claimants amounted to a change in the workforce, since their dismissals were for redundancy.

In the above case, the EAT said that the 'workforce' connotes the whole body of employees as an entity. However, in Spaceright Europe Ltd v Baillavoine and anor EAT 0339/10 the Appeal Tribunal suggested that there is no inherent reason why the 'workforce' should not consist of a single person. Likewise, a reason for dismissal that otherwise constitutes an ETO reason should not be precluded from being so simply because it entails a change in the workforce as regards a single person. However, the EAT concluded on the facts of the particular case that the dismissal of a managing director was not for an ETO reason entailing changes in the workforce because there was no contemplated diminution in the number of employees. The business was always going to need a managing director and it was contemplated that the claimant would be replaced, as indeed he was. Note that the Court of Appeal rejected an appeal in this case (see Spaceright Europe Ltd v Baillavoine and ors 2012 ICR 520, CA), although it did not have to consider specifically the EAT's assumption that the workforce can be a single person.

Transferor cannot dismiss for transferee's ETO reason   4.82
In order to amount to an ETO reason under Reg 7(2), the reason for the dismissal must relate to the future conduct of the business concerned – see Wheeler v Patel and anor 1987 ICR 631, EAT (discussed under 'Economic, technical or organisational reason' above). If it does, the 'ETO defence' can be relied upon in respect of dismissals carried out by either the transferor or the transferee.

That noted, we turn to the question of whether a transferor can establish an ETO reason for dismissal for Reg 7(2) purposes where it dismisses employees, prior to a transfer, for a reason relating to the transferee's future conduct of the business in question. Put another way, can a transferor 'borrow' the transferee's ETO reason, and carry out dismissals prior to the transfer that the transferee would be entitled to carry out after the transfer? Following a number of years of conjecture, the Court of Session in Hynd v Armstrong and ors 2007 SLT 299, Ct Sess (Inner House), answered this question firmly in the negative.

The Hynd case involved Morison Bishop, a law firm with offices in Edinburgh   4.83
and Glasgow, which employed H, a corporate lawyer, in its Glasgow office. The partners in the firm decided to dissolve the partnership with effect from 31 July 2002, with the intention of forming two new firms: an Edinburgh-based firm called Morisons and a Glasgow-based firm called Bishops. Since Bishops was to concentrate on property law and litigation, the Glasgow partners of Morison Bishop anticipated a reduced requirement for corporate lawyers. Acting with the authority of the other partners in the firm, they made H redundant on 31 July 2002 – the date on which the partnership dissolved. On 1 August 2002 Morisons and Bishops each commenced practice. Following his dismissal, H initiated proceedings in an employment tribunal against the former partners of Morison Bishop and the partners of the new entity, Bishops, complaining that his dismissal was by reason of or connected with a relevant transfer, and was automatically unfair under what is now Reg 7(1). The tribunal rejected H's claim. It observed that he had been dismissed by the partners of Morison Bishop (the transferor) in anticipation of the transfer of part of their undertaking to Bishops (the transferee) because the prospective partners in Bishops had decided, for economic and organisational reasons, that H would not be required for the future conduct of the business following the transfer. On that basis, the tribunal concluded that the dismissing employer had established an ETO reason for dismissal, which entailed changes in the workforce, under what is now Reg 7(2). H's appeal to the EAT was refused and he appealed once more, this time to the Court of Session. Before that Court, he argued that since he was dismissed by the transferor prior to the transfer, the 'ETO defence'

379

would only apply if the ETO reason for his dismissal related to the transferor's own future conduct of the business. In other words, the transferor should not be entitled to rely on an ETO reason based on the anticipated future conduct of the business by the transferee.

The Court of Session turned first to the Acquired Rights Directive, holding that it was 'reasonably clear' that Article 4(1) did not permit dismissals by transferors in circumstances such as those in the instant case. With regard to dismissals by a transferor, Article 4(1) was to be naturally construed as limiting the ETO defence to dismissals for reasons that entailed changes in the *transferor's own workforce*. This conclusion was supported by two further considerations. First, if Article 4(1) were interpreted so as to permit a transferor to dismiss employees prior to the transfer because they were surplus to the transferee's requirements, there would be every incentive, where the transferor was insolvent, for redundancies to be effected by the transferor in advance of the transfer so that liabilities with regard to the redundant employees did not pass to the transferee and could, in practice, be avoided. That result would be inconsistent with the Directive's objective of protecting employees. Secondly, in a situation where the combined workforces of the transferor and transferee were greater than the transferee would require after the transfer, and where redundancies would therefore be necessary, such an interpretation of Article 4(1) would enable the selection of employees for redundancy to be made solely from the transferor's workforce, and would thus relieve the transferee of the need, which would otherwise arise, to consider all the employees of the combined workforces on an equal footing.

4.84 Next, the Court considered whether Reg 7(2) – which referred to an ETO reason entailing changes in the workforce 'of either the transferor or the transferee before or after a relevant transfer' – could be construed in line with its preferred interpretation of the Directive. In order to do so, the Court reviewed the relevant authorities. In Wheeler v Patel (above) the EAT had held that a dismissal by the transferor in order to comply with a requirement of the intended transferee could not be an ETO reason for dismissal within the meaning of Reg 7(2). Such a reason did not relate to the conduct of the business; it related simply to the transferor's desire to achieve a sale. This reasoning was later affirmed by the Court of Appeal in Whitehouse v Charles A Blatchford and Sons Ltd 2000 ICR 542, CA, where that Court emphasised that, for an ETO reason to arise where an employee is dismissed by a transferor, the transferor's reason for dismissal must relate to its own future conduct of the business; a condition that could not be met where the transferor had no intention of continuing the business.

Taking these cases on board, the Court of Session concluded that what is now Reg 7(2) could be interpreted in line with Article 4(1) of the Directive. Thus, the right of an employer to dismiss for an ETO reason entailing changes in the workforce arose only where the employer dismissed an employee for a reason of its own, relating to its own future conduct of the business, and entailing a change in its own workforce. Accordingly, the Court held that the tribunal's conclusion that H's dismissal was for an ETO reason was based on a mistaken interpretation of the Regulations. On a correct interpretation, the only conclusion open to the tribunal was that the employer's ETO defence failed, meaning that H's dismissal was automatically unfair.

In reaching its decision, the Court of Session in the Hynd case acknowledged **4.85** that, had H not been dismissed by Morison Bishop prior to the transfer, he could have been fairly dismissed for an ETO reason by Bishops after the transfer. The message from the case to a transferee, then, is a simple one: in the absence of watertight warranties and indemnities from the transferor, where a transferee believes that it has an ETO reason for carrying out dismissals, it should carry out those dismissals itself after the relevant transfer has occurred rather than put pressure on the transferor to dismiss members of the workforce prior to the transfer. Any such dismissals carried out by the transferor are likely to be automatically unfair under Reg 7(1) and, as we shall see under 'Which employer will be liable?' below, liability for such dismissals will pass under TUPE to the transferee in any event.

ETO dismissals deemed to be by reason of redundancy or SOSR **4.86**
Under Reg 7(3)(b), where a transfer dismissal is not rendered automatically unfair by Reg 7(1) – i.e. where the employer is successful with its 'ETO defence' – the reason for dismissal for the purpose of S.98 ERA will be deemed to be either:

- 'some other substantial reason' of a kind such as to justify the dismissal of an employee holding the position which that employee held (SOSR), or

- 'redundancy', where the reason for dismissal fulfils the definition in S.139 ERA, in which case the employee's normal rights on redundancy – such as a redundancy payment and the right to claim that he had been chosen under an unfair redundancy selection – will apply.

Regulation 7(3)(b) addresses an anomaly under the 1981 Regulations, which provided that dismissal for an ETO reason connected to the transfer was always to be treated as being for some other substantial reason, meaning that no redundancy payment was technically required to be paid.

Most cases discussed above in which an ETO defence has been available to an **4.87** employer have involved either the reduction in workforce numbers or dismissals owing to significant changes to job functions. Many of these are likely to meet the statutory definition of redundancy contained in S.139 ERA, in that the requirements of the business for employees to carry out work of a particular kind will have ceased or diminished. Employers wishing to carry out ETO dismissals in connection with a relevant transfer should try to ascertain whether

381

such dismissals will be by reason of redundancy and, if so, ensure that they jump through the necessary hoops to ensure fairness regarding selection, consultation and dismissal processes. If they fail to do this, ETO dismissals are likely to be rendered unfair by virtue of the reasonableness test set out in S.98(4) ERA. For discussion on the definitions of redundancy, redundancy selection and consultation, see IDS Employment Law Handbook, 'Redundancy' (2011).

In some – perhaps more rare – cases, the dismissals of employees after the transfer may arise out of a reorganisation of the workforce without there being any diminished requirement for employees to carry out work of a particular kind. In such cases employers wishing to carry out ETO dismissals in connection with a relevant transfer should follow the steps necessary to ensure fair SOSR dismissals. These are outlined in IDS Employment Law Handbook, 'Unfair Dismissal' (2015), Chapter 8, 'Some other substantial reason', under 'Business reorganisations'.

4.88 Constructive dismissals

Up to this point, this chapter has largely been concerned with *express* dismissals initiated by the *employer* – whether the transferor or the transferee – in a TUPE context, and whether or not such dismissals are automatically unfair by virtue of Reg 7(1) of the TUPE Regulations or for an 'economic, technical or organisational reason entailing changes in the workforce' within the terms of Reg 7(2).

We now examine two routes (envisaged by Reg 4) by which an employee's decision to leave his or her employment, taken in response to the actions of a transferor or transferee, precipitates a 'dismissal', thus giving rise to a potential unfair dismissal claim. In this section we focus on the traditional concept of 'constructive dismissal', which Reg 4(11) acknowledges can arise in a TUPE context; and in the next section we discuss the TUPE-specific concept of 'material detriment' dismissal as defined in Reg 4(9).

4.89 The familiar concept of 'constructive dismissal' as this applies in the context of the statutory protection against unfair dismissal is defined in S.95(1)(c) ERA. A virtually identical definition is set out in S.136(1)(c) in respect of the right to statutory redundancy payments, which are only claimable if the employee has actually been dismissed. Both provisions make it clear that a dismissal will be regarded as having occurred where 'the employee terminates the contract [of employment] under which he is employed (with or without notice) in circumstances in which he is entitled to terminate it without notice by reason of the employer's conduct'. Simplifying the statutory language, and reflecting the way the courts have interpreted S.95(1)(c), this means that a constructive dismissal occurs where the employee resigns, with or without notice, in response to a 'repudiatory breach' of contract on the part of the employer – that is, a breach so significant that it goes to the root of the contract. In such circumstances, even where no express dismissal has occurred, the employee will be treated as having been 'dismissed' and so will be able to bring an unfair dismissal claim under the ERA provided that he or she has the requisite qualifying service – see 'Overview' above.

Many of the cases discussed in the chapter thus far have concerned constructive rather than express dismissals, with such dismissals often arising because of a transferee employer's wish to change transferring employees' contractual terms – see, for example, the leading case of Berriman v Delabole Slate Ltd 1985 ICR 546, CA, discussed at length under 'Dismissals potentially fair for an "ETO reason"' above. For more on changing terms and conditions for a reason connected with a relevant transfer, see Chapter 5, 'Changing terms and conditions'.

4.90 Below, we start by explaining the concept of 'constructive dismissal' in more detail, before considering how such a dismissal is treated by the Regulations. In particular, we examine what might ensue where an employee resigns, prior to a relevant transfer, owing to concerns about changes the transferee might make to his or her contractual terms.

What is a constructive dismissal? **4.91**

The basic elements of a constructive dismissal are reflected in one of the operative definitions of 'dismissal' found in the ERA. By virtue of Ss.95(1)(c) and 136(1)(c), an employer will be regarded as having dismissed an employee if the latter terminates his or her employment contract, with or without notice, in circumstances in which he or she is entitled to terminate it without notice by reason of the employer's conduct.

In Western Excavating (ECC) Ltd v Sharp 1978 ICR 221, CA, the Court of Appeal ruled that the employer's conduct giving rise to a constructive dismissal must involve a repudiatory breach of contract. In other words, it is only in response to a breach serious enough to constitute a repudiation of the contract that an employee is relieved of the obligation to give notice before resigning. As Lord Denning MR put it: 'If the employer is guilty of conduct which is a significant breach going to the root of the contract of employment, or which shows that the employer no longer intends to be bound by one or more of the essential terms of the contract, then the employee is entitled to treat himself as discharged from any further performance. If he does so, then he terminates the contract by reason of the employer's conduct. He is constructively dismissed.'

4.92 What might amount to such a repudiatory breach of contract? Although we do not intend to dwell on this question here – a full discussion of the issues is contained in IDS Employment Law Handbook, 'Contracts of Employment' (2014), Chapter 10, 'Breach of contract' – the following brief points should be noted:

383

- the obligation on an employer to pay employees their salary is so fundamental that a breach of this duty, such as a wage cut (see, for example, RF Hill Ltd v Mooney 1981 IRLR 258, EAT), is likely to be treated as repudiatory

- fringe benefits are commonly regarded as part of employees' remuneration, so a breach of a term relating to such benefits may well be repudiatory (see, for example, Triton Oliver (Special Products) Ltd v Bromage EAT 709/91, where the withdrawal of an employee's right to a company car founded a successful constructive dismissal claim)

- unilateral changes to an employee's job content (outside of those envisaged by the employment contract) and/or to an employee's status are likely to be repudiatory. See, for example, Marconi Radar Systems Ltd v Bennett EAT 793/82, in which B, a quality manager who returned from holiday to find that certain design work had been transferred from himself to his former deputy, was found to have been constructively dismissed

- an increase in or alteration of an employee's hours of work can amount to a repudiatory breach of contract – see, for example, Tawiah v Southern Derbyshire Mental Health Trust ET Case No.11547/94, in which such a breach occurred where the employer insisted that a nurse changed from night shifts to day shifts

- whether or not an employee can claim constructive dismissal when the location of his or her workplace is changed depends largely upon how much mobility is built into the contract. If there is no express or implied mobility clause, the employer may be at risk of a constructive dismissal claim if he tries to relocate the employee. For example, in Strachan St George v Williams EAT 969/94 an employer's moving an audiotypist to an office that was further hour away from where she lived was held to be a repudiatory breach of contract, and

- the common law implies a term into all contracts of employment that employers will not, without reasonable or proper cause, conduct themselves in a manner calculated or likely to destroy or seriously damage the relationship of trust and confidence between the parties – Courtaulds Northern Textiles Ltd v Andrew 1979 IRLR 84, EAT. A breach of this implied term, which can cover a very wide range of behaviour, will amount to a repudiatory breach of contract. It is this term that is most often cited in constructive dismissal claims.

4.93 It is important to note that, whether or not a repudiatory breach of contract has occurred, there will be no constructive dismissal unless the employee 'accepts' that breach by resigning, and thus bringing the contract to an end. The decision whether to accept the breach belongs exclusively to the employee, and often other less drastic options are available. One is that the employee may

384

choose to 'stand and sue' on the contract – meaning that, rather than resign, he or she will take legal action for breach of contract, in which case the contract remains alive as between the contracting parties.

Alternatively, the employee might simply choose to look past the breach – i.e. effectively ignore it. If the employee fails to register any obvious protest about the breach, then at some point he or she is likely to be regarded as having sanctioned it, thereby affirming the contract. In such a case, the employer will no longer be in breach of contract and the employee will thus lose the right to resign and claim that he or she has been constructively dismissed. (That said, the TUPE regime complicates this analysis somewhat, since case law suggests that contractual changes to an employee's detriment are void if made by reason of a relevant transfer, even where the employee in question agrees to those changes – see 'Employee cannot affirm TUPE-connected contractual change' below and, in more detail, Chapter 5, 'Changing terms and conditions', under 'Varying terms in a TUPE context'.)

4.94 In summary, in order to show that he or she has been constructively dismissed, an employee must establish the following:

- that there was a repudiatory breach of contract on the part of the employer

- that it was the employer's breach that actually caused the employee to resign. If there is a different reason for the employee's resignation, such that he or she would have left irrespective of the employer's conduct, then there has not been a constructive dismissal, and

- that the employee did not delay too long before resigning, thus affirming the contract and losing the right to claim constructive dismissal.

Preservation of constructive dismissal rights under TUPE   4.95
The TUPE Regulations expressly provide for the employee's normal constructive dismissal right to be preserved. In this regard, Reg 4(11) stipulates that 'paragraphs (1), (7), (8) and (9) [of Reg 4] are without prejudice to any right of an employee arising apart from these Regulations to terminate his contract of employment without notice in acceptance of a repudiatory breach of contract by his employer'.

In other words, none of the following in any way displace or limit the employee's right to claim constructive dismissal as a result of a repudiatory breach of contract by the employer:

- Reg 4(1), which provides for the automatic transfer of an employee's employment from the transferor to the transferee (see Chapter 2, 'Who transfers?', under 'General effect of transfer on employees – the basic rule: "novation" of the contract')

385

- Reg 4(7) and (8), which concerns the employee's right to object to the automatic transfer of his or her employment (also discussed in Chapter 2, 'Who transfers?', under 'Objecting to transfer'), or

- Reg 4(9), which provides an employee with an additional right to treat his or her contract as having been terminated where the relevant transfer involves or would involve a substantial change to working conditions to his or her material detriment (see 'Material detriment dismissals' below).

4.96 So, where there is a relevant transfer to which TUPE applies, employers who unilaterally seek to make changes to terms and conditions or otherwise to the employer/employee relationship, prompted by the transfer or a reason connected with it, risk provoking employees to resign and claim unfair constructive dismissal. This is the case whether the changes are made prior to the transfer (by the transferor) or after the transfer (by the transferee).

As touched upon under 'What is a constructive dismissal?' above, the kinds of change (or threatened change) that typically lead to employees resigning and claiming constructive dismissal are those that are made to contractual remunerative benefits including pay and other remuneration, holiday, hours of work (including overtime and shift patterns), bonus and commission schemes, profit share, sickness benefit entitlement, pensions, and other fringe benefits such as car provision. Sometimes, however, the changes relate to the work the employees do or the place at which they are employed to do it. Such changes typically affect job descriptions, job functions and/or job status. Unless the scale of the change is minor, then in most cases a unilateral change to any of the above will be regarded as a repudiatory breach of contract entitling the employee to resign with or without giving notice. In addition, if the employer's conduct is such as to destroy or seriously damage the employment relationship, this will amount to a breach of the fundamental implied term of trust and confidence, entitling the employee to resign and claim constructive dismissal.

4.97 Remember that even if a change is not of such a scale as to amount to a repudiatory breach, Reg 4(9) confers a freestanding right for the employee to resign on the ground that the relevant transfer involves or would involve a substantial change in working conditions to his or her material detriment. This right is explored in detail under 'Material detriment dismissals' below.

4.98 **Employee cannot affirm TUPE-connected contractual change**
In the discussion on 'What is a constructive dismissal?' above, we made the point that, generally, where an employee does nothing in response to an employer's repudiatory breach of contract, he or she is likely to be regarded as having sanctioned it, thereby affirming the contract, and will lose the right to resign and claim that he or she has been constructively dismissed.

386

However, owing to case law interpreting the Acquired Rights Directive and the TUPE regime, this analysis does not apply where a change to terms and conditions occurs because of the transfer itself. That is because, as we explain in Chapter 5, 'Changing terms and conditions', under 'Varying terms in a TUPE context', contractual changes to an employee's detriment are void if the principal reason for the variation is the transfer, even where the employee in question purports to agree to them. Logically, then, where a transferee employer reduces a transferring employee's wages, or otherwise alters his or her terms and conditions to his or her detriment as a result of the transfer, the employee will be able, a number of years later, to claim constructive dismissal with regard to the ongoing breach, notwithstanding his or her inaction at the time.

Fairness/unfairness of constructive dismissals 4.99

All that a constructive dismissal accords the employee is the right to regard him or herself as having been dismissed. It does not necessarily follow that the employee in question has been unfairly dismissed.

Assuming that a constructive dismissal has occurred, then, outside of a TUPE context, the following must happen in order for the dismissal to be fair. First, the employer must show that there was a potentially valid reason for dismissal within the terms of S.98(1) and (2) ERA; and, secondly, provided that such a reason is shown, the tribunal must reach the conclusion that, in all the circumstances of the case, the employer had acted reasonably, within the meaning of S.98(4), to dismiss the employee for that reason within the ERA – see 'Overview' above.

What about a constructive dismissal occurring in connection with a TUPE **4.100** transfer? As a general rule, Reg 7(1) and (2) – the provisions dealing with dismissals carried out in a TUPE context, which were discussed at length under 'Automatically unfair dismissal' and 'Dismissals potentially fair for an "ETO reason"' above – apply whether or not dismissals are express or constructive. So, with regard to a constructive dismissal where the sole or principal reason for dismissal is the transfer rather than an ETO reason, the dismissal will be automatically unfair under Reg 7(1) and, assuming that the employee has the necessary continuous service, he or she will be entitled to the usual remedies for unfair dismissal. But if the sole or principal reason for the constructive dismissal is an ETO reason, then, in accordance with Reg 7(2), that reason will be regarded as being either for 'redundancy' or 'some other substantial reason of a kind such as to justify the dismissal of an employee holding the position which the employee held' for the purposes of Ss.98(1) and 139 ERA – see 'Dismissals potentially fair for an "ETO reason" – ETO dismissals deemed to be by reason of redundancy or SOSR' above. In that case, the fairness or otherwise of the decision to dismiss will be assessed by applying the normal reasonableness test set out in S.98(4) ERA.

387

The above applies whether a constructive dismissal occurs while the employee is employed by the transferor prior to the transfer or by the transferee after the transfer.

4.101 Note that it may well be the case in practice that virtually all constructive dismissals which take place within a TUPE context are likely to be found to be by reason of the transfer and thus automatically unfair under Reg 7(1) given the narrow interpretation that has been accorded to the concept of an ETO reason. As discussed under 'Dismissals potentially fair for an "ETO reason"' above, the Court of Appeal in Berriman v Delabole Slate Ltd 1985 ICR 546, CA, concluded that the ETO exception does not apply unless there have been changes in the numbers of the workforce as a whole or in the job functions of members of the workforce. By and large, non-consensual changes to the fundamental terms and conditions of employment are not normally made with a view to changing numbers or functions. And the same is true of most other forms of repudiatory conduct on the employer's part, prompted by the transfer.

However, difficulties are introduced into the otherwise straightforward picture described above where an employee resigns prior to a relevant transfer owing to concerns about what the transferee employer might do after the transfer. As discussed under 'Resignation in anticipation of breach by transferee' immediately below, a combination of various TUPE provisions and the case law interpreting those provisions conspire to make the legal position in this regard rather complex.

4.102 **Resignation in anticipation of breach by transferee**
The normal rule is that, where an employer manifests a clear intention to commit a breach of contract at some date in the future, an employee can resign and claim constructive dismissal in anticipation of the breach of contract. The question is how this plays out in a TUPE context.

There is no confusion where a transferring employee resigns *after* the transfer, in anticipation of a breach of contract by his or her new employer. Here, the normal rule as set out above will apply.

4.103 But can an employee, while still employed by the transferor, anticipate a change being made to his or her fundamental terms and conditions by the transferee and, in view of this, resign and bring a claim of unfair constructive dismissal *prior* to the transfer? And if so, will it be the transferor or the transferee who is liable? It is to these two tricky questions that we now turn.

4.104 **Resignation prior to transfer.** The first appellate case to concern the question of an employee's resignation, prior to the transfer, owing to concerns about what the transferee might do after the transfer, was that of Sita (GB) Ltd v Burton and ors 1998 ICR 17, EAT. This case involved the transfer of services from a local authority to S Ltd. In the weeks leading up to the transfer B and P, who were members of the workforce that was to be transferred, became increasingly concerned about the behaviour of S Ltd, which they believed had no intention of respecting their terms and conditions of employment after the transfer. A few weeks before the transfer, B and P handed in their resignations and brought unfair constructive dismissal claims against both the authority and S Ltd. An employment tribunal found that the behaviour of S Ltd, as the prospective transferee, in the weeks leading up to the transfer, was such as to lead a reasonable employee to suspect that his or her terms and conditions might change substantially after the transfer. This, in the tribunal's view, amounted to a breach of the implied contractual term of mutual trust and confidence, which entitled the employees to resign and claim constructive dismissal. The tribunal went on to hold that, since the sole cause of the employees' resignations was the transfer, their dismissals were in connection with the transfer and were therefore automatically unfair under what is now Reg 7(1). Furthermore, the liability for the dismissals passed to the transferee under what is now Reg 4(1).

S Ltd, however, was successful with its appeal. The EAT held that the tribunal had misdirected itself in law in so far as it held that the employees had been constructively dismissed by the prospective transferee. Since the employees were never employed by the transferee, there never existed any contract of employment which the transferee could have breached. In any event, the tribunal was also in error if its decision, properly understood, was that the transferor had constructively dismissed the employees by proceeding with the transfer in spite of the employees' reservations about the intentions of the transferee. It is only in the rarest of circumstances, the EAT said, that the duty of trust and confidence owed by an employer to an employee can be breached by reason of the actions of third parties. In the context of TUPE transfers, it may be possible that the consequences of the proposed transfer for the employees are so dire, whether in health and safety terms or otherwise, that the transferor's behaviour in going ahead with the transfer could destroy the relationship of trust and confidence with its employees. But it is not possible, as a matter of principle, for such a breach to occur where an employee's concerns relate solely to his terms and conditions following the transfer. The EAT reasoned that, since the 1981 Regulations required the transferee to honour existing terms, they provided a remedy to any attempt by the transferee to alter those terms unlawfully after the transfer. In the light of this protection enjoyed by employees involved in a transfer, the consequences of the transferor's proceeding with the transfer could not be drastic enough to give rise to a breach of the fundamental term of trust and confidence so as to entitle the employee to claim constructive dismissal against the transferor. Accordingly, the EAT overturned the tribunal's decision and rejected the employee's constructive dismissal claims.

The upshot of Sita seemed to be that an employee could not claim constructive **4.105** dismissal prior to a relevant transfer (whether against the transferor or the transferee), in anticipation of the transferee's failure to honour the transferring contractual or other legal obligations. However, the following two cases demonstrate that the position is not, in reality, that simple. In fact, the Humphreys case – a Court of Appeal decision which takes precedence over the EAT's decision in Sita – suggests that an employee can claim constructive dismissal against the transferor on the back of an anticipatory breach of contract by the transferee, as long as the anticipated breach is one of substance:

- **Humphreys v University of Oxford and anor** 2000 ICR 405, CA: The employment of H, an academic with security of tenure, was due to transfer to a new employer under TUPE. H anticipated that, following the transfer, there would be several variations to his terms and conditions, including a fundamental change resulting in a shorter tenure than he had envisaged. Owing to this, he exercised his right under what is now Reg 4(7) to object to the transfer of his employment to the transferee. He combined his objection with a claim for damages for wrongful dismissal, in respect of the unexpired period of his tenure, on the basis that he had been constructively dismissed by the transferor. The transferor – for reasons discussed at length under 'Who is liable – position where employee resigns and objects to transfer' below – denied that H was entitled to claim constructive dismissal against it, and applied for an order that his claim be struck out. This application was rejected by a High Court judge and, on appeal, by the Court of Appeal. However, in allowing the claim to proceed, the Court of Appeal made it clear that, in order for a transferor to be regarded as having constructively dismissed an employee by reason of a transfer entailing an anticipated repudiatory breach, the anticipated breach would have to be one of substance (i.e. a fundamental change in working conditions)

- **Euro-Die (UK) Ltd v Skidmore and anor** EAT 1158/98: S, whose employment was to transfer to a new employer under TUPE, was anxious not to lose his employment protection rights. He refused to work for the new employer in the absence of an assurance from the transferor that his continuity would be protected. When this was not forthcoming, he claimed unfair constructive dismissal against both the transferor and the transferee. An employment tribunal, and thereafter the EAT, upheld his claim, holding that the transferor's failure to reassure the employee as to his continuity of employment was a fundamental breach of the implied term of trust and confidence, entitling him to treat himself as having been constructively dismissed. For reasons expanded upon below, the transferee was held liable for the dismissal, which was by reason of the transfer and thus automatically unfair under what is now Reg 7(1). Note that the EAT (presided over by its then President, Mr Justice Lindsay) acknowledged that the outcome as to the unfairness of the dismissal in the case would have been different had the transferor told S that it was unsure about his rights and would seek advice. In those circumstances, the transferor would not have repudiated the contract by damaging the relationship of trust and confidence, and the employee would not have been found to be constructively dismissed.

It may appear that the Court of Appeal in Humphreys allowed the employee to **4.106** found a claim of constructive dismissal against the transferor on the transferee's anticipatory breach of contract. However, Mr Justice Langstaff's summary of the case in NHS Direct NHS Trust v Gunn EAT 0128/14 suggests that this is not quite accurate. Langstaff P observed in Gunn that, in circumstances where the transferee's proposed actions amount to a substantial and detrimental change to working conditions, the transferor's intention to transfer the employee 'is well recognised as an anticipatory and repudiatory breach of contract (as happened in Oxford University v Humphreys)'. Thus, it seems that what the Court actually decided was that a proposal to transfer an employee to a transferee who would then act in breach of contract is itself an anticipatory breach of contract, and that this was the proper basis for Mr Humphreys' constructive dismissal claim. Therefore, the constructive dismissal claim was founded on the transfer itself as an anticipatory breach, not on the transferee's actions per se.

Who is liable? We saw above that Humphreys v University of Oxford and anor **4.107** (above) and Euro-Die (UK) Ltd v Skidmore and anor (above) suggest that employees can resign and claim unfair constructive dismissal, prior to the transfer, owing to concerns they might have as to what the consequences of the transfer might be. The question arises, then, as to which employer – transferor or transferee – will be liable if such a claim is successful?

It seems that the conclusion in this regard will depend on whether the employee is taken to have formally objected to the transfer. The reasons for this require an analysis of the interplay between the employee's right to object to the transfer under Reg 4(7) and (8) of the Regulations on the one hand, and the preservation of the right arising, apart from the Regulations, to claim constructive dismissal found in Reg 4(11) on the other. Given the importance of the right to object in this context, it will be useful to provide a brief reminder of what this right comprises and its effect on the contract of employment before examining the Humphreys and Euro-Die decisions in more detail.

Background – right to object. The employee's right to object to a relevant **4.108** transfer was considered in detail in Chapter 2, 'Who transfers?', under 'Objecting to transfer'. This right arises out of the general principles that employees cannot be compelled to enter into a contract of employment and an employer may not transfer a contract of employment to a third party without the employee's consent. In Katsikas v Konstantinidis 1993 IRLR 179, ECJ, the European Court held that the Acquired Rights Directive could not be interpreted so as to prevent employees from objecting to the automatic transfer of their contracts of employment. The basis of this decision was that, if the Directive were interpreted as obliging employees to work for the transferee rather than

391

simply permitting them to do so on the terms and conditions agreed with the transferor, this would call into question the fundamental right of employees to select their employer.

The UK Government responded to Katsikas by inserting two new provisions into the 1981 Regulations. Reg 5(4A) provided that an employee's contract of employment would not be transferred automatically on a relevant transfer if the employee informed the transferor or the transferee that he or she objected to becoming the employee of the transferee. And Reg 5(4B) stipulated that, where an employee so objected, the transfer had the effect of terminating the employee's contract of employment with the transferor, but that the employee was not to be treated for any purpose as having been dismissed. Consequently, it seemed, the employee would lose all rights to claim unfair dismissal, wrongful dismissal, redundancy or any other remedy based on his or her having been dismissed by the transferor. However, Reg 5(5) stated that the right to object was 'without prejudice to any right of an employee arising apart from these Regulations to terminate his contract of employment without notice if a substantial change is made to his working conditions to his detriment', while noting that 'no such right shall arise by reason only that… the identity of the employer changes unless the employee shows that, in all the circumstances, the change is a significant change and is to his detriment'.

4.109 Although the wording of these provisions was somewhat altered by the 2006 Regulations, the substance of the specific provisions dealing with the right to object remained essentially the same. Old Reg 5(4A) corresponded to Reg 4(7) of the 2006 Regulations and old Reg 5(4B) corresponded to Reg 4(8). Only in relation to old Reg 5(5) have the changes effected by the 2006 Regulations led to a significant alteration, in that Reg 4(9) and (11) now separate the preserved right in relation to claiming constructive dismissal from the now apparently different right of the employee to treat the contract as having been terminated if a substantial change has been made to working conditions. Previously, Reg 5(5) had bundled these together, which meant that they were seen not as separate rights, but as a single provision aimed simply at preserving the employee's entitlement to claim constructive dismissal if a substantial change was made to his or her employment to his or her detriment as the result of a transfer.

4.110 *Position where employee resigns and objects to transfer.* It was in Humphreys v University of Oxford and anor (above) that the interrelationship between the right to object and the right to claim constructive dismissal by reason of an anticipated repudiation by the transferee was first considered. In essence, the Court of Appeal ruled that the right to claim constructive dismissal based on Reg 5(5) (now Reg 4(11)) survived any objection to the proposed transfer, but that it was the transferor who retained liability in respect of the dismissal.

392

The process of reasoning by which the Court reached this conclusion is fairly complex.

It will be recalled that the employee in that case, H, was an academic with security of tenure. He anticipated that after a relevant transfer there would be several variations to his terms and conditions, including a fundamental change resulting in a shorter tenure. In these circumstances, he objected to the transfer of his employment to the transferee, but also brought a constructive dismissal claim against the transferor. In defending the claim, the transferor conceded that H had formally objected to the transfer and agreed that, in view of Reg 5(4A) (now Reg 4(7)), his employment with it had terminated automatically upon the transfer. However, it denied that H was entitled to claim any damages in respect of the termination, and applied for an order that his claim should be struck out. The transferor's contention centred on the terms of Reg 5(4B) (now Reg 4(8)): it argued that the clear effect of this was to prevent the employee claiming that he had been dismissed 'for any purpose' once he had objected to the transfer of his contract. In other words, an employee who went down the 'objection route' lost the right to claim that the ensuing termination of his employment at the moment of the transfer could be treated for any purpose as a dismissal by the transferor.

4.111 A High Court judge rejected the employer's application to strike out and, on appeal, the Court of Appeal confirmed that he had been right to do so. In its view, H's objection to the transfer had the effect of preventing his contract of employment from automatically passing to the transferee under TUPE. Instead, his contract with the transferor terminated immediately upon the transfer. Since, in those circumstances, the transferee never became his employer, the transferee could not have constructively dismissed him. However, in the Court's view, old Reg 5(5) meant that H's right to claim constructive dismissal against the transferor was preserved. This was because, owing to Reg 5(5), the provision in Reg 5(4B) (now Reg 4(8)) that an employee whose contract terminates following an objection under Reg 5(4A) (now Reg 4(7)) was not to be treated for any purpose as having been dismissed by the transferor, was subject to the right arising 'apart from [the] Regulations' to claim constructive dismissal.

As touched on above, however, the Court made it clear that, in order for the transferor to be regarded as having constructively dismissed the employee by reason of the transferee's anticipated repudiatory breach, the employee's objection to the transfer would have to be one of substance (i.e. a fundamental change in working conditions). If, on the other hand, the employee's objection was merely based on the fact that the identity of his employer was about to change as a result of the imminent transfer, that would not be a repudiatory breach of contract. In these latter circumstances, the employee would simply be left with the legal consequences specified by what is now Reg 4(8) when an objection to the transfer is made – i.e. the relevant transfer would serve

393

automatically to terminate the employee's contract, but he or she would be unable to claim to have been 'dismissed' for any purpose whatsoever.

4.112 In respect of who would be potentially liable for H's constructive dismissal, were his claim to succeed, the Court of Appeal accepted that, before Reg 5(4A) and (4B) were introduced by way of an amendment to the 1981 Regulations, a transferor's liability for a constructive dismissal carried out in connection with the relevant transfer would have passed to the transferee by virtue of Reg 5(2) (now Reg 4(2)) – see Chapter 3, 'What transfers?', under 'Unfair and wrongful dismissal liability – TUPE-related dismissals'. The Court ruled, however, that the effect of Reg 5(4A) and (4B) (now Reg 4(7) and (8)), when read with Reg 5(5) (now Reg 4(11)), was to ensure that, where the employee had objected to the transfer, any liability for the constructive dismissal of that employee would remain with the transferor. In particular, the Court pointed out that where an employee objects to the transfer, what is now Reg 4(7) expressly excludes the comprehensive transfer of rights, obligations and liabilities with regard to the transferring employee's contract, which would otherwise occur under what is now Reg 4(2). It followed that if H had been constructively dismissed by the transferor, any liability would remain with the transferor and not pass across to the transferee. This reasoning of course pre-dated the additional right to resign and complain of detriment on account of a substantial change made to working conditions introduced by the 2006 Regulations and conferred by Reg 4(9) of those Regulations.

Nonetheless, it is submitted that in terms of 'ordinary' constructive dismissal as preserved by Reg 4(11), on the authority of the decision in Humphreys, the analysis above continues to govern the position under the 2006 Regulations. If, for sound reasons, the employee anticipates that the transferee is likely to engage in conduct (such as imposing substantial contractual changes) which would repudiate the contract, and at the same time voices his or her objection to the transfer itself, Reg 4(7) will apply to ensure that the employee's employment is not transferred. Instead, as Reg 4(8) stipulates, the relevant transfer will operate to terminate the contract of employment. And although this same provision makes it clear that such termination will not be regarded as a dismissal for any purpose, the Humphreys ruling drives home the fact that this is 'without prejudice' to the right of the employee enshrined in what is now Reg 4(11) to terminate the contract by reason of a repudiatory breach by the transferor. The Court of Appeal's reasoning as to why the transferor retains liability for the constructive dismissal in these circumstances equally continues to be valid.

4.113 *Position where no objection to transfer accompanies resignation.* The outcome may well be different if an employee claims constructive dismissal prior to a relevant transfer, out of concern about the possible consequences of the transfer, but does not object to the transfer itself within the meaning of Reg 4(7).

In Euro-Die (UK) Ltd v Skidmore and anor (above) an employee, S, who had been anxious not to lose his employment protection rights in the event that his employment was terminated by the transferee, refused to work for the new employer in the absence of an assurance from the transferor that his continuity would be protected. The transferor did not provide this assurance, and S resigned and claimed unfair constructive dismissal against both the transferor and the transferee. A tribunal found that the employee had been constructively dismissed by the transferor and that the transfer was the reason for his dismissal. It held that the dismissal was therefore automatically unfair under Reg 7(1) (discussed at length under 'Automatically unfair dismissal' above) and that liability for the dismissal passed to the transferee by virtue of Reg 4(2) – see Chapter 3, under 'Unfair and wrongful dismissal liability', for details.

The transferee appealed to the EAT. The reasoning of the Appeal Tribunal in **4.114** dismissing the transferee's appeal contained three crucial planks, as follows:

- the transferor's failure to reassure the employee as to his continuity of employment was a fundamental breach of the implied term of trust and confidence entitling him to treat himself as having been constructively dismissed

- the simple fact that he had raised concerns about his continuity of employment did not mean that the employee was to be taken as having objected to becoming employed by the transferee for the purposes of what is now Reg 4(7) such as to prevent the automatic transfer of his contract to the transferee. It was clear that he had no absolute objection to working for the new employer, but had simply declined to do so unless he was given an assurance about the position as to his continuity, and

- the employment tribunal had correctly held that, since the employee's constructive dismissal occurred for a reason connected with the transfer that was not an 'ETO reason', it was automatically unfair under what is now Reg 7(1). Accordingly, liability for unfair constructive dismissal perpetrated by the transferor was transferred to the transferee under what is now Reg 4(2).

As to whether the transferor or the transferee was liable for the constructive dismissal, the EAT was influenced by the fact the transferor's breach consisted not in threatening to change his conditions of employment, or in going ahead with a transfer when the transferee threatened to make such a change, but in failing to reassure the employee that his terms and conditions would be protected by the Regulations following the transfer. Mr Justice Lindsay observed that if the employee's expression of concern in this case had amounted to an absolute objection to the transfer under what is now Reg 4(7), his contract would not have passed to the transferee by virtue of what is now Reg 4(2) and any liability for his constructive dismissal would have remained with the

395

transferor in accordance with the Court of Appeal's ruling in Humphreys v University of Oxford and anor (above).

4.115 **Conclusions and additional points.** Drawing on the above, the following points can be made with regard to an employee's claiming constructive dismissal in anticipation of a repudiatory breach on the part of the transferee employer:

- **Humphreys v University of Oxford and anor** (above), together with Reg 4(11), establishes that an employee who formally objects to a relevant transfer under Reg 4(7) is not precluded from resigning and claiming constructive dismissal. Where a resignation is made in conjunction with an objection to the fact of the transfer itself, however, any constructive dismissal claim will always be against the transferor, even though it may be based on an anticipated breach of contract by the transferee. Furthermore, if such a claim is made out, the transferor will be liable for any damages/ compensation arising from it, as the employee's formal objection will prevent any such liability transferring to the transferee under Reg 4(2). So, if, for example, the transferor employer is insolvent, an employee should avoid formally objecting to the transfer for the purposes of Reg 4(7) if he or she has any designs upon receiving significant compensation for unfair constructive dismissal. In such circumstances, if the employee does not formally object, his or her claim for constructive dismissal is successful and the dismissal is held to be due to the transfer but not for an ETO reason, then the dismissal will be automatically unfair under Reg 7(1), meaning that liability for it will transfer to the transferee under Reg 4(2)

- the rules with regard to which employer – transferor or transferee – will be liable for a pre-transfer constructive dismissal can, at times, yield quirky results. On the one hand, where an employee, owing to his or her anticipating a repudiatory breach by the transferee, both objects to a relevant transfer and successfully claims constructive dismissal, the transferor will be liable for that dismissal through little or no fault of his own (see the Humphreys case). On the other hand, where an employee does not formally object to the transfer but successfully claims unfair constructive dismissal on the back of a failure on the part of the transferor, where the sole or principal reason for such failure is the relevant transfer, liability is likely to pass to the transferee under TUPE, through little or no fault of its own (see Euro-Die (UK) Ltd v Skidmore and anor (above)). This illustrates why it is extremely important that both transferor and transferee consider carefully the nature of the warranties and indemnities that are to be contained in the transfer agreement, under which the parties can essentially decide between themselves who is to bear the liabilities for transfer-connected dismissals. We discuss warranties and indemnities, together with other issues surrounding the transfer agreement, in Chapter 11, 'Practical aspects of transfers'

396

- finally, note that where the anticipated action by the transferee is not sufficient to amount to a repudiatory breach of contract for the purposes of a constructive dismissal claim, the employee might nevertheless be entitled to 'resign' and treat him or herself as dismissed. This is because of the additional protection afforded by Reg 4(9), which takes effect where a relevant transfer involves or would involve a substantial change to a transferring employee's working conditions to his or her material detriment. Such 'material detriment' dismissals are considered under 'Material detriment dismissals' immediately below.

Material detriment dismissals   4.116

Regulation 4(9) of the TUPE Regulations provides that, if a relevant transfer involves or would involve 'a substantial change in working conditions to the material detriment of a person' whose contract of employment is to transfer, 'such an employee may treat the contract of employment as having been terminated, and the employee shall be treated for any purpose as having been dismissed by the employer'.

In this section we explain the background to, and scope and detail of, Reg 4(9), before considering its relationship with the employee's rights to object to a relevant transfer under Reg 4(7), to claim constructive dismissal with reference to Reg 4(11), and to claim unfair dismissal under Reg 7 and the ERA.

Background to introduction of Reg 4(9)   4.117
The first matter that requires consideration is the thinking that lies behind Reg 4(9), since it is substantially different from its predecessor contained in Reg 5(5) of the 1981 Regulations. The old regulation in effect integrated the right to claim constructive dismissal (now separately contained in Reg 4(11) – see 'Constructive dismissals' above) with the right of the employee to terminate his or her contract of employment 'without notice if a substantial change is made in his working conditions to his detriment'.

Position under 1981 Regulations. The origin of what is now Reg 4(9) lies in 4.118
the Acquired Rights Directive, which, in its most up-to-date guise (Directive No.2001/23), stipulates in Article 4(2): 'If the contract of employment or the employment relationship is terminated because the transfer involves a substantial change in working conditions to the detriment of the employee, the employer shall be regarded as having been responsible for termination of the contract of employment or of the employment relationship.' Reg 5(5) of TUPE 1981 was drafted in very similar terms, providing that rules under the Regulations with regard to the automatic transfer of an employee's employment from the transferor to the transferee, and the employee's right to object to the transfer (in respect of both of which, see Chapter 2, 'Who transfers?'), operated 'without prejudice to any right of an employee arising apart from the Regulations

397

to terminate his contract of employment without notice if a substantial change was made in his working conditions to his detriment'. That provision went on to stipulate that 'no such right shall arise by reason only that... the identity of his employer changes unless the employee shows that, in all the circumstances, the change is a significant change and is to his detriment'.

The scope of old Reg 5(5) and the extent to which it gave birth to a new right separate from the right to claim constructive dismissal became the subject of much judicial debate, both domestically and at European level. The main issue was whether the test to be used for interpreting that provision was the same as that used for constructive dismissal, so that there had to be a 'repudiatory breach' by the employer; or whether the provision was to be interpreted less restrictively in that the employee was only required to show a 'substantial change' in his or her working conditions to his or her detriment, so effectively creating another and less stringent test for the purposes of changes implemented to working conditions in a TUPE context.

4.119 In Merckx and anor v Ford Motors Co (Belgium) SA 1997 ICR 352, ECJ, the European Court stated that Article 4(2) of the Directive requires that if the contract of employment is terminated because the transfer involves a substantial change in working conditions to the detriment of the employee (for example, a change in remuneration levels), the employer must be regarded as having been responsible for the termination. This was so even though in that case the employee's pay depended on profit and turnover so that the previous level of income under his employment with the transferor could not be guaranteed – in other words, to use domestic terminology, even though there was not necessarily a repudiatory breach of contract. It seemed for a while that, in the light of Merckx, the courts in the UK had come down in favour of the view that Reg 5(5) provided for something more than merely a consolidation of the right to claim constructive dismissal where either the transferor or the transferee repudiates the contract of employment by changing working conditions to the employee's detriment. In Rossiter v Pendragon plc 2001 ICR 1265, EAT, the Appeal Tribunal concluded that Reg 5(5) had to be interpreted as meaning that, where an employee suffered a substantial change in working conditions to his or her detriment, he or she had the right to claim constructive dismissal even if the employer's actions did not constitute a breach of contract, repudiatory or otherwise. The EAT asserted that such a purposive construction was necessary to give effect to Article 4(2), and was implicit in the ECJ's ruling in Merckx. The EAT also pointed to previous EAT decisions which suggested – albeit tentatively – that a different and less stringent test applied where changes to working conditions were prompted by the transfer of an undertaking compared to the position outside a TUPE situation.

This analysis did not survive, however, when the Rossiter case went to the Court of Appeal, where it was joined with another case, Air Foyle Ltd v Crosby-Clarke.

398

In allowing both appeals – reported as Rossiter v Pendragon plc and another case 2002 ICR 1063, CA – the Court of Appeal was adamant that Reg 5(5) did no more than reiterate the right to claim constructive dismissal on the usual basis. It held that the well-established test for constructive dismissal confirmed in Western Excavating (ECC) Ltd v Sharp 1978 ICR 221, CA (see 'Constructive dismissals' above), applied as much to a case that involves the transfer of an undertaking as it does to a case which does not. In support of that conclusion, Lord Justice Peter Gibson (with whom Jonathan Parker LJ and Sir Christopher Slade agreed) pointed to the particular wording of the regulation in question. Reg 5(5) expressly preserved rights that arose 'apart from these Regulations'. The only right to claim constructive dismissal that arose apart from the 1981 Regulations was the right to terminate the contract 'without notice' in response to an employer's repudiatory breach. If there were to be a right to claim constructive dismissal by reason only of a substantial change in working conditions to the employer's detriment, without there being a breach of contract, that would be a new right arising, not apart from the TUPE Regulations, but by reason of those Regulations. It followed that only conduct by the transferor or transferee amounting to a repudiation of the contract would entitle the employee to terminate the contract and claim constructive dismissal.

In summary, the 1981 Regulations allowed employees to resign and claim **4.120** constructive dismissal if their working conditions were varied to their detriment and that variation amounted to a repudiatory breach. In other words, Reg 5(5) did no more than preserve the common law right to constructive dismissal. A resignation in response to a change which was not so serious as to be repudiatory would not be treated as a constructive dismissal and employees would therefore not have any remedy based on dismissal. That is how the position lay until the enactment of the 2006 Regulations.

Position under 2006 Regulations. As already noted, however, Reg 4(9) of the **4.121** 2006 Regulations now provides that 'where a relevant transfer involves or would involve a substantial change in working conditions to the material detriment of a person whose contract of employment is or would be transferred under [Reg 4(1)]', then 'such an employee may treat the contract of employment as having been terminated, and the employee shall be treated for any purpose as having been dismissed by the employer'. And Reg 4(11) separately provides that the right to object to the transfer (contained in Reg 4(7) and (8)), and the 'automatic transfer of employment' rule in Reg 4(1), 'are without prejudice to any right of an employee arising apart from these Regulations to terminate his contract of employment without notice in acceptance of a repudiatory breach of contract by his employer'. It is immediately apparent that, in contrast to the position under the 1981 Regulations, the 2006 Regulations have separated the provision dealing with substantial changes to working conditions from the employee's right 'arising apart from the Regulations' to resign and claim constructive dismissal.

399

The practical importance of this is that the 2006 Regulations – in line with the Directive and Merckx and anor v Ford Motors Co (Belgium) SA (above) – confers an independent and free-standing right on the employee to resign in the face of a substantial change to working conditions, whether or not this change amounts to a repudiatory breach of contract, and for such resignation to be treated as a dismissal by the employer for all purposes.

4.122 **Scope of right under Reg 4(9)**
The fact that the Reg 4(9) right stands apart from the right of the employee to treat him or herself as 'ordinarily' constructively dismissed indicates that this freestanding right does not require the substantial change to working conditions to amount to a repudiatory breach of contract, or even to a breach of contract at all. All that needs to be shown is that a substantial change has been made to the employee's working conditions causing him or her material detriment.

The clear effect of Reg 4(9), then, is to reverse the Court of Appeal's decision in Rossiter v Pendragon plc and another case 2002 ICR 1063, CA (see 'Background to introduction of Reg 4(9)' above) and to reinstate the position upheld by the EAT in that case – namely, that an employee is entitled to resign and be deemed to have been dismissed where his or her working conditions are substantially changed to his or her detriment irrespective of whether such a change comprises a breach of contract by the employer, repudiatory or otherwise. It is generally accepted that this served to bring the TUPE Regulations back into line with the Acquired Rights Directive, and, in particular, with what Article 4(2) requires. That this was the legislative intention behind Reg 4(9) was expressly acknowledged by the Government in its Public Consultation Document on the draft regulations issued in March 2005.

4.123 The upshot is that the circumstances in which Reg 4(9) can operate are potentially far wider than the normal concept of constructive dismissal. Reg 4(11) continues to give the employee the right to terminate his or her employment without notice in acceptance of the employer's repudiatory breach of contract, but it might prove easier for employees to use the material detriment dismissal provisions, since they entail a less onerous test. However, it will be important to take on board the points made below when considering whether the conditions for claiming a material detriment dismissal under Reg 4(9) have been satisfied.

4.124 **Prerequisites for successful Reg 4(9) claim.** Two conditions have to be satisfied to bring a claim under Reg 4(9): first, the relevant transfer must involve 'a substantial change to working conditions', and secondly, this must be to the 'material detriment of a person whose contract of employment is or would be transferred'. In enacting the 2006 Regulations, the Government took the view that the recasting of these provisions had made it clearer than under the previous 1981 Regulations that the substantial change to working conditions to the employee's material detriment does not necessarily have to be so serious as to amount to a repudiatory breach of contract such as to found a classic case of constructive dismissal.

So far as the first condition is concerned, the question of what amounts to a 'substantial change to working conditions' has been considered by the EAT in two cases: Tapere v South London and Maudsley NHS Trust 2009 ICR 1563, EAT, and Abellio London Ltd (formerly London Travel Ltd) v Musse and ors 2012 IRLR 360, EAT – both of which involved a change in an employee's place of work. The EAT ruled that the phrase 'working conditions' is wider than contractual conditions and therefore is capable of relating to both contractual and physical conditions and that the words are wide enough to cover matters such as a change in the place of work. In Tapere, the EAT held that the transfer of the claimant, who was part of the hospital's procurement team based at Burgess Park, Camberwell, to Bethlem Hospital in Beckenham was a substantial change in working conditions. Similarly in Musse, the EAT upheld the employment tribunal's conclusion that the transferee's requirement that bus drivers change their place of work from Westbourne Park to Battersea was a sufficiently substantial change to come within the scope of Reg 4(9) as it added two hours to the working day in commuting time. This contrasted with the outcome in another case – Cetinsoy and ors v London United Busways Ltd EAT 0042/14 – where the EAT upheld the employment tribunal's conclusion that a change of work location from Westbourne Park to Stamford Brook some 3½ miles away was not sufficient to be 'substantial'.

In relocation cases or cases involving a change in role, it may be relevant to **4.125** consider the terms of any mobility clause that gives the employer the express contractual right to transfer the employee to a different location, or a job flexibility clause that gives the employer the contractual right to change the job role. For different reasons, the mobility clauses in Tapere and Musse were found not to afford the respective employers the contractual right to transfer the employees to a new location but in appropriate cases such as Cetinsoy the existence of such a right may be relevant, though not conclusive. This is reflected in the BIS Guide to the TUPE Regulations, which states that what might constitute a substantial change in working conditions 'will be a matter for the courts and the tribunals to determine in the light of the circumstances of each case. What might be a trivial change in one setting might constitute a substantial change in another. However, a major relocation of the workplace which makes it difficult or much more expensive for an employee to transfer, or the withdrawal of a right to a tenured post, is likely to fall within this definition.' This guidance is supported by the cases referred to above.

Apart from the rulings in Tapere and Musse, the precise parameters of what is meant by 'substantial change to working conditions' is uncertain. Even so, it is clear that the phrase potentially extends to changes to non-contractual terms

401

and conditions. In Merckx and anor v Ford Motors Co (Belgium) SA 1997 ICR 352, ECJ (discussed under 'Background to introduction to Reg 4(9)' above), it will be recalled that this included a change in the employee's amount of remuneration (including a non-contractual bonus scheme). In Nationwide Building Society v Benn and ors 2010 IRLR 922, EAT, the claimants successfully relied on Reg 4(9) when, following the transfer, their job roles and responsibilities were downgraded after they were assimilated into the transferee's existing role structure and the terms of the bonus scheme became less favourable than the scheme operated by the transferor. The EAT confirmed that in these circumstances the employment tribunal had been entitled to conclude that the claimants had been constructively dismissed based either on S.95(1)(c) ERA – which sets out the definition of constructive dismissal for the purposes of claiming unfair dismissal under the ERA – or Reg 4(9).

4.126 So far as the second condition is concerned – showing *'material detriment'* – as previously stated, although the employee may object to the transfer for any reason at all, he or she will only be entitled to rely on the free-standing right to terminate the contract of employment by reason of a substantial change to working conditions falling short of a repudiatory breach if it is shown not just that such a change has been or will be made but also that it is to the employee's material detriment. The effect of the addition of the word 'material' detriment into the phrasing of Reg 4(9) was considered by the EAT in Tapere v South London and Maudsley NHS Trust (above) and Abellio London Ltd (formerly London Travel Ltd) v Musse (above). In both cases it rejected the argument that the issue of 'material' detriment should be considered on an 'objective' basis in the sense of balancing competing arguments of employee and employer and deciding which was the more reasonable. Instead, the correct approach was to consider whether there had been material detriment from the employee's subjective perspective and then should go on to consider whether, objectively, the substantial change was to the disadvantage of the employee. In these cases this entailed considering whether the respective claimants had regarded the change of location as detrimental and, if so, whether that was a reasonable position for them to adopt. The EAT drew an analogy with the approach to 'detriment' in discrimination cases. In Shamoon v Chief Constable of the Royal Ulster Constabulary 2003 ICR 337, HL (a race discrimination case), the House of Lords held that it was unnecessary for a complainant to demonstrate that he or she has suffered some physical or economic consequence in order to prove detriment for the purposes of a race discrimination claim, although an unjustified sense of grievance could not, in their Lordships' view, amount to a 'detriment'.

By holding that 'material detriment' should be interpreted subjectively and in line with Shamoon, the EAT in the Nationwide case has made it relatively easy for an employee to establish a Reg 4(9) dismissal. The focus in such cases is therefore likely to be on the reason for, and fairness of, the dismissal. It is important to remember that, if the principal reason for such a dismissal is the transfer, the dismissal will be automatically unfair under Reg 7(1) – see 'Automatically unfair dismissal' above.

In Tapere, a workplace relocation of just 2½ miles was found to be to the **4.127** claimant's detriment because she lived in Grays in Essex and the change would have materially increased her journey time and affected her childcare arrangements. Similarly in Musse, the relocation was to the material detriment of the bus driver claimants because it added some two hours or more to their journey times.

It should also be noted that, as a result of a change made to Reg 7 by the Collective Redundancies and Transfer of Undertakings (Protection of Employment) (Amendment) Regulations 2014 SI 2014/16, any dismissal – constructive or otherwise – based on the fact that the employee's place of work has changed after a transfer will now be regarded as a 'change in the workforce' for the purposes of the ETO reason – see Reg 7(4A). This amendment applies to any dismissal effective from 31 January 2014 and makes it highly likely that such 'change of workplace' dismissals will not be automatically unfair, but will be regarded as being for 'redundancy' to which the ordinary reasonableness test in S.98(4) ERA will apply to determine the question of fairness. For further details, see 'Dismissals potentially fair for an "ETO" reason – economic, technical or organisational reason' above.

Question of fact. The issue of whether an employee has suffered a substantial **4.128** change to working conditions to his or her material detriment is pre-eminently a question of fact for the employment tribunal to decide having regard to the relevant circumstances of the case. This was confirmed in Europièces SA v Sanders 2001 1 CMLR 25, ECJ, where the European Court stated that it was for the national courts to decide whether the working conditions proposed by the transferee involved or would involve a substantial change to the detriment of the employee. In domestic case law, the EAT has also affirmed that this is the case – see Tapere v South London and Maudsley NHS Trust (above), where His Honour Judge Hand QC stated: 'Whether or not there is a change in working conditions will be a simple question of fact. Whether or not it is a change of substance will also be a question of fact and the employment tribunal will need to consider the nature as well as the degree of the change in order to decide whether it is substantial.'

The following employment tribunal decisions illustrate what amounts to a 'substantial change' to the employee's 'material detriment':

- **Royden and ors v Barnetts Solicitors** ET Case No.2103451/07: the six claimants were employed by LLW, a law firm based in Liverpool. In 2007 they were among 23 staff affected when Barnetts Solicitors (BS) won a £1m contract to provide legal services to the Britannia Building Society, previously held by LLW. The employees worked at LLW's Birkenhead office but, following

403

the transfer, they would have been required to work at BS's Southport office or at the Bradford or Manchester offices of Hammonds, a legal firm that collaborated with Barnetts in fulfilling Brittania work. Southport was the only location to which the claimants would consider relocating but they were reluctant to work there and resigned on 4 June 2007 on the ground that the transfer constituted a substantial change to their working conditions which was to their material detriment. An employment tribunal upheld their claim, concluding that by insisting the employees relocate to its own offices, BS had imposed a substantial and detrimental change to working conditions within the meaning of Reg 4(9) and that the resulting dismissals were unfair

- **Collyer v Boots Opticians Ltd** ET Case No.2602275/08: C's contract of employment with BO Ltd provided that she was entitled to 39 weeks' sick pay, although it also made it clear that the sick pay scheme was discretionary and could be withdrawn at any time. Furthermore, BO Ltd was contractually entitled to withhold sick pay if it thought there were reasons for so doing. In 2008, BO Ltd announced a proposal to transfer the part of its business in which C worked to a new franchise business. When C heard of the proposal she tried to transfer out of the optical side back into the main Boots organisation, where her employment had begun in 1992. Her manager told her that he did not think that she would be allowed to do this as an information pack stated that only those staff for whom a transfer had already been agreed would be allowed to transfer out once a franchise proposal had been announced. The new franchisee proposed that the sick pay scheme be amended to provide for just two weeks' sick pay. When C became aware of this, she lodged a grievance. This was rejected on the day before the transfer and she resigned immediately upon being informed of the outcome of the grievance and claimed unfair dismissal on the basis of Reg 4(9). An employment tribunal held that the change in C's terms of employment was 'substantial' and to her detriment in that, had it not been for the proposed change to the sick pay scheme, she would not have resigned and would instead have transferred to the new organisation. The resulting dismissal was unfair because BO Ltd had failed to show that there was a substantial reason for making the change to the scheme.

4.129 **Change in employer's identity – a substantial change?** There has been a good deal of academic speculation as to the circumstances in which a concern over the changing identity of the employer in a transfer situation might form the basis for an employee claiming a significant change in working conditions to his or her detriment. It is arguable that, if the change in the identity of the employer is materially detrimental to the employee – perhaps where the transferee has a bad reputation in the industry in question – he or she can resign and claim to have been dismissed under Reg 4(9) by reason of a substantial change having been made to his or working conditions, although there is as yet no authority on this point.

Before or after transfer. Regulation 4(9) can apply where the transfer '*involves* **4.130** *or would involve* a substantial change in working conditions' (our stress). This suggests that the employee may rely on Reg 4(9) whether he or she leaves employment before or after the transfer. Any employee who so resigns is deemed to have been dismissed by the employer (i.e. by the transferor or the transferee, depending on whether the effective date of termination is before or after the transfer).

Requirement to give notice? We observed under 'Constructive dismissals' **4.131** above that constructive dismissal is defined in S.95(1)(c) ERA in terms of the employee's right to terminate the contract without notice by reason of the employer's repudiatory conduct. This is the corollary of the employer's right to terminate the contract without notice if the employee repudiates the contract by committing an act of gross misconduct. Just as an act of less serious misconduct does not relieve the employer from the obligation to give full contractual notice before terminating the employee's employment, an employee is not relieved of giving the normal contractual notice before resigning on account of a less serious breach of contract by the employer.

With regard to material detriment – as opposed to constructive – dismissals, Reg 4(9) is silent on the matter of whether the employee should give proper notice before resigning on the basis that the transfer involves or would involve a substantial change to working conditions to his or her detriment. Given that the deemed dismissal is only triggered by the employee's resignation, it is difficult to fathom whether the party who should be giving notice is the employee or the employer. On the one hand, if the employee's resignation is by reason of a substantial change to working conditions that does not amount to a repudiatory breach, the logical position would be that the employee remains obliged to give notice before resigning. On the other hand, this sits uncomfortably with the fact that the resignation is deemed to be a dismissal for all purposes by the employer. Where an employer does the dismissing, it is it (not the employee) who is usually obliged to give notice. Probably the safest view is to assume that an employee is in a position to choose whether to give notice or not before resigning. If, however, he or she gives only partial notice or no notice at all, Reg 4(10) applies to relieve the employer of the obligation to pay wages to the employee in respect of the period of notice not worked. This point is discussed under 'No right to claim damages for lost wages' immediately below.

No right to claim damages for lost wages **4.132**

Regulation 4(10) TUPE stipulates that 'no damages shall be payable by an employer as a result of a dismissal falling within [Reg 4(9)] in respect of any failure by the employer to pay wages to an employee in respect of a notice period which the employee has failed to work'.

405

The effect of this is understandable only in terms of the fact that, where an employee resigns on the ground that a relevant transfer involves or would involve a substantial change in working conditions, such a resignation is deemed to be a dismissal by the employer. Recognising that, normally, an employer would be obliged to give notice before dismissing, Reg 4(10) disentitles the employee from claiming damages for wrongful dismissal in respect of wages not paid during the period of notice in circumstances where the employee chooses not to work out that notice in full or in part. This provision was added only at a late stage in the drafting of the new Regulations, when the Government was persuaded during the public consultation process that it was not right for the employer to be penalised for failing to give notice of termination in a situation where the employee resigned but was treated as having been dismissed by the employer.

4.133 It should be noted that Reg 4(10) speaks of 'any failure by the employer to pay wages'. In the absence of a definition of 'wages', it is arguable that damages for loss of other remunerative benefits (including pension loss, bonuses, profit-related pay and fringe benefits) during the period of notice would be recoverable.

It is not clear, however, whether Reg 4(10) affects compensation for unfair dismissal. In practice, employees who trigger dismissal by resigning within the terms of Reg 4(9) will generally seek to claim unfair dismissal rather than wrongful dismissal. It may be significant that Reg 4(10) states that 'no damages shall be payable', since this could be seen as suggesting that the provision is directed solely at wrongful dismissal claims given that the word 'damages' is usually reserved for the awards payable in respect of claims at common law. However, if 'damages' were to be interpreted more widely to cover any form of monetary compensation, then it is arguable that employment tribunals would have to exclude any unpaid wages for any period of unworked notice from its assessment of the compensatory award for unfair dismissal.

4.134 **Advantages of Reg 4(9) claim over constructive dismissal claim**
As already mentioned, it is apparent that claims based on a Reg 4(9) dismissal can be brought in response to changes to working conditions that fall short of a repudiatory breach of contract. For example, there would be no repudiatory breach of contract (and therefore no basis for a constructive dismissal claim) if an employer changed the place of work in circumstances where the contract contains a mobility clause. But the absence of a repudiatory breach would prove to be no barrier to a Reg 4(9) claim. Employees often regard the circumstances of a transfer as being detrimental, even where the transferor and transferee have fully complied with their legal obligations.

In determining the relative merits and demerits of a constructive dismissal claim and Reg 4(9) material detriment dismissal claim, it is instructive to consider the alleged breaches of contract at issue in the conjoined cases of Rossiter v Pendragon plc and another case 2002 ICR 1063, CA (discussed under 'Background to introduction of Reg 4(9) – position under 1981 Regulations' above). These involved changes to the operation of a commission scheme and changes to a shift pattern and the Court of Appeal found no repudiatory breach of contract in regard to either. Although that was fatal to the claimants' cases of constructive dismissal, it is highly arguable that if these cases were to arise now they would be decided differently in view of the new free-standing right to complain of dismissal where the transfer involves a substantial change to working conditions.

There is also a good case for arguing that a reduction in occupational pension **4.135** benefits following a relevant transfer could be grounds for a Reg 4(9) claim. It is well known that an employee's rights under an occupational pension scheme do not transfer under Reg 4(2) TUPE, save to the extent provided for by the Transfer of Employment (Pension Protection) Regulations 2005 SI 2005/649 – see Chapter 3, 'What transfers?', under 'Occupational pensions'. Furthermore, Reg 10(3) precludes employees from bringing breach of contract or constructive dismissal claims arising out of a loss or reduction in rights under an occupational pension scheme in consequence of a relevant transfer. This exclusion, however, would not appear to apply to claims brought under Reg 4(9), as such claims are not concerned with a breach of contract. There appears to be scope for transferred employees to bring Reg 4(9) claims if the obligations under the Pension Protection Regulations fail to match the pension benefits an employee enjoyed prior to the transfer. That said, just because the employee is treated as having been dismissed after resigning because of a substantial change being made to working conditions does not mean that the dismissal is necessarily unfair. The framework for judging the fairness of Reg 4(9) dismissals is considered under 'Enforcing right to claim unfair dismissal' below.

On the other hand, there are two positive reasons why an employee might wish to claim constructive dismissal in addition to making a claim under Reg 4(9). If a repudiatory breach of contract is made out:

• the employee would be entitled to recover payment of wages in lieu of the unworked notice period. This is not the case in a claim based on Reg 4(9) – see 'No right to claim damages for lost wages' above, and

• the employer might find itself unable to enforce post-termination restrictive covenants. The basic rule is that a repudiatory breach of contract by the employer prevents it from enforcing express clauses in its favour designed to restrict the employee in his or her activities once the contract has ended – see General Billposting v Atkinson 1909 AC 118, HL.

407

4.136 **Interrelationship with right to object**
We saw under 'Constructive dismissals – resignation in anticipation of breach by transferee' above that an employee who objects to a relevant transfer under Reg 4(7) is, in the normal course of events, left high and dry as far as remedies are concerned, because the termination of employment triggered by the objection is not regarded as a dismissal for any purpose – Reg 4(8).

However, Reg 4(8) is expressly made subject to Reg 4(9). This suggests that when Reg 4(9) applies, it overrides Reg 4(8) – meaning that an employee who formally objects to the transfer under Reg 4(7) will be considered dismissed if he or she can show that the transfer would have involved a substantial change in working conditions to his or her detriment. Nevertheless, it would seem (applying the logic of the Court of Appeal in Humphreys v University of Oxford and anor 2000 ICR 405, CA – again, see 'Constructive dismissals – resignation in anticipation of breach by transferee' above) that the employee's Reg 4(7) objection to the transfer has to be respected. The remaining effect of the objection in such circumstances would be to disapply Reg 4(2) – that is, the provision providing for the automatic transfer of the employee's contract and the rights and liabilities arising from it to the transferee. Thus, liability for the dismissal under Reg 4(9) could not transfer under Reg 4(2), meaning that it would be the transferor who retains any liability for it.

4.137 **Enforcing right to claim unfair dismissal**
Regulation 4(9) states that employees who treat the contract as having been terminated in the circumstances covered by that regulation will be treated as if they have been dismissed by the employer even though, technically, they have not. This raises a number of practical and legal uncertainties:

- is the deemed dismissal an 'express' dismissal, a 'constructive' dismissal, or neither?

- do the provisions of Reg 7(1) and (2) dealing with automatically unfair dismissal and ETO reasons for dismissal, discussed at length in this chapter, apply?

Each of these issues will now be discussed in turn.

4.138 **Express or constructive dismissal?** With regard to the type of dismissal that occurs when an employee treats his or her contract as having been terminated by the employer under Reg 4(9), the BIS Guide comments: 'The Regulations merely classify such resignations as "dismissals". This can assist the employee if he subsequently complains [of] unfair dismissal because he does not need to prove he was "dismissed".'

The difficulty left unaddressed by this is that, in order to claim unfair dismissal, the employee has to show that he or she has been 'dismissed' within the terms of the ERA. S.95(1)(a)–(c) of that Act defines three types of dismissal, though only two have any potential relevance for present purposes, namely:

- where 'the contract under which [the employee] is employed is terminated by the employer (whether with or without notice)' – S.95(1)(a) (an express dismissal), and

- where 'the employee terminates the contract... (with or without notice) in circumstances in which he is entitled to terminate it without notice by reason of the employer's conduct' – S.95(1)(c) (a constructive dismissal).

It is by no means clear which of these two types of dismissal applies where an **4.139** employee resigns by reason of a substantial change being made to his or her terms and conditions within the meaning of Reg 4(9).

Given that the resulting dismissal is triggered by the employee's choosing to treat the contract as terminated, it could be argued that the dismissal 'reads' more naturally as a constructive dismissal within S.95(1)(c) rather than an express dismissal under S.95(1)(a). But S.95(1)(c) dismissals are traditionally predicated on the employee's resigning in view of an employer's repudiatory conduct – see 'Constructive dismissals – what is a constructive dismissal?' above. This can be contrasted with the position under Reg 4(9), where the substantial change to working conditions need not entail a repudiatory breach or even a breach of contract at all. Furthermore, S.95(1)(c) speaks of the *employee* terminating the contract. This is not on all fours with Reg 4(9), which provides that the 'employee may treat the contract of employment as having been terminated, and the employee shall be treated for any purpose as *having been dismissed by the employer*' (our stress).

Given the difficulties with regarding a Reg 4(9) 'material detriment' dismissal **4.140** as a constructive dismissal falling within S.95(1)(c) ERA, is it possible to construe such a dismissal as an express dismissal by the employer within S.95(1)(a)? Well, it may be possible, but this would not sit particularly easily with the practical reality of the situation. A decision by an employee to treat his or her contract as having been terminated, for all that it may be deemed to be a dismissal by the employer, is not self-evidently an express dismissal by the employer. Rather, the dismissal is a legal construct over which the employer can hardly be said to have much effective control.

Having said that, a slight alteration to Reg 4(9) would, it seems, be enough to bring such a dismissal within S.95(1)(a). Reg 4(9) states that 'where a relevant transfer involves or would involve a substantial change in working conditions [the employee] may treat the contract of employment as having been terminated, and the employee shall be treated for any purpose as having been dismissed by the employer'. If this were to be read as though an additional comma were inserted after the word 'dismissed – so that it read 'as having been terminated, and the employee shall be treated for any purpose as having been dismissed, by

409

the employer' – it would become clear that the employee could treat the contract as having *been terminated by the employer*. This is exactly the phrase used in the definition of express dismissal in S.95(1)(a).

4.141 A third option would be that, given the 'hybrid' characteristics of a Reg 4(9) dismissal, it may be that tribunals will come to regard this as a new form of statutory dismissal rather than a constructive or express dismissal in the traditional sense. But this would be problematic to employees seeking to bring claims of unfair dismissal under Part X of the ERA, since such claims can only be brought if the employee has been dismissed on one of the bases set out in S.95(1)(a)–(c). It would be expected that tribunals would want to avoid such an outcome since it would clearly be contrary to the legislative intention behind Reg 4(9).

On balance, the stance generally adopted by most legal commentators is that the deemed dismissal provided for by Reg 4(9) is a 'quasi-constructive' dismissal, falling within S.95(1)(c) ERA. This may well be right, but, as we have explained, the language of S.95(1)(c) would need to be stretched somewhat to permit the employee to claim unfair dismissal on that basis.

4.142 **Assessing fairness or unfairness of Reg 4(9) dismissal.** The BIS Guide poses the questions (i) whether it is unlawful for the employer to make substantial changes in working conditions, and (ii) whether it is automatically unfair when an employee resigns because such a change has taken place. In answering 'no' to both these questions, the Guide states that 'to determine whether the dismissal was unfair, the tribunal will still need to satisfy itself that the employer had acted unreasonably, and there is no presumption that it is unreasonable for the employer to make changes'.

There is nothing in the TUPE Regulations to suggest that the rules in Reg 7(1) and (2) dealing specifically with the unfairness of TUPE-connected dismissals – discussed at length in this chapter – do not apply to a Reg 4(9) 'material detriment' dismissal just as much as they apply to express or 'ordinary' constructive dismissals. So, for example, in Nationwide Building Society v Benn and ors 2010 IRLR 922, EAT, the EAT remitted the case to the employment tribunal to consider whether material detriment dismissals which, contrary to the decision of the tribunal, were held to be for an ETO reason, were fair or unfair when judged by the reasonableness test for unfair dismissal set out in S.98(4) ERA.

4.143 It should also be noted that in both Tapere v South London and Maudsley NHS Trust 2009 ICR 1563, EAT, and Abellio London Ltd (formerly London Travel Ltd) v Musse and ors 2012 IRLR 360, EAT, Reg 4(9) unfair dismissal claims arose out of a change in the respective claimants' place of work and these were upheld because the changes of location were found to constitute a substantial change to working conditions to the respective claimants' material detriment.

However, in view of the insertion of Reg 7(3A) into the 2006 Regulations – explained in the section 'Dismissals potentially fair for an "ETO" reason – entailing changes in the workforce' above, under 'Meaning of "changes in the workforce" – change of work location' – it would now be open to the employer to argue that the change in location amounted to an ETO reason and therefore was a potentially fair reason for dismissal on the basis of either redundancy or reorganisation. Nonetheless, the problem for employers is that in many such cases the sole or principal reason for a Reg 4(9) dismissal will be the transfer itself rather than an ETO reason. So, unless the reason for the Reg 4(9) dismissal is found to be entirely unconnected to the transfer or, if transfer-connected, for an ETO reason, the dismissal will be automatically unfair in any event.

Who is liable? It is important to consider whether it would be the transferor or transferee who incurs liability if the employee resigns on the basis of changes in working conditions within the meaning of Reg 4(9).   4.144

Regulation 4(9) states that where a relevant transfer involves or would involve substantial changes to the employee's material detriment, the employee may treat the contract as having been terminated and the employee will be treated as having been dismissed 'by the employer'. The employer in question will, we suggest, be the transferor where the effective date of termination occurs before the transfer takes place, and the transferee where the relevant date falls after the transfer. Subject to what is said below, it is submitted that liability for a pre-transfer dismissal would pass to the transferee in any event under Reg 4(2) and (3) (for details, see Chapter 3, 'What transfers?', under 'Unfair and wrongful dismissal liability') if, as is often likely to be the case, the dismissal is shown to be solely or principally by reason of the transfer under Reg 7(1) – see 'Automatically unfair dismissal' above.

This is subject to a single but important caveat. If an employee formally objects to the transfer, then, as we have seen above, Reg 4(7) operates to preclude the contract of employment and the rights, powers, duties and liabilities under or in connection with it from transferring to the transferee. Thus, where an employee objects formally to the transfer under Reg 4(7) as well as successfully claiming material detriment dismissal under Reg 4(9), liability in these circumstances would not be transferred, but would remain with the transferor.   4.145

Which employer will be liable?   4.146

We finish this chapter by taking a brief look at which employer – transferor or transferee – will be liable for various types of dismissal taking place around the time of, or as a result of, a relevant transfer. This topic is dealt with in more detail in Chapter 3, 'What transfers?', under 'Unfair and wrongful dismissal liability'. To summarise the basic principles:

411

- Reg 4(1) provides that the contract of any person employed by the transferor and assigned to the organised grouping of resources or employees that is subject to the relevant transfer shall have effect after the transfer as if originally made between the person so employed and the transferee. That is, except where the employee in question objects to the transfer in accordance with Reg 4(7)

- all the transferor's rights, powers, duties and liabilities in connection with a transferring contract – including, that is, unfair dismissal liability – will transfer to the transferee

- however, a contract, and liabilities in respect of it, will only transfer under the above rules if the employee in question is employed by the transferor and assigned to the transferring organised grouping *immediately before the transfer*, or would have been so employed *if he had not been dismissed in the circumstances described in Reg 7(1)* – Reg 4(3).

4.147 Where an employee is dismissed by the transferor prior to a relevant transfer, he or she will clearly not be employed by the transferor immediately before the transfer but Reg 4(1)–(3) will nevertheless apply to transfer liability for the dismissal to the transferee if the dismissal was carried out *in the circumstances described in Reg 7(1)*. That is, as we have seen in this chapter, where the dismissal is automatically unfair owing to the sole or principal reason for it being the relevant transfer. Put another way, the transferee will (almost) always be liable for dismissals rendered automatically unfair by Reg 7(1).

The only occasion when this will not be the case is where the automatically unfair dismissal is initiated by the employee – i.e. the employee resigns in the circumstances envisaged by Reg 4(11) (see 'Constructive dismissals' above) or Reg 4(9) (see 'Material detriment dismissals' above), *and* the employee raises an objection to the relevant transfer under Reg 4(7). In such circumstances, the effect of the employee's objection is to disapply the rules in Reg 4 with regard to the transfer of liability to the transferee. In these particular circumstances, residual liability for the Reg 7(1) automatically unfair dismissal will remain with the transferor – see Humphreys v University of Oxford and anor 2000 ICR 405, CA.

4.148 The following general propositions can be made with regard to *pre-transfer* dismissals:

- if the reason for the dismissal is the relevant transfer itself, then the dismissal will be automatically unfair under Reg 7(1) (see 'Automatically unfair dismissal' above) and, owing to Reg 4(1)–(3), liability for the dismissal will pass to the transferee. That is, unless the dismissal was a Reg 4(9) material detriment dismissal or a Reg 4(11) constructive dismissal *and* the employee objected to the transfer within the meaning of Reg 4(7)

- if the sole or principal reason for the dismissal is an ETO reason entailing changes in the workforce, the dismissal will not be automatically unfair under Reg 7(1). In these circumstances, liability for the dismissal (which might be unfair under the reasonableness test set out in S.98(4) ERA) will not pass to the transferee – see, for example, Thompson v SCS Consulting Ltd and ors EAT 0034/00, and

- if the dismissal is unconnected with a relevant transfer – for example, a gross misconduct dismissal which would have occurred whether or not a transfer was on the horizon – the Regulations will have no impact, and liability for the dismissal will remain with the transferor.

Dismissal of employee retained by transferor. What happens if an employee 4.149 claims that he was assigned to the undertaking that was sold and should therefore have transferred to the transferee but he was retained by the transferor and was made redundant a few months after the transfer? Who is liable in such a scenario and when does the limitation period start to run?

We would suggest that the answer to this tricky scenario lies in who has dismissed (or is deemed to have dismissed) the employee. If the employee claims that he should have transferred to the transferee on or after the date of the transfer and the transferee refuses to accept the novation of the employee's contract, then there would be an automatic unfair dismissal claim under Reg 7(1) against the transferee – in which case the claim would have to be brought against the transferee within three months of the date of the transfer. If, however, the employee remains employed by the transferor and is made redundant several months after the transfer, he or she could still potentially make a Reg 7(1) claim against the transferor – such a claim would have to be brought against the transferor within three months of the dismissal (not the date of the transfer). If the unfair dismissal claim against the transferor is successful, it is possible that liability would pass to the transferee under Reg 4(2)(a).

Given these complexities, the transferor and the transferee should always be 4.150 fully aware of any potential liabilities regarding redundancy and unfair dismissal, and consider carefully what warranties and indemnities – which essentially allow the parties to decide who is to bear the costs of liabilities for dismissals connected with the transfer – should be included in the transfer agreement, although this may not be possible in service provision change cases as the new and old contractors are likely to be commercial rivals. The practical issues that the parties involved in a TUPE transfer need to bear in mind are discussed at some length in Chapter 11, 'Practical aspects of transfers'.

5 Changing terms and conditions

It is a basic principle of employment law that an employer can only change a **5.1** contract of employment with the agreement of the employee. Any attempt by an employer to impose a unilateral variation of a fundamental term of a contract would constitute a repudiatory breach entitling the employee to resign and claim constructive dismissal. Even outside the context of a relevant transfer, it is therefore often difficult to change terms and conditions. Given that the purpose of the Transfer of Undertakings (Protection of Employment) Regulations 2006 SI 2006/246 (TUPE) is to protect the rights of employees on a relevant transfer, it is not surprising that transferors and transferees face even greater legal and practical difficulties when seeking to make changes to contracts of employment.

As we have seen in Chapter 2, 'Who transfers?' and Chapter 3, 'What transfers?', employees are protected on a transfer mainly by Reg 4(1) and (2), under which the new employer takes over the employment contracts of all those employed or deemed to be employed immediately before the transfer. The transferee assumes all the rights, powers, duties and liabilities which the transferor had under those contracts and is bound by their terms and conditions as if he were the original employer. This raises the question of whether a transferee can seek to vary the terms and conditions of transferred employees. Although the EU Acquired Rights Directive (No.2001/23) ('the Acquired Rights Directive') does not contain any express provisions relating to changing terms and conditions, it is now well established through case law at both European and domestic level that changes made by reason of the transfer are, for the most part, invalid.

The 2006 Regulations sought to codify this case law by introducing specific **5.2** provision outlining when a contractual variation is prohibited by TUPE, and conversely when such a variation is permitted. These rules were amended by the Collective Redundancies and Transfer of Undertakings (Protection of Employment) (Amendment) Regulations 2014 SI 2014/16 ('the Amendment Regulations'), in relation to all *transfers* occurring on or after 31 January 2014.

415

Knowledge of the old rules cannot be entirely discarded, however, as they still apply to contractual changes in relation to any transfers that took place before that date, and to Northern Ireland. Furthermore, given the limited room for manoeuvre granted by ECJ case law, it may well turn out to be the case that the new rules are interpreted in much the same way as their predecessors.

In this chapter we discuss the basic employment law principles relevant to changing terms and conditions; the types of change to terms and conditions that are permitted under the TUPE Regulations; and the practical considerations that surround this issue.

5.3 Varying terms outside a TUPE context

A contract of employment consists of all the terms and conditions under which the employee works, whether written, oral or implied. Occasionally, a power may be expressed in the contract itself for the employer unilaterally to make (usually minor) changes in terms and conditions (i.e. without the need for the employee's consent). The effect of such a power in the context of a TUPE transfer is considered below under 'Types of change permitted by TUPE – contractual right to vary'.

More commonly, however, the contract will contain no power of variation. In such circumstances, the most straightforward way to vary the contract is to reach agreement with the employee.

5.4 Options if employees refuse to consent to contractual changes

If the desired contractual change cannot be agreed, the employer has three main options:

- to continue seeking the employee's agreement to the change (possibly in return for a financial or other incentive). If the employee continues to work under the new terms and conditions without protest he or she may be deemed to have accepted the change

- to unilaterally impose the required variation and run the risk of breach of contract and/or unfair constructive dismissal claims (see below); or

- to terminate existing contracts by giving contractual notice and combine this with an offer of re-engagement on the revised terms and conditions to come into effect on the day after the old contract expires. In these circumstances, there will be no breach of contract as proper notice has been given. However, the termination of the existing contract may be an unfair dismissal unless the employer can show that the principal reason for dismissal was the potentially fair reason of 'some other substantial reason of a kind such as to justify the dismissal of an employee holding the position which the employee held'. For example, there may be a pressing commercial reason for the changes. In order to be 'fair', the employer would also have had to follow a proper procedure at the very least, and will also have to show that the decision to require changes to the employee's terms was a reasonable one in all the circumstances of the particular case.

The unilateral imposition of a substantial detrimental change to terms and conditions and/or the failure to follow a proper procedure when seeking to reach agreement on new terms may amount to a repudiatory breach of contract entitling the employee to resign and sue in a civil action for wrongful dismissal. Alternatively, so long as the sum claimed for breach of contract does not exceed £25,000 and arises from, or is outstanding on, the termination of employment, the employee is entitled to bring such a claim in the employment tribunal. Damages for wrongful dismissal would usually be limited to the salary and value of remunerative benefits that the employee would have received had he or she been given proper contractual notice. In addition, if the employee has the necessary qualifying service, he or she might choose to bring a complaint of unfair constructive dismissal in the employment tribunal. If such a claim succeeds, the remedy of reinstatement is potentially available, although in practice this is rarely ordered by the tribunal. Any compensation would consist of a basic award calculated according to a set formula equivalent to a statutory redundancy payment and a compensatory award of up to £78,335 or a year's pay (whichever is the lower) based on the employee's proven financial losses.

Constructive dismissal and breach of contract 5.5

A constructive dismissal situation can arise if an employer engages in conduct that is a fundamental (or 'repudiatory') breach of the contract of employment, or which indicates that he no longer intends to be bound by one or more of the contract's essential terms – see Western Excavating (ECC) Ltd v Sharp 1978 ICR 221, CA. Whether the breach of contract by the employer is so significant that it is capable of amounting to a repudiation will depend on the precise facts. Common examples include unilaterally reducing pay or status, changing job function or duties, or withdrawing a significant contractual benefit. In the face of such conduct, the employee is entitled to accept the fundamental breach by resigning from his or her employment with or without notice. In these circumstances he or she is treated as having been constructively dismissed for both common law and statutory purposes, and can therefore claim against his or her employer for breach of contract and, provided there is sufficiently continuous service, unfair dismissal.

The employee does not necessarily have to resign his or her employment to take legal action in respect of a repudiatory breach. One option is to remain in employment and sue in the civil courts for breach of contract or, in a case where the breach in question relates to pay, to bring an employment tribunal claim for unlawful deduction from wages under Part 1 of the Employment Rights Act 1996 (ERA). The availability of this option was confirmed by the House of

417

Lords in Rigby v Ferodo Ltd 1988 ICR 29, HL. If, however, the employee remains in employment after the repudiatory conduct, there is an ever-present risk that he or she will be found to have affirmed the contractual change, with the consequence that the right to bring legal proceedings for constructive dismissal or breach of contract may be lost. For this reason, such an employee is always best advised to signal in the clearest possible terms his or her continuing protest against the breach and to bring legal action at the earliest opportunity.

Note that a more detailed discussion of changing terms and conditions and constructive dismissal can be found in IDS Employment Law Handbook, 'Contracts of Employment' (2014), Chapter 9, 'Variation of contract', and Chapter 11, 'Termination by dismissal', under 'Constructive dismissal'.

5.6 Varying terms in a TUPE context

When variations to an employee's contract of employment are effected by reason of a relevant transfer or for a reason connected to the transfer, the law governing the ability of the employer to enforce such variations is fundamentally affected. Given the complexity of this area, we summarise below the main relevant provisions of TUPE in this regard:

- changes to terms and conditions that are entirely unrelated to a TUPE transfer will not fall within the Regulations, and will instead be dealt with according to the principles outlined above under 'Varying terms outside a TUPE context'

- subject to Reg 4(5), (5A) and (5B) below, any variation of a transferred contract of employment will be void if the sole or principal reason for that variation is the transfer (Reg 4(4))

- even if it is made by reason of the transfer, a variation will not be void where the sole or principal reason for the variation is an economic, technical or organisational reason entailing changes in the workforce, and the variation has been agreed with the employee (Reg 4(5)(a))

- similarly, an employer is not prevented from making a change to terms and conditions, even if by reason of the transfer, if the terms of the contract permit it to make the change (Reg 4(5)(b))

- an employer can vary a term or condition incorporated from a collective agreement, even if the sole or principal reason for the variation is the transfer, provided that (a) the variation takes effect more than a year after the transfer and (b) following the variation, the employee's contract is overall no less favourable to the employee than it was before (Reg 4(5B))

- if a relevant transfer involves or would involve a substantial change in working conditions to an employee's material detriment, he or she is entitled

418

to resign on notice and claim breach of contract or, if he or she has sufficient continuous service, unfair dismissal (Reg 4(9)). However, the employer does not have to pay the employee his or her wages for any period of notice in respect of which the employee fails to work (Reg 4(10))

- nothing in the Regulations affects the employee's general right to resign without notice in response to a repudiatory breach of contract by the employer (i.e. constructive dismissal) (Reg 4(11)); and

- a constructive dismissal or a material detriment dismissal will be automatically unfair if it is found to be by reason of the transfer (Reg 7).

The remedies alluded to above in relation to constructive dismissal and material **5.7** detriment dismissal claims are discussed only in outline below. Full details are given in Chapter 4, 'Unfair dismissal'.

Before examining the variations that are currently prohibited by the TUPE Regulations, it is necessary first to consider the case law and legislation that has led us to this point. As shall become apparent below, this is of more than academic interest to the current provisions – it provides the starting point for, and the boundaries of, their interpretation. We begin by discussing the position under the Acquired Rights Directive.

Position under Acquired Rights Directive 5.8
In Chapter 4 'Unfair dismissal', we saw how Article 4(1) of the Acquired Rights Directive establishes that a transfer of an undertaking 'shall not in itself constitute grounds for dismissal by the transferor or the transferee'. Although it is explicit in prohibiting dismissals by reason of a transfer, the wording of the Directive says nothing about the circumstances in which a transferor or transferee can change the terms and conditions of employees involved in a relevant transfer. Instead, Article 3(1) merely establishes that 'the transferor's rights and obligations arising from a contract of employment or from an employment relationship existing on the date of a transfer within the meaning of Article 1(1) shall, by reason of such transfer, be transferred to the transferee'. Nevertheless, the interpretation given to the Directive by the European Court of Justice demonstrates that there are limits to the types of contractual variation that can be made following a transfer of an undertaking.

The leading case in this regard is Foreningen af Arbejdsledere i Danmark v Daddy's Dance Hall A/S 1988 IRLR 315, ECJ, in which the European Court held that the provisions of the Directive protecting workers' terms and conditions of employment could not be waived by the workers whom they are intended to benefit. This was so even if the disadvantages resulting from the waiver were offset by benefits which, taken together, meant that the worker was not worse off overall. The Court, however, stressed that the objective of the Directive is to achieve only partial harmonisation across EU Member States in respect of the

419

protections accorded to workers on the transfer of an undertaking. Thus, the Directive could be relied upon to ensure that the employee is protected in his relations with the transferee only to the same extent as he or she was in his or her relations with the transferor under the legal rules of the Member State concerned. This meant that if relevant national law allowed the transferor to change terms and conditions in situations other than a transfer of an undertaking, the Directive did not preclude such a change. But this was subject to the rule 'that the transfer of the undertaking itself may never constitute the reason for [the variation]'. The transferee could therefore change terms and conditions for reasons other than the transfer to the extent that the transferor could do likewise under the rules of national law, but the transferee was not entitled to bring about variations to the contract that were prompted by the transfer.

5.9 A similar refrain was taken up by the European Court in Rask and anor v ISS Kantineservice A/S 1993 IRLR 133, ECJ, where it again confirmed that terms and conditions may be altered on a transfer only in so far as national law permits variations in contractual terms outside the context of a transfer, and always subject to the rule that the transfer itself cannot be grounds for such a change. The rationale for the restriction on the transferee's ability to effect changes to a transferred employee's terms and conditions was explained in Langeland v Norske Fabricom A/S 1997 2 CMLR 966, EFTA – a decision of the Court set up to deal with European Free Trade Association disputes. The Court explained that: 'The purpose of the [Acquired Rights] Directive is to ensure that the rights arising from a contract of employment or employment relationship of employees affected by the transfer of an undertaking are safeguarded. Since this protection is a matter of public policy, and therefore independent of the will of the parties to the contract of employment, the rules of the Directive must be considered to be mandatory, so that it is not possible to derogate from them in a manner unfavourable to employees. It follows that employees are not entitled to waive the rights conferred on them by the Directive and that those rights cannot be restricted even with their consent. This interpretation is not affected by whether the employee obtains new benefits in compensation for the disadvantages resulting from an amendment to his contract of employment so that, taking the matter as a whole, he is not placed in a worse position than before.'

The later decision of the ECJ in Martin and ors v South Bank University 2004 ICR 1234, ECJ, is particularly important, because it suggests that changes will be connected to the transfer – and therefore prohibited – if they have no goal beyond harmonisation of transferred employees' terms with those of the transferee's existing workforce. In that case, M and his fellow claimants were lecturers at an NHS nursing college, employed under terms incorporated from a collective agreement. They became employees of the University following a TUPE-transfer in 1994. When, three years later, the University offered them early retirement on terms which were less favourable than those which they had enjoyed as NHS employees, the claimants argued that TUPE entitled them to the benefit of the NHS terms. An employment tribunal – not having the benefit of any specific provision in the then-extant TUPE Regulations to guide it – referred the matter to the ECJ, seeking clarification, among other things, on the extent to which an employer can seek to harmonise terms and conditions. The European Court explained that Article 3 precludes a transferee from offering transferred employees less favourable contractual terms than those they had enjoyed prior to the transfer, and precludes the transferred employees from accepting such terms. Where – as in the instant case – a transferee merely seeks to bring the terms on which it offers early retirement to transferred employees into line with those previously offered to its other employees, the alteration of terms is connected to the transfer and is therefore precluded by Article 3.

In the absence of any specific provision in the Acquired Rights Directive dealing with changes to terms and conditions, it is useful to summarise the principles that have developed in case law: **5.10**

- the Directive does not stand in the way of contractual changes that would be permitted under national law

- this is subject to the proviso that a transfer of an undertaking can never constitute the reason for a contractual variation

- simple harmonisation of terms and conditions with those of the transferee's existing workforce will be regarded as being connected to the transfer and therefore precluded by the Directive, and

- an employee cannot agree to waive his or her acquired rights under the Directive.

Position under TUPE prior to January 2014 **5.11**

In common with the position under the Acquired Rights Directive, the 1981 TUPE Regulations did not include any provisions relating to pre- or post-transfer changes to terms and conditions. However, the decision in Foreningen af Arbejdsledere i Danmark v Daddy's Dance Hall A/S 1988 IRLR 315, ECJ (discussed under 'Position under Acquired Rights Directive' above), was binding on courts in the UK, and was read into domestic law following the obiter comments of the House of Lords in (1) British Fuels Ltd v Baxendale and anor (2) Wilson and ors v St Helens Borough Council 1998 ICR 1141, HL. Prior to this case it was assumed that employers could agree changes with employees on a relevant transfer in accordance with normal contractual principles (see 'Varying terms outside a TUPE context' above). However, the House of Lords in the British Fuels/Wilson cases considered that, even if employees agreed to new terms and conditions on a transfer, they could subsequently reject these and rely on the previous terms as against the new

421

employer. This did not mean that all variations of contractual terms and conditions – whether made at the time of transfer or afterwards – were void: a variation may be prompted for a reason or reasons entirely unconnected to the transfer, in which case it would be valid and enforceable by the transferee, provided it satisfied the normal principles for effecting a lawful variation of contract. The crucial question was whether the transfer was the sole or principal reason for the variation. If it was, then irrespective of whether it was agreed before, at the time of, or after the transfer, it would be void.

Lord Slynn, who gave the leading speech in the British Fuels/Wilson cases, acknowledged that it may sometimes be difficult to determine whether a particular variation is due to the transfer or is attributable to some separate cause, particularly in the case where the variation occurs some time after the date of the transfer. Interestingly, in view of changes introduced by the 2006 TUPE Regulations, his Lordship drew an analogy with the provision in what was then Reg 8(2) of the TUPE Regulations 1981. This provided that where the reason for dismissal, although connected to the transfer, comprised an 'economic, technical or organisational reason entailing a change in the workforce', the dismissal would not be automatically unfair, but rather would be judged according to the normal reasonableness test set out in S.98(4) ERA. Lord Slynn implied that where such an ETO reason prompted a variation of contract, tribunals would be justified in holding that the variation was not caused by the transfer and that accordingly it would not be void.

5.12 In the absence of any statutory provisions, the approach of courts and tribunals was to look for a causal link between the transfer and the variation. In Crédit Suisse First Boston (Europe) Ltd v Padiachy and ors 1998 ICR 569, QBD, three employees entered into restrictive covenants with the transferee, including a three-month non-competition clause. However, the employees resigned to join a competitor in breach of the clause. Even though the employees had received substantial financial inducements to agree to the changes, a High Court judge held that the transferee's attempt to enforce the restrictions failed because the change was in connection with the transfer. In so concluding, the judge specifically relied on the ECJ's ruling in the Daddy's Dance Hall case to the effect that the transfer of an undertaking may not constitute the reason for the variation of a transferred employee's contract of employment.

Similarly, in Crédit Suisse First Boston (Europe) Ltd v Lister 1999 ICR 794, CA, an employee entered into a fresh restrictive covenant after the transfer of a business in return for receiving a retention award of £625,000 in the form of phantom shares and a payment of £2,000 in consideration of agreeing to the new terms. However, the employee sought to leave to work for a competitor, whereupon the transferee brought legal proceedings relying on the restrictive covenant in an attempt to prevent him from doing so. A High Court judge refused to grant an interlocutory injunction and, on appeal, the Court of Appeal upheld that decision. In its view the judge had correctly concluded that the covenant was unenforceable in that the variation of the employee's terms and conditions resulting in the inclusion of the covenant occurred solely or principally by reason of the relevant transfer. This was so notwithstanding the fact that, on a fair view of the contract as a whole, the employee was better off by comparison with his terms and conditions under the transferor.

The basic position under the 1981 Regulations was that changes by reason of **5.13** the transfer were void, even if the employees had agreed to it and even if they were in a better position when their new terms of employment were considered as a whole. Changes unconnected with the transfer, on the other hand, would be permissible provided they complied with the normal rules governing variation of contract. That basic position was carried forward into Reg 4 of the 2006 Regulations.

The 2006 Regulations. Prior to its amendment in January 2014 (as to which, **5.14** see 'Changes made in January 2014' below), Reg 4(4) provided that, subject to the insolvency provisions in Reg 9, any purported variation of a contract that 'is or will be transferred' by Reg 4(1) 'shall be void if the sole or principal reason for the variation is – (a) the transfer itself; or (b) a reason connected to the transfer that is not an economic, technical or organisational reason entailing changes in the workforce'.

Old Reg 4(5) explained the types of variation that were permitted. TUPE would not stand in the way of a variation where the sole or principal reason for it was (a) a reason connected with the transfer which was an economic, technical or organisational reason entailing changes in the workforce or (b) a reason unconnected with the transfer.

The Collective Redundancies and Transfer of Undertakings (Protection of **5.15** Employment) (Amendment) Regulations 2014 SI 2014/16 introduced entirely recast versions of the above provisions which now apply in England, Wales and Scotland. However, the original versions of Reg 4(4) and (5) continue to apply in Northern Ireland. Furthermore, they may still apply to some cases in Great Britain. This is because Reg 6(2) of the Amendment Regulations provides that the new provisions will only apply where '(a) the TUPE transfer takes place on or after 31st January 2014, and (b) that purported variation is agreed on or after 31st January 2014, or, in a case where the variation is not agreed, it starts to have effect on or after that date'. We now turn to outline the provisions that apply from 31 January 2014 onwards.

Changes made in January 2014   5.16
Following its amendment by the Amendment Regulations, Reg 4(4) now states: 'Subject to [Reg 9], any purported variation of a contract of employment that is, or will be, transferred by [Reg 4(1)], is void if the sole or principal reason for the variation is the transfer.'

423

Thus, there is no longer any mention of transfer-connected variations in Reg 4(4). The Government's thinking on this change was set out in its response to the public consultation that preceded the Amendment Regulations. There, it stated: 'Arguably the present wording of the Regulations goes further than the Directive. In order to reduce any risks that the Regulations are interpreted more widely than what is required by the Directive, the Government will amend Regulation 4 to reflect the wording used in the Directive and [ECJ] case law.' Thus, the Government was hoping that a change in wording might lead to greater scope to change terms and conditions. However, the Government appears to have been misinformed, as the Acquired Rights Directive itself has no wording relating to changes to terms and conditions (see 'Position under Acquired Rights Directive' above). Rather, this is an area where the full meaning of the Directive, and the minimum standards it sets down, must be gleaned from the case law. It might be thought at first glance that 'the transfer itself' under old Reg 4(4)(a) and 'the transfer' under new Reg 4(4) are synonymous, and that the limitation on transfer-related variations has therefore been reined in. However, the BIS Guide 'Employment rights on the transfer of an undertaking' ('the BIS Guide') (January 2014) indicates that Reg 4(4) sets down a new test, and since this test implements the UK's obligations under the Directive, it has to be interpreted in line with the ECJ case law. That case law precludes a narrow interpretation of 'the transfer', so if there is any increase in the scope to make variations to terms and conditions, it will be marginal. This is a point we explore further under 'Changes prohibited by Reg 4(4) – are transfer-connected changes still prohibited?' below.

5.17 Regulation 4(4) must be read in conjunction with new Reg 4(5), which provides that Reg 4(4) 'does not prevent a variation of the contract of employment if (a) the sole or principal reason for the variation is an economic, technical, or organisational reason entailing changes in the workforce, provided that the employer and employee agree that variation; or (b) the terms of that contract permit the employer to make such a variation'. The first limb of this provision has merely dropped the words 'a reason connected with the transfer', in keeping with the removal of these words from Reg 4(4). Reg 4(5)(a) is, however, augmented by new Reg 4(5A), which stipulates that 'the expression "changes in the workforce" includes a change to the place where employees are employed by the employer to carry on the business of the employer or to carry out work of a particular kind for the employer' and that the reference to such a place has the same meaning as in the definition of redundancy under S.139 of the Employment Rights Act 1996.

Regulation 4(5)(b) bears no relation to its predecessor, which had stipulated that TUPE did not stand in the way of changes which were 'unconnected with the transfer'. (See 'Types of change permitted by TUPE – changes unrelated to the transfer' below for an explanation of why such changes remain permissible.) The new formulation of this provision – that TUPE 'does not prevent a variation if… the terms of that contract permit the employer to make such a variation' – is merely a clarification of the effect of Reg 4(2), which provides that all rights, obligations and duties arising under the employment relationship will transfer. It does, however, remain unclear whether EU law would permit an employer to exercise a flexibility clause where the reason for doing so is the transfer, or for that matter allow a transferor employer to agree a flexibility clause with employees in contemplation of a future TUPE-transfer. These are points we return to under 'Types of change permitted by TUPE – contractual right to vary' below.

The other entirely new provision is Reg 4(5B). This disapplies the Reg 4(4) restriction in respect of variations that apply to a term or condition incorporated from a collective agreement, provided that (a) the variation takes effect more than a year after the transfer and (b) following the variation, the employee's contract is overall no less favourable to the employee than it was before. This new provision is clearly compatible with the Directive, as changes of this type are permitted by Article 3(3). We discuss this provision below under 'Types of change permitted by TUPE – terms derived from collective agreement'.

Changes prohibited by Reg 4(4)   5.18

As we saw under 'Changes made in January 2014' above, Reg 4(4) of the 2006 Regulations now provides that a variation of contract will be void if the sole or principal reason is 'the transfer'. This statutory wording is relatively recent, having come into force on 31 January 2014 in respect of transfers occurring on or after that date. As a result, there has been no appellate case law considering the current iteration of Reg 4(4) – all cases to date have either considered the 1981 Regulations (under which there were no specific provisions relating to changes to terms and conditions, and courts and tribunals instead adopted a purposive construction in the light of ECJ case law) or the 2006 Regulations as originally drafted. The latter stipulated that a variation would be void where the sole or principal reason for it was (a) the transfer itself or (b) a reason connected to the transfer that was not an economic, technical or organisational reason entailing changes in the workforce.

Until such time as the EAT and appellate courts have had a chance to consider the new wording, there is a degree of guesswork involved in determining whether the sole or principal reason for a variation is 'the transfer'. However, the case law considered above under 'Position under Acquired Rights Directive' acts as a brake on any attempts to significantly widen the scope for transferees to make variations to the contracts of transferring employees. It is for this reason that, in the passages below, we broadly assume that those variations which were prohibited prior to the amendment remain prohibited.

Scope of employment contract to which prohibition applies. The restriction 5.19
on variations under Reg 4(4) is stated to apply 'in respect of a contract of

425

employment that is, or will be, transferred by [virtue of the 'automatic transfer of employment' rule in Reg 4(1)]'. Thus, TUPE will not stand in the way of a transferee making changes to the terms and conditions of its existing workforce. In this respect, the restriction on contractual variations is narrower than the protection from unfair dismissal, which extends to all employees of the transferor and transferee who are dismissed because of the transfer (see Chapter 4, 'Unfair dismissal', under 'The TUPE unfair dismissal regime – which employees are protected?').

Regulation 2(1) provides for a wide-ranging definition of 'contract of employment'. This extends to 'any agreement between an employee and his employer determining the terms and conditions of his employment'. The words 'any agreement' imply that the contract may be express or implied, written or verbal, and are apt to include any collective agreement from which the terms and conditions of individual contracts of employment derive. Thus, detrimental changes made to such an agreement – even if these have been collectively negotiated and agreed by the recognised union or other workplace representational body – will be void in so far as they are incorporated into individual employment contracts and have been prompted by the transfer. This is however, subject to new Reg 4(5B), which gives an employer scope to agree changes to terms incorporated from a collective agreement, provided that (a) a year has passed since the transfer and (b) the employee's position is no less favourable overall – see 'Types of change permitted by TUPE – terms derived from collective agreement' below.

5.20 **Variations before the transfer.** Use of the present and future conditional tenses in Reg 4(4) – 'is or will be transferred' – shows that the prohibition is intended to cover changes to the employee's contract of employment made either by the transferor prior to the transfer or by the transferee after the transfer, and includes the situation where a transferor purports to change terms and conditions because the transferee has insisted on this or in order to make the business more saleable.

The extent to which a pre-transfer variation may be said to be by reason of 'the transfer' where a potential purchaser of a business has yet to be identified has not been the subject of any case law. However, there has been some consideration of the very similar question of whether a dismissal which takes place before a prospective transferee has been identified can be regarded as being by reason of the transfer. The weight of authority suggests that the proper approach is to ask whether a transfer to any transferee who might appear, or a reason connected with such a transfer, was the reason, or principal reason, for the employee's dismissal – see Harrison Bowden Ltd v Bowden 1994 ICR 186, EAT; and Morris v John Grose Group Ltd 1998 ICR 655, EAT. In the latter case, the Appeal Tribunal observed that, in determining whether an employee has been dismissed by reason of 'the transfer' for the purposes of Reg 7(1), no special significance should be attached to the fact that the definite article – 'the' – is used. It is not necessary for the dismissal to relate to the particular transfer that has actually occurred. This interpretation of the relevant words in Reg 7(1) was approved and endorsed by the Court of Appeal in Spaceright Europe Ltd v Baillavoine and ors 2012 ICR 520, CA – for a detailed discussion, see Chapter 4, 'Unfair dismissal', under 'The TUPE unfair dismissal regime – need transferee be identified?'. Although Reg 4(4) is stated by the BIS Guide to set down a 'new test', it is submitted that the same type of reasoning would apply to the use of the words 'the transfer' in that provision.

As a general rule, tribunals are more likely to hold that the provisions of **5.21** Reg 7(1) dealing with automatic unfair dismissal and of Reg 4(4) dealing with contractual variations will apply where the relevant dismissal or variation occurs after the details of a transfer have been agreed between the commercial parties, or at least where it can be shown that such agreement was imminent. If transfer negotiations start weeks or months after the dismissal or variation has taken place, it is far less likely that the necessary causal link will be established between the fact of the transfer and the reason for the variation. In Parmar v Ferranti International plc (in administrative receivership) EAT 710/96 (an unfair dismissal case) the EAT dismissed a claim brought by a former Ferranti employee against the eventual transferee of the business. Its reasoning was that because the employee was dismissed in December 1993 and the transfer did not occur until the end of October 1994, the claim against the transferee was 'almost bound to fail'.

It is suggested that, when determining whether a variation made before the transfer is void under Reg 4(4), the following factors may be relevant:

- the time gap between the date of the variation and the date of the transfer

- the extent to which the variations were required simply to permit the business to carry on trading from a financial point of view

- whether the putative transferor expected or hoped to be able to dispose of the business by way of transfer, and

- if so, how long the transferor envisaged it would take before receiving an offer from a potential transferee.

'Sole or principal' reason. A purported variation is only void under Reg 4(4) **5.22** if the 'sole or principal reason' for it is the transfer. This recognises that an employer may have multiple reasons for seeking to make a contract variation. The test of 'principal reason' means that any reasons for a variation that are unrelated to the transfer must be subsidiary if Reg 4(4) is to render that variation void.

The sole or principal reason for a variation is a question of fact for the employment tribunal, and can therefore only be overturned on appeal if the tribunal's decision was perverse or took account of an irrelevant factor – Smith and ors v Trustees of Brooklands College EAT 0128/11. In that case the EAT upheld the decision of an employment tribunal that changes to part-time teachers' rates of pay were made because of a college official's erroneous belief that there was a mistake in how part-time pay was calculated, and not because the claimants had TUPE-transferred to the college.

5.23 **Changes by reason of transfer itself.** The old wording of Reg 4(4) included the stipulation that variations would be void if they were by reason of 'the transfer itself'. It seems reasonably clear that any such changes will be regarded as being for the sole or principal reason of 'the transfer' under the new wording of Reg 4(4). However, there is a dearth of case law in which the transfer itself is identified as the reason for a variation. Tribunals finding a change to be void (and dealing with the similar question of whether an employee had been dismissed by reason of the transfer) would commonly state that it was due to 'the transfer or a reason connected with the transfer'. Quite understandably, the focus of litigation was on the marginal cases, which were those concerning 'transfer-connected' reasons rather than specifically where the reason for a variation is the transfer itself.

5.24 **Are transfer-connected changes still prohibited?** The TUPE Regulations no longer specify that contractual variations will be void if the sole or principal reason for them is a reason connected with the transfer that is not an economic, technical or organisational reason entailing changes in the workforce. However, case law has yet to address the question of whether such changes remain prohibited under the new wording of Reg 4(4). This provision, as we explained above, now simply prevents variations where the sole or principal reason is 'the transfer'.

At this stage, it seems safe to say that at least some, and possibly all, transfer-connected changes under the old test would fall within new Reg 4(4). The BIS Guide admits as much when it states that 'the new test introduced by the 2014 Regulations is not the same as the old test of the sole or principal reason being the transfer itself. Under the 2014 amendment, the transfer might be the sole or principal reason, even if that reason might previously have been considered to be "connected with" the transfer, rather than the transfer itself. It will depend on the circumstances of any particular case.'

5.25 The view expressed in the BIS Guide will have been influenced by the ECJ's decision in South Bank University v Martin 2004 ICR 1234, ECJ (see 'Position under Acquired Rights Directive' above). There, the European Court held that where a transferee merely seeks to bring the terms and conditions of transferred employees into line with those of its existing workforce, the reason for the change is connected to the transfer, and the change is therefore void. The Martin decision indicates that EU law precludes a narrow interpretation of new

Reg 4(4) – it is simply not open to the UK Government to legislate so as to permit all transfer-connected variations.

Identifying a causal link. Since Reg 4(4) sets down a new test, but does so **5.26** within the constraints of the Acquired Rights Directive, we anticipate that courts and tribunals will be guided by the domestic case law that followed the European Court's ruling in Foreningen af Arbejdsledere i Danmark v Daddy's Dance Hall A/S 1988 IRLR 315, ECJ (discussed under 'Position under Acquired Rights Directive' above). These cases established that a change would be void where there was a causal link between the variation and the transfer. An example:

- **Lansing Linde Severnside Ltd v Spiers** EAT 1490/01: S had TUPE-transferred to LLS Ltd in 1999. Prior to the transfer, his contract had included a clause incorporated from a collective agreement, entitling S to an enhanced redundancy payment in the event of dismissal for that reason. One week prior to the transfer, S agreed new terms with LLS Ltd. Two years later, S was dismissed as redundant. His redundancy payment was calculated by reference to the new terms, which entitled him to no more than his statutory redundancy payment. S then brought an action for breach of contract in the employment tribunal. The employment tribunal referred to the EAT's decision in Wilson and ors v St Helens Borough Council 1996 ICR 711, EAT, where it was held that a tribunal should look for a causal link between the transfer and the variation (a decision which, it should be stressed, remains valid despite the later judgments of the Court of Appeal and House of Lords in respect of other issues in that case). In the tribunal's view, the causal link between the transfer and the variation was inescapable. The EAT upheld that decision on appeal, drawing particular attention to the close proximity of the variation to the date of transfer.

If the new formulation of Reg 4(4) is to narrow the scope of the contractual changes that are prohibited by TUPE, this effect will most likely be seen in marginal cases – i.e. those where the causal link between the transfer and the variation is less strong and where it is therefore more difficult to say that the principal reason for the change was the transfer.

Relevance of effluxion of time. Employers often query how long a period of **5.27** time must pass before it is 'safe' to make changes to TUPE-protected terms and conditions. The straightforward answer is that there is no specific length of time after which it can be guaranteed that the nexus between the variation and the transfer will be broken. A variation remains prohibited if it is by reason of the transfer, no matter how long ago that transfer took place.

Thus, in Taylor v Connex South Eastern Ltd EAT 1243/99 the EAT held that the fact that the claimant's dismissal for refusing to accept contractual variations took place two years after a relevant transfer was not enough to negate the link

429

between the two events. According to the Appeal Tribunal in that case, 'the mere passage of time without anything happening does not in itself constitute a weakening to the point of dissolution of the chain of causation'. A similar conclusion was reached in London Metropolitan University v Sackur and ors EAT 0286/06, in which the EAT upheld an employment tribunal's ruling that employees dismissed two years after a transfer in order to effect harmonisation changes had been dismissed for a reason connected with the original transfer.

Nevertheless, it would appear to be a matter of common sense that the greater the distance in time between the transfer and the variation, the greater the chance that the employer will be able to point to other reasons. As we have seen above, a variation will be prohibited if the sole or *principal* reason for it was the transfer. If it has been some years since a TUPE transfer took place, it will be less likely, albeit not impossible, that the transfer remains the principal reason for a variation.

5.28 So, although there is no automatic cut-off point after which changes can no longer be regarded as having been by reason of the transfer, the effluxion of time is a highly relevant factor when determining the principal reason for a variation. Where a considerable period of time has elapsed, the employer might seek to draw attention to the obiter (i.e. non-binding) comments of Lord Slynn in Wilson and ors v St Helens Borough Council 1998 ICR 1141, HL, where he said: 'I do not accept the argument that the variation is only invalid if it is agreed on as a part of the transfer itself. The variation may still be due to the transfer and for no other reason even if it comes later. However, it seems that there must, or at least may, come a time when the link with the transfer is broken or can be treated as no longer effective.'

Note that the effluxion of time is particularly relevant if the TUPE-transferred term that an employer wants to change has been incorporated into the employee's contract from a collective agreement. This is because of new Reg 4(5B), which gives an employer greater scope to agree changes to such terms if a year has passed since the transfer – see further under 'Types of change permitted by TUPE – terms derived from collective agreement' below.

5.29 ## Types of change permitted by TUPE

As we have seen above, Reg 4(4) now simply prohibits variations where the sole or principal reason is the transfer. So, with that in mind, when can employers agree contractual changes with employees who were, or may be, caught up in a TUPE transfer?

The BIS Guide states that an employer may agree changes to terms and conditions in any of the following situations:

- where the reason for the variation is unrelated to the transfer (see 'Changes unrelated to transfer' below)

- where the reason for the variation is an ETO reason entailing changes in the workforce (see 'ETO reasons entailing changes in workforce' below)

- where the terms of the contract permit the employer to make the variation (see 'Contractual right to vary' below)

- where the varied terms are incorporated from a collective agreement, it is over a year since the transfer, and the changes result in the contract being overall no less favourable than it was before the variation (see 'Terms derived from collective agreement' below)

- where the changes are entirely positive (see 'Are beneficial changes void?' below), and

- in certain insolvency situations.

We now consider the first five of these circumstances. The question of when **5.30** changes can be made in insolvency situations is considered in Chapter 6, 'Transfer of insolvent companies', under '"Relevant insolvency proceedings" – changing terms and conditions'.

Changes unrelated to transfer   5.31
Following its amendment by the Amendment Regulations, Reg 4 TUPE no longer makes any mention of changes 'unconnected with the transfer'. However, this does not necessarily mean that the position in respect of such contractual variations is any different. As we have seen under 'Varying terms in a TUPE context – changes prohibited by Reg 4(4)' above, Reg 4(4) simply specifies that changes will be void if the sole or principal reason for the variation is the transfer. Thus, if the sole or principal reason for the change is entirely unconnected with the transfer, it will not fall within Reg 4(4) and will not be rendered void.

Examples given in the BIS Guide of reasons unrelated to the transfer are:

- the sudden loss of an expected order by a manufacturing company

- an upturn in demand for a particular service, and

- a change in a key exchange rate.

These examples suggest that a reason for a variation will probably be regarded **5.32** as being entirely unconnected with the transfer if it is unforeseen, unexpected and out of the control of the transferor and transferee. In Lorimer v Aberdeenshire Council EAT 0055/02 the EAT said that the question was whether there was evidence of a 'wholly separate cause unrelated to' the

431

transfer, rather than whether, 'but for' the transfer, the contractual variation would have taken place.

A later division of the EAT considered that, if a variation is unconnected with the transfer, it should be possible to say that it would have happened irrespective of the fact of the transfer – Smith and ors v Trustees of Brooklands College EAT 0128/11. There, employees who transferred to the College had unusual salary entitlements, whereby they worked between 22 and 25 hours per week but were paid as if they worked a 36-hour week. This arrangement had been agreed with the transferor. Following the transfer, the HR director of the transferee discovered these arrangements and assumed them to be a mistake. She accordingly secured agreement with the transferred employees for a phased reduction of their salary. They then brought tribunal claims of unauthorised deductions from wages, asserting that the salary reduction – albeit contractually agreed – was rendered void by Reg 4(4) TUPE. An employment judge rejected that argument and the EAT upheld his decision on appeal. The employment judge had found, as a fact, that the reason for the change in salary was the HR director's belief that the claimants were being overpaid by mistake, and that their pay did not conform to the sector norm. This was a permissible finding for him to make, having assessed relevant factors, including the time that had elapsed between the transfer and the variation. The judge had then, also permissibly, decided that this was not a reason connected to the transfer. Although case law has established that simple harmonisation of contractual terms is always a transfer-connected reason, this was not a harmonisation case. The steps taken by the College could have been taken at any stage, irrespective of TUPE.

5.33 It is clear from the Brooklands College case that identifying the reason for a contract variation (or a dismissal) is a question of fact. However, the EAT may interfere on appeal with an employment tribunal's finding on this question if its conclusion is at odds with the evidence. For example, in Enterprise Managed Services Ltd v Dance and ors EAT 0200/11 the EAT overturned a tribunal's majority decision that a transferee varied contract terms, and dismissed employees who refused to accept them, for a transfer-connected reason. EMS Ltd held a contract to provide maintenance services at Ministry of Defence accommodation. After the MoD raised concerns about maintenance standards and cost, EMS Ltd introduced a performance-related pay system for staff working on that contract. It then won another MoD contract in circumstances that amounted to a TUPE transfer and so took on a group of transferred employees, to whom it sought to apply the same performance-related pay arrangements. The majority in the tribunal – the two lay members – thought that EMS Ltd's reason for acting was harmonisation and that any improvement in productivity was a consequence of that. The minority – the employment judge – saw it the other way round, concluding that the desire to improve performance had the unlooked-for consequence of harmonising terms and conditions. On appeal, the EAT preferred the judge's approach and held that the majority's decision was flawed. The majority had clearly accepted that EMS Ltd did not look to harmonise out of a simple wish for tidiness, for example, but was driven by the success of the productivity changes that pre-dated the transfer. That could not logically stand with its conclusion that improved productivity was a mere consequence of harmonisation. In the EAT's view, there was a 'straight line' linking the success of the productivity changes that EMS Ltd had put in place for its employees before the transfer and what it put in place for transferred employees after the transfer. Since it is open to an employer to effect productivity changes in accordance with the ordinary law, such changes do not become unlawful simply because there has been a relevant transfer.

It is important to remember that just because the reason for a contractual variation is unconnected with the transfer does not mean that the variation is necessarily lawful. The normal rules relating to variation – as explained under 'Varying terms outside a TUPE context' above – still apply. Accordingly, the consent of the employee(s) in question will be necessary before any such variation is imposed. If, in spite of the employer's best efforts, such consent is not forthcoming, it will be necessary to terminate the contract(s) on proper notice and offer re-engagement on the desired terms (see 'Alternative strategies for effecting changes' below).

ETO reasons entailing changes in workforce 5.34

Regulation 4(5)(a) provides that TUPE will not stand in the way of a contract variation if the sole or principal reason for the variation is 'an economic, technical or organisational reason entailing changes in the workforce' (an ETO reason). The first thing to note about this provision is that it does not derive from either the wording of the Acquired Rights Directive or the ECJ case law considered under 'Varying terms in a TUPE context – position under Acquired Rights Directive' above. Rather, the Government has assumed that, because the Directive permits transfer-related dismissals to take place where the reason for dismissal amounts to an ETO reason (Article 4(1)), the same should apply with regard to contractual variations. The BIS Guide explains: 'It would not be logical for the Directive to permit dismissals for such a reason, which is a greater interference with employee rights, but not the lesser interference of agreeing changes to terms and conditions where there is such a reason.'

It is, however, arguable that the Directive – as interpreted by the European Court – in fact precludes any changes where the main operating reason behind such variation is the transfer. The European Court's ruling in Foreningen af Arbejdsledere i Danmark v Daddy's Dance Hall A/S 1988 IRLR 315, ECJ (discussed under 'Varying terms in a TUPE context – position under Acquired Rights Directive' above), specifically established that a transfer of an undertaking itself may never constitute the reason for a variation in an employee's terms and conditions to his or her detriment. Nothing in the ECJ's

433

ruling in that case or in any of the subsequent decisions where the Daddy's Dance Hall principle has been endorsed suggests that even a limited exception to this rule is permissible. Accordingly, it may be that the Regulations are, on a strict reading, incompatible with the Directive. However, this point has yet to be tested in case law, perhaps reflecting the narrow interpretation that has been given to the expression 'an economic, technical or organisational reason entailing changes in the workforce' by the UK courts (see 'Definition of "ETO reason entailing changes in the workforce"' below), which consequently has made it very difficult for employers to show that variations that are connected to a transfer are, in fact, for an ETO reason.

5.35 **Changes must be agreed with employee.** Regulation 4(5)(a) stipulates that a variation for an ETO reason entailing changes in the workforce will be permissible 'provided that the employer and employee agree that variation'. Thus, an employer cannot rely on that provision to *impose* changes for an ETO reason.

5.36 **Definition of 'ETO reason entailing changes in the workforce'.** In order to understand the meaning of the phrase 'economic, technical or organisational reason entailing changes in the workforce', it is now necessary to refer to a combination of legislation, case law and non-statutory guidance. The first part of the phrase – 'economic, technical or organisational reason' – is fairly self-explanatory. As the BIS Guide observes, economic reasons relate to market and financial performance, technical reasons relate to equipment and process, and organisational reasons relate to management and structure. Most reasons an employer would have for varying contracts would fall within these three broad categories. It is the second part of the phrase that raises more debate – when does such a reason 'entail changes in the workforce'?

The leading case on this point is the Court of Appeal's decision in Berriman v Delabole Slate Ltd 1985 ICR 546, CA, where it held that for an ETO reason to 'entail changes in the workforce' in the context of dismissals connected with the transfer, there must be a change in the job functions or numbers of the workforce as a whole. In Manchester College v Hazel and anor 2014 ICR 989, CA, Lord Justice Underhill distilled these categories into the readily understandable shorthand of 'redundancies or redeployment'. The Amendment Regulations introduced a third circumstance in which an ETO reason will 'entail changes in the workforce': namely, where there is 'a change to the place where employees are employed by the employer to carry on the business of the employer or to carry out work of a particular kind for the employer' – Reg 4(5A). The reference to such a place is stated to have the same meaning as in the definition of redundancy under S.139 of the Employment Rights Act 1996 (for which, see IDS Employment Law Handbook, 'Redundancy' (2011), Chapter 2, 'Redundancy', under 'Closure of workplace').

The Berriman test. The Court of Appeal emphasised in Berriman v Delabole 5.37
Slate (above) that the reason for the constructive dismissal relied upon by the
transferee in that case – namely, to produce standardisation of pay terms – did
not involve any change in either the number or the functions of the workforce
as a whole. The most that could be said was that such an organisational reason
might (not must) lead to the dismissal of any employees who did not fall into
line, coupled with the filling of the vacancies thereby caused by new employees
prepared to accept the conditions of service. This was not enough to establish
a change in numbers or job functions for two reasons. First, the phrase
'economic, technical or organisational reason *entailing changes in the
workforce*' (our stress) required that the change in the numbers or job functions
be an integral part of the economic, technical or organisational reason relied
upon by the employer. In other words, the employer must deliberately plan to
bring about changes in the workforce rather than that being merely a
consequence of, or incidental to, the employer's objective. Secondly, a change
in the identity of the individuals who make up the workforce did not constitute
a change in the workforce itself where the overall numbers and functions of the
employees looked at as a whole remain unchanged. The word 'workforce'
connoted in this context the whole body of employees as an entity, and
corresponded to phrases such as 'the strength' or 'the establishment'. It followed
from this that the dismissal of one employee followed by the engagement of
another in his or her place does not bring about a 'change in the workforce' for
the purposes of establishing an ETO reason.

One important aspect of the decision in Berriman was later clarified in Crawford
v Swinton Insurance Brokers Ltd 1990 ICR 85, EAT (another unfair dismissal
case). The EAT made it clear that 'changes in the workforce' for the purposes
of the ETO defence can also encompass changes in the functions of personnel
without necessarily involving a reduction in overall numbers. Where the same
employees are kept on after a relevant transfer but are required to perform
entirely different jobs, the EAT confirmed, such an organisational change will
'entail a change in the workforce'.

Job functions. As stated above, the Berriman test requires a wholesale change 5.38
in the numbers or functions of members of the workforce in order for such a
change to 'entail changes in the workforce' and thus come within the ETO
exception. As we have seen, this hurdle is unlikely to be met in most transfer
situations because rarely will the impetus behind effecting transfer-related
contractual variations be to reduce the numbers of the workforce or to
substantially alter an employee's job functions.

That said, it is possible to envisage situations where, for economic, technical or
organisational reasons, the employer may be forced to change the job
descriptions of employees who are or will be transferred. If such a reason is the
sole or principal reason for the change, then, provided that the employee agrees

435

to it, the variation will be for an ETO reason and therefore valid. Furthermore, if, in these circumstances, the employee were to refuse to consent to the change and be dismissed on notice for so refusing, then provided that he or she is offered re-engagement on new terms, the dismissal will not be automatically unfair under Reg 7(1). The employer will be able to rely on there being an ETO reason for dismissal, and in that case the fairness or otherwise of the dismissal will be judged according to the normal reasonableness test set out in S.98(4) ERA. The same reasoning applies if the employee were to resign and claim constructive dismissal as a result of a transferee's insistence that his or her basic job function change.

5.39 A key question in this regard is how wide-reaching a change to an employee's job description must be in order to amount to a change in his or her 'function', and thus to a 'change in the workforce' for the purposes of the employer's ETO defence. We explored this matter at some length, with reference to a considerable body of case law, in Chapter 4, 'Unfair dismissal', under 'Dismissals potentially fair for an "ETO reason" – entailing changes in the workforce'. Although that discussion concerned when an employer might establish an ETO defence under Reg 7(2) with regard to a transfer-related dismissal, rather than under Reg 4(5) with regard to a transfer-related change to terms and conditions, we suggest that the same considerations will apply here.

5.40 **Regulation 4(5A) – change of workplace.** Most variations in terms and conditions do not involve changes in either general job functions or the numbers of the transferred workforce as a whole. Thus, the scope for making changes under the test as formulated in Berriman is limited. In RR Donnelley Global Document Solutions Group Ltd v Besagni and ors and another case 2014 ICR 1008, EAT, Mrs Justice Slade considered it arguable 'that changes in numbers or functions referred to in Berriman may not be the only "changes in the workforce" falling within TUPE', but nevertheless held that a change in location of the workplace clearly did not fall within that phrase. That said, her judgment recognised that, in respect of transfers occurring after 31 January 2014, the position has been reversed by the express words of Reg 4(5A), which was introduced by the Amendment Regulations 2014. These specifically include a change in the location of the workplace within the meaning of 'entailing changes in the workforce'. In its response to the consultation which preceded the amendments, the Government stated that the new provision 'might be helpful where there is a change in the location of the work and the employee actually wants to move to the new location rather than be made redundant: the contract could be varied by agreement to provide for the new location to be the place of work'.

If we assume for the moment that extending the meaning of 'entailing changes in the workforce' in this way is compatible with the Acquired Rights Directive, it follows that the scope for employers to agree changes for ETO reasons has been significantly increased. Changes of workplace are particularly common where a transfer takes place by way of a service provision change (SPC). Many large employers, for example, have outsourced IT or back-office functions to more remote locations, where office space is cheaper. The majority of SPCs will fall within the scope of TUPE (see Chapter 1, 'Identifying a "relevant transfer"', under 'Service provision changes'), so the ETO exception could now be of more practical use.

Alternative means of changing workplace. Note that the ETO exception is not **5.41** the only route by which a transferee can change the workplace of transferring employees. Depending on how the terms of the contracts are drafted, the employer may be able to direct the employees to a new workplace without requiring a contractual variation – for example, some contracts specify that the place of work will be within reasonable commuting distance of a particular location. As we explain immediately below, TUPE provides that the benefit of such a power to vary the contract will pass to the transferee.

Contractual right to vary   **5.42**
Contractual working conditions or practices may be changed by an employer if the change is authorised by a term of the employment contract. In short, contractual terms may give an employer the right to make changes if:

- they are wide enough to be construed or interpreted so as to cover proposed changes, or

- they are explicitly phrased in order to give employers a wide discretion to make changes, such as flexibility or mobility clauses.

A full consideration of an employer's contractual right to vary falls outside the scope of this Handbook, and is instead found in IDS Employment Law Handbook, 'Contracts of Employment' (2014), Chapter 9, 'Variation of contract', under 'Contractual right to vary'. The important thing to note for TUPE purposes is that Reg 4(4) – which, as we have seen, stipulates that a contractual variation is or will be void if the sole or principal reason for it is the transfer – will not prevent a variation if 'the terms of that contract permit the employer to make such a variation' – Reg 4(5)(b). Reg 4(5)(b) – which was introduced by the Amendment Regulations and applies to transfers occurring on or after 31 January 2014 – in reality does not introduce anything new but amounts to a clarification of the effect of Reg 4(2). This provides that all rights, obligations and duties arising under the employment relationship will automatically transfer to the new employer. Thus, the benefit of any clause that afforded the transferor the power to vary the employment contract will survive the transfer by being passed to the transferee, and this would have been the case even in the absence of Reg 4(5)(b). The key question will be whether the variation power in question covers the particular change implemented by the transferee. In this regard, it needs to be borne in mind that the courts habitually

437

interpret contractual rights to vary narrowly in an employment context as they are chary of allowing employers to use general powers to make sweeping unilateral changes to terms and conditions. This point is amplified in the discussion on 'Drafting issues' below.

5.43 **Compatibility of Reg 4(5)(b) with EU law.** As we have seen under 'Varying terms in a TUPE context – position under Acquired Rights Directive' above, Foreningen af Arbejdsledere i Danmark v Daddy's Dance Hall A/S 1988 IRLR 315, ECJ, established that the Directive stands in the way of changes made by reason of the transfer. This principle was elaborated upon in Rask and anor v ISS Kantineservice A/S 1993 IRLR 133, ECJ, a case involving cleaners in Denmark whose service had been outsourced to a new employer, which then made changes to their wages. The ECJ held that: 'Article 3 of the Directive is to be interpreted as meaning that, upon a transfer, the terms and conditions of the contract of employment or employment relationship relating to wages, in particular those relating to the date of payment and the composition of wages, cannot be altered even if the total amount of the wages remains the same. The Directive does not, however, preclude an alteration of the employment relationship with the new employer in so far as the applicable national law allows such an alteration to be made in situations other than the transfer of an undertaking.'

Taken on its own terms, the final sentence in the quoted paragraph above might indicate that if the transferor employer could lawfully have made the change to the employment relationship, so can the transferee, no matter its reason. The second interpretation, however, is that this statement of law is subordinate to the previous sentence, the broad effect of which is that upon the transfer, terms cannot be altered. Thus, changes to the employment relationship, even if authorised under national law, can only be made by a transferee for reasons *other than* the transfer. To explore the point further, it is worth quoting in full another passage of the ECJ's decision in Rask. There, the Court extracted the following principles from the Daddy's Dance Hall case:

5.44 '[T]he Directive is intended to achieve only partial harmonisation, essentially by extending the protection guaranteed to workers independently by the laws of the individual Member States to cover the case where an undertaking is transferred. It is not intended to establish a uniform level of protection throughout the Community on the basis of common criteria. Thus the Directive can be relied on only to ensure that the employee is protected in his relations with the transferee to the same extent as he was in his relations with the transferor under the legal rules of the Member State concerned.

Consequently in so far as national law allows the employment relationship to be altered in a manner unfavourable to employees in situations other than the transfer of an undertaking, in particular as regards their terms and conditions of remuneration, such an alteration is not precluded merely because the

438

undertaking has been transferred in the meantime and the agreement has therefore been made with the new employer. Since by virtue of Article 3(1) of the Directive the transferee is subrogated to the transferor's rights and obligations under the employment relationship, that relationship may be altered with regard to the transferee, to the same extent as it could have been with regard to the transferor, *provided that the transfer of the undertaking itself may never constitute the reason for that amendment'* (our stress).

This analysis is problematic when applied to a contractual power to vary. On **5.45** the one hand, it states that the Acquired Rights Directive is not intended to give the transferring employees any greater protection than they had enjoyed when employed by the transferor. That would suggest that any contractual power the transferor could exercise before the transfer can be exercised by the transferee upon or after the transfer. Indeed, much of the above quote is entirely consistent with the Directive not standing in the way of a variation which is authorised by an existing term in the contract. However, the ECJ then throws a large spanner in the works when it asserts in the italicised part of the final sentence of the passage quoted above that the transfer of the undertaking itself can *never* constitute the reason for that variation. This, again, suggests that a transferee employer must have a reason entirely separate from the transfer itself for exercising a contractual power to amend the terms and conditions of employment in order for a variation to be valid.

It should be noted that the ECJ's formulation of the rule in Foreningen af Arbejdsledere i Danmark v Daddy's Dance Hall A/S and Rask and anor v ISS Kantineservice A/S (above), permitting post-transfer contractual variations to the same extent as such variations could have been made prior to the transfer has been reiterated word-for-word in several subsequent rulings, including the decisions of the European Free Trade Association Court in Langeland v Norske Fabricom A/S 1997 2 CMLR 966, EFTA, and Viggósdóttir v Íslandspóstur HF 2002 IRLR 425, ECJ. Additionally, the formulation was reiterated by the ECJ in Martin and ors v South Bank University 2004 ICR 1234, ECJ. In all of these cases, the respective courts repeated the specific proviso that appears at the very end of the quoted passage from Rask above; namely, that 'relationship may be altered with regard to the transferee, to the same extent as it could have been with regard to the transferor, provided that the transfer of the undertaking itself may never constitute the reason for that amendment'.

If the principle that a transfer can never constitute the reason for a contractual **5.46** variation is subject to no exceptions, then Reg 4(5)(b) – which directly cuts across that principle by permitting an employer to make a change by reason of the transfer where it is authorised by a term of the contract – is prima facie incompatible with the Acquired Rights Directive. Thus, where a transferee has unilaterally altered terms upon a TUPE transfer to an employee's detriment, and has done so by relying on a contractual power to vary, the

439

affected employee might choose to bring an employment tribunal claim for breach of the Regulations, relying on a purposive construction in light of EU law. The employee's argument would go that, despite the presence of a clause in his or her contract of employment which purported to give the transferee authority to make that variation, the variation is void because the reason for it was the transfer.

The BIS Guide overlooks the question of whether new Reg 4(5)(b) is compatible with the Directive. The only indication that it has been considered by the Government comes from the official response to the 2013 consultation on the TUPE Regulations (URN BIS/13/1023). There, when announcing the intention to amend Reg 4, it stated: 'The amendment will also seek to provide that unilateral variations to contracts are permissible where they are pursuant to a contractual provision (for example, a mobility clause) and where such a change would be permitted had there not been a transfer. This is to deal with any doubt as to whether such changes would be permitted. The Government considers this is compatible with the Directive.'

5.47 No further explanation of that position has been provided, so doubts remain despite the statutory amendment. It is questionable whether there is any scope to legislate for an exception to the prohibition on changes by reason of the transfer. To return to the quote from Rask and anor v ISS Kantineservice A/S 1993 IRLR 133, ECJ (above), the way the ECJ expressed itself there is more consistent with a contractual power to vary being *subordinate* to the overriding principle that changes by reason of the transfer itself are prohibited. Thus, despite the fact that Reg 4(5)(b) gives a transferee employer apparent freedom, upon a TUPE transfer, to exercise a contractual power to vary the terms of the contract, a change made under this provision could turn out to be unenforceable if the Government has overstepped the mark in terms of the minimum standards of EU law.

If, however, there is no issue of compatibility with the Directive, then the scope to make changes under Reg 4(5)(b) is in any event not particularly broad. This is because clauses affording a power to unilaterally vary a contract of employment are generally interpreted in a narrow fashion, as we outline further below.

5.48 **Clauses agreed ahead of transfer.** In order to make a business more attractive to potential purchasers, a transferor may be tempted to insert a contractual power to vary into the contracts of those employees it expects to transfer. The problem here is that the insertion of the power to vary may itself be regarded as a change made by reason of the transfer, and therefore void under Reg 4(4). As we outlined above in the section 'Varying terms in a TUPE context' under 'Changes prohibited by Reg 4(4) – variations before the transfer', the prohibition applies to a term which 'is or will be' transferred under TUPE.

440

As the transferee will be landed with liability for any breach of contract, the due diligence process should include an examination of when any relevant contractual power to vary was inserted into the employees' contracts, and of any contemporaneous reasons given by the employer. If there is a close temporal link to the transfer, or there is a clear lack of reasons (other than a potential TUPE-transfer) for the insertion of the power to vary, there may be an increased risk that changes made under that power will subsequently be rendered void by Reg 4(4). One way of a transferee mitigating that risk is to seek an indemnity or warranty from the transferor in the event that pre-transfer changes to terms and conditions are rendered void – see Chapter 11, 'Practical aspects of transfers', in the sections 'Warranties' and 'Indemnities'.

Drafting issues. Although a contractual power to vary – such as a mobility or **5.49** flexibility clause – will pass to a transferee, it could turn out to be of little use if it is drafted in terms that are specific to the transferor. An example:

- **Tapere v South London and Maudsley NHS Trust** 2009 ICR 1563, EAT: T was employed by Lewisham Primary Care Trust. Her place of work was stated to be Camberwell, but the contract included a mobility clause which stated: 'There may be occasions when you are required to perform your duties either temporarily or permanently at other locations within the Trust.' T's employment TUPE-transferred to South London and Maudsley NHS Trust, which purported to rely on the mobility clause to move T to a new workplace in Beckenham. She subsequently resigned and claimed, among other things, that she had been constructively dismissed. In concluding that T's contract had not been breached by the change in work location, an employment tribunal found that the words 'within the Trust' did not add anything – an employer with a mobility clause would only transfer an employee to other locations which that employer itself owned or operated. In the employment tribunal's view, the clause was not restricted, post-transfer, to Lewisham Primary Care Trust's geographical location. Instead, the benefit of the clause transferred under TUPE so that South London and Maudsley NHS Trust was entitled to transfer T to any of the locations at which it operated. On appeal, the EAT held that the words 'within the Trust' in the mobility clause were not otiose or meaningless; they were vital words of definition which defined the scope of the mobility clause. Since the contract fell to be construed at the time that it was entered into, it was plain that there was no contractual right to move the claimant to a place of work outside those operated by the transferor, and the transferee was in breach of contract when it purported to do so.

The above case demonstrates the restrictive approach that courts and tribunals have taken to the construction of mobility and flexibility clauses, and underlines the fact that the practical difficulties experienced by a transferee cannot be invoked to override or modify an employee's contractual rights. Given this

441

approach, a more generalised form of drafting may make it more likely that a transferee will be able to benefit from a contractual power to vary. On the other hand, a clause which is too widely drafted may be considered too ambiguous and therefore unenforceable. Although a TUPE transfer will put such drafting issues to the fore, they are not exclusive to the TUPE context, and are instead given a thorough examination in IDS Employment Law Handbook, 'Contracts of Employment' (2014), Chapter 9, 'Variation of contract', under 'Contractual power to vary – restrictions on flexibility clauses'. The discussion there also touches on another point which could be relevant to a transferee's exercise of a contractual power to vary – the fact that a widely drafted power may be moderated by one or more implied terms.

5.50 **Material detriment dismissals.** If an employer exercises a contractual power to make changes which are to an employee's detriment, the right under Reg 4(9) could prove particularly important. As we outlined in Chapter 4, 'Unfair dismissal', under 'Material detriment dismissals', this provides that 'where a relevant transfer involves or would involve a substantial change in working conditions to the material detriment of a person whose contract of employment is or would be transferred under [Reg 4(1)], such an employee may treat the contract of employment as having been terminated, and the employee shall be treated for any purpose as having been dismissed by the employer'. Few cases have arisen to define what amounts to a 'substantial change in working conditions' or 'material detriment', although the EAT in Tapere v South London and Maudsley NHS Trust (above) did find that, if the change in work location had been authorised by the terms of the contract, the claimant would nevertheless have been entitled to treat it as a substantial change to her material detriment.

5.51 **Terms derived from collective agreement**

Although trade union membership is well below its heyday in the 1970s and 80s, many contracts of employment continue to contain terms which are incorporated from a collective agreement. In the context of TUPE, recent changes to the Regulations have the effect of temporally confining the restriction on effecting contractual variations connected to a relevant transfer. Reg 4(5B), which was inserted as part of the 2014 amendments, provides that the Reg 4(4) prohibition on variations will not apply in respect of a variation of a term or condition incorporated from a collective agreement provided (a) the variation takes effect more than a year after the transfer and (b) following the variation, the employee's contract is overall no less favourable to the employee than it was before. Thus, the fact that a term in an individual employee's contract derives from a collective agreement means that, so long as a year or more has passed since the transfer, the employer has greater scope to agree a variation of that term.

This provision reflects Article 3(3) of the Acquired Rights Directive, which provides that: 'Following the transfer, the transferee shall continue to observe the terms and conditions agreed in any collective agreement on the same terms applicable to the transferor under that agreement, until the date of termination or expiry of the collective agreement or the entry into force or application of another collective agreement. Member States may limit the period for observing such terms and conditions with the proviso that it shall not be less than one year.'

Regulation 4(5B) goes further than the Directive in one important respect – **5.52** changes under that provision must leave the employee in a situation where his or her contract is 'overall no less favourable' than it was before the changes. There is as yet no case law to demonstrate an approach to the question of when a contract will be regarded as being less favourable overall, but the BIS Guide has set out the following view: 'The employer could seek to agree effective variations to terms and conditions incorporated from a collective agreement, which may result in those particular terms being less favourable to the employee, provided that the employee gets some other more favourable terms, so that overall, the employee is in a no less favourable position after the variation compared to immediately before it.'

The above guidance suggests that tribunals will need to carry out a balancing act – weighing the detrimental effect of the variation against the positive effect of the term or terms offered as a quid pro quo. Presumably, the decision as to whether the contract is 'no less favourable overall' is a question of fact for the tribunal. However, we may not see much litigation on this point – the fact that any such variation will need to be agreed with the employee leaves limited room for disputes to end up in employment tribunals.

The BIS Guide also states: 'It is only the terms incorporated from a collective **5.53** agreement which the employer can seek to make less favourable under this exception, although the employer could agree to new individual terms which are entirely beneficial to the employee to offset the less favourable changes.' This highlights the limited scope of Reg 4(5B) – it only works in one direction, and does not permit a transferee to use a collective agreement as the mechanism to introduce detrimental changes to terms and conditions that were previously negotiated between the transferor and the employee.

A full consideration of how collectively agreed terms become incorporated into individual contracts can be found in IDS Employment Law Handbook, 'Contracts of Employment' (2014), Chapter 5, 'Incorporated terms'.

Are beneficial changes void?   5.54
In Crédit Suisse First Boston (Europe) Ltd v Lister 1999 ICR 794, CA – a case which was determined under the 1981 TUPE Regulations – the Court of Appeal upheld a High Court judge's decision that a restrictive covenant introduced into the employee's contract by the transferee at the time of the transfer was void because the contractual variation had occurred for a reason connected to

443

the transfer. Lord Justice Clarke, who gave the Court of Appeal's judgment, acknowledged that a number of difficult questions arose from the basic premise that a transfer-related variation cannot be enforced by the transferee. Chief among these was whether an employee would have the right to enforce any terms that were more favourable to him or her where these have been agreed by reason of the transfer. Although his Lordship did not provide the answer to this question as it did not directly arise for decision in that case, the weight of informed legal opinion has always been that there was nothing in the Acquired Rights Directive or TUPE to prevent the enforcement of varied terms which are to an employee's advantage, even if those terms comprise the quid pro quo for the employee agreeing to other terms that are to his or her detriment and which are therefore unenforceable.

This interpretation was endorsed by the Court of Appeal in Power v Regent Security Services Ltd 2008 ICR 442, CA, where an employee was held to be entitled to enforce a beneficial contractual variation agreed immediately prior to the transfer. The variation in question concerned the employee's normal retirement age. The transferee had sent the employee a letter shortly before the transfer in July 2005 informing him that his contractual retirement age was to be increased from 60 to 65. However, two months later the transferee told the employee that he would be retired on his 60th birthday in November 2005. The employee brought a claim of unfair dismissal, in response to which the transferee contended that the variation did not apply since the employee had reached his normal retirement age of 60, with the result that he was barred from claiming unfair dismissal by virtue of S.109 ERA. An employment tribunal ruled that the contractual variation of the retirement age to 65 was void and so could not be relied upon by the employee. On appeal, the EAT ruled that the tribunal had erred. It agreed with the employee's submission that nothing in the Acquired Rights Directive was aimed at protecting the interests of the employer; nor was there any public policy reason why the employee should be barred from relying upon the variation. In the EAT's view, 'it would be inconsistent with the aim of protecting the workforce to refuse them benefits conferred by the transferee'. The EAT's decision, and the reasoning on which it was based, was subsequently upheld by the Court of Appeal.

5.55 The Court of Appeal in the Power case observed that the decisions in Foreningen af Arbejdsledere i Danmark v Daddy's Dance Hall A/S 1988 IRLR 315, ECJ, and Crédit Suisse First Boston (Europe) Ltd v Lister 1999 ICR 794, CA (above), merely established that, where an employee wishes to rely on a term in his or her contract with the transferor, rather than a term in a varied agreement with the transferee, he or she will be entitled to do so, and there is no need for an objective assessment of whether the original term is more beneficial to the employee. Similarly, where an employee considers a new term to be more favourable, there is no reason why he or she should be prevented from relying on it. In the words of Lord Justice Mummery: 'The safeguarding of an

444

employee's acquired rights on the transfer of an undertaking means that a transferred employee, who wishes to take the benefit of the original retiring age of 60 agreed with the transferor, is entitled to do so as against the transferee. If the retiring age is then varied by agreement with the transferee, the employee must be treated as obtaining an additional right not as waiving an acquired right. His acquired right to retire at the original retiring age of 60 is transferred by [TUPE]. The acquired right cannot be removed by his agreement on the transfer of the undertaking or by reason of it. There is, however, nothing in the EU or domestic legislation to prevent the employee from obtaining an additional right. Neither the public policy reflected in the Directive and the Regulations nor the reasoning in the authorities cited by Regent prevent an employee from reaching an agreement with the transferee employer under which he obtains an additional right by reason of the transfer. The transferred employee can then choose between enforcing the transferred acquired right or the newly obtained right.' This meant, in the instant case, that the employee was entitled to rely on the contractual variation increasing his retirement age to 65 and was therefore eligible to pursue his claim of unfair dismissal.

In common with the Crédit Suisse case, the decision in Power v Regent Security Services Ltd (above) was made under the 1981 TUPE Regulations, but there is no good reason to suppose that the same reasoning would not apply to contractual variations governed by the 2006 Regulations. It is true that, taken at face value, Reg 4(4) appears to render void any and all variations – whether beneficial or detrimental – which are by reason of the transfer. However, given the purposive interpretation applied to TUPE by the Court of Appeal in the Power case, and the fact that the Court referred expressly to both the Directive and the ECJ case law governing the matter, the overriding principle established in Lord Justice Mummery's judgment – that an employee should not be barred from enforcing more favourable terms – would apply just as much to Reg 4(4). In consequence, only changes that, from the employee's point of view, are detrimental will be void. The BIS Guide, which was issued to coincide with the 2014 amendments, reflects the stance in the Power case. It asserts that 'the underlying purpose of the Regulations is to ensure that employees are not penalised when a transfer takes place. Changes to terms and conditions agreed by the parties which are entirely positive are not prevented by the Regulations.'

Harmonising terms and conditions   5.56

Harmonisation, in the context of TUPE, is a process by which the transferee varies the terms and conditions of transferred employees so as to put them on the same contractual footing as those employed in its existing workforce. However, the law places a major obstacle in the way of an employer seeking to effect harmonisation of terms and conditions. The BIS Guide neatly summarises the position when it states: 'If the new employer wishes merely to bring into

445

line the terms and conditions of transferred staff with those of existing staff, then the transfer would be the reason for this change (due to the way in which the courts have interpreted the Acquired Rights Directive).'

The BIS Guide is no doubt referring to the decision in Martin and ors v South Bank University 2004 ICR 1234, ECJ. The European Court there confirmed that Article 3 of the Acquired Rights Directive – which requires the transfer of all the transferor's rights and liabilities existing on the date of the transfer to be transferred to the transferee – precluded the transferee from offering transferred employees less favourable terms in respect of early retirement than those provided by the transferor, and further precluded the transferred employees from accepting inferior terms. The Court ruled that the Directive does not prevent a transferred employee and the new employer from making an agreement to amend the employment relationship, provided the transfer of the undertaking does not constitute the reason for the amendment. Where, however, a transferee merely seeks to align the terms on which it offers early retirement to transferred employees with those of its other employees, it is clear that the alteration of terms is connected to the transfer and will therefore be precluded by Article 3. In these circumstances, any consent given by the transferred employees to the unfavourable alteration is invalid.

5.57 When consulting on the 2014 amendments to TUPE introduced by the Amendment Regulations, the Coalition Government made it clear that it would have liked to have gone further in allowing parties to change contracts for the purpose of harmonisation, so long as employees were no worse off overall, and that it would in the future like to see the Acquired Rights Directive amended to allow this. However, the Government reluctantly concluded that, in view of the relevant case law, there was a very serious risk that widening the ability of parties to agree to vary contracts for the express purpose of harmonisation would be incompatible with the Directive as currently drafted. For that reason, it decided not to include a provision in the 2006 Regulations permitting post-transfer harmonisation.

5.58 **Harmonisation does not fall within Berriman test.** It might be thought at first glance that, rather than falling within the prohibition on changes by reason of the transfer in Reg 4(4), harmonisation of terms and conditions is an 'economic, technical or organisational reason entailing changes in the workforce', and therefore a type of change that is permitted, with the employee's agreement, by Reg 4(5)(a). However, in cases decided under the 1981 TUPE Regulations, the courts established that post-transfer harmonisation does not constitute an ETO reason under the test in Berriman v Delabole Slate Ltd 1985 ICR 546, CA (see 'Types of change permitted by TUPE – ETO reasons entailing changes in workforce' above). The process of harmonisation is invariably related to the transfer and, even if for an organisational reason, the standardisation of terms will not 'entail changes in the workforce' in terms of numbers or job functions as required by Berriman.

The facts of the Berriman case eloquently demonstrate how little room for manoeuvre a transferee has to harmonise terms and conditions if this causes disadvantage to the transferred employees. The case concerned B, who was employed as a quarry worker and whose contact of employment guaranteed him a weekly wage of £100. Following the transfer of the undertaking in which he worked, the transferee sought to alter B's pay terms in order to standardise his terms of employment with those of the transferee's existing staff. As a result, he was offered an hourly rate of £1.94 (equating to £77.60 a week) and an anticipated weekly bonus of around £22 in accordance with the transferee's current agreement with the TGWU. B refused the offer, gave notice of termination of his employment and claimed unfair constructive dismissal. An employment tribunal held that although he had been constructively dismissed and the dismissal was connected to the transfer, B's dismissal was not unfair because it was for an ETO reason and satisfied the reasonableness test under S.98(4) ERA. On appeal, the EAT reversed the tribunal's decision, holding that the reason for the dismissal (to produce standardisation of pay) did not entail changes in the workforce, so that the dismissal was automatically unfair under what is now Reg 7(1). In upholding that decision, the Court of Appeal, as has been seen, laid down crucial guidance as to how the phrase 'economic, technical or organisational reason entailing a change in the workforce' should be interpreted.

The Court of Appeal accepted that its narrow interpretation would have **5.59** adverse consequences on transferees' reorganisation programmes. The Court reasoned, however, that although unfair dismissal law outside the transfer context was generally sympathetic to business reorganisations, one of the main aims of TUPE was to safeguard employees' rights over a transfer, and that had to prevail in a transfer situation.

Change of workplace. The case law which established that harmonisation is **5.60** not an ETO reason entailing changes in the workforce was decided solely under the Berriman test. As we have seen under 'Types of change permitted by TUPE – ETO reasons entailing changes in workforce' above, Reg 4(5A) now stipulates that the expression 'entailing changes in the workforce' includes the situation where there is 'a change to the place where employees are employed by the employer to carry on the business of the employer or to carry out work of a particular kind for the employer'. This, when read with the ETO exception in Reg 4(5)(a), would appear to provide an employer with scope to harmonise one aspect of transferring employees' terms and conditions – the clause or clauses relating to place of work. However, it is doubtful that these provisions could be used to effect wider harmonisation of terms and conditions upon or following a TUPE-transfer. Reg 4(5)(a) and 4(5A) will need to be in interpreted in line with ECJ case law, and in particular Martin and ors v South Bank University (above).

5.61 **Wider scope of dismissal protection.** Regulation 4(4) only applies to the contracts of employees who have transferred under TUPE (or those who will transfer). However, the protection from dismissal in Reg 7(1) applies to all employees of the transferor or transferee who are dismissed by reason of the transfer, and who have the two years' qualifying service to claim unfair dismissal – see Chapter 4, 'Unfair dismissal', under 'The TUPE unfair dismissal regime – which employees are protected?'. This further limits the ability of an employer to harmonise the terms and conditions of the workforce following a TUPE-transfer. If, for example, the transferee wished to move the terms and conditions of its pre-existing workforce into line with those who transferred to it under TUPE, then, although this would not fall within the prohibition on Reg 4(4), the dismissal of any employees (with sufficient qualifying service) who refuse to accept the changes would still be a dismissal by reason of the transfer under Reg 7(1) and therefore automatically unfair (assuming the employees in question have at least two years' continuous service).

5.62 Alternative strategies for effecting changes

Some employers have tried alternative methods of changing terms and conditions in an attempt to avoid the restrictions of TUPE. The most common of these strategies are outlined below. However, since the courts and tribunals will be wary of allowing any changes that are contrary to the basic premise that a variation will be void where the sole or principal reason is the transfer, none of the alternative methods are likely to meet with much success. Employers should therefore ensure that they are aware of the legal risks if they agree changes with employees which are not expressly permitted under TUPE.

5.63 Offering inducements/incentives

The transferee might seek to offer transferred employees financial or other inducements (such as a one-off payment, extra holiday or enhancements to fringe benefits) to encourage them to agree to the required changes in their terms and conditions. Harmonisation exercises outside a TUPE context often involve this kind of quid pro quo. The hope, so far as the transferee is concerned, is that such inducements will reduce the risk of claims being brought, especially if they result in employees being better off (or at least no worse off) overall.

But reducing the risk is not the same as extinguishing it. It may well be that an employee who accepts both the advantageous and disadvantageous variations will lose the right to treat the contract as terminated and claim unfair dismissal on the basis that he or she has suffered a substantial change in working conditions to his or her material detriment within the meaning of Reg 4(9) – for a detailed discussion of such dismissals, see Chapter 4, 'Unfair dismissal', under

448

'Material detriment dismissals'. But whether or not this particular option is closed off to employees, there is still the prohibition in Reg 4(4) to consider. Any detrimental changes would, in accordance with that provision, be void unless made for an ETO reason within the terms of Reg 4(5)(a), regardless of whether the employee has accepted an incentive or inducement in return for consenting to the change. In consequence, the transferee may well find that somewhere down the track it ends up in disputes with employees who claim that they can rely on their pre-transfer terms and conditions.

The abiding hope for employers in this situation is that, for an employee to be **5.64** entitled to enforce the terms of the original contract, he or she would have to relinquish any advantages he or she received in return for consenting to new detrimental changes. When the case of Power v Regent Security Services Ltd 2008 ICR 442, CA (discussed in detail under 'Types of change permitted by TUPE – are beneficial changes void?' above), was before the EAT, it intimated that, if an employee had been given additional benefits in return for any changes to terms and conditions, he or she might have to give up those benefits before being entitled to object to the detrimental changes at a later stage. But these remarks were made only in passing in the context of a judgment whose main thrust was that the transfer-related changes to the benefit of the employee are not void. Nor did the Court of Appeal provide any further elucidation when the Power case was appealed. It may well be that future case law will develop the EAT's thinking in the Power case. But until then, employers should be cautious in assuming they can enforce terms to which the employee has agreed as part of a suite of transfer-related changes containing both new benefits and new detriments so far as the employee is concerned.

'Red-circling' TUPE-protected staff   5.65
The obligation under TUPE is to maintain rather than improve terms and conditions. If the transferee cannot obtain the consent of the transferred employees to contractual changes, it may agree to 'red-circle' their terms. This would entail agreeing to honour their better terms vis-à-vis the inferior terms of the transferee's existing workforce, but freezing the transferred terms by not paying annual increases until such time as the terms of the existing workforce have caught up. This option, however, assumes that the introduction of red-circling would not itself constitute a breach of contract. If the transferred employee's contract provides for a guaranteed annual pay increase or uplift of financial benefits – as it might do, either expressly or as a result of custom and practice – then the act of freezing increases or uplifts would itself be a breach of contract. In that case, the imposition of red-circling would amount to a unilateral variation of the employee's terms and conditions and would be invalid on normal contractual principles. Even were the employee to consent to the change, the detrimental variation would still be void if the sole or principal reason for it was the transfer.

449

There are legal dangers for the employer even if there is no absolute contractual guarantee of pay or benefit increases. It has been established that pay reviews must be carried out in good faith and in a reasonable manner – see Clark v Nomura International plc 2000 IRLR 766, QBD. And in Glendale Managed Services v Graham and ors 2003 IRLR 465, CA, the Court of Appeal held that a transferee who was bound by an implied term concerning wage rises owed the general duty of trust and confidence to employees when exercising that term. A breach of that duty – for example, by acting capriciously in the matter of awarding basic pay increases or discretionary bonuses – would afford the employee grounds for claiming unfair constructive dismissal. In such a case, were the dismissal shown to be for a reason connected to the transfer that is not an ETO reason, then the dismissal would be automatically unfair under Reg 7(1).

5.66 Dismissal and re-engagement on new terms

It should be remembered that employees with less than two years' continuous service will not – as the law currently stands – be entitled to bring a complaint of unfair dismissal. This means that a transferee who wishes to effect post-transfer variations in respect of short-service employees may do so with relative impunity by terminating their contracts and offering re-engagement on the revised terms – provided, of course, that the notice necessary to ensure that termination occurs lawfully expires before the employee notches up two years' continuous service. It should be borne in mind that any previous service with the transferor is likely to be added to the employee's service with the transferee when calculating the total period of continuous service.

In any case, the strategy of dismissal followed by re-engagement is not one that should be embarked upon lightly. An employee in this situation has the option to resign with a view to claiming unfair constructive dismissal while at the same time accepting the new contract under protest. Alternatively, he or she may simply allow the employer to terminate the existing contract on notice, accept the new contract at the end of the notice period and then claim unfair dismissal in respect of the terminated contract – see Hogg v Dover College 1990 ICR 39, EAT (constructive dismissal); and Alcan Extrusions v Yates and ors 1996 IRLR 327, EAT (express dismissal). The employee's requested remedy is likely to be reinstatement on his or her old terms and conditions. Or, if pay or financial benefits have been varied, the employee might seek compensation to the value of the difference between the old and new terms. The fairness of the dismissal will be judged on normal principles – i.e. whether a sufficient business reason has been made out to comprise 'some other substantial reason of a kind such as to justify the dismissal' within the meaning of S.98(1) ERA, and, if so, whether the decision to dismiss the employee for that reason was reasonable in all the circumstances within the meaning of S.98(4). For further detail of the law relating to unfair dismissal in

450

this situation, see IDS Employment Law Handbook, 'Unfair Dismissal' (2015), Chapter 8, 'Some other substantial reason'.

It is also possible that if the employer seeks to use a settlement agreement as a mechanism for preventing an employee from commencing or continuing with a tribunal claim, a tribunal might view this as an attempt to exclude the operation of TUPE, contrary to Reg 18 (see 'Settlement agreements' below).

Transferees should always take on board that it is they who are likely to incur **5.67** any costs associated with a 'termination followed by offer of re-engagement' strategy. This is so even if the dismissals are effected by the transferor prior to the transfer. Unless the dismissals are for an ETO reason, they will almost certainly be automatically unfair for being by reason of the transfer (Reg 7(1)). As such, the dismissed employees will be 'deemed' to have been employed in the transferred undertaking immediately before the transfer for the purposes of Reg 4(3), which means that Reg 4(2) will apply to transfer any liability arising from their dismissals to the transferee – see Chapter 3, 'What transfers?', under 'Contractual rights and liabilities'.

Settlement agreements   5.68
Settlement agreements may be used on termination of employment in order to preclude the bringing of tribunal claims by employees arising from that termination. In Solectron Scotland Ltd v Roper and ors 2004 IRLR 4, EAT, the Appeal Tribunal rejected the argument that settlement agreements entered into by employees who had been made redundant within months of their employment being transferred following a relevant transfer and who contended that they remained entitled to an enhanced redundancy package they had enjoyed with their original employer were rendered invalid because the agreements infringed the express restriction on excluding or limiting the operation of the TUPE Regulations in what is now Reg 18. The EAT accepted that an employer cannot, after a transfer, vary the terms of an employee's contract if that variation is by reason of the transfer. In the instant case, however, the effect of the settlement agreements was solely to compromise the financial claims that the employees had on the termination of their employment. The employer was not thereby trying to vary the employees' contracts, but to compromise a dispute as to their value. The fact that the dispute arose because of uncertainty as to the precise nature and scope of the terms transferred did not make the settlement agreements themselves ones which effected a detrimental variation in the terms of the contracts solely or even mainly by reason of the transfer.

However, if, in contrast to the Solectron case, employment with the transferee were to continue on revised terms, and the settlement agreement is used to secure the employee's agreement to re-engagement on such terms, there is a high risk that a tribunal would regard this as a strategy to avoid the effect of

451

Reg 4(4). This would go against Reg 18, which prohibits agreements that exclude or limit the operation of TUPE.

5.69 Delaying the change

Waiting for a period following the transfer before making contractual changes may not successfully reduce the risk of claims because the test is whether the change is connected to the transfer, and the effluxion of time does not necessarily break that link – see 'Relevance of effluxion of time' under 'Varying terms in a TUPE context – changes prohibited by Reg 4(4)' above. There does, in all probability, come a point in time when a variation will no longer be regarded as connected with the original transfer, but precisely when that point is will vary from case to case. This makes the matter very difficult to judge with any degree of certainty.

5.70 Exploiting the employee's right to object

Some transferees have tried to secure a variation of terms and conditions by the rather counterintuitive route of getting employees formally to object to the transfer for the purposes of Reg 4(8). Such an objection, as we have seen in Chapter 2, 'Who transfers?', under 'Objecting to transfer', means that the employee's employment is not transferred to the transferee but rather is terminated in circumstances where the termination is not treated as a dismissal for any purpose. In theory, therefore, the employee could then be taken back on by the transferee on new terms and conditions without the protections of Reg 4 applying.

However, there are a number of major stumbling blocks to this TUPE-avoidance strategy. First, there is no reason to suppose that a break of continuity would occur unless there is a substantial gap between the date of termination and the date of re-engagement – see further Chapter 7, 'Continuity of employment', under 'Relationship between TUPE and ERA'. Secondly, and more importantly for present purposes, exploiting the right to object in this way would appear to be contrary to the EAT's decision in Senior Heat Treatment Ltd v Bell and ors 1997 IRLR 614, EAT, in which it was held that any objection must be genuine and not a device to evade the TUPE Regulations. In that case, employees were held not to have 'objected' to becoming employed by the transferee in circumstances where they accepted the transferor's option of 'opting out' of the transfer of the business in return for receiving severance packages. Since the employees had, before the date of the transfer, entered into contracts of employment with the transferee to take effect immediately after the transfer, the EAT held that it was open to the employment tribunal to find that, notwithstanding their agreement to 'opt out' of the transfer, they had not objected to it. In consequence, the employees' contracts of employment were automatically transferred to the transferee and their continuity of employment

452

remained unbroken for the purposes of claiming redundancy payments and compensation for unfair dismissal against the transferee.

Lastly, it should be noted that the BIS Guide suggests that it is only the transferor **5.71** who, following an employee's objection to the transfer, could 're-engage the employee on whatever terms they agree'. Any instance of an employee exercising the right to object, and then becoming employed by the transferee, is likely to be approached with extreme suspicion by employment tribunals.

Effecting variations – practical considerations **5.72**

Even if a proposed variation falls within one of the categories of 'permitted' changes (for which see 'Types of change permitted by TUPE' above), the employer should consider carefully the strategy for effecting the change. Most importantly, it should be remembered that the general legal principles governing changes to terms and conditions will apply – see 'Varying terms outside a TUPE context' above. A failure to observe these requirements will mean that the employer may become liable for breach of contract and/or unfair constructive dismissal claims.

In addition, there are a number of general points that should be kept in mind when considering changing terms and conditions in the context of TUPE:

- potential contractors should be wary of pricing tenders for the supply of services on the basis that changes are going to be made to the acquired workforce's terms and conditions (for example, reductions in pay or benefits). If their bid is successful, it may prove impossible to effect the desired changes and/or be too expensive in terms of legal claims

- the transferee should always ensure that proper due diligence is carried out. This will include obtaining information on collective bargaining procedures, terms and conditions, details of all benefits and pension arrangements, pay reviews and other changes that may have been promised to employees. This will ensure that costs and potential liabilities can be quantified

- the reasons for any change should be considered very carefully to establish whether it is permitted under TUPE. Assuming the change is for an ETO reason or for a reason entirely unconnected with the transfer, this should be emphasised in the consultation process. There should be a proper paper trail and evidence of the employer's reasoning in this regard. In Banger v Pall Mall Services EAT 395/97 the transferee's argument that changes in terms and conditions were made for reasons other than the transfer was rejected because there was no documentary evidence of this

- the legal implications of employees not agreeing to a change must be properly considered. Imposed changes of a fundamental nature may constitute a repudiatory breach of contract entitling the employee to resign

453

and claim constructive dismissal. But even changes of a lesser kind that are nonetheless a substantial change to working conditions to the employee's material detriment may result in claims of unfair dismissal

- the transferee should devise a plan of action in the event that employees do not agree to the proposed changes. In the absence of consent, the employer may need to resort to dismissal on notice followed by re-engagement on the proposed new terms (see 'Varying terms outside a TUPE context' above). Other methods of obtaining agreement may also be tried (see 'Alternative strategies for effecting changes' above), but it should always be borne in mind that the courts and tribunals are unlikely to allow an employer to use any method that is in reality a device to avoid the effect of TUPE

- even where a variation of contractual terms has been agreed by an employee, such agreement will not stop the varied terms being rendered void if the change is to the employee's detriment and the sole or principal reason for the variation is the transfer. This principle applies even if the employee has received substantial consideration for agreeing to the change. Depending on the nature of the contractual change in question, it may be that the employer will only seek to enforce the varied term a long while after the transfer occurred – for example, a clause relating to permanent health insurance. Even so, if the term has been rendered void by Reg 4(4), then it remains incapable of being enforced; and

- both transferor and transferee have a duty to inform and consult with workplace representatives of affected employees about any 'measures' that either party envisages taking in connection with the transfer, or in relation to any affected employee (Reg 13(2)(c)). The transferor is under the additional duty to inform and consult the representatives about the measures, in connection with the transfer, that he envisages the transferee will take in relation to any affected employees who will become employees of the transferee after the transfer by virtue of Reg 4 (Reg 13(2)(d)). Both these duties would include any planned dismissals or changes in terms and conditions. In the absence of elected workplace representatives, the employer must provide the requisite information to the affected employees themselves. Failure to inform and consult properly could result in a tribunal awarding compensation to employees. It is crucial, therefore, that a realistic timetable be set out for the consultation process. Employees would have to be made aware of any time limits for agreeing to changes and the consequences of declining to agree. For full details of the information and consultation rights and duties in the TUPE Regulations, see Chapter 8, 'Information and consultation'.

5.73 If the employer decides to adopt a strategy of dismissing and re-engaging employees on new terms and conditions, then depending on the number of employees to be dismissed, the employer would also need to follow a collective redundancy consultation procedure. Full contractual notice would also have to be given to each employee, and new contracts issued to take effect when that notice expires. Details of the collective consultation procedure can be found in IDS Employment Law Handbook, 'Redundancy' (2011), Chapter 11, 'Collective redundancies'.

6 Transfer of insolvent companies

European law background

Types of insolvency procedure

Outline of insolvency provisions in TUPE

Bankruptcy and liquidation proceedings

'Relevant insolvency proceedings'

Dismissal by insolvency practitioners

Information and consultation

Notification of employee liability information

An insolvency situation arises when a business, or an individual, is unable to **6.1** meet its financial liabilities. This difficulty can arise for many reasons – for example, under-capitalisation, imprudent business judgement or unforeseen circumstances such as loss of a crucial order or client. The type of insolvency proceedings used in each case depends mainly on the level of debt and whether or not the business can be continued as a going concern. However, in most types of proceedings a qualified insolvency practitioner is appointed to maximise the recovery of assets for the benefit of creditors. Depending on the type of procedure, the insolvency practitioner will generally be a liquidator, administrative receiver, receiver or administrator.

At the time the original TUPE Regulations were enacted in 1981, the UK Government clearly intended that the protections contained in them should apply to transfers of undertakings in the context of insolvency just as they applied to any other type of relevant transfer. The only provision that was made to deal specifically with insolvency was Reg 4, which dealt with transfers by receivers, liquidators and administrators in a 'hiving down' situation. This is an insolvency procedure by which employees are retained within the insolvent company while the assets of that company are transferred to the outside purchaser.

The position that now obtains under the Transfer of Undertakings (Protection **6.2** of Employment) Regulations 2006 SI 2006/246 (TUPE) is radically different. It remains the case that if a business cannot be continued and is wound up, the employment of all employees employed in that business will be terminated and there will be no question of the TUPE Regulations applying. However, where a business, or the underlying profitable part of it, is continued and subsequently sold, the TUPE Regulations may apply. In practice this happens quite often. Although it is rare for the insolvency practitioner to sell the entire company

457

itself because a potential purchaser will be put off by the fact that, as a corporate legal entity, it will remain liable for all the debts owed to its creditors, the viable part of the company is often sold off so that it can continue to trade under new ownership as a going concern.

A detailed analysis of insolvency law and insolvency procedures is beyond the scope of this Handbook and specialist advice should always be sought in respect of these matters. However, an overview of the procedures is given below, since certain of these trigger application of the provisions contained within Regs 8 and 9 TUPE. These in effect modify the normal TUPE rules in the event of a relevant transfer occurring of an insolvent business or part of a business. This chapter therefore discusses the following issues:

- the way in which the 1981 Regulations applied to insolvency proceedings and the changes introduced by Regs 8 and 9 of the 2006 Regulations

- the main types of insolvency proceedings and the extent to which these have an effect on the employment contracts of those employed in the insolvent business

- the specific limitations contained in Reg 8 regarding the transfer of employee debts and liabilities to the transferee in respect of where the transferor is subject to certain insolvency proceedings, and the disapplication of the automatic transfer of employment rule in Reg 4 and the provisions dealing with unfair dismissal in Reg 7 in respect of certain insolvent liquidations

- the special provision made in Reg 9 for permitting employees' terms and conditions of employment to be varied where the transferor is subject to certain insolvency proceedings

- the extent to which the unfair dismissal provisions of Reg 7 apply in the case of employees who are dismissed by insolvency practitioners, and

- the practical issues relevant to information and consultation and the notification of employee liability information when the transferor is subject to insolvency proceedings.

6.3 European law background

The EU Acquired Rights Directive 1977 (No.77/187) ('the 1977 Directive') and its implementation in the UK through the TUPE Regulations 1981 is outlined in the introduction to this Handbook. In this section we consider how the 1977 Directive applied to the disposition of businesses that were subject to insolvency proceedings. This background is relevant to the way in which the Directive was amended to deal with transfers of insolvent undertakings, and accordingly to the interpretation of the TUPE Regulations 2006, which give effect to those amendments.

The 1977 Directive initially made no express provision in relation to businesses which were transferred in the context of insolvency proceedings. This led to a substantial amount of case law concerning the scope of the Directive with regard to such transfers. The first major consideration of this issue by the European Court of Justice was in Abels v Administrative Board of the Bedrijfsvereniging voor de Metaalindustrie en de Electrotechnische Industrie 1987 2 CMLR 406, ECJ. According to the ECJ, the Directive did not apply to the transfer of an undertaking where the transferor has been declared insolvent with a view to the realisation and distribution of the undertaking's assets on behalf of its creditors. The Court reasoned that, as the paramount purpose of the Directive was to protect the rights of workers, that aim in the context of insolvency would not be best achieved by applying the provisions to sales of insolvent businesses by liquidators because potential purchasers might be deterred by the prospect of having to take on all the workers employed by the insolvent company. However, the Court qualified this by confirming that the Directive was applicable to a judicially controlled procedure where the primary aim was to protect the assets of the undertaking and to ensure that it continued to trade by means of an agreement to suspend payment of the transferor's debts. This created some confusion about whether it was the degree of control exercised by the judicial or administrative authority over the transfer, or the purpose of the insolvency procedure in question, which determined whether the Directive applied.

The position was clarified by the ECJ in its subsequent ruling in D'Urso and ors **6.4** v Ercole Marelli Elettromeccanica Generale SpA (in special administration) and ors 1992 IRLR 136, ECJ. There, the Court held that the 1977 Directive did, in fact, apply to the transfer of an insolvent business where the purpose of the insolvency procedure was to enable the undertaking to continue trading. The only circumstances in which it did not apply was in the context of compulsory liquidation proceedings designed to dispose of an insolvent company's assets rather than of the business (or part business) as a going concern. In Jules Dethier Équipement SA v Dassy and anor 1998 ICR 541, ECJ, the European Court reiterated that the 1977 Directive would apply where the substance and form of the insolvency proceeding was to allow the business to trade with the aim of making it commercially viable in the longer term.

New 'rescue culture' options   6.5
Amendments to the 1977 Directive made by EU Directive 98/50 codified the position as confirmed by the case law of the European Court discussed above. In particular, new Article 4A provided that: 'Unless Member States provide otherwise, Articles 3 and 4 [providing for transfer of employment liabilities on a relevant transfer] shall not apply to any transfer of an undertaking, business or part of an undertaking or business where the transferor is the subject of bankruptcy proceedings or analogous insolvency proceedings which have been

459

instituted with a view to the liquidation of the assets of the transferor and are under the supervision of a competent public authority (which may be an insolvency practitioner authorised by a competent public authority).' This wording was retained when the Directive was reissued in 2001 (the EU Acquired Rights Directive (No.2001/23) ('the Acquired Rights Directive')). The provision – which is now to be found in Article 5(1) of the 2001 Directive – is considered in detail under 'Bankruptcy and liquidation proceedings' below.

In addition to the right in Article 5(1) to exclude application of the normal protections on a transfer in a situation where the transferor is subject to bankruptcy or analogous insolvency proceedings, Article 5(2) of the 2001 Directive confers on EU Member States scope for enacting limitations on the protections otherwise guaranteed by the Directive in cases where insolvent businesses (or parts of businesses) are sold or otherwise disposed of. The policy objective behind these options is to increase the chances that the viable parts of insolvent businesses can be sold as going concerns, and therefore maximise the chance that some employees will be retained in those businesses. In this regard, Member States are given the following two options:

- to legislate to prevent the transferor's pre-existing debts towards affected employees from passing to the transferee – Article 5(2)(a); and/or

- to allow the transferor, transferee or insolvency practitioner and employees' representatives to negotiate changes to terms and conditions of employment (in so far as current national law permits) if this is done with a view to ensuring the survival of the business and the preservation of jobs – Article 5(2)(b).

6.6 These options were introduced in response to the trend across Europe towards legislating to promote a 'rescue culture' for insolvent businesses. As we shall see, the provisions of Article 5(1) and 5(2) provide the platform for the new regime put into place by the 2006 Regulations for dealing with relevant transfers of businesses within an insolvency context.

6.7 Implementation of Article 5 options into UK law

In the light of European case law interpreting the Acquired Rights Directive (see 'European law background' above), there is no doubt that the 1981 Regulations were in harmony with the requirements of the Directive as it applied at that time. The Regulations applied to any transfer of an insolvent business as a going concern and that is what the Directive also required, as confirmed by the European Court in D'Urso and ors v Ercole Marelli Elettromeccanica Generale SpA (in special administration) and ors, ECJ (above), and Jules Dethier Équipement SA v Dassy and anor 1998 ICR 541, ECJ (outlined under 'European law background') above.

The only issue that remained unclear was the extent to which the TUPE Regulations applied to liquidations designed to dispose of the assets of an insolvent company.

460

Initially, the EAT's view – as expressed in Belhaven Brewery Co Ltd v Berekis and ors EAT 724/92 – was that a relevant transfer occurred when individuals running a business were declared bankrupt and a trustee in bankruptcy was appointed to manage their affairs. A further transfer then occurred when the trustee subsequently transferred the business to new management. However, in the later decision of Perth and Kinross Council v Donaldson and ors 2004 ICR 667, EAT, the Appeal Tribunal concluded that, since the ECJ had made it clear that the Directive did not apply in a case of irretrievable insolvency and cessation of business, neither could the 1981 TUPE Regulations apply in that situation. The fact that the Directive was implemented into UK law by subsidiary legislation meant that that legislation (i.e. the TUPE Regulations) could not go beyond the scope of the protection provided by the Directive. There was accordingly no relevant transfer when a local council took back work that it had contracted out to a company that had been subject to liquidation proceedings and had ceased to trade.

The EAT's reasoning in the Perth case is open to question in view of later **6.8** decisions confirming that it is permissible for statutory regulations made under the powers conferred by S.2 of the European Communities Act 1972 to confer wider protection than that provided for by the EU Directives on which the TUPE Regulations are based – see Numast and anor v P & O Scottish Ferries Ltd and ors EAT 0060/04. But in any event this controversy has now been overtaken by the adoption of the 'rescue culture' options contained in the Acquired Rights Directive.

When enacting the 2006 Regulations, the Government chose to take up all of the options available to it under Article 5 of the Acquired Rights Directive as outlined under 'European law background' above. In so doing, it introduced a radically different legislative regime from the one that applied under the predecessor Regulations, which (apart from the specific provision covering hiving-down situations mentioned above) contained no special provisions dealing with insolvency transfers. In its consultation and guidance papers on the 2006 Regulations, the Government stressed that its main objective as regards the insolvency changes was to promote the 'rescue culture'. With more flexibility in the application of TUPE and a reduction of the financial burden on the transferee, insolvent businesses had a better chance of remaining viable, with a resulting saving of jobs. The changes also took into account the leading TUPE cases decided under the 1981 Regulations relating to insolvency proceedings.

Types of insolvency procedure

6.9

If a business gets into extreme financial difficulties, an insolvency practitioner can be appointed either to wind up the business or to keep it running with a view to the sale of the whole or part of it as a going concern. Once appointed, the insolvency practitioner will normally want to sell the business as soon as possible to avoid a depletion in its value. As we shall see, the nature of the

461

particular insolvency proceedings is the determining factor in ascertaining whether and to what extent the key protections in the TUPE Regulations apply when an insolvency practitioner disposes of an insolvent business to an outside purchaser.

6.10 Personal bankruptcy

Bankruptcy only applies to insolvent individuals (although individuals in a partnership can be made bankrupt). The TUPE Regulations are not usually relevant to these situations unless a sole trader or other individual is the employer and his or her business is sold to an outside purchaser in the course of bankruptcy proceedings. For this reason, and also because the definition of 'relevant insolvency proceedings' in Reg 8(7) specifically refers to bankruptcy, it is appropriate to briefly consider personal bankruptcy here.

Bankruptcy proceedings commence when a bankruptcy order is made by the court following a petition usually presented by a creditor who is owed more than £750 or the individual himself, on the grounds that he or she cannot pay his or her debts. Once the order is made, control over the bankrupt's assets passes to a trustee in bankruptcy whose function is to collect in those assets and distribute them to creditors. The trustee in bankruptcy has very wide powers, including the power to sell the bankrupt's assets and carry on his or her business as well as wide investigatory powers. The bankrupt loses any rights to that property other than those required to meet his or her basic domestic and business needs. Creditors are paid in the preferential order prescribed by law: the costs of the bankruptcy proceedings first, followed by payment of debts owed to secured and preferential creditors, and then, if there are sufficient funds, payments to unsecured creditors. The bankrupt is normally discharged from bankruptcy automatically after one year, or earlier if appropriate.

6.11 The appointment of a trustee in bankruptcy does not necessarily terminate the contracts of employment of anyone personally employed by the bankrupt – see Thomas v Williams 1834 1 Ad & EL 685, Ct of King's Bench – although this may be the effect if the court appoints a receiver over the bankrupt's affairs – see Reid v Explosives Co Ltd 1887 19 QBD 264, CA. If the trustee opts to carry on the business, this may well constitute a TUPE transfer of the business to the trustee in the sense that the responsibility for operating the business has changed hands. This assumes that what has transferred is an economic entity. In this situation, it might be thought that the usual TUPE protections would apply to any employee employed by the transferor (i.e. the person declared bankrupt) and assigned to the business, and, indeed that is precisely what the position was under the 1981 Regulations – see Belhaven Brewery Co Ltd v Berekis and anor EAT 724/92. However, as we shall see, Regs 4 and 7 (which deal with the transfer of employment and special protection against unfair dismissal in a TUPE context) would now be excluded by virtue of Reg 8(7) of the 2006 Regulations – see 'Bankruptcy and liquidation proceedings' below. This would

462

also be true if the bankrupt's insolvent business is subsequently sold on by the trustee as a going concern.

An individual who is in financial difficulties can also ask his or her creditors to agree to an individual voluntary arrangement, which will provide some protection in relation to those creditors for a specified period of time, normally one to five years – see 'Voluntary arrangements' below.

Liquidation (winding-up)   6.12

As well as being a stand-alone procedure, liquidation, or winding up, can be used following a receivership or administration. The main tasks of a liquidator are to take over the powers of the directors and management of the business, realise the assets of the business, and use the proceeds to pay the debts of the business in the order prescribed by insolvency legislation. As soon as the winding-up commences, the liquidator is permitted to carry on the business only so far as may be necessary for its 'beneficial winding-up' – S.167 Insolvency Act 1986 (IA) read in conjunction with para 5, Schedule 4 IA. In practice, he or she will generally run the business down while liquidating its assets, with the result that all contracts of employment will eventually be terminated. Once the liquidation process is completed, the company is dissolved and struck off the Companies Register at Companies House.

There are three different types of liquidation. These are:

- *compulsory liquidation:* this is commenced by a court petition presented by the company itself, its directors or its creditors, normally on the ground that the company is unable to pay its debts (Ss.122 and 123 IA). If the court makes a winding-up order, then the only person who can be appointed to act as a liquidator (unless the compulsory liquidation has followed a company voluntary arrangement or an administration) is the Official Receiver. This person is a civil servant who will rarely (and certainly not without the court's consent) continue to trade the company. Following a creditors' meeting, another person may be appointed to act as liquidator with the consent of the majority of the creditors and contributors voting. The liquidator's main responsibility is to secure the assets of the company and distribute these to the creditors and shareholders. In accordance with Part XII of the Employment Rights Act 1996 (ERA), should employees not be retained in employment by the liquidator, they are eligible to receive specific protected payments (such as wages of up to eight weeks' pay and pay in lieu of untaken holiday entitlement) as well as statutory redundancy payments from the National Insurance Fund

- *members' voluntary liquidation:* this type of winding up (also known as a 'solvent voluntary liquidation') is put in train by a special resolution of the members of a company (i.e. its shareholders and any 'contributors') and is appropriate where the company is genuinely able to meet its liabilities with the prospect of a surplus left over for distribution among the members once its debts have been paid. The directors must be in a position to make a statutory declaration stating that the company is solvent and will be able to pay its debts in full within 12 months, in which case the shareholders will appoint the liquidator. A members' voluntary winding up arises for reasons other than insolvency – for example, if there is no further use for the company or shareholders want to extract their capital. Such liquidations often occur in respect of subsidiaries in a group of companies, where the dissolution of the subsidiary is required on account of structural corporate change. The insolvency provisions in Regs 8 and 9 TUPE are therefore not relevant, but there may be a 'relevant transfer' if the business of the company is transferred by the appointed liquidator to an external purchaser, in which case the normal TUPE provisions would apply; and

- *creditors' voluntary liquidation:* this form of winding up (also known as an 'insolvent voluntary liquidation') is by far the most common form. It occurs if the directors are not in a position to make a statutory declaration of solvency or the company is unable to pay its debts as they fall due. In that case, the creditors will convene a meeting, appoint the liquidator and be in effective control. They may also appoint a 'liquidation committee', the purpose of which is to ensure that the liquidator complies with his or her duty to act in the interests of the creditors as a whole. The basic purpose of the appointment of a liquidator is always to realise the company's assets and, after the payment of costs, distribute the proceeds among the creditors and shareholders according to their respective rights and interests – S.107 IA. Again, dismissed employees are eligible for redundancy and insolvency payments in accordance with Part XII of the ERA.

6.13 **Effect of appointment on contracts of employment.** A liquidator in either of the two types of voluntary winding up is regarded as an agent of the company so that his or her appointment does not, of itself, automatically terminate existing contracts of employment – see Midland Counties District Bank Ltd v Attwood 1905 1 Ch 357, ChD. The rationale for this is that there is no change in legal identity of the employer when such a liquidator is appointed because the assets remain under the control of the company liquidator, who is an officer of the company. The general rule is that, subject to any contrary specific terms of a contract of employment, the passing of the resolution to wind up in a creditors' voluntary liquidation does not constitute notice of termination of employment of all employees. This is certainly the case if the purpose of the winding up is to reconstitute the business under new management – Barnes and ors v Leavesley and ors 2001 ICR 38, EAT. However, on the authority of Deaway Trading Ltd v Calverley and ors 1973 ICR 546, NIRC, it may be that if the effect of a creditors' voluntary winding up is to bring about the immediate cessation of the company's activities, this could constitute a repudiatory breach that brings employees' contracts to an immediate end. But the accuracy of the Deaway decision is debatable. It would certainly have to be questioned whether the reality in that case was that it was not so much the appointment of the liquidator that brought the contracts of employment to an end as the cessation of the business.

In the specific case of a members' voluntary liquidation, since the company is not, by definition, insolvent, the appointment of a receiver has no discernible effect on employees' contracts unless and until the liquidator chooses to terminate these expressly. In practice, however, the process of corporate restructuring is likely to have begun even prior to the appointment of the receiver, and, as part of this, employees may well have already been transferred to another subsidiary or have had their employment terminated. If this happens, then it is possible that these manoeuvres themselves constitute a 'relevant transfer', in which case the general principles of the TUPE Regulations will apply.

The position as described above in respect of voluntary liquidation is to be **6.14** contrasted with a compulsory liquidation where the winding-up order is issued by the court. The Official Receiver or any subsequently appointed liquidator is an agent of the court, not of the company. Since the effect of his or her appointment is to place the control of the company and its assets in the hands of a court-appointed outside party, this comprises a repudiatory breach that automatically and immediately terminates the contracts of employment of all employees – Re Oriental Bank Corporation 1886 32 Ch 366, Ch D. This is so even where employment is continued after the order to facilitate the liquidation. However, it is possible that the rule is different where the business continues. In that case, the continued employment of employees may militate against the automatic termination of their contracts – Re English Joint Stock Bank 1867 LR 2 Eq 341, Ch D. In practice, however, it will be very rare indeed for the Official Receiver or any other liquidator in a compulsory winding up to continue trading. To do so, he or she would need to obtain the permission of the court and show that this is necessary for the beneficial winding up of the company – S.145 IA.

Where employees are dismissed as soon as the liquidator is appointed, they will be entitled to claim damages for wrongful dismissal based on the notice of termination they should have received. In addition, they will be eligible to receive certain guaranteed sums out of the National Insurance Fund in accordance with Part XII of the ERA – for example, up to eight weeks' arrears of pay and up to six weeks' holiday pay (subject to the statutory cap on a week's pay), as well as statutory redundancy payments. Although there is nothing to prevent those with sufficient qualifying service claiming unfair dismissal, their chances of recovering any compensatory award that may be ordered should they succeed in their claims is usually minimal: rarely are there sufficient assets recovered from a liquidation to pay off the claims of unsecured creditors, which is what employees are in respect of the compensatory award of unfair dismissal.

6.15 **Does appointment of liquidator constitute a TUPE transfer?** In the light of the above, it is relevant to consider the situation where a liquidator does choose to carry on trading the business after his or her appointment. To what extent does this, in itself, constitute a 'relevant transfer'? The position appears to be clear cut in relation to a members' or creditors' voluntary liquidation. Since contracts are not automatically terminated, and the appointed receiver acts as an agent of the company, there is no reason to assume that any change in the person responsible for operating the company occurs when the liquidator is appointed. Hence, there is no relevant transfer at that stage. If the business or the commercially viable part of it (as opposed to merely its assets) is subsequently sold to an outside purchaser, then that is likely to constitute a relevant transfer. The test, as always, is whether an economic entity has been transferred – see Chapter 1, 'Identifying a "relevant transfer"', for details. If a relevant transfer does occur, it will be important to consider the extent to which employees' rights are affected by the insolvency provisions of the Regulations – see '"Relevant insolvency proceedings"' below.

Where, however, the Official Receiver or other liquidator in the course of a compulsory liquidation continues to trade (with the court's consent) after appointment, it is possible that a relevant transfer could be regarded as taking place at that stage. This is because, unlike in a voluntary liquidation, the liquidator acts as an agent not of the company but of the court. As a result, it could be argued that the continued trading by the liquidator in this case represents a change in the legal or natural person responsible for carrying on the economic entity in the capacity of employer. Since that is the test determining whether there has been a relevant transfer of an undertaking to another person of an economic entity within the meaning of Reg 2(1)(a) – see Chapter 1, 'Identifying a "relevant transfer"', under 'Business transfers – transfer "to another person"' – it is conceivable that a TUPE transfer of the insolvent company's business to the liquidator would be regarded as having occurred.

6.16 There does not appear to be any direct case authority confirming the above proposition – which probably testifies to how rare it is for a liquidator to continue the business in a compulsory liquidation context. However, in the context of personal bankruptcy, the EAT in Belhaven Brewery Co Ltd v Berekis and anor EAT 724/92 held that the appointment of a trustee in bankruptcy in a case where an individual employer was subject to bankruptcy proceedings had the effect of causing a TUPE transfer of the business to the trustee. This was on the basis that, on appointment, legislative provisions (now contained in S.306 IA) applied to vest the bankrupt's estate (property, assets and legal rights) in the trustee and that, since he had continued to operate the bankrupt's public house business and retained the staff, this constituted a change in the person

466

operating the business for the purposes of TUPE. Given the similarities in the status of liquidators in a compulsory winding up and trustees in bankruptcy in personal bankruptcy proceedings, it seems logical to extend the EAT's reasoning in Belhaven to cases where a compulsory liquidator continues to run the business after being appointed.

Even if the TUPE Regulations were to apply, however, it seems reasonably clear that employees would not receive a great deal of benefit from their application. Compulsory liquidation is almost certainly a form of insolvency proceedings 'instituted with a view to the liquidation of the assets of the transferor' within the meaning of Reg 8(7). As such, the protections in relation to transfer of contracts of employment in Reg 4 and unfair dismissal in Reg 7 are disapplied – see "'Relevant insolvency proceedings'" below.

Receivership and administrative receivership 6.17
The purpose of receivership and administrative receivership is to protect the whole or part of the business and assets of a company from the actions of creditors while seeking to realise those assets for the benefit of secured and other creditors. A receiver can be appointed in three ways: by the court; by the holder of a fixed charge attaching to specific property under the Law of Property Act 1925 (LPA), also known as a 'fixed charge receiver' or 'LPA receiver'; or by the holder of a floating charge secured over the whole or substantially the whole of a company's assets under the terms of a debenture or other loan agreement ('administrative receiver'). The main functions of the receiver in the latter case are to realise sufficient assets to pay off the secured creditor by whom the receiver was appointed and the costs of the receivership. In order to achieve this, the receiver normally takes over the day-to-day running of the company with a view to either selling the assets piecemeal or disposing of the business as a going concern.

Administrative receivers. In practice, many receivers are administrative 6.18 receivers appointed by a bank under the terms of a debenture agreement with the company following the company's breach of the terms of its borrowing. However, with the coming into force of S.250 of the Enterprise Act 2002, the appointment of administrative receivers under qualifying floating charges created on or after 15 September 2003 was abolished. This was part of the then Government's drive to encourage the use of administration (see 'Company administration' below). The power to appoint such administrative receivers continues in respect of capital market arrangements, public-private partnerships, utilities, urban regeneration projects, project finance, financial markets, registered social landlords and protected railway companies. Except in these cases, any power to appoint an administrative receiver under the terms of a floating charge created on or after 15 September 2003 will no longer be exercisable and, instead, the debenture holder will have the right to seek the appointment of an administrator.

467

In so far as the appointment of administrative receivers continues to occur, such receivers have much wider powers and duties than an LPA/fixed charge receiver. These include not only the contractual powers contained in the relevant security document but also statutory powers set out in Schedule 1 IA (Schedule 2 in Scotland) embracing the power to take possession of the company's property, manage its business, borrow money, hire staff and sell the business.

6.19 An administrative receiver is deemed to be the agent of the company unless and until that company goes into liquidation (S.44 IA). This means that there is no change in employer on his or her appointment because any employees who are not expressly dismissed continue to be employed by the company. Subject to a 14-day grace period, an administrative receiver will be taken to have 'adopted' contracts of employment of any employees he or she continues to retain, in which case he or she will owe a personal liability to the employees in respect of certain 'qualifying liabilities' set out in S.44(2A) IA. The provisions for adoption and the definition of qualifying liabilities are virtually identical to those that apply to administration (again, see 'Company administration' below).

6.20 **LPA/fixed charge receivers.** If a company defaults on the terms of a fixed charge, such as a mortgage over a property or a charge over fixed assets (such as plant and machinery, intellectual property or interests in equities and securities), the holder of the charge may appoint a receiver to recover its property. Technically a fixed charge receivership is a method of enforcing security, not an insolvency proceeding, and the receiver has a contractual relationship with the company that is determined by the terms of the charge and/or the limited powers set out in S.109 LPA. There is normally no direct effect on employees arising from the appointment of an LPA receiver.

If receivers who are not administrative receivers permit contracts of employment to continue for 14 days or more, they will be deemed to have adopted the contracts and thereby assume personal liability for sums incurred (such as wages) in respect of those contracts from that point onwards – S.37(2) IA. A detailed discussion of this is beyond the scope of this Handbook, although the issues are briefly outlined under 'Company administration' below.

6.21 **Court-appointed receivers.** Most receivers are appointed by debenture holders as described above (see 'Administrative receivers'). The courts do have a discretionary power to appoint a receiver in limited circumstances – for example, to enforce a judgment – but this is rarely exercised. A receiver who is the appointee of the court is an officer of the court and so is not regarded as acting as the company's agent. His or her appointment therefore automatically terminates the contracts of employment of all employees working in the business – see Reid v Explosives Co Ltd 1887 19 QBD 264, CA. If the receiver keeps the employees on in order to keep the business viable, he or she becomes their employer. The same argument can therefore be made that this constitutes a relevant transfer of the insolvent business to the receiver as that which applies to personal bankruptcy and compulsory liquidations (see 'Personal bankruptcy' and 'Liquidation (winding-up)' above).

Company administration   6.22

Administration orders are specifically intended to assist companies that are insolvent but have a good chance of being rescued. A simpler administration procedure was introduced by the Enterprise Act 2002 with effect from 15 September 2003, the relevant provisions of which are now contained in Schedule B1 to the IA. An administrator can be appointed by the court, as was always the case prior to the coming into force of the Enterprise Act. However, as part of the simplified procedures that now apply, the administrator can also be appointed by the holder of a qualifying floating charge over the assets of the business, or the shareholders/directors of the insolvent company, and in both cases without the need to apply to the court first (paras 14 and 22 of Schedule B1). The main limitation on the right of the company or directors to appoint an administrator is that, before doing, they must notify the holders of a qualifying floating charge of their intention to appoint an administrator and then wait at least five days before doing so (para 26 of Schedule B1). This gives the holder of the floating charge time to appoint its own administrator should it so desire. (A qualifying floating charge is one that expressly states that para 14 of Schedule B1 applies to it or, if made prior to the coming into force of the provisions of Schedule B1, expressly empowers the holder of the charge to appoint an administrator or administrative receiver – para 14(2), Sch B1.) It is a cardinal principle of administration that irrespective of who appoints him or her, the administrator owes a duty to act in the interests of all the company's creditors – para 3(2), Sch B1.

Objectives of administration. Paragraph 3(1) of Schedule B1 sets out three 6.23 potential objectives of an administration. Whereas the administrator was previously at liberty to choose which of these to prioritise, he or she is now obliged to observe a strict order of priority. The primary objective is to rescue the company as a going concern, with as much of its business intact as possible, if that would provide the best result for the company's creditors as a whole. If this is not possible, the second objective is to achieve a better return for creditors than would be achieved if the company was simply wound up. This may entail keeping the business trading while seeking a purchaser of a viable part of its business or of its key assets. For example, the saleable assets of a loss-making part of the business may need to be disposed of to enable the rest of the business to continue. Only if the administrator cannot meet the first or second objectives does the third come into play, which is to realise the assets in order to make a distribution to secured and preferential creditors.

During the currency of an administration, a moratorium applies, which means that creditors are prevented from taking steps to have the company wound up

469

or enforce any security they hold over the company's property – para 42, Sch B1. Furthermore, legal proceedings against the company cannot be commenced or continued except with the leave of the administrator or the court – para 43, Sch B1. This moratorium is crucial as it provides a breathing space during which the possibility of some form of rescue or arrangement with creditors can be explored.

6.24 An administration must normally be concluded within one year, unless extended with the agreement of creditors or the court – para 76, Sch B1. There are several possible outcomes of the administration. The company may be returned to the control of its directors and management; it may be dissolved if there are insufficient funds for distribution to unsecured creditors; a voluntary arrangement agreed during the administration may be continued; or it may be wound up, in which case the administration will cease and a process of liquidation will commence.

6.25 **Status of administrator.** The formal status of the administrator is that of an officer of the court, regardless of whether it was the court that appointed him or her – para 5, Sch B1. But, crucially, in exercising his or her principal functions, the administrator acts as the company's agent – para 69, Sch B1. On being appointed, he or she takes custody and control of all the property to which he or she believes the company is entitled, and is empowered to do anything necessary or expedient for the management of its affairs, property or business – paras 59 and 67, Sch B1. The administrator's specific powers (as set out in Schedule 1 to the IA) include taking possession of, collecting or getting in the property of the company and selling or otherwise disposing of it; raising or borrowing money and granting securities over the property of the company; employing and dismissing employees; bringing or defending legal proceedings in the name of the company; establishing subsidiaries and transferring the business or property of the company (in whole or in part) to subsidiaries; removing and appointing directors; and carrying on the business – paras 1, 2, 3, 5, 11, 14, 15, and 16, Sch 1.

6.26 **Effect of appointment on contracts of employment.** Since the administrator is an agent of the company, no question arises of employees' contracts of employment being automatically terminated on his or her appointment. If, subsequently, the administrator does terminate the employment of employees, then the resulting act of dismissal will be regarded as having been done on behalf of the company.

6.27 **Adoption of employment contracts.** Special provision is made under the IA for administrators (and, for that matter, administrative receivers) to 'adopt' contracts of employment. This is seen as a necessary facility given that the usual aim of an administration is to keep the insolvent business trading until the whole (or any viable part of it) can be sold as a going concern, as distinct from

470

breaking up the company's assets. Normally, to achieve this goal, it is essential that administrators can call upon the continued service of all or most of the employees employed in the business. In this case, all debts incurred by the company after entry into such insolvency proceedings are classified as an expense of the insolvency proceedings and are payable ahead of the fees of the insolvency practitioner. Adoption is a necessary tool to enable employees to become entitled to have their wages prioritised in this way.

The adoption of employment contracts by administrators is governed by the provisions in the IA dealing with the priority given to payment of employees' remuneration paid out during the course of the administration over and above the administrator's own fees payable when he vacates office. In this regard, S.19(6) IA and para 99(4) and (5) of Schedule B1 stipulate that liability in respect of 'wages or salary' arising under a contract of employment that has been 'adopted' by the administrator is chargeable on and payable out of the property of which the administrator has custody and control in priority to the administrator's own remuneration and expenses. 'Wages or salary' for these purposes are defined in para 99(6) as including holiday entitlement, sums paid in lieu of holiday, sickness pay, sums in respect of any period that would be treated as earnings during that period for the purposes of social security, and contributions to an occupational pension scheme.

It should be noted in passing that Part 7 of Schedule 6 to the Deregulation Act **6.28** 2015 (DA 2015) has removed from the definition of 'wages or salary' holiday entitlement accrued under what are known colloquially as 'year-in-hand schemes' in respect of which employees accrue holiday entitlement for the year ahead. For social security purposes, such entitlement has always been counted as being accrued in the year it was earned and, by virtue of S.19(10) IA and para 99(6)(d) of Schedule B1, the definition of 'wages and salary' (prior to repeal) included any sum which would be treated as earnings for the purposes of an enactment concerned with social security. Employees could therefore expect their holiday entitlement under a year-in-hand scheme to be paid as a prioritised expense of the administration. However, in view of the fact that such schemes are no longer legally permissible under the Working Time Regulations 1998 SI 1989/1833, which stipulates that paid annual leave entitlement has to be taken in the actual year in which it is accrued, the Government used the opportunity presented by the DA 2015 to repeal S.19(10) and para 99(6)(d) as part of its general initiative to rid the statute book of 'red tape' measures that cause unnecessary burdens to businesses.

Although the IA contains no definition of 'adoption', para 99(5)(a) of Schedule B1 expressly stipulates that any action taken by the administrator within the period of 14 days after his or her appointment shall not be taken to amount to the adoption of a contract. Thus, any wages or salary payable during this grace period do not attract priority over the administrator's remuneration and expenses. In Powdrill and anor v Watson and anor and other cases 1995 ICR 1100, HL, the House of Lords considered what might demonstrate that 'adoption' has occurred after the expiry of the 14-day grace period and whether it was possible for an administrator to expressly contract out of adoption in respect of employees who are retained by the insolvent company. The relevant provisions at the time of that decision were contained in S.19 IA, but have since been transferred in slightly amended form to Schedule B1. Their Lordships concluded that if employment is continued for more than 14 days after the administrator's appointment, it inevitably follows that the whole of the employee's contract is to be regarded as having been adopted. In Lord Browne-Wilkinson's words: '[The word "adoption"] can only connote some conduct by the administrator or receiver which amounts to an election to treat the continued contract of employment with the company as giving rise to a separate liability in the administration or receivership.' Thus, adoption in essence denotes nothing more than a decision to allow a pre-existing contract of employment to continue. The House of Lords went on to confirm that it was not possible for the administrator to avoid this result or alter the consequences that the IA specifies where a contract of employment has been adopted by informing employees that he or she is not adopting their contracts or is only doing so on specific terms.

6.29 By contrast, in the later case of Allsop v Christiani and Nielsen Ltd (in administration) EAT 0241/11 the EAT held that there had been no adoption of the contract of an employee who was absent from work at the time the administration commenced. It referred to the High Court's decision in Re Antal International Ltd 2003 EWHC 1339, Ch D, which indicated, citing Powdrill, that what is required for adoption is some conduct by the administrator that amounts to an election to treat the continued contract of employment as giving rise to a separate liability in the administration. In the present case, the claimant was on long-term sick leave at the time the employer went into administration and the administrator appeared to have assumed that he would be able to claim a redundancy payment. The administrator did not pay the claimant any sick pay or salary after he assumed control of the company. In these circumstances, the EAT could see no evidence suggesting an intention on the administrator's part to adopt the claimant's contract of employment.

It is clear from Lord Browne-Wilkinson's definition of 'adoption' that even where the administrator retains the services of employees after 14 days he or she does not personally become their employer. Their contracts of employment continue to be with the company. As a result, no TUPE transfer occurs at that point. If the administration eventually results in the disposal of the business or part of it as a going concern, then a relevant transfer will occur at that stage, and this will trigger the special provisions in Regs 8 and 9 TUPE modifying the application of the normal protections guaranteed under the Regulations – see '"Relevant insolvency proceedings"' below.

Voluntary arrangements

6.30

A debtor (whether an individual or a company) in financial difficulties can enter into a voluntary arrangement with his or its creditors. If a company, such arrangement may well enable it to continue as a going concern – for example, by arranging reduced or delayed debt repayment terms (Ss.1–7 IA). The arrangement will normally last from two to four years. Usually the directors of the company appoint an insolvency practitioner to consider and report on the proposals they have made for the voluntary arrangement. Shareholders and creditors then vote on whether to approve it. If at least 75 per cent in value of creditors approve the arrangement, it is binding on all the company's creditors. The function of the insolvency practitioner is simply to supervise the arrangement. Since the business normally continues to trade while subject to the voluntary arrangement, there is no automatic termination of contracts of employment, and the TUPE Regulations will not normally be relevant. A voluntary arrangement can be run at the same time as an administration.

Outline of insolvency provisions in TUPE

6.31

The way in which the TUPE Regulations apply to the sale of an insolvent business or part thereof is set out in Regs 8 and 9. In places these provisions are difficult to interpret, often because they require familiarity with concepts that are not contained in the Regulations themselves, including insolvency procedures and the statutory payment provisions relevant to employees of insolvent companies. There has been much criticism of the complexity and drafting of the insolvency provisions, in particular by insolvency specialists such as R3 (the Association of Business Recovery Professionals), who were concerned that the provisions may not work well in practice. On 3 May 2006 an application to revoke the new TUPE Regulations was made in the House of Lords by Lord Hunt of Wirral on behalf of R3, defended by Lord Sainsbury of Turville for the Department of Trade and Industry. The motion was defeated by just two votes. Key points of the debate are considered below in the context of the relevant insolvency provisions. In his conclusion, Lord Sainsbury said that the Government would monitor closely how the 2006 Regulations operate in practice, and if problems emerge it will consider the case for amending them.

In broad outline, the key changes introduced by Regs 8 and 9 of the 2006 Regulations were:

- the wholesale disapplication of Regs 4 and 7 where the transferor is subject to bankruptcy or analogous insolvency proceedings instituted with a view to liquidating the transferor's assets under the supervision of an insolvency practitioner. In such cases, employees will not be accorded the normal protections in respect of the automatic transfer of their employment and attendant rights, duties, powers and liabilities on a relevant transfer, nor the

473

protections against detrimental variation of contracts or unfair dismissal by reason of the transfer – Reg 8(7)

- the non-transfer of liability by the transferor for certain core debts (such as statutory redundancy payments, payments in lieu of notice and unpaid holiday pay of up to six weeks) where the transferor is the subject of 'relevant insolvency proceedings'. Rather than debts being 'inherited' by the transferee in the usual way by virtue of Reg 4, they will become payable by the Secretary of State for Trade and Industry out of the National Insurance Fund – Reg 8(5); and

- the legal right – subject to certain procedural safeguards – for the transferor, transferee or insolvency practitioner to negotiate variations to terms and conditions with employee representatives where the transferor is subject to 'relevant insolvency proceedings' even if the reason for the changes is connected with the transfer and is not an economic, technical or organisational reason entailing changes in the workforce – Reg 9.

6.32 The second and third of these provisions – which are specifically drawn from the 'rescue culture' options conferred on Member States by Article 5(2) of the Acquired Rights Directive – involve a significant modification to the application of Reg 4. Both only apply in a case where the transferor is subject to 'relevant insolvency proceedings', defined in Reg 4(6) as being 'insolvency proceedings which have been opened in relation to the transferor not with a view to the liquidation of the assets of the transferor and which are under the supervision of an insolvency practitioner'. This is to be contrasted with the first of the provisions outlined above – drawn from Article 5(1) of the Directive – which provides for the wholesale disapplication of Regs 4 and 7 where the particular insolvency proceedings to which the transferor is subject has the aim of liquidating the transferor's assets.

Although there has been a considerable amount of confusion and debate about the wording of these different sets of provisions, it seems to be reasonably clear that the types of proceedings to which Reg 8(7) is intended to apply are mutually exclusive to those that are intended to come within the definition of 'relevant insolvency proceedings' to which the remainder of Reg 8 and the whole of Reg 9 apply. In other words, each of the different types of insolvency procedure discussed under 'Types of insolvency procedure' above will be caught either by Reg 8(7) or by Regs 8(1)–(6) and 9, unless the procedure is not a genuine 'insolvency' procedure, in which case it will be caught by neither. The key criterion for determining into which category a particular procedure falls is whether or not the insolvency proceedings in question were instituted with a view to liquidating the assets of the transferor's business. The wording of the Regulations leave plenty of scope for argument as to whether the aim of one or another particular proceeding is to liquidate the transferor's assets. However, as we shall see when we examine Regs 8 and 9 in detail – starting with Reg 8(7)

474

below – it is possible to reach a commonsensical view about this, particularly if it is accepted that the point at which the aim of the proceedings has to be determined is their commencement rather than at any later date.

Bankruptcy and liquidation proceedings 6.33

Regulation 8(7) stipulates that: 'Regs 4 and 7 do not apply to any relevant transfer where the transferor is the subject of bankruptcy proceedings or any analogous insolvency proceedings which have been instituted with a view to the liquidation of the assets of the transferor and are under the supervision of an insolvency practitioner.' Where it applies, this provision has a much more dramatic effect on the rights of employees than the provision in Reg 8(5) limiting the transfer or specific liabilities payable to relevant employees under a relevant statutory scheme (see '"Relevant insolvency proceedings"' below). However, the reach of Reg 8(7) is much narrower because its application is limited to where the transferor is subject to insolvency proceedings that aim to liquidate the business rather than keep it trading with a view to its sale or disposition as a going concern. As we shall see, this means that in practice Reg (7) only applies to compulsory and creditors' voluntary liquidations.

Proceedings 'under the supervision of' insolvency practitioner 6.34
Before considering Reg 8(7) in detail, it should be noted that the insolvency proceedings have to be under the supervision of an 'insolvency practitioner'. Such a person is defined in Reg 2 TUPE in terms of the meaning given by S.388 IA, which states that, in relation to a company, a person acts as an insolvency practitioner when he or she acts as its liquidator, administrator, administrative receiver, or supervisor of a voluntary arrangement. Subsequent sections set out various requirements that must be met for an insolvency practitioner to be validly appointed. For example, all insolvency practitioners must be members of a recognised professional body or otherwise properly authorised. This means that they must be appointed by one of the chartered accountancy bodies, the Law Society, the Insolvency Practitioners Association, or the Department of Trade. Note that the definition of insolvency practitioner does not cover court-appointed receiverships or LPA receiverships, as these are not true insolvency proceedings.

A person will only 'act' as an insolvency practitioner for the purposes of Reg 8(7) once he or she has actually been appointed to that role, as the EAT made clear in Ward Brothers (Malton) Ltd v Middleton and ors EAT 0249/13. There, BT Ltd was in severe financial difficulty and ceased trading on a Friday. On the following Monday, WB Ltd started to perform BT Ltd's major contracts, using BT Ltd's ex-employees. However, WB Ltd argued that TUPE did not operate so as to require it to take on BT Ltd staff because, at the time of the transfer, BT Ltd was 'under the supervision of an insolvency practitioner'

475

within the meaning of Reg 8(7). The EAT rejected this argument, holding that the insolvency practitioners that were at BT Ltd's premises at the time of the transfer acted merely in an advisory capacity. In order for Reg 8(7) to apply, a person must be appointed to act as a company's insolvency practitioner. This interpretation was consistent with S.388 IA and the EAT's decision in Secretary of State for Trade and Industry v Slater and ors 2008 ICR 54, EAT (discussed under '... which have been instituted with a view to the liquidation of the assets' below). Accordingly, as insolvency practitioners, different from those who were present at the time of the transfer, were only formally appointed a week after the transfer, Reg 8(7) did not apply and BT Ltd's employees transferred to WB Ltd.

6.35 'Timing' issues of a different kind arose in the two cases below:

- **Coyne and ors v Reed Presentation Ltd and ors** ET Case No.2500843/10: a private company, RP Ltd, purchased another company, HFW, in 2007, following which HFW continued to trade. However, HFW's debts began to pile up. On 10 December 2009 it wrote to inform its employees that it intended to apply for a creditors' voluntary winding-up in due course, that it would cease to trade on 11 December, and that the employees' contracts would be summarily terminated on that date. At the same time RP Ltd acquired plant and equipment owned by HFW and began to deploy this from 14 December. It was not, however, until 15 January 2010 that a creditors' meeting was convened for the purposes of appointing a liquidator and around that time 26 of HFW's former employees were invited to start working for RP Ltd as it had decided to use the plant and equipment previously owned by HFW to carry on the HFW business. Some of the former HFW employees subsequently brought employment tribunal claims contending that there had been a relevant transfer from HFW to RP Ltd, that the principal reason for their dismissals was the transfer, and that the dismissals were therefore automatically unfair under Reg 7 TUPE. RP Ltd sought to defend the claims on that basis that, as HFW had gone into liquidation, Reg 8(7) applied to exclude the operation of Reg 7. In rejecting that defence, the tribunal held that on 14 December 2009 the economic entity that was HFW had been transferred to RP Ltd and that this constituted a relevant transfer. It further held that the insolvency proceedings applicable to HFW could not be said to have been under the supervision of an insolvency practitioner until 15 January 2010 at the earliest given that it was only then that a creditors' meeting had taken place with a view to appointing a liquidator. Since the transfer had already occurred by then, Reg 8(7) had no application, with the consequence that Reg 7(1) applied to render the claimants' dismissals unfair. Furthermore, Reg 4(2) also applied to transfer the liability for the unfair dismissals to RP Ltd

476

- **Jug and ors v APR Media Ltd (in liquidation) and ors** ET Case No.1702008/12: APRM Ltd was a distributor of media products whose business was exclusively conducted through Amazon and eBay. The business ran into difficulties in 2012 and in September of that year its accountants advised that the company was insolvent and should be liquidated. All APRM Ltd's employees were dismissed as redundant on 1 October 2012. However, around the same time the sole director of APRM Ltd purchased its assets and sold these to TM Ltd, a company that he had incorporated in 2008. Thereafter, TM Ltd began trading with the benefit of the purchased assets, took on several of APRM Ltd's former employees, leased part of the premises formerly occupied by APRM Ltd and continued to use eBay and Amazon as its vehicle for trading. Furthermore, TM Ltd e-mailed customers of APRM Ltd implying that it was a successor business. J, a former employee of APRM Ltd, brought an employment tribunal claim asserting, among other things, that a TUPE transfer had occurred and that he had been unfairly dismissed by reason of that transfer contrary to Reg 7 TUPE. Rejecting the claim, the tribunal held that part of APRM Ltd's business had transferred over a period from 15 October to 1 November 2012, and that during that time APRM Ltd had been subject to insolvency proceedings with a view to the liquidation of its assets and was under the supervision of an insolvency practitioner within the terms of Reg 8(7). Consequently, Regs 4 and 7 were excluded.

Transferor 'the subject of bankruptcy proceedings or any analogous insolvency proceedings...' 6.36

The language of Reg 8(7) is imported word-for-word from Article 5(1) of the Acquired Rights Directive. Both provisions speak of the disapplication of the rules dealing with transfer of contractual rights and protection against unfair dismissal by reason of the transfer 'where the transferor is the subject of bankruptcy proceedings or any analogous insolvency proceedings which have been instituted with a view to the liquidation of the assets of the transferor'. The problem is that 'bankruptcy' in UK insolvency law has a special and very narrow meaning connoting personal rather than corporate insolvency, whereas there is a sense in the context of the Directive that the word is intended to carry a wider and less specific meaning. This was recognised by Advocate General Sir Gordon Slynn in Abels v Administrative Board of the Bedrijfsvereniging voor de Metaalindustrie en de Electrotechnische Industrie 1987 2 CMLR 406, ECJ, when explaining his choice of terminology in the written Opinion he gave to the European Court: 'Since in English "bankruptcy" and "liquidation" have technical meanings, one referring to the insolvency of individuals or partnerships, the other to the winding up of companies... I use the words "liquidator" and "liquidation" as covering also "a trustee in bankruptcy" and "bankruptcy".' In view of this, it would seem fairly clear that, in the context of corporate insolvency, the type of proceedings that comes closest to personal bankruptcy

— 477

is liquidation – certainly compulsory liquidation and probably creditors' voluntary liquidation. Although there is no question of the legal interest in the debtor's assets becoming vested in the liquidator (unless the court specifically so orders) – as happens when a trustee in bankruptcy is appointed – the insolvent company's assets nevertheless become entirely controlled by the liquidator. The notion that this brings liquidations into the scope of Reg 4(7) is further strengthened by the next clause of that regulation, considered below.

6.37 **'... which have been instituted with a view to the liquidation of the assets'**
In order to determine which of the insolvency procedures discussed under 'Types of insolvency procedure' above are caught by Reg 8(7), it is necessary to dissect the meaning of 'proceedings which have been instituted with a view to the liquidation of the assets'.

The first thing to note is the words 'which have been instituted'. The proceedings that are covered by Reg 8(7) have to have been instituted with a view to the liquidation of the assets. Rather oddly, the word is not used in the Reg 8(6) definition of 'relevant insolvency proceedings', which refers to 'proceedings which have been opened in relation to the transferor'. Why the difference? Unfortunately, none of the official guidance on the TUPE Regulations offers an explanation. But there is no obvious reason why the words should be interpreted differently. Therefore, unless and until the courts discover a nuance of practical or legal import that is not immediately apparent, it seems safe to assume that 'instituted' in Reg 8(7) and 'opened' in Reg 8(6) simply mean 'commenced' – that being the word usually applied by insolvency practitioners when insolvency proceedings are begun.

6.38 **Date for determining purpose of insolvency proceedings.** Case law suggests that, in order for the consequences set out in Reg 8(7) to apply, it is necessary that bankruptcy or analogous proceedings have already commenced by the time the transfer takes place. If this is not the case, then Reg 4 will apply unabated, which means that the transferee will acquire the contract of employment and all liabilities thereunder of any employee employed immediately before the transfer. The transferee will also be subject to the full rigour of Reg 7 should any such employee be dismissed for a reason connected to the transfer.

In Secretary of State for Trade and Industry v Slater 2008 ICR 54, EAT, the Appeal Tribunal had to consider whether Reg 8(7) applied in circumstances where the appointment of a liquidator was imminent at the time a relevant transfer occurred. Faced with financial difficulties, the directors of C Ltd decided on 25 July 2006 to put the company into voluntary liquidation. Since it was insolvent, a creditors' voluntary winding up was the appropriate type of insolvency proceedings, and the directors appointed a firm of accountants to assist in preparing for this. The following day, R (an employee of the

478

accountants), gave the staff notice of redundancy. C Ltd's assets and goodwill were then purchased by a new company, CFGN Ltd, on 27 July in circumstances that were found to amount to a TUPE transfer. C Ltd was formally put into liquidation on 16 August at a meeting of the shareholders, who passed a resolution to wind up the company. The creditors then appointed R and another person as joint liquidators. C Ltd's employees, who were taken on by CFGN, sought payment of back pay and holiday pay from their new employer on the basis that it had acquired those liabilities following the transfer. CFGN, however, denied liability, relying on Reg 8(6), or alternatively Reg 8(7). An employment tribunal agreed with the transferee that the insolvency procedure in this case fell under Reg 8(6) and went on to find that the insolvency proceedings had been opened on 25 July – two days before the transfer – when the directors had resolved to call the shareholders' meeting to wind up the company. Since those proceedings had been opened before the transfer, liability did not pass to the transferee and, instead, the Secretary of State was liable to make the payments out of the National Insurance Fund.

6.39 On appeal to the EAT by the Secretary of State, certain concessions were made by the parties, which meant that the question of whether the case fell within Reg 8(6) or Reg 8(7) was no longer specifically relevant. The sole remaining issue was whether the insolvency proceedings in question had commenced prior to the transfer. In this regard, the EAT held that neither Reg 8(6) nor Reg 8(7) applied given that, as a consequence of the creditors' voluntary winding up, the resulting insolvency proceedings – whether these were taken to commence at the time of the resolution of the members or with the subsequent decision reached at a creditors' meeting – were begun only after the transfer had occurred. But even if those proceedings had been in place when the business was transferred, those proceedings were not – as at the date of the transfer – under the supervision of an insolvency practitioner, as required by both Reg 8(6) and Reg 8(7). This was despite the fact that it was apparently assumed that the accountant appointed by the transferor was an insolvency practitioner from the moment he was first asked to assist the company. The definition of an insolvency practitioner in S.388 IA made it plain that it was not until he was appointed liquidator that he could be so described. He was of course qualified to act as an insolvency practitioner, but he was not acting in that capacity with respect to the transferor. As a result, since neither Reg 8(7) nor Reg 8(6) applied to limit the operation of the automatic transfer of contractual liability rule in Reg 4, the transferee, CFGN, was responsible for the payment of the debts owed to the transferred employees.

6.40 The EAT's decision makes it clear that preparatory steps for a winding up – there, the appointment of accountants – do not mean that insolvency proceedings have been formally commenced. Similar reasoning has been adopted in subsequent cases, as the following tribunal decisions make clear:

- **Darlington v Marlin Group Ltd (in administration) and anor** ET Case No.2401949/09: D was employed by MG Ltd as a senior art worker, dealing with off-the-page advertising for a major client, P. MG Ltd suffered the loss of a number of contracts in 2008, and, in particular, lost P's contract at the end of September 2008. At that point, D was informed that he was to be made redundant with effect from 21 November. On 23 November, MG Ltd was advised that the company could not be saved and administration should be considered. Some two weeks before this, a new company, MDI Ltd, was set up and incorporated on 6 November 2008 and a senior employee of MG Ltd (W) was appointed director of that company on 26 November. On 28 November W met MG Ltd's liquidator and agreed to purchase that company's outstanding debts and goodwill, together with its equipment. Following a break of one week, MDI Ltd commenced operation of a slightly different service, and approached various clients of MG Ltd who had been acquired as part of its purchase by MDI Ltd. The question arose as to whether the dismissal of D (who was not taken on following the transfer) was caught by Reg 8(7) TUPE. MDI Ltd contended that it was, with the consequence that neither Reg 4 nor Reg 7 applied. In rejecting this contention, an employment tribunal ruled that in this case the insolvency proceedings instituted by MG Ltd had not commenced prior to the date of the transfer. It followed that Reg 8(7) had no application, so that the unfair dismissal provisions of Reg 7 applied. As D was dismissed for a reason connected with the transfer that was not for an ETO reason, Reg 7 operated to render his dismissal automatically unfair

- **Dearing v Pentagon Glass Tech Ltd (in liquidation) and ors** ET Case No.3302313/08: D was employed by PGT Ltd as a workshop manager and controller. The company encountered financial difficulties and decided that these could not be resolved. Even so, some employees, including D, were told that their jobs were secure, whereas others were made redundant. D's employment continued until 31 May 2008, when PGT Ltd ceased trading. He had been told he would be given a new contract to do the same job in a new location but with a 10 per cent reduction in salary. One of PGT Ltd's directors had been looking for alternative premises from which the business could be run. When these were found, they had to be fitted out and a newly incorporated company, PG Ltd, set up. This did not begin trading until 20 July 2008. Eight days later, PGT Ltd went into voluntary liquidation and the final transfer of assets from it to PG Ltd was made by invoice dated 22 September. In the meantime, D had refused the offer of the new contract because of the proposed pay cut and claimed he was entitled to be paid a redundancy payment by PGT Ltd (the liability for which had been transferred to PG Ltd). An employment tribunal held that the relevant date of the transfer was 31 May – the date that PGT Ltd ceased to trade. As at that date, no insolvency process had been instituted, which meant that

Reg 8(7) did not apply. It followed that PG Ltd was the only appropriate respondent to the tribunal proceedings and D was entitled to proceed with his claim.

Which insolvency procedures are analogous to bankruptcy? Assuming, then, **6.41** that liquidation or analogous proceedings have been commenced by the time the transfer occurs, the next – and very significant – issue concerns the question of the point in time at which the aim of the proceedings in question has to be assessed. The proceedings have to have been instituted 'with a view' to the liquidation of the assets. As mentioned above, it would seem that the determining factor as to whether a particular insolvency procedure falls within Reg 8(7) as opposed to the definition of 'relevant insolvency proceedings' in Reg 8(6) is the extent to which, at the time it is commenced, its object is the liquidation of the transferor's assets. The difficulty here is that all of the insolvency procedures available under UK law to a greater or lesser extent entail realising the value of the transferor's assets and all can end up in the disposal of the insolvent business as a going concern (or the viable parts of the business). Clearly, a distinction is intended to be drawn between those types of proceedings which, by their nature, drive towards the disposal of the business or part of it as a going concern (or at least see this as ensuring the best realisation of the assets) and those that have as their usual goal merely the realisation of the assets and the beneficial distribution of the proceeds to creditors. For reasons explained under '"Relevant insolvency proceedings"' below, it is clear that the point at which to judge the nature of the insolvency proceedings is at the outset of those proceedings. So, on this basis, proceedings that have as their usual aim the liquidation of the transferor's assets would be caught by Reg 4(7) even if, in a particular case, the insolvency practitioner happened to end up selling the viable part of the insolvent business as a going concern.

In determining whether a particular insolvency procedure is to be regarded as instituted with a view to liquidation of the transferor's assets as distinct from keeping the business operating with a view to its sale as a concern, it is useful to remember that the language of Article 5(1) of the Acquired Rights Directive (which Reg 8(7) replicates) was drawn from the decisions of the European Court in Abels v Administrative Board of the Bedrijfsvereniging voor de Metaalindustrie en de Electrotechnische Industrie 1987 2 CMLR 406, ECJ, and in D'Urso and ors v Ercole Marelli Elettromeccanica Generale SpA (in special administration) and ors 1992 IRLR 136, ECJ (discussed under 'European law background' above). An examination of those cases is accordingly instructive in elucidating the wording of Reg 8(7). In D'Urso the ECJ noted that Abels was concerned with whether the transfer of a business arising out of a Dutch insolvency procedure known as a 'surséance van betaling' was covered by the Directive. This procedure entails the national court giving leave to insolvent companies to suspend payments to their creditors while options for rescue are investigated. The ECJ summarised the ruling in Abels as follows:

481

'The Court held that the Directive did not apply to transfers effected in bankruptcy proceedings designed to liquidate the transferor's assets under the supervision of the competent judicial authority… [However], the Directive was applicable to a procedure like a "surséance van betaling" (suspension of payments), although that procedure did have some features in common with liquidation proceedings.' The Court considered that the reasons which justified not applying the Directive in the case of liquidation proceedings were not valid when the procedure in question involved court supervision more limited than in liquidation proceedings and when its purpose was primarily to safeguard the assets and, where possible, to continue the business of the undertaking by means of a collective suspension of the payment of debts with a view to reaching a settlement which would ensure that the undertaking was able to continue operating in the future. The ECJ in D'Urso then went on to point out that the extent of court supervision of the insolvency procedure in question was not itself determinative of whether the Directive applies. Rather, 'the decisive test is… the purpose of the procedure in question'.

6.42 The particular insolvency procedure under scrutiny in D'Urso and ors v Ercole Marelli Elettromeccanica Generale SpA (in special administration) and ors (above) was an Italian one called 'amministrazione straordinaria delle grandi imprese in crisi' ('special administration procedure for large undertakings in critical difficulties'). The characteristics of this procedure differed according to whether the national court decreed that the insolvent undertaking should be compulsorily liquidated or should continue trading. If the former, then in the ECJ's view the aim of the special administration procedure would be comparable to that which had led the Court to conclude in Abels v Administrative Board of the Bedrijfsvereniging voor de Metaalindustrie en de Electrotechnische Industrie (above) that the Directive did not apply to transfers of an undertaking (or part transfers). That was because it would be primarily designed to liquidate the debtor's assets in order to satisfy the body of creditors. On the other hand, as was apparent from the relevant Italian national law, when the court authorised the undertaking to continue trading under the supervision of an insolvency practitioner, the primary purpose of the special administration procedure would then be to give the undertaking some stability, allowing its future activity to be safeguarded. In that case, the ECJ concluded, the Directive would apply to any transfer effected in the course of the procedure in question.

Returning to the position under UK domestic law, the following employment tribunal decision specifically focused on whether the insolvency proceedings in question attracted the application of Reg 8(7):

- **Bowater and ors v NIS Signs Ltd (in liquidation)** ET Case No.1901191/09: in 2009 the group of which NS Ltd was a part encountered serious financial difficulties. A management buyout was proposed, and a new company – NS(L) Ltd – was incorporated for this purpose on 8 April 2009. At the same time the entire group of companies was about to be put into insolvency administration. NS(L) Ltd took legal advice, as a result of which it was advised that it should purchase NS Ltd from a liquidator rather than an administrator so that Reg 8(7) TUPE would be engaged. This would have the beneficial effect, so far as NS(L) Ltd was concerned, of disapplying the entirety of Regs 4 and 7 with regard to the former employees of NS Ltd. On 22 April NS Ltd passed a resolution voluntarily winding up the company and on the same day the liquidator sold that company to another subsidiary, LS Ltd. Following claims brought by B and others, an employment tribunal was called upon to consider whether Reg 8(7) applied – and, in particular, whether a creditors' voluntary liquidation (CVL) was analogous to bankruptcy or analogous proceedings and whether the CVL in this case was a mere sham. It held that, under UK domestic insolvency law, the liquidation of assets is the only possible outcome of a CVL. The tribunal accepted that, in this case, the liquidation was undertaken solely with a view to precluding the operation of TUPE. However, on closer inspection of the facts, the tribunal discovered that this objective was primarily aimed at securing the commercial interests of NS Ltd's principal creditor – namely, its bank, which had advanced the money to enable the purchase of NS Ltd's business by LS Ltd. By engineering the situation to avoid liabilities that would otherwise have been transferred under TUPE, the bank was thus able to transfer its investment to an independent viable concern away from a financially fragile group of companies. The CVL was therefore not a sham, and the fact that the CVL was not the only option available did not mean that the tribunal could mitigate the clear effect of Reg 8(7).

A more controversial finding was reached by the EAT in Oakland v Wellswood 6.43 (Yorkshire) Ltd 2009 IRLR 250, EAT. In that case, a company facing severe financial difficulties appointed joint administrators under what has become known as the 'pre-pack administration' – see 'Relevant insolvency proceedings – meaning of "relevant insolvency proceedings"' below for further details. Prior to their appointment, the managing director of the company had discussions about the possibility of a major supplier purchasing the company. Reluctant to take on the company's debts, the supplier decided to set up a subsidiary for the purposes of purchasing purely the company's assets and premises and employing several of its staff, including the claimant. The joint administrators were appointed on the same day as the sale of assets to the new subsidiary. Just short of a year later, the claimant was dismissed and sought to claim unfair dismissal. Before the tribunal, the question arose as to whether Reg 8(7) applied to exclude the normal protections afforded by Regs 4 and 7. This depended on whether the joint administration comprised 'bankruptcy or analogous proceedings' within the meaning of Reg 8(7) or 'relevant insolvency proceedings which have been opened in relation to the transferor not with a view to the liquidation of the assets of the transferor' within the meaning of

483

Reg 8(6). If the latter, then the operation of Regs 4 and 7 would not be excluded. The employment judge found that, in this case, the appointment of joint administrators was made with a view to the eventual liquidation of the assets of the transferor company, within the meaning of Reg 8(7), and that Reg 4 was therefore disapplied, with the consequence that the claimant's employment was not transferred to the transferee.

On appeal, the EAT upheld the employment judge's decision. His Honour Judge Peter Clarke (sitting alone) reasoned that the question of whether particular insolvency proceedings are to be characterised as having been instituted with a view to the liquidation of the transferor company's assets, within the meaning of Reg 8(7), is a question of fact for the employment tribunal; it is not purely a question of domestic insolvency law. Where joint administrators continue to trade the business with a view to its sale as a going concern, any relevant transfer in those circumstances will attract the Reg 4 protection for employees (apart from the specific carve-out in respect of debts that are payable under the National Insurance Fund). However, that is not what happened in the instant case. The administrators of the company had concluded that the first objective of rescuing the company as a going concern was not achievable and had taken immediate steps to sell the assets. This was seen as the best course for realising the optimum return for creditors in the final liquidation of the company. On those facts the tribunal had been entitled to conclude that the appointment of joint administrators was with a view to the eventual liquidation of the assets of the company.

6.44 It should be pointed out that the EAT's decision in Oakland was, in fact, successfully appealed to the Court of Appeal, but on the basis of reasoning that was entirely unrelated to the Reg 8(6)/8(7) issue – see Oakland v Wellswood (Yorkshire) Ltd 2010 ICR 902, CA. The Court of Appeal ruled that the courts below had overlooked the fact that the claimant was, in fact, able to establish the necessary continuity of employment to claim unfair dismissal against the transferee without needing to resort to the TUPE Regulations at all – see Chapter 7, 'Continuity of employment', under 'Residual application of ERA – insolvency'. But notwithstanding that the TUPE issues were out-of-scope on the appeal, Lord Justice Moses made the following obiter remarks concerning those issues: 'It would seem to me most unwise for us to give a binding pronouncement on the correctness or otherwise of the contention that administration necessarily excludes the application of Reg 8(7). I would only, for my part, wish to emphasise that that is a strongly arguable point, and the only reason I agree that it should not be resolved today is that the Secretary of State is not here and, since [the respondent] is in the process of being liquidated almost as we speak, and therefore has no representation here today, it would be unwise to reach and pronounce upon any definitive conclusion.'

A definitive conclusion has since been pronounced – one that establishes beyond doubt that Lord Justice Moses was correct to see force in the suggestion that administration necessarily excludes the application of Reg 8(7). In OTG Ltd v Barke 2011 ICR 781, EAT – a case which comprised five separate tribunal decisions joined on appeal – the EAT essentially had to determine whether it is always a question of fact whether administration comprises proceedings 'analogous to bankruptcy' for the purposes of Reg 8(7) or whether there is an absolute rule that administration is not analogous to bankruptcy. For reasons elaborated upon under 'Relevant insolvency proceedings – meaning of "relevant insolvency proceedings"' below, the EAT – presided over by its then President, Mr Justice Underhill – decisively ruled that administration is not analogous to bankruptcy proceedings, and Reg 8(7) cannot therefore ever apply to that particular procedure. Although it accepted that, in some cases, administration ends up with the liquidation of the insolvent business's assets, the EAT was persuaded that the essential purpose of this particular insolvency procedure is to operate within the context of the rescue culture and requires the appointed administrator, at the point of commencement of the administration, to consider whether the primary object of rescuing the company as a going concern can be achieved. This is because, as previously noted, an administrator when appointed is expected to identify one out of three different but strictly ranked objectives set out in para 3(1) of Schedule B1 to the IA, the principal one of which is the rescue of the company as a going concern. Only if this is not considered to be viable will he or she select one of the alternative objectives entailing the realisation of assets in order to make a distribution to the company's secure and preferred creditors – see 'Types of insolvency procedure – company administration' above.

The Court of Appeal subsequently dismissed an appeal in one of the cases **6.45** heard by the EAT in the OTG litigation, confirming the EAT's 'absolute' approach and rejecting the fact-based analysis adopted in Oakland. In Key2Law (Surrey) LLP v De'Antiquis and anor 2012 ICR 881, CA, the Court held that it would be unsatisfactory if the triggering of Reg 8(7) depended on evidence of events leading up to the appointment of the administrator. Such an analysis might well produce an uncertain picture as to the objective intended. Given that all options are open to an administrator and that the original intention of an administration may never be realised, it could not be said that the appointment of an administrator is made 'with a view' to the liquidation of the company's assets. That may be what happens in practice, and it may in many cases be apparent from the outset that that is what is going to happen, but it is not always so.

Summary. In the light of the above, the following types of insolvency **6.46** proceedings would appear to come within the scope of Reg 8(7) as being analogous to bankruptcy proceedings 'which have been instituted with a view to the liquidation of the assets':

- *personal bankruptcy*: Regulation 8(7) expressly states that 'Regulations 4 and 7 do not apply to any relevant transfer where the transferor is the subject of bankruptcy proceedings' – a provision that receives its legitimacy from the explicit mention of 'bankruptcy' in Article 5(1) of the Acquired Rights Directive. Therefore if a trustee in bankruptcy sells a business that was run by the bankrupt, the employees' contracts of employment do not automatically pass to the purchaser and the employees will be redundant. They would be eligible for redundancy and insolvency payments payable by the Secretary of State in accordance with Parts XI and XII of the ERA

- *compulsory liquidation*: clearly, an order by a court for the compulsory winding up of an insolvent company would be 'analogous' to bankruptcy and is instituted with a view to the liquidation of the assets of the transferor. Reg 8(7) would therefore apply; and

- *creditors' or members' voluntary liquidation*: such proceedings are commenced with a view to winding up the company and are also 'analogous' to bankruptcy. This view concurs with the stance taken in the BIS Guide, 'Employment rights on the transfer of an undertaking' ('the BIS Guide') (last updated in January 2014), which, in contrasting these forms of insolvency proceedings with those constituting 'relevant insolvency proceedings' within the terms of Reg 4(6), states: 'It is the Department's view that "relevant insolvency proceedings" mean any collective insolvency proceedings in which the whole or part of the business or undertaking is transferred to another entity as a going concern. That is to say, it covers an insolvency proceeding in which all creditors of the debtor may participate, and in relation to which the insolvent office holder owes a duty to all creditors. The Department considers that "relevant insolvency proceedings" does not cover winding-up by either creditors or members where there is no such transfer.'

Administration, on the other hand, will fall within Reg 8(6) as comprising 'relevant insolvency proceedings' rather than proceedings analogous to bankruptcy instituted with a view to the liquidation of the assets within the meaning of Reg 8(7). This is so regardless of whether the administrator strives from the outset to keep the business running while taking steps to sell off its viable parts as a going concern, or decides instead that this primary objective is unlikely to be achieved and so seeks to realise and distribute the assets, leading to the dissolution of the failed business.

6.47 As has previously been noted, the appointment of the Official Receiver in a compulsory winding up automatically terminates the contracts of employees employed in the insolvent business – see 'Types of insolvency procedure – liquidation (winding-up)' above. Although the same is not necessarily true in a creditors' voluntary winding up, in practice liquidators will often take immediate steps to terminate employees' contracts of employment because their continued employment will not be in the best interests of creditors. Since

486

the special protection against unfair dismissal in Reg 7 is disapplied as a consequence of Reg 8(7) applying, such dismissals would not be automatically unfair but may be unfair on normal principles. Employees would be eligible to receive redundancy and insolvency payments from the National Insurance Fund in accordance with the provisions of Parts XI and XII of the ERA. If, in the comparatively rare event of the liquidator retaining the services of employees and subsequently selling the viable parts of the insolvent business as a going concern, although this would be a relevant transfer to which the TUPE Regulations apply, Reg 8(7) would operate to prevent the automatic transfer of the employees' employment to the transferee (see immediately below).

Consequences of disapplication of Regs 4 and 7   6.48

When it applies, the effect of Reg 8(7) is to disapply the whole of Regs 4 and 7 in respect of employees who are employed by the transferor at the time of the relevant transfer. So far as Reg 4 is concerned, this means that such employees will not be entitled to the automatic transfer of their employment to the new employer; nor will the new employer acquire the rights, duties, powers and liabilities under or in connection with the employees' contracts. If the employees are taken on by the new owner, they will not be entitled to the protection against detrimental variation of their terms and conditions by reason of the transfer, which would normally be guaranteed by Reg 4(4).

As for the disapplication of Reg 7, the consequence of this is that employees will be deprived of the special protections against unfair dismissal normally applicable to dismissals by reason of a relevant transfer. Thus, employees who are dismissed by the liquidator or trustee in bankruptcy prior to the relevant transfer will not be able to claim that they have been automatically unfairly dismissed for a reason connected to the transfer that is not an economic, technical or organisational reason entailing changes in the workforce. The same applies if they are taken on by the new employer but subsequently dismissed for a transfer-connected reason. However, it is important to note that this is not to say that unfair dismissal rights are entirely excluded. There is nothing to prevent an employee who qualifies for the right to claim unfair dismissal from bringing a claim against the transferor and/or insolvency practitioner personally prior to the transfer, or, if taken on, the new employer after the transfer. In such a case, the unfairness of any such dismissal would be judged according to normal principles of unfair dismissal law.

Although the disapplication of Regs 4 and 7 means that the key provisions of 6.49 the TUPE Regulations do not apply, it is also important to note that the Regulations' other key substantive provisions do so. Thus, employees will be entitled to the protection in respect of the transfer of collective agreements in Reg 5 and the transfer of union recognition in Reg 6 (see Chapter 3, 'What transfers?', under 'Collective rights and liabilities'). The provisions dealing with employee liability information in Reg 11 and information and

487

collective consultation in Regs 13–16 will also apply (see Chapter 8, 'Information and consultation').

Finally, it should be noted that an employee who is taken on by the transferee is likely to retain his or her continuity of employment notwithstanding the operation of Reg 8(7). By virtue of S.218(2) ERA, where a business or undertaking 'is transferred from one person to another' an employee's period of employment in the trade, business or undertaking at the time of the transfer is deemed to count as a period of employment with the transferee, and the transfer will not break the continuity of the period of employment. This provision – which is discussed in detail in Chapter 7, 'Continuity of employment' – sits entirely outside of the TUPE Regulations, which means that the disapplication of Reg 4 has no effect on an employee's continuity.

6.50 'Relevant insolvency proceedings'

Regulation 8(1) provides that the provisions of Reg 8(2)–(6) will apply 'if at the time of a relevant transfer the transferor is subject to relevant insolvency proceedings'. Reg 8(5) stipulates: 'Reg 4 shall not operate to transfer liability for the sums payable to the relevant employee under the relevant statutory schemes.' The phrases 'relevant employee' and 'relevant statutory schemes' in this context are defined by Reg 8(2) and (4). The overall effect of Reg 8(5) can be summarised as providing that, in a case where the transferor is subject to relevant insolvency proceedings, its liability to employees for some types of statutory payment will be excluded from the liabilities that pass to the transferee on a relevant transfer, and instead that liability will be paid to the employee out of the National Insurance Fund.

Regulation 9(1) provides: 'If at the time of a relevant transfer the transferor is subject to relevant insolvency proceedings these Regulations shall not prevent the transferor or transferee (or an insolvency practitioner) and appropriate representatives of assigned employees agreeing to permitted variations.' Sub-paragraphs (2)–(7) flesh out what is meant by 'appropriate representatives', 'assigned employees' and 'permitted variations' in this regard.

6.51 It will be noted that both of these provisions are only triggered where the transferor is subject to 'relevant insolvency provisions' as defined in Reg 8(6). This raises the question: which types of insolvency procedure outlined earlier in this chapter fall within the scope of this definition? This is a crucial matter to which we shall now turn.

6.52 Meaning of 'relevant insolvency proceedings'

The starting point in considering the application of Regs 8(5) and 9 is the meaning given to 'relevant insolvency proceedings'. Reg 8(6) defines these as being 'insolvency proceedings which have been opened in relation to the transferor not with a view to the liquidation of the assets of the transferor and which are under the supervision of an insolvency practitioner'. It should be noted that the insolvency proceedings have to be under the supervision of an 'insolvency practitioner'. This point has also been made in respect of Reg 8(7) – see 'Bankruptcy and liquidation proceedings – proceedings "under the supervision of" insolvency practitioner' above.

Attention has also already been drawn to the slight difference in wording between Reg 8(6) and Reg 8(7), in that the former speaks of 'proceedings which have been opened', whereas the latter speaks of 'proceedings which have been instituted'. As outlined previously, we can find no clear explanation for this difference in wording and do not believe that it has any significance in practice – see the discussion under 'Bankruptcy and liquidation proceedings' above. What is identical between the two provisions is that both use the words 'which have been', denoting the past tense. As was made clear by the EAT in Secretary of State for Trade and Industry v Slater 2008 ICR 54, EAT, in order for either Reg 8(6) or Reg 8(7) to be engaged, it is necessary for the insolvency proceedings in question to have actually been opened/instituted prior to the date of the relevant transfer. If the proceedings commence after the transfer had occurred, then the TUPE Regulations will apply in full, not just the reduced protections provided for in Reg 8(6) or Reg 8(7). For a fuller discussion of the Slater decision, see 'Bankruptcy and liquidation proceedings – "… which have been instituted with a view to the liquidation of the assets"' above.

Criticism of drafting of Reg 8(6). Turning to the types of proceedings that 6.53 will qualify as 'relevant insolvency proceedings' under Reg 8(6), it is immediately apparent that a straightforward list is not provided. This lack has been criticised in some quarters. However, the DTI in its Public Consultation Document on the draft regulations in March 2005 gave a number of reasons for not simply listing the proceedings to which Reg 8(5) (and, for that matter, Reg 9) was intended to apply. These included that the lack of a list made the provision much simpler, given that there are different (albeit largely equivalent) procedures in England and Wales, Scotland and Northern Ireland, and that this ensured beyond doubt that the UK has not extended the coverage of the exclusionary provision more widely than the Acquired Rights Directive allows.

Identifying main purpose of the insolvency proceedings. Whatever may be 6.54 the drafting ambiguities, it seems reasonably clear that in assessing whether the limitation provided for by Reg 8(5) applies, the most important factor to consider is the purpose of the proceedings – in particular, whether they have been opened with a view to the liquidation of the assets of the transferor. The BIS Guide asserts that '"relevant insolvency proceedings" means any collective insolvency proceedings in which the whole or part of the business or undertaking is transferred to another entity as a going concern'. In this context, the BIS Guide makes it clear that a 'collective' insolvency proceeding means

489

'an insolvency proceeding in which all creditors of the debtor may participate, and in relation to which the insolvency office-holder owes a duty to all creditors'. The Guide expressly states that this would exclude a situation where the insolvent company is wound up as a result of a members' or creditors' voluntary liquidation.

It has to be said that this interpretation is not immediately apparent from the language of the Regulations. In any event, in order to clarify the Government's approach, more specific guidance was issued in June 2006 by the Insolvency Service to coincide with the coming into force of the 2006 Regulations. This guidance stated that the determining factor is the main or sole purpose of the procedure rather than its outcome in a specific instance. This fits in with the words 'opened with a view to' in the definition of 'relevant insolvency proceedings' in Reg 8(6), which implies that the key factor is the aim at the outset of the proceedings. Although the guidance is sufficient to enable insolvency practitioners to understand how Regs 8 and 9 apply to most straightforward types of insolvency proceedings, problems of interpretation may still arise in more complex scenarios – particularly where different types of insolvency proceedings overlap, or where the purpose of the insolvency proceedings changes.

6.55 **Which insolvency procedures comprise 'relevant insolvency proceedings'?** It is possible to be fairly confident that certain of the kinds of insolvency proceedings discussed under 'Types of insolvency procedure' come within the definition of 'relevant insolvency proceedings' in Reg 8(6). This is because they are opened for a purpose other than the liquidation of the assets, and are under the supervision of an insolvency practitioner. The proceedings in question are:

- *a company voluntary arrangement:* the objective of this type of insolvency arrangement is to enable the company to continue as a going concern under the supervision of an insolvency practitioner. As the insolvency guidance points out, in a voluntary arrangement the debtor is left in control of the assets and the function of the insolvency practitioner is merely to supervise the arrangement

- *administrative receivership:* since an administrative receiver is appointed to realise assets to pay off secured creditors but not to liquidate all the company's assets, it would seem that this form of insolvency proceeding comes within Reg 8(6) as it would 'have been opened... not with a view to the liquidation of the assets of the transferor'; and

- *administration:* for reasons discussed in detail immediately below, it has been a matter of some controversy whether administration falls within the definition of 'relevant insolvency proceedings' in Reg 8(6) or whether, in some cases at least, it is a form of proceedings analogous to bankruptcy instituted with a view to the liquidation of the assets to which Reg 8(7) accordingly applies. The matter had been the subject of conflicting case law at EAT level, but it was established beyond doubt by the Court of Appeal in Key2Law (Surrey) LLP v De'Antiquis and anor 2012 ICR 881, CA, that administration is invariably to be regarded as falling within Reg 8(6) rather than Reg 8(7).

Administration (including 'pre-pack administration'). As has already been 6.56 seen, the provisions in the IA governing administration require the objective of the administration to be identified according to a strictly prioritised order – see 'Types of insolvency procedure – company administration' above. The first two objectives seek to avoid a winding up, and it is only if these are unachievable that an administrator is entitled to select the third option – namely, the realisation of the assets in order to make a beneficial distribution to secured and preferred creditors. Since the administrator is required to identify his or her aim at the outset of the administration, it seemed arguable that if he or she chose the third option at the outset the administration might fall outside the definition of 'relevant insolvency proceedings' for the purposes of Reg 8(6) and instead comprise 'proceedings that are "analogous" to bankruptcy' which are 'instituted with a view to the liquidation of the assets' within the meaning of Reg 8(7). This, indeed, was the approach taken by the EAT in Oakland v Wellswood (Yorkshire) Ltd 2009 IRLR 250, EAT – discussed in detail in the context of Reg 8(7) under 'Bankruptcy and liquidation proceedings – "… which have been instituted with a view to the liquidation of the assets"' above. The Appeal Tribunal in that case ruled that the question of whether administration is instituted with a view to the liquidation of the assets so as to bring Reg 8(7) into play was a question of fact for the employment tribunal to decide, and that this decision should essentially be predicated on the objectives of the administration in the particular case and the decisions taken by the administrator as to the viability of keeping the business functioning as a going concern.

However, this approach has since been comprehensively disapproved, first by a different division of the EAT and then by the Court of Appeal. In OTG Ltd v Barke 2011 ICR 781, EAT, the Appeal Tribunal, presided over by its then President, Mr Justice Underhill, declined to follow the Oakland decision and held instead that there is an absolute rule that administration in every case attracts the operation of Reg 8(6) as opposed to the more draconian provisions of Reg 8(7). In legal parlance, the EAT sanctioned a 'bright line' rule being applied to administration in preference to the 'question of fact' approach taken by the EAT in Oakland.

The Court of Appeal then dismissed an appeal in one of the cases heard by the 6.57 EAT. In Key2Law (Surrey) LLP v De'Antiquis and anor (above), it endorsed Underhill P's 'absolute' approach and rejected the fact-based analysis adopted in Oakland. Lord Justice Rimer, giving the fullest judgment of a unanimous

491

court, noted that it would be unsatisfactory if the triggering of Reg 8(7) depended on the evidence leading up to the appointment of the administrator. Such an analysis might well produce an uncertain picture as to the objective intended. As the EAT had noted, the 'absolute' approach had the benefit of legal certainty.

Like Underhill P in the EAT, the Court based its conclusion on a comparison of the procedures and obligations of the administration scheme with the purpose of Article 5(1) of the Acquired Rights Directive, which Reg 8(7) implements. Rimer LJ noted that Article 5(1) is concerned with proceedings 'which have been instituted' with liquidation in mind, i.e. with the objective of the insolvency proceedings at the point they are instituted. He agreed with the EAT that this requires a consideration of the purpose of an administration order when actually made, rather than a consideration of what the applicants for the order hoped to achieve by it if it were to be made. In this regard, he noted that under the IA, when an administrator's appointment takes effect, his or her first obligation is to work towards the rescue of the company, unless he or she thinks it not reasonably practicable or that a better result could be achieved for the company's creditors. As the EAT pointed out, even though it may immediately be clear that a rescue of the company is not feasible, the matter must nevertheless be formally considered. Rimer LJ did not think that this could realistically be described as an appointment made 'with a view' to the liquidation of the transferor's assets, within the scope of Article 5. While liquidation may be what is envisaged, and what eventually happens, that is not always so given the requirement on the administrator formally to engage with the alternatives.

6.58 Much of the case law outlined above concerned so-called 'pre-pack' administrations. This is a process that has become quite common in recent years, involving an administrator who, prior to his appointment, works with the insolvent business to secure its sale immediately upon the formal commencement of the administration. Pre-packs are used where the degree of insolvency is such that there will be no surplus available from the proceeds of sale for distribution to the company's unsecured creditors and the proposed sale is likely to be advantageous by comparison with what might be yielded if the statutory formalities associated with post-administration sales – for example, the requirement to hold a creditors' meeting – have to be observed. The procedure has been viewed by some as controversial, since it seems to pay mere lip service to the formal requirements of the IA. Its legitimacy has, however, been upheld by the courts – see, for example, DKLL Solicitors v HM Revenue and Customs 2007 BCC 908, ChD. The EAT in OTG Ltd v Barke (above) made it clear that even pre-pack administrations do not fall within Reg 8(7), and although the Court of Appeal did not expressly focus its conclusions in the Key2Law appeal on pre-pack arrangements, its reasoning – based on the statutory scheme underpinning all administrations rather than on the circumstances specific to any particular administration – means that the full extent of the EAT's conclusion is still sound. Pre-pack administrations, and administrations in general, do not trigger Reg 8(7) and TUPE protection therefore applies in full, subject to the application of Reg 8(6).

Foreign insolvency proceedings. In the rare event of a relevant transfer **6.59** occurring in Great Britain where the business or undertaking is subject to foreign insolvency proceedings, it would be necessary to consider whether those proceedings come within the definition of 'relevant insolvency proceedings'. If they do, then the provisions of Regs 8(5) and 9 as described below would apply.

Liability for sums payable under statutory scheme   **6.60**

Under the 1981 TUPE Regulations, the liabilities in respect of employees transferring from an insolvent business passed to the transferee in accordance with the same principles as those applicable to any other type of TUPE transfer. However, under the 2006 Regulations, Reg 8(5) provides that certain liabilities in respect of transferring employees that would ordinarily attach to the transferee will instead be met by the payments out of the National Insurance Fund where the transferor is subject to 'relevant insolvency proceedings' as described under '"Relevant insolvency proceedings"' above. This is in keeping with the Government's desire to encourage the rescue of more insolvent businesses.

As previously mentioned, Reg 8(5) reflects the option given in Article 5(2)(a) of the Acquired Rights Directive. This allows EU Member States to provide that the transferor's debts arising from any contracts of employment or employment relationships and payable before the transfer or the opening of the insolvency proceedings need not be transferred to the transferee, provided that employees' rights in this regard are protected by payments from state guarantee institutions that are at least equivalent to those required by the EU Insolvency Directive (No.2008/94). The categories of debt guaranteed under the relevant UK provisions satisfy this condition, since they are more extensive than those required under the Directive itself.

Regulation 8(5) stipulates that 'Reg 4 shall not operate to transfer liability for **6.61** the sums payable to a relevant employee under the relevant statutory schemes'. As explained under '"Relevant employee"' below, Reg 8(2) and (4) define 'relevant employee' and 'relevant statutory schemes' for this purpose. Taken together, these provisions essentially aim to ensure that where a relevant transfer takes place in the context of 'relevant insolvency proceedings', liabilities in respect of certain debts and payments payable to employees do not transfer – as they normally would – but remain with the transferor. However, in view of the transferor's insolvency, responsibility for payment is taken on by the Secretary of State for Trade and Industry out of the National Insurance Fund. Whenever

493

such a payment is made, all rights and remedies of the employee with respect to that payment are transferred to the Secretary of State. Under insolvency law, such payments will usually attract preferential status, and so the Secretary of State will often seek to recover sums paid from the proceeds of sale or other realisation of the insolvent business's assets.

6.62 **'Relevant employee'.** Regulation 8(5) only applies in respect of a 'relevant employee'. Such a person is defined as an employee of the transferor whose contract of employment transfers to the transferee by virtue of the operation of the TUPE Regulations (Reg 8(2)(a)); or whose employment with the transferor is terminated before the time of the relevant transfer in circumstances where he or she has been automatically unfairly dismissed by reason of the transfer or for a reason connected to it within the meaning of Reg 7(1) (Reg 8(2)(b)).

In OTG Ltd v Barke 2011 ICR 781, EAT, the EAT explained that Reg 8(2) therefore creates two categories of 'relevant employee' and that the effect of the application of Reg 8(1)–(6) with regard to the liabilities for which the Secretary of State ends up being responsible can be different depending on which of the categories applies in a particular case. For details, see 'Which liabilities for debts and payments do not transfer?' below.

6.63 **'Relevant statutory schemes'.** The liabilities that are not transferred to the transferee by virtue of Reg 8(5) are specifically those sums payable under 'the relevant statutory schemes'. These are defined in Reg 8(4) as the statutory insolvency payments provisions in Part XII of the ERA and the statutory redundancy payments provisions in Chapter VI of Part XI of the ERA (and their equivalent under the statutory provisions applicable to Northern Ireland). The specific debts and payments covered by these provisions are listed under 'Which liabilities for debts and payments do not transfer?' below.

Part XII of the ERA (or Part XIV of the Employment Rights (Northern Ireland) Order 1996) covers 'Insolvency of Employers' and provides that an employee can apply to the Secretary of State for payment of certain debts out of the National Insurance Fund if the employee can demonstrate that the employer is insolvent, that his or her employment has been terminated, and that he or she was entitled to the whole or part of the debt in question on the 'appropriate date' (S.182 ERA). The appropriate date for the purposes of a claim for arrears of pay is the date on which the employer became insolvent, and for the purposes of other debts to which Part XII applies (including holiday pay and payments in lieu of notice) is the date of the employer's insolvency or the date of termination of the employee's employment, whichever is the later – S.185(a) and (c) ERA. However, these requirements are modified by Reg 8(3) TUPE, which provides that the normal qualifying condition for payment of these debts – namely, that the employee's employment has actually been terminated by the insolvent employer or insolvency practitioner – does not apply to a relevant employee as defined in Reg 8(2). Thus, such employees do not have to show

494

that their employment has been terminated to be eligible for payments out of the Fund in respect of the debts in question. Reg 8(3) also deems that the date of the transfer is to be treated as the date of termination and the transferor is to be treated as the employer.

As mentioned above, the EAT in OTG Ltd v Barke 2011 ICR 781, EAT, held **6.64** that the scope of the Secretary of State's liability under the appropriate statutory schemes for picking up the relevant debts and payments may depend on which of the two categories of 'relevant employee' (as defined in Reg 8(2)) applies to the claimant – see '"Relevant employee"' above. The EAT pointed out that the Secretary of State is liable only for 'past liabilities', i.e. for liabilities that have crystallised at the 'appropriate date' as defined above. This effectively means that in respect of a 'relevant employee' who has not been dismissed prior to the transfer, and whose employment is therefore automatically transferred to the transferee under Reg 4, liabilities under Part XII of the ERA will only be met if the employee's actual date of termination coincides with the 'appropriate date'. Since the appropriate date for these purposes is the date of the insolvency or the date of the transfer (whichever is the later), the termination of employment of an employee who has been transferred to the transferee will need to coincide with the date of the insolvency or transfer for the transferee to be relieved of liability for making the relevant payments and for that liability to be picked up by the Secretary of State instead. (Note that one of the cases considered by the EAT in the OTG litigation was the subject of a further appeal to the Court of Appeal – Key2Law (Surrey) LLP v De'Antiquis and anor 2012 ICR 881, CA. That appeal concerned only the application of Reg 8(7) and so does not affect the EAT's decision as to who is a relevant employee under Reg 8(1)–(6).)

On the particular facts of the OTG case, the transfer occurred on the same day that the company was put into administration. There were two claimants: L (a woman) was found to have been dismissed prior to the transfer/insolvency, and B (a man) was dismissed the day after the transfer/insolvency. Upholding the decision of the employment tribunal, the EAT ruled that the transferee rather than the Secretary of State was liable for B's payment in lieu of notice and unpaid holiday pay. Since these termination debts/payments had not yet accrued on the 'appropriate date', the reality was that the provisions of Reg 8(1)–(6) did not apply to relieve the transferee of liability to meet them.

However, the position was different in respect of L. In her case, the Secretary of **6.65** State conceded that she had been dismissed for redundancy prior to the date of the transfer/insolvency. As such, she came within the other category of 'relevant employee' defined in Reg 8(2). Outside of an insolvency context, where an employee has been dismissed prior to the transfer for a non-ETO reason connected to the transfer, he or she would be deemed to be employed at the date of the transfer, with the consequence that the transferee would inherit liability for all the termination debts payable to the employee. But this is

495

precisely the circumstance that is modified in an insolvency situation to which Reg 8(6) applies. L's was such a case. Reg 8(1)–(5) operated to relieve the transferee of liability for the debts/payments owed to her (in so far as these were ones payable under the relevant statutory scheme). The EAT accepted that, since L had been dismissed before the date of the transfer/insolvency, liability for the relevant termination payments was deemed to have accrued on the 'appropriate date', with the consequence that it was the Secretary of State who was liable to pick up the tab for satisfying the debts/payments claimed.

The EAT's conclusion in the OTG case that liabilities incurred in respect of a transferring employee after the transfer cannot, under Reg 8, be attached to the Secretary of State applies even where the employee is dismissed on the same day as the transfer. In Pressure Coolers Ltd v Molloy and ors 2012 ICR 51, EAT, M was employed by MI Ltd. On 13 January 2009, at 11 am, MI Ltd went into administration and there was a TUPE transfer of its business, and of M's employment, to PC Ltd. At 3 pm on the same day M was dismissed by PC Ltd, in circumstances later found by a tribunal to have been unfair. The EAT held that PC Ltd, as transferee, and not the Secretary of State, was liable for M's basic award and notice pay. Reg 8 is designed to relieve the transferee only of liabilities incurred towards transferring employees by the transferor before the transfer. Since M was unfairly dismissed by the transferee after the transfer, liability to pay the basic award and notice pay could not sensibly be said to constitute a liability incurred by the transferor.

6.66 A similar situation arose in Secretary of State for Business, Innovation and Skills v Dobrucki and ors EAT 0505/13. There, a company, RFM, got into financial difficulty and administrators were appointed on 14 June 2011. Two hours later they sold the business as a going concern to S, the principal shareholder. The business continued to trade but only for three days, ceasing trading on 17 June. When employees of RFM sought payments from the National Insurance Fund, an employment judge awarded them sums in respect of unpaid wages, notice pay and (in one case) a redundancy payment on the basis of their dismissals on 17 June. On appeal by the Secretary of State, the EAT held that the judge was wrong to do so. The relevant transfer occurred on 14 June and, following the Pressure Coolers case (above), only those debts that had accrued prior to or coincident with the transfer potentially attached to the Secretary of State. It followed that the Secretary of State had no liability for arrears of pay after 14 June or for any sums in respect of notice pay or redundancy pay.

Chapter VI of Part XI of the ERA (Ss.166–170) (and the equivalent Part VI of Part XII of the Employment Rights (Northern Ireland) Order 1996) deals with 'Payments by Secretary of State'. The payments in question are redundancy payments. In summary, it provides that, where an employee has not been paid a redundancy payment that is due to him or her from an insolvent employer, he or she can apply to the Secretary of State for payment of it out of the National Insurance Fund (S.166 ERA). It should be noted that the provision in Reg 8(3) deeming a 'relevant employee' to have been dismissed for the purposes of payment of debts under the statutory scheme in Part XII of the ERA does not apply in respect of payments of statutory redundancy pay. Relevant employees will not therefore be deemed to have been dismissed if they have not actually been so in order to enable them to claim redundancy payments.

Under both statutory schemes, it is the insolvency of the employer that triggers **6.67** entitlement to claim for the respective debts or payments from out of the National Insurance Fund. An employer is regarded as being 'insolvent' under either scheme if: (a) a winding-up order has been made or a resolution for winding up has been passed; (b) an administration order has been made; (c) a receiver or manager of the company's undertaking has been appointed; (d) possession has been taken by or on behalf of the holders of any debentures secured by a floating charge, of any property of the company comprised in or subject to the charge; or (e) a voluntary arrangement has been approved under Part I IA (Ss.166(7) and 183(3) ERA). For the reasons mentioned under 'Meaning of "relevant insolvency proceedings"' above, it would seem likely that (b)–(e) would come within the definition of 'relevant insolvency proceedings' and so would trigger the application of Reg 8(5), but that a winding-up order or resolution for winding up would not. Instead, Reg 8(7) – providing for the disapplication of Reg 4 in its entirety – would apply (see 'Bankruptcy and liquidation proceedings' above).

Which liabilities for debts and payments do not transfer? The payments **6.68** included in the relevant statutory schemes are set out below. (Note that all of these are subject to the statutory cap on a week's pay – currently (from 6 April 2015) £475. This is uprated annually):

- up to eight weeks' arrears of pay, owed as at the date the employer became insolvent (subject to a current maximum (from 6 April 2015) of £3,800). 'Arrears of pay' includes a guarantee payment, payment for time off for carrying out trade union duties or the duties of a public office, payment when an employee is suspended on medical or maternity grounds, and a protective award made under S.189 of the Trade Union and Labour Relations (Consolidation) Act 1992 (TULR(C)A)

- pay in lieu of notice up to the statutory minimum notice periods (up to a current maximum (from 6 April 2015) of £5,700)

- up to six weeks' accrued but unpaid holiday pay (to a current maximum (from 6 April 2015) of £2,850). The holiday must have accrued in the last 12 months

- the basic award of compensation for unfair dismissal (up to a current maximum (from 6 April 2015) of £14,250), due on the later of the date the

497

employer became insolvent, the date of termination of employment or the date the award was made

- a reasonable sum as reimbursement for any fee or premium paid by an apprentice or articled clerk (which is not subject to the current limit on a week's pay)

(all payable by virtue of S.174 ERA); and

- a statutory redundancy payment (up to a current maximum (from 6 April 2015) of £14,250) – S166 ERA.

6.69 It must be borne in mind that, in order for any of the above payments to be payable, the employee has to be entitled to it. Generally, so far as redundancy is concerned, if the transferor or insolvency practitioner dismisses an employee for a transfer-connected reason comprising an economic, technical or organisational reason entailing changes in the workforce within the meaning of Reg 7(2), the dismissal will be regarded as being for redundancy and will thus trigger entitlement to a statutory redundancy payment (provided the employee has at least two years' continuous service) – see Chapter 4, 'Unfair dismissal', under 'Dismissals potentially fair for an "ETO" reason – ETO dismissals deemed to be by reason of redundancy or SOSR'. In such a case, if the employee is a relevant employee as defined by Reg 8(2) – see '"Relevant employee"' above – then his or her statutory redundancy payment will be met by the Secretary of State via a payment out of the National Insurance Fund. If, however, the employee is dismissed solely or mainly because of the transfer or for a reason that is not an ETO reason, the reason for the dismissal will not be 'redundancy', and no entitlement for a payment out of the Fund will arise. Of course, as the dismissal is unfair and the employee is likely to be entitled to compensation, he or she would be entitled to a basic award, which is calculated according to the same formula as used for statutory redundancy payments. However, the Fund would not pay out the compensatory award. This was made clear in guidance previously issued by the Insolvency Service and now archived entitled 'Redundancy and Insolvency – A Guide for Insolvency Practitioners to employees' rights on the insolvency of their employer' (URN 08/550). That said, it may be that, following a finding of unfair dismissal, a tribunal's decision to award sums in respect of unpaid holiday and the statutory minimum notice period as elements of the compensatory award would provide evidence that these debts, which as we have seen are recoverable from the Fund, were owed by the insolvent transferor to the employee. Any payment already made by the Secretary of State in respect of these particular matters by the time of the remedies hearing would fall to be offset against the compensatory award.

Similar reasoning would apply if an employee is taken on by the transferee. In that case, he or she will not be entitled to a redundancy payment, as such a payment is only payable if (a) the employee had been dismissed, and (b) the reason for dismissal satisfies the definition of redundancy in S.139 ERA. If such a payment is made despite the fact that the employee does not meet the above conditions, then the rule in S.214(2) ERA, that the payment of a statutory redundancy payment serves to break the employee's continuity of employment for redundancy pay purposes, will not apply – Senior Heat Treatment Ltd v Bell and ors 1997 IRLR 614, EAT. The same view was adopted by the Insolvency Service's insolvency guidance on Regs 8 and 9, which stated: 'Where an employee's contract of employment is transferred pursuant to Reg 4 and his employment continues with the transferee, no redundancy payment will be payable as the employee has not been dismissed.' (It is worth reiterating that the provision in Reg 8(3) deeming employees to have been dismissed, which is discussed under '"Relevant statutory schemes"' above, does not apply to redundancy payments paid by the Secretary of State out of the National Insurance Fund under Chapter VI of Part XI of the ERA.)

Other debts that do transfer. Regulation 8 will result in fewer liabilities **6.70** transferring to a transferee, and should in theory make the business more attractive to a potential purchaser. However, there are still liabilities over and above those included in the 'relevant statutory schemes' which will transfer to the transferee in the usual way. These include:

- statutory and contractual debts and liabilities that fall outside the categories payable under the relevant statutory schemes (see Chapter 3, 'What transfers?'), and

- sums owed to employees which exceed the statutory upper limits on the statutory payments (since these payments are subject to the statutory cap on a week's pay, currently (from 6 April 2015) £475). This would include, for example, arrears of pay in excess of eight weeks. In Connor v Secretary of State for Trade and Industry EAT 0589/05 the EAT held that the eight-week limit in this regard was not contrary to the requirements of either the Insolvency Directive or the EU Collective Redundancies Directive (No.80/987).

Changing terms and conditions
6.71

Under the 1981 TUPE Regulations there was some confusion over whether an employee's terms and conditions could be varied by agreement where the reason for the variation was a TUPE transfer. This confusion stemmed partly from the decisions of the House of Lords in (1) British Fuels Ltd v Baxendale and anor (2) Wilson and ors v St Helens Borough Council 1998 ICR 1141, HL. The position is clarified in the 2006 Regs in relation to a non-insolvency TUPE transfer by Reg 4 and in relation to transfers that take place in the course of relevant insolvency proceedings by Reg 9. For a detailed discussion of the normal TUPE rules regarding the ability to vary contracts of employment, see Chapter 5, 'Changing terms and conditions'. This section looks at the

499

special rules on changing terms and conditions of employment in 'relevant insolvency proceedings'.

Summarising the position as it applies outside an insolvency context, Reg 4(5) stipulates that contracts of employment can only be varied by agreement between the transferee and transferred employees if the sole or principal reason for the change is (a) a reason connected with the transfer that is an economic, technical or organisational reason entailing changes in the workforce ('ETO reason'); or (b) a reason altogether unconnected with the transfer. It follows that if the reason for a detrimental change is the transfer itself or is a reason connected to the transfer that is not an ETO reason, that change will be void (and so cannot bind the employee even if he or she has acquiesced to the change by word or deed) – see Reg 4(4). As a result of amendments introduced by the Collective Redundancies and Transfer of Undertakings (Protection of Employment) (Amendment) Regulations 2014 SI 2014/16 ('the Amendment Regulations'), these restrictions have been somewhat modified in the case of amendments to contractual terms incorporated from collective agreements or which are made pursuant to a pre-existing variation term in the contract of employment (Reg 4(5B)). But outside of these specific circumstances, the capacity to vary contractual terms for a reason connected to the transfer is – in a non-insolvency context – severely restricted.

6.72 The special provisions of Reg 9, however, reflect the Government's policy to promote the 'rescue culture' that underlies the insolvency provisions of the Regulations as a whole. In accordance with this policy, the Government took advantage of the option given to Member States in Article 5(2) of the Acquired Rights Directive designed to promote the sale of insolvent businesses as going concerns. This allows Member States to permit employers and employee representatives to agree alterations to employees' terms and conditions of employment provided those alterations are designed to safeguard jobs by ensuring the survival of the undertaking or part of the undertaking. Reg 9 enacts this option, with the additional requirement that the changes must be agreed with appropriate employee representatives and in writing. Changes to terms and conditions can therefore now be agreed even in the absence of an ETO reason subject to compliance with these procedural safeguards. In theory Reg 9 should make it easier for insolvency practitioners to achieve a sale of a going concern by allowing employees to transfer on inferior terms and conditions, and by enabling transferees to harmonise terms and conditions. Under the 1981 TUPE Regulations this would not have been possible. Having said that, the procedural steps required to effect the changes may, in practice, prove so time-consuming that Reg 9 will not assist insolvency practitioners in securing the sale of insolvent businesses as much as was hoped.

6.73 **Procedural requirements.** Regulation 9(1) stipulates that: 'If at the time of a relevant transfer the transferor is subject to relevant insolvency proceedings these Regulations shall not prevent the transferor or transferee (or an insolvency practitioner) and appropriate representatives of assigned employees agreeing to permitted variations.' The remainder of Reg 9 sets out the criteria that must be met for the changes to terms and conditions to be valid:

- the transferor must be subject to 'relevant insolvency proceedings' at the time of the relevant transfer (Reg 9(1)) (see '"Relevant insolvency proceedings"' above)

- the change must be a 'permitted variation' as defined in Reg 9(7)

- the permitted variations must be agreed between the transferor, the transferee or an insolvency practitioner and 'appropriate representatives' of assigned employees as defined in Reg 9(2) – see 'Appropriate representatives' below. In essence, these are union representatives if there is a recognised independent trade union or, if there is no recognised trade union, employee representatives who have been elected either specifically for the purposes of Reg 9 or for other purposes, provided they have authority to agree changes to contracts of employment on behalf of employees (Reg 9(2) and (3))

- the permitted variations must be agreed with representatives of 'assigned employees' – defined in Reg 9(7) as those employees assigned to the organised grouping of resources or employees that is the subject of the relevant transfer. The overarching requirement for employees to be assigned to the business or undertaking being transferred in order for Reg 4 to apply is discussed in detail in Chapter 2, 'Who transfers?', under '"Assigned" to undertaking transferred'; and

- if employees are represented by non-trade union representatives, the permitted variations must be in writing and signed by each representative. In addition, before the agreement is signed, the employer must provide all employees to whom it is going to apply with a copy of the agreement and any guidance that they may need in order to understand it fully (Reg 9(5)).

'Permitted variations'. Regulation 9 applies only if the variation comprises a **6.74** 'permitted variation'. Following amendment introduced by the Amendment Regulations, this is defined in Reg 9(7) as 'a variation to the contract of employment of an assigned employee where – (a) the sole or principal reason for it is the transfer and not a reason referred to in Regulation 4(5)(a)' (i.e. an economic, technical or organisational reason entailing changes in the workforce); and (b) it is designed to safeguard employment opportunities by ensuring the survival of the undertaking, business or part of the undertaking or business that is the subject of the relevant transfer'.

The first thing to note is that, in the light of the first limb of Reg 9(7), the variation in question must not be one where the sole or principal reason for it is an ETO reason. This is in order to distinguish 'permitted variations' that may

501

arise in the course of relevant insolvency proceedings from the kind of variation of contract that is permissible outside of an insolvency context as governed by Reg 4(5). An ETO reason for a variation is valid provided that the normal non-TUPE rules governing variation of contract are adhered to – see Chapter 5, 'Changing terms and conditions', under 'Types of change permitted by TUPE – ETO reasons entailing changes in workforce'. A Reg 9 'permitted variation', on the other hand, attracts the special rules and procedures discussed in this section, and can only arise in an insolvency context.

So, for example, a variation to which Reg 9 might apply but Reg 4(5) would not would be changes entailing employees accepting lower pay or holiday entitlement, giving up a company car or other benefit, or changes made in order to harmonise terms and conditions. None of these are likely to comprise an ETO reason since, as we have seen in Chapter 5, they do not 'entail changes in the workforce'. That said, any new terms and conditions agreed by way of a permitted variation must not breach any other statutory entitlements – for example, a change in contractual pay terms must not be set below the national minimum wage.

6.75 The second limb of Reg 9(7) makes it clear that the objective of agreeing the permitted variation must be to safeguard employment opportunities by ensuring the survival of the undertaking or business. The wording of this requirement may cause difficulties in practice, as the transferee will need to be able to show that the business could not survive without those particular changes. In reality, the effect of the change may not be as clear cut as envisaged by this definition.

Once agreed, a permitted variation takes effect as a term or condition of the assigned employee's contract of employment in place (where relevant) of any term or condition which it varies – Reg 9(6). This raises the question of whether the contractual terms of individual employees who decline to give their consent to the proposed variation are overridden so long as all the procedural requirements, including the reaching of agreement with appropriate representatives, have been honoured. This matter is discussed under 'What if the employee does not agree?' below.

6.76 **'Appropriate representatives'.** The requirements to appoint and elect employee representatives for the purposes of Reg 9 closely mirror those required to appoint and elect employee representatives for information and consultation purposes which are set out in Reg 14. This procedure is discussed in detail in Chapter 8, 'Information and consultation', under 'Informing and consulting appropriate representatives – appropriate representatives'. But the two sets of requirements are not identical, as we shall see below.

As defined in Reg 9(2), 'appropriate representatives' are:

- if the employees are of a description in respect of which an independent trade union is recognised by their employer, representatives of the trade union. It seems likely that union representatives must have the right to agree changes to terms and conditions on behalf of their members, a right which will usually be found in collective agreements or will arise out of custom and practice; or

- in any other case, whichever of the following employee representatives the employer chooses: (i) employee representatives appointed or elected by the assigned employees other than for the purposes of Reg 9, who nevertheless have authority to agree variations to contracts of employment on their behalf; (ii) employee representatives elected by assigned employees for the purposes of Reg 9, in an election satisfying the requirements set out in Reg 14 in respect of information and consultation.

There are two significant differences between these provisions and those that **6.77** apply in respect of the employer's duty to inform and consult. First, in respect of non-trade union representatives, the employee representatives under Reg 9 can only be elected by 'assigned employees' (in other words, employees who are assigned to the undertaking or business or part that is the subject of the relevant transfer). This is in contrast to the position in respect of electing employee representatives to deal with the information and consultation duties. Such representatives are electable by all 'affected employees' – i.e. employees of either the transferor or the transferee who may be affected by the transfer or measures connected with it, whether or not they are assigned to the undertaking or part transferred. Secondly, in the case of Reg 9 representatives, a specific term of office does not need to be determined by the employer, in contrast to the position of Reg 14 representatives, in respect of whom the employer must determine a period of office sufficient to ensure that the representatives are properly informed and consulted – Reg 9(2)(b)(ii).

The remaining requirements are identical for both sets of representatives. Indeed, the same individual may be an appropriate representative for the purposes of both agreeing permitted variations under Reg 9 and participating in the information and consultation process under Regs 13–15. All representatives are entitled to the same protections so far as dismissal and detriment for carrying out their respective duties are concerned – Ss.47(1)(a) and 103(2) ERA. And all such employees (including candidates for an election, not just those who are actually elected) have the right to a reasonable amount of paid time off to enable them to carry out their duties – S.61(1) ERA and, in the case of union representatives, S.168(1)(c) TULR(C)A.

Additional procedural requirements for non-trade union representatives. **6.78** Where assigned employees are represented by non-trade union representatives there are additional requirements designed to give the employees greater protection with regard to permitted variations of their terms and conditions. In its Public Consultation Document on the Regulations published in March 2005, the Government stated that the additional safeguards included in Reg 9

503

are based on similar provisions relating to working time agreements under the Working Time Regulations 1998 SI 1998/1833 (see IDS Employment Law Handbook, 'Working Time' (2013), Chapter 1, 'Scope and key concepts', for details). They are designed to take into account the fact that non-union representatives are not normally involved in negotiating changes to employees' terms and conditions, and are likely to be less experienced and knowledgeable than union representatives. Reg 9(5) accordingly stipulates that:

- the agreement recording a permitted variation must be in writing, and

- signed by each of the representatives who have made it or, where that is not reasonably practicable, by a duly authorised agent of that representative, and

- the employer must, before the agreement is made available for signature, provide all employees to whom it is intended to apply on the date on which it is to come into effect with (i) copies of the text of the agreement and (ii) such guidance as those employees might reasonably require in order to understand it fully.

It has yet to become clear from case law how tribunals will interpret the requirement for guidance – for example, how wide its scope needs to be and whether employees should be advised on what to do if they do not agree to the proposed variation. Clearly these additional requirements add another procedural hurdle for an insolvency practitioner, taking up time and resources in the quest to sell the viable parts of the insolvent business as a going concern. On the other hand, given the potential significance of the changes for an individual employee, the additional procedural requirements may help to reduce the risk of the insolvency practitioner (on behalf of the transferor) or the transferee having to face legal challenges from members of a disenchanted workforce. Although not strictly a requirement within the scope of Reg 9, it may be advisable to obtain from employees their individual written consent for permitted variations that are negotiated and agreed with their representatives. This could be achieved by issuing new contracts containing the amended terms and asking employees to sign these.

6.79 **What if the employee does not agree?** Even if an agreement to vary contracts of employment is negotiated with employee representatives, there may be problems if individual employees do not agree to those changes. The circumstances of insolvency proceedings are such that the negotiated changes will normally involve employees taking a pay cut or a reduction in benefits. While ultimately such changes, in order to be valid, have to be shown to be designed to save jobs, obviously there may be some employees who are unhappy about them. Assuming the procedure has been followed correctly, in theory the permitted variation takes effect nonetheless as a term or condition of their contracts of employment.

It should also be borne in mind that the TUPE Regulations accord employees the right to resign where a relevant transfer involves or would involve a substantial change in working conditions to their material detriment – Reg 4(9). This right – which has been extensively analysed in Chapter 4, 'Unfair dismissal', under 'Material detriment dismissals' – appears to allow the employees to regard themselves as having been dismissed if they resign on the basis of a change that need not amount to a fundamental breach of contract or even to a breach of contract at all. It is, as yet, far from clear how (if at all) Reg 4(9) ties in with the ability to agree permitted variations in the course of insolvency proceedings under Reg 9. However, there is a risk that individual employees who are disgruntled with the outcome agreed on their behalf by their representatives might utilise the right in Reg 4(9) to challenge permitted variations. Presumably, the hope is that employees will weigh up the risk of losing their employment altogether – which is a considerable risk if the prospects for sale of the business are reduced owing to concern about legal challenges to the validity of agreed contractual changes.

Practical issues. There may be situations where negotiating permitted variations **6.80** does safeguard employment opportunities and ensure the survival of the company. However, the business of complying with the procedure may not be straightforward in practice. This is because:

- it can take time to appoint appropriate representatives, particularly if all employees are not covered by recognised trade unions and elections need to be arranged

- the negotiations to seek agreement to changes in terms and conditions may take some time and even then may not result in an agreement. In particular, it will be hard for insolvency practitioners to manage this process if there are ongoing negotiations with several potential purchasers, each with different ideas about the changes which need to be made to safeguard the business

- the second limb of the definition of a 'permitted variation' (Reg 9(7)(b)) may in practice limit its scope, since it will have to be demonstrated that the change directly ensures the survival of the business. Although there is no prescribed time limit for the change to take place, it therefore seems likely that in order to come within the definition of 'permitted variations', a change should be effected as close to the transfer as possible; and

- it is possible to agree permitted changes after the transfer has taken place. However, due to the uncertain financial position of the insolvent company, a prospective purchaser may not be willing to take on the business without knowing that the changes it requires can be effected. A conditional sale agreement may solve the problem, but this may not be acceptable to the insolvency practitioner.

505

6.81 Dismissal by insolvency practitioners

Except in the case of a compulsory liquidation, the appointment of an insolvency practitioner will not, in itself, have any effect upon contracts of employment. This means that employees will continue to be employed by the insolvent company unless and until their employment is terminated – for example, because the insolvency practitioner forms the view that the dismissal of some or all of the workforce is necessary in order to achieve an optimum realisation of the insolvent company's assets.

Dismissals of employees in the context of a TUPE transfer are governed by Reg 7, which is discussed in Chapter 4, 'Unfair dismissal', under 'The TUPE unfair dismissal regime'. These general principles also apply where dismissals occur during the course of relevant insolvency proceedings. In summary, Reg 7(1) provides that where the sole or main reason for dismissal is the transfer, the dismissal is automatically unfair. Reg 7(2) provides that where the sole or main reason for the dismissal is an economic, technical or organisational reason entailing changes in the workforce ('ETO reason') the dismissal is potentially fair by reason of redundancy or 'some other substantial reason' of a kind such as to justify the dismissal. An ETO reason can apply to a dismissal effected by either the transferor or the transferee whether before or after a relevant transfer, and such a dismissal will only be unfair if it fails to satisfy the usual 'reasonableness test' for unfair dismissal as set out in S.98(4) ERA.

6.82 Under Reg 4(3), transferring employees include any employees who would have been employed immediately before the transfer had they not been automatically unfairly dismissed under Reg 7(1). This provision reflects the House of Lords' judgment in Litster and ors v Forth Dry Dock and Engineering Co Ltd (in receivership) and anor 1989 ICR 341, HL (see Chapter 2, 'Who transfers?', under 'Employed "immediately before" transfer').

6.83 Is relevant transfer sole or principal reason for dismissal?

Any dismissal that is solely or principally by reason of a relevant transfer will be automatically unfair by virtue of Reg 7(1). Previously, it had been the case that, if the reason for the dismissal was a reason connected with the transfer that is not an ETO reason, this too would have been automatically unfair. However, following amendments introduced by the Amendment Regulations, Reg 7(1) was amended with effect from 31 January 2014 to remove this category of automatically unfair dismissal. For full details of this change and its practical consequences, see Chapter 4, 'Unfair dismissal', under 'The TUPE unfair dismissal regime – changes to Reg 7(1) made in January 2014'. In view of Reg 7(1), if an insolvency practitioner dismisses employees immediately prior to selling the viable parts of an insolvent business, the question will inevitably arise as to whether the sole or principal reason for those dismissals is the transfer, and in many cases the conclusion will be that that is the reason. If so, the purchaser will inherit the contracts of the employees and all related liabilities, including liability for those dismissals, subject to the provisions of Reg 8 (see '"Relevant insolvency proceedings" – liability for sums payable under statutory scheme' above).

It may be, however, that the insolvency practitioner decides shortly after his or her appointment that the dismissal of some or all of the workforce is unavoidable because no potential sale of the business seems likely and its continuation would merely serve to deplete the realisable assets available for distribution to creditors. Dismissals may also be necessary because certain parts of the business entirely lack commercial viability. In either case, the dismissals will be for redundancy in that there will be a cessation of the business or a diminution in the requirements of the business for employees. If it should later transpire that, against expectations, the insolvency practitioner does manage to sell some or all of the business in circumstances constituting a 'relevant transfer', employees who were dismissed previously would not be entitled to rely on Reg 7(1) because their dismissals will be regarded as having been for a valid ETO reason.

6.84 It can be much more difficult where dismissals are effected at a time when tentative plans to sell the business exist, but the sale does not actually happen until a much later date. It is often hard to say whether such dismissals are connected with the subsequent transfer. Each case will be decided on its own distinct facts and circumstances. A body of case law, however, has accrued concerning the question of whether it can be said that the principal reason for dismissal is the transfer in circumstances where no specific purchaser has been identified at the time the dismissal takes place. Virtually the entirety of this case law – which is discussed in detail in Chapter 4, 'Unfair dismissal', under 'Automatically unfair dismissal – need transferee be identified?' – has arisen in the context of insolvency transfers. Suffice to say here that the Court of Appeal has now cleared up the inconsistency in the approach adopted by the EAT in earlier cases when in Spaceright Europe Ltd v Baillavoine and ors 2012 ICR 520, CA, it resoundingly endorsed an employment tribunal's decision that the dismissal of a chief executive officer by the administrators of his company was for a reason connected with its subsequent transfer, even though no specific transferee had been determined at the time of dismissal. The same conclusion was reached in another decision of the Court of Appeal in Kavanagh and ors v Crystal Palace FC Ltd and anor 2014 ICR 251, CA.

European case law lends tacit support to the position described above. In P Bork International A/S (in liquidation) v Foreningen af Arbejdsledere i Danmark and ors 1989 IRLR 41, ECJ, the European Court ruled that the proper approach to the issue of whether dismissals are made in connection with a transfer is to consider what happened in retrospect. Applying that approach, the fact that no transferee could be identified at the moment of the dismissal would not necessarily prevent an employee's rights from being protected by the Acquired Rights Directive.

6.85 Notwithstanding the above, it remains possible for a detailed scrutiny of an insolvency practitioner's motive in dismissing employees prior to a disposal of the viable part of a business to reveal that the principal reason was not, in fact, the transfer. For example, in Page and anor v Lakeside Collections Ltd (t/a Lavender Hotels) and anor EAT 0296/10 a company was put into administration on 3 February 2009 following the breakdown of negotiations over the sale of part of its business to a potential transferee. The administrator dismissed the claimants on the same day. On 13 February, the transferee submitted a revised offer and the sale of the business was completed on 10 March. An employment tribunal found that the dismissals were unfair on procedural grounds. However, they were held not to be automatically unfair under Reg 7(1). The EAT upheld this decision, finding that the administrator's reason for dismissing the claimants was a reduced need for senior managers during the administration – i.e. a redundancy. Furthermore, there had been no collusion between the administrator and the transferee. As such, even although the dismissals had occurred before the transfer and after a buyer had been identified, the reason for them was not the transfer itself or a reason connected to the transfer.

6.86 **Is dismissal for 'ETO' reason?**
As previously intimated, dismissals that are for an ETO reason are potentially fair under Reg 7(2) and (3). The scope of this defence is considered fully in Chapter 4, 'Unfair dismissal', under 'Dismissals potentially fair for an "ETO reason"'. In the specific context of insolvency, it can be very difficult to determine whether dismissals by insolvency practitioners prior to a transfer are for an economic, technical or organisational reason 'entailing changes in the workforce'. It has to be shown that the ETO reason necessitated a reduction in the numbers of the workforce or a change in the job functions of those employed – Berriman v Delabole Slate Ltd 1985 ICR 546, CA.

So, for example, harmonising terms and conditions would not normally involve a change in numbers or job functions, and nor will dismissals aimed at enhancing the prospects of a sale by freeing an insolvent business of its encumbrances. In this regard, in Wheeler v Patel and anor 1987 ICR 631, EAT, the Appeal Tribunal held that the dismissal of employees for the purpose of enhancing the sale price of an insolvent business did not constitute an 'economic... reason... entailing changes in the workforce' because the reason did not relate, as the EAT held it must, to the conduct of the business. This decision was approved in Gateway Hotels Ltd v Stewart and ors 1988 IRLR 287, EAT, where another division of the EAT ruled that the dismissal of a

508

workforce at the behest of the transferee as a condition for agreeing to the sale of the business was not for an ETO reason.

In Longden and anor v Ferrari Ltd and anor 1994 ICR 443, EAT, the Appeal **6.87** Tribunal held that employees had not been dismissed by receivers in connection with the transfer of the insolvent business where there was evidence that, despite the original intention of the receivers to keep all employees on and to sell the business as a going concern, it became necessary to effect some dismissals and to rationalise costs in order to minimise trading losses and to meet the pressure being applied from the bank to close the business down. This was treated as a genuine redundancy situation.

Where dismissals occur at an early stage of the insolvency at a time when a future sale is neither contemplated nor expected, it is generally easier to demonstrate that this is a genuine redundancy situation. The nearer the dismissals are made to a subsequent relevant transfer, the more difficult it will be for the insolvency practitioner to argue that the dismissals were for an ETO reason that necessitated reductions in the workforce as part of the conduct of the insolvent business.

The Court of Appeal in Kavanagh and ors v Crystal Palace FC Ltd and anor **6.88** 2014 ICR 251, CA, confirmed that it is legitimate to draw a distinction between dismissals effected in order to preserve a business as a going concern (which may be fair for an ETO reason), and those effected in order to make the business more attractive to transferees (which may not). The claimants were 'non-core' employees of a football club in administration who had been dismissed when the administrator decided to 'mothball' the club during the closed season. The administrator was at the time working towards achieving a sale of the club, which did eventually occur, and the claimants argued that their dismissals were unfair under Reg 7 because they were connected to the eventual transfer and there was no ETO reason. The employment tribunal found that the dismissals were for an economic reason; namely, keeping the club alive as a going concern. Although the administrator did have the longer-term aim of selling the club, this was not the reason for the dismissals. The EAT allowed an appeal against this decision but the Court of Appeal restored the tribunal's judgment. It had been right to draw a distinction between the administrator's reason for these particular dismissals and his ultimate objective. The case could be distinguished from Spaceright Europe Ltd v Baillavoine and ors 2012 ICR 520, CA, where Lord Justice Mummery stated that an ETO reason is not available where employees are dismissed to make a business more attractive to prospective transferees. There, the CEO was dismissed on day one of the administration as no purchaser would require his services. Thus, he was dismissed not because the money had run out but to make the business more attractive to purchasers. The facts of the instant case were significantly different.

509

6.89 **Information and consultation**

The requirements to inform and consult appropriate employee representatives in connection with an actual or proposed TUPE transfer are fully explained in Chapter 8, 'Information and consultation'. These requirements apply equally in any insolvency situation to which TUPE applies, whatever the nature of the insolvency proceedings. In this section, we consider the practical issues which can arise in this context.

Briefly, Reg 13(2) requires that the representatives of employees who are affected by a transfer be informed of specified information about the transfer, and consulted about any measures which are envisaged by the employer in relation to those employees. The prescribed information must be provided long enough before a relevant transfer to enable consultation to take place, and consultation must take place with a view to seeking the agreement of employee representatives to the intended measures (Reg 13(6)). The Regulations themselves do not give further guidance on these timescales. In many cases it will also be necessary to factor in time for the election of employee representatives.

6.90 The main problem for insolvency practitioners is the very tight timescale normally involved in the transfer of an insolvent business, which means that in practice it is often impossible to comply fully with the information and consultation requirements. In addition, an insolvency practitioner may not have sufficient information to inform and consult employees properly in any event. However, the cases decided under the 1981 Regulations (which are still relevant) have consistently held that these obligations apply even in insolvency situations unless there are very sudden unforeseen circumstances. The best course of action for an insolvency practitioner, and the potential purchaser, is to make every effort to comply with the information and consultation requirements, and to bear in mind that the steps they have taken may come under the scrutiny of a tribunal.

The risks inherent in failing to take steps to comply with the Regulations are considerable. Potential liability for failure to inform and consult is an award of up to 13 weeks' pay per employee (with no limit on the amount of a week's pay). In the context of insolvency proceedings, particularly where there are large numbers of employees, this could amount to a liability significant enough to influence whether the transfer actually goes ahead. It seems clear that if no attempt is made to comply with the requirements, in many cases maximum compensation will be awarded by the tribunal. In Sweetin v Coral Racing 2006 IRLR 252, EAT, the Appeal Tribunal reiterated that compensation for failure to inform and consult on a TUPE transfer is intended to punish the employer for default, so non-compliance is taken very seriously. However, in Baxter and ors v Marks and Spencer plc and ors EAT 0612/05 the EAT did not award compensation for a minor technical breach where employees suffered no detriment.

The TUPE Regulations provide for joint and several liability between **6.91** transferor and transferee (Reg 15(9)). This means that employees have a greater chance of recovering any compensation. Although liability for failure to inform and consult may be covered in sale documentation, the transferor and transferee are best advised to cooperate to minimise the likelihood of expensive tribunal claims.

Notification of employee liability information   6.92

Under Reg 11 the transferor is obliged to notify the transferee of certain employee liability information of any employee who is assigned to the transferring business. This obligation applies to any relevant transfer, including relevant insolvency proceedings. The meaning of employee liability information and the notification procedure are considered in Chapter 8, 'Information and consultation', under 'Employee liability information'. In brief, these are:

- 'employee liability information' means the following information relating to each employee: his or her identity and age; statutory particulars of employment; details of disciplinary procedures taken against him or her and grievance procedures taken by him or her in the previous two years, in either case, where the statutory dispute resolution procedures apply; employment claims or actions brought against the transferor in the last two years or which the transferor has reasonable grounds to believe may be brought against the transferee, arising out of the employee's employment with the transferor; and information on transferring collective agreements (Reg 11(2))

- the information must be supplied in writing or made available to the transferee in a 'readily accessible form' (Reg 11(1))

- the information must be provided at least 28 days before the transfer or, if special circumstances make this not reasonably practicable, as soon as reasonably practicable thereafter (Reg 11(6))

- notification can be given in instalments and indirectly, through a third party (Reg 11(7)). However, the transferor remains liable if the third party does not pass the information on

- information must be correct as at a specified date which must be not more than 14 days before the date on which the information is notified to the transferee (Reg 11(3))

- the information also has to be provided in respect of any employee who would have been employed by the transferor had he or she not been unfairly dismissed under Reg 7(1) (Reg 11(4))

511

- the transferor must notify the transferee of any changes in the employee liability information (Reg 11(5))

- it is not possible to contract out of the notification obligations although Regs 11 and 12 can be covered in any relevant sale indemnities; and

- failure to comply with Reg 11 will normally lead to minimum compensation for the transferee of £500 per employee (Reg 12). This can be reduced if it is just and equitable in all the circumstances, having particular regard to any loss sustained by the transferee and to the terms of any relevant indemnities in the sale documentation. However, there is no upper limit.

6.93 These obligations appear to be fairly onerous for insolvency practitioners, who are normally trying to conclude a sale as quickly as possible and may not have a detailed knowledge of the business, its employees or its internal information systems. The Government has argued that, in most cases, the information will be available from payroll and personnel records. However, in an insolvency context, even simply collating the information may be more time-consuming than usual, making it harder to comply with the time limits. The requirement to provide information about claims which the transferor has reasonable grounds to believe an employee may bring against the transferee, arising out of his or her employment with the transferor, may also be harder to comply with in the context of insolvency proceedings, not only because of the practical difficulties, but also because there may be more potential claims.

There is some flexibility in Regs 11 and 12 which may assist insolvency practitioners. The BIS Guide notes that it may not be practicable to comply with the time limit if the transferor does not know the identity of the transferee until very late in the process, which might be relevant where there are competing bids to buy the business, or where the transfer takes place at very short notice because it is the only option for saving the business and therefore jobs. These examples would be relevant to many insolvencies, but the Guide is not binding on tribunals, and all cases will be decided on their particular facts. In any event, the insolvency practitioner will need to be able to demonstrate to the satisfaction of a tribunal that he or she notified the transferee of the employee liability information as soon as was reasonably practicable.

6.94 Insolvency practitioners may also be able to persuade the tribunal that lower compensation should be awarded because it is 'just and equitable in all the circumstances'. Although the facts of each insolvency are different, the special circumstances involved in the transfer of an insolvent company may well discourage large awards. This is likely to depend on whether the transferor is able to demonstrate that he has in fact made every reasonable effort to comply with TUPE. Doing nothing to comply is likely to be expensive unless there are very exceptional circumstances.

7 Continuity of employment

An employee's entitlement to many statutory employment rights is dependent **7.1** upon his or her having been engaged for a particular period of continuous employment. For example, the right to claim unfair dismissal under the Employment Rights Act 1996 (ERA) (other than in cases of 'automatically' unfair dismissal) applies to employees who have been continuously employed for at least two years at the time of dismissal. Similarly, the right to claim a redundancy payment under the ERA applies only to employees with two years' continuous employment when dismissed. Moreover, even where an employee has sufficient continuous service to bring a claim, his or her period of continuous employment will often affect the value of the right claimed; for example, the amount of statutory redundancy pay or statutory notice entitlement will increase in proportion to length of service. For these reasons, establishing the length of an employee's period of continuous employment can be crucial. The rules governing the computation of continuous employment are set out in detail in IDS Employment Law Handbook, 'Continuity of Employment' (2012). In this chapter, we focus on the application of those rules where a business or undertaking is transferred from one employer to another.

Parallel provisions
7.2

In the absence of statutory provision to the contrary, continuity of employment would be broken on any change of employer. At common law, following the principle established in Nokes v Doncaster Amalgamated Collieries Ltd 1940 AC 1014, HL – that an employee must be free to choose his or her employer – there is no automatic transfer of an employment contract from one employer to another and no transfer at all without the employee's consent. A change of employer would therefore have the effect of terminating the employee's contract with the transferor and any employment with the transferee would involve a fresh contract. However, the TUPE Regulations effectively reverse this common law position in specified circumstances. Furthermore, S.218(2) ERA applies to preserve continuity of employment where 'a trade or business, or an undertaking... is transferred from one person to another'.

—————————————————————————— **513**

Difficulties have arisen in this area since the introduction of the original TUPE Regulations in 1981, which were replaced by the Transfer of Undertakings (Protection of Employment) Regulations 2006 SI 2006/246 (TUPE) in respect of relevant transfers taking place on or after 6 April 2006 (or relevant service provision changes taking place on or after 4 May 2006). The central difficulty is that, while the cornerstone of the Regulations (in both their 1981 and 2006 guises) is the automatic transfer of employees' contracts from the transferor to the transferee, the Regulations do not expressly mention continuity of employment or alter or amend S.218(2) in any way. However, the EU Acquired Rights Directive (No.2001/23) on 'the approximation of the laws of the Member States relating to the safeguarding of employees' rights in the event of transfers of undertakings, businesses or parts of undertakings or businesses' ('the Acquired Rights Directive'), which the TUPE Regulations implement in the UK, is arguably intended to cover employees' rights based on continuity of service in the same way as any other rights. Indeed, if employees' rights on transfers were prejudiced by the statutory concept of continuity in the ERA, the Regulations would almost certainly be in breach of the Directive.

7.3 Much of the debate has centred on whether the TUPE Regulations themselves are effective in preserving continuity or whether S.218(2) is to be applied. The matter has been resolved to the extent that there is now little doubt that continuity of employment will be preserved on the transfer of an undertaking in the vast majority of cases. What remains to be definitively clarified is the means by which this is achieved, which may be an important question in determining whether or not continuity is preserved in certain situations.

While some courts and tribunals have proceeded on the basis that the Regulations themselves preserve continuity, others have chosen to apply S.218(2) ERA. This may well be because S.218(2) clearly states that its purpose is to preserve continuity, while the Regulations are silent on the point (although the reasons given vary from one judgment to the next). A difficulty could arise for an employee relying solely on S.218(2) if the concept of a 'transfer' were to be more restrictively defined under that section than under TUPE: this would leave a residual category of relevant transfers under the Regulations to which S.218(2) would not apply. Employees transferring by virtue of such transfers would not, therefore, enjoy the benefit of preserved continuity of employment.

7.4 However, in light of the scope and aims of the Acquired Rights Directive, it would be surprising if a tribunal were to deny continuity in a case where TUPE applies, given that the Regulations must be interpreted purposively in a manner consistent with the Directive (see Litster and ors v Forth Dry Dock and Engineering Co Ltd (in receivership) and anor 1989 ICR 341, HL). Therefore, in the majority of cases it is unlikely to matter whether the tribunal applies S.218(2) or TUPE (although it should be noted that the Regulations apply to the whole of the UK (England, Scotland, Wales and Northern Ireland) while the ERA only applies to Great Britain (England, Scotland and Wales only)). The basic position is that continuity of employment on a transfer is very likely to be preserved, if not by one regime then by the other (or by both). Indeed, there is authority from the EAT in D36 Ltd v Castro EAT 0853/03 (discussed under 'Relationship between TUPE and ERA' below) to the effect that the two sets of provisions must be interpreted consistently with one another, at least as far as each defines a 'transfer'. However, there is conflicting EAT authority on the point so until the issue is resolved at Court of Appeal level, both regimes need to be considered. Below, we address how the two schemes have been applied in practice, first focusing on the TUPE Regulations and then considering the relationship between the Regulations and S.218(2). We then discuss the residual application of S.218.

Continuity under TUPE 7.5

Regulation 4(1) TUPE, which provides for the automatic transfer of contracts to the transferee, states that 'a relevant transfer shall not operate so as to terminate the contract of employment of any person employed by the transferor and assigned to the organised grouping of resources or employees that is subject to the relevant transfer, which would otherwise be terminated by the transfer, but any such contract shall have effect after the transfer as if originally made between the person so employed and the transferee'.

The first thing to note about this provision is that it does not mention continuity of employment. Nor does it expressly provide that an employee's accrued period of employment is transferred along with his or her contract. However, the fact that it provides that the transferred contract shall have effect 'as if originally made between the [employee] and the transferee' would appear to support the view that the employee's continuity of employment will not be broken by the transfer and, consequently, it may well be that the TUPE Regulations alone preserve continuity. This argument appeared to be accepted by the Court of Appeal in Royal Ordnance plc v Pilkington 1989 ICR 737, CA, where Lord Justice Neill observed that the effect of Reg 4(1) was 'to require a person whose employment has been transferred to be treated as though employed throughout by the transferee company'. However, this opinion was obiter – i.e. not strictly necessary to decide the case and therefore not binding on other courts.

The guidance issued by the Department for Business, Innovation and Skills, 7.6 'Employment rights on the transfer of an undertaking' (January 2014) ('the BIS Guide'), states that: 'An employee's period of continuous employment is not broken by a transfer and, for the purposes of calculating entitlement to statutory employment rights, the date on which the period of continuous employment started would usually be the date on which the employee started work with the

515

old employer.' However, it does not make it clear whether it is the Regulations themselves that preserve continuity. Thus, the question as to which set of provisions has the desired effect remains unanswered. This question is discussed further under 'Relationship between TUPE and ERA' below. However, it would not arise at all if continuity of service could be shown to form part of the 'rights, powers, duties and liabilities' that transfer with the employee under the Regulations and so we turn to this issue first.

7.7 Continuity as a 'right, duty or liability'

Regulation 4(2)(a) TUPE fleshes out the novation principle enunciated in Reg 4(1) by specifying what exactly is 'transferred' in respect of the employment contract. It states that 'without prejudice to [Reg 4(1)]… on the completion of a relevant transfer… all the transferor's rights, powers, duties and liabilities under or in connection with any such contract shall be transferred by virtue of this regulation to the transferee'. In Green-Wheeler v Onyx (UK) Ltd EAT 925/92 (discussed further under 'Relationship between TUPE and ERA' below) the transferor's 'liabilities' were held by the EAT to include an employee's right not to be unfairly dismissed where that right had already accrued before the date of the transfer. Since, by virtue of S.108(1) ERA, qualification for that right is (generally speaking) dependent upon an employee having the requisite period of continuous employment, it would seem that the EAT was implying that continuous employment could be regarded as a 'liability' under the contract of employment which is transferred on a relevant transfer.

However, it is difficult to see how a statutory right such as the right not to be unfairly dismissed can be conflated with the period of continuous employment necessary to qualify for such a right. Continuity of employment is merely a calculation of the length of an employee's service. The statutory rights that may flow from a period of continuous service can, of course, comprise liabilities that are transferred to the transferee under Reg 4(1). But that is not, in our view, the same as saying that the period of continuous service itself is a liability. It is not possible to maintain that statutory continuity in a general sense will be transferred by virtue of Reg 4(2) as a liability under or in connection with a transferred contract without undue straining of the statutory language.

7.8

This view is reinforced by the EAT's subsequent decision in Nicholas v Grant (t/a Sandancers Café) EAT 0198/06. In that case the EAT stated in clear terms that continuity is 'not aptly described as a right or an obligation and so does not fit within [Reg 4]'. The EAT held further that it is S.218(2) ERA that is effective in preserving continuity in the event of a transfer, which has the added implication that the calculation of an employee's continuity of employment following a transfer will be in accordance with the detailed rules contained in Ss.210–219 ERA. However, the EAT's reasoning does not mean that the TUPE Regulations prevent, or are irrelevant to, the preservation of an employee's accrued service post-transfer: it merely rules out one mechanism by which it might occur. The other means by which TUPE and S.218(2) may be effective in preserving continuity are considered below.

Relationship between TUPE and ERA   7.9

Section 218(2) ERA provides that: 'If a trade or business, or an undertaking... is transferred from one person to another – (a) the period of employment of an employee in the trade or business or undertaking at the time of the transfer counts as a period of employment with the transferee, and (b) the transfer does not break the continuity of the period of employment.' 'Except in so far as the context otherwise requires', the term 'business' includes 'a trade or profession and... any activity carried on by a body of persons (whether corporate or unincorporated)' – S.235(1).

There have been remarkably few cases where both S.218(2) ERA and the TUPE Regulations have been at issue and those that have considered the relationship between them show marked inconsistencies in approach.

In Green-Wheeler v Onyx (UK) Ltd EAT 925/92 G-W, who had been employed **7.10** since 1975, was dismissed for redundancy from his job as driver of a council refuse-collection vehicle on Friday 6 December 1991. He was re-employed on the following Monday by O (UK) Ltd, the day on which O (UK) Ltd took over the refuse collection service. He was dismissed shortly thereafter and the question for the employment tribunal was whether G-W had the necessary qualifying service to proceed with his unfair dismissal claim. The tribunal dismissed G-W's claim and he appealed to the EAT. The EAT addressed the question of whether, if there had been a relevant transfer under the Regulations, G-W's past service with the Council could be carried forward to establish the necessary continuity of employment. Having found that the breadth of the word 'transfer' in the Regulations is wider than in S.218(2), the EAT held that where there is a transfer situation to which the latter does not apply, an employee who has accrued the necessary continuous service prior to the transfer may rely on the alternative route provided by the Regulations in order to transfer his or her right not to be unfairly dismissed. In the EAT's view, the statutory right not to be unfairly dismissed fell within the scope of the word 'liabilities' contained in Reg 4(2), which states that 'all the transferor's rights, powers, duties and liabilities under or in connection with any [employment] contract shall be transferred by virtue of this Regulation to the transferee'. In reaching this conclusion, the EAT relied on a speech given by Lord Lyle in the House of Lords when the 1981 Regulations were passing through Parliament (Hansard, 10 December 1981, paras 1482–1500) to find that it had been the intention of the legislature to include continuity of employment in the rights and liabilities that transferred under the Regulations.

517

The EAT also had to consider G-W's contention that S.218(2) should be construed in accordance with the Acquired Rights Directive. In support of this argument, he cited the ECJ's decision in Marleasing SA v La Comercial Internacional de Alimentacion SA 1992 1 CMLR 305, ECJ, as interpreted by the House of Lords in Webb v EMO Air Cargo (UK) Ltd 1993 ICR 175, HL. In that case their Lordships stated that the principle established in Marleasing meant that 'a national court must construe a domestic law to accord with the terms of a Directive in the same field only if it is possible to do so. That means that the domestic law must be open to an interpretation consistent with the Directive whether or not it is also open to an interpretation inconsistent with it.' However, the EAT thought that it was inappropriate to construe S.218(2) in line with the ECJ decisions on the Directive on three grounds: (i) the rights provided by the ERA did not have any parallels in any EU Directives; (ii) the provisions of Part XVI ERA (which include S.218) were only relevant to determining the jurisdiction of a UK court; and (iii) the EAT considered itself bound by a long succession of Court of Appeal cases giving clear guidance on the meaning of that section.

7.11 While it is perhaps understandable that the EAT chose not to apply the ECJ's rulings on the meaning of a transfer under the Acquired Rights Directive to the definition of a transfer for the purposes of the continuity provisions under the ERA (as these were not introduced specifically to implement the Directive), we would nonetheless argue that the law should operate consistently. To allow for one definition of a transfer in the context of continuity of employment and another in the more general context of the TUPE Regulations is likely to lead to inconsistencies, in that it could create situations in which there is a relevant transfer but continuity is not preserved. For example, it may transpire after judicial elucidation that the definition of a transfer is wider under the 2006 Regulations than it was under the 1981 Regulations by virtue of their specific inclusion of 'service provision changes' (see Chapter 1, 'Identifying a "relevant transfer"'). If that is the case, then unless the courts and tribunals take the view that the meaning of 'transfer' under S.218(2) is to be read consistently with the Directive and the TUPE Regulations and has evolved accordingly (or at least is no narrower), there will be cases where there is a relevant transfer under the Regulations but where the transferring employees' continuity of employment is not preserved, because there will not have been a transfer for the purposes of S.218(2).

Furthermore, while the EAT in Green-Wheeler v Onyx (UK) Ltd (above) may have avoided the problem in that case by finding that the employee's right not to be unfairly dismissed (which he had gained by accruing the then requisite two years' continuous employment with the Council) was a 'duty or liability under or in connection with' the transferring employee's contract, the same reasoning would not apply to an employee seeking to establish continuity for other purposes, such as the calculation of a redundancy payment or basic award. Nor would it apply to an employee who has not accrued the required period of continuous service for claiming unfair dismissal by the time of the transfer. In this situation, the reasoning in Green-Wheeler would leave such an employee vulnerable to losing any continuity built up with the transferor and having to start again with the transferee, simply by virtue of not having accrued enough continuity to claim unfair dismissal at the date of the transfer.

A different division of the EAT took a more holistic view in the case below, **7.12** holding that the TUPE Regulations go further than merely transferring the right not to be unfairly dismissed by establishing a presumption that continuity is preserved for all purposes. In Harrison Bowden Ltd v Bowden 1994 ICR 186, EAT, B had been employed by NGS Bowden for over two years when he was dismissed for redundancy by the company's receivers. The dismissal took place at a time when the receivers had advertised the sale of the business as a going concern and had received a positive response from HB Ltd. Three days after his dismissal, B went to work for HB Ltd to 'help them get into the saddle' and formally commenced employment with them one week later. One month later, he was dismissed. The main issue for the employment tribunal was whether B's dismissal for redundancy by the receivers was a dismissal in connection with the transfer to HB Ltd for the purposes of the Regulations. The tribunal took the firm view that if this was a dismissal in connection with a transfer, the legal significance was that B's employment continued and HB Ltd would have responsibility for his contract as though it had employed him since 1988, when he was originally taken on by NGS Bowden. The tribunal went on to find that the dismissal was in connection with the transfer and HB Ltd appealed to the EAT. Before the EAT, HB Ltd argued that the tribunal's approach was wrong on the basis that the reference in Reg 7(1) to dismissals in connection with 'the' transfer meant that there must be a transfer in existence, or at least a prospective transferee, at the time of the dismissal. The EAT rejected this argument on the basis that such an interpretation would 'open a loophole in [the Regulations] which *presumes continuity of employment* and attempts to ensure the protection of workers when undertakings are transferred' (our stress).

In the course of its judgment the EAT noted that there was another route by which the tribunal could have reached the same conclusion on continuity of employment, namely under S.218(2), as interpreted by the EAT in Macer v Abafast Ltd 1990 ICR 234, EAT (see 'Breaks in employment' below). However, as the tribunal had not considered this route, the EAT said no more on this issue.

However, the route was taken by the EAT in the case below, where it expressly **7.13** applied S.218(2), although it also relied heavily on the ECJ's definition of a 'transfer' under the Acquired Rights Directive, thereby implicitly finding that the definition of a 'transfer' under S.218(2) was the same as under TUPE.

519

In Farmer v Danzas (UK) Ltd EAT 858/93 F was employed by his own transport business, F Ltd, which he set up in 1988. In essence, his business was to supply D Ltd with lorries and drivers so that D Ltd could provide a transport service called Eurapid to its customers. F leased and maintained the lorries and had office accommodation on D Ltd's premises. In 1991 D Ltd decided to move the Eurapid service to its main site and offered F the position of manager of the Eurapid service on condition that he ceased to operate his own business. F agreed but was dismissed just over five months later. The preliminary issue for the employment tribunal was whether F had the necessary continuity of service to bring an unfair dismissal claim. This depended on whether there had been a transfer of F's business within the meaning of S.218(2). The tribunal decided that there had been no such transfer on the ground that F's business had been integrated into that of D Ltd and had not, therefore, retained its identity after the transfer. The EAT disagreed and decided to adopt the ECJ guidelines as to the proper interpretation of what constitutes a transfer of an undertaking. In the EAT's view, there was nothing in the ECJ's decisions to suggest that a business ceased to retain its identity merely because its activities had been absorbed into the transferee's business. Accordingly, the EAT held that, as there had been a relevant transfer, F had the necessary continuity to bring a claim.

7.14 What is particularly interesting about the Farmer case is that, while the EAT expressly stated at the beginning of the judgment that it was concerned with S.218(2), it had substantial regard to the decisions of the ECJ on the scope of the Acquired Rights Directive and concluded by finding that the transfer in question was covered by TUPE. This analysis runs directly counter to that adopted in Green-Wheeler v Onyx (UK) Ltd (above), where the EAT was of the view that the interpretation of the Directive was irrelevant for the purposes of construing S.218(2). The Appeal Tribunal in that case did go on to find, however, that the right not to be unfairly dismissed could be transferred by the TUPE Regulations, which must themselves be interpreted in line with the Directive. It should be noted that the EAT in the Farmer case did not appear to have been referred to Green-Wheeler, but the underlying proposition in Farmer is clearly that S.218(2), the Regulations and the Directive are to be interpreted consistently with one another.

Indeed, in D36 Ltd v Castro EAT 0853/03 the EAT upheld an employment tribunal's view that the provisions of S.218(2), the TUPE Regulations and the Acquired Rights Directive should be treated as part of a 'single scheme'. There, C began working at the Windsor office of McCann Erickson ('McCann'), an advertising agency, as senior art worker on 2 April 2001. In December the Windsor office was closed and C was transferred to D36 Ltd, which was solely engaged in conducting work for McCann on a sub-contract basis. C received a letter from D36 Ltd dated 18 December 2001 confirming that from 1 January 2002 his employment would be with D36 Ltd and stating that his continuity of employment would be protected from 2 April 2001. A draft contract was also supplied, which gave the date of commencement of his employment as 2 April 2001. C was subsequently dismissed for redundancy by D36 Ltd in September 2002 and at a preliminary hearing an employment tribunal found that C had sufficient continuity of employment to bring a claim. In rejecting the employer's appeal, the EAT agreed with the tribunal that S.218(2) and TUPE should be seen as a single scheme for preserving continuity in the event of a business transfer. The EAT noted that neither S.218(2) nor S.235 ERA (the definition section) offers any explanation of the meaning of the word 'transfer' used in S.218(2). Reg 2(1), on the other hand, defines a 'relevant transfer' as 'a transfer... to which these Regulations apply' and Regs 3 and 4 provide further guidance on what constitutes a transfer and what rights are transferred. The EAT observed that there was no further definition of 'transfer' in the Regulations themselves, and that there was no reference anywhere in them to the concept of continuity of employment. The question the EAT posed for itself was whether there was anything in the domestic case law militating against applying the definition of 'transfer' in the Regulations to S.218(2), and found that there was not. It held that such an approach was consistent with judgments of the Court of Appeal in Celtec Ltd v Astley and ors 2002 ICR 1289, CA (which was subsequently affirmed by the House of Lords in North Wales Training and Enterprise Council Ltd (trading as Celtec Ltd) v Astley and ors 2006 ICR 992, HL), and the European Court in Sánchez Hidalgo and ors v Asociación de Servicios Aser and anor and another case 2002 ICR 73, ECJ, and Collino and anor v Telecom Italia SpA 2002 ICR 38, ECJ, to the effect that the Directive preserves continuity of employment upon a relevant transfer.

Thus case law shows a head of steam developing in favour of the view that the **7.15** separate regimes for preserving continuity under TUPE and S.218(2) should be construed consistently as a single scheme. However, the matter cannot be regarded as conclusively resolved, since a differently constituted EAT appeared to reject that proposition in Nicholas v Grant (t/a Sandancers Café) EAT 0198/06. In that case N started work for F as a griddle cook at the Sandancers Café in April 2004. On 14 February 2005 the café was taken over by a new concessionaire, G. Prior to the transfer N had a meeting with G to agree new terms of employment and she then tendered her resignation to F on 7 February 2005, giving one week's notice. N was later dismissed by G in May 2005 and she presented a claim for unfair dismissal. Rejecting her claim, the employment tribunal found that, because of her resignation, N had not been employed in the undertaking immediately before the transfer and that as a result she had taken up new employment with G under new terms. That employment had commenced on 14 February, meaning that N had not accrued the requisite period of continuous employment to enable her to bring an unfair dismissal claim. On appeal, the EAT held that the tribunal had made an error of law in failing to have regard to the test laid down by the ECJ in Botzen and ors v Rotterdamsche Droogdok Maatschappij BV 1986 2 CMLR 50, ECJ, requiring

521

it to consider whether N had been assigned to the undertaking transferred. The EAT found on applying that test that N was employed by the café at the time the transfer took place. For the EAT, the essential issue was whether N had sufficient continuity of employment, and that was a matter to be determined by reference to S.218(2) and not TUPE. It accepted that unless there had been a relevant transfer, N had insufficient service to present a claim. However, it emphasised that 'the resolution of whether there was a transfer for the purposes of the Regulations can only be described as an aid to what was the essential task of determining whether there was continuity of employment for the purposes of the [ERA]'.

If the EAT had only had to consider this one point, the position following Nicholas would have been clear and could have been reconciled with the decision in D36 Ltd v Castro (above), despite the latter case not having been referred to in Nicholas. The position would be that, applying Castro, the definition of a 'transfer' would be the same under both TUPE and S.218(2) (or at least no *narrower* under the latter). Indeed, the EAT in Nicholas said that the case 'was correctly decided to be a relevant transfer for the purposes of TUPE. The claimant was employed at the relevant time and her contract of employment went over. We would have made the same decision if it were necessary for us to do so under S.218.' This would mean that in the event of a relevant transfer for the purposes of the Regulations, there would always be a transfer for the purposes of S.218(2), but it would be S.218(2) that would actually have the effect of preserving continuity. This would also appear to be the approach implicitly taken by the EAT in Farmer v Danzas (UK) Ltd (above). However, there is a further hurdle which must be overcome before continuity will be preserved under S.218(2), even if the definition of a transfer is the same for both sets of provisions: whether the employee was employed in the transferring entity at the time of the transfer.

7.16 **'At the time of' or 'immediately before' transfer**
The ERA and the TUPE Regulations use slightly different wording in respect of the point at which the employee must have been employed in the entity transferred. S.218(2) ERA applies to employees employed in the trade or business or undertaking 'at the *time* of the transfer' (our stress), whereas the Regulations require employees to be employed in the entity transferred '*immediately before* the transfer' – Reg 4(3) (our stress). Although the EAT did not cite these phrases in Nicholas v Grant (t/a Sandancers Café) EAT 0198/06 (discussed under 'Relationship between TUPE and ERA' above), it clearly considered them to be distinct concepts, noting that there 'will rarely be cases that do not satisfy both but, in any event, we hold that using the language of TUPE Reg [4] and of S.218, the claimant was in the employment of the café at the time that the transfer came about'.

522

On the facts, the claimant in Nicholas was employed both immediately before and at the time of the transfer. N had given seven days' notice, which (applying West v Kneels Ltd 1987 ICR 146, EAT) ended on 14 February, the date of the transfer. But, continued the EAT, even if the West case had been wrongly decided, '[N] would still have been employed on the day immediately before the transfer, 13 February'. Albeit obiter, the clear implication here is that had N been unable to rely on West, she would not have been employed 'at the time of the transfer' for the purposes of S.218(2).

Thus, it appears that there may in theory still be cases where there is a relevant **7.17** transfer under both TUPE and S.218(2) and where the employee was employed in the entity transferred 'immediately before' the transfer (so that his or her contract will have transferred under the Regulations), but was *not* so employed 'at the time of the transfer' for the purposes of S.218(2). Had N handed in her notice a day earlier, for example (so that it would have expired on 13 February, the day before the transfer), she would have fallen into this category. She would have been employed on the day immediately before the transfer and would have transferred under TUPE, but her continuity of employment would have been at risk for the purposes of any subsequent claim in respect of dismissal by the transferee.

On its face, this formulation ignores the effect of Macer v Abafast Ltd 1990 ICR 234, EAT, in which the Appeal Tribunal held that S.218(2) should not have a restrictive meaning and that since a transfer can take place over a period of time, any gap will be inconsequential if it can be said to be part of the 'machinery of the transfer'. However, this case must now be treated with some caution following North Wales Training and Enterprise Council Ltd (trading as Celtec Ltd) v Astley and ors 2006 ICR 992, HL, where the House of Lords held that transfers under the Acquired Rights Directive (and therefore, by implication, the TUPE Regulations) occur at a fixed point in time (see 'Breaks in employment' below).

The situation would be different if the end of the first employment came about **7.18** by *dismissal*, with the employee then taking up subsequent employment with the transferee and being dismissed a second time by the transferee. The House of Lords in Litster and ors v Forth Dry Dock and Engineering Co Ltd (in receivership) and anor 1989 ICR 341, HL, held that Reg 5(3) of the 1981 Regulations deemed an employee to have been employed immediately before a transfer where he or she was unfairly dismissed close to the transfer for a reason connected with it. This statement of law has now been codified in Reg 4(3) of the 2006 Regulations. It does not mean, however, that the employee is deemed to have transferred, only that he or she is able to claim unfair dismissal against the transferee – see (1) British Fuels Ltd v Baxendale and anor (2) Wilson and ors v St Helens Borough Council 1998 ICR 1141, HL, where the House of Lords clarified that such dismissals cannot be a nullity. In other words, liability

523

for the dismissal passes to the transferee under Reg 4. The question of continuity would not normally arise in these circumstances, as the claim would be one of automatically unfair dismissal under what is now Reg 7(1), for which no continuity of service is required. Continuity up to the point of dismissal would not be affected in any event, but there would be a serious question mark over its preservation in respect of any subsequent employment under a new contract.

On one view, it would not be preserved, because employment with one employer will have ceased and employment with a completely different employer will have commenced and the employee will not have transferred. Continuity would only begin to run from the date of employment with the transferee, thereby preventing the employee from bringing a claim for non-automatic unfair dismissal in respect of any subsequent dismissal taking place within two years of that date. However, it could be argued that this is a somewhat simplistic view. For S.218(2) to operate to prevent the transfer breaking continuity it requires there to have been a transfer; for there to be employment with the transferee; and for there to have been employment in the transferor's business at the time of the transfer. It does not require the individual employee to have actually transferred, provided the transfer has occurred. It could therefore be argued that an employee who does not transfer under Reg 4 because he or she was dismissed shortly before the transfer may still have continuity of employment preserved by S.218 if he or she subsequently takes up employment with the transferee under a new contract. Whether continuity is in fact broken would then depend on the existence of any non-counting week and whether Macer v Abafast Ltd (above) remains good law – see 'Breaks in employment' below.

7.19 The scenario discussed above is fairly common in transfer situations: the employees of the transferor are dismissed before the transfer and then re-employed by the transferee, perhaps on a selective basis, after the transfer. Another common scenario involves the dismissal of employees by the transferor and re-engagement by the transferee before the transfer takes place. In other cases, there is no express dismissal and the employee is simply transferred by agreement over to the transferee ahead of the actual time when the transfer is completed (with or without a gap in employment). In all these situations, continuity has to be determined.

7.20 Breaks in employment
Where an employee resigns, is dismissed or is transferred before the transfer two questions arise: will he or she be regarded as not being employed 'at the time of the transfer' under S.218(2) ERA, so that his or her continuity is broken because of the change of employer? And even if the answer to that question is 'no', does the gap between employments break continuity if it lasts for more than one 'non-counting week' under the rules governing the computation of continuity in Ss.210–219 ERA? (Note that a 'non-counting week' is one that

ends on a Saturday and, unless it is covered by one of the exceptions in S.212, e.g. sickness or temporary cessation of work, breaks continuity of service – see IDS Employment Law Handbook, 'Continuity of Employment' (2012), Chapter 2, 'Breaks in employment where there is no contract', and Chapter 3, 'Non-counting weeks that do not break continuity'.) Both these questions are considered below.

Employment 'at the time of the transfer'. In Brook Lane Finance Co Ltd v **7.21** Bradley 1988 ICR 423, EAT, the EAT held that in order for continuity to be preserved under S.218(2) it was necessary for the employee to be employed by the transferor at the moment of the transfer. As a result, B, who had left the employment of the transferor prior to the date of the transfer and began working for the transferee two days after the transfer, did not have continuity of employment preserved. The EAT thought that the phrase 'at the time of the transfer' in S.218(2) should be read strictly, in the same way that the phrase 'immediately before the transfer' in what is now Reg 4(3) had been read by the Court of Appeal in Secretary of State for Employment v Spence and ors 1986 ICR 651, CA (a decision which was not overruled by the decision of the House of Lords in Litster and ors v Forth Dry Dock and Engineering Co Ltd (in receivership) and anor – see '"At the time of" or "immediately before" transfer' above – on that point).

Previously, there had been some divergence of opinion on the issue in the Court of Appeal in Teesside Times Ltd v Drury 1980 ICR 338, CA. In that case, Lord Justice Goff thought that 'at the time of the transfer' did in fact mean at the moment of transfer. But Lord Justice Stephenson felt that it referred to the period of the transfer, and that a gap between dismissal and transfer followed by re-employment after the transfer would be acceptable as long as it did not fall foul of the general continuity provisions in the ERA (i.e. that there be no non-counting weeks). More radically, Lord Justice Eveleigh stated that, where 'the dismissal was a step towards the re-engagement', any break in employment was immaterial and that the two periods of employment could simply be added together. However, all these views were obiter (i.e. not binding) as the case was decided on different grounds.

A couple of years after Brook Lane Finance Co Ltd v Bradley (above), a **7.22** differently constituted EAT, in Macer v Abafast Ltd 1990 ICR 234, EAT, disposed of both the non-counting week problem and the narrow interpretation of 'at the time of the transfer' on the basis of legal reasoning that attracted some criticism. In that case, M had been employed by CTR Ltd for four years when its business was transferred to a subsidiary of A Ltd called CTR (Recruitment) Ltd ('Recruitment'). M and the other employees of CTR Ltd were dismissed by CTR Ltd and offered re-engagement with Recruitment but A Ltd managed to engineer a gap of 12 days between M leaving CTR Ltd and joining Recruitment. Exchange of contracts on the transfer took place about a

525

month *after* M joined Recruitment and completion was finally achieved a year after that. However, M was dismissed prior to the date of completion and he brought an unfair dismissal claim against A Ltd. The EAT held that Reg 4 did not apply to M's employment contract, but that S.218(2) preserved continuity nonetheless. Mr Justice Wood stated that a broad interpretation of S.218(2) had to be applied and that there was no reason that the phrase 'at the time of the transfer' should be read to mean the same as 'immediately before the transfer'. Furthermore, he took a similar view to that taken by Eveleigh LJ in the Teesside Times case – holding that an interval between employments, however long, did not matter for continuity purposes as long as it related to the 'machinery' of the transfer. Wood J concluded, therefore, that the Brook Lane case was wrongly decided and should not be followed. In reaching this conclusion, he was influenced by the reasoning behind Litster and ors v Forth Dry Dock and Engineering Co Ltd (in receivership) and anor (see '"At the time of" or "immediately before" transfer' (above)), where the House of Lords extended the meaning of employees 'employed immediately before the transfer' in the old Reg 5(3) (now rewritten in Reg 4(3)) to include, for the purposes of claiming unfair dismissal, employees who would have been so employed had they not been dismissed for a reason connected with the transfer.

The EAT's decision in Macer abandons entirely the restrictive construction of S.218(2) adopted in Brook Lane Finance. Wood J, who examined the various analyses of that provision by the Court of Appeal in Teesside Times Ltd v Drury (above), concluded that the reasoning of Eveleigh LJ was the most persuasive since he properly focused on the fact that the wording of S.218(2) requires 'the period of employment... at the time of the transfer' to be counted as a period of employment with the transferor rather than requiring the employee actually to be employed at the time of the transfer. Eveleigh LJ rationalised his construction by pointing out that Ss.210–219 ERA are primarily concerned with the computation of periods of employment, not with the circumstances in which rights or benefits may arise. He also showed himself to be alive to the policy behind S.218(2), i.e. the protection of employees' rights on the transfer of the business in which they are employed. He therefore eschewed any restrictive interpretation of the relevant provision that would enable employers easily to defeat that policy by causing a break in continuity to occur simply by dismissing employees prior to completion and re-engaging them after the transfer.

7.23 The EAT's endorsement in the Macer case of Eveleigh LJ's interpretation of S.218(2) gives effect to the presumed legislative intention behind that provision. If correct, then the questions of whether a transfer occurs on completion or on exchange, and whether it necessarily occurs at a specific point in time or can extend over a period, become, strictly speaking, irrelevant for the purposes of the ERA. Instead, what matters is that the period of employment vested in the employee at the time of the transfer falls to be included in the total period of

526

reckonable service with the transferee. And, as Wood J pointed out, any gap between these two periods of employment will, in most cases, be kept within reasonable proportions given that commercial interests usually dictate that employees be re-engaged as soon after a transfer as possible in order for the business to continue normally.

Non-counting weeks. There is, however, one major problem with the decision 7.24 in Macer v Abafast Ltd 1990 ICR 234, EAT, that was not covered at all by the EAT in that case. In order to deal with the non-counting week, Wood J relied on S.218(1). However, this is an ambiguous provision that can be interpreted in diametrically opposed ways. It actually states: 'Subject to the provisions of this section, this Chapter relates only to employment by the one employer.' This can mean either that S.218(2) is subject to the rule on non-counting weeks in the same way as employment with only one employer is subject to the rule or that, since S.218(2) applies to more than one employer, it takes effect without any reference at all to the other provisions of the Chapter (i.e. Ss.210–219). Wood J preferred the latter interpretation. However, in order for this argument to stand up it would have to apply to Ss.218(3)–(9) as well – all of which cover situations involving more than one employer. Unfortunately, the decision of the Court of Appeal in Minetti v DVK Executive Hotels Ltd, unreported 22.11.88, CA, is authority to the contrary, at least in relation to S.218(6), which covers the transfer of employees between associated employers.

The EAT's generously purposive approach to the interpretation of S.218(2) in Macer was followed by another division of the EAT in Justfern Ltd and ors v D'Ingerthorpe 1994 ICR 286, EAT, where it held that S.218(2) can bridge gaps in employment of longer than one week provided the gap relates to the 'machinery' of the transfer. The EAT also rejected any suggestion that the decision in Macer be limited to situations in which there was evidence of collusion between the transferor and the transferee to avoid the operation of TUPE. In the Justfern case D was employed by EM as a college lecturer until the business was closed on 10 October 1988 due to financial difficulties. D was paid until 7 October and sent home. The following day he applied for unemployment benefit. Shortly after the closure, J Ltd bought the college and it was reopened on 24 October. D was re-employed by J Ltd but resigned and claimed constructive dismissal seven months later. The employment tribunal had to decide whether D had the requisite continuous service to proceed with his claim when there had been a two-week gap between his employment and re-employment. On the basis that the sale of the college was a transfer within S.218(2), the tribunal held that D's employment with EM had been preserved over that transfer. J Ltd appealed unsuccessfully to the EAT.

The EAT rejected the contention that D's employment with EM should not be 7.25 carried over because he was not employed by EM 'at the time of the transfer'. The EAT noted that Wood J in Macer said that the words 'at the time of the

527

transfer' did not mean that there had to be one identifiable point in time when the transfer took place – a transfer of a business is something which takes time and 'the time' of the transfer means a period of time rather than a specific moment. The EAT found further support for this wide interpretation in S.210(5), which provides that: 'A person's employment during any period shall, unless the contrary is shown, be presumed to have been continuous' (but see 'Residual application of ERA – presumption of continuity' below).

J Ltd tried to distinguish Macer by contending that the termination of D's employment with EM was for commercial reasons of insolvency rather than as a step in a transfer of the business. The EAT rejected this line of argument on the ground that the issue is whether there is a transfer of a business in relation to which an employee's employment can be regarded as also transferred. EM's motive for terminating D's employment was, in its opinion, irrelevant. All S.218(2) required was that the business and the employment of the relevant employee should survive sufficiently to be capable of transfer to the transferee, i.e. that there should be enough of the original business left to transfer. Thus, if the first employer closed down the business so completely that the new employer was effectively starting a new business, S.218(2) would not apply. However, the tribunal did not consider that that had happened here and the EAT saw no reason to challenge that view.

7.26 The most difficult aspect of the case for the EAT was D's application for, and receipt of, unemployment benefit for more than one week during the gap in his employment. Claiming unemployment benefit may indicate that the employee has severed the link with the former employer, thus breaking continuity. However, the EAT saw a major distinction between taking on a new job on the one hand and applying for benefit when wages are no longer being paid on the other. In D's particular case, his claim did not mean that he was unavailable for work in the college. Furthermore, re-employment was still a possibility. While acknowledging that there was uncertainty in the situation, the EAT saw no reason why S.218(2), which was capable of bridging a period of more than one week, could not also bridge a period of uncertainty. It concluded that D's receipt of benefit did not break his continuity.

What is the position if an employee remains in the employment of the transferor after the transfer but then goes to work for the transferee, who subsequently dismisses him or her? Will the fact that the employee is retained by the transferor (albeit for only a short period) mean that when he or she begins work with the transferee this will be regarded as new employment, with the consequence that continuity of employment is broken? The answer depends on whether the employee is considered to have been employed 'at the time of the transfer' for the purposes of S.218(2). The EAT sought to tackle this thorny issue in A and G Tuck Ltd and anor v Bartlett 1994 ICR 379, EAT. B had worked for two associated companies, S and H, since 1989, although he remained an employee of S throughout. On 10 August 1992, he discovered that S had been sold to C (trading under the name of A&GT Ltd) while he was on holiday. B was not transferred to C but on 12 August C invited B to go and work for him. B started work for C two weeks later but was subsequently dismissed. C maintained that B's continuity had been broken when he remained in his previous employment for two weeks after the transfer. The main question for the EAT was whether B was employed 'at the time of the transfer'. The EAT rejected C's argument that the Macer case did not apply because it was concerned with a gap in employment before the transfer, not after. The issue, following Macer, was whether the gap in B's employment related to the 'machinery' of the transfer and whether that could extend beyond the date of legal completion of the sale. The EAT decided that the employment tribunal had taken the right course when refusing to limit the transfer to that moment in time when the legal documentation was completed. The members of the tribunal were also correct in taking into account their experience of industrial life and the fact that the normal problems associated with business takeovers could extend the actual machinery of the transfer beyond the actual date of transfer. Moreover, the way the tribunal had interpreted S.218(2) was consistent with the intention of Parliament and with the requirements of justice.

7.27 It would appear, therefore, that unless and until a higher authority overrules Macer v Abafast Ltd (above), the problem of the 'non-counting' week has ceased to be an issue, provided the gap in employment can be considered to be part of the machinery of the transfer. This will be a question of fact in each case, although obviously the longer the gap the less likely it will be considered a part of that machinery.

7.28 **Effect of Celtec.** The approach in Macer v Abafast Ltd 1990 ICR 234, EAT, has been applied in a number of subsequent cases and was adopted by the Court of Appeal in Clark and Tokeley Ltd v Oakes 1999 ICR 276, CA. However, a potential difficulty has arisen since the decisions of the ECJ and the House of Lords in North Wales Training and Enterprise Council Ltd (trading as Celtec Ltd) v Astley and ors 2006 ICR 992, HL ('Celtec'), which effectively confirmed the view taken by the Court of Appeal in Secretary of State for Employment v Spence and ors 1986 ICR 651, CA (although without referring to it), that – for the purposes of TUPE at least – a transfer can only take place at a specific point in time. It could be argued, of course, that the same does not necessarily apply under the ERA and that courts and tribunals are perfectly entitled to continue to apply the Macer line of cases for the purposes of S.218(2). But this would lead to a rather unsatisfactory situation in which 'at the time of the transfer' under the ERA would have to be given a wider meaning than 'immediately before' the transfer in the Regulations. Moreover, it is difficult to see how this could be consistent with D36 Ltd v Castro EAT 0853/03 (discussed under 'Relationship between TUPE and ERA' above), where it was held that the same definition of a 'transfer' applies across both sets of provisions. The two positions could be reconciled if the view is taken that Castro only requires a definition of 'transfer' under the ERA that is *no narrower* than that under the Regulations, but this may be to strain the words of the EAT in that case.

It would seem, therefore, that there is a very serious issue to be determined by the courts in the light of Celtec. If the House of Lords' approach in Celtec and a strict view of Nicholas v Grant (t/a Sandancers Café) EAT 0198/06 (that continuity is a matter to be determined by reference to S.218(2), not TUPE – see 'Relationship between TUPE and ERA' above) are applied, rather than the Macer line of cases, the result could potentially be catastrophic for employees, particularly those with long service with the transferor. It would mean that if an employee was not employed at the exact moment of the transfer, S.218(2) simply would not apply to preserve continuity, regardless of the nature and/or duration of any gap between employments (but see 'Residual application of ERA – breaks in employment covered by S.212(3) ERA' below). It is equally arguable, however, that in order for S.218(2) to preserve continuity, the individual employee does not actually need to transfer so long as a transfer occurs and he or she takes up employment with the transferee. If Macer prevails, employees employed at the time of the transfer in its wider sense will be protected by S.218(2), provided the interval between employments related to the machinery of the transfer.

7.29   Authority for following the Macer line of cases can be found in the case of Services for Education (S4E Ltd) v White and anor EAT 0024/15. There, the EAT declined to apply the 'time of the transfer' approach set down in Celtec, noting that the TUPE Regulations and the continuity provisions of the ERA have distinct purposes. It upheld an employment tribunal's decision that W, a teacher who was employed by Birmingham City Council on a succession of fixed-term contracts, each of which lasted for the academic year (1 September to 31 July) separated by a temporary cessation of work under S.212(3)(b) ERA, benefited from continuous employment under the ERA provisions when the Council outsourced the services to S4E Ltd. The EAT accepted that the tribunal had, in fact, erred in finding that S.212(3)(b) ERA could bridge the gap between the end of W's last fixed-term contract with the Council on 31 July 2013 and the start of his employment by S4E Ltd on 3 September, since S.218(1) clearly provides that the continuity provisions generally only apply to employment by the one employer. But the tribunal had nonetheless come to the correct overall conclusion in that W's continuity was preserved by the special protection available in the case of a business transfer under S.218(2), which applies where the employee is employed by the transferor 'at the time of the transfer'. The EAT noted that, following the Court of Appeal's decision in Clark and Tokeley Ltd v Oakes (above), such a transfer can be a process in respect of which the precise identification of 'the time of the transfer' is a question of fact and degree. The tribunal was entitled to find that, although W's employment with the

Council ended on 31 July and the transfer did not take place until 1 September, W was nonetheless employed by the Council 'at the time of the transfer'.

The EAT's approach was based on there being two different concepts of timing for the purposes of, on the one hand, being transferred under TUPE, and, on the other, being transferred for the purposes of calculating continuous service under the ERA. For an employee to be the subject of a TUPE transfer he or she must be employed immediately before the transfer, which, as held in Celtec, is a distinct point in time. However, for the purposes of the continuous service provisions in the ERA, the time of the transfer is a far more nebulous concept that potentially stretches back some months before the transfer actually or formally takes place. Provided that the employee is employed by the transferee at some point during the period over which the process of the transfer takes place, then his or her continuity of employment will be preserved.

Employee objection to transfer
7.30

Regulation 4(1) and (2) TUPE provides that the contract of employment of anyone employed by the transferor will be automatically transferred to the transferee. However, this is subject to the employee's right to object to being transferred. This right is provided for in Reg 4(7), which states that paras (1) and (2) will not operate to transfer the contract of employment of an employee who informs the transferor or transferee that he or she objects to becoming employed by the transferee. Reg 4(8) goes on to provide that where there is an objection under Reg 4(7), the transfer will have the effect of terminating the employee's contract but he or she will not, for any purpose, be considered to have been dismissed by the transferor.

Regulation 4(7) and (8) should be read in conjunction with Reg 4(9) and (11), however. Reg 4(9) states that where a transfer involves or would involve a substantial change in the employee's working conditions that is to his or her material detriment, the employee may treat the contract as having been terminated and he or she will be treated for any purpose as having been dismissed by the employer. Furthermore, nothing in paras (1), (7), (8) or (9) prejudices an employee's right to terminate his or her contract without notice in acceptance of a repudiatory breach by the employer and claim constructive dismissal – Reg 4(11).

In Humphreys v University of Oxford and anor 2000 ICR 405, CA, the Court 7.31 of Appeal held that an objection under Reg 4(7) (which, according to the Court, must relate to the actual identity of the transferee to be valid) and a claim under Reg 4(11) can be made together in advance of the transfer. The same is likely to be true of claims based on Reg 4(9), which protects employees from being subject to substantial detrimental changes to their working conditions as a consequence of a transfer. This means that an employee may treat him or herself as dismissed prior to the transfer and claim constructive

531

dismissal (or 'material detriment dismissal') against the transferor, with the dismissal taking effect at the date of the transfer (as per Reg 4(8)). Alternatively – although the Humphreys case did not decide the point – if an employee does not object under Reg 4(7) but simply waits until after the transfer to bring a claim under Reg 4(9) or 4(11), Reg 4(8) will not operate so as to make the transfer date the point at which the contract is terminated: the employee will transfer and the date on which he or she treats the contract as having terminated will be the date of dismissal.

It seems clear, based on the well-reasoned decision of the High Court in New ISG Ltd v Vernon and ors 2008 ICR 319, ChD, that if an employee is kept in the dark about a transfer and is therefore given no opportunity to object to the new employer's identity before the transfer takes place, he or she can make an objection at a later stage once he or she becomes aware of the transfer. This means that the objecting employee's employment will not be regarded as having transferred to the transferee, and he or she will be left with those rights under Reg 4(9) and (11) enforceable against the transferor. Thus the normal rule is that any objection to a transfer has to be made *before* the transfer occurs – see Capita Health Solutions Ltd v McLean and anor 2008 IRLR 595, EAT (discussed under 'Secondments and employees who go to work for transferee' below). However, according to the High Court in the New ISG case, there is an exception to this rule where the employee does not know the identity of the transferee before the date of the transfer. To hold that such an employee had lost his or her right to object to the transfer would be to 'undermine the fundamental freedom of the employee to chose his employer'. It was therefore necessary to adopt a purposive construction of Reg 4(7) to permit an objection to be made once the identity of the transferee had become known.

7.32 An employee's right to object to a transfer, and the interrelationship between Reg 4(7) and (8) and Reg 4(9) and (11), is discussed in detail in Chapter 2, 'Who transfers?', under 'Objecting to transfer'. In this chapter, we consider the effect of those provisions on an employee's continuity of employment.

7.33 **What is an objection?** It is not precisely clear what sort of conduct will be sufficient to constitute a Reg 4(7) 'objection', although in Hay v George Hanson (Building Contractors) Ltd 1996 IRLR 427, EAT, the EAT stated that the word in this context effectively means 'a refusal to accept the transfer', and that this state of mind 'must be conveyed to either the transferor or transferee'. Logically, it would seem that an objection in these circumstances cannot consist simply of the act of resigning from employment or the giving of notice of resignation. This is because, under basic contractual principles, the resignation itself would terminate the contract on the date of its occurrence, whereas Reg 4(8) stipulates that where there is a Reg 4(7) objection it is the date of the transfer that constitutes the date of the termination. The effect of Reg 4(7) and (8) is that after the employee has manifested an objection, he or she continues in employment until the date of the transfer, at which point he or she is deemed to have been dismissed by the transferor. Of course, it may be that in the context of transfers, a resignation in such circumstances will not have the usual contractual effect, meaning that if the resignation is in opposition to the identity of the transferee, the transfer itself will terminate the contract (rather than the resignation). But up to now no case has specifically held this to be so.

A resignation on other grounds *would* have the usual effect, with the proviso that if notice is given and the notice period extends up to or beyond the date of the transfer, the employee will transfer to the transferee (see Nicholas v Grant (t/a Sandancers Café) EAT 0198/06). In these circumstances, the employee's continuity would not be affected because, if he or she transfers, there can be no issue as to whether or not he or she was employed 'at the time of the transfer'. Continuity problems arise where the notice period expires *before* the transfer occurs and the employee then takes up employment under a new contract with the transferee. Continuity in these circumstances will depend on two things: first, that the EAT's reasoning in Macer v Abafast Ltd 1990 ICR 234, EAT, continues to be applicable (post North Wales Training and Enterprise Council Ltd (trading as Celtec Ltd) v Astley and ors 2006 ICR 992, HL), and that any gap between the two employments is seen as part of the 'machinery of the transfer'; and, secondly, that it is accepted that, for the purposes of S.218(2), the individual employee does not need to transfer so long as he or she can be said (pursuant to Macer) to have been employed in the transferor's business at the time of the transfer (see 'Breaks in employment' above).

7.34 Judicial clarification is needed as to the true effect of a resignation on the date of termination where the resignation is based on an objection to the identity of the transferee. This is especially so since the BIS Guide to the 2006 Regulations appears to take the orthodox contractual position, stating that: 'The objection terminates the contract of employment and the employee is not treated for any purpose as having been dismissed by either the transferor or the [transferee]'. However, this is inconsistent with the actual words used in the Regulations, which state at Reg 4(8) that: 'Subject to paragraphs (9) and (11), where an employee... objects, the *relevant transfer* shall operate so as to terminate his contract of employment with the transferor but he shall not be treated, for any purpose, as having been dismissed by the transferor' (our stress). There is therefore a divergence between the Regulations and the Guide, and it is submitted that the Guide is unreliable in this regard.

The distinction is crucially important for continuity purposes. If the *objection* terminates the employment, this will generally be in advance of the transfer. This means that there would be a serious risk of the employee being found not to have been employed 'at the time of the transfer', so that even if employment is subsequently taken up with the transferee (on a new contract), continuity would not be preserved. This could well be so even if the Macer line of cases is

533

followed, since the reasoning in those cases applies where the employee is *dismissed* prior to the transfer and re-engaged by the transferee. A Reg 4(7) objection means there is no dismissal 'for any purpose', despite the contract having been terminated by the transfer – Reg 4(8).

7.35 If, however, as Reg 4(8) suggests, the *transfer* terminates the contract, this means that the employee would be employed 'at the time of the transfer', since it would be the event of the transfer itself that would bring about the end of the employment contract. The fact that the individual does not transfer does not mean that the transfer itself does not occur. In these circumstances, an employee making a Reg 4(7) objection in advance of the transfer could have continuity of employment preserved by S.218(2) if subsequently employed by the transferee under a new contract. (This would be subject to the proviso that any gap between the employments did not break continuity, although even this proviso may not apply if Macer v Abafast Ltd (above) remains good law – see 'Breaks in employment' above.)

7.36 Secondments and employees who go to work for transferee
There are situations in which, far from objecting to the transfer, the employee may be unaware that a transfer has even taken place. The decision of the House of Lords in North Wales Training and Enterprise Council Ltd (trading as Celtec Ltd) v Astley and ors 2006 ICR 992, HL (implementing that of the ECJ reported at 2005 ICR 1409) ('Celtec'), has implications for the preservation of continuity of employment in circumstances where the transferor purports to second employees to another entity in an attempt to avoid their being transferred. In that case, civil servants employed by the Department of Employment were seconded in 1990 to a Training and Enterprise Council (TEC) that later became Celtec. It was common ground that Celtec was an emanation of the state. In 1993, the civil servants opted to become employees of Celtec and resigned from the Department. In their letters of engagement, they were told that their periods of continuous employment would re-start from that point and that their periods of service with the Department would no longer count. When a redundancy situation later arose, the claimants sought a declaration from an employment tribunal that their continuous service included service in the Department. The employment tribunal upheld the claims under both S.218 ERA and the EU Acquired Rights Directive (No.77/187). After appeals to the EAT, the Court of Appeal, the House of Lords and a referral to the ECJ, the House of Lords concluded that the tribunal had reached the correct decision, albeit via different reasoning. Their Lordships held by a majority (Lord Mance dissenting) that the claimants were deemed to have transferred in 1990 when they were initially seconded, despite the fact that none of the parties was aware of this at the time or intended that to be the legal effect of the arrangement. The claimants' contracts therefore passed to the transferee on the date they were seconded and their continuity of

employment was preserved by Article 3(1) of the 1977 Directive (subsequently re-enacted as Article 3(1) of the 2001 Directive). The claimants had also relied on S.218, but the majority of their Lordships took the view that in this case it was only necessary to consider the Directive.

The fact that the House of Lords in the Celtec case did not address S.218 does not mean, however, that that provision is no longer effective to preserve continuity within the context of a transfer of an undertaking. The events in Celtec occurred before the 1981 Regulations were amended in 1993 to extend the definition of an undertaking to non-commercial entities by S.33 of the Trade Union Reform and Employment Rights Act 1993. Thus the claims, while clearly analogous to claims under the Regulations, were technically claims brought directly under the Acquired Rights Directive. What the case means is that, even outside the context of pre-1993 transfers between state entities, the Directive requires domestic legislation to preserve the continuity of employment of employees when they are deemed to have transferred at the point of their initial secondment. Although the TUPE Regulations were passed in order to transpose the Directive, UK law will not be in breach of its requirements if continuity is preserved by other means, i.e. by S.218(2).

On the face of it, the Celtec case would seem to suggest that employees are **7.37** saddled with the consequences of their employment having automatically transferred simply because they remained in employment until the date of the transfer, even where they knew nothing about the change in the identity of their employer and would have exercised their right to object had they been in a position to do so. In most cases, of course, employees in this situation would prefer their continuity to be preserved since, sometime down the track, they may well wish to maximise their period of continuous service with their 'new' employer. For example, if they are made redundant, their entitlement to and scale of statutory redundancy payments will depend on the amount of continuous employment they have accrued. In such cases, S.218 operates to preserve continuity notwithstanding the lack of any objection or even the opportunity to object. But what is the position if the employee genuinely would not have wished his or her employment to transfer had he or she been informed of the imminent change of employer?

This was the situation in New ISG Ltd v Vernon and ors 2008 ICR 319, ChD, discussed under 'Employee objection to transfer' above. There, the employee was kept in the dark about the identity of his new employer following the sale of the transferor's business by joint administrators. When, two days after the transfer, he learned of the identity of the transferee, he resigned and subsequently went to work for a competitor. The new transferee immediately sought to enforce restrictive covenants in the employee's contract, contending that this had been transferred automatically in accordance with Reg 4 of TUPE. Initially, the transferee was successful in obtaining a temporary injunction restraining

535

the employee from working for the competitor. However, on review, a High Court judge lifted the injunction on the basis that the employee, by resigning as soon as he found out about the transfer, had in effect objected to the transfer within the meaning of Reg 4(7). This had the consequence that his contract of employment had not transferred, so the transferee was not in a position to enforce the restrictive covenants contained within it. The judge rejected the transferee's argument that the employee's objection was ineffective because it was made after the transfer had occurred. The employee had not known of the identity of the transferee before the date of the transfer and had submitted a letter of resignation within two working days of the transfer. In those circumstances, while the wording of Reg 4(7) envisaged that an employee must object before or at the time of the transfer of the undertaking for the objection to be valid, the judge reasoned that a purposive approach was necessary to give force to the principle behind the right to object.

7.38 There are limits, however, to the extent to which the courts will allow an employee to object after a transfer has occurred. In Capita Health Solutions Ltd v McLean and anor 2008 IRLR 595, EAT, an employee employed by the BBC had deep reservations about the imminent transfer of her employment as an occupational nurse to CHS Ltd, which was due to take over the entirety of the BBC's HR department, including its occupational health service. These reservations were expressed by way of a grievance alleging that the change of employer entailed a significant change to the employee's role and pension benefits. However, in subsequent dealings, the employee and the BBC agreed that she would go to work for CHS Ltd for the six-week period during which she was working out her notice of resignation, and that she would continue to be paid by the BBC during this period. At the end of the six weeks, the employee duly resigned and claimed unfair dismissal against both CHS Ltd and the BBC and the issue arose as to whether the transferor – i.e. the BBC – should be regarded as a proper respondent to the proceedings. This depended on whether the employee had validly objected to the transfer: if not, her employment would have transferred to CHS Ltd, making it the sole respondent potentially liable for the unfair dismissal.

The EAT ruled that the act of going to work for the transferee under a temporary secondment arrangement in circumstances where the employee was fully aware of the change in the identity of the employer was wholly inconsistent with having evinced an objection to the transfer. What, in fact, the employee's approach showed was that she was agreeable to working for CHS Ltd, albeit for only six weeks: this was wholly inconsistent with her claim that she had objected to the transfer. In the EAT's view, the intention of the parties, while a relevant consideration, was not determinative of the question whether an objection within the meaning of Reg 4(7) had been made. This was entirely an objective matter to be decided not by the intention of the parties but by the facts and circumstances of the case at issue. Furthermore, the fact that the BBC

536

had continued to pay the employee during the secondment period was irrelevant, as was the fact that the employee was working out notice given prior to the transfer. In Lady Smith's judgment, 'if... it had been intended that objecting employees be required or able to work out notice periods that ran on after the date of the transfer, it is more than reasonable to have expected that to be provided for in the Regulations... That is not to say that an objecting employee cannot be employed by the transferor employer after the transfer date, but the transferor is not obliged to retain such an employee in his employment. Any such employment would be under a new contract.'

Residual application of ERA   7.39

In D36 Ltd v Castro EAT 0853/03 the EAT made it clear that the TUPE Regulations and S.218(2) ERA should be interpreted consistently as part of a 'single scheme' for preserving continuity in the event of a transfer. This view is arguably supported indirectly by the ERA itself, in that it provides that the definition of 'business' under S.235 ERA can adapt according to the context; for example, according to the definition applied for the purposes of the Regulations.

It may even be the case that a wider definition of 'transfer' applies for the purposes of S.218(2) than it does for TUPE. In Dabell v Vale Industrial Services (Nottingham) Ltd and ors 1988 IRLR 439, CA, the Court of Appeal found that a transfer under the ERA had occurred despite the fact that only an informal agreement to a transfer had ever been reached. The decision in D36 Ltd v Castro (above) is not necessarily inconsistent with this as it can be interpreted as simply requiring that the definition of 'transfer' under the ERA should be no narrower than that under the Regulations. This leaves open the possibility that there may be situations that would constitute a transfer for the purposes of S.218(2) but not amount to a relevant transfer under TUPE. In other words, falling within the definition of a 'relevant transfer' would be a sufficient, but not a necessary, requirement for a transfer to exist under S.218(2).

Thus, it seems that S.218(2) will apply to preserve continuity in all cases where **7.40** there has been a relevant transfer under the TUPE Regulations (subject to the question of whether the employee was employed in the entity transferred 'at the time of' the transfer – see 'Relationship between TUPE and ERA – "at the time of" or "immediately before" transfer' above). However, there are a number of situations in which the ERA applies entirely independently of the Regulations to preserve continuity of employment and these are now considered.

Redundancy pay and continuity   7.41
It is not uncommon for employees to receive a statutory redundancy payment from the transferor despite taking up employment with the transferee. S.214 ERA states that continuity of employment is broken by receipt of a redundancy payment but only for the purposes of the statutory redundancy scheme. This

means that employees start acquiring a new period of continuity so far as future entitlement to redundancy payments is concerned as soon as their continuity has been formally broken by the receipt of a statutory redundancy payment – but not for other purposes (provided, of course, that their continuity has not otherwise been broken on some other basis). S.214 applies where the employee's contract was renewed or the employee was re-engaged under a new contract, whether by the same or by another employer.

However, it is crucial to note that, in order for S.214 to apply, the transferor must have been liable to pay a redundancy payment under the legislation. If an employee is paid a redundancy payment by the transferor where there is a relevant transfer, his or her dismissal, if connected with the transfer within the meaning of Reg 7(1), will be automatically unfair unless the reason for the dismissal constitutes an ETO reason under Reg 7(2). In such circumstances, the payment made by the transferor will not have been in respect of a true liability because there will not have been a true redundancy situation. Therefore, S.214 would not apply and continuity for the purposes of calculating a future redundancy payment could be preserved.

7.42 There is one exception to the rule that S.214 will not apply if a payment is made in respect of a dismissal that is not a genuine redundancy. S.167 ERA essentially provides that where an employee is dismissed by an insolvent company by reason of redundancy, the Secretary of State will make a redundancy payment out of the National Insurance Fund. In Lassman and ors v Secretary of State for Trade and Industry and anor 2000 ICR 1109, CA, the Court of Appeal examined a situation where the Secretary of State made redundancy payments to employees dismissed by an insolvent company where the dismissals were later found to have been by reason of a relevant transfer and automatically unfair under Reg 7(1) rather than by reason of redundancy. L and others were employed by R Ltd, which became insolvent in 1988. On 29 March 1988 T Ltd signed an option agreement with R Ltd's receivers to purchase R Ltd. Two days later the employees were dismissed. However, they subsequently accepted jobs with T Ltd to commence on the next working day. They later received redundancy payments in respect of their dismissals by R Ltd from the Secretary of State, who was unaware that TUPE applied. Some years later, when T Ltd also became insolvent, the employees were again dismissed. They claimed that they were entitled to redundancy payments calculated by reference to their periods of employment with both employers. They argued that, since TUPE applied to the 1988 transaction, the Secretary of State should not have made redundancy payments at the time and that, accordingly, S.214 had not operated to break their continuity of employment for redundancy purposes.

The Court of Appeal stated that the case turned on whether the payments made by the Secretary of State in 1988 were valid in the sense that they were payments which, under the relevant legislation, the Secretary of State was empowered to make. S.214(5) provides: 'For the purposes of this section a redundancy payment shall be treated as having been paid if... (c) the Secretary of State has paid a sum to the employee in respect of the redundancy payment under S.167.' S.167(1) provides that the Secretary of State must make a payment where he or she 'is satisfied that the requirements specified in subsection (2) are met'. One requirement set out in S.167(2) is that the employee is entitled to the employer's payment. The Court pointed out that S.167 does not require an employee to be entitled to a redundancy payment for that payment to be valid. Rather, it requires the Secretary of State to be satisfied that the employee is so entitled. This is a subjective test, not an objective one. The Court believed that the Secretary of State could have properly concluded (on the basis of the decision in Secretary of State for Employment v Spence and ors 1986 ICR 651, CA – which was the leading authority at the time) that the employees concerned were not employed immediately before the transfer and, therefore, were not affected by TUPE. Accordingly, the Secretary of State could properly have concluded that the employees were entitled to a redundancy payment. Therefore, the Court held that S.214 had operated in 1988 to break the employees' continuity of employment for redundancy purposes.

Insolvency   7.43

Regulation 4 TUPE (automatic novation of contracts) does not apply where the transferor is the subject of bankruptcy proceedings or other insolvency proceedings commenced under the supervision of an insolvency practitioner *with a view* to the liquidation of the transferor's assets – Reg 8(7). If, however, despite the initial aims of the insolvency proceedings, the trustee in bankruptcy or liquidator ends up selling the business as a going concern, this may well be a relevant transfer under the TUPE Regulations but the employee's employment will not automatically transfer under Reg 4. This does not necessarily mean that the employees will not be taken on voluntarily by the transferee but it does mean that their terms and conditions of employment will not be protected by the Regulations. However, for the purposes of continuity of employment this is unlikely to matter since, applying Nicholas v Grant (t/a Sandancers Café) EAT 0198/06 (see 'Relationship between TUPE and ERA' above), it is S.218(2) ERA that actually preserves continuity where there has been a business transfer (provided continuity has otherwise been preserved).

For example, in Belhaven Brewery Co Ltd v Berekis and ors EAT 724/92 BB Co Ltd owned the pub in which B and his fellow claimants worked. It went into bankruptcy and the pub, as one of its assets, became vested in the trustee in bankruptcy. The pub remained open, but management responsibility was transferred to a new management company. As well as holding that there had been a relevant transfer for the purposes of the 1981 TUPE Regulations (both when the trustee in bankruptcy had been appointed and again when the new managers had taken over), the EAT held that the employees' continuity of employment had been preserved by S.218(2).

7.44 Note that if the same facts were to be considered under the 2006 Regulations, the tribunal would first have to decide whether BB Co Ltd had entered into bankruptcy and appointed trustees in bankruptcy with a view to liquidating the assets (and therefore whether Reg 8(7) would apply to prevent Reg 4 from having effect). However, this issue would arguably have no impact on that part of the EAT's decision concerned with the preservation of the employees' continuity of employment and it is submitted that Berekis remains good law on that particular point.

This has subsequently been reinforced by the Court of Appeal in Oakland v Wellswood (Yorkshire) Ltd 2010 ICR 902, CA. Both the employment tribunal and the EAT in that case concentrated on the issue of whether Reg 8(7) applied to exclude the operation of the automatic transfer of employment rules in Reg 4 and the automatic unfair dismissal provisions of Reg 7 in the context of a transfer that took place following a so-called 'pre-pack' administration. The specific issue in the case was whether the employee had the requisite one year's continuous service (since increased to two years) to claim unfair dismissal against the transferee. When the matter reached the Court of Appeal, it cut through all the complex issues surrounding Reg 8(7) to point out that continuity was simply dependent on whether there had been a transfer of a trade, business or undertaking from one person to another within the meaning of S.218(2). On that basis, it had little difficulty in concluding that there had been such a transfer. Accordingly, the employee's period of continuous employment with the transferor was added to his period of employment with the transferee, with the result that he had sufficient continuous service to bring an unfair dismissal claim.

For a detailed discussion of transfers in an insolvency context, see Chapter 6, 'Transfer of insolvent companies'.

7.45 Breaks in employment covered by S.212(3) ERA
In Macer v Abafast Ltd 1990 ICR 234, EAT, Mr Justice Wood stated that a broad interpretation of S.218(2) ERA had to be applied and that an interval between employments, however long, did not matter for continuity purposes provided it related to the 'machinery' of the transfer (see 'Relationship between TUPE and ERA – breaks in employment' above). This meant that the normal continuity rules governing 'non-counting' weeks in Chapter I of Part XIV (i.e. Ss.210–219) of the ERA were not relevant to transfer situations provided the gap in employment could be considered a part of the machinery of the transfer. A similar approach had been adopted by the Court of Appeal in Clark and Tokeley Ltd v Oakes 1999 ICR 276, CA, where it was made clear that, for the purposes of the continuity provisions, a transfer could be regarded as extending

540

over a period of time and, provided the employee was employed by the transferee at any point during that period, his or her continuity would be preserved by virtue of what is now S.218(2).

At first glance it might be thought that the Macer and Oakes decisions would now need to be treated with some caution in the light of the House of Lords' subsequent decision in North Wales Training and Enterprise Council Ltd (trading as Celtec Ltd) v Astley and ors 2006 ICR 992, HL. In that case, their Lordships held that transfers under the Acquired Rights Directive (and therefore, by implication, TUPE) occur at a fixed point in time rather than across a period of time. If the same principle were to be applied to S.218(2), then there would be greater scope for continuity issues to arise as a result of gaps occurring between whichever specific date a transfer is found to have occurred and the date when employees begin working for the transferee. In such cases the non-counting week rules in the ERA would have to be closely considered. In a transfer context, these would potentially deprive employees of continuity under S.218(2) where there is a gap of more than a week between the ending of the employee's employment with the transferor and the beginning of his or her employment with the transferee.

7.46 However, as we have seen, the EAT in Services for Education (S4E Ltd) v White and anor EAT 0024/15 has held that the decision in Celtec is confined to the interpretation of 'transfer' in the TUPE Regulations. Mrs Justice Laing in that case ruled that the decision in Oakes remains sound authority for a more flexible approach being taken to the concept of 'transfer' for the purposes of S.218(2) – see under 'Relationship between TUPE and ERA – breaks in employment' above.

What also emerges from the White decision is that S.218(2) is the only continuity provision within the ERA that can be utilised to preserve continuity in respect of employees affected by a transfer of the business in which they work. Previously, there was some authority for the view that the 'bridging' provision in S.212(3) ERA could, if need be, be utilised to preserve continuity across gaps between the date of the transfer and the date of re-employment by the transferee. This lists the circumstances in which an otherwise non-counting week counts as a period of employment, notwithstanding the absence of an employment contract. It provides, inter alia, that any week counts in computing the employee's period of employment if, during the whole or part of that week, an employee is absent from work –

- on account of a temporary cessation of work – S.212(3)(b), or

- in circumstances such that, by arrangement or custom, he or she is regarded as continuing in the employment of his or her employer – S.212(3)(c).

7.47 In Robert Elliot Ltd v Edgar EAT 581/85 the EAT suggested that a temporary cessation of work within the meaning of S.212(3)(b) might preserve continuity during an interval on a transfer. This could be where there is no work available for employees to do while the business is being transferred. It was alternatively suggested that an agreement whereby employees were asked to keep themselves available for employment by the transferee could qualify as an 'arrangement' for the purposes of S.212(3)(c). However, in White and anor v Services for Education (S4E Ltd) (above) the EAT was adamant that these alternative bases for establishing continuity were not possible. Laing J pointed out that, subject to specific exceptions dealing with change of employer scenarios set out in S.218 (including a transfer of business under S.218(2)), the continuity provisions in Ss.210–219 ERA are predicated on the employee being employed by a single employer. This is made explicitly clear by S.218(1) when it states: 'Subject to the provisions of this section, this Chapter relates only to employment by the one employer.' Since the bridging provisions of S.213(2) do not concern a 'change of employer' scenario, these can only be used to preserve continuity between gaps of employment with the *same* employer. The upshot of this forceful reasoning – which was also adopted by the EAT in Secretary of State for Employment v Cohen and anor 1987 ICR 570, EAT, in respect of the continuity provisions when they were previously contained in Schedule 13 to the Employment Protection (Consolidation) Act 1978 – is that the suggestions made by the EAT in Robert Elliot Ltd v Edgar do not hold water.

The general effect of S.212(3) is discussed in detail in IDS Employment Law Handbook, 'Continuity of Employment' (2012), Chapter 2, 'Breaks in employment where there is no contract'.

7.48 Changes in employer where no business transfer occurs

It is important to note that specific statutory provisions apply in respect of preserving continuity of employment where an employee's employment transfers between two 'associated' employers – see S.218(6) ERA. Such a transfer does not usually constitute a transfer of a business or undertaking and therefore application of the provisions of S.218(2) is inappropriate.

There are similar provisions in S.218 which provide for preservation of continuity in other non-transfer situations where there has for some reason been a change of employer. These cover:

- statutory changes of employer – S.218(3)

- the death of an employer – S.218(4)

- a change in the partners making up an employing partnership – S.218(5)

- transfers of employees between local education authorities and governing bodies of local authority-run schools – S.218(7), and

- transfers of relevant employment between Health Service employers – S.218(8). 'Relevant employment' for these purposes means employment where the individual is undergoing professional training which involves him or her being employed successively by a number of different health service employers and which is specified in an order made by the Secretary of State – S.218(9).

These provisions are considered in greater depth in IDS Employment Law **7.49** Handbook, 'Continuity of Employment' (2012), Chapter 4, 'Changes of employer'.

Note that there are also specific provisions contained in other legislation preserving continuity in particular circumstances or for particular professions. For example, continuity of employment for local government employees in a redundancy situation is governed by the Redundancy Payments (Continuity of Employment in Local Government, etc) (Modification) Order 1999 SI 1999/2277 (as amended). This provides that the whole of local government is treated as a single employer when computing the period of continuous employment for the purpose of calculating redundancy payments.

Presumption of continuity
7.50

Section 210(5) ERA lays down a presumption that continuity is preserved 'unless the contrary is shown'. However, S.218(1) states that: 'Subject to the provisions of this section, this Chapter [i.e. Ss.210–219] relates only to employment by the one employer'. According to the EAT in Secretary of State for Employment v Cohen and anor 1987 ICR 570, EAT, this means that the presumption applies only to employment by the one employer unless the case can be brought within one of the exceptions in S.218 (e.g. S.218(2)). However, it is sometimes unclear from the facts what exactly has taken place. In the Cohen case, C worked for F Ltd until it became insolvent. F Ltd was succeeded by W Ltd as C's employer. When W Ltd in turn became insolvent, B Ltd became C's employer. B Ltd then went into liquidation and C was made redundant. C's entitlement to a redundancy payment depended on whether there had been transfers of businesses between successive employers so as to preserve his continuity of employment through his successive employments by F Ltd, W Ltd and B Ltd. There was scant evidence on the nature of the transactions that had taken place between the three companies. An employment tribunal decided to apply the presumption of continuity and to hold that C was entitled to a redundancy payment, which was payable by the Department of Employment because of the insolvency of C's last employer. The Secretary of State appealed. The EAT held that the statutory presumption of continuity applies only to employment with one employer unless the case can be brought within one of the statutory exceptions. It follows that the existence of a statutory exception must be demonstrated before the presumption of continuity can be applied.

This ruling means that in cases of transfers between employers the employee must show that the provisions on transfers and continuity contained in S.218(2) are applicable without resort to the presumption of continuity. It is only after

543

it has been shown that there has been a transfer of a business that the presumption may be applied in the employee's favour. This may operate to the disadvantage of employees, who will often not have access to the information which could help to establish the nature of the transfer.

8 Information and consultation

Employee liability information

Informing and consulting appropriate representatives

In this chapter we turn our attention to the specific rules in the Transfer of **8.1**
Undertakings (Protection of Employment) Regulations 2006 SI 2006/246
(TUPE) that govern the provision of information and employee consultation on
a TUPE transfer. We divide these into two categories:

- the duty on the transferor to provide information to the transferee about
  the employees who are to transfer under TUPE (see 'Employee liability
  information' below), and

- the duty on both the transferor and the transferee to inform and consult
  appropriate representatives of employees who may be affected by a relevant
  transfer (see 'Informing and consulting appropriate representatives' below).

The Department for Business, Innovation and Skills (BIS) has issued guidance
on the issues raised by the provisions considered in this chapter entitled
'Employment rights on the transfer of an undertaking' ('the BIS Guide'), which
was last updated in January 2014. We refer to this guide throughout the
chapter where relevant.

Employee liability information
8.2

In Chapter 2, 'Who transfers?', and Chapter 3, 'What transfers?', we explain
that, when a relevant transfer occurs, the contracts of employment of certain
members of the transferor's workforce, together with all the transferor's rights,
powers, duties and liabilities under or in connection with such contracts, will
(if the employees in question do not object) transfer automatically to the
transferee as a result of Reg 4 TUPE.

It is clear that a transferee will want to be aware, prior to a relevant transfer, of
the employees and the liabilities that it is about to take on. To this end, it will
usually expect the transferor to provide the relevant information and to sign up
to warranties in respect of it (see Chapter 11, 'Practical aspects of transfers', for
further details). However, some smaller firms might have insufficient bargaining
power to negotiate the appropriate contractual safeguards. Moreover, where
TUPE applies to a service provision change following a retendering exercise,
the incoming contractor (the transferee) does not normally have a contractual
relationship with the outgoing contractor (the transferor), and thus, historically,
has had no simple means of ascertaining the extent of the liabilities that are

_____

545

about to transfer. As we shall see, however, the TUPE regime has sought to ameliorate transferees' difficulties in this regard.

Article 3(3) of the EU Acquired Rights Directive (No.2001/23) ('the Acquired Rights Directive') gives Member States the option to introduce provisions 'to ensure that the transferor notifies the transferee of all the rights and obligations which will be transferred to the transferee... so far as those rights and obligations are or ought to have been known to the transferor at the time of the transfer'. This option, not available under the previous version of the Directive, was taken up by the UK Government in the 2006 Regulations (which replaced the Transfer of Undertakings (Protection of Employment) Regulations 1981 SI 1981/1794 ('the 1981 Regulations'), and as a result transferors are now obliged to notify transferees about so-called 'employee liability information'. As discussed below, Regs 11 and 12 of the Regulations lay down rules as to the manner, extent and timing of the notification that the transferor must give to the transferee, and the remedy for failure to observe the requirements.

In the 2005 consultation document that accompanied the 2006 Regulations, the Government expressed the view that 'the introduction of these new provisions will ensure that transferees are entitled to full, accurate information about the employees, and the associated rights, obligations etc, that they are taking on in a relevant transfer, and so are well placed to honour those rights, obligations etc'. Furthermore, it continued, 'it will help to ensure transparency in the transfer process and to prevent instances of sharp practice – such as where, shortly before a transfer is completed, the transferor changes the terms and conditions and/or the composition of the workforce assigned to the undertaking in question, to the disadvantage of the transferee'.

8.3 Information in respect of transferring employees

Regulation 11(1) TUPE specifies that 'the transferor shall notify to the transferee the employee liability information of any person employed by him who is assigned to the organised grouping of resources or employees that is the subject of a relevant transfer'. Reg 11(4) clarifies that the Reg 11(1) duty 'shall include a duty to provide employee liability information of any person who would have been employed by the transferor and assigned to the organised grouping of resources or employees that is the subject of a relevant transfer immediately before the transfer if he had not been dismissed in the circumstances described in regulation 7(1)'.

Put more simply, the transferor must supply the transferee with 'employee liability information' – for which, see 'Definition of "employee liability information"' below – in respect of the following two categories of employee:

- those whose contracts of employment will, subject to the employees' right to object, transfer to the transferee under Reg 4(2) – see Chapter 2, 'Who transfers?', and

546

- those whose contracts would have transferred under Reg 4(2) had they not been automatically unfairly dismissed under Reg 7(1) by reason of the relevant transfer, or for a reason in connection with the relevant transfer that was not 'an economic, technical or organisational reason entailing changes in the workforce' – see Chapter 4, 'Unfair dismissal'.

Technically therefore, Reg 11 does not cover anyone who had been dismissed **8.4** by the transferor for a non-TUPE related reason or who objected to the transfer – see, for example, G4S Secure Solutions (UK) Ltd v Carlisle Security Services Ltd ET Case No.3400150/14. However, where there is a dispute over whether an employee is covered, the safest course may be to provide the information on a 'without prejudice' basis because, if the tribunal concludes that the employee was among the group of employees assigned to the undertaking or the service, the transferor will in all probability be found to be in breach of its duty to inform. Alternatively, it may be open to the transferor to argue that, in such circumstances, the tribunal should not exercise the discretion to make an award conferred on it by Reg 12(3)(b) or that it would be just and equitable to make a lesser award under Reg 12(5) (see 'Remedy for failure to notify' below).

The duty is on the transferor to provide the information to the transferee and its accuracy cannot be challenged by the transferring employees (or, where appropriate, their representatives) under Reg 11 as the remedy in Reg 12 is given to the transferee (see 'Remedy for failure to notify' below).

Definition of 'employee liability information' 8.5
The list of information that must be provided in respect of the transferring employees is set out in Reg 11(2), which defines 'employee liability information' as:

- the identity and age of an employee

- the particulars of employment that an employer is obliged to give to an employee pursuant to S.1 of the Employment Rights Act 1996 (ERA)

- 'information of any (i) disciplinary procedure taken against an employee; (ii) grievance procedure taken by an employee, within the previous two years, in circumstances where a Code of Practice issued under Part IV of the Trade Union and Labour Relations (Consolidation) Act 1992 which relates exclusively or primarily to the resolution of disputes applies'

- 'information of any court or tribunal case, claim or action brought by an employee against the transferor, within the previous two years' and of any court or tribunal case, claim or action 'that the transferor has reasonable grounds to believe that an employee may bring against the transferee, arising out of the employee's employment with the transferor', and

547

- 'information of any collective agreement which will have effect after the transfer, in its application in relation to the employee, pursuant to Reg 5(a)'.

8.6 **Identity and age.** In WGC Ltd v Resource (UK) ET Case No.2302094/09 an employment tribunal decided that there is no material difference between providing employees' dates of birth and providing ages. Accordingly, where the transferee requested dates of birth, it should have been provided with them. As to employees' identities, a tribunal in Kentklean Ltd v Southern Cleaning and Support Services Ltd ET Case No.1100807/08 held that this does not include a requirement to provide employees' addresses. The tribunal thought addresses could to some extent be regarded as sensitive, private information, and that if such information were required to be given, the Regulations would have said so expressly.

8.7 **Particulars of employment.** As stated above, under Reg 11(2) the transferor must provide the transferee with the transferring employees' S.1 ERA particulars of employment. These will include reasonably extensive information about the employees' terms and conditions, dealing with job title, remuneration, hours, holidays, terms relating to incapacity for work due to sickness or injury (including sick pay), pensions, when employment began, length of notice, place of work, relevant collective agreements and overseas working. For more details, see IDS Employment Law Handbook, 'Contracts of Employment' (2014), Chapter 6, 'Written particulars'.

In many cases, it will be relatively easy to comply with this obligation provided the current particulars of employment have been kept up to date but difficulties may arise where there have been a succession of service providers and the particulars have not been updated following a previous transfer or if the particulars are not accurate for some other reason. In G4S Secure Solutions (UK) Ltd v Carlisle Security Services Ltd ET Case No.3400150/14, for example, the tribunal found that the transferor had failed to provide accurate information in respect of eight employees who transferred to the transferee under a contract for security guarding services that was awarded to the transferee by the London Borough of Hackney. The 'Hackney eight' (as they were referred to by the tribunal) had previously worked for the Council. The tribunal concluded that the information which had been provided to the transferee by way of a spreadsheet did not provide sufficient information relating to a shift allowance which was payable to some but not all of the eight employees. The tribunal also found that the information regarding overtime was incorrect as the information provided suggested that the 'Hackney eight' were entitled to be paid overtime at time and a half whereas the tribunal found that overtime was not payable at all, although they were entitled to an enhanced payment for working at weekends.

8.8 The transferor's obligation under Reg 11(2)(b) is limited to the information required by S.1 ERA. This does not cover all benefits or other rights that may

548

be set out in a contract of employment or statutory particulars as these will often go beyond the minimum statutory requirements. For example, there is no statutory obligation to give particulars relating to benefits like company cars or maternity rights even though these are commonly referred to in particulars of employment or employment contracts. Two examples:

- **WGC Ltd v Resource (UK)** ET Case No.2302094/09: an employment tribunal held that information such as the employee's marital status, nationality, attendance record and right to work in the UK is not required under Reg 11(2). However, information about sickness absence was necessary to enable the transferee to calculate accurately the employees' entitlement to contractual or statutory sick pay. (Note that the tribunal's ruling on this latter point may be open to doubt because S.1(4)(d)(ii) ERA only requires an employer to provide particulars of terms and conditions relating to sickness absence and any provision for sick pay. There is no obligation to provide details of an employee's *entitlement* to sick pay – see also the G4S Secure Solutions case below)

- **G4S Secure Solutions (UK) Ltd v Carlisle Services Ltd** (above): a tribunal ruled that the obligation to provide information on holiday entitlement did not extend to providing 'information about the amount of holiday which employees had taken in the leave year'. The tribunal's conclusion is supported by the fact that the reference to accrued entitlement in S.1(4)(d)(i) ERA only applies to holiday accrued on termination of employment and under the 'automatic transfer' principle in Reg 4(1) there is no termination of employment where there is a 'relevant transfer' for TUPE purposes.

The requirement to provide particulars does extend, however, to any terms and conditions relating to occupational pension schemes even though such schemes do not transfer under the TUPE Regulations – see Chapter 3, 'What transfers?', under 'Occupational pensions'. So, for example, in G4S Secure Solutions (UK) Ltd v Carlisle Services Ltd (above) the tribunal found that the transferor had failed to provide pension details in respect of one salaried employee who transferred. But this will not ordinarily include benefits such as death in service payments unless these form part of a pension entitlement. So, in Weston Aviation Support Ltd v Signature Flight Support UK Regions Ltd ET Case No.1201434/12 the tribunal ruled that the transferor was not in breach of its obligation under Reg 11(2)(b) in not providing information in relation to a 'death in service scheme' that was a free-standing benefit.

Disciplinary and grievance procedures. The transferor must also provide information about any disciplinary procedure instituted in respect of a transferring employee, and about any grievance procedure instituted by a transferring employee, within the previous two years to which a Code of Practice issued under Part IV of the Trade Union and Labour Relations (Consolidation) Act 1992 applies. The only relevant Code currently in force is **8.9**

the recently updated Acas Code of Practice on Disciplinary and Grievance Procedures (2015) – see IDS Employment Law Supplement, 'Disciplinary and Grievance Procedures' (2009), for details. Given that the transferor will be required to provide details on any disciplinary action it has taken in the previous two years, disciplinary policies providing for a shorter retention period for expunged disciplinary sanctions will need to be reviewed to ensure that adequate records are kept in the employee's personnel file for the relevant two-year period.

8.10 The following points should also be considered:

- the transferor is only obliged to provide details of occasions when a disciplinary or grievance procedure has actually been instituted – not about occasions on which a procedure should have been instituted but was not

- there is no indication in the TUPE Regulations or the BIS Guide of how much detail the transferor is obliged to provide in respect of the disciplinary or grievance proceedings in question. This might, in time, be ironed out by case law. In the meantime, we suggest that a transferor should, at the very least, state when and why the procedure was followed, and what the outcome was

- it would seem from the wording of Reg 11(2) that the transferor is obliged to provide information about *any* disciplinary or grievance procedure instituted by or in respect of a transferring employee within the previous two years, whether such procedure involved the transferor itself or a previous employer. Where the employee in question transferred to the transferor from a previous employer under TUPE – meaning that any liabilities arising from such previous employment passed to the transferor and will, in turn, pass to the transferee – it makes sense that the transferee should be made aware of this information. It makes less sense, however, if the employee's employment with the previous employer did not transfer to the transferor under TUPE and was not otherwise continuous. In such circumstances, anything that happened in the employee's previous employment could not, via the transferor, lead to liability on the part of the transferee; and thus the provision of information about the employee's previous employment would seem to be beyond the scope of Article 3(2) of the Acquired Rights Directive and outside the purpose of Reg 11; and

- information need only be provided in respect of proceedings taken 'within the previous two years'. The date on which the two-year period starts is clear: it is the date on which the disciplinary or grievance procedure was instituted – that is, the date on which the employer or employee respectively complied with the first step of the relevant procedure. But on which date the two-year period ends is less clear. Is it the date of the relevant transfer? Is it the date on which the employee liability information is provided? Or is it the specified date in respect of which the employee liability information is accurate? In the absence of any guidance on this issue, and in order to ensure compliance, transferors should probably assume that the third alternative is correct, as it would involve the earliest of the three possible 'end dates' – see 'How and when should information be provided?' below for further details.

Claims and prospective claims. Regulation 11(2) states that a transferor must **8.11** provide information about any legal action that a transferring employee has brought against it within the previous two years, and about any legal action that the transferor has reasonable grounds to believe that a transferring employee may bring against the transferee arising out of the employee's employment with the transferor.

Again, this raises questions about how much detail the transferor is obliged to provide, and what might amount to 'the previous two years'. In this regard, the points made above (see 'Disciplinary and grievance procedures') apply equally here. It is interesting to note that under Reg 11(2) the transferor must provide information of any court or tribunal case, claim or action brought by an employee against the *transferor* within the previous two years, as opposed to against the transferor or a previous employer. This should be contrasted with the wording with regard to information about disciplinary and grievance procedures discussed above. The logic behind this difference is unclear.

The obligation on the transferor is to provide information about any legal **8.12** action that it has 'reasonable grounds' to believe that a transferring employee may bring against the transferee, arising out of the employee's employment with the transferor. This raises the question of what might amount to 'reasonable grounds'. The first point to make is that it is irrelevant whether the prospective claim is itself 'reasonable'. It might be utterly hopeless. The key question is whether the transferor has reasonable grounds to believe that a claim might be brought. In this regard, the BIS Guide states: 'This is a matter of judgment and depends on the characteristics of each case. So, where an incident seems trifling – say, where an employee slipped at work but did not take any time off as a result – then there is little reason to suppose that a claim for personal injury damages would result. In contrast, if a fall at work led to hospitalisation over a long period or where a union representative raised the incident as a health and safety concern, then the transferor should inform the transferee accordingly.' In Eville and Jones (UK) Ltd v Grants Veterinary Services Ltd (in liquidation) ET Case No.1803898/12 the tribunal held that the transferor, which had been experiencing financial difficulties prior to the transfer on 1 April 2012, should have disclosed the non-payment of salaries in the period from 19 March to the date of the transfer as there were reasonable grounds for believing that the non-payment of salaries might lead to claims for unlawful deductions under Part II ERA.

551

8.13 **Collective agreements.** The final category of employee liability information covered by Reg 11(2) is 'information of any collective agreement which will have effect after the transfer, in its application in relation to the employee, pursuant to Regulation 5(a)'.

We shall not discuss the intricacies of Reg 5(a) here, as it is dealt with at length in Chapter 3, 'What transfers?', under 'Collective rights and liabilities'. Essentially, it provides that where at the time of a relevant transfer the transferor recognises a collective agreement with a trade union which covers a transferring employee, that agreement shall, in respect of that employee, have effect after the transfer as if made between the trade union and the transferee.

8.14 **Additional information.** Note that although the employee liability information listed in Reg 11(2) will clearly be useful, it is limited and the transferee will usually wish to receive information that is far more extensive than that covered by the provision. We discuss what additional information the transferee might consider requesting in Chapter 11, 'Practical aspects of transfers', under 'Due diligence'.

8.15 **How and when should information be provided?**
Having discussed the types of employee liability information that are covered by Reg 11, we now consider how and when that information should be provided. In this regard, Reg 11 provides:

- the transferor must notify to the transferee the employee liability information 'in writing' or shall make it available to the transferee 'in a readily accessible form' – Reg 11(1)

- the notification under Reg 11(1) must contain employee liability information 'as at a specified date not more than fourteen days before the date on which the information is notified to the transferee' – Reg 11(3)

- once the information has been provided, the transferor must notify the transferee of any changes to it – Reg 11(5). The transferor was found to be in breach of this provision in All Square Ltd v Guardian Facilities ET Case No.3104115/08 when, having initially stated that no claims had been brought against it, it subsequently found that three employees had brought proceedings for unpaid wages but failed to advise the transferee of this change

- a notification under Reg 11 'shall be given not less than 28 days before the relevant transfer or, if special circumstances make this not reasonably practicable, as soon as reasonably practicable thereafter' – Reg 11(6). (For transfers that took place before 1 May 2014, this minimum period was 14 days); and

- a notification may be given in more than one instalment, and may be given indirectly through a third party – Reg 11(7).

In writing or 'readily accessible form'. Under Reg 11(1) the employee liability **8.16** information must be notified in writing or made available in readily accessible form. In this regard, the BIS Guide states: 'The information must be provided in writing or in other forms which are accessible to the [transferee]. So, it may be possible for the transferor to send the information as computer data files as long as the [transferee] can access that information, or provide access to the transferor's data storage. Likewise, in cases where a very small number of employees are transferring and small amounts of information may be involved, it might be acceptable to provide the information by telephone. However, it would be a good practice for the transferor to consult the [transferee] first to discuss the methods which he can use.' The Guide goes on to point out that it is open to the transferor to supply some information in the form of staff handbooks, sample contracts or the texts of collective agreements 'if it would assist'.

Timing of notification. Whereas the original draft of the Regulations proposed **8.17** that notification should be given 'in good time' before the transfer, the final form of the 2006 Regulations was more specific, requiring that the information be given at least 14 days before the transfer or, if this is not reasonably practicable owing to special circumstances, as soon as is reasonably practicable (Reg 11(6)). This minimum period has now been increased to 28 days before the transfer by Reg 10 of the Collective Redundancies and Transfer of Undertakings (Protection of Employment) (Amendment) Regulations 2014 SI 2014/16. The BIS Guide, however, suggests that 'the transferor and transferee and any client on whose behalf the transferor may be providing services may consider whether earlier disclosure of some information should be made', noting that 'it will often be helpful if the transferor provides the necessary employment liability information at an early stage to the transferee. This may not necessarily be all of the information which will ultimately be required and it may need to be on an anonymised basis, or in a way which complies with other appropriate data protection safeguards' (see 'Data protection' below).

The BIS Guide is vague as to what might qualify as 'special circumstances', saying that 'these would be various depending on circumstances'. It does, however, go on to give a specific example, saying 'clearly, it would not be reasonably practicable to provide the information in time, if the transferor did not know the identity of the [transferee] until very late in the process, as might occur where service contracts are re-assigned from one contractor to another by a client, or, more generally, when the transfer takes place at very short notice'. It is likely that, by reference to case law under the redundancy consultation regime, such 'special circumstances' must exist at the time the obligation to provide employee liability information arises (see E Ivor Hughes Educational Foundation v Morris 2015 IRLR 696, EAT).

553

8.18 When the Reg 11(2) notification is given, it should specify the date at which the information in question was accurate. This date does not have to be the same as the date of notification, but must not be more than 14 days before it – Reg 11(3). In order to guard against the information becoming out of date, Reg 11(5) states that following notification, 'the transferor shall notify the transferee in writing of any change in the employee liability information'. Unlike the initial notification, changes must be notified in writing.

At first glance, Reg 11(5) gives no indication of the timescale within which notification of changes has to be provided. However, since such a notification is, presumably, 'a notification under this regulation', it would seem that Reg 11(6), discussed above, applies. In other words, notification of the changes shall be given not less than 28 days before the relevant transfer or, if special circumstances make this not reasonably practicable (e.g. where the change itself takes place after that deadline), as soon as reasonably practicable thereafter.

8.19 **Provided through third party.** The specified information may be given to the transferee indirectly through a third party – Reg 11(7). The BIS Guide states: 'For example, where a client is re-assigning a contract from an existing contractor to a new contractor, that client organisation may act as the third party in passing the information to the new contractor.'

8.20 **Data protection.** Several respondents to consultation on the draft 2006 Regulations were concerned about a potential conflict between the provision of employee liability information and the Data Protection Act 1998 (DPA), which places limits on the disclosure of personal information. The Government suggested, in its response to consultation, that the disclosure of employee liability information would be fully compliant with the DPA. The Government's logic would seem to be as follows. S.35 DPA states that the Act's provisions with regard to the non-disclosure of 'personal data' will not apply 'where the disclosure is required by or under any enactment'. Thus, where transferors provide the information required by Reg 11 TUPE, they would not be acting in breach of the DPA.

This analysis, on its face, seems to make sense. However, the reality is more complicated. If, when providing employee liability information, the transferor provides slightly more than is 'required' by Reg 11, the provision of this additional information will fall outside the S.35 exception to the DPA. As we have seen, Reg 11(2) does not go into great detail as to how much information need be provided. Thus, a transferor wishing to ensure compliance with Reg 11 is almost certainly going to end up providing more information than is strictly necessary, and as a result the DPA may come into play. Transferors should therefore take note of the Information Commissioner's Employment Practices Code, which provides guidance for employers on data protection compliance. In particular, paras 2.11 and 2.12 of the Code provide the following advice about publishing information about workers in the context of a transfer or merger situation:

- ensure that there is a legal obligation to publish the information, that the information is clearly not intrusive, that the worker has consented to disclosure, or that the information is in a form that does not identify individual workers

- ensure, wherever practicable, that information handed over to another organisation in connection with a prospective acquisition, merger or business reorganisation is anonymised

- only hand over personal information prior to a final merger or acquisition decision after securing assurances that it will be used solely for the evaluation of assets and liabilities, will be treated in confidence and not be disclosed to other parties, and will be destroyed or returned after use

- unless it is impracticable to do so, tell workers if their employment records are to be disclosed to another organisation before an acquisition, merger or reorganisation takes place. If the acquisition, merger or reorganisation proceeds, make sure workers are aware of the extent to which their records are to be transferred to the new employer; and

- where a merger, acquisition or reorganisation involves a transfer of information about a worker to a country outside the European Economic Area (EEA), ensure that there is a proper basis for making the transfer.

Contracting out   8.21
Regulation 18 TUPE, which restricts contracting out of the Regulations' provisions, applies to the transferor's obligation to provide employee liability information. This is reflected in the BIS Guide, which notes that the transferor and transferee cannot agree between themselves that the Reg 11 employee liability information should not be provided since 'that would disadvantage the employees involved'. We discuss Reg 18 and its implications in Chapter 10, 'Contracting out of TUPE'.

Remedy for failure to notify   8.22
Regulation 12(1) TUPE gives transferees the right to complain to an employment tribunal, 'on or after a relevant transfer', where the transferor has failed to comply in whole or in part with any of the notification requirements set out in Reg 11. The complaint has to be made to the tribunal before the end of the period of three months beginning with the date of the relevant transfer, or within such further period as the tribunal considers reasonable in a case where it is satisfied that it was not reasonably practicable for the complaint to be presented before the end of that period – Reg 12(2). The time limit may also be extended to allow for early conciliation – Reg 12(2A).

555

Where the tribunal finds that the complaint is well founded, it must make a declaration to that effect and may make an award of compensation to be paid by the transferor to the transferee – Reg 12(3). Under Reg 12(4), 'the amount of the compensation shall be such as the tribunal considers just and equitable in all the circumstances... having particular regard to (a) any loss sustained by the transferee which is attributable to the matters complained of; and (b) the terms of any contract between the transferor and the transferee relating to the transfer under which the transferor may be liable to pay any sum to the transferee in respect of a failure to notify the transferee of employee liability information'. This latter provision means that, in deciding whether or not to make an award, the tribunal is entitled to take account of any warranties or indemnities provided for in the contract between the transferor and the transferee.

8.23 The meaning of the term 'any loss sustained by the transferee which is attributable to the matters complained of' was considered by the employment tribunal in G4S Secure Solutions (UK) Ltd v Carlisle Security Services Ltd ET Case No.3400150/14, where the transferee sought to recover its losses over the entire contractual term. The employment tribunal, in declining to make such a substantial award, ruled that those losses were not attributable to the transferor's breaches because G4S had 'won the contract having bid on the basis of pricing information provided to it by Hackney [Council]' and had been warned by the Council to check its pricing assumptions before it made the bid. It was also the Council, rather than the transferor, who had failed to advise bidders that one of the transferring employees was a salaried employee and therefore entitled to a pension. The tribunal concluded that while the transferee 'took risks that its exposure to staffing costs might be greater than it had envisaged, this was in no way attributable to the quality of the employment liability information provided by Carlisle after G4S won that bid'. In the alternative, but for the same reasons, the tribunal concluded that it would not be 'just and equitable' to award compensation for the 'special loss' claimed by the transferee.

A tribunal is required by Reg 12(6) to consider whether or not the transferee has made any attempt to mitigate its loss (for which, see IDS Employment Law Handbook, 'Contracts of Employment' (2014), Chapter 10, 'Breach of contract', under 'Deductions from damages – duty to mitigate'). Interestingly, in the G4S Secure Solutions case the tribunal did not think it was unreasonable for the transferee to seek a ruling from the tribunal before it sought to renegotiate its contract with Hackney Council.

8.24 Finally, Reg 12(7) provides that S.18 of the Employment Tribunals Act 1996, which concerns Acas conciliation, applies to claims under Reg 12 as it applies to the rights conferred by and to proceedings under that Act. (See IDS Employment Law Handbook, 'Employment Tribunal Practice and Procedure' (2014), Chapter 3, 'Conciliation, settlements and ADR', under 'Acas-conciliated (COT3) agreements'.)

Amount of award. Regulation 12(5) provides that, subject to the duty to **8.25** mitigate, the amount of compensation awarded under Reg 5(3) (assuming that the tribunal decides to make an award), must be at least £500 per employee in respect of whom the duty to inform arose 'unless the tribunal considers it just and equitable, in all the circumstances, to award a lesser sum'. The BIS Guide suggests that 'trivial or unwitting' breaches may lead the tribunal to depart from the minimum award.

It has been suggested that, subject to the tribunal's power to award a lesser sum where it is just and equitable to do so, Reg 12(5) is a penal provision to penalise transferees who do not comply with the requirements of this provision. Some support for this view is found in the BIS Guide, which states that under these provisions, 'the level of compensation must be no less than £500 for each employee for whom the information was not provided, or the information was defective'. This 'guidance' was followed by the employment tribunal in Eville and Jones (UK) Ltd v Grants Veterinary Services Ltd (in liquidation) ET Case No.1803898/12, where the tribunal awarded £500 in respect of each of the 131 employees who transferred, making a total award of £65,500 even though the total management costs were said to be in the region of £42,000. The tribunal stated that 'whilst the costs of management time and other costs would not reach the £65,000 level, such costs were not insignificant and would indeed have been of a material sum'. The tribunal concluded that 'in all the circumstances, the tribunal does not view it to be just and equitable to make an award of less than £500 per employee'. On the other hand, in G4S Secure Solutions (UK) Ltd v Carlisle Security Services Ltd (above), the tribunal took a slightly different approach, ruling that Reg 12(3)(b) 'does not make provision for payment of a penalty'. Nonetheless, the tribunal accepted that as a result of the transferor's failure to comply with its obligations, the transferee had suffered additional administrative costs associated with the transfer. It therefore awarded £500 in respect of nine employees 'to reflect the difficulties for a transferee in proving the particular loss caused by a transferor's breach of Reg 11'.

Informing and consulting appropriate representatives

8.26

It is one of the central pillars of the Acquired Rights Directive, and hence of TUPE, that transferor and transferee must inform, and usually also consult with, appropriate representatives of employees who might be affected by a proposed transfer.

At European level, the relevant provisions are found in Article 7 of the Directive (previously Article 6). Article 7(1) provides that the transferor and transferee 'shall be required to inform the representatives of their respective employees affected by the transfer' of the date or proposed date of the transfer, the reasons

557

for it, the 'legal, economic and social implications' for the employees, and 'any measures envisaged in relation to the employees'. In this regard, Article 7(1) continues, the transferor shall be required to give the information to appropriate representatives in good time before the transfer is carried out. Similarly, the transferee shall be under a duty to provide the information to appropriate representatives in good time and, in any event, before its employees 'are directly affected by the transfer as regards their conditions of work and employment'. Article 7(2) goes on to state that 'where the transferor or the transferee envisages measures in relation to his employees, he shall consult the representatives of [his] employees in good time on such measures with a view to reaching an agreement'.

8.27 Article 7 is given effect by Regs 13, 14, 15 and 16 of the TUPE Regulations, which are discussed at length below. These are in largely the same form as the corresponding provisions in the previous version of the Regulations – Regs 10–11A 1981 Regulations.

8.28 Affected employees

Regulation 13 only obliges transferors and transferees to inform and consult in respect of 'affected employees'. This term is defined in Reg 13(1), which states: 'In this Regulation and Regs 14 and 15 references to affected employees, in relation to a relevant transfer, are to any employees of the transferor or the transferee (whether or not assigned to the organised grouping of resources or employees that is the subject of a relevant transfer) who may be affected by the transfer or may be affected by measures taken in connection with it.'

This means that, in order to be an 'affected employee', an individual must be:

- an 'employee' for the purposes of the TUPE Regulations. 'Employee' is defined by Reg 2(1) as being 'any individual who works for another person whether under a contract of service or apprenticeship or otherwise but does not include anyone who provides services under a contract for services'. For a full discussion of this definition, see Chapter 2, 'Who transfers?', under 'Who is an "employee" for TUPE purposes?'

- an employee of either the transferor or the transferee (not a third party), and

- someone who may be affected by the transfer or by measures taken in connection with it. It is important to note the use of the word 'may' rather than 'will' – meaning that an employer does not have to be sure that an employee will be affected in order for Reg 13 to be triggered in respect of that employee. We consider the meaning of 'measures taken in connection with a transfer' under 'Duty to consult' below.

8.29 It is clear from the above that it is not only the employees scheduled to transfer under TUPE who can be 'affected employees' for the purposes of Reg 13. A relevant transfer may also have repercussions for the employees of parts of the transferor's undertaking that are not transferred, and for the transferee's existing workforce. So, as is reflected in the BIS Guide, there are three possible categories of 'affected employees'. They are, '(a) those individuals who are to be transferred; (b) their colleagues in the transferor employer who will not transfer but whose jobs might be affected by the transfer; or (c) their new colleagues in employment with the [transferee] whose jobs might be affected by the transfer'.

The EAT considered this guidance in Unison v Somerset County Council and ors 2010 ICR 498, EAT. There, two Councils decided to transfer the bulk of the work of their resources directorates to a joint venture company, SWO Ltd. Employees 'in scope' were given the option of either transferring to SWO Ltd or remaining as employees of the relevant Council and being seconded to SWO Ltd. A dispute arose over the Councils' compliance with Reg 13 in relation to SWO Ltd's proposed recruitment policy following the transfer. The union initially hoped to secure agreement that in-scope employees would receive preferential treatment for any future vacancies that might arise within SWO Ltd; that existing employees of the Councils would be second in order of preference; and only then, if that failed to fill the post, would vacancies be advertised externally. SWO Ltd could not accept this arrangement. It agreed to give preference to in-scope employees but reserved the right to advertise posts to the world at large if that produced no successful applicant. The union asserted that this meant non-transferring employees of the Councils were 'affected employees' for the purposes of Reg 13(1), since their prospects of securing future employment with SWO Ltd, if vacancies became available, were adversely affected.

8.30 The EAT rejected that argument, holding that the 'affected employees' on these facts were:

- employees who will or may be transferred

- employees whose jobs are in jeopardy by reason of the proposed transfer, and

- employees who have job applications within the undertaking subject to the transfer pending at the time of the transfer.

The EAT could not accept that 'affected employees' included everyone in the transferor's workforce who may apply for a vacancy at some point in the future with the transferred part of the organisation. We would suggest that, where the BIS Guide states that affected employees include non-transferring employees whose jobs might be affected by the transfer, it should be read with the EAT's qualification in mind.

8.31 The meaning of 'affected employees' was also considered by the EAT in I Lab Facilities Ltd v Metcalfe and ors 2013 IRLR 605, EAT. There, the transferor,

ILUK Ltd, had two substantially discrete parts to its media production business, one part dealing in 'rushes' work and the other involved in 'post-production'. When ILUK Ltd got into financial difficulties it hoped to sell both parts. However, only the sale of the 'rushes' part went ahead, giving rise to a TUPE transfer. The 'post-production' part of the business closed down and the employees assigned to that part were dismissed. A tribunal awarded 'post-production' employees a protective award on the basis that they had not been informed and consulted before the transfer of the 'rushes' part. The EAT overturned that award on appeal, holding that the 'post-production' employees were not 'affected employees' in relation to the transfer.

The EAT stated that, in a straightforward case where a single employer has two wholly self-contained plants or businesses, or two parts of the same undertaking, A and B, the sale of A does not as such 'affect' employees in B. The same is true even if at the same time as selling A, the employer closes B. Even if the closure of B is indirectly the result of the sale of A, that does not mean that B's employees are affected by the transfer within the meaning of Reg 13. While a transfer may well affect employees who do not transfer, such that Reg 13 is engaged, it does not do so simply because the transfer leaves the remaining part of the business less viable. The EAT went on to reject the 'post-production' employees' argument that the situation was different because ILUK Ltd had originally proposed transferring their part of the business as well and had told seven of them that they would be dismissed and rehired on new contracts. The EAT noted that the Reg 13 duty does not arise when the transferor first envisages a TUPE transfer; it only arises 'long enough before' a transfer for consultation to take place. If there is in the end no transfer and no affected employees, then there is no breach of Reg 13.

8.32 Appropriate representatives

In attempting to give effect to the mandatory provisions of what was then Article 6 (and is now Article 7) of the Acquired Rights Directive, the 1981 Regulations, as originally enacted, imposed a duty on transferors and transferees to inform and consult with representatives of any independent trade union recognised in respect of affected employees. However, in Commission of the European Communities v United Kingdom 1994 ICR 664, ECJ, the European Court of Justice (ECJ) decided that, in limiting the scope of those whom employers had to inform and consult to trade union representatives, the 1981 Regulations were defective.

The UK Government responded to the ECJ's ruling by introducing the Collective Redundancies and Transfer of Undertakings (Protection of Employment) (Amendment) Regulations 1995 SI 1995/2587, which gave employers a choice whether to consult representatives of a recognised trade union or other employee representatives. This, however, proved exceedingly unpopular with trade unions, as it gave employers the opportunity to bypass them with regard to information and consultation under TUPE even where they were recognised in the workplace. This situation was rectified by further amendments, activated by the Collective Redundancies and Transfer of Undertakings (Protection of Employment) (Amendment) Regulations 1999 SI 1999/1925. These produced the current state of affairs, whereby an employer must consult with trade union representatives where the union is recognised with regard to affected employees, and with 'employee representatives' in other circumstances.

This position is set out in Reg 13(3) of the 2006 Regulations, which provides **8.33** that, for the purposes of the TUPE information and consultation rules, 'appropriate representatives' of affected employees are:

- if the employees are of a description in respect of which an independent trade union is recognised by their employer, representatives of the trade union – Reg 13(3)(a), or

- in any other case, whichever of the following employee representatives the employer chooses – (i) employee representatives appointed or elected by the affected employees otherwise than for the purposes of Reg 13, who (having regard to the purposes for, and the method by which, they were appointed or elected) have authority from those employees to receive information and to be consulted about the transfer on their behalf; (ii) employee representatives elected by any affected employees for the purposes of Reg 13, in an election satisfying the requirements of Reg 14(1) – Reg 13(3)(b).

There is one exception to the requirements in Reg 13(3) contained in Reg 13A. This applies to 'micro-businesses' that employ fewer than ten employees and allows employers to inform and consult directly with affected employees in certain specified circumstances. This provision – introduced in 2014 – is discussed under 'Micro-businesses' below.

Under Reg 13(2) and (6), an employer who is acquiring or transferring a **8.34** business must inform and consult with 'appropriate representatives' of affected employees (see 'Duty to inform' and 'Duty to consult' below). We now consider in more detail who the relevant union/employee representatives might be, and look at what other rules in the TUPE Regulations and elsewhere apply in respect of them.

Independent and recognised trade union. As we explain directly above, **8.35** Reg 13(3)(a) states that where affected employees are represented by a recognised, independent trade union, the employer *must* inform and consult representatives of that trade union, as opposed to other employee representatives. This is reflected and expanded upon in the BIS Guide, which states that 'where employees who may be affected by the transfer are represented by an independent trade union for collective bargaining purposes, the employer must inform and consult an authorised official of that union. This may be a shop steward or a district union official or, if appropriate, a national or regional official.

_____ **561**

The employer is not required to inform or consult any other employee representatives in such circumstances, but may do so if the trade union is recognised for one group of employees, but not for another.'

This raises the questions of when a trade union is independent, and when such a union is recognised. These questions are dealt with in IDS Employment Law Handbook, 'Trade Unions' (2013), and shall not be examined at length here. The basics, however, are set out below.

8.36 *Independence.* The law acknowledges that, for trade unions to carry out their functions properly, they must be truly independent of employers. For example, house unions or staff associations to which management may belong or to whom they may provide funds might not, owing to management's apparent control, robustly defend the interests of their members.

There is a statutory definition of independence, found in S.5(1) of the Trade Union and Labour Relations (Consolidation) Act 1992 (TULR(C)A), which provides that a union is independent if it is:

- not under the domination or control of an employer, and

- not liable to interference by an employer (arising out of the provision of financial or material support or by other means) tending towards such control.

8.37 Note that a listed trade union – that is, one found on the list of unions maintained by the Certification Officer – may apply to the Certification Officer under S.6(1) TULR(C)A for a certificate stating that it satisfies the statutory definition of independence.

For further details, see IDS Employment Law Handbook, 'Trade Unions' (2013), Chapter 1, 'Trade unions', under 'Independence'.

8.38 *Recognition.* Put simply, 'recognition' is the process by which an employer accepts a trade union as being entitled to act on behalf of a particular group (or groups) of workers for some purpose.

Regulation 2(1) TUPE provides that 'recognised' has the meaning given to it by S.178(3) TULR(C)A. Thus, a recognised trade union for the purposes of the Reg 13 information and consultation rules is one that is recognised 'by an employer, or two or more associated employers, to any extent, for the purposes of collective bargaining'. 'Collective bargaining', also defined by S.178 TULR(C)A, means negotiations relating to or connected with one or more of the following:

- terms and conditions of employment, or the physical conditions in which any workers are required to work

- engagement or non-engagement, termination or suspension of employment

- allocation of work between workers or groups of workers

- disciplinary matters

- a worker's membership or non-membership of a trade union

- facilities for trade union officials, and

- machinery for negotiation or consultation, and other procedures, relating to any of the above matters, including the recognition by employers or employers' associations of the right of a trade union to represent workers in such negotiation or consultation or in the carrying out of such procedures.

Recognition can be either voluntary on the part of the employer or compulsory **8.39** under the complex scheme contained in Schedule A1 to the TULR(C)A. For further details, see IDS Employment Law Handbook, 'Trade Unions' (2013), Chapter 5, 'Trade union recognition', and Chapter 6, 'Statutory recognition'.

Is union recognised in respect of all affected employees? Where there is an **8.40** independent trade union that is recognised in the workplace, it will be important for the transferor or transferee in question to determine whether that union is recognised in respect of all of the employer's 'affected employees'. Union representatives only act for those in the recognised bargaining unit – Independent Insurance Co Ltd (in provisional liquidation) v Aspinall and anor 2011 ICR 1234, EAT, a case involving the similarly worded provisions of Ss.188 and 189 TULR(C)A. Where there are a number of unions recognised in respect of different bargaining units, it is important that the employer inform and consult with each of the recognised unions – see, for example, British Medical Association v Secretary of State for Health and anor ET Case No.2409047/13. If there are any employees not covered by a recognition agreement, the employer will need to inform/consult separately with 'employee representatives' of those employees.

Employee representatives. Where employees who may be affected by the **8.41** transfer are not represented by a recognised, independent trade union, the employer must inform and consult employee representatives of those employees – Reg 13(3)(b). Employee representatives only represent those employees who have elected them (or could have elected them if they had chosen to participate in the election) – Independent Insurance Co Ltd (in provisional liquidation) v Aspinall and anor (above). In Games-Thomas v UBS AG and anor ET Case No.2201962/09 the claimant alleged that there had been a breach of Reg 13(3)(b) because he was working overseas at the time the election took place. Dismissing the claim, the employment tribunal ruled that Reg 13(3)(b) conferred an entitlement to vote, not a requirement to do so.

Under Reg 13(3)(b) the employer has a choice between informing and consulting existing employee representatives or new ones especially elected for TUPE purposes.

8.42 *Existing employee representatives.* One option, then, is for the employer to inform and consult 'employee representatives appointed or elected by the affected employees otherwise than for the purposes of this regulation, who (having regard to the purposes for, and the method by which they were appointed or elected) have authority from those employees to receive information and to be consulted about the transfer on their behalf' – Reg 13(3)(b)(i).

If existing employee representatives are to be informed and consulted, then it is obviously important that they meet the above description. As the BIS Guide puts it, 'their remit and method of election or appointment must give them suitable authority from the employees concerned'. The question of whether the existing representatives have such authority is to be answered with 'regard to the purposes for, and the method by which they were appointed or elected'. With this in mind, the BIS Guide states: 'It would not, for example, be appropriate to inform and consult a committee specially established to consider the operation of a staff canteen about a transfer affecting, say, sales staff; but it may well be appropriate to inform and consult a fairly elected or appointed committee of employees, such as a works council, that is regularly informed and consulted more generally about the business's financial position and personnel matters.' In our view, this suggests that a committee established under the Information and Consultation of Employees Regulations 2004 SI 2004/3426 for the purposes of information and consultation on a number of workplace issues would suffice (for details, see IDS Employment Law Supplement, 'Information and Consultation Regulations 2004' (2005)).

8.43 Note that Reg 15(3) provides that if tribunal proceedings are brought in relation to an employer's alleged failure to inform or consult under Reg 13 and in the course of those proceedings a question arises as to whether an employee representative was an appropriate representative for the purposes of Reg 13, it will be for the employer to show that the employee representative had the necessary authority to represent the affected employees.

8.44 *Electing new employee representatives.* In the absence of a recognised trade union, and whether or not there are appropriate existing employee representatives, an employer caught up in a relevant transfer may choose to inform and consult employee representatives elected by the affected employees specifically for the purposes of Reg 13 – Reg 13(3)(b)(ii). Any such election must be conducted in accordance with Reg 14 – see 'Election of employee representatives' below.

Before turning to the method of election itself, however, there is a significant issue that first needs to be addressed. That is, where there is neither a recognised trade union nor existing employee representatives in place with regard to 'affected employees', must the employer concerned proactively invite the affected employees to elect employee representatives for the purposes of Reg 13, or can it simply sit back and do nothing?

564

Perhaps unsurprisingly, the majority of EAT case law suggests that the employer **8.45**
does need to take action of some sort. We discuss the relevant cases below, but
first it is necessary to set out a number of Reg 13 provisions not yet touched
upon in this chapter that have been central to the EAT's reasoning on this issue:

- Reg 13(9) states that 'if in any case there are special circumstances which
  render it not reasonably practicable for an employer to perform a duty
  imposed on him by [Reg 13(2)–(7)], he shall take all such steps towards
  performing that duty as are reasonably practicable in the circumstances'

- Reg 13(10) provides that 'where (a) the employer has invited any of the
  affected employees to elect employee representatives; and (b) the invitation
  was issued long enough before the time when the employer is required to
  give information under [Reg 13(2)] to allow them to elect representatives by
  that time, the employer shall be treated as complying with the requirements
  of this regulation in relation to those employees if he complies with those
  requirements as soon as is reasonably practicable after the election of the
  representatives'

- and finally, Reg 13(11) makes it clear that 'if, after the employer has invited
  any affected employees to elect representatives, they fail to do so within a
  reasonable time, he shall give to any affected employees the information set
  out in [Reg 13(2)]'.

In Russell v Bacon's College and anor EAT 98/99 a transferor employer failed
to inform R (an affected employee) or any representative of R about an
imminent TUPE transfer. R brought a claim in respect of this failure before an
employment tribunal. At the hearing, the transferor made the point that its
obligations under Reg 13 were to inform and consult appropriate representatives.
In its view, it followed that where, as in this case, there were no appropriate
representatives in place, no obligation under TUPE to inform and consult had
arisen. The employment tribunal accepted the transferor's argument, noting
that 'there appears to be no duty to inform and consult individual employees
when no representative has been elected'. R appealed to the EAT, referring the
Appeal Tribunal to R v Secretary of State for Trade and Industry ex parte
Unison 1996 ICR 1003, QBD, a case in which the High Court had considered
whether the Acquired Rights Directive was properly implemented in the UK.
There, expressing satisfaction with the way in which the Regulations were
structured, Lord Justice Otton stated that compliance with the Directive was
achieved by the Regulations' imposing a primary duty on the employer to
inform and consult appropriate representatives. If there are no such
representatives in place, he continued, the employer is bound to be in breach of
this primary duty unless it can show that it falls within one of the specified
exceptions in the Regulations.

565

8.46 Mr Justice Burton, giving judgment in the instant case, affirmed the above comments of Otton LJ and, in light of what is now Reg 13 TUPE, made the following comments:

- there is a 'primary' duty on employers to inform employee representatives under Reg 13(2) – see 'Duty to inform' below

- if employers do not inform appropriate representatives they are, on the face of it, in breach, whether or not such representatives exist

- this is not imposing a statutory obligation to do the impossible. Reg 13(10) provides that where an employer has invited any employees to elect employee representatives, the employer's duty is fulfilled if it informs and consults those representatives, and

- furthermore, Reg 13(9) states that where special circumstances render it not reasonably practicable to comply with TUPE's information and consultation duties, the employer should take all such steps towards performing that duty as are reasonably practicable in the circumstances.

In the instant case, the transferor employer had not informed appropriate representatives and thus, on the face of it, was in breach of the Regulations. The question for Burton J was whether the employer could rely on the 'special circumstances' defence set out in Reg 13(9). Turning to this, he acknowledged that 'it is quite plain that one special circumstance which renders it not reasonably practicable for an employer to perform a duty to consult an employee representative is if there are no employee representatives'. However, he continued, 'it is equally clear that the step which is reasonably practicable to resolve that problem is for the employer to invite an employee to appoint a representative under [Reg 13(10)]'. If an employer does invite affected employees to elect representatives under Reg 13(10) then, if no representatives are in fact appointed, 'the employer is entitled to perform its duty... by informing the employee himself or herself, and thus avoid what would otherwise be a breach of the [absolute] duty to inform a representative'. In the circumstances, then, where the respondent transferor did not invite the affected employees to elect representatives, it had not taken all reasonably practicable steps towards complying with its information and consultation duties, and was thus in breach of them.

8.47 In Howard v Millrise Ltd (in liquidation) and anor 2005 ICR 435, EAT, the EAT went even further. There, contrary to the previous decision of the EAT in Ashford School and anor v Nixon and ors EAT 666/00, the Appeal Tribunal held that, where no appropriate representatives already exist, the employer in question is actually under a statutory obligation to invite the affected employees to elect such representatives. In that case H brought a claim in respect of M Ltd's failure to inform and consult prior to the transfer. An employment tribunal rejected his complaint, taking the view that the information and consultation provisions 'appear to apply only to appropriate representatives, as defined by the Regulations'. Since H had at no time been an appropriate representative, his claim could not succeed. He appealed to the EAT, which overturned the tribunal's decision.

The EAT stated that where there are no recognised trade union or other employee representatives in place for information and consultation purposes, Reg 13 provides for the election of representatives for the purpose of the required consultation. Furthermore, Reg 13(11) provides that where an employer has invited affected employees to elect representatives but they fail to do so, the employer must give the required information about the transfer to each individual affected employee. This provision would be rendered pointless, the EAT continued, if the employer (assuming there were no recognised trade union or other appropriate representatives in place) were not obliged to set the ball rolling by inviting affected employees to elect representatives. The EAT concluded that in this case it was unnecessary to determine whether H's claim related to the employer's failure to take any steps to invite the election of representatives, the failure to give information to such representatives, or, in default of election, the failure to give information to the claimant himself. It was clear that H's complaint was well founded and his case was remitted to the employment tribunal for compensation to be determined.

So, it seems that an employer will be in breach of Reg 13 where, in the absence **8.48** of existing appropriate representatives, it fails to invite affected employees to elect representatives for the purposes of information and consultation. The next question, then, is when such an invitation should be issued.

The simple answer is that the invitation to elect employee representatives should be issued in accordance with the timescale suggested by Reg 13(10). That is, long enough prior to the time when the employer is required to provide information under Reg 13(2) for the representatives to be elected. Since, as discussed under 'Duty to inform' below, the relevant information must itself be provided to the representatives long enough before the transfer to enable consultation to take place, the invitation to elect would ideally be issued some time before the transfer. There will, of course, be times when this is not reasonably practicable to achieve, in which case the employer may be able to throw itself upon the mercy of the Reg 13(9) 'special circumstances' defence.

Note that we discuss Reg 13(9), (10) and (11) further under 'Employers' defences' below.

Election of employee representatives. If there are no existing appropriate **8.49** representatives who can be consulted about a relevant transfer, or if there are existing employee representatives that the employer does not wish to use, then – as explained immediately above – the employer should invite the election of

567

employee representatives. Any election that ensues should be conducted in accordance with the requirements set out in Reg 14, which are as follows:

- the employer must make such arrangements as are reasonably practicable to ensure the election is fair – Reg 14(1)(a)

- the employer must determine the number of representatives to be elected so that there are sufficient representatives to represent the interests of all the affected employees, having regard to the number and classes of those employees – Reg 14(1)(b)

- the employer must determine whether the affected employees should be represented either by representatives of all the affected employees or by representatives of particular classes of those employees – Reg 14(1)(c)

- before the election, the employer must determine the term of office of an employee representative so that it is of sufficient length to enable information to be given and consultations to be completed – Reg 14(1)(d)

- the candidates for election as employee representatives must be affected employees on the date of the election – Reg 14(1)(e)

- no affected employee should unreasonably be excluded from standing for election – Reg 14(1)(f)

- all affected employees on the date of the election are entitled to vote – Reg 14(1)(g). (Note that in Games-Thomas v UBS and anor ET Case No.2201962/09 an employment tribunal held that the elected representative was appropriate in respect of a particular employee, even though that employee had not taken part in the election process as he was working abroad at the relevant time. It held that while the TUPE Regulations grant all affected employees an entitlement to vote, they do not impose a requirement that they do so)

- the employees entitled to vote may vote for as many candidates as there are representatives to be elected to represent them or, if there are to be representatives for particular classes of employees, may vote for as many candidates as there are representatives to be elected to represent their particular class of employee – Reg 14(1)(h), and

- the election itself must be conducted so as to ensure that (i) so far as reasonably practicable, those voting do so in secret, and (ii) the votes are accurately counted – Reg 14(1)(i).

8.50 Furthermore, according to Reg 14(2), where an employee representative is elected in accordance with these rules but ceases to act as such and as a result any affected employees are no longer represented, then another election must be held – in accordance with Reg 14(1)(a), (e), (f) and (i) – to elect a new employee representative.

While the above requirements are detailed, they do not answer all the questions that employers will have about organising elections. As the BIS Guide explains, 'the legislation does not specify how many representatives must be elected or the process by which they are to be chosen. An employment tribunal may wish to consider, in determining a claim that the employer has not informed and consulted in accordance with the requirements, whether the arrangements were such that the purpose of the legislation could not be met. An employer will therefore need to consider such matters as whether:

- the arrangements adequately cover all the categories of employees who may be affected by the transfer and provide a reasonable balance between the interests of the different groups;

- the employees have sufficient time to nominate and consider candidates;

- the employees (including any who are absent from work for any reason) can freely choose who to vote for;

- there is any normal company custom and practice for similar elections and, if so, whether there are good reasons for departing from it.'

8.51 Note that Reg 15(4) provides that where a tribunal claim is brought in respect of an employer's alleged failure relating to the election of employee representatives, it shall be for the employer to show that the requirements of Reg 14 have been satisfied. In Shields Automotive Ltd v Langdon and anor EATS 0059/12 the EAT held that an employer did not comply with Reg 14 when it announced an election at 2 pm and required all votes to be cast by 5 pm on the same day. It made no allowance for the fact that one of the 18 employees entitled to vote was off that day. The EAT noted that the duty on employers under Reg 14 is not absolute, in that the employer is only required to make such arrangements as are 'reasonably practicable' to ensure the fairness of an election, but that it is for the employer to show that what it did was reasonable. So if there is a reason why an election has to be rushed and cannot be extended over a longer period – such as, in this case, by allowing votes to be cast up to the end of the following day – then it is for the employer to put that reason before the tribunal. Furthermore, although the requirement in Reg 14(1)(g) is that all affected employees should be 'entitled' to vote, not that they are given the opportunity to vote, the ideal is that all employees should be able to vote and, again, if there is a reason why that is impracticable to arrange, it is for the employer to show it. The EAT went on to hold that the employer was also in breach when it decided, without consultation, to select as a representative one of two employees who had received the same number of votes on the basis that the other had a regular day off on the day that consultation meetings were expected to take place. The EAT held that this undermined the fairness of the election as the effect was that, although the employees had a voice in the election, the ultimate selection was made not by them but by the employer.

8.52 **Micro-businesses.** Regulation 13A, which was introduced by Reg 11 of the Collective Redundancies and Transfer of Undertakings (Protection of Employment) (Amendment) Regulations 2014 SI 2014/16, makes special provision for micro-businesses. These are defined as businesses where an employer has fewer than ten employees at the time when the obligation to inform and consult arises, i.e. 'long enough before the transfer for consultation to take place' – see 'Duty to inform' and 'Duty to consult' below. In such circumstances, the employer may inform and consult affected employees directly provided there is no recognised trade union or appropriate representatives within the meaning of Reg 13(3) and the employer has not invited any affected employees to elect employee representatives.

The BIS Guide explains that a micro-business can comply with the duties to inform and consult by 'dealing with each of the affected employees as if they were an appropriate representative or invite the employees to elect representatives' but the guide makes it clear that if there are existing representatives then the duty to inform and consult applies in the ordinary way.

8.53 Regulation 13A applies to transfers which take place on or after 31 July 2014. If there is a dispute as to whether Reg 13A applies, Reg 15(3A) provides that the burden of proof is on the employer to show that it does.

8.54 **Rights of appropriate representatives.** Under Reg 13(8), an employer must allow 'the appropriate representatives' (who, as we have seen, may include elected representatives and/or trade union representatives) access to any 'affected employees' and to 'such accommodation and other facilities as may be appropriate'. Undeniably, as the BIS Guide states, 'what is "appropriate" will vary according to circumstances'. These circumstances, presumably, will include the size and complexity of the transfer. We suggest that appropriate 'accommodation and other facilities' should generally include access to a room, photocopier, telephone and IT equipment. Furthermore, an employer might wish to consider whether, in certain circumstances, inexperienced representatives need to be afforded facilities for training.

In addition, most employee representatives and candidates for election will have certain statutory rights and protections to enable them to carry out their functions properly. We say 'most' rather than 'all' because such protections are provided by the ERA only to 'employees' within the meaning of S.230 of that Act. As discussed at length in this Handbook, particularly in Chapter 2, 'Who transfers?', 'employees' for ERA purposes comprises a narrower grouping than 'employees' for TUPE purposes. It follows that some 'affected employees' under Reg 13 who become 'employee representatives' under Reg 14 might not be 'employees' capable of attracting the ERA protections set out below.

8.55 The rights and protections in question are essentially the same as those granted to trade union representatives under the TULR(C)A (for which, see IDS Employment Law Handbook, 'Trade Unions' (2013)), and are as follows:

570

- an employee has the right not to be subjected to any detriment by any act or deliberate failure to act by his or her employer done on the ground that, being an employee representative for the purposes of TUPE, or a candidate in an election in which any person elected will become such an employee representative, he or she performed or proposed to perform any functions or activities as such an employee representative or candidate – S.47(1) ERA. He or she has the right to complain to an employment tribunal that he or she has been subjected to such a detriment – S.48(1) ERA. The complaint must be presented (a) before the end of the period of three months beginning with the date of the act or failure to act or, where that act or failure is part of a series, the date of the last of them, or (b) within such further period as the tribunal considers reasonable where it is satisfied that it was not reasonably practicable for the complaint to be presented in time – S.48(3) ERA. (The time limit may also be extended to allow for early conciliation or cross-border mediation – S.48(4A))

- an employee who is dismissed shall be regarded as unfairly dismissed if the reason or principal reason for dismissal is that the employee, being an employee representative (or a candidate for election as an employee representative) for the purposes of TUPE performed or proposed to perform any functions or activities as such an employee representative or candidate – S.103 ERA. The qualifying period of service usually required by the ERA unfair dismissal regime does not apply to this type of automatically unfair dismissal – S.108 ERA. Any such claim should be brought (a) before the end of the period of three months beginning with the effective date of termination, or (b) within such further period as the tribunal considers reasonable where it is satisfied that it was not reasonably practicable for the complaint to be presented in time – S.111(2) ERA. (The time limit may also be extended to allow for early conciliation or cross-border mediation – S.111(2A)); and

- an employee who is an employee representative (or candidate for election as an employee representative) is entitled to reasonable, paid time off during working hours in order to perform his or her functions as an employee representative or candidate or in order to undergo training to perform such functions – Ss.61 and 62 ERA. Where this right has been breached, the employee can bring a tribunal claim under S.63 ERA. The claim must be brought (a) before the end of the period of three months beginning with the day on which the time off was taken or should have been permitted, or (b) within such further period as the tribunal considers reasonable where it is satisfied that it was not reasonably practicable for the complaint to be presented in time – S.63(2). (The time limit may also be extended to allow for early conciliation or cross-border mediation – S.63(2A)).

Note that similar protection with regard to detriment (S.47(1A) ERA) and **8.56** dismissal (S.103(2) ERA) is afforded to any 'employee' for ERA purposes, where such detriment is done or dismissal carried out on the ground of his or her participation in an employee representative election.

8.57 Duty to inform

Having examined who 'affected employees' and 'appropriate representatives' might be, we now turn to the substance of the duty to inform under TUPE. This is contained in Reg 13(2), which provides that 'long enough before a relevant transfer to enable the employer of any affected employees to consult the appropriate representatives of any affected employees, the employer shall inform those representatives' of the following:

- the fact that the transfer is to take place, the date or proposed date of the transfer and the reasons for the transfer – Reg 13(2)(a)

- the 'legal, economic and social implications' of the transfer for any affected employees – Reg 13(2)(b)

- the 'measures which he envisages he will, in connection with the transfer, take in relation to any affected employees or, if he envisages that no measures will be so taken, that fact' – Reg 13(2)(c), and

- if the employer in question is the transferor, 'the measures, in connection with the transfer, which he envisages the transferee will take in relation to any affected employees who will become employees of the transferee after the transfer by virtue of regulation 4 or, if he envisages that no measures will be so taken, that fact' – Reg 13(2)(d).

In addition, following amendments made by the Agency Workers Regulations 2010 SI 2010/93, the employer must provide 'suitable information' relating to its use of agency workers. This requirement is discussed under 'Information on use of agency workers' below.

8.58

The information must be as accurate as possible and not be misleading. In Hagen and ors v ICI Chemicals and Polymers Ltd and ors 2002 IRLR 31, QBD, which concerned the transfer of the central engineering resource section of ICI, the parties to the proposed sale realised, prior to the transfer, that the transfer could not take place successfully if the relevant group of staff could not be persuaded to accept it. Various promises were given and representations made by the transferor and transferee to the employees, especially about occupational pension arrangements after the transfer. After the transfer, employees believed that the promises had not been honoured and that they had been misled, and so sued. The High Court held that a transferor is under a duty in contract in tort to take reasonable care to ensure that information provided in accordance with TUPE is accurate, and that statements of intent are capable of being fulfilled. The Court decided that the transferor had been guilty of negligent misstatement in respect of pension arrangements and so was in breach of its duty of care. The employees had reasonably relied on the transferor's representations and, in this unusual case, where the transfer depended on employee approval, damages could be recovered for negligent misstatement on the basis of what would have happened if the correct information had been given.

The wording of Reg 13(2) carries the strong implication that the duty to inform and the duty to consult are interlinked – information is provided 'to enable the employer of any affected employees to consult'. As we shall see below, the statutory duty to consult under Reg 13(6) only arises if the employer of an affected employee envisages that it will take 'measures' in relation to the transfer. However, this does not mean that the duty to provide information depends on the statutory duty to consult applying – see Cable Realisations Ltd v GMB Northern 2010 IRLR 42, EAT, discussed under 'Duty to consult' below.

Fact of, date of and reasons for transfer. Under Reg 13(2)(a) the employer **8.59** must inform the appropriate representatives of:

- the fact that the transfer is to take place
- the date or proposed date of the transfer, and
- the reasons for the transfer.

The first requirement under this head is normally quite straightforward. It is not always so easy, however, to determine when the transfer will take place – see further Chapter 1, 'Identifying a "relevant transfer"', under 'When does transfer occur?'. The third requirement is also normally quite straightforward, although it is not entirely clear how detailed the reasons should be. In LLDY Alexandria Ltd (formerly Loch Lomond Distillery Co Ltd) v Unite the Union and anor EATS 0002/14 the union had been in discussion with LLDY about a pay rise. The pay rise offered by LLDY was rejected. Thereafter, following a further rejection of the offer, LLDY said that it had 'no option but to subcontract the work'. However, LLDY did not refer to the pay dispute as one of the reasons for the transfer. The union complained that it had not been given the reasons for the transfer and that the company had not complied with its obligations under Reg 13(2)(a). The employment tribunal upheld the complaint on the basis that the employers had not provided the 'real' reason for the transfer. Dismissing the appeal, the EAT ruled that the tribunal had been entitled to reach this conclusion on the facts. Thus, it would appear that it is not enough simply for the employer to inform appropriate representatives of the principal reason, or just one of the reasons, for the transfer. It must inform the representatives of all the reasons (if more than one) for the transfer in order to comply with Reg 13(2)(a).

Legal, economic and social implications. The phrase 'legal, economic and **8.60** social implications', which is copied verbatim from the Directive, is clarified by neither the TUPE Regulations themselves nor the BIS Guide. We imagine that

573

'legal' implications will cover the impact of the transfer on employment contracts, statutory rights and collective agreements. 'Economic' implications may refer to any effect on employees' remuneration, benefits and future prospects, including potential redundancies. In this context, it should be noted that 'benefits' includes pension benefits as there is no exclusion for occupational pension schemes from the information and consultation obligations under Reg 13. This is because the exclusion in Reg 10 only applies to Reg 4 (the automatic transfer principle) and Reg 5 (the effect of a relevant transfer on collective agreements).

According to an employment tribunal in NALGO v British Waterways Board ET Case No.11548/88, the 'economic implications' requirement also means that sufficient information should be given about the new employer to enable the employees to assess its 'worth'. Another tribunal subsequently went further. In Grindrod v Excel Europe Ltd and anor ET Case No.2702651/06 the transferor operated a frozen food facility at Heathrow Airport and until 2004 its sole customer was Safeway. The second respondent took over Safeway in 2004 and in due course decided that its own employees would carry out frozen food distribution from a purpose-built facility in Corby. It gave notice to the transferor to terminate the contract in March 2006. Only one employee transferred from Heathrow and G was made redundant in October 2006. The tribunal held that the transferor had failed to provide information on the economic and social implications of the transfer. In its view, the obligation extended to providing the affected employee with information on the housing market in Corby, the nature and availability of schools and education, the job market, comparability of wage rates and the future of the second respondent's business and its investment in the Corby area.

8.61 Note that in providing the necessary information, the employer does not warrant either its legal accuracy or the accuracy of the legal implications of the transfer. In Royal Mail Group Ltd v Communication Workers Union 2010 ICR 83, CA, RMG Ltd transferred certain Post Office businesses to WHS. RMG Ltd genuinely believed that, although TUPE would apply, no contracts would automatically transfer since the affected employees would all either take voluntary redundancy or be redeployed. It therefore informed and consulted on that basis under Reg 13. The issue that eventually came before the Court of Appeal was whether information and consultation on the basis of a mistaken but genuine belief as to the legal implications of a transfer was an automatic breach of Reg 13. The Court held that it was not. Lord Justice Waller noted that 'the language of Reg 13(2) was not the language of strict liability or warranty'. 'The language of Reg 13(2)(b) obliges the employer to describe what he genuinely believes to be the legal, social and economic implications' but no more. Although an employer must inform employees' representatives of its 'considered view' as to the legal implications for employees prior to a transfer of its business to another, the employer is not required in effect to warrant the accuracy of the law in this regard.

Envisaged measures. The employer – whether transferor or transferee – must **8.62** inform representatives of whether or not it 'envisages' that it will take 'measures' in relation to any of its affected employees, and if so, what those measures are. Neither 'measures' nor 'envisages' is defined in the TUPE Regulations, but the following cases cast some light on what these words might mean in the context of Reg 13:

- **Institution of Professional Civil Servants and ors v Secretary of State for Defence** 1987 IRLR 373, ChD: two dockyards at Rosyth and Devonport were privatised by transfer to commercial management in April 1987. This was achieved by the Dockyard Services Act 1986, which re-enacted the TUPE information and consultation provisions almost word for word. The IPCS brought a High Court action claiming that the duty to inform and consult under the 1986 Act had not been fulfilled. In the course of giving judgment, Mr Justice Millett discussed the meaning of 'measures' and 'envisages' in the relevant provisions. In his opinion, 'measures' is a word of the widest import and includes any action, step or arrangement. 'Envisages' simply means 'visualises' or 'foresees'. He went on to state that the phrase 'measures which he envisages he will... take' is apt to exclude mere hopes and possibilities. So, 'it is not enough that there should be some possibility in contemplation; the company must have formulated some definite plan or proposal which it has in mind to implement'. Turning to the facts, he concluded that manpower projections were not 'measures', but that positive steps to achieve planned reductions in manpower levels would be

- **Baxter and ors v Marks and Spencer plc and ors** EAT 0162/05: M&S decided to outsource its 'profit protection operation', which was concerned with preventing theft, to Securicor. This outsourcing amounted to a TUPE transfer. A group of employees brought tribunal claims, some of which related to the Regulations' information and consultation provisions. These claims were largely unsuccessful and the employees appealed on a number of points. Before the EAT, the employees argued that the refocusing of their work from 'internal theft' to 'external theft' was a 'measure' for the purposes of the information and consultation rules. The EAT disagreed. The change in question was simply a change of emphasis within the employees' agreed job description. Furthermore, the detail of the different procedural steps that employees would have to take as a result of their being employed by Securicor rather than by M&S 'was not something which could be regarded as a "measure in connection with the transfer" but simply an inevitable administrative consequence of the transfer'

- **Todd v Strain and ors** 2011 IRLR 11, EAT: an employment tribunal upheld a complaint of breach of Reg 13 on the basis that the transferor, T, had failed to inform employees affected by the sale of a care home of certain proposed administrative changes. These included arrangements for payment for work done in the three days prior to the transfer and for untaken holiday, and information that some staff would receive a tax rebate that was to be reclaimed by the transferee the following month. On appeal, T argued that these were not 'measures', being merely administrative consequences of the transfer. The EAT rejected that argument. It held that at least two of the proposals – changing the normal payment date and the payment for untaken holiday – represented a departure from what would otherwise have occurred. They were not, therefore, an inevitable consequence of the transfer itself, but measures taken by the transferor. Furthermore, the fact that the change envisaged with regard to pay dates was not to the disadvantage of the employees in question was irrelevant to the issue of whether it constituted a measure for TUPE purposes. Nothing in the legislation requires a measure to be disadvantageous (or indeed of a particular level of materiality) for it to be 'envisaged' by either transferor or transferee and so trigger the information and consultation obligations of TUPE.

8.63 In addition, a change in the proposed depot from which employees worked was held to be a 'measure' in GMB v Eastleigh Borough Housing and anor ET Case No.3102915/08, as was a change in the employee's role and work location in Sullivan v Make Room and anor ET Case No2401578/12.

We saw above that the EAT in Baxter and ors v Marks and Spencer held that a change was not a 'measure' for the purposes of Reg 13 where it was simply a change of emphasis falling within the employees' job descriptions. We should point out, however, that it is universally accepted that the duty to inform (and consult) under Reg 13 applies not only to measures resulting in changes to contractual terms and conditions of employment. Other measures covered could include those relating to non-contractual benefits, collective issues and occupational pensions (notwithstanding that pension rights do not transfer under TUPE – see Chapter 3, 'What transfers?', under 'Occupational pensions').

8.64 As set out above, if the employer who is doing the informing is the *transferor*, it must inform the appropriate representatives of the measures which the transferee envisages taking in relation to the affected employees in connection with the transfer; and if the transferee does not envisage taking any measures, the transferor must inform the representatives of that fact – Reg 13(2)(d). In order that the transferor will be in a position to comply with this requirement, Reg 13(4) provides that 'the transferee shall give the transferor such information at such a time as will enable the transferor to perform the duty imposed on him by virtue of paragraph (2)(d)'. (Note, however, that the transferring employees who are entitled to be informed by the transferor have no remedy directly against the transferee if it fails to provide the transferor with the relevant information under Reg 13(4) – Allen and ors v Morrisons Facilities Services Ltd

2014 ICR 792, EAT. This case is discussed further under 'Claims for failure to inform or consult' below.)

When should information be provided? In contrast with the TULR(C)A, **8.65** which lays down a clear timetable as to when information with regard to collective redundancies should be passed on, the TUPE Regulations are vague as to when information about a TUPE transfer should be provided. Reg 13(2) simply states that the employer must provide the information long enough before the relevant transfer to enable consultation with the representatives of affected employees. Common sense suggests that information concerning larger and more complex transfers will need to be provided earlier in the process than information about smaller transfers.

The issue arose for consideration in Cable Realisations Ltd v GMB Northern 2010 IRLR 42, EAT. There, CR Ltd had been making a loss since late 2006 and in May 2007 made a decision to either close or sell off its cable business. It received a non-binding purchase offer from an India-based company on 31 May 2007, which CR Ltd's holding company decided to pursue on 28 June. CR Ltd first met with the GMB union, representing the affected employees, on 3 July. However, at that stage, it felt that it was not in a position to reveal the identity of the purchasing company. By 15 August, the purchasing company was happy to reveal itself and had informed CR Ltd that it did not envisage taking any 'measures' in connection with the transfer. CR Ltd provided that information, along with the other information required by Reg 13(2), to the GMB that same day and held a 'consultation' meeting on a voluntary basis. It held a further 'consultation' meeting on 17 August but then, on 20 August, the company's annual two-week shutdown began. The transfer eventually took place on 3 September. The GMB complained to a tribunal that CR Ltd had not met its obligations under Reg 13(2). The tribunal upheld the complaint. On appeal to the EAT, CR Ltd argued for the first time that, since no consultation was prescribed under Reg 13(6) (as no measures were envisaged), there was no requirement to provide information at all. The EAT rejected that contention. While the EAT recognised that such a submission may seem logical as a matter of construction, it was plainly wrong in light of the industrial relations rationale behind TUPE. Reg 13(2) is designed to allow the representatives of affected employees to engage in informed consultation about a wide range of matters relating to a TUPE transfer, whether that consultation is entered into voluntarily or as a result of Reg 13(6). The EAT therefore upheld a tribunal's decision that, while providing the required information over two weeks before the transfer looked, on the face of it, 'long enough', the company shutdown changed matters. In order to engage in meaningful consultation it is essential that union representatives are available to speak with management and that those representatives can communicate with the members whom they represent. This was not possible when around 90 per cent of the affected employees were on holiday.

577

8.66   It might be thought that, when the transfer has minimal or no implications for affected employees, the required information need be given only a short time before it takes effect. However, a tribunal in Spencer and ors v Somerset Crane and anor ET Case No.1701703/08 decided that information given the day before a transfer cannot be given 'long enough before' the transfer even when no measures are proposed.

Note that, under Reg 13(9), if there are special circumstances which make it not reasonably practicable for an employer to provide the requisite information in time, the employer shall take all such steps towards performing that duty as are reasonably practicable in the circumstances – see 'Employers' defences' below.

8.67   **How should information be provided?** According to Reg 13(5), the Reg 13(2) information should be delivered to the appropriate representatives or sent by post to an address notified by them to the employer, or, in the case of trade union representatives, sent by post to the trade union at the address of its headquarters or main office. This wording suggests that the information must always be provided in writing.

Note that in Institution of Professional Civil Servants and ors v Secretary of State for Defence 1987 IRLR 373, ChD, the High Court held (about an identical provision in the Dockyards Services Act 1986) that the unions were not entitled to the particular documents from which the information was extracted, but only to the information itself.

8.68   **Decision resulting in transfer taken by third party.** Note that Reg 13(12) provides that the duty on employers to inform under Reg 13(2) will apply regardless of whether the decision resulting in the transfer is taken by the employer or a person controlling the employer.

8.69   **Information on use of agency workers.** When the Agency Workers Regulations 2010 SI 2010/93 came into force on 1 October 2011, they amended Reg 13 TUPE to introduce information requirements relating to an employer's use of agency workers. In addition to the details set out in Reg 13(2), Reg 13(2A) requires the employer to provide 'suitable information' relating to its use of agency workers. Suitable information is defined by Reg 13(2A)(b) as:

- the number of agency workers working temporarily for and under the supervision and direction of the employer

- the parts of the employer's undertaking in which those agency workers are working, and

- the type of work those agency workers are carrying out.

These provisions raise some questions of interpretation. Reg 13(2A)(a) requires the provision of 'suitable information relating to the use of agency workers (if any) by that employer'. The use of the bracketed words 'if any' suggests that the obligation only arises if the employer does actually use agency workers – if not, there is presumably no requirement even to state that fact in writing. Potentially more problematic is the scope of Reg 13(2A)(a), in that it requires information about the use of agency workers 'by that employer'. There is nothing to limit the scope of this requirement to information about agency workers used in the undertaking or establishment affected by the transfer. Without express restriction, this wording appears to require the provision of information relating to the use of agency workers anywhere in the employer's business. So, for example, it seems that an employer who transfers a factory in Manchester, where no agency workers are engaged, would have to inform the appropriate representatives of the fact that it employs agency workers to do cleaning at its factory in Newcastle. This interpretation has been applied to the collective redundancy provisions in Ss.188 and 189 TULR(C)A by the employment tribunal in Unison v Capita Business Services Ltd ET Case No.2341219/12, where the employment judge stated: 'I can see no reason for limiting that class of individuals to those working at any specific place, nor to those who may be somehow affected by the proposed redundancies, nor indeed by another other criterion or limitation.'

8.70 Given that failure to provide the information required under Reg 13 can attract a remedy of up to 13 weeks' pay for each affected employee, employers would be well advised to err on the side of caution and comply with Reg 13(2A) in its full breadth, regardless of how irrelevant information about agency workers might appear. However, it is worth noting that while the penalty for breach of Reg 13 is intended to be punitive, the tribunal must have regard to the nature and extent of the employer's default. An employer who has failed to provide full information regarding agency workers at establishments and undertakings other than the one affected by the transfer could presumably argue that the failure was trivial in its effect on the employees and seek a reduction in the award.

Duty to consult
8.71

The employer's duty to consult with appropriate representatives of affected employees (for the meaning of 'appropriate representatives' and 'affected employees', see 'Appropriate representatives' and 'Affected employees' above) is contained in Reg 13(6) and (7) TUPE. Reg 13(6) states that 'an employer of an affected employee who envisages that he will take measures in relation to an affected employee, in connection with the relevant transfer, shall consult the appropriate representatives of that employee with a view to seeking agreement to the intended measures'. And Reg 13(7) adds that 'in the course of those consultations the employer shall (a) consider any representations made by the appropriate representatives; and (b) reply to those representations and, if he rejects any of those representations, state his reasons'.

Envisaged measures. Unlike the duty to inform, the duty to consult under **8.72** Reg 13(6) does not arise in every transfer situation. Rather, it does so only where

579

a transferor or transferee 'envisages that he will take measures' in respect of one or more affected employees. The meaning of the words 'envisages' and 'measures' in the context of Reg 13 was discussed under 'Duty to inform' above.

We should emphasise that the duty to consult arises only where the employer in question envisages that it will take measures in respect of its own affected employees. Thus, where a transferor envisages that the transferee will take measures in respect of the transferring employees, the transferor will not be obliged to consult in respect of such measures. As we saw under 'Duty to inform' above, however, it will be required to inform the appropriate representatives of any measures it envisages that the transferee will take – Reg 13(2)(d).

8.73 **Must transferee consult in respect of transferring employees?** We have explained that Reg 13(6) does not place the transferor under a duty to consult the transferring employees about measures that will be taken, post-transfer, by the transferee. But will the transferee be under a duty to consult about such measures, either before or after the transfer takes place?

It was generally accepted that, under the 1981 Regulations, the transferee was not obliged to consult representatives of the transferor's employees prior to the transfer. The relevant rule, old Reg 10(5), stated that the consultation duty only arose 'where an employer of any affected employees envisages that he will, in connection with the transfer, be taking measures in relation to any such employees'. The only employees referred to in this rule, it was thought, were the relevant employer's employees, and not anybody else's.

8.74 However, owing to a slight change in wording, the position under Reg 13(6) of the 2006 Regulations appears rather more complicated. As we have seen, Reg 13(6) provides that the consultation duty arises where 'an employer of an affected employee... envisages that he will take measures in relation to an affected employee, in connection with the relevant transfer'. On the face of it, this wording would seem to cover some situations where transferees envisage taking measures in respect of transferors' employees. Consider the following: a transferee has an existing workforce, some of whom are to be affected by the relevant transfer and are thus 'affected employees' for the purposes of Reg 13 (see 'Affected employees' above). In such circumstances, the transferee is clearly 'an employer of an affected employee' within the meaning of Reg 13(6). Prior to the transfer, the transferee envisages that it will take measures in respect of one (or more) of the employees who is to transfer from the transferor under TUPE. That employee is also, clearly, 'an affected employee'. Thus, again within the meaning of Reg 13(6), the transferee 'envisages that he will take measures in relation to an affected employee'. It does not appear to matter that the affected employee of whom the transferee is the employer, and the affected employee in respect of whom measures are envisaged, are not the same person. Arguably, then, the effect of Reg 13(6) in this situation would be to place the transferee under a duty to consult in respect of the transferor's employee.

It remains to be seen whether the courts agree with this analysis. Since the wording of Reg 13(6) is unclear, one pertinent question they might ask is whether the Government intended the position under the 2006 Regulations to be different to that under the 1981 Regulations. In this regard, the fact that the new wording was not specifically referred to in the BIS Guide or in the 2005 consultation document suggests that any substantive change to TUPE's consultation requirements was inadvertent. Moreover, the Acquired Rights Directive itself only requires the transferee to consult representatives of its own employees, and not representatives of the transferor's employees: Article 7(3) of the Directive, which Reg 13(6) is intended to implement, states that 'where the transferor or the transferee envisages measures in relation to *his employees*, he shall consult the representatives of [those] employees' (our stress). With this in mind, the courts might be disinclined to conclude that transferees' consultation duties have been extended.

On balance, then, it seems that the transferee is not obliged to consult **8.75** representatives of the transferor's employees prior to the transfer. But when the transfer occurs, the transferring employees will no longer be the transferor's employees, but will be the transferee's employees. This raises the question of whether, at the point of the transfer or thereafter, the transferee becomes obliged to consult representatives of the transferred employees in respect of measures it envisages taking in respect of those employees.

Such post-transfer consultation does not generally happen. And case law suggests it need not. In Sweetin v Coral Racing 2006 IRLR 252, EAT, for example, the EAT stated categorically that 'the obligation is to consult in advance of the transfer'. However, there is nothing obvious in Reg 13, or indeed in the Acquired Rights Directive, that suggests that the duty to consult cannot arise upon or after the date of the transfer. Indeed, there seems no reason at all why post-transfer measures that the transferee envisages taking in respect of a transferred employee could not amount to 'measures in relation to an affected employee, in connection with the transfer' within the meaning of Reg 13(6), triggering the duty to consult. Indeed, as explained in Chapter 4, 'Unfair dismissal', and Chapter 5, 'Changing terms and conditions', 'transfer-connected' events have been held to take place some years after the transfer date.

Furthermore, the EAT has found that the Acquired Rights Directive does – at **8.76** least implicitly – bring the duty to consult to a halt at the date of the transfer. Lady Smith, presiding over the Scottish EAT in UCATT v Amicus and ors and another case 2009 ICR 852, EAT, held that the Directive does not oblige a transferee employer to consult, after the transfer, about measures that it envisages taking in respect of transferred employees. Several factors supported this conclusion. In particular, Lady Smith noted that the obligation in Article 7(1) to provide information clearly looked forward to the date of the transfer, and that any post-transfer duty to consult would not therefore be

581

supported by any corresponding duty to inform. Furthermore, if the Directive did impose a post-transfer duty to consult, which would have to be read into Reg 13, this would create an entirely open-ended consultation duty, since it is well established that measures taken by a transferee years after a transfer can still be 'transfer-connected', and so potentially within the duty to consult. Lady Smith noted that 'the logical extension of the union's argument would also be that such an employer could not safely put any measures in connection with the transfer into effect in advance of the transfer even if it had consulted with its existing workforce about them because it [was] required to wait and consult with the transferring employees about them once they had transferred into its employment'. That, said Lady Smith, 'would be wholly unworkable. It was not... for TUPE to continue to control the transferee's operation of its employment relationships post-transfer.'

Lady Smith's reasoning is open to question as it would appear to be inconsistent with the Directive's purpose of safeguarding employee rights and it is suggested that any continuing obligation to consult would only be open-ended to the extent that the measure was envisaged by the transfer itself. Nonetheless, her conclusion is supported by the EAT's ruling in Allen and ors v Morrisons Facilities Services Ltd 2014 ICR 792, EAT, that there is no independent cause of action against the transferee for its failure to inform or consult (see the section 'Claims for failure to inform or consult', under 'Which employer is liable? – transferee's failure to provide information' below).

8.77 Finally, Lady Smith endorsed the view given in the 2007 edition of this Handbook that the Reg 15(12) time limit for claims relating to a failure to consult points away from a duty on the transferee to consult post-transfer. Reg 15(2) states that any claim in relation to a failure to consult must be brought within three months of the relevant transfer (or, where not reasonably practicable, within such further period as the tribunal considers reasonable). Unlike Reg 13(6), then, Reg 15(12) seems to suggest that the date of the transfer is significant with regard to the duty to consult, perhaps forming some kind of cut-off point. In other words, it implies that all consultation has to take place prior to the transfer, meaning that the transferee will be under no obligation, post-transfer, to consult representatives of its newly acquired workforce. Lady Smith thought that this indicated that the drafter of the Regulations – rightly in her view – clearly read the Directive as envisaging no post-transfer duty on the transferee to consult.

8.78 **Consultation with view to seeking agreement.** As initially drafted, the 1981 Regulations omitted the requirement that consultation needed to take place with a view to reaching agreement. As this was specified in Article 6(2) (now Article 7(2)) of the Acquired Rights Directive, the ECJ, in Commission of the European Communities v United Kingdom 1994 ICR 664, ECJ, concluded that the 1981 Regulations were defective in this regard. This deficiency was rectified by the Trade Union Reform and Employment Rights Act 1993, which introduced the phrase 'with a view to seeking agreement' into what eventually became Reg 13(6).

The European Court of Justice considered the meaning of the phrase 'with a view to reaching agreement' in Junk v Kühnel 2005 IRLR 310, ECJ, stating that it imposes an obligation to negotiate to try to reach an agreed solution. Although this case was concerned with the EU Collective Redundancies Directive (No.98/59), it is likely that the same words in the Acquired Rights Directive (and the similar words in the 2006 Regulations) should be given the same meaning. In essence, then, it would seem that an employer should discuss the proposed measures with an open mind and negotiate with the appropriate representatives about them. This is backed up by Reg 13(7)(a), which states that in the course of consultations the employer must consider any representations made by the appropriate representatives. It is not the case, however, that the employer is necessarily obliged to change its position. In fact, Reg 13(7)(b) acknowledges that an employer may reject representations, provided that it gives reasons.

Timing of consultation. The TUPE Regulations do not lay down a timetable **8.79** for consultation under Reg 13. At first glance, it would seem that consultation must begin long enough before the measures are to be taken to allow a meaningful consultation process to be carried out. However, as stated above, Reg 15(12) states that any claim in relation to a failure to consult must be brought within three months of the relevant transfer (or, where that is not reasonably practicable, within such further period as the tribunal considers reasonable). This, together with the not particularly extensive case law in this area, seems to suggest that all consultation under Reg 13(6) should be completed before the transfer takes place, regardless of when the measures are scheduled to be taken.

If 'measures' are not 'envisaged' until the last minute, meaningful consultation within the appropriate time frame might not be possible. Here, the employer has two alternatives: delay the transfer until consultation has taken place, or rely on the Reg 13(9) 'special circumstances' defence – see 'Employers' defences' below.

Decision resulting in transfer taken by third party. As with the rules regarding **8.80** the provision of information, Reg 13(12) states that the duty on employers to consult under Reg 13(6) will apply whether the decision resulting in the transfer is taken by the employer or by a person controlling the employer.

Employers' defences   8.81

Before looking at the remedies available for a failure to inform or consult (see 'Claims for failure to inform or consult' below), we consider two ways in which employers who have not followed Reg 13(2) (information) or Reg 13(6) (consultation) to the letter may nonetheless be able to avoid liability.

8.82 **'Special circumstances' defence.** As explained under 'Appropriate representatives' above, under Reg 13(9) employers have an excuse for not complying with the duties to inform or consult if there are 'special circumstances which render it not reasonably practicable' to do so. They must, however, take all such steps to fulfil the duty as are reasonably practicable in the circumstances. If the question of reasonable practicability reaches a tribunal, the onus is on the employer to show that the special circumstances defence should apply – Reg 15(2).

We should note here that this 'special circumstances' defence is not provided for in the Acquired Rights Directive, a fact that has led to speculation that TUPE does not implement the Directive properly. But it is perhaps significant that when the European Commission commenced infraction proceedings against the UK Government with regard to aspects of the 1981 Regulations that it believed were in breach of the Directive, which led to the ruling in Commission of the European Communities v United Kingdom 1994 ICR 664, ECJ, the 'special circumstances' defence was not one of the objections taken by the Commission. It may be, therefore, that the defence is accepted as being a reasonable proviso to the duty to inform and consult so long as it is narrowly construed.

8.83 And in fact, case law suggests that the defence *will* be narrowly construed. The wording of Reg 13(9) is similar to that of S.188(7) TULR(C)A, which sets up a 'special circumstances' defence when an employer has failed to carry out the statutory duty to consult trade union representatives about proposed redundancies. Case law on the meaning of 'special circumstances' in the context of redundancy consultation is therefore likely to be applicable in the context of information and consultation about proposed transfers. The basic principle is that circumstances are only 'special' if they are 'exceptional or out of the ordinary' – Clarks of Hove Ltd v Bakers' Union 1978 ICR 1076, CA. Appellate courts have applied this strictly, as illustrated by the fact that neither insolvency (if it was reasonably foreseeable) nor the need for confidentiality will normally be viewed as a special circumstance in this regard – see IDS Employment Law Handbook, 'Redundancy' (2008), for further details.

Case law on the 'special circumstances' defence in the context of redundancy consultation has also established that 'special circumstances' must exist at the time the obligation to inform and consult arises rather than as an explanation given with hindsight (see E Ivor Hughes Educational Foundation v Morris 2015 IRLR 696, EAT) and it is likely that the same approach applies to the defence under Reg 15(2). In the Morris case, the EAT upheld the employment tribunal's decision that the employer's fear that it was inevitable that the information would be leaked did not amount to a 'special circumstance' within the meaning of S.188(7) TULR(C)A.

584

Below we set out some examples, from case law and the TUPE Regulations, of **8.84** situations that may or may not amount to 'special circumstances' for the purposes of Reg 13(9):

• Reg 15(6) provides that a failure by a person controlling the employer, whether directly or indirectly, to provide information necessary for the employer to fulfil its duties to inform and consult will *not* constitute special circumstances rendering it not reasonably practicable for the employer to comply with the statutory requirements. Thus, for example, the possible defence of a subsidiary company that its parent company kept it in the dark about the transfer will not succeed

• in NATTKE v Rank Leisure Ltd COET 1388/134 an employer attempted to rely upon the defence of 'special circumstances' where the need to speed through the transfer was a pertinent factor influencing the employer's failure properly to inform and consult. In September 1982 negotiations for the sale of a West End cinema owned by R Ltd took place with a view to ensuring that its transfer as a going concern was achieved within a month. NATTKE, representing a transferred employee, complained to a tribunal that R Ltd had failed to consult and inform it adequately before the transfer. The tribunal held that the speed with which the transaction had to be completed was a 'special circumstance', but that R Ltd had not taken all reasonable steps in trying to inform the union. It could have written to the union a day earlier and delivered the letter by hand instead of posting it

• in Unison v Somerset County Council and ors 2010 ICR 498, EAT, the Appeal Tribunal endorsed a tribunal's finding that 'fast moving events and [an] approaching deadline' were special circumstances where the transferee sought to unpick an agreement it had reached in principle with the transferor over future staffing policy. However, the EAT appeared to have been influenced by the fact that the consultation up to that point on other matters had been 'lengthy and exemplary', the proposed transfer having been known about and consulted on for two years

• in Scott and ors v Guardian Facilities and anor ET Case No.2330014/08 the claimants complained that the transferor had failed to consult them about their transfer to the second respondent. The transferor argued that it had only one hour's notice of the transfer and that in these circumstances it was not reasonably practicable to consult. However, the tribunal found that, although the transfer had happened very quickly, the loss of business at short notice was neither exceptional nor extraordinary and that the transferor had been on notice that the contract was at risk for seven months. There were therefore no special circumstances within the meaning of Reg 13(9).

585

8.85 Another 'special circumstance' that might well be alleged in transfer situations is that information cannot be provided and consultation cannot take place because of the need to keep the transfer process secret. This may be so particularly where, for example, it is claimed by a company in financial difficulties that the transfer would not take place without strict maintenance of confidentiality. However, if tribunals are too ready to accept such arguments, the whole purpose of Reg 13 will be defeated. In NALGO v British Waterways Board ET Case No.11548/88 the tribunal saw no reason why commercially sensitive information could not be omitted from an agreement to transfer with only the remaining parts being disclosed to the union. European law may be of particular relevance on this point. One of the basic principles on which the Acquired Rights Directive is based is that the rights of employees must generally prevail over commercial considerations.

Note that Reg 15(5) suggests that the Reg 13(9) 'special circumstances' defence, or at least a variant of it, is available to the transferor where it was not reasonably practicable for it to provide the Reg 13(2) information to representatives because the transferee had failed to provide it with the information specified by Reg 13(4) (see 'Duty to inform' above). Reg 15(5) provides that, in these circumstances, the transferor must notify the transferee that it intends to give this reason for non-compliance with Reg 13(2) to an employment tribunal. The effect of giving the notification is to add the transferee as a party to the tribunal proceedings, which, if the transferor's argument is successful, may lead to the transferee paying compensation to affected employees under Reg 15(8).

8.86 **'Invitation to elect' defence.** If an employer fails to inform or consult appropriate representatives in accordance with Reg 13(2) and (6) this is, generally, a breach of TUPE. But if there are no appropriate representatives, what should an employer do? As we saw under 'Appropriate representatives' above, it can invite affected employees to elect such representatives, but what if the employees decline to do so or fail to do so in good time?

Regulation 13(10) and (11) provide comfort for employers in such circumstances. Reg 13(10) provides that 'where (a) the employer has invited any of the affected employee[s] to elect employee representatives; and (b) the invitation was issued long enough before the time when the employer is required to give information under [Reg 13(2) – see 'Duty to inform' above] to allow them to elect representatives by that time, the employer shall be treated as complying with the requirements of this regulation in relation to those employees if he complies with those requirements as soon as is reasonably practicable after the election of the representatives'. Reg 13(11) then states that 'if, after the employer has invited any affected employees to elect representatives, they fail to do so within a reasonable time, he shall give to any affected employees the information set out in [Reg 13(2)]'.

586

In the light of these provisions, we make the following points concerning the **8.87** situation where there are no appropriate representatives in the workplace:

- if the employer invites the affected employees to elect employee representatives in accordance with the time limit set down in Reg 13(10), it will not be in breach of Reg 13 if it complies with its information and consultation duties as soon as is reasonably practicable after the representatives are elected. Although Reg 13(10) does not expressly state that the consultation process can be curtailed in such circumstances owing to the election taking longer than expected, this might well be the provision's intention; and

- if the affected employees fail to elect representatives within a reasonable time, having been invited to do so by the employer, under Reg 13(11) the employer must give the information required by Reg 13(2) to the affected employees themselves. Again, this is worded as an obligation on the part of the employer, rather than as a defence, but we suggest that the purpose of Reg 13(11) is to relieve the employer of its consultation obligations in such circumstances. However, it is important to stress that in these circumstances an individual does not act as a representative of other affected employees – Independent Insurance Co Ltd (in provisional liquidation) v Aspinall and anor 2011 ICR 1234, EAT.

We have dealt, then, with the situation where there are no existing appropriate **8.88** representatives in place. But what of the situation where there are such representatives? As discussed under 'Appropriate representatives' above, if the existing appropriate representatives are recognised trade union representatives, the employer will be obliged to inform and consult them. But if they are employee representatives elected or appointed for some other purpose, the employer is entitled to choose, under Reg 13(3), to ignore them and instead inform and consult new representatives elected for TUPE purposes. If the employer chooses to consult new representatives to be elected in such circumstances, the following propositions with regard to Reg 13(10) and (11) seem to make sense:

- if the employer is to invite affected employees to elect new representatives, it must give them sufficient time to do so. If it does not (where the transfer is imminent, a timely invitation might not be possible) the invitation to elect will not fall within Reg 13(10). In such circumstances, the Reg 13(10)/(11) defence will not be available and the employer will be obliged to inform and consult the existing representatives; and

- if the employer invites in accordance with Reg 13(10) – that is, invites all affected employees, in time, to elect employee representatives for TUPE purposes – Reg 13(10) and 13(11) would seem to apply regardless of whether there are already employee representatives in existence. So, for example, if

587

the employees fail to elect new employee representatives within a reasonable time, the employer will be able to provide the information required by Reg 13(2) to the individual affected employees under Reg 13(11), and will not, it seems, be obliged to inform or consult the existing employee representatives at all.

8.89 Claims for failure to inform or consult
Complaints that an employer – whether the transferor or the transferee – has failed to comply with Reg 13 (the duty to inform and consult) or Reg 14 (the election of employee representatives) are governed by Reg 15 TUPE. The sanctions imposed by the Regulations are similar to those prescribed by the TULR(C)A in respect of a failure to inform and consult about collective redundancies – see IDS Employment Law Handbook, 'Redundancy' (2011), Chapter 12, 'Collective redundancies', under 'Complaints about breach of S.188'.

8.90 Who can bring claims? Where it is alleged that an employer has failed to comply with any requirement of Reg 13 or Reg 14, then only certain persons can bring a complaint to the employment tribunal:

- in the case of a failure relating to the election of employee representatives, by any of the employer's employees who are affected employees – Reg 15(1)(a)

- in the case of any other failure relating to employee representatives, by any of the employee representatives to whom the failure related – Reg 15(1)(b)

- in the case of failure relating to representatives of a trade union, by that trade union – Reg 15(1)(c), and

- in any other case, by any of the employer's employees who are affected employees – Reg 15(1)(d).

The issue of whether employees can directly enforce breaches of Reg 13, when no appropriate representatives are already in place or have been elected, was discussed in Howard v Millrise Ltd (in liquidation) and anor 2005 ICR 435, EAT. There it was held that an affected employee had standing to bring a claim for breach of Reg 13 where an employer had failed to invite affected employees to elect representatives or, in the absence of any election, to provide the requisite statutory information to the employee him or herself. Furthermore, it was unnecessary to decide under which particular section of Reg 15 the complaint should be made. This decision was followed in Hickling (t/a Imperial Day Nursery) and ors v Marshall EAT 0217/10, where the EAT acknowledged that individual entitlement to claim is not obvious under Reg 13, since only Reg 13(11) imposes obligations on an employer in respect of individual employees. However, the Appeal Tribunal held that the case was 'on all fours' with Howard and upheld the tribunal's decision that M could bring a claim for breach of the employer's obligations under Reg 13.

However, it must be stressed that it is not open to an individual employee to **8.91** claim compensation on behalf of a group of affected employees – Independent Insurance Co Ltd (in provisional liquidation) v Aspinall and anor 2011 ICR 1234, EAT. In that case, which was decided under the similarly worded provisions of Ss.188 and 189 TULR(C)A, the EAT ruled that an employment tribunal can only make an award to the individual (or individuals) who actually bring the claim.

Furthermore, it should be noted that both Howard and Hickling were concerned with the entitlement of individual employees to bring claims where no appropriate representatives were in place. In Nationwide Building Society v Benn and ors 2010 IRLR 922, EAT, the EAT made it clear that where appropriate representatives are in place, only they may seek remedies for breaches of Regs 13 and 14 on behalf of the affected employees. In reaching this conclusion, the EAT relied on the Court of Appeal's decision in Mercy v Northgate HR Ltd 2008 ICR 410, CA, which set down the same rule in relation to failures under the information and consultation regime for collective redundancies under Ss.188 and 189 TULR(C)A.

Where non-trade union representatives are in place, it should not simply be **8.92** assumed that they will have authority to bring claims on behalf of the affected employees. In Jackson Lloyd Ltd and anor v Smith and ors EAT 0127/13 the EAT held that it is necessary to apply Regs 13, 14 and 15 purposively and that their clear purpose is to ensure that employees give meaningful consent to those who are nominated to represent them collectively. In that case, appropriate representatives were elected for a 12-month term. At the date of the transfer, their term of office had expired and election of a new committee had been deferred. Consequently, the EAT upheld the tribunal's finding that there was no one mandated to represent the affected employees and that they were entitled to bring claims in their own names.

Time limits. As discussed under 'Duty to consult' above, Reg 15(12) provides **8.93** that any claim under Reg 15(1) must be brought before the end of the period of three months beginning with the date on which the relevant transfer is completed, or within such further period as the tribunal considers reasonable where it is satisfied that it was not reasonably practicable for the complaint to be presented within this time frame. (The time limit may also be extended to allow for early conciliation – Reg 15(13)).

In South Durham Health Authority v Unison 1995 IRLR 407, EAT, the Appeal Tribunal considered an appeal by an employer that a claim for lack of information and consultation had been premature, and thus that it should not be heard, in that it was brought before the transfer was completed. The EAT rejected the appeal, noting that TUPE only specified an end date – the end of the period of three months beginning with the date on which the transfer is completed – and did not prohibit a tribunal from considering a claim before

589

any particular date. The EAT concluded that the claim in this case was not premature, as it had not been made before there was something to complain about. Thus, a tribunal had jurisdiction to hear the claim.

8.94 **Compensation.** Where a tribunal finds a complaint under Reg 15(1) to be well founded, it must make a declaration to that effect, and may order the relevant employer to pay 'appropriate compensation to such descriptions of affected employees as may be specified in the award' – Reg 15(7) and (8).

'Appropriate compensation' is defined by Reg 16(3) as 'such sum not exceeding thirteen weeks' pay for the employee in question as the tribunal considers just and equitable having regard to the seriousness of the failure of the employer to comply with his duty'. Under Reg 16(4), a 'week's pay' for this purpose is to be determined by reference to Ss.220–228 ERA (see IDS Employment Law Handbook, 'Wages' (2011), Chapter 10, 'A week's pay'). Note that a week's pay for this type of award is not subject to the limit (currently, from 6 April 2015, £475) imposed by the ERA – Zaman and ors v Kozee Sleep Products Ltd t/a Dorlux Beds UK 2011 IRLR 196, EAT.

8.95 The nature of the compensation to be awarded under Reg 15 was considered by the EAT in Sweetin v Coral Racing 2006 IRLR 252, EAT. There, mirroring the approach taken in the collective redundancy regime (see Susie Radin Ltd v GMB and ors 2004 ICR 893, CA), the EAT held that the award is intended to be punitive and therefore the amount of the award should reflect the nature and extent of the employer's default. The EAT stated that while the tribunal is entitled to have regard to any loss sustained by the employees caused by the employer's failure, the focus of the award 'requires to be the penal nature which governs it and proof of loss is neither necessary nor determinative of the level at which to fix the award'. In essence, therefore, the employment tribunal should consider the seriousness or gravity of the default and any mitigating circumstances. Such circumstances might exist, for example, where the tribunal rejects the 'special circumstances' defence but acknowledges that there were none the less mitigating circumstances.

In Susie Radin Ltd v GMB and ors (above) the EAT held that the employment tribunal had erred in awarding affected employees the equivalent of six weeks' pay calculated on the basis that this was what they had lost as a consequence of the employer's failure to consult. Given that the employer's failure to consult had been complete, and given the absence of any mitigating circumstances, a maximum award of 13 weeks' pay was appropriate. It follows that the 13 weeks' maximum may be regarded as the starting point but the EAT has stressed, both in TUPE cases like Todd v Strain and ors 2011 IRLR 11, EAT (see below), and in cases under the collective redundancy regime like London Borough of Barnet v Unison EAT 0191/13, that tribunals should not approach this provision in a mechanical manner, particularly where some information has been given and some consultation has taken place. The award is therefore likely to be small where the failure is not deliberate. So, for example, in GMB v Eastleigh Borough Council ET Case No.3102915/08 (see below) the employment tribunal awarded just £200 per affected employee where the employer's failure to advise the union of the transferee's proposed change to the depot from which the employees worked was not 'deliberate'.

Four illustrations of circumstances that have been taken into account in determining the appropriate award: **8.96**

- **Cable Realisations Ltd v GMB Northern** 2010 IRLR 42, EAT: CR Ltd provided the appropriate representative GMB union with the information required by Reg 13(2) and met with union representatives two days before the company's annual two-week shutdown began. The transfer took place a few days after the return to work. A tribunal upheld the GMB's complaint of failure to give information long enough before the transfer. In the light of the annual shutdown, during which around 90 per cent of the union members were not at work, there had been insufficient time for proper consultation. The tribunal awarded three weeks' pay to each of the union's affected members, an amount that the EAT agreed on appeal was 'just right'

- **Todd v Strain and ors** (above): the EAT reduced the employment tribunal's award from 13 to seven weeks' pay per employee on the basis that the failure was not at the most 'extreme end of the scale so as to justify a maximum award'. The transferor had not arranged the election of employee representatives, but had informed a group of approximately one third of the affected employees of the impending sale and confirmed that their jobs were safe, the intention being that they would inform their colleagues of the position. The transferor had also made clear that the transferee would not be reducing staff numbers or changing terms and conditions

- **GMB v Eastleigh Borough Council and anor** (above): the transferor had provided all the information to the employees, albeit in instalments and not all of it in writing. The tribunal found that oral discussions with the employees, forewarning them of the inevitability of a transfer, were sufficient to satisfy Reg 13. However, the transferor had not provided information in writing of the measures that the transferee proposed to take; namely, to change the depot from which the employees worked. As that failure was not deliberate, and deemed to be a technical failure only, each employee was awarded £200

- **Commercial Motors (Wales) Ltd v Howley** EAT 0491/11: the EAT upheld the employment tribunal's award of 13 weeks' pay where there had been no attempt to invite employees to elect employee representatives.

Which employer is liable? It has always been clear – and this remains the case **8.97** – that where the transferee fails to inform or consult in accordance with Reg 13, it is the transferee, and not the transferor, that will be liable in respect of the

591

default. However, the situation is more complicated where it is the transferor who fails to inform or consult.

8.98 *Joint and several liability.* Under the 1981 Regulations it was unclear whether the transferor or the transferee should be liable where the transferor failed to inform or consult, prior to the transfer, in respect of transferring employees. The debate in this regard focused on Reg 5(2) of the 1981 Regulations (now, with minor changes, Reg 4(2) of the 2006 Regulations), which provided that 'on the completion of a relevant transfer (a) all the transferor's rights, powers, duties and liabilities under or in connection with [a contract of a transferring employee] shall be transferred by virtue of this Regulation to the transferee; and (b) anything done before the transfer is completed by or in relation to the transferor in respect of that contract or a person employed in that undertaking or part shall be deemed to have been done by or in relation to the transferee'. The key question was whether liability for the transferor's failure to inform or consult was capable of transferring to the transferee under this provision. In the following two cases, the EAT reached different conclusions:

- **Transport and General Workers' Union v James McKinnon, JR (Haulage) Ltd and ors** 2001 ICR 1281, EAT: the EAT held that the transferor's liability to pay compensation for its failure to inform and consult representatives prior to a relevant transfer did not pass to the transferee under old Reg 5(2). TUPE should be construed in a way that ensures that a transferor has an incentive to comply with the information and consultation obligations imposed upon it during the transfer process. This required the conclusion that the transferor would retain the liability to pay compensation for its own failure to consult

- **Alamo Group (Europe) Ltd v Tucker and anor** 2003 ICR 829, EAT: the EAT held that where a transferor fails to comply with its duty to inform or consult under TUPE, liability for that failure will pass to the transferee by virtue of old Reg 5(2). Had the legislature intended to exclude liability in respect of the obligation to inform and consult from the scope of Reg 5, then it would have expressly done so.

Recognising that there was conflicting case law on this point, the Government wished to make the position clear when drafting the 2006 Regulations. Its chosen solution, found in Reg 15(9), was to make the transferor and transferee jointly and severally liable – that is, both collectively and individually liable – where a transferor has failed to inform or consult in respect of affected employees. In deciding upon this course of action, the Government, in the 2005 consultation document, reiterated the EAT's concern in the TGWU case that if liability were to pass wholly to the transferee, there would be little or no statutory incentive for the transferor to comply with the information and consultation requirements.

The 2006 version of the BIS Guide explained how the new system of joint and **8.99** several liability was intended to work. It noted that it would be for the appropriate representatives or individual employees seeking redress to choose whether to take action against the transferor, the transferee or both. Furthermore, a party who was a sole respondent in such an action would have the possibility of joining others who were jointly liable in respect of the same liability. When this occurred, it would be for the tribunal to apportion the compensation between the two respondents fairly. Alternatively, the Guide continued, if judgment was given against a sole respondent, that respondent might be able to recover a contribution from others who were jointly liable in respect of the same liability by suing them in the civil courts where liability would then be apportioned fairly in line with the provisions of the Civil Liability (Contribution) Act 1978.

It has since been held that the 2006 Guide was wrong to suggest that a tribunal is able to apportion compensation between two respondents and this guidance has been omitted from the 2014 version of the Guide. In Country Weddings Ltd v Crossman and ors EAT 0535/12 the EAT stated that the suggestion that tribunals may apportion liability themselves is incorrect. The terms of Reg 15(9) are unequivocal and the EAT's decision in Todd v Strain and ors 2011 IRLR 11, EAT, is clear authority requiring tribunals to order compensation for breach of Reg 13 on a joint and several basis. If liability is to be apportioned between the transferor and transferee(s), it must be done by the ordinary courts under the 1978 Act. (The same approach has been taken to the analogous provisions under Ss.188 and 189 TULR(C)A – see London Borough of Barnet v Unison EAT 0191/13.)

To our knowledge there has been no High Court case where a transferor or **8.100** transferee has sought to apportion liability and it is doubtful whether in fact such a claim could be brought given that employment tribunals have exclusive jurisdiction to determine complaints under Reg 12. By way of analogy, in Brennan and ors v Sunderland City Council and ors 2012 ICR 1183, EAT, an equal pay case, the EAT stated that there was no power to apportion liability under the Equal Pay Act 1970 (now consolidated into the Equality Act 2010) either in the tribunal or in the High Court. However, if a court is empowered to apportion liability, it is likely to focus on the extent of each respondent's responsibility for the damage in question. Since joint and several liability only arises in respect of the *transferor's* failure to inform and consult, and not the transferee's, one would imagine that the transferor will usually be required to pay most if not all of the compensation awarded. (Note that, regardless of how liability is apportioned by the court, the transferor and transferee may well have agreed between themselves, by way of indemnities, who will actually bear the cost for any failure on the part of the transferor to inform or consult – see Chapter 11, 'Practical aspects of transfers', under 'Indemnities', for details.)

593

Before moving away from Reg 15(9) we should point out one rather odd aspect of it. As we have seen, the debate under the 1981 Regulations centred on whether liability for the transferor's failure to inform or consult passed to the transferee under Reg 5(2). Whatever the right answer to that question was, it was abundantly clear that such a transfer of liability could only be possible where the transferor's failure was in respect of the employees who transferred to the transferee.

8.101 But, as stated earlier in this chapter under 'Affected employees', it is not necessarily only the transferring workforce in respect of which the transferor is obliged to inform/consult. The transferor may well be under a duty to inform/consult in respect of members of its workforce who will not transfer to the transferee, but will nevertheless be affected in some way by the transfer situation.

It was clear under the 1981 Regulations that the transferor would itself be liable if it failed to inform/consult in respect of non-transferring employees. And this clearly makes sense. However, Reg 15(9), which provides for the joint and several liability of the transferor and transferee, does not distinguish between the transferor's failure to inform/consult in respect of the transferring employees and its failure to inform/consult in respect of the employees whom it is to retain. In other words, Reg 15(9) provides that whenever a transferor fails to comply with its TUPE information and consultation obligations, it will be jointly and severally liable with the transferee for the compensation awarded. So, in theory, the transferee could be liable for the transferor's failure to inform/consult employees in respect of whom the transferee will never have an employment relationship. This cannot have been the Government's intention and hopefully common sense will prevail.

8.102 *Transferee's failure to provide information.* Note that there is one situation in which the transferee could be solely liable for the transferor's failure to inform transferring employees. Reg 15(8)(b) states that where the transferor (after giving notice to the transferee in accordance with Reg 15(5) – see 'Employers' defences' above) shows that its failure to inform was due to the transferee's failure to provide the information specified in Reg 13(4) (see 'Duty to inform' above), the tribunal may order the transferee to pay appropriate compensation to such descriptions of affected employees as may be specified in the award.

However, the application of this provision is conditional on the transferor being or remaining a party to the proceedings and the complaint having been upheld against the transferor. In Allen and ors v Morrisons Facilities Services Ltd 2014 ICR 792, EAT, the claimants brought various claims alleging breaches of the information and consultation duties under Reg 13. However, they settled, or withdrew, their claims against the transferor. The EAT held that an order may only be made against the transferee if the tribunal has upheld a complaint against the transferor and the transferor has shown that the transferee failed to perform its obligations under Reg 13(4). There is no mechanism by which transferred employees can bring the claim against the transferee directly in relation to its failure to provide the transferor with information before the transfer. The EAT noted that Reg 13(4) imposes no obligation on either the transferor or the transferee as regards their employees. Reg 13(4) requires the transferee to give the transferor such information as will enable it to perform the duty placed on it by Reg 13(2)(d), i.e. to inform appropriate representatives of the measures in connection with the transfer the transferor envisages the transferee will take in relation to any affected employees who will become employees of the transferee after the transfer. The EAT rejected the argument that the Acquired Rights Directive requires the Regulations to be interpreted so as to provide for a direct claim by employees against the transferee. The only route for affected employees of a transferor to obtain compensation from a transferee who had failed to provide information would be to pursue a claim against the transferor for breach of Reg 13(2)(d), for the transferee to be made a party to the proceedings pursuant to Reg 15(5), and for the tribunal to find the allegations well founded. In the present case, as the transferred employees had withdrawn their claims against the transferor before the claim against the transferee was heard, the tribunal was in no position to make the necessary findings that would enable an award to be made under Reg 15(8)(b).

8.103 *Failure to comply with compensation order.* If a tribunal makes an award of compensation under Reg 15 and the employer in question fails to pay it, either wholly or in part, the affected employee concerned (as opposed to an appropriate representative) may complain to a tribunal – Reg 15(10). If the tribunal upholds such a complaint, it must order the employer to pay the complainant(s) the amount owed – Reg 15(11). The combined effect of Reg 15(9) and Reg 15(11) means that the order can be made against the transferor or the transferee jointly and severally.

The time limit for bringing a Reg 15(10) claim is three months after the date of the tribunal's order, or within such further period as the tribunal considers reasonable where it is satisfied that it was not reasonably practicable for the complaint to be presented within this time frame – Reg 15(12). (The time limit may also be extended to allow for early conciliation – Reg 15(13).)

8.104 The time limit in Reg 15(12) may be extended where there is an appeal. In Dillon and ors v Todd and anor EATS 0010/11 the EAT held that the time limit began running from the date of a successful appeal against a tribunal's order, not from the date of the original order. The appeal had succeeded on questions of quantum (the EAT reduced the award from 13 weeks' pay to seven) and scope (the EAT added a jointly liable respondent). The EAT had, in effect, exercised the tribunal's power to make an order, which it was permitted to do under S.35 of the Employment Tribunals Act 1996. The order made by the EAT could therefore be treated as 'the tribunal's order' referred to in Reg 15(12) for the purpose of calculating the limitation period. The EAT did not speculate

595

on what the outcome would have been had the appeal failed but in these circumstances the EAT has no cause to exercise the tribunal's power to make an order and so the only date capable of setting time running would be the date of the original order. Thus, it would perhaps be prudent for employees who have not been paid to lodge a Reg 15(10) complaint even if the order is under appeal. The complaint could be stayed while the appeal is determined.

It should be noted that even this simple scheme can have bizarre consequences. Reg 15(9) states that 'the transferee shall be jointly and severally liable with the transferor in respect of compensation payable under sub-paragraph 8(a) [the transferor's failure to inform or consult] *or paragraph 11*' (our stress). Paragraph 11 – that is, Reg 15(11) – is the provision under which the tribunal shall order the transferor or transferee, as applicable, to pay the sum owed where the employer in question has failed to comply with a tribunal's order for compensation.

8.105 Why is this bizarre? Consider, for example, the following situation: the transferee recognises, prior to a relevant transfer, that members of its existing workforce (as opposed to the transferring workforce) may be affected by that transfer, rendering them 'affected employees' for the purposes of the TUPE information and consultation rules. It fails miserably to inform and consult in respect of those employees, whose representatives bring a tribunal claim seeking compensation. The tribunal upholds the claim and makes a compensatory award, which the transferee fails to pay. The employees themselves then bring a claim under Reg 15(10), pointing out that the transferee has failed to pay, and the tribunal rules in their favour. Accordingly, in line with Reg 15(11), the tribunal orders the transferee to pay what is due. At this point – that is, at the point where compensation becomes payable under Reg 15(11) – according to Reg 15(9) the transferee and the transferor become jointly and severally liable for the amount due. This is so even though the transferor has at no point had any relationship with the employees in question and was not liable for the original award that the transferee failed to pay. This, again, is surely not what the Government intended. And, again, we hope (and indeed imagine) that tribunals will not apply the letter of the law strictly in this regard.

9 Transnational issues

The increasingly global nature of the economy means it is common for business **9.1** acquisitions and outsourcing exercises to span more than one country. It is not unusual, for example, to read that a call-centre or IT support function is being outsourced to India, where there is a surfeit of highly qualified English-speakers available for a fraction of the cost of their UK counterparts. Of course, an outsourcing exercise such as this is extremely unlikely to result in the transfer of the relevant UK workforce to India. The companies involved in such exercises tend to proceed on the basis that the Transfer of Undertakings (Protection of Employment) Regulations 2006 SI 2006/246 (TUPE) do not apply, and simply treat the UK-based workforce as redundant.

It is not necessarily the case, however, that the TUPE regime has no part to play with regard to cross-border transfers. Thus, an employer's simple assumption that the Regulations do not apply in such circumstances could potentially lead to legal difficulties. This might particularly be so where the transfer in question takes place from the UK to another EU Member State. After all, employees might well be willing to move from one Member State to another, and there would be no impediment to their doing so as free movement of workers is a fundamental aspect of the function of the EU.

Despite the fact that cross-border transfers are becoming more common, **9.2** however, neither the EU Acquired Rights Directive (No.2001/23) ('the Acquired Rights Directive') nor the TUPE Regulations are clear as to whether their provisions apply to such transfers or, if they do apply, what exactly this might mean. In this chapter, we examine the wording of the Directive and the Regulations (so far as there is any) in this regard, and provide a brief analysis of some of the issues involved. We should point out, however, that this is simply an overview. A detailed exposition of the principles of private international law that might come into play if the Directive/Regulations do apply to cross-border transfers is beyond the scope of this Handbook. For further details, see the document prepared for the European Commission by the CMS Employment Practice Area Group, entitled 'Study on the application of Directive 2001/23/EC to cross-border transfers of undertakings' ('the 2006 Study'), available on the European Commission website.

597

Also in this chapter, turning to an issue that can arise with regard to transfers taking place within the UK, we consider the extent of the protection bestowed by TUPE upon employees who spend some or all of their time working overseas.

9.3 Transfers from and to United Kingdom

As stated in the introduction to this chapter, neither the Acquired Rights Directive nor the TUPE Regulations contain much information as to their application to cross-border transfers. And, perhaps owing to many employers and employees being wary of taking the transfer rules into account where a cross-border relocation takes place (a wariness presumably fuelled partly by uncertainty), there has been virtually no case law on the subject until the EAT's decision in Holis Metal Industries Ltd v GMB and anor 2008 ICR 464, EAT, which is helpful to some degree but unfortunately of persuasive authority only. This case is discussed under 'Application of TUPE Regulations' below.

Below, we examine what the Directive and TUPE do manage to say on the matter.

9.4 Application of Directive to cross-border transfers

Each EU Member State and member of the European Economic Area (EEA) is required to implement the Acquired Rights Directive. But the Directive says little as to whether or how its rules apply to transfers between Member States, or to transfers from a Member State to a country not covered by the Directive.

9.5 Scope of Directive. The Acquired Rights Directive states that it applies 'where and in so far as the undertaking, business or part of the undertaking or business to be transferred is situated within the territorial scope of the Treaty [of Rome]' – Article 1(2). Thus, provided that the business to be transferred is located within the EU, the application of the Directive does not depend on the transferee also being located in the EU.

This is the view taken by the CMS Employment Practice Area Group in the 2006 Study, referred to in the introduction to this chapter. As to the Directive's scope, the Study states that 'the provisions of the Directive cover each transfer in the boundaries of the Member States having signed or acceded to the Treaty establishing the European Community, i.e., cross-border transfers from one Member State to another... are subject to the Directive. Moreover, since the Directive only refers to the place of origin of the business unit "to be transferred" and gives no regard to the destination of the transfer, the Directive is – according to its wording – also applicable to transfers outside the territory of the European Union (EU).' The Directive does not apply, however, 'where the undertaking is situated outside the EU originally, even if the transferor, transferee or both of them are domiciled in the EU'.

Transferring entity must retain its identity. So, it seems that the Acquired **9.6** Rights Directive is *capable* of applying to cross-border transfers. But before highlighting some of the practical difficulties its application might cause, there is another important matter to consider. That is, regardless of the theoretical scope of the Directive to apply to such transfers, its provisions will only apply in practice where there is a transfer of an 'economic entity which retains its identity' (Article 1(1)(b)) – see Chapter 1, 'Identifying a "relevant transfer"', under 'Business transfers – when does an economic entity retain its identity?'.

It is therefore pertinent to ask whether it is possible for an entity to retain its identity, and thus to be covered by the Directive, where the entity moves from one country to another. If this is not possible, then the debate with regard to the application of the Directive to cross-border transfers will be nipped in the bud. Unfortunately, there is not as yet any ECJ case law on this point. The case of Merckx and anor v Ford Motors Co (Belgium) SA 1997 ICR 352, ECJ, is helpful to an extent, in so far as the ECJ confirmed that the fact that an economic entity operates at a different location post-transfer does not necessarily mean that its identity has not been retained. But this case was concerned not with a cross-border transfer, but with a transfer taking place within Belgium.

So, can an entity retain its identity when it transfers to a different country? In **9.7** order to answer this question we must first return briefly to the seminal ECJ case of Spijkers v Gebroeders Benedik Abattoir CV and anor 1986 2 CMLR 296, ECJ, discussed at length in Chapter 1, 'Identifying a "relevant transfer"', under 'Business transfers'. In Spijkers, the European Court set out a number of factors (none of which was to be decisive) that a court or tribunal should consider in order to determine whether an economic entity has retained its identity. These factors included, for example, the type of business or undertaking, the transfer or otherwise of tangible assets such as buildings and stocks, whether the majority of the staff are taken over by the new employer, the transfer or otherwise of customers and the degree of similarity of activities before and after the transfer.

In many cross-border relocation situations, we imagine that certain key factors of the Spijkers 'retention of identity' test will not be present. Often, neither tangible assets nor the transferor's workforce will relocate. In such circumstances, the Acquired Rights Directive is unlikely to apply, and the relocation will be viewed as a business closure rather than as a transfer of an undertaking. In the UK, this would result in a redundancy situation.

Nevertheless, there will be *some* cross-border transfer situations in which, in **9.8** essence, the Spijkers 'retention of identity' test will be fulfilled. Where this is so, the 2006 Study takes the view that the fact that the entity in question is transferred to a different country will not preclude the Acquired Rights Directive's application. It states that where, aside from the fact that the transfer has an international aspect, the transferring entity retains its identity, 'the relocation of a business to another country constitutes a transfer of business within the meaning of the Directive. To this [extent] the question of distance of the relocation is of minor importance.' This view is backed up by one of the few decided cases concerning cross-border transfers, the 'Englischer Dienst' case (Hamburg Labour Appeal Court – 22 May 2003). There, the Court held that the transfer of a German news agency to Ireland did constitute a relevant transfer under German business transfer law. The Court had particular regard to the distance between the transferor and the transferee, but stated: 'Although great geographical distance generally militates against the preservation of economic entity, this is not the case here because the activities of news editing and news dissemination are determined much more by the information systems used than by the location of the establishment.' In the event, the claimants were able to succeed with their claims in respect of their dismissals by the transferor employer.

The 2006 Study does acknowledge, however, an alternative proposition that the application of the Acquired Rights Directive to cross-border transfers 'might be doubtful because of the radical changes that would necessarily result from a cross-border transfer (change of country and general language, change in the legal, economic and social context), threaten per se the identity of the transferred economic entity'. This, the Study notes, was the view taken by the French Supreme Court in respect of a relocation from France to Brazil.

9.9 On balance, we suggest, in line with the Englischer Dienst decision, that there will be at least some cross-border transfers with regard to which the 'retention of identity' test will be satisfied. We now turn to some of the difficulties that the application of the Acquired Rights Directive to such a transfer might pose.

9.10 **Difficulties arising from Directive's application.** Although it might well be the case that the Acquired Rights Directive is capable of applying to a cross-border transfer, its application in practice would lead to many difficult legal and practical conundrums.

As the 2006 Study notes, the Directive simply provides a framework with regard to the law on the transfer of undertakings, meaning that Member States have a wide margin of discretion regarding implementation. It follows that the transfer rules applicable in different countries vary quite considerably, and that there are no uniform rules that apply throughout the EU. Moreover, the transfers law of some countries (such as Spain) expressly covers EU transfers into those countries, whereas the law of others (such as the UK, as we shall see below) does not. All this raises complex questions as to which country's law might apply to one or more of the parties at the various stages of the transfer process, and, indeed, how parties in different locations might go about bringing and enforcing claims. These are questions that, in the absence of any assistance from the Directive, can only be answered with reference to the complex rules of private international law.

Furthermore, the purpose of the Directive is, in a nutshell, to preserve acquired **9.11** employment rights. However, just as the laws of the Member States differ with regard to the application of the Directive, they differ – and even more so – with regard to employment rights generally. So how, in reality, will employment rights be preserved following a cross-border transfer? For example, the TUPE Regulations preserve and augment the transferring employees' right not to be unfairly dismissed under the Employment Rights Act 1996 (ERA). But how will such rights conceivably be maintained where employees of a UK operation transfer to a country whose dismissal law is completely different?

Moreover, consider the situation where employees who transfer have their pay adjusted to reflect the cost of living in the country to which they have been relocated. Would a reduction in pay in such circumstances be contrary to the transfer rules and thus void? As the 2006 Study states: 'A remuneration calculated as adequate for a work assignment in the City of London will certainly not mirror the adequate remuneration for an assignment in Naples and vice versa. A rule of law that does not consider this and does compel employers to maintain the remuneration agreed upon in the employee's contract concluded at the employee's place of origin, does not foster mobility and is unfair, because it treats different matters the same.'

The 2006 Study proposals. Owing to the Acquired Rights Directive's silence **9.12** with regard to cross-border transfers, and to the numerous difficulties this silence gives rise to, the 2006 Study was prepared for the European Commission by the CMS Employment Practice Area Group. It begins by examining the different ways in which Member States have implemented the Directive. It then considers how 'existing legal instruments of international private law' (some of which we touch upon under 'Enforcement of cross-border transfer claims within EU' below) might provide solutions to some of the jurisdictional and conflict of laws problems arising. The Study concludes by setting out proposals as to how the Directive might be amended in order 'to establish a seamless legal framework for cross-border transfers', which might well form the basis of any amendment to the Directive ultimately proposed by the Commission.

We do not intend to go into any great depth about the Study's proposals. However, some of the main ones suggest that the Acquired Rights Directive should:

- provide either that it can apply to transfers from one Member State to another or that it only applies to transfers within a Member State. If the latter option is taken, specific rules relating to cross-border situations could be drawn up

- set out whether or not a Member State's national law should cover transfers into that state

- provide that the law of the Member State applicable to the transferor will apply to define the central concepts of 'employee' and 'representative', determine what will transfer, and determine the extent to which the transferor must provide information to the transferee

- determine that employees are not deprived of their rights and remedies in connection with a termination of/substantial change to their contracts where they either object to or opt in to a cross-border transfer

- provide that the place of work where the employee has effectively and regularly rendered his services shall determine the jurisdiction in which he or she can sue the transferee – that is, the jurisdiction in which he or she worked for the transferor, unless the employee has started to work at the transferee's site

- introduce rules aimed at determining the law applicable to employment contracts where there is a conflict of laws between Member States, and

- determine whether a change of place of work can, in fact, be changed automatically in connection with the transfer of the business.

9.13 Following the 2006 Study proposals, however, there has been a distinct lack of progress. No further action has yet been taken to amend the Directive, or to introduce specific rules covering cross-border transfers. The uncertainties over the Directive's application in cross-border transfers will therefore continue.

9.14 Application of TUPE Regulations

As we outlined in Chapter 1, 'Identifying a "relevant transfer"', the TUPE Regulations expressly apply where, prior to the transfer, the entity or group of employees to transfer is situated in the UK. They are far more ambivalent, however, on the issue of how they apply when a UK-based entity or group is transferred abroad.

The relevant provisions in this regard are contained in Reg 3(1). Reg 3(1)(a) stipulates that 'these Regulations apply to a transfer of an undertaking, business or part of an undertaking or business situated immediately before the transfer in the United Kingdom to another person where there is a transfer of an economic entity which retains its identity'. Then, Reg 3(1)(b) and 3(3) extends the application of the Regulations (beyond the scope of the Acquired Rights Directive) to service provision changes where, among other things, 'immediately before the service provision change there is an organised grouping of employees situated in Great Britain'.

9.15 Employees in Northern Ireland are not covered by the service provision change rules in the TUPE Regulations, but they are provided with an equivalent level of protection by the Service Provision Change (Protection of Employment) Regulations (Northern Ireland) 2006 SI 2006/177, Reg 3 of which largely mirrors Reg 3(1)(b) and 3(3) TUPE, in respect of organised groupings of employees situated in Northern Ireland.

Regulation 3(4)(b) TUPE emphasises the mandatory nature of the Regulations in respect of transfers falling within Reg 3(1), providing that the rules will apply 'notwithstanding (i) that the transfer... is governed... by the law of a country or territory outside the United Kingdom... (ii) that the employment of persons employed in the undertaking... is governed by any such law'.

Transfers from UK. There has been much discussion, but precious little **9.16** agreement, as to whether all this means that the TUPE Regulations are capable of applying to a transaction resulting in a business/service moving overseas. One argument against TUPE applying to such a transfer is based on the presumption that UK legislation does not have extra-territorial effect unless it expressly provides otherwise. Some believe that the Regulations do not do enough to rebut this presumption, in that they do not expressly refer to their application to cross-border situations.

In addition, those opposed to the application of transfer rules in such circumstances point out that this would not be practical, post-transfer. For example, Reg 4(2) provides that upon a relevant transfer 'all the transferor's rights, powers, duties and liabilities' in connection with transferring employees' contracts (and this includes UK statutory employment rights) shall be taken on by the transferee employer. However, the transferee's country might well have a very different statutory employment regime, meaning that the transferring employees' statutory rights would almost certainly change. Moreover, it might prove difficult for jurisdictional reasons, which we discuss below, for any employees who have transferred abroad to succeed with claims against their foreign employer under TUPE.

On the other hand, those who argue that TUPE can apply to cross-border **9.17** transfers point out, as we did above, that Reg 3(1) requires only that the transferring entity or group of employees be situated in the UK prior to the transfer. Since the rule stipulates no requirement as to where that entity or group is to be transferred, the argument goes, the clearly stated intention of the Regulations is that they can apply to cross-border transfers. Proponents of this argument tend also to point to the similar wording of the Acquired Rights Directive, contending that it is intended to apply to at least those cross-border transfers involving Member States. They accept that there are practical difficulties with bringing claims post-transfer, but argue that it would be wrong to consider these in conjunction with the question of whether the Regulations are capable of applying. The fact of TUPE's application to the transfer situation itself should be sorted out first, and the practical difficulties of such application examined afterwards.

Moreover, those who believe that TUPE applies in such circumstances argue that, in reality, such a transfer does not even require the extra-territorial application of the Regulations. This argument proceeds thus: under TUPE, the transferee inherits the transferring workforce under their pre-transfer terms and conditions. Generally, those terms will involve the workers performing their jobs in the UK. So, the transfer, in essence, takes place within the UK (and is thus covered by TUPE), and the employees only move abroad as a result of the transfer.

9.18 Although there has been much theorising on the application of TUPE to transfers from the UK, the only appellate case to have considered the matters arising is Holis Metal Industries Ltd v GMB and anor 2008 ICR 464, EAT. N Ltd ran a track, pole and blind manufacturing business from a factory in Tamworth. In February 2006 the company informed its staff that the track and pole part of the business was to be purchased by H Ltd, an Israeli company, on 9 April of that year. The track and pole employees were told that, unless they agreed to relocate to Israel, they would be made redundant following the sale. In the event, none of the employees wished to relocate so they were dismissed. For administrative reasons, the redundancy payments were made through N Ltd rather than through the Israeli purchaser. The GMB, a union recognised by N Ltd for collective bargaining purposes, brought a claim before an employment tribunal alleging that both N Ltd and H Ltd had breached the duty under Reg 13 TUPE to consult employee representatives about a relevant transfer. In response, H Ltd applied to have the claim struck out on the basis that the TUPE Regulations did not apply to what it termed an 'off-shoring situation'.

An employment judge refused the strike-out application – a decision subsequently upheld on appeal. The EAT (His Honour Judge Ansell sitting alone) decided that, in this particular case, both the business transfer and the redundancy dismissals took place within the UK. As such, the question of the application of TUPE to employees of a business transferred outside the UK was, strictly speaking, not a matter that needed to be determined for the purposes of this particular case. However, HHJ Ansell did address the extra-territorial issue. He held that 'the wording of both the [Acquired Rights Directive] and Regulation 3 is precise in setting the application of the regulation to transfers of undertakings situated immediately before the transfer in the UK. Set against the purpose of protecting the rights of workers in the event of change of employer... a purposeful approach requires that those employees should be protected even if the transfer is to be across borders outside the EU. It is not a case of either the UK or the EU seeking to legislate outside their jurisdictions without good reason.' He went on to say that 'the service provision changes brought into the 2006 Regulations, where again the only limitation is that there should have been an organised group of employees situated in Great Britain immediately before the service provision change, is clearly aimed at the modern outsourcing of service provision, particularly call centres, whether inside or outside the EU'.

Given the Holis decision, there is now some judicial guidance, albeit of **9.19** persuasive authority only, that TUPE can potentially apply to a transfer from the UK to a non-EU entity in the event that, upon transfer, the undertaking does not remain in the UK. The impact of the Holis decision may be limited in practice, as a key component in determining whether there has been a TUPE transfer under Reg 3(1)(a) is whether the economic entity transferred retains its identity (see Chapter 1, 'Identifying a "relevant transfer"', under 'Business transfers – when does an economic entity retain its identity?')

Transfers to UK. As we have seen, in order for a relevant transfer to occur for **9.20** the purposes of TUPE, the transferring business must be situated in the UK immediately before the transfer – Reg 3(1)(a). Alternatively, for a transfer by way of an SPC to occur, the group of employees must be situated in Great Britain (for the purposes of Reg 3(1)(b) TUPE) or Northern Ireland (for the purposes of Reg 3 of the Service Provision Change (Protection of Employment) Regulations (Northern Ireland) 2006 SI 2006/177). Thus, it is clear that these Regulations do not apply (regardless of whether the Acquired Rights Directive wishes them to) to transfers into the UK from elsewhere, whether or not the business in question is transferred from a fellow Member State.

It is possible that employees moving to the UK might glean protection from the transfers law of their own country, but their bringing and enforcing claims against the UK employer in that regard will depend on the nature of the law in question, and on some of the principles touched on under 'Enforcement of cross-border transfer claims within EU' below.

Difficulties arising from TUPE's application. Even if one concludes that the **9.21** TUPE Regulations can apply to a cross-border transfer, in practical terms, a 'place of work' redundancy situation will normally arise in this type of scenario given that the statutory definition of redundancy in S.139(1) ERA includes the situations where the employer 'intends to cease to carry on the business in the place where the employee was... employed' or where the requirements of the business 'for employees to carry out work of a particular kind in the place where the employee was employed by the employer have ceased or diminished or are expected to [do so]'. Employees are often paid redundancy payments on this basis and any further complications in respect of TUPE are ignored or overlooked. But while the lack of a body of case law on cross-border transfers suggests that parties are often happy to assume that TUPE does not apply when an undertaking, or part of one, moves abroad, employers would be unwise simply to put their heads in the sand and ignore the Regulations in such situations. If TUPE does apply, the common practice of the transferor making the affected employees redundant becomes risky, as any dismissals effected in connection with the transfer are likely to be automatically unfair under Reg 7.

Also, employers might fall foul of the additional information and consultation obligations that TUPE imposes.

As for transferring employees, they will rarely want to follow their jobs abroad and will be likely to take redundancy or a similar settlement where offered. However, if negotiations are not going well – perhaps because their current employer insists that TUPE applies – the employees might find themselves in a tricky situation. They are not, however, without options. If the Regulations do apply, as a last resort they could 'object' to the transfer under Reg 4(7) and argue that the forthcoming move abroad would amount to a fundamental breach of contract entitling them to resign and claim constructive dismissal under common law principles, or to a substantial change in terms and conditions to their material detriment, entitling them to resign and claim unfair dismissal under Reg 4(9). Case law including Humphreys v University of Oxford and anor 2000 ICR 405, CA, suggests that, in such circumstances, employees can claim against the UK-based transferor, thus avoiding the tricky problem of enforcing UK law against the foreign transferee.

9.22 Employees who wish to bring claims against the foreign transferee in another EU Member State will need to consider international laws. We now turn to look, briefly, at how some of these matters might be sorted out.

9.23 ## Enforcement of cross-border transfer claims within EU

In this section we touch on some of the principles that might apply where an employee involved in a cross-border transfer wishes to bring claims against the transferor or, perhaps more problematically, the transferee. At the outset we should point out that we do not seek to provide a thorough exposition of what is an extremely complicated area of law, but intend simply to give a flavour of the types of issue that might crop up. We focus our attention on transfers from the UK to other EU Member States, in that, as discussed in the section 'Transfers from and to United Kingdom', under 'Application of TUPE Regulations – transfers from UK' above, such transfers are arguably capable of attracting the application of TUPE.

Before attempting to reach some conclusions, it is necessary to consider the scope of:

- the Recast Brussels Regulation, which deals with matters of international jurisdiction within the EU, and

- the Rome Convention, the terms of which determine which Member State's law applies to an employment contract.

Recast Brussels Regulation 9.24

The Recast Brussels Regulation (Council Regulation No.1215/2012) – which applies in respect of all proceedings commenced, and judgments handed down, on or after 10 January 2015 – sets out mandatory rules as to jurisdiction and the enforcement of judgments within the EU. Whereas its predecessor – the Brussels I Regulation (Council Regulation No.44/2001) – did not apply to Denmark, the Recast Brussels Regulation now applies to all EU Member States.

Articles 20–23 are concerned with jurisdiction over individual contracts of employment. Article 21(1) provides for a default position whereby a claim must be brought in the courts of the country where the respondent employer is domiciled. Article 63(1) provides that the domicile of the employer will be where its 'statutory seat', 'central administration' or 'principal place of business' is located. Article 60(2) further provides specifically for the UK, Cyprus and Ireland that 'statutory seat' means 'the registered office or, where there is no such office anywhere, the place of incorporation or, where there is no such place anywhere, the place under the law of which the formation took place'. If the employer is domiciled outside the EU but has a 'branch, agency or establishment' in a Member State, that Member State will be deemed to be the employer's domicile by virtue of Article 20(2).

Article 21(2) of the Recast Brussels Regulation provides, however, that the **9.25** employee can choose instead to institute proceedings against the employer in the courts of the Member State where the employee 'habitually carries out his work' or where he or she 'last did so'. If the employee does not or did not carry out his or her work habitually in any one country, he or she may commence proceedings in the state where the business that engaged him or her is or was situated.

The Recast Brussels Regulation goes on (in Articles 36–57) to set out formalities which, if complied with by the claimant, will result in a judgment against an employer being recognised and enforced in another Member State.

Rome Convention 9.26

With regard to disputes within the EU, the question of which country's law will cover an employment relationship (as opposed to the question of which country a claim should be brought in) will be determined with reference to the 1980 Rome Convention on the law applicable to contractual obligation. This was implemented into UK law by the Contracts (Applicable Law) Act 1990.

The basic rule of the Convention is that the parties can choose (a choice that must be expressed on the face of the contract or otherwise demonstrated with reasonable certainty) which law should govern the contract – Article 3. However, the parties' choice of law cannot have the effect of depriving the employee of the protection afforded by the 'mandatory rules' of the country with which the contract is otherwise most closely connected. So, for example, an employee working in Germany will not be deprived of certain German employment rights simply because the parties have decided that UK law will apply to his or her employment contract.

9.27 In the absence of a choice of law, Article 6 of the Convention provides that a contract is to be governed by the law of the country in which the employee habitually carries out his or her work, even though he or she may be temporarily employed in another country. If the employee does not habitually work in any one country, the contract is governed by the law of the country in which the place of business that employs him or her is situated, or the law of another country if, in the circumstances of the case, the contract is more closely connected with that other country.

9.28 Dismissal by transferor prior to or upon transfer
The usual ploy adopted in cross-border transfers is for the transferor to proceed as if the employment of the relevant workforce is terminated upon the transfer by reason of redundancy. This will work perfectly well until somewhere along the line one of the parties to the transfer decides that there is no redundancy situation and that it is more advantageous to argue that TUPE applies. For example, the transferor might decline to make redundancy payments on the basis that the workforce should transfer to the transferee; or an employee might wish to pursue an unfair dismissal claim in the hope of obtaining compensation. To an extent, this risk can be mitigated by including appropriate guarantees and warranties in the transfer agreement – see Chapter 11, 'Practical aspects of transfers'. Nevertheless, there are bound to be circumstances where there are no such contractual protections to fall back on.

With that in mind, we now consider whether an employee involved in a cross-border transfer situation from the UK to another EU Member State might claim unfair dismissal where: (i) he or she is treated as redundant by the UK transferor upon the transfer, (ii) the transferor does not treat the employee as redundant and the transferee refuses to take the employee on, and/or (iii) the employee is not treated as redundant by the transferor and the transferee does wish to take him or her on.

9.29 Employee treated as redundant. In situation (i) – where the transferor purports to make the employee redundant – the employee might seek to bring unfair dismissal claims in a UK employment tribunal against both the transferor and the transferee. In this regard, we should make the following points:

- presuming that the TUPE Regulations applied to the cross-border transaction in question, the redundancy dismissal would be automatically unfair owing to Reg 7(1) (see Chapter 4, 'Unfair dismissal', under 'Automatically unfair dismissal') unless the transferor carried it out for an 'economic, technical or organisational reason entailing changes in the workforce' (see Chapter 4 under 'Dismissals potentially fair for an "ETO reason"')

- if the transferor can establish such an 'ETO reason' then, so long as the redundancy was carried out fairly, there would be no unfair dismissal. If the transferor can establish an ETO reason but the redundancy dismissal was carried out unfairly, then the dismissal would be unfair for the purposes of the ERA, and liability for that dismissal would lie with the transferor

- case law has established that a transferor cannot dismiss for the transferee's ETO reason (see Chapter 4, 'Unfair dismissal', under "Dismissals potentially fair for an "ETO reason" – transferor cannot dismiss for transferee's ETO reason'). This makes it unlikely that an ETO reason for dismissal could be established under the test as set down in Berriman v Delabole Slate Ltd 1985 ICR 546, CA, since that test requires a change in job numbers or job functions, and any such changes would only apply in respect of the transferee. The transferor might, however, be able to rely on Reg 7(3A), which provides that the expression 'entailing changes in the workforce' includes the situation where there is a change of workplace. If the transferor is unable to rely on Reg 4(5A) to establish an ETO reason, it is likely that the dismissal would be automatically unfair under Reg 7(1)

- by virtue of Reg 4(2), liability for the automatically unfair dismissal would pass to the transferee (see Chapter 3, 'What transfers?', under 'Unfair and wrongful dismissal liability'). This is why the employee would wish to claim against the transferee as well as the transferor, and this is where the Recast Brussels Regulation (see 'Recast Brussels Regulation' above) would come into play

- if the transferee employer, although running an overseas business, is domiciled in the UK, then Article 21(1) of the Recast Brussels Regulation would allow the employee to bring a claim in the employment tribunal (or industrial tribunal in Northern Ireland)

- in any event, we suggest that, since the employee's last habitual place of work was the UK, he or she would be entitled to rely upon Article 21(2) of the Recast Brussels Regulation to bring a claim in the UK against a foreign transferee. The transferee, however, might dispute that this conclusion is correct. It might point out that since the transferor dismissed the employee, and since the dismissal was effective, the transferee did not at any point have an employment relationship with the employee. As a result, it might contend, the 'habitual place of work' provision of Article 21(2) is not available to the employee, meaning that the tribunal should not accept jurisdiction; and

- if the employee is successful with his or her unfair dismissal claim against the transferee, the tribunal's judgment will be capable of being enforced in the courts of the transferee's Member State, in accordance with Articles 36–57 of the Recast Brussels Regulation.

609

9.30 **No redundancy payment, but transferee refuses to take employees on.** As with situation (i) above, in situation (ii) – where the transferor declines to make a redundancy payment in the belief that the employee will pass to the transferee under TUPE, but where the transferee refuses to take the employee on – the employee might wish to bring claims in the employment tribunal against both the transferor and the transferee. Some of the considerations with regard to situation (ii) are the same as those in situation (i), but note the following:

- the employee would argue that if the TUPE Regulations did not apply, he or she was unfairly dismissed by the transferor under the normal provisions of the ERA (in which case the transferor would retain liability). In the alternative, the employee would contend that the Regulations did apply, and that he or she was unfairly dismissed by the transferee contrary to Reg 7; and

- if there was a relevant transfer in this situation, the employee would, we suggest, be able to proceed with an unfair dismissal claim in the UK against the transferee. The employee's contract, under which he or she last habitually performed work in the UK, would be deemed by TUPE to have transferred from the transferor to the transferee. Since the transferee became the employee's employer, and since the employee habitually worked in the UK, the employment tribunal would, owing to Article 21(2) of the Recast Brussels Regulation, more than likely have jurisdiction to hear the claim. Furthermore, the employee, who never actually worked abroad, would be able to satisfy the territorial test for bringing an unfair dismissal claim.

9.31 **Employee reluctant to transfer.** If the employee in situation (iii) does not wish to transfer to the transferee, yet both employers insist that TUPE will apply to transfer his or her employment, he or she does have some options, as the following demonstrates:

- the employee could refuse to transfer and bring a tribunal claim against the transferor, arguing that TUPE did not apply. Thus, the argument would go, he or she will have been unfairly dismissed by the transferor, who would be liable for the dismissal

- alternatively, if the employee accepts that TUPE applies, he or she could resign prior to the transfer and claim constructive dismissal (envisaged by Reg 4(11)) or material detriment dismissal (within the meaning of Reg 4(9)). These types of claim are discussed at length in Chapter 4, 'Unfair dismissal', under 'Constructive dismissals' and 'Material detriment dismissals' respectively. Put simply, in many cases a transferee's requirement that an employee move abroad to continue with his or her job would leave the way open for the employee to bring one of these claims, if not both

- as also explained in Chapter 4, 'Unfair dismissal', under 'Which employer will be liable?', the question of which employer (transferor or transferee) is landed with liability for a constructive or material detriment dismissal might depend on whether the employee has (in addition to resigning) made a formal objection to the transfer within the meaning of Reg 4(7) – for further details about objection see Chapter 2, 'Who transfers?', under 'Objecting to transfer'. Cases including Humphreys v University of Oxford and anor 2000 ICR 405, CA, suggest that where an employee has objected to the transfer, liability for a constructive or material detriment dismissal will remain with the transferor; but where the employee has not so objected, any such liability will pass to the transferee

- so, in most cases, an employee who wishes to resign when faced with a cross-border transfer situation would be best served by objecting to the transfer as well as claiming constructive or material detriment dismissal. That is because liability might well remain with the transferor, meaning that no complicated matters of international jurisdiction will arise; and

- if the employee has not objected to the transfer – perhaps the employee actually wants liability to pass to the transferee, owing to the fact that the transferor is insolvent – similar considerations with regard to the Recast Brussels Regulation will arise to those set out with regard to situation (i) above.

Dismissal or contractual variation by transferee after transfer 9.32
We now consider the situation where the employee has transferred under TUPE, and as a result has gone to work for the transferee in another Member State. What can the employee do if, some time after the transfer, he or she is dismissed by the transferee or subjected to post-transfer contractual variations? The following points are relevant in this regard:

- unless the transferee is domiciled in the UK, a UK employment or industrial tribunal will not be able to accept jurisdiction to hear any claim arising from the employee's post-transfer employment. This is because, for the purposes of Article 21(2) of the Recast Brussels Regulation, the employee's habitual place of work will no longer be the UK

- we assume, in any event, that the employee would not be protected, with regard to a post-transfer dismissal, by the unfair dismissal rules contained in Reg 7. This is because the employee would (other than in peculiar circumstances) presumably fall outside the territorial scope of the right to claim unfair dismissal (see 'Employees working outside United Kingdom' below); and

- in the absence of a choice of law, the law of the country in which the employee habitually works will apply to his or her employment contract (Article 6(2) of the Rome Convention). So, generally, the contract of an employee who

611

transfers to another Member State on a permanent basis would attract the law of that Member State as soon as the employee moves there.

In conclusion, this means that in most cases an employee who has transferred to another Member State under TUPE will, in respect of the post-transfer conduct of the transferee employer, need to seek recourse in the Member State in which he or she is working. Furthermore, the protection that he or she is afforded will depend to a large extent on the law of the Member State in question.

9.33 Employees working outside United Kingdom

The question we pose in this section is whether, and to what extent, the TUPE Regulations can afford protection to employees working abroad. As we saw earlier in this chapter, this question is relevant to cross-border transfers, in that it might impact upon the ability of an employee who has transferred from the UK to another jurisdiction to bring a claim against his or her new employer. In addition, the question is relevant to a TUPE transfer taking place within the UK, where some of the workforce assigned to the business or service to be transferred spend some or all of their time working in another country. We shall focus on the latter situation here.

9.34 TUPE can apply to overseas employees

The first thing to note is that the TUPE Regulations can apply to a transfer of a business or service whether or not there are employees assigned to that business or service who work outside the UK. This is made clear by Reg 3(4)(c), which provides that, as long as the transferring business or service can be said to be situated in the UK immediately prior to the transfer, the Regulations will apply to 'a transfer of an undertaking, business or part of an undertaking or business (which may also be a service provision change) where persons employed in the undertaking, business or part transferred ordinarily work outside the UK'.

The guidance issued by the Department for Business, Innovation and Skills, 'Employment rights on the transfer of an undertaking' (January 2014) ('the BIS Guide') elaborates: 'If there is a transfer of a UK exporting business, the fact that the sales force spends the majority of its working week outside the UK will not prevent the Regulations applying to the transfer, so long as the undertaking itself (comprising, amongst other things, premises, assets, fixtures & fittings, goodwill as well as employees) is situated in the UK.'

9.35   The above example clearly envisages a 'business transfer' under Reg 3(1)(a), but the BIS Guide provides a further example of how an employee working abroad could transfer by way of a service provision change under Reg 3(1)(b): 'Where a contract to provide website maintenance comes to an end and the client wants someone else to take over the contract, if in the organised grouping of employees that has performed the contract, one of the IT technicians works from home, which is outside the UK, that should not prevent the Regulations applying to the transfer of the business.'

Extent of protection 9.36

It is clear that the TUPE Regulations can apply where some members of the transferring workforce perform their duties overseas. But what protection is bestowed on such employees? The right to bring a claim under Reg 15 for a failure to inform and consult is free-standing. Given the position discussed under 'Enforcement of cross-border transfer claims within EU – Recast Brussels Regulation' above, it seems reasonably clear that an employee who is working abroad for an employer based in the UK could bring an employment tribunal claim for failure to inform and consult. Article 21(1) of the Recast Brussels Regulation, as we have seen, means that a claim can be lodged in the place where the employer is domiciled, regardless of whether the employee actually worked in that location.

Other rights in the TUPE Regulations operate through the medium of the contract of employment. Thus, Reg 4(1) modifies the contractual parties, so that the transferee steps into the shoes of the transferor as employer, and Reg 4(4) renders a variation of contract as void when the sole or principal reason for it is the transfer. Where the contract is governed by the law of England and Wales, Scotland, or Northern Ireland, and the employer is domiciled in the UK, there are no obstacles to claiming in an employment tribunal or industrial tribunal. Even if the contract is governed by the law of another EU Member State, the principles of the Rome Convention (considered under 'Enforcement of cross-border transfer claims within EU – Rome Convention' above) prevent the parties from contracting out of the mandatory rules of the country with which it is most closely connected. The TUPE Regulations arguably constitute part of the mandatory rules of the UK, and would therefore be applicable if the contract was most closely connected with it rather than any other country.

Limited scope of dismissal rights. Regulation 7(1) does not contain a free- 9.37 standing protection from being dismissed because of a TUPE transfer. Instead, it stipulates that such a dismissal will be *deemed* to be unfair for the purposes of Part X of the Employment Rights Act 1996 (ERA). Thus, in order to benefit from the TUPE protections regarding unfair dismissal, an employee must be entitled to bring a claim of unfair dismissal under the ERA. We assume that, in a cross-border transfer case, the employee would have to satisfy the test of jurisdiction laid down in respect of ordinary unfair dismissal law. A full discussion of the territorial reach of the right to claim unfair dismissal falls outside the scope of this Handbook, and can instead be found in IDS Employment Law Handbook, 'Employment Tribunal Practice and Procedure' (2014), Chapter 2, 'Tribunals' jurisdiction', in the section 'Territorial limitations', under 'Territorial reach – unfair dismissal and other ERA rights'. What we set out here are the essential points that apply in a TUPE context.

The basic rule is that the ERA only applies to employment in Great Britain – Lawson v Serco Ltd and two other cases 2006 ICR 250, HL. However, in exceptional circumstances it may cover working abroad. As summarised by the Court of Appeal in Bates van Winkelhof v Clyde and Co LLP and anor 2013 ICR 883, CA:

- where an employee works partly in Great Britain and partly abroad, the question is whether the connection with Great Britain and British employment law is sufficiently strong to enable it to be said that Parliament would have regarded it as appropriate for the employment tribunal to deal with the claim – Ravat v Halliburton Manufacturing and Services Ltd 2012 ICR 389, SC

- where an employee works and lives wholly abroad, it will be more appropriate to ask whether his or her employment relationship has much stronger connections both with Great Britain and with British employment law than with any other system of law – Duncombe v Secretary of State for Children, Schools and Families (No.2) 2011 ICR 1312, SC.

9.38 The above tests focus on the connection with Great Britain. However, where the TUPE Regulations are concerned, there is an added complicating factor. Reg 1(3) provides that the Regulations extend to Northern Ireland. In that territory, the right to claim unfair dismissal is not contained in the ERA but in very similar provisions set out in Part XI of the Employment Rights (Northern Ireland) Order 1996 SI 1996/1919. To our knowledge, no appellate cases have considered the territorial reach of the 1996 Order, but it is generally interpreted consistently with the ERA. Thus, it is assumed that, for the purposes of Reg 7(1) TUPE, the test of territorial reach would need to be modified so that the claimant must demonstrate the requisite connection with the UK (rather than merely Great Britain) and UK employment law rather than the law of Great Britain.

In our view, the majority of the employees of a UK business who could be said to be 'assigned' to such a business for the purposes of the automatic transfer of employment rule contained in Reg 4 TUPE (as to which see Chapter 2, 'Who transfers?', under '"Assigned" to undertaking transferred') will be able to satisfy the 'employment in the UK test' explained above. Take the example used in the BIS Guide concerning a UK exporting business whose sales force spends the majority of its working week outside the UK. Here, the relevant test of territorial reach is that set down in Ravat v Halliburton Manufacturing and Services Ltd (above). Since the business for which the sales force work is situated in the UK, the strength of the connection is obvious, and it seems likely that members of the sales force would be entitled to claim unfair dismissal under Reg 7.

Even if the sales staff were based permanently outside the UK, if they were **9.39** performing their roles for the UK business, and were assigned to that business for the purposes of Reg 4 TUPE, it would seem that they would stand a good chance of fulfilling the test set down in Duncombe v Secretary of State for Children, Schools and Families (No.2) (above). Similar considerations would apply to the second example provided in the BIS Guide, of an IT technician working from home, outside the UK, as part of an organised grouping of employees situated within the UK. That said, the fact that an employee works entirely outside the UK does leave open the possibility that there is a greater connection with the country in which the work is carried out. Here it is perhaps relevant that the question of whether, on given facts, a case falls within the territorial scope of an employment right is a question of law; but it is also one of degree – Ravat v Halliburton Manufacturing and Services Ltd (above). As such, the employment tribunal's role as primary fact-finder will be crucial.

It is also worth noting that the European origin of the TUPE Regulations may require courts and tribunals to construe the rules of territorial jurisdiction generously. Cases such as Bleuse v MBT Transport Ltd 2008 ICR 488, EAT, and Kücükdeveci v Swedex GmbH and Co KG 2010 IRLR 346, ECJ, suggest that national laws must be set aside if they conflict with EU laws in order to give effect to the directly effective rights under European law. Having said that, we are not aware of any cases that indicate that the Acquired Rights Directive is capable of direct effect, and there are strong grounds for arguing that it is not: the Directive is addressed to Member States, and is aimed at achieving partial rather than total harmonisation of rules across the EU.

10 Contracting out of TUPE

Waiver of rights

Validity of contracting-out clauses in transfer agreement

As one would expect, the Transfer of Undertakings (Protection of Employment) **10.1** Regulations 2006 SI 2006/246 (TUPE) contain an express provision restricting the capacity of any party to a transfer – transferor, transferee or employee – to contract out of the employment protection provisions contained within the Regulations. These provisions are mandatory in that they operate irrespective of the parties' wishes in the matter. So, for example, in MRS Environmental Services Ltd v Dyke and anor EAT 93/96 the EAT ruled that the automatic transfer of employment rule in what is now Reg 4 TUPE imported a statutory novation that has effect regardless of whether the parties consented or had knowledge of each other's identity. This meant that a relevant transfer occurred and the consequences which TUPE provides on such a transfer followed irrespective of the fact that the employees had not agreed to the transfer and had not been informed of the identity of the transferee.

Similarly, in relation to variation of terms and conditions, the European Court of Justice has also made it clear that it is not open to employees to waive rights conferred on them by the EU Acquired Rights Directive (No.2001/23) ('the Acquired Rights Directive') guaranteeing protection against adverse variations. In Foreningen af Arbejdsledere i Danmark v Daddy's Dance Hall A/S 1988 IRLR 315, ECJ, a question was referred to the ECJ as to whether a worker may waive these rights even if the disadvantages to him of agreeing to detrimental changes to contractual terms as a result of the transfer were offset by the offer of more advantageous terms, so that he was not left in a worse position overall. In answer to that question, the Court ruled that: 'The workers concerned do not have the option to waive the rights conferred on them by the Directive and... it is not permissible to diminish these rights, even with their consent. This interpretation is notwithstanding the fact that, as in the instant case, the worker, to offset disadvantages arising for him from a change in his employment relationship, obtains new advantages so that he is not, overall, left in a worse position than he was before.'

Regulation 18 TUPE reflects the mandatory nature of the Acquired Rights **10.2** Directive's provisions by stipulating that: 'Section 203 of the [Employment Rights Act 1996 (ERA)] (restrictions on contracting out) shall apply in relation to these Regulations as if they were contained in that Act, save for that section shall not apply in so far as these Regulations provide for an agreement (whether a contract of employment or not) to exclude or limit the operation of these

617

Regulations.' In essence, what this does is apply the same restrictions on contracting out as apply to substantive claims contained within the ERA (such as unfair dismissal and unlawful deductions from wages), with the exception of where the TUPE Regulations expressly provide for a right to contract out of, or limit the application of, specific provisions of the Regulations.

It follows that, in order to determine the precise ambit of Reg 18, it is necessary to understand two things: (i) what is the scope for contracting out (or waiver) of the provisions of the ERA as set out in S.203 of that Act? And (ii) what specific exceptions are made in the Regulations to allow for their protections to be disapplied or limited?

10.3 Waiver of rights

Section 203 ERA – to which Reg 18 TUPE refers – contains a wide-ranging restriction on the capacity of employers to enforce agreements entered into by employees to compromise or waive their substantive rights conferred by or under that Act. In particular, S.203(1) provides that: 'Any provision in an agreement (whether a contract of employment or not) is void in so far as it purports – (a) to exclude or limit the operation of any provision of this Act, or (b) to preclude a person from bringing any proceedings under this Act before an employment tribunal.' S.203(2) then goes on to qualify the general position set out in S.203(1) by providing for specific exceptions in which any agreement to preclude a person from bringing or continuing tribunal proceedings is allowed. Two of these exceptions are relevant for present purposes. These are:

- where the agreement in question is one in respect of which an Acas conciliation officer has taken action under any of Ss.18A–18C of the Employment Tribunals Act 1996. These sections refer to Acas's powers and duties to attempt to conciliate employment disputes, including under the 'early conciliation' scheme introduced in April 2014 – S.203(2)(e); or

- where the agreement is a settlement agreement that (a) satisfies the conditions for validity set out in the ERA, and (b) relates to the settlement of proceedings in respect of contravention or alleged contravention of one of the specific statutory provisions in the ERA listed in S.18(1) of the Employment Tribunals Act 1996 – S.203(2)(f)(i).

10.4 Acas-conciliated agreements

Thus, the first way in which an agreement to refrain from continuing or bringing proceedings may be effective is where it has been reached through Acas conciliation. S.18 ETA sets out a comprehensive list of the types of claim or proceedings in respect of which a conciliation officer may 'take action' to help parties to settle such claims or proceedings. Included in that list are claims or proceedings brought under provisions of the ERA relating to unlawful deductions from wages or unfair dismissal (S.18(1)(b)) and breach of contract claims arising on, or outstanding at, the termination of employment (S.18(1)(g) and (h)).

The claims most relevant in S.18 in a TUPE context are claims for unfair dismissal and unlawful deduction from wages. Thus, where a conciliated settlement settles claims relating to the employee's unfair dismissal rights under Reg 7 or provides for compromise of a wages claim against the transferor or transferee, this will be both effective and binding on all parties.

The same is true in respect of settlement of claims of breach of the employee **10.5** liability notification obligations in Reg 11 and the duty to inform and consult appropriate representatives of employees affected by the relevant transfer under Regs 13–16 TUPE. Although neither of these claims are specifically mentioned in S.18(1) as being claims over which an Acas conciliation officer is entitled to take action, express provision is made in the TUPE Regulations themselves for Ss.18A–18C to apply. Accordingly, Reg 12(7) in respect of a claim of failure to comply with the employee liability obligations provides: 'Section 18A to 18C of the [ETA] (conciliation) shall apply to the right conferred by this regulation and to proceedings under this regulation as it applies to the rights conferred by that Act and the employment tribunal proceedings mentioned in that Act.' Reg 16(1) provides likewise in respect of claims concerned with breaches of the duty to inform and consult.

Note that some claims under TUPE, such as unfair dismissal, must be brought against the transferee, whereas claims for failure to inform and consult may be brought against the transferee and transferor on a joint and several basis. It is therefore important for any settlement to be drafted so as to preclude claims against all of the appropriate parties. In Tamang and anor v ACT Security Ltd and anor EAT 0046/12 the EAT held that an employment tribunal misconstrued an Acas-conciliated agreement with the transferor, R, relating to liability for failure to inform and consult. The tribunal had been wrong to find that the agreement also released the joint respondents ACTS Ltd and ESUK Ltd, whom it was claimed were the transferees, from claims of failure to inform and consult and unfair dismissal. It is established legal principle that a release of one joint tortfeasor from liability is a release of all of them. However, properly construed, the conciliated agreement was not an unqualified release but a covenant not to sue R. The tribunal had incorrectly noted that liability for unfair dismissal is joint and several as between transferor and transferee and this error may have infected its construction of the conciliated agreement. The EAT ordered that the claims against the alleged transferees could go ahead.

There is some doubt about the correctness of the Tamang decision in so far as **10.6** it relates to a claimant's ability to bring an independent complaint against a transferee for a failure to inform and consult where the claim against the transferor has been settled or withdrawn. The EAT's subsequent decision in

619

Allen and ors v Morrisons Facilities Services Ltd 2014 ICR 792, EAT, asserted that the only route for affected employees of a transferor to obtain compensation from a transferee who had failed to provide employee liability information under Reg 12 would be to pursue a claim against the transferor for breach of Reg 13(2)(d), for the transferee to be made a party to the proceedings pursuant to Reg 15(5), and for the tribunal to find the allegations well founded; and that, as the claimants' claims against the transferors in that case had been settled or withdrawn, it had not been open to the tribunal to make the necessary findings for an order requiring the transferee to pay compensation under Reg 15(8)(b). The reasoning in the Allen case is discussed in detail in Chapter 8, 'Information and consultation', under 'Informing and consulting appropriate representatives – claims for failure to inform or consult'. However, it should be pointed out that the approach adopted by the EAT in the Tamang case with regard to compromising claims against all parties had been similarly adopted by the EAT in the context of an Acas-conciliated settlement of unfair dismissal proceedings in the earlier case of Thompson and ors v Walon Car Delivery and anor 1997 IRLR 343, EAT. There, WCD successfully won a Saab car distribution contract from the transferor, BRS. Although T and his colleagues were dismissed prior to the transfer, BRS negotiated settlement terms before the date of the transfer that led to the signing of an Acas COT3 agreement once the transfer had occurred. WCD, however, was not a party to that agreement. When T and others brought an unfair dismissal claim against WCD, an employment tribunal initially ruled that the settlement terms amounted to a variation of contract which debarred the claimants from bringing claims against WCD as the transferee. Overturning that ruling, the EAT held that, since the dismissals were effected because of the transfer and were therefore automatically unfair under what is now Reg 7, liability passed to WCD under what is now Reg 4(2) and that the Acas-conciliated settlement agreed by the BRS with the employees after the transfer could not be relied upon by WCD because it was not a party to the agreement. There is no reason to suppose that the same principle would not be applied in a case where a claim is settled by way of a settlement agreement (see 'Settlement agreements' below).

10.7 Settlement agreements

The second means by which it may be possible to refrain from continuing or bringing proceedings concerned with rights provided by the TUPE Regulations is through a valid settlement agreement. As mentioned above, S.203(2)(f) ERA exempts the general prohibition against contracting out of the ERA's provisions in S.203(1) where a settlement agreement relates to claims/proceedings of the kind listed in S.18(1)(b) ETA, provided that the agreement also complies with the validity conditions specified in the ERA. The list in S.18(1)(b) refers to a large number of statutory provisions within the ERA, but the only ones of relevance so far as TUPE is concerned are S.13 (the right not to suffer unlawful deductions from wages) and S.111 (unfair dismissal).

620

It is important to note that, unlike the position in respect of conciliated agreements, it is not possible to use a settlement agreement to compromise TUPE claims relating to employee liability information or the duty to inform and consult. This is because the provisions dealing with these matters in regulations are not mentioned in S.18(1)(b) ETA. The fact that Regs 12(7) and 16(1), as we have seen, specifically state that Ss.18A–18C shall apply to the rights conferred by relevant regulations and to proceedings brought to enforce those rights is not sufficient to enable these matters to be compromised. S.18(1)(b) itself restricts the scope for use of settlement agreements specifically to tribunal proceedings and claims under or arising out of the particular ERA provisions that it lists. Any claim that is not listed cannot therefore be the subject of a valid settlement agreement.

In respect of the TUPE claims that can be settled by settlement agreements, it is **10.8** necessary, in order to be valid, that any such agreement also complies with the stringent conditions specified in S.203(3)–(4) ERA. These are discussed in detail in IDS Employment Law Handbook, 'Employment Tribunal Practice and Procedure' (2014), Chapter 3, 'Conciliation, settlements and ADR', under 'Settlement agreements – statutory requirements'. Essentially, they require the agreement to be in writing, relate to 'particular proceedings', and to have been made only after the employee has received advice from a relevant independent adviser as to the terms and effect of the proposed agreement. In University of East London v Hinton 2005 ICR 1260, CA, the Court of Appeal interpreted the requirement for the agreement to 'relate to particular proceedings' to mean that the relevant proceedings had to be specifically identified. Thus, there had to be either a reference to the relevant statutory provisions or a phrase generically describing each type of claim (e.g. 'unfair dismissal' or 'unlawful deductions from wages') that the parties intended to compromise. What was not acceptable was to use a rolled-up expression such as 'all statutory rights'.

Waiver of contractual claims
10.9

We have seen above that statutory claims such as unfair dismissal or deduction from wages can be settled by an Acas-conciliated settlement or a settlement agreement, and that, in addition to these, claims relating to breach of Reg 11 and 13 duties can also be settled, but only via an Acas-conciliated settlement. But what of breach of contract claims? Owing to the constraints that the TUPE Regulations themselves impose with regard to varying contractual terms and conditions, the capacity of the parties to reach valid compromises of breach of contract actions and claims is severely limited. Such claims do not fall within the categories of claim or proceeding capable of being settled by way of a settlement agreement, since they are not listed in S.18(1)(b) ETA, which is the provision that establishes the scope for making potentially valid settlement agreements (see 'Settlement agreements' above).

621

By way of contrast, breach of contract claims arising on termination of employment do come within the remit of an Acas conciliation officer's powers to take action to help the parties reach a conciliated settlement. This is because S.203(2)(e) ERA empowers a conciliation officer to take such action in respect of all the types of claim set out in S.18(1) rather than – as is the case in respect of settlement agreements – merely those set out in S.18(1)(b). S.18(1)(g) and (h) specifically refer to a conciliation officer's powers to conciliate in relation to 'proceedings on a contract claim' under Article 6 of the Employment Tribunals Extension of Jurisdiction (England and Wales) Order 1994 SI 1994/1623 and the Employment Tribunals Extension of Jurisdiction (Scotland) Order 1994 SI 1994/1624.

10.10 However, there are two important factors that, in practice, limit the scope of parties to use the services of a conciliation officer to settle a breach of contract claim in a TUPE context. First, only claims for breach of contract arising or outstanding on termination of employment up to the value of £25,000 fall within the jurisdiction of the employment tribunal. It would have to be questioned, therefore, whether a conciliation officer would be acting within his or her powers (or in any case would be willing to take action) in respect of claims that exceed such an amount. Secondly, and more importantly, the scope for making valid and binding agreements to compromise claims based on changes to contractual terms and conditions brought about by a relevant transfer is limited. The general rule, as outlined immediately below, is that a TUPE-related variation will be void even if the employee agrees to the variation or enters into a conciliated settlement or settlement agreement restricting his or her right to bring action based on breach of contract to enforce his or her original terms.

10.11 Express exceptions enabling waiver of rights

Chapter 5, 'Changing terms and conditions', was concerned with explaining the limited ability of the parties to negotiate valid changes to terms and conditions where it is the relevant transfer that prompts such changes. As we saw in that chapter, Reg 4(4) – which applies, along with the entirety of Reg 4, to employees who are employed by the transferor and assigned to the undertaking or organised grouping of resources being transferred immediately before the transfer – renders void any purported variation if the sole or principal reason for the variation is the transfer. However, Reg 4(4) does not prevent a variation in the contract if:

- the sole or principal reason for variation is an economic, technical, or organisational reason entailing changes in the workforce ('an ETO reason'), provided the employer and employee agree that variation – Reg 4(5)(a); or

- the terms of the employment contract permit the employer to make such a variation – Reg 4(5)(b).

622

The meaning of 'ETO' and 'changes in the workforce' is discussed in Chapter 5, 'Changing terms and conditions', under 'Types of change permitted by TUPE – ETO reasons entailing changes in workforce'. Since the 2014 TUPE amendments introduced by the Collective Redundancies and Transfer of Undertakings (Protection of Employment) (Amendment) Regulations 2014 SI 2014/16, 'changes in the workforce' now includes a change to an employee's place of work (Reg 4(5A)).

10.12 One significant further exception to the rule that purported variations for transfer-related reasons are void is where such variations are made in the course of insolvency proceedings. In this regard, Reg 8(7) provides for the entirety of Reg 4 to be disapplied where the relevant transfer occurs while the transferor is the subject of bankruptcy proceedings or any analogous insolvency proceedings that have been instituted with a view to the liquidation of its assets – see Chapter 6, 'Transfer of insolvent companies', under 'Bankruptcy and liquidation proceedings'. Furthermore, Reg 9 provides that, in the case of 'relevant insolvency proceedings' – i.e. proceedings that have been opened in relation to the transferor but not with a view to the liquidation of its assets – the transferor, transferee or insolvency practitioner can agree 'permitted variations' with appropriate representatives of employees assigned to the transferred undertaking that would otherwise be rendered void by Reg 4(4) – see Chapter 6, 'Transfer of insolvent companies', under '"Relevant insolvency proceedings" – changing terms and conditions'.

The only other way in which an employer may effectively bring about transfer-related variations is to dismiss employees and re-engage them on new terms. Obviously, the employer risks such dismissals being automatically unfair under Reg 7(1) for being principally by reason of the transfer, but even if the dismissals are unfair, they will be effective to bring the old contract to an end. Any re-engagement will be on the new terms and will be valid, subject to the power of the employment tribunal subsequently ordering reinstatement on the previous terms as one of the remedies available for unfair dismissal – see Chapter 5, 'Changing terms and conditions', under 'Alternative strategies for effecting changes – dismissal and re-engagement on new terms'.

10.13 Pulling all these strands together, the position can be summarised as follows: the employer (whether it be the transferor pre-transfer or the transferee post-transfer) can implement binding contractual terms and conditions only if one of the following sets of circumstances obtain:

- there is a TUPE transfer but any variation to contractual terms and conditions is not transfer-related

- the variation to contractual terms is for an ETO reason

- the terms of the contract expressly permit the variation in question

623

- the variation occurs while the transferor is subject to bankruptcy or analogous insolvency proceedings opened with a view to liquidation of its assets, or, in respect of other insolvency proceedings, comprises a 'permitted variation' negotiated with appropriate representatives

- a new contract of employment based on new terms is entered into following the termination of the previous contract. However, the employer is likely to be liable for unfair dismissal under Reg 7(1) unless the reason for dismissal can be shown not to relate to the transfer at all or, if it was so related, comprised an ETO reason within the meaning of Reg 7(2), and

- the transferring employee has not expressly objected to the changes and has affirmed the contract by continuing to work for the new employer. In such circumstances, it is arguable that any actionable claim for breach of contract in the courts is lost at common law, although it is unclear whether this would apply to a variation which was rendered void by virtue of Reg 4(4).

In the absence of one of these legitimate bases for effecting variations, any Acas agreement to settle a claim in relation to a non-ETO transfer-related variation in terms would be void under Reg 18(1) TUPE and S.203 ERA.

10.14 The difficulty in securing a valid settlement of a breach of contract claim in relation to a subsisting contract was underlined in Solectron Scotland Ltd v Roper and ors 2004 IRLR 4, EAT. The Appeal Tribunal in that case ruled that the precursor of Reg 18 – Reg 12 of the 1981 Regulations – would apply to exclude an agreement where employees formally retained their rights under TUPE but simply gave up their right to enforce those rights in the courts or tribunals. In the EAT's view, the retained rights would be of no value at all if they could not be enforced in a court of law. Thus, a settlement agreement could not be used as a back-door route to effect a transfer-related variation by purporting to compromise a claim for breach of contract in relation to the transferor's or transferee's failure to comply with the original terms.

However, the EAT did accept that if the settlement agreement related to the re-engagement of employees on new terms following the prior termination of their employment, the agreement would be valid. On the facts of the Solectron case, the EAT ruled that settlement agreements signed by employees who were made redundant within months of their employment being transferred under TUPE were not rendered invalid by what is now Reg 18. While it was true that, under TUPE, an employer cannot, after a transfer, vary the terms of an employee's contract if that variation is solely by reason of the transfer, in this case the effect of the settlement agreements was solely to compromise the financial claims that the employees had on the termination of their employment. The employer was not thereby trying to vary the employees' contracts, but to compromise a dispute as to their value. The dispute arose as to the sums due on termination of employment because there was disagreement as to whether the enhanced redundancy payments were still part of the employees' contracts. The fact that the dispute arose because of uncertainty as to the precise nature and scope of the terms transferred did not make the settlement agreements ones that had given rise to a variation in the terms of the contracts solely or even mainly by reason of the transfer.

It has been argued that the Solectron decision opens up the possibility of an **10.15** employer securing valid and consensual variations in terms and conditions by a process of terminating the employment to bring the contract to an end, and then entering a compromise of claims upon dismissal. But we would sound a note of caution about this. There remains a high risk that in a case where employment with the transferee continues on the revised terms after the settlement agreement has been signed (which is not what happened in the Solectron case), a tribunal would regard this as a strategy to avoid the effect of Reg 4(4). In that case, it could be contended that this strategy was in breach of Reg 18, with the result that the settlement agreement would be void so far as the breach of contract claims are concerned. There is also the point – not considered by the EAT in Solectron – that a settlement agreement cannot in any event be used to compromise an employee's right to bring a breach of contract claim over which an employment tribunal has jurisdiction under Article 6 of the Employment Tribunals Extension of Jurisdiction (England and Wales) Order 1994 (or its Scottish equivalent). If this is so, then even if the 'termination followed by re-engagement strategy' were possible, the parties would need to compromise any breach of contract claims through an Acas-conciliated settlement.

Validity of contracting-out clauses in transfer agreement **10.16**

The scope of Reg 18 extends to the commercial transaction between transferor and transferee. Thus, the non-contracting out rule will apply to the obligation on the transferor to notify the transferee of employee liability information under Reg 11. If the transferor fails to do so, the transferee can make a claim in the employment tribunal.

One consequence of the non-contracting out provision is that, even if a commercial agreement expressly stipulates that the transferee will waive its right to require this information, such waiver will not be capable of being relied upon should the transferee subsequently seek to bring a complaint to the employment tribunal regarding a failure to supply the relevant information. That said, Reg 12(4)(b) provides that, in assessing compensation payable for failure under Reg 11, a tribunal shall have a particular regard to 'the terms of any contract between the transferor and the transferee'. In the light of this, the tribunal would no doubt take on board what the parties had previously

625

agreed between themselves in assessing what was just and equitable to award by way of compensation.

10.17 Regulation 15 TUPE also contains provisions concerning complaints to an employment tribunal where an employer – whether the transferor or the transferee – is alleged to have failed to comply with Reg 13 (the duty to inform and consult) or Reg 14 (the election of employee representatives) – see Chapter 8, 'Information and consultation', under 'Informing and consulting appropriate representatives'. Reg 15(9) makes the transferor and transferee jointly and severally liable whenever a transferor has failed to inform or consult in respect of affected employees or where the transferee has failed to comply with its duty relating to the election of employee representatives. Although the commercial parties will often apportion liability in respect of such failures as between themselves in the form of indemnities in the transfer agreement, Reg 18 operates to preclude them avoiding joint and several liability to pay any compensation due to employees.

As always, transferors and transferees should ensure that, in relation to the provisions where contracting out is prohibited, appropriate mutual warranties and indemnities are drafted in their commercial agreements. This will clarify upon whom the financial burden falls if there is any failure to comply with mandatory provisions of the TUPE Regulations.

11 Practical aspects of transfers

The course of a sale and purchase transfer

Due diligence

Common practical transfer issues

Conditions precedent

Warranties

Restrictive covenants

Indemnities

It is now more than 30 years since the passing of the Transfer of Undertakings **11.1** (Protection of Employment) Regulations 1981 SI 1981/1794. When, in 2006, those Regulations were repealed and replaced by the Transfer of Undertakings (Protection of Employment) Regulations 2006 SI 2006/246 (TUPE), the changes then introduced were fairly modest or simply sought to codify the developed case law on particular aspects of the predecessor Regulations. The Government's declared aims when enacting the 2006 Regulations were to:

- assist with the smooth management of necessary business restructuring and public sector modernisation by securing the interests and commitment of the employees affected

- promote a cooperative partnership approach towards change; and

- help create a level playing field and reduce transaction risks and costs in business acquisitions and in contracting operations in the business services sector.

Many had hoped that the review of the law in this area would lead to substantial improvements in the operation of the Regulations, but nobody would suggest that the 2006 Regulations have, in practice, made transfer of undertakings law much simpler than it was before. Indeed, it is clear from the foregoing chapters of this Handbook that the Regulations continue to represent a minefield to those involved in the sale or purchase of a business, or to those involved in a service provision change. That minefield will almost inevitably claim as victims those parties to small-scale transfers who innocently believe their transaction to be a simple one. The same mistake would be inexcusable on the part of professionals, such as lawyers, receivers and accountants, who may be engaged by the parties to effect the sound transfer of a larger business. There may, of course, be other ways of structuring the transfer so that it is not covered by the Regulations, the most common method being by way of a share acquisition.

627

However, a share transfer is not always practical for a variety of reasons and, in any case, recent case law has blurred the distinction between a TUPE transfer and a pure share acquisition – see Print Factory (London) 1991 Ltd v Millam 2007 ICR 1331, CA, discussed in detail in Chapter 1, 'Identifying a "relevant transfer"', under 'Business transfers – transfers "to another person"'). It is also sometimes the case that, in order to prepare a large business for a share acquisition, elements of it have to be restructured in a way that attracts the TUPE Regulations.

11.2 Much of the lawyer's task, particularly in business acquisitions, will be the drafting of an agreement that protects the party by whom he or she is instructed from unexpected liabilities. These may arise as a direct consequence of TUPE or they may be inherent in the nature of a business transfer itself. The commercial parties will also need to know whether and to what extent they may contract as between themselves or with employees who are assigned to the undertaking or grouping of resources to be transferred to contract out of the key protections guaranteed by the Regulations. Some of these 'inquiries' are now mandatory even in the context of service provision change transfers as a result of the transferor's duty to notify the transferee of employee liability information. There is also a need to address particular issues in staff transfer agreements (considered under 'Common practical transfer issues – service provision changes (outsourcing)' below).

In this chapter we outline some practical tips as to the kind of matters which will need to be considered during the negotiations leading to the transfer of an undertaking. Careful planning prior to the transfer will ensure that significant issues are not overlooked, and will ensure that a timescale for the transfer is considered at an early stage. In all transfers the vital factors are likely to be the time and knowledge available – knowledge not just about the TUPE Regulations but also about the undertaking or activities to be transferred. This Handbook focuses mainly on the employment aspects of relevant transfers. While employment law issues are just one among many of the matters that need to be considered, their proper handling of the employment relations issues will reduce legal claims and can address some of the natural concerns of affected employees so that the new employer has a more committed workforce. This process takes time, and time is often in short supply.

11.3 ## The course of a sale and purchase transfer

Purchasers, incoming contractors and other transferees will need to learn as much as possible about what precisely they are acquiring before being able to anticipate accurately the various liabilities that may arise. Once the risks are assessed, the precautions (in the form of conditions, warranties, restrictive covenants and indemnities) can then be taken. The old maxim 'caveat emptor'

628

remains true, as one of the basic thrusts of the TUPE Regulations is to pass employee liabilities on a TUPE transfer from the transferor to the transferee.

As we have seen in Chapter 1, 'Identifying a "relevant transfer"', the TUPE Regulations cover three different types of transaction. These are:

- a group reorganisation, where the businesses in a group are restructured and come under the ownership of different legal entities but are all ultimately controlled by the same parent

- the sale or disposal of a business to a third party, including the creation of joint ventures, company takeovers and privatisations, and

- outsourcing (service provision change) where an activity previously performed in-house is contracted out to a third party (outsourcing), or where such a contract is re-let, or where it is taken back in-house (insourcing).

These are very different transactions where different considerations will apply **11.4** in practice, but in any commercial transaction based on a sale and purchase of a business the three principal variables are price, warranties and indemnities. In relation to outsourcing agreements, a further significant variable is the duration of the service contract. If the potential liability for employment claims can be identified precisely and quantified, then the simple way to deal with such liability is through a variation in the price of the business. However, things are seldom so clear cut. For example, the commercial negotiations may not be straightforward and the relative bargaining strength of the parties may not allow for significant price negotiation. Furthermore, even if the liabilities can be identified and precisely quantified, there is no guarantee that all the potential employment claims will actually be brought, let alone succeed. Thus a reduction in the price of the maximum amount of the potential claims may be unrealistic. It might, however, be possible to hold back part of the purchase price until an agreed date (e.g. until the expiration of the statutory time limits for claims) and/or to deal with this through indemnities and warranties.

Typical stages of a transfer   11.5

The degree of complexity involved in a transfer will principally depend, of course, upon the size of the undertaking being transferred. It will also depend on the corporate or organisational structure into which the newly acquired business is to be fitted. Typically, however, a more involved transfer in the form of the sale and purchase of a business will have the following stages:

- *pre-contractual negotiations*: the intending transferee will attempt to determine, in general terms, whether the undertaking has the trading position and reputation which the transferor claims for it. The transferee may involve his solicitors and accountants in examining published accounts and other statutory information as well as making company searches. The negotiations at this stage will usually determine the form that the transfer will take; the price to be paid; preparation of the commercial sale agreement; disclosure of information by the transferor; and exchange of contract

- *post-contract investigation and approval*: the transferee will probably instruct his accountants to investigate the accounting and financial aspects of the business to a greater depth than previously, with a view to their verifying the warranties, representations and disclosures made by the transferor prior to exchange. The transferee's solicitors will further investigate the business's freehold and leasehold properties and may ask the transferor's solicitors to compose a report as to title and vouch for the accuracy of that report. In a case where prior shareholders' approval is necessary, a condition precedent will be drawn up which will make purchase of the business conditional upon such approval being obtained. Usually, the approval of shareholders to the transaction is required where the value of the assets being acquired by the transferee equals or exceeds 25 per cent of the value of the assets of the acquiring company

- *completion*: this will usually include a special meeting of the transferor's board of directors; delivery of statutory books, title deeds and other completion documents; and payment of any cash consideration. The transferee and his accountants will usually meet after the transfer in order to determine whether there is any need to bring claims for breach of warranty by the transferor. Human Resources will normally issue TUPE transfer letters to the transferring employees and ensure that any relevant TUPE objection letters have been provided by the transferor

- *post-completion integration*: on completion, the transferee will need to ensure the successful integration of the new business into its existing activities. This will entail communication with the transferring employees, managing cultural differences and implementing changes to the target company after completion. Human Resources may need to deal with any post-transfer redundancy dismissals and manage the tricky process of harmonising the terms and conditions of employment of the transferring employees with the rest of the workforce. A post-acquisition audit may also be carried out to monitor the success of the business transfer.

11.6 It is a common experience that transfers do not fully follow this pattern because negotiations and investigations become greatly protracted. Sometimes this causes the date for exchange of contracts to be postponed so that the exchange occurs at the same time as completion. The danger of this is that both parties are left free to pull out of the negotiations. On the one hand, the transferee may find that he has been gazumped after having incurred substantial and irrecoverable costs during the process of the negotiation and investigation by his solicitors and accountants. On the other, the transferor may find that it has put all its eggs in one basket and has let other opportunities for a lucrative sale slip by. Also, the exposure for a protective award is high as there would be no opportunity to carry out TUPE information and consultation. One way to avoid the expense and inconvenience of such disappointments is for the transferee to exchange contracts at the earliest possible stage on the basis of the transferor's representations and warranties. A deferred completion date can then be arranged to allow for full pre-completion investigations to take place in order to verify the transferor's claims. The sale agreement, in such circumstances, usually preserves the transferee's right to bring claims for breach of warranty after completion even where his investigations before completion had not disclosed any breach.

Due diligence 11.7

Due diligence is the process by which formal investigations are carried out in relation to the company or undertaking that is subject to the TUPE transfer prior to its transfer. The essential purpose is for the transferee to obtain as much information as possible about the target business. If carried out thoroughly, the process will help the transferee to identify any potential problems and avoid any unexpected costs and liabilities following completion of the sale or other disposition. Whether the transfer is the sale and purchase of a business or a service provision change, the disclosure of information that forms a key part of due diligence is essential.

Regulation 11 lists the employee liability information that has to be notified by the transferor to the transferee (see Chapter 8, 'Information and consultation', under 'Employee liability information'). This provision is particularly designed to reduce uncertainty in second generation outsourcing arrangements, where the lack of a direct connection between outgoing and incoming contractor can make it difficult for a transferee to obtain information about the employee liabilities for which it will become responsible. However, the obligation will apply to all transfers and is not limited to outsourcing situations. As stated in Chapter 8, other than in special circumstances, employee liability information must be given at least 28 days before the transfer. Although the guidance issued by the Department for Business, Innovation and Skills, 'Employment rights on the transfer of an undertaking' (January 2014) ('the BIS Guide') recommends that it may be 'helpful' if it is given sooner, when this occurs there is a residual obligation to update the information prior to the transfer – see Chapter 8, 'Information and consultation', under 'Employee liability information – how and when should information be provided?'.

In some simple small-scale cases, this employee liability information may be 11.8 sufficient, and in some service provision changes, this may be all the information that is received. However, in most cases a transferee would want more information at an earlier date than merely that which is required by Reg 11, not least because this may affect the price the purchaser is prepared to pay to buy the business or the price assumptions made in tendering for the provision of a service.

The many decisions that have to be taken by the transferee in the course of negotiations leading to the purchase of a business can only be effectively made once it has acquired accurate information about the target undertaking or activities. Also, the transferee will only be in a position to assess the prospects of the business and the risks and costs involved once such information has been fully disclosed. It is important that the information is not just collated but is analysed to assess risks. The analysis can identify 'hidden' costs and problems for the transferee. For example, specific deal-breaker issues that can arise from disclosure are: occupational pension problems; enhanced redundancy pay arrangements that are very expensive where rationalisation is essential; and health and safety issues and discrimination issues, where there are serious and extensive problems that may not only prove very expensive but may adversely impact on the reputation of the transferee if the deal proceeds.

11.9 Subject to Reg 11, how much information is disclosed is clearly a matter of balance depending on each particular transaction: too much, and the transferee may feel flooded with information that it cannot properly assess; too little, and the transferee may miss vital data that has serious commercial implications.

11.10 Types of information disclosed as part of due diligence

In commercial transactions, the due diligence process is often initiated by the buyer sending the seller a questionnaire covering the kinds of information set out below, whereas in service provision change cases the relevant information will often be disclosed as part of the tendering process. As a general rule, the transferee should, through its lawyers and accountants, seek the kinds of information set out below.

11.11 Employee details

- names and addresses
- ages
- sex, race, disability
- dates from which continuous employment began
- identification of which employees are key personnel
- details of employees who are in active service and those who are on leave of absence (e.g. family leave, sabbatical or secondment)
- resignation letters
- amounts of salaries/wages
- other remunerative benefits (e.g. commissions, bonuses)
- normal working hours and overtime arrangements

- notice entitlements

- holidays and holiday pay

- job grades

- sickness absence, sick pay and permanent health insurance entitlements

- membership of or participation in other benefit schemes (e.g. private health plans, life assurance, pension, company car provision or car allowance)

- restrictive covenants, confidentiality agreements and intellectual property agreements

- details of any grievance raised by employees or any disciplinary action taken over the last two years, and

- details of any court or tribunal claims brought by employees over the last two years (including health and safety/personal injury claims) or any outstanding claims of this nature.

The purpose of these details is to determine the entitlements of each employee (both financially and in terms of employment rights), and to assess the extent to which variation or harmonisation of contractual terms may have to be considered following the transfer. These details, combined with the employment data set out below, can also be used to build up a picture of how flexible the terms and conditions of employment are, and whether there are any particular problems.

Non-employee details. This would include details – including their terms of engagement – of any atypical workers such as consultants, workers and agency workers, so that the transferee can determine their employment status and termination arrangements. **11.12**

Demographics **11.13**

- numbers of weekly and monthly paid employees

- salary bands and total employment costs

- number of temporary and part-time staff

- number of consultants, trainees, apprentices, and casual and self-employed workers

- number and identity of employees on maternity, paternity and dependant leave or off work due to long-term sickness

- absence records

- ethnic breakdown of workforce

- sex breakdown of workforce

633

- age breakdown of workforce, and

- job evaluation structures in force.

The purpose of these enquiries is to identify any latent discrimination or equal pay problems, to ascertain potential problems of incompatibility with the transferee's existing business(es), and to establish who is working in the business and in what capacity, and whether there are any significant absenteeism problems. The process of due diligence should be used to enable the transferee to identify which employees are assigned to the undertaking or grouping of workers at the time of the transfer, and an accurate list of the names of such employees should be linked to an appropriate indemnity protecting the transferee in respect of costs or liabilities arising from the transfer of employees who are not on the list.

11.14 **Contractual documentation.** The written contracts of all employees (including directors) will be valuable, especially where the transferee intends to implement job changes or changes to other terms and conditions after the transfer. If this would be too onerous in terms of the sheer number of employees who are liable to be transferred, then sample contracts should be asked for and supplied. The following documents might contain contractual provisions or evidence of them in the absence of a comprehensive written contract of employment:

- written statement of terms and conditions (required under S.1 ERA)

- sample offer letters

- job descriptions

- company rules and policies (e.g. whistleblowing, computer misuse, family-friendly policies, drugs and alcohol, data protection)

- disciplinary and grievance procedures, and

- staff handbooks.

11.15 **Pay and benefits**

- basic pay

- pension schemes

- employee share schemes

- company cars/petrol or other travel allowances (including loans)

- bonus/profit-sharing/commissions/long-term incentive plans

- equipment hire schemes

- staff discounts

634

- insurance-based benefits, such as permanent health insurance and private health plans (e.g. BUPA)

- mortgage subsidies and relocation packages

- redundancy schemes, and

- contractual sick pay arrangements.

Many of the above arrangements will be contractual, with the consequence that entitlement to the benefits of such schemes will continue if employees' contracts of employment are transferred. The financial implications of this therefore ought to be considered. Even if the benefits are non-contractual (e.g. discretionary), any discontinuation or change in the basis on which, or level at which, they are paid may provide grounds for an employee to resign and claim that he or she has suffered a substantial change to working conditions to his or her material detriment within the meaning of Reg 4(9). In that case, the employee will be regarded as having been dismissed and will, it seems, be entitled to bring a claim of unfair dismissal on that basis – see Chapter 4, 'Unfair dismissal', under 'Material detriment dismissals'. In the case of pension schemes, although Reg 10 excludes such schemes from the operation of automatic transfer of contracts provided for by Reg 4, this exclusion is tightly circumscribed and there are now minimum statutory legal requirements that have to be met to ensure continued pension provision following a transfer – see Chapter 3, 'What transfers?', under 'Occupational pensions'. While occupational pension issues can involve substantial sums of money, there are often other contentious issues, such as company car arrangements.

Directors and senior executives   11.16

- names of all executives and non-executive directors

- details of directors' fees paid within a prescribed period and due to be paid in the current year

- details of all directors' other interests

- copies of senior executives' service agreements

- copies of confidentiality agreements, restrictive covenants and intellectual property agreements

- details of special benefits (e.g. company apartments, golden parachutes and special bonus or share option schemes), and

- change of control clauses (sometimes directors and senior employees will become entitled to certain specified payments if there is a change of control of the business).

635

The employment contracts will need to be examined in detail with a view to assessing employment costs, potential termination costs and how such contracts will operate in the context of the transferee's business.

11.17 Collective issues

- details of trade union presence within the undertaking and union recognition
- any applications for statutory trade union recognition
- industrial dispute history
- arbitration awards
- wages and salary review dates
- current state of employer-union negotiations
- details of any consultation committees
- health and safety policies and related matters, such as health and safety representatives and committees, with a record of any prohibition or improvement notices
- collective and workplace agreements, including working time opt-outs, and
- requests made under the Information and Consultation of Employees Regulations 2004 SI 2004/3426.

11.18 Miscellaneous matters

- tied accommodation commitments
- loans to employees
- lay-off and guarantee payment provisions
- actual and potential employment-related litigation, as well as investigations and inquiries by the Commission for Equality and Human Rights; this information should include personal injury as well as employment law claims
- policies on equal opportunities, data protection, redundancy, and family-friendly policies
- disabled staff and details of reasonable adjustments that have been made or requested
- contractual retirement age(s), if any, and details of its/their objective justification, and
- flexible working arrangements (including part-time, job-sharing and homeworking).

It needs to be borne in mind that business and financial 'due diligence' extends well beyond information relating to employees, staff terms and conditions and human resources information.

Method of disclosure 11.19

The ways in which this type of information is disclosed vary. For example, sometimes the 'due diligence' information is prepared by way of a due diligence report with additional information attached to it or, as recommended by the Information Commissioner, the information may be put into a data room by the transferor for inspection by potential transferees. Provision may also be made for the transferor to respond to the transferee's questions in open correspondence. The latter method is intended to help ensure compliance with data protection law (as to which, see 'Confidentiality and data protection' below). In more straightforward transactions or service provision change cases, the transferor may give the transferee an open letter that makes all the general and specific disclosures of information.

Confidentiality and data protection 11.20

Typically, a seller will require prospective buyers to enter into a confidentiality agreement as part of the commercial transaction or tendering process. Given that, as a result of the 'due diligence' process, the buyer will become aware of the terms and conditions of staff, particularly 'senior employees', there is a real risk that the buyer may seek to 'poach' key employees if the negotiations are unsuccessful. For this reason, particularly in larger transactions, in addition to confidentiality obligations there will normally be restrictions on 'poaching' senior staff that continue to apply for a period of time if the deal does not go ahead.

So far as the Data Protection Act 1998 (DPA) is concerned, to the extent that information is disclosed in order to meet the obligation to disclose 'employee liability information' under Reg 11, such disclosure of itself will be lawful by virtue of S.35 DPA. For a while there had been uncertainty as to whether the DPA required information relating to employees to be disclosed only on an anonymous basis, and a practice of doing this was adopted. However, the UK Information Commissioner has confirmed that the DPA does allow employers to disclose personal employee data on a named basis as required by TUPE – see 'Employment Practices Code – Supplementary Guidance' (June 2005), p.72. Even so, while the disclosure of such data is lawful, consideration should still be given to the application of the eight data protection principles regarding the disclosure of personal data and to the recommendations in the Information Commissioner's Code of Practice (the relevant provisions of which are summarised below).

Data protection issues will also arise where information in excess of that 11.21 required by TUPE is provided under either a due diligence or a tendering

637

process. Specific regard should be had to the relevance and application of the data protection principles in these circumstances. In addition, transferors should consider imposing confidentiality obligations in the sales agreement and/or during negotiations requiring the return of personalised information if the sales transaction falls through. It is also advisable for transferors to ensure that explicit consent for the transfer of data in the event of a sale of the business (within Great Britain and, where appropriate, outside of the European Union) has been obtained from the employees in their contracts of employment. Even more significant data protection issues will arise if 'sensitive' personal data, as defined by S.2 DPA, is disclosed as part of the due diligence or tendering process. Such data includes health records and information relating to racial or ethnic origin or disability. Where possible, such information should be anonymised and be subject to confidentiality obligations. In the case of health records or information relating to disability and reasonable adjustments, it may well be necessary to seek the employee's explicit consent before making disclosure.

11.22 The Employment Practices Code (2011) issued by the Office of the Information Commissioner makes the following general recommendations in cases of mergers and acquisitions:

- ensure that those responsible for negotiating the merger/acquisition are aware of the provisions of the Code

- assess any request for personal information from the other organisation. If at all possible, limit the information given to anonymised details

- only hand over personal information after receiving assurance that it will be used solely for the evaluation of assets and liabilities, that it will be treated in confidence, not disclosed to other parties and will be destroyed or returned after use

- remind those negotiating that they must receive assurances about how personal information will be used and what will happen to it should discussions end

- consider setting up a 'data room' with accompanying rules of access

- unless impractical to do so, tell workers that their employment records are to be disclosed to another organisation before acquisition or merger and make workers aware of the extent to which their records will transfer to the new employer; and

- where mergers/acquisitions involve the transfer of personal information about a worker outside the European Economic Area (to which the EU Data Protection Directive (No.95/46) applies), ensure that there is a proper basis for making the transfer and that adequate safeguards are in place.

Given the specific requirements to provide employee liability information under Reg 11 TUPE, all potential transferors – but most particularly contractors – should ensure that their data protection policies allow for the retention of personal data so that they are in a position to retrieve the requisite information if necessary for a reasonable period after the transfer.

Common practical transfer issues 11.23

The transferor and transferee need to consider how to handle the employment aspects of the transfer. The key to successful TUPE transfers lies in good planning, including identifying key risks at an early stage and holding a genuine dialogue with employees about the sale of the business and the impact this is likely to have on the workforce. Fear of change is a natural human instinct and frank communication from the management is essential to ensure the business transfer proceeds smoothly. For example, what will be the attitude of affected employees and their representatives to the transfer? Have they the power to disrupt the deal, and what concessions or promises may have to be made to them?

Issues to be managed on transfer 11.24

Set out below are the common practical challenges that need to be managed by transferors and transferees:

Representations to affected employees. The decision in Hagen and ors v ICI 11.25 Chemicals and Polymers Ltd and ors 2002 IRLR 31, QBD, is an excellent example of the dangers of making promises to ease the deal which are then not kept. That case concerned occupational pensions, which, along with redundancies, is the area usually of most concern to employees who may be affected by the transfer. Representations, if inaccurate or negligent, may give rise to claims in contract or tort or claims under the Misrepresentation Act 1967. While the decision in the Hagen case was about misrepresentation, the decision in Gill and ors v Cape Contracts Ltd 1985 IRLR 499, QBD, is about breach of warranty when the prospective employer does not deliver on promises made. In this non-TUPE case, the employees were induced to give up their employment at Harland and Wolff in Northern Ireland on the basis of a representation that they would be employed at Sullom Voe in the Shetland Islands by Cape Contracts on much higher wages. However, after they had left Harland and Wolff but before they started work at Sullom Voe, Cape Contracts cancelled the offers of employment due to threat of industrial action by employees at Sullom Voe. The High Court held that the representation was a warranty in the collateral contract between Cape Contracts and the employees to give up their existing work and go to work at Sullom Voe, and this warranty had been broken, entitling the employees to damages.

639

Employees or their representatives sometimes ask for guarantees of no compulsory redundancies within specified periods of time after a transfer, and for guarantees by the transferor to pay redundancy payments if the transferee becomes insolvent. If such concessions are made, they can be included in the commercial agreement, but often the best way of the transferor guaranteeing redundancy payments in the event of transferee insolvency is to make the promise directly with the employees through their representatives as part of the collective consultation process.

11.26 **Identifying employees who are 'in scope'.** Although it may seem obvious and easy to resolve, there are often problems surrounding exactly who the transferred employees are. The supply of a provisional list of transferring employees prior to exchange of contracts and the provision of a finalised list prior to completion are therefore indispensable. This requires the transferor to plan and organise in advance exactly who is and who is not going to transfer, but the transferee should also take steps to ensure that it is clear about the individual identity of the transferred workforce and to clear up discrepancies in this regard. So, for example, in some transfer situations – particularly where an integrated large business is being broken up – there will be those who do some work for the undertaking or activity being transferred but do other work for other parts of the transferor organisation. There will also be situations where an employee is employed by the company due to be sold but is seconded to another subsidiary within the group structure. Some employees (especially managers) may provide key services to different parts of the organisation.

All these scenarios raise the question of which employees are assigned to the undertaking or part of it that is being transferred – see Chapter 2, 'Who transfers?', under '"Assigned" to undertaking transferred'. In such cases, it must be decided what will happen to these employees when there is a transfer, and if some are to transfer, which ones will do so and which will remain with the transferor. Obviously the views of the transferee may be important, but it is common in larger transfers for employees providing common services to be allocated to a specific business in advance of any transfer. Therefore if that specific business is transferred then the employees allocated to it will transfer. This process of allocation is not without risks of breach of employment contract, and the process itself will alert employees and their representatives as to what is being planned and precipitate the need for information and consultation. In practice, it is usually the employees who believe they will be transferred who will be the most concerned, as employees normally prefer to stay with their existing employer rather than transfer to the unknown.

11.27 Another common problem concerning the identity of those employees who are to be transferred arises with larger and more complex organisations. This is that there are employees working full time in the business to be transferred who should transfer except that they are not employed by the transferor but by some associated organisation or company. In these cases, the employees may need to be moved from employment with the associated company into the employment of the transferor prior to the transfer.

The issue of identifying who transfers may raise particular difficulties in service provision change cases where the outgoing contractor may seek to 'dump' certain employees on the incoming contractor – for example, those with poor attendance or performance records. This practice was quite common in the past but a transferor's ability to do this is now perhaps more limited as a result of 'exit' provisions commonly now contained in outsourcing contracts that serve to restrict or even prohibit staff reassignment during a specified period prior to the contract coming to an end. The disclosure obligations under Reg 11 also now help to prevent such nefarious manoeuvres.

Insurance-based benefits. If employees who are to be transferred are away on **11.28** long-term sickness leave and in receipt of benefits under insurance-based sickness or disability policies, then the transferee will inherit the duty to make equivalent payments. Ever since the Court of Appeal's decision in Martin v Lancashire County Council and another case 2001 ICR 197, CA, transferees have been helped in this regard by being entitled to claim indemnity under the transferor's insurance policy – see Chapter 3, 'What transfers?', under 'Tortious and other civil liabilities – personal injury insurance cover'. Obviously, it makes sense for issues concerning long-term sickness absence to be aired prior to the transfer so that any necessary liaison with the relevant insurance company can be undertaken.

Restrictive covenants. The restrictive covenants in employees' contracts of **11.29** employment will have been drafted to be appropriate to the circumstances of the transferor prior to the transferee. They may, however, be inappropriate and unenforceable in the circumstances of the transferee after the transfer (see Chapter 3, 'Who transfers?', under 'Obligations specifically tailored to transferor's identity – restrictive covenants and implied duty of fidelity'). If such covenants are of real importance to the transferee, and there is a real risk that the existing covenants will be unenforceable or inappropriate, then the issue needs to be resolved either at the time of the transfer or soon afterwards with the individuals concerned. Difficulties can arise, however, with variations to contractual terms and conditions made before or after a relevant transfer as a result of which new or varied restraint clauses are inserted. If the reason for the variation is the transfer itself, any new restrictions that are to the detriment of the employee may well be rendered void – see Chapter 5, 'Changing terms and conditions', under 'Varying terms in a TUPE context'.

Redundancy. If the transferee plans redundancies soon after the transfer and **11.30** the deal only makes commercial sense if there is major rationalisation, then disclosed information that shows that the redundancy exercise will be very expensive will be a problem. For example, the disclosed information may show

641

that there is an enhanced redundancy payments scheme that has become incorporated into individuals' contracts of employment and/or that there is an agreement about redundancy procedures or redundancy selection criteria that the transferee does not wish to follow. It is, of course, very difficult to negotiate successfully to reduce such benefits, or to change redundancy procedures or redundancy criteria, and so there will often be a discussion about how the transferor may help the transferee with the cost of the redundancies. This could be by varying the price or by sharing the cost of redundancies when they arise. The transferor would need to take care as to the precise basis on which it makes any promise to contribute to redundancy costs. The amount of a redundancy payment is dynamic in the sense that it is based on wages and service at the time of dismissal over which the transferor will have no control once the transfer has been completed.

11.31 **'Piggy backing' on transferor's redundancy consultation.** Where the transferee operates from a different geographical location, a 'place of work redundancy' may well arise in relation to the transferring employees. Many transferees in such a situation will need to effect the redundancy dismissals on the day of the transfer and so will not be in a position to consult with the affected employees for 30 or 45 days as the case may be prior to the first dismissal. The commercial solution is for the transferee to ask the transferor to effect collective consultation on its behalf to avoid the risks of protective awards. As the legality of such 'piggy back' arrangements has yet to be tested in the tribunals, appropriate indemnities should be negotiated by the transferor.

11.32 **Pensions.** Occupational pension rights will always be an issue of great concern to affected employees and their representatives and the sums of money involved can often have a major impact on the deal. Although benefits under occupational pension schemes are excluded by Reg 10 from automatic transfer to the extent that they relate to rights to old-age, invalidity or survivors' benefits, this does not mean that transferees are free of all obligations to make continuing pension provision. The position is set out in detail in Chapter 3, 'What transfers?', under 'Occupational pensions'.

11.33 **Bonus and share option schemes.** It is likely that there will be problems about the automatic transfer of these arrangements from the transferor to the transferee (see Chapter 3, 'What transfers?', under 'Contractual rights and liabilities – express and implied terms' in respect of bonuses, and 'Obligations specifically tailored to transferor's identity – share option schemes' in respect of share options. The practical issues are likely to be how to replicate comparable benefits that make sense in the circumstances of the transferee's business or whether to buy out such arrangements.

11.34 **Changes to pay and benefits prior to transfer.** Transferees will want to be kept advised of any pay negotiations in progress leading up to the transfer and the outcome of those negotiations. This will also be important in service provision change cases where any pay increase could potentially have an adverse impact on the pricing assumptions in the tender document.

Harmonisation. Transferees for a variety of reasons often wish to harmonise **11.35** the terms and conditions of employment of the transferred employees with their existing workforces. The information disclosed by the due diligence exercise will show how different the terms and conditions of employment are between the transferred employees and the existing employees of the transferor and thus reveal the scale of the problem. All methods of achieving harmonisation, including 'red-circling', agreed variation of employment contracts and dismissal and re-engagement with a settlement agreement, involve significant risks (see Chapter 5, 'Changing terms and conditions', under 'Harmonising terms and conditions' and 'Alternative strategies for effecting changes').

Accrued holiday pay and loans. At the time of transfer, there will probably be **11.36** transferring employees who have accrued holiday pay that they have not taken. There may also be outstanding loans made by the transferor to some employees. Unless specific apportionment arrangements are made, the transferee is likely to benefit from the repayment of employee loans rather than the transferor, but the transferee will have to grant holiday and holiday pay for holidays accrued while the employees were working for the transferor. The importance of these issues will depend on the circumstances of each proposed transfer but in the case of TUPE transfers comprising service provision changes, the size of the sums involved can often be substantial.

Transferee's access to transferring employees before transfer date. It is not **11.37** uncommon for the transferee to request access to the transferor's workforce prior to the transfer date in order to discuss the business transfer. A transferor who is willing to agree to such arrangements will need to ensure that measures are put in place to protect itself from any pre-transfer dismissals by vetting the proposed communications and contents of any corporate presentations and by negotiating appropriate indemnities.

Service provision changes (outsourcing)   11.38
There are a number of important differences between the sale and purchase of a business and outsourcing, even though both are covered by TUPE. Particular issues tend to arise in an outsourcing context, and these are highlighted below.

When there is a sale and purchase of a business there will be a contract between the transferor and transferee, but there is no such contractual link between one contractor and a successor contractor where there is a service provision change. The contractors are likely to be rivals and may be reluctant to cooperate where one may be losing the contract and the other winning it. It is for this reason that the disclosure of employee liability information provision in Reg 11 is important, as it should ensure the flow of basic employee information where there is a service provision change. As mentioned under 'Due diligence' above, the

BIS Guide suggests that it will be helpful if this information is provided to the transferee at an early stage (although if this is done, it is important to bear in mind the obligation to update the information prior to the actual transfer and the potential compensatory liability if the information is inaccurate).

11.39 In any event, the client remains in the central position. The client will have the contractual and financial links when granting and administering the commercial contract to control the relationship between the outgoing and incoming contractors. Thus the commercial contracts between the client and respective contractors often contain 'employment entry provisions' at the start of the contract and 'employment exit provisions' when the contract is terminated so as to better regulate the handover procedure to be observed when a change of contractor is imminent.

Unlike a sale and purchase, the client often wishes to provide in the commercial contract that the contractor cannot sub-contract or assign, but must do the work itself. Furthermore, the client will often want to control through the commercial contract the terms and conditions of employment of those of the contractor's employees who are employed on the client's contract. This is frequently to help the client control costs, maintain standards and prevent manipulation of the contract, particularly where there may be a change of contractor.

11.40 Another difference between a sale and purchase agreement and an outsourcing agreement is that the client may wish through the commercial contract to have some degree of control over the quality and number of personnel employed to service the particular contractual activity and over changes to such personnel. The reasons for this are that the client will want to maintain service standards and retain staff who might have special knowledge of the client's work, as well as preventing contractors about to lose contracts from removing good staff from the contract and replacing them with poor staff. Also, in sensitive working environments such as the financial services industry, governmental bodies, prisons and schools, the client might wish to retain a veto over who is allowed access to its premises. On the other hand, contractors themselves will usually look for some degree of flexibility over the issue of who they assign to work on a particular contract to enable them to move employees from one contract to another as business needs demand.

The client in outsourcing arrangements will often have the contractor's staff working on the client's premises and this raises a number of special issues that can be covered in the commercial contract. For example, the client may wish to specify that, while working on the client's premises, the contractor's staff comply with the client's policies on, for example, discrimination, data protection, professional code of conduct and any compliance issues imposed by a regulator (e.g. the Financial Services Authority). The client may also require the contractor's staff to comply with the health and safety and security arrangements established by the client when the contractor's staff are on the client's premises. In some cases the client may want to have the right to require the contractor to remove any of its staff who are in breach of these policies, and replace them with staff who will comply with the client's policies.

So-called 'standstill' provisions are also normally found in an outsourcing **11.41** agreement restricting the outgoing contractor's ability to effect changes between the period when notice for termination of the contract has been given by the client and the expiry of the contract. Typical restrictions include:

- increasing the total number of the contractor's personnel save for the purposes of fulfilling certain projects or assignments previously agreed with the client

- changing the terms and conditions of employment of the contractor's personnel

- increasing the proportion of working time spent by the contractor's personnel without the consent of the client

- replacing any of the contractor's personnel with other persons engaged to provide the services

- terminating the employment of the contractor's personnel, and

- introducing any new contractual or customary practice concerning the making of lump sum payments on the termination of employment of the contractor's personnel.

Warranties and indemnities are sometimes to be found in 'first generation' outsourcing agreements – i.e. where the service is outsourced for the first time – but are less common on retendering thereafter. The outsourcing agreement will usually make provision for when the liabilities of the outgoing contractor will cease and incoming contractor will commence. For example, where there is an equal pay claim or discrimination claim, it is not uncommon for the transferor to be liable for claims prior to the transfer and the transferee to be liable for claims after the transfer. More difficult is who bears the liabilities for continuing claims. Sometimes, as an alternative to indemnities, the outsourcing agreement will provide for a price adjustment mechanism if the information set out in the tender document is wrong but very often, particularly in the public sector, the client or customer will not be willing to give warranties or indemnities and the new contractor will be expected to assume the risk if the information turns out to be incorrect. Even in private sector contracts, the customer may prefer to offer specific adjustments to the price rather than deal with open-ended warranties or indemnities.

11.42 Conditions precedent

The transferee (and occasionally the transferor) may well wish to make the purchase of the business conditional upon certain events happening. To this end, conditions precedent can be inserted into the sale agreement which will have to be satisfied before completion takes place. Where such conditions are not met, the sale or disposition of the business will fall through, and the transferee will be entitled to claim damages (unless agreement to the contrary has been made). Such conditions may include the following:

- that the transferor continue to conduct the business in the ordinary way until completion

- that the transferor will not, prior to completion, do anything which may materially prejudice the business or any of the assets to be transferred

- that a full opportunity be afforded by the transferor to the transferee and its advisers to investigate and verify the business and assets to be transferred

- that the sale agreement be submitted for approval by an ordinary resolution of shareholders of the transferee at a duly convened general meeting of the transferee to be held by a specified date, and

- that the transferee reimburse all of the transferor's reasonable expenses in the event that the transferee's shareholders fail to approve the transfer; and further, that the transferor reimburse all the transferee's reasonable costs in the event that the latter rescinds the agreement on account of breach of condition by the transferor.

Sometimes the transferee will want the transferor to make changes to the business being transferred before it is transferred. These types of change may be sufficiently important to be made conditions precedent in the commercial agreement. If these changes involve pre-transfer dismissals of employees and/or variations of employment contracts by the transferor to suit the transferee, then it will be important to bear in mind that the dismissal may well be unfair under Reg 7 and the attempted variations of employment contracts may be rendered void by virtue of Reg 4(4) (see Chapter 4, 'Unfair dismissal', and Chapter 5, 'Changing terms and conditions', respectively).

11.43 Warranties

Investigation under a 'due diligence' process is not a substitute for contractual protection. The transferee, and to a lesser extent the transferor, will need to feel confident that the representations made by the other side are true and accurate. Disclosure of information and due diligence will, if thorough, go a long way towards establishing this and the warranties given by the transferor will often mirror and confirm the accuracy of the information disclosed as part of the due diligence process. But there is always the danger of an item being overlooked, undiscovered, and even sometimes deliberately disguised. For this reason, the parties will often make express written warranties that vouchsafe the statements each has made to the other concerning the important aspects of the transaction.

General purpose of warranties   11.44

A warranty is a contractual assurance from the transferor to the transferee. It is a subsidiary or collateral provision to the main purpose of the transfer agreement. Thus, in the event that the representations made prove false or inaccurate, the innocent party will be entitled to sue to recover damages as a result. Warranties may be given in the form of an absolute guarantee of the accuracy of the information given in the course of the negotiating process or may be qualified by words like 'reasonably practicable', or 'so far as the seller is aware'. Warranties therefore serve two main purposes:

- to provide the buyer with a remedy (a claim for breach of warranty) if the statements made about the business prove to be incorrect and the value of the business is thereby reduced, and

- to encourage the seller to disclose all known problems to the buyer. For this reason, warranties are normally limited to the information disclosed by the seller.

However, the transferor will only be responsible for the loss and damage that is a reasonably foreseeable result of the breach of warranty. This involves a high degree of probability. The onus is on the buyer to show both a breach and that there is a quantifiable loss as a result of the breach. Furthermore, breach of a warranty does not afford the transferee the right to rescind the contract as in the case of a breach of condition.

The use of warranties is common in commercial transactions and is not **11.45** necessarily limited to the information provided about staff or HR-related issues. The nature of the warranty in a particular case will depend on the nature of the deal, the bargaining strengths of the parties and the disclosure process. Whereas transferees, if they can, will seek extensive warranties to back up disclosure, transferors will be pulling in the opposite direction to limit their warranties; for example, by words that qualify the warranty. Often, a minimum liability floor is agreed (particularly in relation to individual claims) whereby only sums in excess of the specified minimum will trigger indemnity payments. It is also common to agree whether the transferor's liability for breach of warranty should be capped on a 'per claim' or 'aggregate claim' basis. Sometimes, there is an overall limit or maximum cap on the amount that can be claimed for breach of warranty. Other limitations include

647

provisions to prevent double recovery where, for example, the loss is recoverable under an insurance policy; and provisions that exclude liability for acts carried out after the sale; and provisions for changes in legislation after the acquisition.

11.46 Typical warranties

The kinds of warranty that typically may be made are:

- that all the employees listed in [specify letter or document] will transfer but no other employees and that there have been no TUPE transfers during a specified period prior to the sale

- that the appropriate representatives have been informed and consulted by the transferor in accordance with Reg 13

- that the disclosed data (including the employee liability information under Reg 11) is full and accurate

- that there is no threatened or impending industrial dispute

- that there is no recognised trade union except that which has been disclosed and that there are no outstanding applications for recognition

- that there are no outstanding claims to tribunals or other courts or facts which could give rise to such claims

- that all relevant contracts of employment or service agreements have been disclosed

- that there has been no change of terms of employment since a specified date and no promises of future changes especially in relation to remuneration

- that no contract or service agreement exists which cannot be lawfully terminated on less than [three] months' notice

- that no profit share or bonus agreements are in force other than those already disclosed

- that the transferee warrants that it has informed the transferor of all measures the transferee will take in respect of transferred employees

- that all PAYE, national insurance, pension contributions, remuneration and expenses are paid up to the transfer date

- that there have been no resignations or dismissals in connection with the relevant transfer (other than those which may have already been disclosed)

- that all details of formal and informal agreements have been disclosed

- that the transferor has complied with all recommendations made by Acas in relation to the transferring employees and with all awards and declarations made by the Central Arbitration Committee in relation to the transferring employees

- that employee liability information has been provided by the transferor in a readily accessible form and is true and accurate in all material respects

- that the transferor has obtained all necessary proofs of legal status for the purposes of the Immigration, Asylum and Nationality Act 2006, and

- that there is not at present a claim, occurrence or state of affairs which may give rise to a claim against the transferee arising out of the employment or termination of employment of the transferring employees for compensation for loss of office or employment.

Short form of warranty   11.47

In more simple cases, a short and general warranty might be appropriate. If, however, it is used to cover a multitude of sins, then the transferor may put himself at risk of incurring substantial liabilities. The short form of warranty may approximate to the following: 'The Vendor warrants to the Purchaser: (1) that the accounts have been correctly prepared in accordance with good accounting practice and make full provision and reserve for all accruing and accrued liabilities and commitments of the Vendor in relation to the business at the balance sheet date, and show a true and fair view of the profitability and assets and liabilities of the Vendor employed in the business; and (2) that there are no adverse matters apparent from the accounts and which have not been disclosed in a disclosure letter dated [insert date] from the Vendor's solicitors to the Purchaser.'

Duration of warranties   11.48

Warranties only 'guarantee' the accuracy of the information at the time the warranty is given unless the warranty is expressly stated to cover a longer period.

From the transferor's point of view, warranty clauses may prove (or at least threaten) to be a millstone round its neck. The normal period for which a breach of warranty is actionable is six years – the standard limitation period for claims for breach of contract under the Limitation Act 1980 – but, in order to place some tighter limit upon the period for which he remains liable for the representations made in the sale agreement, the transferor will usually insist upon a clause providing for a period (e.g. 12 months from the date of completion) in which it must be notified of any claim(s) for breach of warranty intended to be brought by the transferee. It is also not uncommon for a term to be inserted on the transferee's part, waiving any claim or claims which do not in aggregate amount to or exceed a specified sum.

649

11.49 Restrictive covenants

Restraint of trade clauses are important means, especially for smaller businesses providing services, by which the transferee of a business may seek to prevent the transferor (or the transferor's former employees) from setting up in direct competition against it.

The presence of such restrictive covenants is a good indication that the transferee has acquired the goodwill of the transferor's business. In general terms, courts are more willing to enforce such restrictions between vendors and purchasers of a business than restrictions contained in employment contracts. However, the practicability of their enforcement depends greatly upon the extent to which they are drawn circumspectly in order to meet the legitimate and reasonable needs of the business and no more. Breach of any covenant can be remedied by way of injunction and/or damages to the extent that the terms of the covenant are reasonable in the circumstances.

11.50 A typical covenant may impose the following kinds of restraint:

'(1) The Vendor shall observe (and shall procure its officers and use bona fide endeavours to procure the employees to observe) strict confidence in relation to the Business and the Assets Transferred to the extent that and for so long as information relating to the Business and Assets Transferred is confidential and not in the public domain.

(2) For a period of [X] months following completion the Vendor shall not, either alone or jointly with others or directly or indirectly and whether as principal, agent, or employee, invest or otherwise be directly or indirectly engaged or concerned or interested within the area specified in (3) below in any business which competes directly or indirectly with the Purchaser's continuance of the Business in succession to the Vendor.

(3) The area referred to in (2) above is: (a) [X] miles radius of the premises; and (b) any other part of the United Kingdom in which any director or employee of the Vendor has had a territorial responsibility for sales or customer service within the [X] months prior to completion; and (c) any other part of the [European Union] in which the Vendor has had an active trading interest with which any director or employee of the Vendor was actively and personally engaged within the [X] months prior to completion.'

It is also not uncommon to insert clauses that require the transferor to procure that the directors and certain named key employees enter into new restrictive covenants with the transferee so that the terms of the covenant are contemporary and of particular relevance to the business of the transferee, thus increasing the chances of being enforceable in the courts (see Chapter 3, 'What transfers?', under 'Obligations specifically tailored to transferor's identity – restrictive covenants and implied duty of fidelity'). However, in so far as this may involve varying terms of employment, it is important to bear in mind the difficulties of effecting contractual variations in a TUPE context – see Chapter 5, 'Changing terms and conditions'.

Indemnities   11.51

Very often contingencies arise that may cause loss to the transferor or transferee. In order to protect against such eventualities, the parties to a transfer deal will usually deploy contractual indemnities. Unlike a warranty, an indemnity is a promise to reimburse the other party in respect of a particular type of liability, should it arise. The purpose of an indemnity is to provide guaranteed compensation to the other party in circumstances in which a breach of warranty would not necessarily give rise to a claim for damages or to provide a specific remedy that might not otherwise be legally available.

Typical liabilities (depending on the nature of the event indemnified) include claims for damages, legal costs, compensation, expenses, fines, court awards and penalties. The basic aim is to apportion the financial liability between the parties for employment costs associated with the transfer. Frequently, the indemnity will be in respect of a particular risk disclosed by the transferor either during due diligence or in a disclosure letter, e.g. where information reveals the risks of certain employee grievances leading to discrimination claims. The indemnity will give the transferee in this instance an ability to be recompensed without necessarily having to sue in the civil courts. It may be, for example, that the parties agree to hold a specified sum of money in the joint names of their solicitors for a fixed period of time out of which any indemnity can be made. There is also a role for indemnities in a service provision change, but as explained earlier, these have been arranged through the client's contracts with the outgoing and incoming contractors, as no contract will exist between the outgoing contractor (transferor) and incoming contractor (transferee).

The range and scope of indemnities largely depend on the relative bargaining **11.52** strength of the respective parties. The nature of the indemnities will also reflect decisions that the parties have had to make in the course of negotiations concerning on whose shoulders the burden lies in respect of compensating for events that cause loss. When indemnities are used, the parties will have to agree between themselves whether full recompense is to be made or merely a percentage of the loss actually incurred. In some cases, a maximum (or cap) is agreed either on a per-employee basis or as a total covering liabilities in respect of all the employees transferred. Sometimes, instead of indemnities being used, the purchase price or price for the provision of the service will be adjusted in accordance with decisions about, for example, who is to pay redundancy payments or monies in lieu of notice. But the complexity and uncertainties of

651

many business transfer situations and the ever-present danger of nasty surprises more often than not make the process of detailed indemnification an essential commercial exercise.

11.53 Specific issues in second generation outsourcing

There is usually a consensus among the parties to the transfer that the transferor will indemnify the transferee for all acts and omissions prior to the transfer date, and that the transferee will likewise indemnify the transferor for all acts and omissions after the transfer date – so called 'mirror indemnities'. The same arrangement is perfectly possible as between a client and contractor in a first generation change of service provider. However, difficulties arise in the case of a second generation change of service provider as there will be no commercial contract between the outgoing and incoming contractors. A solution is for the client to impose on both contractors mutual 'own watch' indemnities whereby each contractor agrees to hold the client and any predecessor or successor contractor indemnified against all employment liabilities relating to the period for which it is or was responsible for operating the service contract. In other words, the 'mirror indemnities' agreed between the client and the contractor are replicated and cascade downwards in the event of a subsequent service provision change. In practice, the preponderance of the liability risk tends to be with the transferee because of the automatic transfer of employment provisions in Reg 4, which means that it will usually be the transferee who is the most assiduous in ensuring that appropriate indemnities are agreed.

11.54 Typical indemnities

Indemnities can cover a very wide variety of matters. For example, an indemnity might specifically deal with the legal expenses incurred as a result of, or in connection with, the transfer, and both commercial parties will have an interest in securing their position in this regard. This is because it is common in employment litigation relating to transfers for employees to bring proceedings against both parties, and even if a party is wrongly joined it may prove costly to establish this. Furthermore, if legal expenses are to be indemnified, these should be precisely defined, as with the other liabilities covered by the indemnity. A party granting an indemnity against legal expenses needs to consider whether to set some financial limit on the amount indemnified, or whether to have some right to control the legal proceedings in order to ensure that legal claims are dealt with as economically as possible.

Like warranties, indemnities are only as good as the financial position of the party giving them: where there are doubts about the creditworthiness of the seller, the buyer may want some kind of additional security; for example, part of the purchase price may be held in a special account for a period of time after completion of the transfer as security against breach of an indemnity and the loss that may flow from this.

652

The following are the kinds of event for which indemnities may prove a **11.55** wise precaution:

- *late completion*: it is common for late completion to be one contingency covered by some kind of indemnity. This may, for example, take the following form: 'In the event that completion is delayed beyond the completion date for any reason not attributable to default or delay of the Vendor in performing its obligations under this agreement, interest shall be payable to the Vendor in respect of the consideration due under Clause [X] of this Agreement at the rate of [X] per centum over [X] Bank plc's base rate current from time to time, such interest to be calculated on a daily basis and to be compounded at monthly intervals'

- *uncompleted contracts*: the transferee may agree to indemnify the transferor in respect of losses, costs and claims arising from uncompleted contracts, but usually with exemption for such losses, etc, which are attributable to acts or omissions of the transferor prior to the completion date

- *general indemnity against acts or omissions*: the sale agreement may include a general indemnity clause which purports to indemnify against losses, costs and claims arising from acts or omissions of the parties. So far as the transferor's indemnity is concerned, the transferee will usually insist that the period covered includes the completion date, although an exemption may be made if the transferor has acted on the express written request of the transferee. In his turn, the transferee will probably undertake to indemnify the transferor against losses which the latter incurs as a result of the former's acts or omissions after the completion date

- *general indemnity about any inaccuracies in the disclosed information*: this clause will indemnify the transferee and be given by the transferor supplying the information

- *specific indemnity for employee liability information*: this clause will indemnify the transferee where no statutory information has been disclosed by the transferor at all prior to completion or where the information that has been disclosed proves to be inaccurate and causes loss to the transferee. (It should be borne in mind that, by virtue of Reg 12(4)(b), the existence of such an indemnity can be taken into account by an employment tribunal in assessing compensation for the failure by the transferor to notify the transferee of accurate and up-to-date employee liability information)

- *specific indemnity for redundancy and unfair dismissal claims arising out of the transfer and associated legal costs*: the indemnity clause will deal with who will pay for these claims. In particular, it will be important to stipulate whether the indemnity covers pre- and post-transfer dismissals and for how long; what level of severance pay will be covered by the indemnity clause, e.g. statutory redundancy pay only or enhanced redundancy pay; what

653

types of unfair dismissal claim will be covered, e.g. express and constructive dismissal claims, including claims based on a substantial change to working conditions based on Reg 4(9); the termination procedure that will need to be adopted; what levels of unfair dismissal compensation will be covered by the indemnity; and who bears the legal costs associated with dealing with tribunal claims. With specific regard to Reg 4(9), transferors might seek a specific indemnity from transferees to protect against liability arising from the dismissal that is deemed to occur where an employee resigns prior to the transfer as a result of a proposal by the transferee to make substantial changes to working conditions

- *specific indemnity for other employment claims*: the indemnity clause will deal with who will satisfy any compensation liability and associated legal costs in respect of claims such as wrongful dismissal, breach of contract, discrimination and equal pay and other legal claims such as personal injury for which liability transfers under TUPE or for which liability may be inherited by the transferee under the commercial agreement. It will deal with who will pay for any identifiable and potential claims such as discrimination, wrongful dismissal and breach of contract before and after the transfer, and for how long. The clause will also identify who is responsible for any associated legal costs in connection with such claims

- *specific indemnity for protective awards under Reg 13*: the penalty for failure to comply with the duty in Reg 13 to inform and consult employees affected by a relevant transfer is up to 13 weeks' pay per affected employee (which is not subject to any cap on weekly pay) – see Chapter 8, 'Information and consultation', under 'Informing and consulting appropriate representatives'. In light of this, the parties may wish to address and apportion financial liability for any failure to inform and consult through an appropriately worded indemnity depending on any timescales imposed and by whom

- *specific indemnity for failure to elect 'appropriate representatives' under Reg 14*: the penalty for this failure is set out in Reg 15 – see Chapter 8, 'Information and consultation', under 'Claims for failure to inform or consult'

- *specific indemnity for payment of emoluments*: this will address who is responsible for salaries, expenses, NI contributions, pensions and other benefits up to the completion date. This is a particularly important question where the transferee begins to assume de facto control over the business before completion of the transfer takes place; and

- *'wrong pocket' indemnity*: this will deal with who is to indemnify whom if some employees who should have been on the list of transferring employees are left off the list, or if some personnel (e.g. atypical workers) are on the list of transferring employees but should not be.

Case list

(Note that employment tribunal cases are not included in this list.)

A

ADI (UK) Ltd v Willer and ors 2001 IRLR 542, CA	1.70
AEEU and ors v Lyndon Scaffolding plc EAT 1242/99	1.55
ALHCO Group Ltd v Griffin and anor EAT 0007/14	1.102
A and G Tuck Ltd and anor v Bartlett 1994 ICR 379, EAT	2.170, 7.26
Abbey National plc v Holmes EAT 406/91	3.20
Abdulla and ors v Birmingham City Council 2012 ICR 1419, SC	3.126
Abellio London Ltd (formerly London Travel Ltd) v Musse and ors 2012 IRLR 360, EAT	2.145, 4.124, 4.126, 4.143
Abels v Administrative Board of the Bedrijfsvereniging voor de Metaalindustrie en de Electrotechnische Industrie 1987 2 CMLR 406, ECJ	1.140, 1.141, 3.66, 6.3, 6.36, 6.41, 6.42
Abernethy v Mott, Hay and Anderson 1974 ICR 323, NIRC	4.43
Abler and ors v Sodexho MM Catering GmbH and anor 2004 IRLR 168, ECJ	1.58, 1.76
Ackinclose and ors v Gateshead Metropolitan Borough Council 2005 IRLR 79, EAT	3.143
Adams and ors v Lancashire County Council and anor 1996 ICR 935, ChD	3.82
Addison and ors v Denholm Ship Management (UK) Ltd and ors 1997 ICR 770, EAT	1.80
Alamo Group (Europe) Ltd v Tucker and anor 2003 ICR 829, EAT	3.110, 3.160, 3.199, 8.98
Albron Catering BV v FNV Bondgenoten and anor 2011 ICR 373, ECJ	2.17, 2.20, 2.33, 2.89, 2.90, 2.94, 3.18
Alcan Extrusions v Yates and ors 1996 IRLR 327, EAT	5.66
Alemo-Herron and ors v Parkwood Leisure Ltd 2010 ICR 793, CA; 2013 ICR 1116, ECJ	3.144, 3.145, 3.147, 3.148
Allen and ors v Amalgamated Construction Co Ltd 2000 ICR 436, ECJ	1.18
Allen and ors v Morrisons Facilities Services Ltd 2014 ICR 792, EAT	8.64, 8.76, 8.102, 10.6
Allonby v Accrington and Rossendale College and ors 2004 ICR 1328, ECJ	2.26
Allsop v Christiani and Nielsen Ltd (in administration) EAT 0241/11	6.29
Angus Jowett and Co Ltd v National Union of Tailors and Garment Workers 1985 ICR 646, EAT	3.168, 3.169
Argyll Coastal Services Ltd v Stirling and ors EATS 0012/11	1.114, 2.110
Argyll Training Ltd v Sinclair and anor 2000 IRLR 630, EAT	1.36
Armstrong and ors v Newcastle upon Tyne NHS Hospital Trust EAT 0158/04; 2006 IRLR 124, CA	3.116
Ashby and ors v Birmingham City Council 2012 ICR 1, QBD	3.126
Ashford School and anor v Nixon and ors EAT 666/00	8.47
Associated Newspapers Ltd v Wilson and anor 1995 ICR 406, HL	3.157
Astle and ors v Cheshire County Council and anor 2005 IRLR 12, EAT	1.56, 1.71

B

BET Catering Services Ltd v Ball and ors EAT 637/96	3.144
BSG Property Services v Tuck and ors 1996 IRLR 134, EAT	1.36

657

H

I

659

J

J Murphy and Sons Ltd v Fox and anor EAT 1222/96   2.109, 2.111
J Sainsbury Ltd v Savage 1981 ICR 1, CA   2.66, 2.124
JNJ Bricklaying Ltd v Stacey and ors EAT 0088/03   2.25
Jackson Lloyd Ltd and anor v Smith and ors EAT 0127/13   1.8, 8.92
Jakowlew v Nestor Primecare Services Ltd (t/a Saga Care) and anor EAT 0431/14   1.122, 2.74, 2.124
James v Greenwich London Borough Council 2008 ICR 545, CA   2.32
Jefferies v Powerhouse Retail Ltd EAT 1328/95   3.15, 3.16, 3.19
Jinks v London Borough of Havering EAT 0157/14   1.92
Johnson Controls Ltd v Campbell and anor EAT 0041/12   1.86, 1.108
Jones and anor v Darlows Estate Agency EAT 1038/96; 1998 EWCA Civ 1157, CA   2.44, 2.80, 2.98
Jouini v Princess Personal Service GmbH 2008 ICR 128, ECJ   1.32
Jules Dethier Équipement SA v Dassy and anor 1998 ICR 541, ECJ   1.140, 6.4, 6.7
Junk v Kühnel 2005 IRLR 310, ECJ   8.78
Justfern Ltd and ors v D'Ingerthorpe 1994 ICR 286, EAT   7.24

K

Karalia Ltd v Eracli EAT 453/97   1.21
Katsikas v Konstantinidis 1993 IRLR 179, ECJ   2.133, 2.135, 2.176, 4.108
Kavanagh and ors v Crystal Palace FC Ltd and anor 2014 ICR 251, CA   4.37, 4.52, 4.62, 6.84, 6.88
Kavanagh v Coral Racing Ltd and anor EAT 231/97   2.79
Kelly and anor v Northern Ireland Housing Executive 1998 ICR 828, HL   2.31
Kerry Foods Ltd v Creber and ors 2000 ICR 556, EAT   3.169
Key2Law (Surrey) LLP v De'Antiquis and anor 2012 ICR 881, CA   6.45, 6.55, 6.57, 6.64
Kimberley Group Housing Ltd v Hambley and ors and another case 2008 ICR 1030, EAT   1.83, 1.85, 1.107, 1.109
Kirtruna SL and anor v Red Elite de Electrodomésticos SA and ors 2008 ECR I-7907, ECJ   3.8
Klarenberg v Ferrotron Technologies GmbH 2009 ICR 1263, ECJ   1.53
Kücükdeveci v Swedex GmbH and Co KG 2010 IRLR 346, ECJ   9.39

L

LLDY Alexandria Ltd (formerly Loch Lomond Distillery Co Ltd) v Unite the Union and anor EATS 0002/14   8.59
Ladies' Health and Fitness Club Ltd v Eastmond and ors EAT 0094/03   2.154
Landsorganisationen i Danmark v Ny Mølle Kro 1989 ICR 330, ECJ   1.10, 1.14, 1.51, 2.55, 3.134
Langeland v Norske Fabricom A/S 1997 2 CMLR 966, EFTA   5.9, 5.45
Langton v Secretary of State for Health 2014 ICR D2, EAT   3.193
Lansing Linde Severnside Ltd v Spiers EAT 1490/01   5.26
Lassman and ors v Secretary of State for Trade and Industry and anor 2000 ICR 1109, CA   7.42
Law Society of England and Wales v Secretary of State for Justice and Office for Legal Complaints 2010 IRLR 407, QBD   1.59, 1.148
Lawson v Serco Ltd and other cases 2006 ICR 250, HL   4.5, 9.37
Learning and Skills Council v Barfoot and ors EAT 0621/03   3.12

661

N

O

P

Index

667

677

681

691